REVOLUTIONARY CONSTITUTIONALISM

This book, the result of a major international conference held at Yale Law School, contains contributions from leading scholars in public law who engage critically with Bruce Ackerman's path-breaking book, *Revolutionary Constitutions: Charismatic Leadership and the Rule of Law*. The book also features a rebuttal chapter by Ackerman in which he responds directly to the contributors' essays.

Some advance Ackerman's theory, others attack it, and still others refine it – but all agree that the ideas in his book reset the terms of debate on the most important subjects in constitutionalism today: from the promise and perils of populism to the causes and consequences of democratic backsliding, from the optimal models of constitutional design to the forms and limits of constitutional amendment, and from the role of courts in politics to how we identify when the mythical 'people' have spoken. A must-read for all interested in the current state of constitutionalism.

Revolutionary Constitutionalism

Law, Legitimacy, Power

Edited by
Richard Albert

•HART•
OXFORD • LONDON • NEW YORK • NEW DELHI • SYDNEY

HART PUBLISHING
Bloomsbury Publishing Plc
Kemp House, Chawley Park, Cumnor Hill, Oxford, OX2 9PH, UK
1385 Broadway, New York, NY 10018, USA

HART PUBLISHING, the Hart/Stag logo, BLOOMSBURY and the Diana logo are trademarks of Bloomsbury Publishing Plc

First published in Great Britain 2020

A catalogue record for this book is available from the British Library.

Library of Congress Cataloging-in-Publication data

Names: Revolutionary Constitutionalism Conference (2018 : Yale Law School) | Albert, Richard (Law professor), editor.

Title: Revolutionary constitutionalism : law, legitimacy, power / edited by Richard Albert.

Description: Oxford ; New York : Hart, 2020. | Includes bibliographical references and index.

Identifiers: LCCN 2019051906 (print) | LCCN 2019051907 (ebook) | ISBN 9781509934577 (hardback) | ISBN 9781509934584 (Epub)

Subjects: LCSH: Constitutional law—Congresses. | Ackerman, Bruce A. Revolutionary constitutions—Congresses.

Classification: LCC K3165.A6 R48 2020 (print) | LCC K3165.A6 (ebook) | DDC 342—dc23

LC record available at https://lccn.loc.gov/2019051906

LC ebook record available at https://lccn.loc.gov/2019051907

ISBN: HB: 978-1-50993-457-7
ePDF: 978-1-50993-459-1
ePub: 978-1-50993-458-4

Typeset by Compuscript Ltd, Shannon
Printed and bound in Great Britain by CPI Group (UK) Ltd, Croydon CR0 4YY

MIX
Paper from responsible sources
FSC® C013604

To find out more about our authors and books visit www.hartpublishing.co.uk. Here you will find extracts, author information, details of forthcoming events and the option to sign up for our newsletters.

TABLE OF CONTENTS

NOTES ON CONTRIBUTORS

Bruce Ackerman is Sterling Professor of Law and Political Science at Yale University.

Richard Albert is the William Stamps Farish Professor in Law and Professor of Government at the University of Texas at Austin.

Andrew Arato is Dorothy Hirshon Professor in Political and Social Theory at the New School for Social Research, New York.

Denis Baranger is Professor of Public Law at Université Panthéon Assas (Paris 2).

Marta Cartabia is Full Professor of Constitutional Law and President of the Constitutional Court of Italy.

Alessandro Ferrara is Professor of Political Philosophy at the University of Rome Tor Vergata.

James Fowkes is Professor of Foreign and International Law at the University of Muenster.

Stephen Gardbaum is MacArthur Foundation Professor of International Justice and Human Rights at UCLA School of Law

Roberto Gargarella is Senior Researcher at the National Research Council (CONICET).

Tom Ginsburg is the Leo Spitz Professor of Law at the University of Chicago, and Research Associate at the American Bar Foundation.

Dieter Grimm is a former Justice of the Federal Constitutional Court of Germany and a Permanent Fellow of the Wissenschaftskolleg zu Berlin (Institute for Advanced Study).

Menaka Guruswamy is a Senior Advocate at the Supreme Court of India, and was formerly the BR Ambedkar Research Scholar and Lecturer in Law at Columbia Law School from 2017 to 2019.

Daniel Halberstam is Eric Stein Collegiate Professor of Law and Associate Dean for Faculty & Research at the University of Michigan Law School.

Alon Harel is Mizock Professor of Law at The Hebrew University and a member of the Federmann Center for the Study of Rationality.

Yasuo Hasebe is Professor of Constitutional Law at Waseda Law School.

Maciej Kisilowski is Associate Professor of Law and Public Management at Central European University.

Mitchel Lasser is the Jack G Clarke Professor of Law and Director of Graduate Studies at Cornell Law School.

Aziz Rana is Professor of Law at Cornell Law School.

Neil Walker is Regius Professor of Public Law and the Law of Nature and Nations at the University of Edinburgh.

Introduction: A Global Tour of Constitutionalism

RICHARD ALBERT

Nearly 25 years ago, Bruce Ackerman uncovered a series of contrasts and convergences among the constitutions of the world, opening our eyes to new possibilities for understanding how the many peoples in our modern day have arrived at their particular form of constitutionalism.[1] Ackerman's essay-length study on *The Rise of World Constitutionalism* distinguished two patterns in constitutional creation and the attendant roles of courts, taking readers on a global tour of constitutions to identify the impulses behind their founding and to theorise how their beginnings would later compel or constrain future constitutional politics.

Ackerman's provocative and innovative analysis was an early expositor of what Ran Hirschl has described as comparative constitutional studies – inquiries across jurisdictions that go beyond doctrinal analysis and deep into other spheres, for instance, history or political science, to explain the differences and similarities uncovered in law.[2] Public law scholars the world around had hoped that Ackerman would one day expand his essay into a book-length treatment of the fundamental questions he had raised and begun to answer. Ackerman has delivered just that and more in his new book, *Revolutionary Constitutions: Charismatic Leadership and the Rule of Law*,[3] the first instalment in what will be a multi-volume study on the foundations of constitutionalism.

From populism to democratic retrogression, from constitutional design to constitutional amendment, and from the role of courts in constitutional democracy to the promise and peril of popular constitution-making, Ackerman's new book forces us to rethink all of these subjects and others, putting him at the centre of the essential questions of our time. Is the US Constitution exceptional in the world? What are the historical origins of the popular movements that have achieved great successes in rights and freedoms – the same rights that are now

[1] Bruce Ackerman, *The Rise of World Constitutionalism*, 83 Va. L. Rev. 771 (1997).

[2] Ran Hirschl, Comparative Matters: The Renaissance of Comparative Constitutional Law (2014).

[3] Bruce Ackerman, Revolutionary Constitutions: Charismatic Leadership and the Rule of Law (2019).

under pressure in every corner of the globe? What threats do charismatic leaders pose to the rule of law and what institutional design choices can they make to reinforce its values? To answer these and other pressing questions, Ackerman serves as our guide across East and West: France, India, South Africa, Iran, Italy, Israel, the US – along with Burma and Poland, countries in the midst of dramatic constitutional transformations. Ackerman identifies an as-yet-unidentified thread that runs through the constitutions of each of these countries: they are revolutionary constitutions. He defines these constitutions as 'revolutionary' in contrast to two other types of constitutions: establishmentarian (for instance, those in Great Britain, Australia and Canada) and elite constructions (for example, those in Germany, Japan and Spain). As he explains in his introductory chapter of *Revolutionary Constitutions*, what distinguishes these three constitutional archetypes are the paths each takes to constitutionalism and the competing sources of authority and legitimation that sustain their local constitutional orders. *Revolutionary Constitutions* is focused squarely on the revolutionary model of constitutionalism. The two other models will form the basis of future volumes in his comprehensive study of constitutionalism – an extraordinarily wide-ranging study that few others in the world are capable of executing and even fewer still of executing well.

A Celebration and a Challenge

In August 2018, just after Ackerman put the finishing touches to his manuscript for *Revolutionary Constitutions*, 20 of the world's leading scholars in public law gathered at the Yale Law School for a two-day conference to debate the themes in the book. The conference offered the first structured opportunity to engage critically with Ackerman's new project. Some advanced his thesis, others attacked it and still others refined it – but all agreed that the ideas in the book will reset the terms of debate on the most important questions in constitutionalism today. The conference was an occasion both to celebrate the completion of a work that will become a focal resource in the field and also to test its groundbreaking ideas. The papers delivered at that conference have since been revised and updated, and they now appear as chapters in this volume.

In this Volume

This volume opens with a chapter by Dieter Grimm, whose chapter on 'A Political, Not a Legal History of the Rise of Worldwide Constitutionalism' formed the core of his remarks as the keynote speaker at the conference on Ackerman's book. Grimm identifies six fundamental choices that Ackerman makes in his first volume to shape his study and to organise the universe of revolutionary constitutions, from those concerning time and space, to perspective and politics, to sequence and scale. A former Justice of the Federal Constitutional Court of Germany and a Permanent Fellow of the Wissenschaftskolleg zu Berlin (Institute for Advanced Study), Grimm offers an invaluable analysis of the book's many contributions to the study of public law in general and to constitutionalism in particular.

The rest of the volume is divided into four parts. Part I, 'The Legitimating Foundations of Revolutionary Constitutionalism', features five chapters. Alon Harel's chapter on 'A Defence of Non-representational Constitutionalism: Why Constitutions Need Not Be Representational' offers a direct challenge to Ackerman's central presupposition in *Revolutionary Constitutions* that legitimation flows from representation. Harel suggests and defends reason-based legitimation as an alternative justification. Denis Baranger's chapter on 'Constitutionalism and Society: Ackerman on Worldwide Constitution-Making and the Role of Social Forces' is next, describing *Revolutionary Constitutions* as a 'eulogy of "political constitutionalism"'. Roberto Gargarella's chapter, entitled 'Bruce Ackerman's Theory of History', critiques several items in *Revolutionary Constitutions*, including Ackerman's reliance on 'We the Judges' instead of 'We the People', his legal formalism, and among others his concealed incorporation of normative evaluation into his descriptive account of revolution. Aziz Rana identifies in his chapter on 'Constitutionalism and the Predicament of Postcolonial Independence' what he understands as a 'potential cost of Ackerman's approach', namely that Ackerman does not inquire into the broader international contexts in which constitution-making occurs. This part of *Revolutionary Constitutionalism* closes with Andrew Arato's chapter on 'Revolution on a Human Scale: Liberal Values, Populist Theory?' Arato outlines the common ground he shares with Ackerman, but explains why, in the end, he and Ackerman situate episodes of constitutional founding differently – Ackerman as revolutions and Arato as negotiations.

Part II is entitled 'Constitutional Evolutions and Transformations'. Tom Ginsburg's chapter on 'Charismatic Fictions and Constitutional Politics' presses Ackerman on his use of charisma in social analysis and also suggests an alternative, perhaps more conventional, way of understanding the phenomena Ackerman identifies in *Revolutionary Constitutions*. Stephen Gardbaum argues in 'Uncharismatic Revolutionary Constitutionalism' that Ackerman misses an important variation on revolutionary constitutions: leaderless, movementless, but nonetheless spontaneous constitutionalist revolutions. These 'uncharismatic' revolutions, he writes, locate their legitimacy in an alternative source. In the chapter by Alessandro Ferrara, 'Unconventional Adaptation and the Authenticity of the Constitution', the author homes in on the authenticity of a constitution and its foundations, explaining that how we perceive authenticity need not be rooted in political autonomy. The next chapter, 'Constitutional Revolution, Legal Positivism, and Constituent Power' by Yasuo Hasebe, theorises the difference between Ackerman's understanding of constitutional revolution and positivist conceptions of revolution, while also elaborating the similarities between Ackerman's charismatic figures at the head of revolutionary movements and Jean-Jacques Rousseau's famed 'Lawgiver'. Part II closes with a chapter by Richard Albert entitled 'The Traditions of Constitutional Change', in which Albert identifies the peculiar problems and pathologies in each of the three paths to constitutionalism and explains how some jurisdictions merge elements of all three paths.

Parts III and IV of the volume turn to jurisdiction-specific commentary on Ackerman's analysis in *Revolutionary Constitutionalism*. Part III examines 'The Future of Europe' and features three chapters. In the first chapter in this part, entitled 'Constitutional Crossroads: A View from Europe', Neil Walker introduces the intentionally paradoxical idea of a managed revolution to navigate readers through the crossroads at which the British establishmentarian tradition finds itself amid the tradition of elite construction in the European Union (EU) – a subject that Ackerman touches upon in the book, but for which he offers a different diagnosis. In his chapter on 'How Europe Brought Judicial Review to France: A Response to Bruce Ackerman (and Others Who Think the French Did This on Their Own)', Daniel Halberstam resists the conventional narrative that the EU's Member States compromised their domestic constitutions to grow the European project and instead shows – with France as a case study of a larger cross-jurisdictional dynamic – how Europe itself shaped and reinforced the Member States' own national constitutions. The final chapter in this part, 'Constituting the Judiciary, Constituting Europe' by Mitchel Lasser, examines the reconstruction of the European Court of Justice and the European Court of Human Rights to illustrate that the constitutional diversity in Europe is even broader and richer – and therefore perhaps more problematic – than Ackerman suggests.

Part IV, 'The Law and Politics of Revolution', probes the revolutionary experiences specifically in India, Italy, Poland and South Africa. In her chapter on 'Sustaining Revolutionary Constitutions: From Movement Party to Movement Court', Menaka Guruswamy enriches and contests Ackerman's account of India by illuminating the consequences of the institutional design of the Indian Supreme Court, namely its expansive powers arrogated at the expense of the executive and legislative branches. Marta Cartabia's chapter on 'The Italian Constitution as a Revolutionary Agreement' brings readers to the origins of the modern Italian Republic to highlight the centrality of the context around which the constitution came to be: the destruction of two great wars, the toll of a generation of fascism, and the imperative to rebuild and reunify the peoples of the country. The volume turns next to Poland with Maciej Kisilowski's chapter on 'Constitutional Strategy for a Polarised Society: Learning from Poland's Post-revolutionary Misfortunes', in which he builds on Ackerman's analysis to illustrate how the current trajectory on which Poland finds itself could well serve as a cautionary model for constitutional designers in divided societies. James Fowkes contributes the last chapter in this part entitled 'Revolution as a Human Tale: Lessons from South Africa's Undecided Constitutionalism'. His provocative chapter takes a very different view from that of Ackerman on the country's revolutionary constitution. Fowkes declares that we do not yet know whether South Africa actually had a revolution. What results is a chapter that grapples with the past and present of South Africa, and what they tell us about the possible futures for the country.

This volume closes with a response by Bruce Ackerman. In 'The Race against Time', he responds to each of the chapters directed at his field-shaping contribution to the study of constitutionalism. His chapter is itself an important exposition of the paths of constitutionalism, in particular of the revolutionary track, as it offers him the occasion to strengthen and clarify his arguments in *Revolutionary Constitutions* and also to rebut and neutralise criticisms that he sees as misplaced. Ackerman's chapter has an additional virtue: it points the way to some of his early thinking on the shape that future volumes will take as he continues to develop his multi-volume study of constitutionalism.

A Word of Thanks

There are many thanks to give for making this volume and its associated conference possible. Renee DeMatteo, Barbara Corcoran, Trish Do and Jennifer Marshall ensured the smooth operation of the programme and gave all participants a memorable experience that will not soon be forgotten. Members of the Yale faculty – including Jack Balkin, Mirjan Damaška, Paul Kahn, Daniel Markovits, Samuel Moyn, Cristina Rodriguez, Jed Rubenfeld and James Whitman – chaired the many sessions in the conference, and with their comments and questions seeded a fascinating set of conversations over the course of the conference. And Heather Gerken, Dean of the faculty, hosted us on the Law School campus and opened the conference with inspiring words of welcome. The biggest thanks belong to Bruce Ackerman, author of *Revolutionary Constitutions*, a revolutionary study that will enrich our understanding of modern constitutionalism for years to come.

1

A Political, not a Legal History of the Rise of Worldwide Constitutionalism

DIETER GRIMM

Nobody will have expected that the author of *We the People*, in his turn from American constitutionalism to comparative constitutional law, would content himself with petty questions like the number of constitutional court judges in various jurisdictions or the length of the bills of rights of various national constitutions. His subject is the worldwide rise of constitutionalism in several volumes, of which we hold volume 1 in our hands. This opens up a vast and intricate field. How can we structure it in such a way that the project remains manageable? And which questions should be addressed to the material so that the result is not a mere juxtaposition of case studies, but an explanation of a development that deserves the name 'worldwide constitutionalism'? Choices have to be taken and selections have to be made, knowing that each of them excludes other options.

Bruce Ackerman makes several choices to handle the sheer number of cases, but also to give his work a distinctive face. I count six fundamental choices that characterise his work. The first is *temporal* and follows from the purpose to describe and explain the rise of *worldwide* constitutionalism. Worldwide constitutionalism in the sense of universal acceptance of the constitution as a way to legitimate and organise public authority is a rather recent phenomenon. It spread only after the Second World War. Ackerman's book is limited to this period. The beginnings of modern constitutionalism in the eighteenth century in North America and France, the struggle for constitutions in the nineteenth century in Europe and later also in Latin America are left out, as well as the constitutional movements in the first half of the twentieth century, most of which ended in failure.

The second choice is *spatial*. 'Worldwide constitutionalism' cannot mean every constitution in the world. For this we have the Chicago data bank. Nevertheless, Ackerman makes an enormous effort. The critique of many comparative works that their basis is too small does not apply to his work. Ten cases are analysed in volume 1. More will follow. No continent is left out and not only the usual candidates for comparison show up. Think of Burma and Iran in volume 1. It seems almost inevitable that there will be readers who find that an important country is missing. I do not want to join them. Instead, I am impressed by the number and variety of the cases and the in-depth analysis that each of them gets. The reading considerably broadened my constitutional horizon.

The temporal and spatial choices narrow the field. What is needed next is a perspective on the material. This is the third choice. Ackerman is interested in constitutions as a means to *legitimate* political rule. The very first sentence of the book reads: 'Law legitimates power.'[1] He understands constitutionalism as a new pattern of legitimation and, indeed, for the longest period of time, the legitimation of power had sources other than constitutions. Power derived its legitimacy from God, from tradition or from the belief that those who governed (monarchs mostly) had superior insight in the common good. In modern times, these sources have lost much of their persuasiveness. In the absence of absolute truths, constitutions, agreements on shared values and practices, took their place. But there is no guarantee that they will succeed in legitimating power. Constitutionalism has more or less established itself. Constitutions are fragile constructions.

What is it that enables constitutions to legitimate public power? The quality of the text? It is unlikely that a bad text will generate legitimacy. But a good text does not necessarily entail legitimacy either. Legitimacy is not an inherent quality of constitutions; rather, it comes as an ascription. Legitimacy is ascribed to a constitution if, in Ackerman's words, the revolutionaries 'can hammer out a Constitution that is plausibly related to the vision of the public good that animated their long struggle'.[2] He presumes that this has something to do with the beginnings of a constitution. This explains his fourth choice. He classifies constitutions not according to their legitimating principle, democracy or other, not according to the type of government they establish, federal or unitary, parliamentarian or presidential, or whatever other classification may come to mind, but according to their *origin*.

There are, of course, as many beginnings as there are constitutions. Ackerman believes that they can be reduced to three *ideal types*, called revolutionary, establishmentarian and elitist constitutionalism. They are described as 'different pathways through which constitutions have won legitimacy'.[3] In the course of the book, this connection becomes more differentiated. Each of the three beginnings creates special conditions for the success of the project 'legitimacy through law'. But each also goes along with special risks or dangers. Many succeed, others fail. Is this a convincing choice? We will be able to answer this question only after having read all the volumes, because only then will we be in a position to tell whether the constitutions assembled under the three ideal types justify the classification or whether there are constitutions that do not fit into this framework, which would mean that it is not comprehensive, but incomplete.

[1] Bruce Ackerman, Revolutionary Constitutions: Charismatic Leadership and the Rule of Law 1 (2019).

[2] *Id.* at 34.

[3] *Id.* at 1.

Volume 1 is limited to cases of revolutionary constitutionalism. The specific risk of this ideal type is that it may end up in totalitarianism. 'Totalising' revolutions[4] want to change everything. Ackerman calls them 'the worst pathologies of the 20th century',[5] which have led many countries into deep catastrophe. Totalitarian systems may have constitutions, but they do not set legal limits to political power. The alternative is a 'revolution on a human scale'.[6] Revolutions of this type set out to change certain sectors of political and social life, but not everything. For Ackerman, this type of revolutions succeeds if it '*fundamentally* reorganises dominant beliefs and practices in a *relatively* short period of time'.[7] Here, constitutions play an important role because they establish the particular transformations. So, the fifth choice is to treat only constitutions on a *human scale* in volume 1.

The group that is assembled under this common denominator consists of nine countries with 10 constitutions. Their pathways towards legitimation of power are the object of comparison. The author is, of course, aware that the ways are not necessarily linear and that their result is not necessarily stable. The 'constitutional moment' can be missed. A once successful legitimation can get into trouble or fade away. In order to give his comparison a structure that takes the dynamics into account, Ackerman makes his last and perhaps most ingenious choice by dividing the process of legitimation that a revolutionary beginning has set in motion into a *sequence* of stages that he assumes repeat themselves in every case of revolutionary constitutionalism.[8]

Time 1 ('mobilised insurgency') is the stage where outsiders challenge the legitimacy of the existing political and social order, and fight under risk for life and liberty for a better order. Time 2 ('constitutional founding') is the stage where the revolutionaries gain popular support for their programme and replace the old order by a new one – constitutionalising charisma. Time 3 ('succession crisis') is the time when the departure of the charismatic leaders of time 1 and time 2 leaves a legitimacy gap and politicians less charismatic and less devoted to the constitutional principles quarrel over the succession. Time 4 ('consolidation') is the stage where judges, who had remained in the background as long as the charismatic founders were in power, assume the role of defining the revolutionary principles vis-a-vis the mediocre successors of the revolutionary heroes.

The gains of this approach are obvious. The common denominator 'revolutionary constitutions' allows a meaningful comparison of very diverse systems. It structures the comparison of seemingly unrelated cases without levelling the differences. On the contrary, it makes differences as well as similarities visible, which would otherwise have gone unnoticed or appeared as the peculiarities of

[4] *Id.* at 27.
[5] *Id.* at 28.
[6] *Id.*
[7] *Id.*
[8] *Id.* at 43.

a single case. The illuminating and often surprising insights of this book are a fruit of the four stages. Who would have expected that a comparison between, say, Iran and Israel or Italy and India is eye-opening? Although Ackerman does not attempt to give a complete causal account of the conditions under which revolutionary constitutional projects succeed or fail – external events not related to the type of revolutionary constitutionalism may intervene – he can explain a lot of developments through his four-phase dynamics that characterises this type of constitutionalisation.

At the same time, the analysis of countries united under the rubric of revolutionary constitutionalism calls into question the realistic approach to the phenomenon, which came into fashion recently.[9] For realists, the constitutional world is dominated by rational actors who have nothing else in mind than maximising their profit in whatever currency. The actors of revolutionary constitutionalism, on the contrary, gained their credit in time 1 because they were ready to sacrifice life, liberty and property in the interest of a higher ideal, a just political and social order. This was the legitimacy resource on which they could build in time 2. This is not to say that the realistic explanation of the rise of constitutionalism is completely wrong. We will almost certainly encounter cases that support this theory in the following volumes. But Ackerman's work shows that it is not the exclusive explanation for the success of constitutionalism, as some realists would have it.

It remains to be seen whether a similar ingenious pattern capable of analysing and explaining the constitutional development of the other two ideal types will be available. We will know that in due time. My question for today is rather what the costs of Ackerman's choice are, given the fact that even the best choice excludes alternatives. Are there aspects of revolutionary constitutionalism that remain unexplored or neglected in *Revolutionary Constitutions*? Ackerman's focus on revolutionary constitutionalism is the legitimation of political rule. Legitimation is without doubt an important function of constitutions. But it is not the only and not even the foremost function. Before a constitution can legitimate public power, it has to establish and organise public power and to regulate its exercise. This is its immediate concern, achieved through the medium of law.[10]

However, Ackerman does not write a *legal* history, but a *political* history of the rise of worldwide constitutionalism. This is, of course, justifiable, first because political analyses are much smaller in number than legal ones and, second, because constitutions are political phenomena. They are products of political decisions and they have an impact on politics. Time 1 in Ackerman's sequence is a completely political stage. There may be a constitution in time 1, but if so, it is the constitution

[9] Protagonists are Ran Hirschl, Towards Juristocracy (2007); and Tom Ginsburg, Judicial Review in New Democracies (2012).

[10] See Dieter Grimm, Constitutionalism: Past, Present, and Future (2016) 3.

of the enemy. It is legally in force, but its legitimacy is challenged by the revolutionaries, whereas their own concept of legitimate rule is not legally in force. It is at best a constitutional project, waiting for transformation into law. But the transformation is the goal because 'law legitimates power',[11] as Ackerman said in the beginning, and a new power that succeeds in overthrowing the old power sees a heightened need of legitimation because of the illegality of its action.

Hence, the constitutional project renders its legitimating service to the new order simply by becoming *law*. Legitimation presupposes legality. Legitimation by constitution depends on the successful submission of politics to law. This cannot be reached by a few fundamental principles. In order to be able to bind politics effectively, these principles must translate into specific rules. But rules are not enough. Legality is a necessary but not a sufficient condition of legitimacy. It also matters how the rules are designed and whether they take effect in practice. The legitimacy that constitutions transmit is a result of their *continuous* relevance for the political process after adoption. From time 2 onwards, the constitution must prove its relevance as law. A constitution that is notoriously disregarded or is circumvented whenever constitutional requirements collide with political interests will not convey legitimacy on politics.

Ackerman does not ignore this. For him, it characterises constitutions that they impose 'significant legal constraints on top decision-makers'.[12] This distinguishes constitutionalism from dictatorship. Dictatorships may have constitutions, but they do not impose constraints on politics. Ackerman even insists that enlightened autocracy remains an autocracy and is not a constitutional state. When I say that Ackerman writes a political instead of a legal history of constitutionalisation, I mean that he is more interested in the process than the product, and insofar as the product plays a role, he is more interested in the political system established by the constitution than in the legal constraints for day-to-day government and their implementation. He leaves this to the 'positivists', whom he regards with a certain disdain because they have nothing to say about the question that in his view really matters, namely legitimation.[13]

In this respect, Ackerman almost follows the Schmittian concept of constitutionalism. I dare say this is because every reader of Ackerman's works knows that he is immune to succumbing to Schmittian temptations. Schmitt distinguishes between constitution and constitutional law.[14] 'Constitution' means the decision of a political entity about the type and form of its political order. He calls this decision 'existential'. It is neither taken by identifiable actors nor in a certain procedure and it is nowhere textually fixed. All this follows when the existential decision is transformed into constitutional law. But what counts is the constitution, not

[11] ACKERMAN, *supra* note 1 at 1.
[12] *Id.* at 2.
[13] *Id.* at 36 f.
[14] CARL SCHMITT, VERFASSUNGSLEHRE (1928) 20 ff. (§ 3).

constitutional law. Constitutional law derives its validity not from a vote taken by a constituent assembly or even the people themselves, but from the existential constitution, and it is legally binding only insofar as it is compatible with the constitution.

Unlike Schmitt, Ackerman does not mystify the fundamental decision.[15] But this decision is what he too is interested in, not the provisions and institutional arrangements in a particular constitutional text. It may be that he feels exonerated from going into the legal details of a constitution and its functioning because he decided to deal only with revolutionary constitutions on a human scale, what I understand as constitutions with a certain democratic and liberal quality. For Ackerman, revolutions on a human scale seek to prevent a backsliding into the previous system and to establish the fundamental principles of the new order. He adds: 'This point is sufficient for my purpose.'[16] But is it? The question arises at the latest when Ackerman irritatingly includes a country like Iran in the category of constitutions on a human scale.

The Iranian Constitution undoubtedly falls in the category of revolutionary constitutionalism. But Iran is the only country in Ackerman's list that is Islamic, yet, with a constitution that, in Ackerman's interpretation, is not based on the will of God, but on the will of the people. However, the most powerful position in this constitutional order is held by the Supreme Leader, an unelected cleric chosen by the high clergy. Below the Leader, there is a President who derives his position from general elections. But his decisions are subject to a veto by the Supreme Leader and also by the Guardian Council, whose task is to guarantee the conformity of legislation with Islamic principles. The Leader may also issue binding orders. Yet, Ackerman argues that the Leader may hesitate to use his powers against a President who enjoys strong support from the electorate. So the pendulum may swing 'from democratic to religious authority and back again'.[17]

To be on the constitutional side, it is sufficient for Ackerman that no single power centre exists in a country, which can legitimately impose its commands in a top-down manner. As soon as there are 'institutional rivals for the final say over the future course of political development',[18] we are within the constitutional universe. But is hesitation to exercise a certain power an equivalent to a legal constraint of that power? And what if one of the rivals is in a clearly hierarchical position or if the rivalry remains within the small circle of the ideological leadership? Here, it appears to be a disadvantage that Ackerman does not articulate his understanding of 'constitution' more closely. To be sure, it would be unwise to limit comparative constitutional research prematurely by a narrow definition, but Ackerman's understanding may be overly broad. What remains in the end is that a constitution contains some legal constraints on top decision-makers.

[15] See a brief discussion of Schmitt in ACKERMAN, *supra* note 1 at 42.
[16] *Id.* at 34.
[17] *Id.* at 356.
[18] *Id.* at 360.

However, legal constraints on politics are nothing new. They existed long before the modern constitution emerged. Even the absolute state was much less absolute than it may have seemed. It had to accept legal limitations of its power. If legal limits to political power are sufficient for the existence of constitutionalism, the groundbreaking novelty of constitutions, which Ackerman himself emphasised at the beginning of his book, is obfuscated. Unlike the older legal bonds of political rule, constitutions are a particularly ambitious form of submitting politics to law. It is this specific ambition that explains the stunning success of modern constitutionalism, which finally led to the rise of worldwide constitutionalism. Ackerman's understanding, on the contrary, is a rather thin notion of constitutionalism, compared to what I used to call 'the achievement of constitutionalism'.[19]

Is it a consequence of Ackerman's preference for a political rather than a legal history of the rise of world constitutionalism that time 4 gets the least attention of all four stages in the case studies? If we reformulate the stages in terms of the relationship between law and politics, time 1 is the stage of pure politics. Insurgents attack the old system, and this does not give way, but strikes back. Time 2 is the stage of constitutional politics. The revolutionaries use their newly acquired power to hammer out a constitution as law. But it is not yet the time of judicial politics. As the comparison shows, the deference of the French Conseil constitutionnel during President de Gaulle's lifetime is not the exception, but the rule. The exception is the South African Constitutional Court, which did not hesitate to rule against the charismatic leader. Time 3 is again a stage where politics dominate. Second-generation politicians fight for the succession of the charismatic leaders. Only time 4 is mainly law.

At time 4, the judges dominate. Still, Ackerman is not so much interested in what they do as in how they gain their dominant role. He criticises traditional comparative constitutional research for being court-centred or, perhaps more precisely, jurisprudence-centred, while he wants to explore the dynamic process through which courts establish themselves as actors capable of legitimating political power under post-charismatic conditions. The ground is laid in time 3. There, the professionalisation of constitutional law begins. It is increasingly treated as law like private or criminal law. Increasingly confident judges confront increasingly normalised politicians who lack the revolutionary credentials of the charismatic leaders and are less devoted to the constitutional principles. In this situation, judges can credibly claim that they, not the parliamentarians, are 'the more legitimate guardians of the constitutional legacy of the Revolution'.[20]

However, this does not mean that the legitimation problem which is central for Ackerman is solved; it is only reformulated. How can courts fill the 'legitimacy vacuum'[21] that the charismatic leaders leave? Their only means consists in deciding

[19] Dieter Grimm, *The Achievement of Constitutionalism and its Prospects in a Changed World, in* Grimm, *supra* note 10 at 357.

[20] Ackerman, *supra* note 1 at 161 f.

[21] *Id.* at 8.

the cases brought before them. And they cannot hope to legitimate the political system by showing that they are the better politicians than the elected representatives of the people; on the contrary, they must convince citizens that what they do is *not* politics, but the enforcement of constitutional law. So, the jurisprudence demands attention. Ackerman would not deny this, but he gives it a specific political twist. The success of courts depends on what he calls 'judicial statesmanship'.[22] This is something quite different from legal doctrine. Statesmanship requires a clever selection of a few cases by which the judiciary can demonstrate its superiority over politics in defending the revolutionary principles.

As a matter of fact, decisions of this sort can be found in many jurisdictions. But they are rare incidents, whereas legitimation of power is a permanent process. Will a few early statesman-like judgments be sufficient or does the impression that the judges are faithful to constitutional law matter? If this is so, who guarantees their faithfulness and what does 'faithful' mean? Constitutional norms are notoriously open-ended. They cannot be applied straight away to controversial cases. There is a gap between the general and abstract norm and the individual and concrete case, which has to be bridged by interpretation. Interpretation determines the meaning of constitutional norms with regard to a certain problem. It is not only a cognitive but also a creative operation. It does not uncover a meaning that is inherent in the text of the constitution from the time of enactment. The meaning is at least partly construed, especially when the courts have to cope with problems that were unknown at the time of enactment.

The legal device to secure faithfulness is the method of interpretation. To be sure, legal methods vary greatly, but all share the purpose to separate legal from non-legal arguments and thereby contribute to the legitimacy of adjudication. Realists would probably argue that method is just a camouflage, while judges do something different from what they say they do. And certainly, there is ample evidence to support this suspicion. But one should make clear that these are pathological cases.[23] The legitimation of political power by courts in time 4 cannot be dissolved from the way in which they understand and enforce the constitution. However, adjudication is not in the foreground of Ackerman's work unless he encounters an open controversy between the political and the judicial institutions, like when the Indian Supreme Court developed the basic structure doctrine to limit the amendment power of parliament.

Furthermore, legitimation by the judiciary raises the question why post-charismatic politicians tolerate the judicial interference in politics. Have only the politicians departed from the revolutionary principles, not the general public, so that the judges who uphold these principles enjoy the backing of the citizenry and thus make it too costly for politicians to disregard court rulings? Realists would

[22] *Id.* at 159.

[23] See Dieter Grimm, *What Exactly is Political about Constitutional Adjudication?*, *in* Judicial Power 307 (Christine Landfried ed., 2019).

probably answer that politicians have no reason to disregard judgments because they instrumentalise courts for the purpose of shielding their power against competitors. They see judicial review as a 'hegemonic' project.[24] This may be so in a number of instances, and the French Fifth Republic is an example of this. But constitutional courts do not always render judgments that please the elected representatives. There are enough incidents where judges severely frustrate political plans. Hence, the question of why the post-charismatic politicians more or less comply with judgments even if they dislike them suggests itself.

Ackerman's analysis of constitutional dynamics ends with time 4. He does not want to think beyond this point, although he admits that time 4 will not necessarily be the end and a time 5 or a new time 1 will begin. Could it be that we have already entered this stage? The author himself remarks that some 20 years after its culmination, constitutionalism is in a crisis. In a number of democracies with various pathways towards constitutional legitimacy, constitutions are being transformed from rules of the game for democratic competition into instruments in order to shield the majority party from competition and critique. And courts are the first targets. In his chapter on France, Ackerman assumes that an attempt by a new movement party to take over the constitutional system would take years, simply because of the existence of judicial review. Countries like Poland and Hungary have shown that a few months are enough. Has the rise of world constitutionalism come to a halt?[25]

[24] See Ran Hirschl, The New Constitutionalism and the Judicialization of Pure Politics Worldwide, 75 Fordham L. Rev. 721, 745 (2006); Ran Hirschl, *The Judicialization of Mega-politics and the Rise of Political Courts*, 11 Annual Review of Political Science 93 (2008).

[25] Mark A. Graber, Sanford Levinson & Mark Tushnet (eds.), Constitutional Democracy in Crisis? (2018); Tom Ginsburg & Aziz Huq, How to Save a Constitutional Democracy (2018).

PART I

The Legitimating Foundations of Revolutionary Constitutionalism

2

A Defence of Non-representational Constitutionalism

Why Constitutions Need not be Representational

ALON HAREL

I. Introduction

Ackerman's *Revolutionary Constitutionalism* is among the few books in constitutional theory that transcend the boundaries of a single jurisdiction and makes a bold effort to explore the underlying logic of constitutionalism as such (rather than constitutionalism of a particular jurisdiction). After exposing some of its virtues, I turn to challenge the underlying presupposition of *Revolutionary Constitutionalism* that legitimation rests exclusively on representational grounds, eg, on the fact that the constitution represents central values of the polity and/or that it plays a constitutive role in the formation of the political community. It is here that I believe that Ackerman advances a position which rests on the US parochial experience and, consequently, fails to acknowledge the multiplicity of the ways in which legitimation can be achieved. More specifically, I differentiate between two types of legitimation – representational legitimation and non-representational or reason-based legitimation – and show that some of the puzzles raised by Ackerman can be resolved by acknowledging the significance of the latter type of legitimation. To put it provocatively, the legitimation of a constitution need not rest on the conviction that it represents the people whom it governs; it may simply rest on the belief that it is a good or just constitution. Representational legitimacy is only one form of legitimacy, but not the only one.

Revolutionary Constitutionalism has many virtues, but let me point out two prominent virtues. By highlighting these virtues, I hope to urge future theorists (including myself) to follow Ackerman's lead in these respects. *Revolutionary Constitutionalism* resists two seductive temptations which often inflict constitutional theory: monism on the one hand and normative judgementalism on the other. Monism refers to the view that there is a single theory that can capture all forms of constitutionalism. The seductiveness of monism rests on its theoretical elegance and its aesthetic simplicity. Yet, as Ackerman realises, the costs of yielding to the seductiveness of monism are often greater than its benefits, as it comes at the expense of distorting the multi-faceted realities of constitutional evolution. Normative judge-mentalism is also a common seductive trap. Constitutional theorists often use their own normative commitments to interpret, understand or explain constitutional realities. Ackerman wisely distances himself from engaging in evaluative judgments. In examining the underlying shared features of revolutionary constitutionalism (or constitutionalism more generally), Ackerman believes one should focus on the shared structural features of revolutionary constitutions rather than on the merits of particular constitutions or even the merits of constitutionalism as such. As Ackerman pronounces at the outset of his book:

> I will be bracketing my own philosophical commitments to make a different point. Regardless of whether they are 'right' or 'wrong' revolutionary movement-parties confront *the same* series of legitimation problems in constitutionalising their charisma over time.[1]

By avoiding both the trap of monism on the one hand and judge-mentalism on the other, Ackerman shows sensitivity to the complexity of constitutionalism and its multi-faceted structure. In particular, he exposes the fact that that both 'good' and 'bad' constitutions need to be legitimated and that the process of legitimation has its own logic independently of the merits of the resulting constitutions or the liberal or illiberal sentiments of the founders of the constitution. I will show at the end of this chapter that in these two respects, I follow Ackerman's method and even (dare to) argue that I am more faithful to these virtues than Ackerman himself.

Ackerman's point of departure is legitimation. Founders of constitutions strive to realise legitimation and it is this impetus which provides the key to the understanding of their decisions. The primary challenge of the founders of political revolutions is how to reach legitimation. Legitimation is crucial for the success of any constitutional order, but it is particularly crucial at the time of political revolutions and yet, as Ackerman pointed out, legitimation of revolutionary constitutions is a tricky process. After all, the revolutionaries disrupt the existing constitutional order; such disruption is often the byproduct of delegitimising an established existing legal order. On what basis can the revolutionaries succeed in establishing legitimacy of their own constitutional order? How can they address the challenge that their new proposed constitutional order is not better than that of the former constitutional order or is not better than an alternative constitutional order proposed by another group of revolutionaries which is equally worthy? This is the core question addressed by Ackerman and in this respect too, I will follow his lead.

[1] Bruce Ackerman, Revolutionary Constitutions: Charismatic Leadership and the Rule of Law 36 (2019).

In this chapter I wish to complement Ackerman's analysis by differentiating between two modes of legitimation: *representational legitimation* and *non-representational* or *reason-based legitimation*. I will argue that differentiating between these two modes of legitimation can shed better light on some of Ackerman's own observations and can successfully address some puzzles raised by him. Let me briefly summarise my main claims.

Legitimacy is representational if it rests upon the conviction that the constitution is representative of the people, that it is constitutive of their collective identity, that it promotes their distinct values as a nation and that it is being sustained by the active engagement of citizens with the constitution. Legitimacy is non-representational or reason-based if it rests upon the conviction that the (procedural, institutional or substantive) aspects of the constitutional order promote justice, the protection of rights, stability and/or well-being.

Given Ackerman's previous normative work it is not surprising that *Revolutionary Constitutionalism* emphasises and, at times, gives exclusivity to the representational mode of legitimation. I shall argue that an understanding of constitutional evolution can be greatly enriched by understanding the role that these two modes of legitimation play in the evolution of constitutions. Most importantly, in order to be legitimated, the constitution need not be representational. The current conflict between populists on the one hand and liberals on the others can be better understood as a debate between advocates and opponents of representational constitutionalism. I shall also argue that Israel can provide an example: the contemporary controversies concerning the so-called 'constitutional revolution' rest partly upon a conflict between these two modes of legitimation.

II. The Representational and the Reason-Based Modes of Legitimation

Constitutions, I shall argue, can be legitimated in two ways: representational legitimation and reason-based legitimation. Representational legitimation grounds legitimacy in claims concerning popular will, consent, voluntary endorsement, active engagement, participation etc. The constitution is binding because we want it; we have agreed to it, we have voted for it, it reflects our identity as a community etc. To put it crudely, it is binding because it is *our* constitution – the constitution to which we agreed and which we cherish; most typically, it is also the constitution which we (or, at least our representatives) ratified on the grounds that it entrenches the values that are constitutive of our political or collective identity.[2]

[2] In his previous work, Ackerman has contributed more than anybody to the understanding of representational legitimation. See Bruce Ackerman, *The Storrs Lectures: Discovering the Constitution*, 93 YALE L.J. 1013 (1984).

Non-representational or reason-based legitimation rests on judgements concerning the institutional, procedural or substantive justness, correctness or usefulness of the constitution. The constitution is binding because it establishes good institutions, entrenches just norms and is worthy therefore of our allegiance. In short, under representational legitimation, the constitution merits our allegiance because it is ours, while under reason-based legitimation, it is ours because it merits our allegiance.

When I do not write academic articles, I read theology. The similarity between the concern I raise here and a classical puzzle in theology is evident. One of the classical concerns of theologists has been to address the relations between God and goodness. According to one view, whatever God wills is good by virtue of its being willed by God. This view is often labelled 'theological voluntarism'.[3] What is shared by all theological voluntarists is the view 'that entities of some kind have at least some of their moral statuses in virtue of certain acts of divine will'. In contrast, anti-voluntarists adhere to the view that goodness precedes God's will. The tradition of intellectualism in theology suggests that God wills the good because it is judged by God to be good. Crudely speaking, according to the first view, the good is good because it is willed by God, while according the latter view, it is willed by God because it is good. It is precisely this classical distinction between voluntarism and the so-called intellectualism which I wish to import from theology to constitutional theory. I suggest that the legitimation of constitutions may be grounded in voluntarism (will-based legitimation or representational constitutionalism) or in intellectualism (reason-based legitimation or non-representational constitutionalism).

Under the representational mode of legitimation, the constitution is legitimate because it is ours and it is ours because we created, we committed ourselves to it and because our values are entrenched in it. Typically, constitutions that are legitimated in this way are subject to a referendum and constitutional debates are central to the public life of the polity. In contrast, under the reason-based mode of legitimation, we endorse the constitution because it is just or effective. In such cases, the constitution need not be ceremonially accepted by citizens and it need not guide them in their public life. In reality, almost or perhaps all constitutions gain their legitimacy both in representational and in non-representational manner. Yet, as I will show below, some constitutions are more representational than others.

Let me provide an analogy: compare the type of engagement that an individual has with her private garden and the engagement that an engineer has with his enterprise of building a bridge. The owner of the garden aims to shape her garden in a way that addresses her own needs, tastes, sensibilities and preferences. She wants the garden to appeal *to her* aesthetic judgements. She can assert truthfully that other gardens are equally or even more beautiful than hers and nevertheless

[3] See Mark Murphy, *Theological Voluntarism, in* Stanford Encyclopedia of Philosophy, https://plato.stanford.edu/entries/voluntarism-theological.

she prefers *her* garden to that of others. In contrast, an engineer who builds a bridge aims at building *a good bridge* rather than a bridge *that appeals to him*. An engineer typically does not say that he builds a bridge to satisfy his own inclinations or to appeal to his own aesthetic judgements; the bridge simply ought to be a good, safe, solid and even a beautiful bridge, but not one that is designed specifically to appeal to its creator. Representational legitimation can be analogised to the case of the garden; it rests on the conviction that the constitution is a constitutive component in the lives of the polity. Consequently, it ought to represent the collective values, ideals and aspirations of the political community. In contrast, reason-based legitimation rests not on the conviction that the constitution is constitutive of our collective identity, but simply on the conviction that it is a good constitution; it serves our interests and/or effectively promotes our well-being.

As indicated above, the conventional reservations applying to any dichotomy (except perhaps in logics) should also apply here as well. The dichotomy between the two modes of legitimation is not a sharp dichotomy; it is often the case that legitimation rests on both representational and reason-based modes of legitimation. Often the judgement that a constitution is legitimate on representational grounds and the judgement that it is legitimate on reason-based grounds are interrelated. Typically, different political and social movements use both representational arguments and reason-based arguments to justify their allegiance to a particular constitutional order. Further, the balance between these two types of legitimation can shift in time such that a constitution that has been primarily legitimated on reason-based grounds may eventually be transformed and be legitimated on representational grounds and vice versa.

Although there is no direct reference to these concepts in *Revolutionary Constitutionalism*, Ackerman thinks of legitimation primarily in terms of representational legitimation. This is not surprising given that the US is perhaps the primary example of a constitution that is legitimated on representational grounds; it is the will of the American people which provides the foundations for the normative force of the US Constitution. To illustrate the representational force of the US Constitution, Ackerman analogised the US Constitution to a non-realistic picture which may represent the deeper dimensions of one's identity – ones which may not be represented by a photograph.[4] Representational legitimation hinges on popular endorsement. In order to be genuinely representative, the constitution needs to be accepted by the public and to be constantly present in the public sphere; its meaning needs to be constantly debated and used in political debates. Such an

[4] Ackerman, *supra* note 1 at 1028. Ackerman differentiates there between mimetic representation and semiotic representation. He describes the difference between the two as follows: 'On the one hand you may find somebody with photographic aspirations, who might provide an image of you as you appear at the present moment [mimetic representation]. This mimetic kind of representation has familiar advantages and disadvantages … Perhaps an artist who self-consciously appreciates that he *cannot* reduce your living reality to a piece of paper-that he is *only* providing a representation-will paint a portrait that, while less realistic, will nevertheless convey a deeper meaning to its audience [semiotic representation].'

understanding of constitutions is deeply ingrained in the US constitutional law scholarship.

Needless to say, what counts as popular endorsement (sufficient for representation) is controversial. Populists believe that ideally, representation requires the representative to accurately mirror the actual preferences and judgements of her constituents. In his previous work Ackerman effectively rebutted this view.[5] Recently, Ofer Malcai and I supported his view and argued that this view fails to acknowledge the complexity of preferences and judgements; for instance, the prevalence of conditional and second-order preferences. More specifically, we argued that representation may require the representative to decide (or vote) against the view of the represented as long as the decision is justifiable to the represented.[6] Representation is about taking seriously *the perspective of the represented*, looking at the world from *the standpoint of the represented* etc. Theories of representation differ in terms of what they perceive to be the authentic perspective of the represented, but they all aim to capture what it means for one person to act in the name of another. Representational constitutionalism cherishes the view that the constitution is ultimately legitimated by representing the people.[7]

But representation is not the only mode of constitutional legitimation. Reason-based constitutions are legitimate, despite not being representational. They are legitimated by virtue of being perceived as good, just, efficacious or desirable on other grounds that do not presuppose representational legitimacy. It is therefore the (perceived) virtues of the constitution and/or its justness rather than the active endorsement of the constitution by the people which provides the basis for legitimation.

Before illustrating the significance of this distinction, let me draw a distinction between two types of reason-based legitimation: substantive reason-based legitimation and institutional/procedural reason-based arguments. Substantive reason-based legitimation rests on the conviction that the *content* of the constitutional provisions is just, that these provisions protect the right values and entrench the right norms etc. The justness of these norms is the reason why one should adhere to them and be guided by them. Institutional/procedural legitimation rests on the belief that the constitutional form in itself is desirable. Hence, the constitution is valuable not only or primarily because it protects or promotes the right values, but also because it protects these values in the right way.[8]

[5] See Ackerman, *supra* note 1.

[6] Alon Harel & Ofer Malchai, Populism, Elitism and Private Reason (unpublished manuscript).

[7] For a classical work differentiating between different conceptions of representation, see Hana Pitkin, The Concept of Representation (1972).

[8] The first type of reason-based legitimation (substantive reason-based legitimation) needs no special explanation. In order to be legitimated, constitutional documents need to include provisions which are perceived to be just or at least not to be perceived as unjust. Most typically, the constitution is understood often as entrenching pre-political rights – rights that existed prior to the polity and the constitution merely entrenches them within the legal order. The more interesting and less obvious reason-based legitimation is the procedural/institutional reason-based legitimation. In *Why Law Matters*, I argued that the *constitutional* protection of rights that rests on the binding normative

To sum up the discussion so far, I argued that there are two modes of legitimation: representational legitimation and non-representational or reason-based legitimation. The former rests on the conviction that the constitution is an embodiment of the values of the polity. Under representational legitimation, our allegiance to the constitution rests upon the fact that it is our constitution, that we participated in shaping it, that it reflects the values that constitute us as a community etc. The latter simply maintains that the constitution is grounded in reason. Under reason-based legitimation, our allegiance to the constitution rests upon the fact that it promulgates the right values both substantively and procedurally/institutionally.

To show the relevance of reason-based legitimation (and perhaps more accurately the incompleteness of accounts that rest purely on representational legitimation), the next section considers two examples illustrating the usefulness of the distinction drawn above between the two forms of legitimation.

III. Illustrations: Germany and Israel

This section uses the dichotomy between representational and reason-based legitimation to shed light on three major issues. I first examine the grounds for the success of the German Constitution and argue that the German Constitution is a non-representational one. I later show the relevance of this dichotomy in shedding light on the contemporary debates between populists and liberals. Lastly, I use the distinction between representational and non-representational legitimation to investigate the contemporary debates in Israel concerning the status of the Israeli basic laws and the powers of the court.

force of constitutions is superior not because it is more effective in protecting rights or protecting democracy or realising any other contingent ends, but because it protects these ends for the right reasons or in the right way. The key element in this analysis is what I labelled 'binding constitutionalism'. Constitutional entrenchment of rights facilitates public recognition that the protection of rights is the state's duty rather than a mere discretionary gesture on its part, namely that the state has no discretion but to honour these rights. The rationale underlying binding rights-based constitutionalism is grounded in the significance of the public recognition of rights-based duties binding the legislature. It rests on the importance of the publicly salient differentiation between discretionary legislative decisions (namely those decisions that are grounded in the legislature's inclinations/preferences/taste and judgments) and those decisions that are grounded in the legislature's rights-based duties. It is one thing to be granted a right because the people regard it as desirable and wish to grant you the right or even believe it is mandatory on their part to give you the right; however, it is another thing to be granted a right by a constitution or by a court which, in effect, pronounces that the people have no power to deprive you of the right because it is a right that is so fundamental that it is not subject to the contingencies of majoritarian legislation. Constitutional entrenchment is appealing not because it successfully entrenches *the right values*, but because it successfully *entrenches* the right values. The Constitution is legitimate because it is the right form by which our rights should be respected (rather than because we chose it). This analysis can be classified as a reason-based source of legitimacy of constitutions. For a detailed exposition of this view, see Alon Harel, Why Law Matters (2014) 147–90.

A. The German Constitution

Ackerman describes the German Constitution (as well as other 'elitist' constitutions) as a constitution that was constructed 'by elites at a time when the masses were overwhelmed by the defeat in the war'.[9] He continues to ask: what is the source of legitimation of these constitutions? Why is the German Constitution which has never been properly endorsed by the German people so stable and robust?

Perhaps Ackerman exaggerates the German case. Admittedly, as he notes, the outlines of the German Constitution were dictated by the Allies. The conditions set by the Allies included the requirement that the constitution be democratic, establish a federal order and protect basic rights. But it was also understood by the Allies that if the new constitution were to succeed, it ought to be established in cooperation with the German people rather than imposed on them.[10] Yet, despite this qualification, Ackerman is right that the German Constitution was not the exclusive product or creation of the German people. The Constitution that was ultimately adopted was subject to the approval of the Allies, who used their powers to dictate changes in it. Ackerman asks the following question: how can a constitution that was endorsed under these conditions be legitimated? In addressing this puzzle, he says:

> But in some cases, this question is buried so deeply in political consciousness that it fails to provoke collective anxiety. This is precisely the situation in Germany today. How has the country avoided a serious confrontation with the fact that its Basic Law of 1949 created under military conditions that severely compromised its claims to authenticity?[11]

I am keen to know how Ackerman would address this puzzle, but to find out, we should wait for the future volumes of his monumental enterprise. In a rare attempt to address this puzzle, one of the former Justices of the German Court asserted that: 'Allied intervention did not succeed in branding the basic law with the stain of an instrument imposed by the occupying powers.'[12] Here I wish to suggest an answer that is simpler than that realised by Ackerman; the German Constitution is legitimated not by virtue of popular assent or endorsement that rests on the conviction that it is constitutive of German values or on a ceremonial referendum that conveys the voluntary allegiance of the German people to the constitution or on any other form of representational legitimacy. Instead, it is legitimated on the grounds that it is believed to be desirable on both substantive and institutional

[9] Ackerman, *supra* note 1 at 7.
[10] See David P. Currie, The Constitution of the Federal Republic of Germany 9–10 (1994).
[11] Ackerman, *supra* note 1 at 19.
[12] *Id.* at 10.

reasons. The German Court has explicitly sided with the reason-based view when it argued:

> Laws are not constitutional merely because they have been passed in conformity with procedural provisions … They must be substantively compatible with the highest values of a free and democratic order, i.e. the constitutional order of values, and must also conform to unwritten fundamental constitutional principles as well as the fundamental decisions of the Basic Law.[13]

Acknowledging that not all constitutions are representational explains a fundamental difference between US citizens' and German citizens' attitude to constitutionalism. The former hail the Constitution as a great achievement of their own; they study its provisions in school, debate its meanings in the media and often justify their political positions on constitutional grounds. It is the constant popular engagement with the constitutional provisions which facilitates the constitutional patriotism that is characteristic of the US. In contrast, traditionally German citizens are not engaged in debating the substantive provisions of their constitution; instead, they defer to the expertise of the Constitutional Court and accept its determinations as binding.[14] Their deference to the Court relies at least in part on the German (understandable) distrust of representative institutions. History has taught the German people that representative institutions may fall prey to brutal extremism and the deference to the Court rests on the conviction that the Court is an institution that may protect the polity from such risks.[15]

I suggest that this difference in attitudes between US citizens and German citizens is also attributable to the difference between the two forms of legitimation: representational legitimation in the US context and reason-based legitimation in the German context. Representational legitimation requires constant engagement with the constitution; after all, the legitimacy of the constitution hinges on the *enduring* commitment of the people to the constitution. Commitment presupposes knowledge, understanding and constant engagement. In contrast, non-representational legitimation may rest upon trust in the judgements of elite institutions such as the court. After all, non-representational constitutions do not rest upon the active endorsement of the constitution, but upon a judgement that the constitution is conducive to the right values. To the extent that the Court is trusted, active engagement with the constitution is not necessary for its legitimacy.

[13] 6 BverfGE 32 [109]. For a translation of this case, see: https://law.utexas.edu/transnational/foreign-law-translations/german/case.php?id=610.

[14] Research has shown that the German Constitutional Court is very popular and enjoys broad public support. See, eg, James L. Gibson et al, *On the Legitimacy of High Courts*, 92 Am. Pol. Sci. Rev. 343–58 (1998). For the distinct attitudes of Germans towards their Constitution and the Constitutional Court, see also *German Constitutional Culture in Transition*, 14 Cardozo L. Rev. 711, 724–25 (1992); James L. Gibson & Gregory A. Caldeira, *Defenders of Democracy? Legitimacy, Popular Acceptance and the South African Constitutional Court*, 65 J. Pol. 1, 5 (2003).

[15] See, eg, Georg Vanberg, The Politics of Constitutional Review in Germany 8–12 (2005).

The fundamental difference between the US and the German Constitution can be further understood given the different timings in the history of the nations that the respective constitutions were written and ratified. The US Constitution was accepted at a time of great confidence in the virtues of the American people and their ability to govern themselves. In contrast, the German Constitution was written not only after military defeat but also at a time in which the Germans distrusted the virtues and even the sanity of their own nation. As a matter of fact, the German Constitution can be regarded as a tool to counter all attempts to embody a national entity; it can therefore be described as an anti-representational constitution. When the German Constitution was established, the most urgent task was to distance the new state from the nation establishing it (rather than represent it).

The ideal of representation rests upon a conviction in the prior existence of some pre-existing entity that is *worth representing* and there was no such entity to represent in Germany in 1949. The less representative the constitution was, the better. In contrast, at the time that the US Constitution was ratified, the US nation had traditions which it was willing to endorse and entrench, hence the establishment of a representational constitution.

The US Constitution is legitimate because it is the constitution of the people of the US – one which they shaped in light of their own distinctive values and aspirations and which they sustain by virtue of their allegiance to these values. In contrast, the German Constitution is legitimate simply because it is a good and a stable constitution. It is good both in its substantive content, but, more importantly, it is also good because of the stability and trustworthiness of the institutions it created and that are in charge of interpreting it.

B. Populism, Liberalism and the Israeli Constitutional Revolution

Let me use a second example illustrating the contrast between representational legitimacy and reason-based legitimation. To do so, I will first make a broad generalisation and later turn to explore the ways in which the two modes of legitimation operate in the Israeli context.

A prominent characteristic of contemporary democracies is the persistent conflict between populism and liberalism.[16] The traditional concern of populists is the concern for representation. I will argue that the current cultural and political conflicts concerning populism and liberalism can often be conceptualised as a conflict between representational and reason-based legitimation. Populism considers political representation to be a substitute for direct, personal democratic

[16] The contrast was examined and investigated by Margaret Cannovan, *Trust the People! Populism and the Two Faces of Democracy*, XLVII Political Studies 2 (1999). For another recent and influential attempt to capture the contrast between the two, see Jan-Werner Muller, What is Populism? (2016).

participation; it purports to give effect to the people's actual will and its primary ambition is to represent the people as realistically as possible.[17] In the language of Ackerman, populists care about mimetic representation.[18]

Populism is not the only theory of representational legitimacy, but it is a theory that cherishes a certain form of representation under which representatives are (presumptively) required to make the very same decisions as members of the public would make were they to occupy a political office. This explains why populism is highly critical of intermediate institutions (such as activist courts, the media or non-governmental organisations (NGOs)) which place limits on representatives, labelling such institutions as elitist.[19] On this view, courts exercising judicial review illegitimately obstruct representation, while the media and NGOs distort the people's authentic voice.[20] It is the duty of deputies in a democracy to take the duty of representation seriously, ie, to take seriously the convictions and preferences of voters. It is this 'democratic' intuition that explains the appeal of contemporary populist politics.[21]

In contrast, many liberals retort that representation may conflict with other central concerns of the liberal state: equality and/or freedom, protection of minorities, dignity etc. Liberals also emphasise the centrality of intermediate institutions which are not purely representative: courts, the media etc. The ambition to represent the people is often mitigated by the recognition that there are values that limit the powers of the people, hence the common accusation that liberal institutions suffer from a 'democratic deficit', that they fail to be responsive to popular sentiments or, in other words, that they fail to be representative.

I do not claim that there is a complete convergence between, on the one hand, populist arguments and representational legitimation and, on the other, between liberals and reason-based legitimation. Liberals often raise representational arguments; more particularly, they challenge the populist understanding of representation.[22] For instance, it is argued that representation requires differentiating

[17] G. Hermet, Les populismes dans le monde. Une histoire sociologique. XIXe–XXe siècle 50 (2001), cited in Cesare Pinelli, *The Populist Challenge to Constitutional Democracy*, 7 Eur. Const. L. Rev. 5, 11 (2011).

[18] See Ackerman, *supra* note 1.

[19] See Muller, *supra* note 16 at 2.

[20] Israeli politicians frequently make the accusation that the media is 'leftist' and that NGOs act as 'moles', even prompting legislation aimed to constrain the ability of NGOs to raise funds. See Ruth Eglash and William Booth, *Israeli NGOs Decry 'Deeply Anti-democratic Move' as New Law Approved*, Washington Post, July 12, 2016, https://www.washingtonpost.com/world/israeli-ngos-decry-deeply-anti-democratic-move-as-new-law-approved/2016/07/12/a07b1bdb-a431-4fce-b76d-d0a35dfca519_story.html?utm_term=.0987f3bc7028.

[21] This does not imply that populist leaders conform to the ideals they cherish. In an ironic reaction to the pretension of President Trump to speak for the people, the political scientist Cas Mudde argued that: 'Where populist leaders claim to be vox populi, the voice of the people Trump is the voice of Trump.' See Cas Mudde, *The Blog: The Power of Populism? Not Really!*, Huffpost, Feb. 13, 2016, www.huffingtonpost.com/cas-mudde/the-power-of-populism-not_b_9226736.html. Hence, Mudde concludes that Trump cannot be classified as a populist.

[22] See Harel & Malchai, *supra* note 6.

between deeper and more long-standing convictions which merit greater respect than mere short-term whims. According to this view, intermediate institutions such as courts can be more representational than traditional representational entities such as the legislature.[23] It is also the case that sophisticated populists sometimes raise reason-based arguments. For instance, it is claimed that the people have the intellectual tools and the wisdom necessary to render the right decisions.[24] Yet, as I show, the Israeli experience suggests that populists often use representational arguments, while liberals are often inclined to use reason-based arguments.

The most vocal opponents of the Israeli constitutional revolution of the 1990s use predominantly representational arguments. In their view, the Israeli constitutional revolution – in particular, the enactment of the two basic laws protecting rights and conferring the power of judicial review to the courts – is wrong because these basic laws have never been accepted or endorsed by the citizenry of the country.[25] In contrast, the most vocal proponents of the constitutional revolution use reason-based arguments. They argue that the constitutional revolution protects minorities, promotes justice, is conducive to freedoms etc. They also argue that courts are better institutions to make such decisions than legislatures.

The representational arguments opposing the granting of the power of judicial review have been raised in the Knesset prior to the legislation of the basic laws. The Knesset members themselves raised the concern that entrenching a constitution may be anti-democratic. Thus, it was argued:

> How could it be that we would enact such a law in the Knesset without being aware that the idea in the background is usurpation, taking the powers of the Knesset and the legislature and granting them to the Supreme Court.[26]

The representational argument against judicial review is described by Shuki Segev as follows:

> [T]he new basic laws were enacted by a very small majority, they did not engage the positive aspect of constitutional making. No special procedures were followed and no special majority was formed that could have overcome past disagreements about how to achieve popular ratification or how to symbolize the formation of a broad consensus.[27]

Segev and other opponents of the constitutional revolution therefore presuppose that the legitimacy of a constitution must be representational. They thus preclude

[23] For such a view, see, eg, Robert Alexy, *Balancing, Constitutional Review and Representation* 3 International Journal of Constitutional Review 572 (2005). Alexy believes that 'the only way to reconcile constitutional review with democracy is to conceive of it, too, as representation of the people'.

[24] This is the view of the Israeli Minister of Justice Ayelet Shaked in her manifesto. See Ayelet Shaked, *The Path to Democracy and Governance* 1 Hashiloach 37, 54 (2016, in Hebrew).

[25] For a discussion of these basic law and their constitutional ramifications, see David Kretzmer, *The New Basic Laws on Human Rights: A Mini-Revolution in Israeli Constitutional Law* 26 Israel L. Rev. 238 (1992).

[26] DK Knesset member Michael Ethan (1991) 1247 (Isr.).

[27] Joshua Segev, *Who Needs a Constitution? In Defense of the Non-constitution Constitution-Making Tactic in Israel*, 70 Albany L. Rev. 409 (2007).

the very legitimacy of a constitution such as the German Constitution, which does not rest on representational grounds.

Politicians also frame their opposition to the Court and also to the discretion of public officials in terms of representational legitimation. Minister of Justice Ayelet Shaked argued:

> I believe that the people and their representatives are those who ought to express the will of the people and that they ought to have the final say in the public sphere. The government is no one's contractor. It is committed only to the people a majority of whom voted for it … [The government] is committed to a people who seeks to determine its fate *directly* and through its representatives.[28]

The most forceful and rhetorically powerful expression of this view was made by Justice Cheshin in his concurrence in the highly important case which first established the power of the Israeli court to review legislation. In *United Mizrachi Bank v Migdal*, Justice Cheshin argued:

> Indeed, even those supporting the adoption a constitution should tread carefully … Let a constitution be drafted and submitted for a referendum. Let the constitution be adopted in a process of six readings spread out over the two Knessets. Let any act be done, provided that it involves a substantial deviation from regular legislative proceedings, and provided that the people are involved in the enactment of the constitution. All of these are legitimate acts, and we will acquiesce to them and cherish them. But with all my might I will oppose our recognition of the Knesset's authority to enact a constitution by force of a judicial ruling, via a legal analysis of a document dating back forty seven years, in reliance on disputed conceptions which have no firm roots in Israeli society. And where is the people? Should we not ask its opinion? On the contrary, let us call the people and consult them … I cannot agree to enacting a constitution without consulting the people.[29]

In contrast, Chief Justice Barak – the most vocal representative of the constitutional revolution argued on reason-based grounds that:

> In my opinion every branch of government, including the judiciary, must use the power granted to it to protect the constitution and democracy. The judiciary and each of its judges must safeguard both formal democracy, as expressed in legislative supremacy and substantive democracy, as expressed in basic values and human rights.[30]

Justice Aharon Barak also believes that: 'Democracy has its own internal morality, based on equality and dignity of all human beings.'[31] Hence, in his view:

> [T]here is no (real) democracy without recognition of basic values and principles such as morality and justice. Above all democracy cannot exist without the protection of

[28] See Shaked, *supra* note 24 (emphasis added).

[29] CA 6821/93 United Mizrahi Bank v. Migdal Cooperative Village. For the decision in English, see: http://versa.cardozo.yu.edu/opinions/united-mizrahi-bank-v-migdal-cooperative-village.

[30] Aharon Barak, *A Judge on Judging: The Role of the Supreme Court in a Democracy*, 116 Harv. L. Rev. 16, 26 (2002).

[31] *Id.* at 39.

> individual human rights – rights so essential that they must be insulated from the power of the majority.[32]

To amplify this hypothesis, let us also mention the response of Justice Aharon Barak to the procedural requirements set by Justice Cheshin:

> It is true that no special appeal was made to the public to approve the text of the Basic Laws, as it developed in the course of the Knesset debates over the years. But such an appeal was not necessary. It may be desirable, but it is not indispensable. Direct appeal to the nation is one method of adopting a constitution, and perhaps the most desirable. But this is not the only method and it involves considerable difficulty. The constitutional history of many nations recognizes constitutions that derived authority from the nation but were not presented for direct national approval.[33]

It is evident that Justice Barak believes at least partly in the necessity of a non-representational constitution – a constitution whose value rests on its just content, hence the concern raised by representational constitutionalists such as Justice Cheshin that the constitution must rest on the will of the people is constrained by the conviction that reason sets limits to the will of the people. Consequently, the symbolic procedural requirements indicating popular acceptance such as a referendum or 'six readings spread over two Knessets' that are regarded by Justice Cheshin as essential are not regarded as such by Justice Barak.[34]

Therefore, it seems that the debate between, on the one hand, Justice Cheshin and other jurists who claim that the Israeli Basic Laws do not grant the courts the power of judicial review and, on the other hand, Justice Barak and the jurists who claim that the basic laws empower the court to invalidate legislation should be (at least partly) conceptualised as a dispute between representational constitutionalists and non-representational constitutionalists. This also explains why the former regard popular referenda and other rituals of this sort as essential, while the latter deny the significance of such ceremonial gestures.

Note again some qualifications to these observations. First, I do not claim that there is a necessary connection between liberalism and reason-based legitimation on the one hand and populism and representational legitimation on the other. At most, we can speak of a natural disposition which is reflected in the Israeli public discourse. Second, I do not claim that as an empirical matter, liberals use only reason-based arguments and populists use only representational arguments. Associating populism with representational legitimacy and liberalism with reason-based legitimation is a generalisation, but it is a generalisation that is supported by observing the Israeli public discourse concerning the constitution. Third, the populist opponents of the constitutional revolution have been shown not to be

[32] *Id.*

[33] *Supra* note 26.

[34] Interestingly, to support his view, Justice Barak mentions the German Constitution and the fact that it was not endorsed by the people in accordance with the requirements regarded as necessary by Justice Cheshin.

consistent in their own urge for representational legitimacy. Recent developments in Israel indicate that the opponents of the constitutional revolution are not always faithful to their own convictions.

Just a few months before this chapter was written, the Knesset has adopted a new basic law which was supported by precisely those populists who complained bitterly about the non-representational foundations of the constitutional revolution: Basic Law: Israel as the Nation-State of the Jewish People (2018). The law that is supposed to entrench Israel as a Jewish state was passed by a very small margin (62 in favour and 55 against). So while most of the supporters of this law complain about the small margin in which the previous basic laws have been passed (and draw the conclusion that they are not sufficiently representational and therefore illegitimate), they have not followed their own judicial philosophy: short-term interests, hypocrisy and most likely intellectual dishonesty of monstrous magnitude led the supporters of the new Basic Law to act against their own philosophical inclinations. But these reservations do not undermine the basic observation that opponents of the constitutional revolution seem to adhere to the conviction that only representation can lend legitimacy to the constitution and that the basic laws and, in particular, the judicial interpretations of these laws are not sufficiently representational. They therefore deny (or, more accurately, ignore the very possibility of reason-based legitimation).

Underneath the conflict between liberals and populists lurks a disagreement concerning the philosophical question whether ultimately the constitution ought to be legitimated on representational or reason-based grounds. In a previous engagement with the work of Ackerman, I argued that:

> The debate between Ackerman and myself is a very old debate: the debate between reason and will as the foundation of law. Thomas Aquinas believed that law is 'an ordinance of reason'. Jean Jacques Rousseau equated the law with the general will and argued that the general will can never be wrong. It seems that legal theory will continue in different ways to move from one pole (reason) to the other (general will). I urge you (despite the seductive beauty of Rousseau prose) to join Aquinas' camp – the camp of law as an ordinance of reason.[35]

It seems to me that ultimately the debate between the two modes of legitimation is a reincarnation of this earlier debate. Admittedly, the previous debate was a normative debate, while the current debate is a descriptive debate, but the structural features of these debates is similar. Ackerman presupposes that legitimation must rest on representational grounds. While his perception of representation is a sophisticated one, the force of the constitution needs to be grounded in the conviction that it is *our* constitution, that it is *we* who created it and therefore that we are bound by it. In contrast, I argue that a different source of legitimation

[35] See Alon Harel, *Why Constitutional Law Matters: Between Popular Sovereignty and Reason: Comments on We the People Vol III*, 13 Jerusalem Review of Legal Studies 31 (2016).

is that the constitution is just both substantively and institutionally/procedurally. The controversy concerning the Israeli constitutional revolution is to a large extent (although not exclusively) not only a practical or a legal debate about the powers of courts and judicial review; it is also a philosophical debate as to the groundings of legitimation. Should legitimation rest on representational grounds or can legitimation rest on reason-based grounds? I urge Israelis to join the latter camp.

This comment is based on the lessons of Ackerman's own work. Like Ackerman, this comment rejected monism and it showed that there are two types rather than one type of legitimation. It also rejected the other vice condemned by Ackerman: judge-mentalism. Ackerman, I believe, has not been fully faithful to his own view under which one has to separate sharply between the descriptive and the normative aspects of constitutionalism. Ultimately his allegiance to representational legitimation rests on his own normative commitments stemming from his experience as a great scholar of the US Constitution. I therefore follow Ackerman's lead with respect to each of the virtues I identified at the outset of this comment: the rejection of monism and the rejection of judge-mentalism. I believe my analysis of the two modes of legitimation follows strictly Ackerman's own lead – perhaps even more strictly than he does.

3

Constitutionalism and Society

Ackerman on Worldwide Constitution-Making and the Role of Social Forces

DENIS BARANGER

I. Republican Narratives

A. On Constitutionalism

Revolutionary Constitutions raises important questions about constitutionalism. Ackerman is an unapologetic supporter of the classical principles of constitutionalism. He makes no mystery of the fact that his standpoint is a defence of those core values for which, as he says in passing, he has fought all his life. There remains, it seems, some hope of establishing 'Enlightenment political order[s]',[1] Ackerman's own version of what Locke – at the dawn of the constitutionalist era – had chosen for his part to call 'well-ordered commonwealths'. The book reads as a eulogy of 'political constitutionalism'. The very nature of Ackerman's project – of which *Revolutionary Constitutions* is only, we are told, the first instalment – is to discuss the destiny of the principles, values and core mechanisms of constitutionalism in the modern world. In the course of the twentieth century, some key events took place outside the perimeter of 'liberal democracies'. In Central and Eastern Europe, communist regimes collapsed after 1989 and the opportunity was given to countries of the former Eastern Bloc to develop their own domestic version of constitutionalism. In non-Western countries – very well represented in *Revolutionary Constitutions* by South Africa, India, Burma and Iran – new working versions of constitutionalism have had to be devised in original contexts.

[1] Bruce Ackerman, Revolutionary Constitutions: Charismatic Leadership and the Rule of Law (2019) 296.

A major virtue of *Revolutionary Constitutions* consists in the fact that it enables us to incorporate those new experiences into our approaches. Comparative constitutional law becomes a richer and more diverse enterprise – and also a much more intellectually challenging one – for it. The key to all the experiments depicted in the book is Ackerman's ability to identify 'revolutions' in several contemporary contexts for which that denomination is not self-evident, as in the case of de Gaulle's France in 1958 or Israel during the 1990s. Ackerman does a convincing job of showing these revolutions as meaningful developments in the wider history of constitutionalism. This is not trivial. The standard approach in constitutional law seems to treat the American or the French eighteenth-century events as the only 'revolutions' deserving to be analysed in textbooks and scholarly research. Few of us would have thought it necessary to factor in the case of Khomeini's Iran, Mandela's South Africa or the Burmese constitutional experiment. Yet constitutional law is inherently a comparative subject. Any constitutional development in any given country is likely – at least potentially – to shed light on the meaning of the discipline's core concepts. However, in the light of the generalisation of the idea and practice of written constitutions, evidence had to be shown that a variety of political systems around the world needed to be considered. This is what *Revolutionary Constitutions* accomplishes with its several comparative case studies, all the more so as some of these sample countries have 'repudiated western constitutionalism'[2] or at least 'downplayed' Western constitutional values. The book thus offers a rich and meaningful discussion of the destiny of constitutionalism in the global (or at least 'pre-global') era. I say 'pre-global' as there is precious little in the book that would convince us that such constitutional experiments are anything but *domestic* ones. Ackerman's larger project may be about the 'global constitution', but so far there is little in *Revolutionary Constitutions* to support the views of the followers of the cosmopolitan cult. In a much subtler way – and, to my mind, closer to the true reason why constitutional law is indeed a global experiment – the book shows how constitutional values and mechanisms are at the same time universal and in need of local adaptations. This is an old lesson, from Aristotle's natural law to Montesquieu's *expériences universelles*. Yet old lessons need to be taught again when they are lost sight of. This is one of the book's most significant accomplishments. What, then, has happened to constitutionalism in this process of worldwide expansion? At least two things.

First, Enlightenment values have not lost their appeal. Ackerman shows how Western constitutional values have spread outside of – and sometimes against the will of – Western countries. They may even have been revived in the process. This is the lesson from some impressive restatements of revolutionary constitutional values, as in the case of South Africa. Ackerman rightly insists on the remarkable statement by Albie Sachs on the need to let the people decide on their own constitution and not let a 'group of experts' draft it once and for all at a time when

[2] *Id.* at 324.

the South African people is not able to express their will. 'It is hard', as Ackerman notes, 'to imagine a more self-conscious statement of the core principles of revolutionary constitutionalism.'[3]

Second, these various constitutional experiments shed an important light on the meaning of constitutionalism generally speaking. Ackerman makes the point that Western constitutional values are not all there is to constitutionalism. Rather, a certain principled practice of power seems to be more characteristic of constitutionalism than the acknowledgement of the values of the American or French Revolutions of the eighteenth century. This is certainly one of the book's key lessons: constitutionalism 'is not synonymous with liberalism'. In this regard, the Iranian case study could not have been better chosen. Where do you find a nation in which Western values have been so strongly repudiated, yet in which institutional checks and balances, in addition with a carefully designed representative system, have been more consciously established? The Iranian case is relevant because it allows us to analytically distinguish *values* and *mechanisms* in constitutional law. There has been constitutional law ever since it has been understood that power was necessary to balance power and thus to avoid arbitrariness, which stems from confusion and concentration of power. Liberal pluralist democracy and human rights are not the necessary premises of this mode of reasoning; it existed before their generalisation in Europe and America's 'constitutional revolutions', and it can exist without them. 'The rise of world constitutionalism' can thus thrust its roots in those constitutional mechanisms without entailing adhering to Western values. There might be a limit to this and one would be tempted to think that separation of powers and Western individualist values (enshrined in our declarations of human rights) are tightly bound together, in such a way as to make the one quite dependent on the other. Yet the Iranian regime might well be a good example of 'weak' (or low-key) separation of powers in a non-Western context.

B. Constitutional Change

The quality and sheer breadth of Ackerman's narratives – which at times make the book read like a chain of historical monographs or a series of captivating political short novels – should not make us underestimate the underlying conceptual structure that he carefully puts in place in the book. This may be *political* history, but at the same time this is always *conceptual* history, and this is why *Revolutionary Constitutions* can be a valuable contribution to *constitutional* history. In fact, in its style and purpose, the book is reminiscent of traditional 'constitutional history' as it was practised in nineteenth-century (especially *English*, not to say typically *Whig*) European scholarship, at the time as that kind of intellectual pursuit was central to constitutional law. The way in which Ackerman sets out the comparative

[3] *Id.* at 88.

history of certain political regimes over the course of their modern history even has something in common with what used to be called 'philosophical history' in the eighteenth century, a type of scholarly exercise epitomised, for instance, in the work of David Hume or Adam Ferguson, hence the unapologetic historicism displayed in *Revolutionary Constitutions*, as is evidenced by the 'four steps' theory of how political regimes are exposed to change.

How do constitutions evolve? This question stands at the centre of *Revolutionary Constitutions*, as well as perhaps the entire Ackermanian corpus: 'the point of this book is to show how revolutionary dynamics … leads actors to straddle the positivist line in unconventional ways … mixing legal and illegal appeals … to establish their authority'.[4] As a matter of fact, this is of course the very same underlying question as the one which stood at the very core of *We the People*: what is constitutional change? Should we not consider constitutions as multi-faceted phenomena that are by no means sufficiently explained by the classical skills of lawyers studying 'lawyers' law'? Rather, should not a constitution be analysed as a historical object, subject to a complex process of constitutional change in which political and social factors play a major role, while the ordinary 'legal' (or 'conventional') instruments – such as constitutional amendments, superstatutes or landmark cases – appear to mark moments of consolidation rather than moments of historical creativity?

Revolutionary Constitutions answers that very same question with a carefully chosen set of historical case studies. Ackerman has faith in political narrative as a useful heuristic device in comparative constitutional law. He does not have recourse to such a stylistic device for its own sake, but rather with a view to developing a scheme of constitutional change and constitutional stabilisation, which, the author claims, is similar in otherwise vastly different political systems. The book's purpose is to set up a common framework for comparing 'constitutional revolutions of the twentieth century'. One cannot underestimate the quality of Ackerman's political and historical analyses. They are reminiscent of the political chronicles of classical republican authors, from the Roman chroniclers to Machiavelli, especially as they emphasise the role of *Fortuna* in the making of political institutions. One does not have to choose between the two options famously adumbrated in Hamilton's first *Federalist Letter*: conscious choice versus historical contingencies. Certainly, the book shows that, in the words of Publius, 'societies of men are really capable or not of establishing good government from reflection and choice'. The book, from beginning to end, is a meditation on this very theme and a eulogy of those heroic founding men and women who have done so across the world. At the same time, Ackerman does not rule out the possibility that, despite Hamilton's hopeful words, communities of men might in fact be 'destined to depend for their political constitutions on accident and force'. Historical accidents, as well as the limits of men's historical intelligence and moral virtue, also participate in shaping

[4] *Id.* at 313.

human institutions. History is contingent, and this is precisely why it matters to constitutional law. Constitutionalism has a history – it *is* a history – and one which is not only made up of landmark cases and formal amendments to entrenched constitutions. No amount of casuistic exegesis or Langdell-like Socratic teaching will apprise us of the fate of a constitution in times of peril and upheavals. Doing so is not an exercise that should be confined to the columns of daily newspapers or to historical monographs. *Revolutionary Constitutions* shows why (and how) great twentieth-century political crises were at the same time constitutional ones.

In order to do so, Ackerman narrates how revolutions occur in republican polities. With *Revolutionary Constitutions*, one is reminded of those English republican writers of the early eighteenth century who, like Robert Molesworth in his *Account of Denmark*, exerted so much influence on the American Revolution. The analogy may seem a little far-fetched, yet there is a distinctively classical republican flavour to *Revolutionary Constitutions*. This should not come as a surprise to the Ackermanian reader. The reader meets again old acquaintances, such as those 'mobilized citizenries' (a neo-Harringtonian[5] vocabulary which Caroline Robbins' English *commonwealthmen* and Gordon Wood's American founding fathers would certainly not have disapproved of) which had already mattered so much in *We the People*. As a matter of fact, *Revolutionary Constitutions* significantly expands this portrait gallery of historical actors whose destiny it is to establish political communities and manoeuvre the ship of the state in hard times. The lesson of classical republicanism is that those perilous moments are also ripe with opportunities. In the course of a nation's history, it is the responsibility of men – great individuals, 'movement-parties', as well as entire societies – to build their own polity. Yet *Fortuna* is always likely to strike: things can go wrong or conversely chance can lend a benevolent hand. Or maybe both things can happen at the same time. There can be, in Ackerman's own words, 'lost moments' or conversely times at which windfall profits are reaped thanks to good timing. In any case, constituent power never takes the form of a single moment; it is an ongoing process which is dependent on circumstances (see the case of Israel). In certain cases, countries get 'lost in time' (Poland and South Africa) and miss their chance to constitutionalise human rights or put down in writing a more favourable arrangement of power or forces. 'Races against time'[6] are sometimes successful (Iran) or, maybe more often, they end up with a defeat (Burma, Poland and Israel) due to the blindness or lack of virtue of some otherwise towering personalities. This is, for instance, the lesson of Ackerman's admirable portrait of Ben-Gurion, which has reminded me of an

[5] I do not think I have ever seen the adjective 'neo-Harringtonian' being used outside the writings of J.G.A. Pocock: see especially JOHN GRENVILLE AGARD POCOCK, VIRTUE, COMMERCE AND HISTORY (1985) and of course THE MACHIAVELLIAN MOMENT FLORENTINE POLITICAL THOUGHT AND THE ATLANTIC REPUBLICAN TRADITION (1975). The adjective refers to the use by republican writers and politicians of some republican themes (such as the dread of standing armies, rotation of power or the eulogy of active citizens' involvement in politics) by eighteenth-century readers of James Harrington.

[6] ACKERMAN at 289.

anecdote once told by an Israeli friend: at the end of Ben-Gurion's life, an Israeli newspaper published a satirical cartoon showing the great man, a big hammer in his hand, busy crushing his own statue. In a sense, destroying one's own achievement and ruining one's claim to posterity is also what de Gaulle did after 1968, not to speak of some of the more disreputable associates of Mandela who went on to run South Africa after his departure from power. This is an inherent danger of charisma.

II. Constitutions at the Level of Society

A. Revolution and Society

There is a Weberian atmosphere to *Revolutionary Constitutions* which is apparent in the use it makes of the concept of 'constitutionalisation of charisma', one which Ackerman acknowledges is a derivation from Weber's own 'bureaucratization of charisma'. The notion of charisma is drawn from Weber's theory of legitimacy. Legitimacy is a concept that draws a nexus between individuals bearing power and communities. *Revolutionary Constitutions* frequently emphasises the role of 'great men' and 'women' in constitutional developments. This goes so much against the tide of most of contemporary writing in the field of constitutional law that we could almost think that Ackerman has decided to move away from his past accomplishments and engage in more banal, political biography of the kind available in any airport newsstand. It goes without saying that the book does nothing of the kind. What goes on here is a continuation of Ackerman's meditation on constituent power and constitutional change which took place in the three volumes of *We the People*. In his theory of constituent power, Ackerman establishes a pattern of continuity between revolutionary founding fathers (de Gaulle, Mandela, Ben-Gurion, Begin, Aung San, Nehru etc) and the political institutions they have created or inspired. That there is continuity at all is a hypothesis that deserves a closer look. For instance, Ackerman insists that constitutional courts have more often than not attempted to 'preserve core revolutionary principles once the founding generation has left the scene'.[7] This idea of an 'intergenerational framework'[8] is what makes Ackerman's narrative possible.

For all practical purposes, contemporary constitutional lawyers or their counterparts in the politics department make precious little use of the concept of revolution. It is certainly not unworthy of our attention, then, that such a towering figure as Ackerman should point to this very concept and that he should use it so imaginatively. Constitutional law is in constant danger of losing contact with politics and becoming 'normalised' as just another technical subject. The outcome

[7] *Id.* at 318.
[8] *Id.* at 318.

is that politics and law come to be seen as realities that do not communicate. As a result, the promise of a 'government of laws and not of men' becomes unintelligible and more remote every day. Ackerman never falls victim to this temptation of entirely separating law and politics. The concept of revolution is central to his account of constitutional law because it accounts for precisely that reality: politics shape law as much as law shapes politics. In the constitutional model, politics has come first, as a moment of creation and through moments where the state is unsettled, sometimes entirely destroyed by social forces. As much as institutions try to control society – ie, to govern it – this government is always subject to society's power to upend governmental structures and establish new ones. The core lesson of the modern art of government (and most of our public law) is that government shapes society. Public law *qua* administrative law could do perfectly well without a concept of revolution. But this cannot be the case of constitutional law, as the core lesson of constitutionalism is that government is the offspring of society. Yet there is more than one way for society to establish or reconstitute government. This is the purpose of Ackerman's three 'scenarios' to account for these various relations between state and society.

All the case studies described in the book are 'revolutions on a human scale', a concept directly opposed to that of the Jacobin model of revolutions as 'totalizing reconstruction[s] of society'.[9] In a sense, the whole book reads like a meditation on the meaning of the expression 'revolution on a human scale'. Yet the reader cannot help musing over the exact meaning of each of these words: why 'revolutions'? Why a 'human' scale? I do not mean to say that Ackerman avoids these questions.[10] Yet the book induces the reader to keep asking herself those very same questions.

It is common knowledge that the concept of 'revolution' is one that has a 'negative' side (upending the existing political system) as well as a 'positive' one (revolution as the making of a new state, a new constitution, a new 'table of values'). It is the classical (essentialist) account of society that has enabled these two meanings of 'revolution' to become coherent. This was as true of liberal 'bourgeois' revolutions' of the nineteenth century as of the modern communist regimes in Eastern Europe and Asia. Even the creation of new regimes in Eastern and Central Europe after the fall of the USSR followed this pattern – but not anymore. The social structure underpinning nineteenth-century Europe has largely disappeared. The idea of a homogeneous society, master of its own political destiny, may well be a feature of the past. Our contemporary concept of society is based on identity politics and fragmentation. This 'new' society cannot be expected as a matter of course to adhere to the values of classical liberalism (individual liberty, privacy, political representation by legitimate elites). Ackerman is not unaware of this phenomenon and of its political as well as constitutional effects. In fact, the

[9] *Id.* at 28.
[10] See especially *id.* at 39 f. and 67.

idea of a 'revolution on a human scale' might be interpreted as showing that the changing nature of society has a deep impact on the constitution and the political regime. *Revolutionary Constitutions* sheds new light on these new forms of constitution-making, both by expanding the scope of comparison to new parts of the world and by offering new paradigms that make it possible to understand informal constitutional change. A good example is the case of Poland and the role of the 'Solidarity' movement. According to Ackerman, Solidarity represented one of the greatest revolutionary mobilisations of modern times.[11] But it seems that Solidarity did not have the means to transform itself easily into a political party, even less into an engine of constitutional change. By 1995, says Ackerman, 'voters were disgusted' and vowed to replace Solidarity leaders with former communists. Another case study of the complex interactions between society and the making of a new frame of government is of course South Africa after the end of apartheid.

B. Rethinking Society in Constitutional Law

A revolution, as a constitution, is a collective enterprise, but in order to take place at the 'human' scale, it must also concern individuals. This is one of the core questions of theoretical sociology: how does one reconcile (if at all) the 'micro-social' level (individuals) and the 'macro' level of social institutions, discourses and representations? The question has a constitutional dimension: how (if at all) does one harmonise individual autonomy and rights with collective autonomy, and the right of political communities with self-government? At the end of the day, this appears to be the core question of constitutional law. Individual and collective autonomy are not self-evidently compatible with each other and this is why any modern political 'regime' is nothing other than an ongoing, structurally instable, political revolution trying to draw the curtain and, in French parlance, 'terminer la Révolution' ('bring the revolution to an end'). In modern constitutional government, revolution is inevitable, not in the sense of a single Bolshevik *grand soir*, but of a permanent instability of the relationship between rulers and governed. What is the right 'scale' at which this ongoing 'revolution' should take place? Should we sacrifice sovereignty (collective autonomy) to the furthering of the human rights' project, or at least tip the balance more in the direction of individuals (like the Barak court in the 1990s or the French constitutional court in the 1970s)? Or should we, as seems to be the case of the contemporary anti-liberal movements in Poland, Hungary or Turkey – and quite possibly the British 'hard Brexiteers' as well – sacrifice human rights and individual welfare in the name of collective autonomy?

[11] *Id.* at 52.

In any case, this goes some way towards proving that there exists a deep underlying connection between constitutional law and the idea of society. This may not have been Ackerman's main project in writing *Revolutionary Constitutions*, but I would tend to think that the book invites us to apprehend under a new light the role of societies in reshuffling political regimes and bringing about constitutional change. Constitutional law needs to rethink its own internal sociology and *Revolutionary Constitutions* is there to show us why (and how). Constitutional law relies on a certain social ontology. Classical constitutionalism, to begin with, was predicated upon an essentialist account of society. Its blueprint had been defined in Locke's *Second Treatise of Government* and it did not change much in eighteenth- and nineteenth-century political liberalism. Society – as a community of free individuals – was a concrete agent of historical change and the bearer, in its own right, of natural 'rights'. It had both the power to trigger formal constitution-making and to generate informal constitutional change. In this fashion, society was already apprehended in such a way as to make constitutional law possible: it was an 'agent' which could, through a revolution and the use of constituent power, give itself a government (in the classical liberal view) and/or generate a 'state' (in the German and French tradition of 'general theory of the state', in which the state was defined as the impersonation of the 'nation').

For that reason, and whatever their own political agendas and the various ideological axes they wish to grind, most constitutional lawyers have remained – at least for the sake of their professional pursuits – classical liberals. They are theory-bound to be so. This vision of society, however, has come under attack by modern sociology and normative political philosophy. In particular, leftist and progressive social theory – the Frankfurt School, the anti-totalitarian schools of 'socialisme et barbarie' in France or the 'radical democratic' school dominated by Ernesto Laclau, Judith Butler and Chantal Mouffe – has insisted that society should be understood in a different way. While these sociological changes have been acknowledged for quite some time in several fields of social sciences and in normative political philosophy, constitutional law and comparative government have yet to take them fully into account. Yet, Ackerman's work is there to remind us that this update is long overdue and that the consequences of the current neglect are far from trivial. For that reason, it is at the same time a classical account, in the sense that it envisages comparative government as one of the legitimate purposes of constitutional law, and a revisionist one, in the sense that *Revolutionary Constitutions* challenges the existing typologies and theoretical accounts of comparative political regimes. This is the very purpose of Ackerman's 'evolutionist framework' and his four-step pattern of mobilised insurgency, constitutional founding, succession crisis and eventually consolidation.

Constitutional law has done little to adjust to this change and to the legitimate attacks which these progressive schools of thought – quite independently of their own political agendas – have built against the traditional idea of society that was formerly dominant in the social sciences. On the other side of the political spectrum, neo-conservatives and neo-liberals have in fact mounted a theoretical assault which aimed at bringing down the very idea of society – asserting in a Thatcherite way that it 'does not exist' – rather than modernising it. In the classical 'Lockean' approach, society exists as a 'thing' – a reality that we are able to talk about – even before it establishes a 'government' and is potentially able, should such a government fail to protect the fundamental rights of its members, to react to tyranny and maladministration by creating or re-creating a new form of government. This supposes that society – or, in the French tradition, the 'nation' – exists prior to government and the constitution. This raises two questions: (1) what is society (the 'ontology of the social')?; and (2) how should society be represented in positive governmental and legal arrangements? As a matter of fact, this way of posing the question appears to be inadequate. There are not two questions, but just one. The account of society that we make use of is already institutionalised (or at least we need it to be so), while at the same time constitutions incorporate a certain image of society.

There are considerable evidence of this phenomenon in *Revolutionary Constitutions*. Written constitutions contain an image of society through, for instance, the rights – individual and collective – that they declare, through the way in which they institutionalise political representation and make major choices in terms of constitutional arrangements (the number and nature of houses of parliament, the choice of an electoral system, referendums or the absence thereof), through the insistence on sovereignty or, then again, as in the British or American case, the relative absence of that concept in positive law, and finally through the role of constitutional courts as 'forums of principles' but also as 'representatives' of civil society. We were already indebted to Ackerman for showing in *We the People* that constitutional courts participate in the wider exercise of 'higher lawmaking' in the sense that they acknowledge and 'consolidate' constitutional moves already triggered by political movements and other political institutions. *Revolutionary Constitutions* gives them a similar role in consolidating 'revolutions on a human scale' that were triggered by national heroes and/or 'movement-parties'. The book draws a pattern of constitutional change in which a richer meaning is attributed to the idea that constitutional courts 'represent' society. They do so through their potential ability to interpret major historical changes in constitutional terms. France's Conseil constitutionnel did so after May 1968 and de Gaulle's death. The Barak court did so in Israel in the 1990s in order to make good on the fact that Israel's founding fathers (especially Ben-Gurion and the Mapai party) had chosen *not to have* a written constitution protecting fundamental rights (the so-called 'Harari decision'). The question here is not to identify a 'general will' that one could ascribe to society. Rather, on a more 'human scale', sociological changes (like the shift in mores in the West after 1968), historical events (the USSR's downfall in 1991) and 'great men' enrich and qualify the choices that societies makes. These choices simply 'happen'. It is then the responsibility of certain state institutions and normative procedures to set them in constitutional stone (or, in constitutional parlance, to 'entrench' them). This is where the magic of the Ackermanian framework operates again. Beyond 'general will' or some sort of delusional Schmittian 'constitutional decisions', Ackerman is there to remind us that constitutional change is made up of such historical developments that were at the same time anticipated by founding generations and only made possible by social changes that no one – even some enlightened and authoritative founders – could have anticipated. In this sense, 'political representation' means the ability to construe social changes and interpret the meaning of the ongoing revolution. The South African Revolution, for instance, is aptly described as a 'struggle' for a 'just society'[12] which begun with the repudiation of apartheid and is far from finished today. In a sense, despite his claims to the contrary, Ackerman comes close to the vision of society put forward by radical democrats when they make the claim that various social struggles (environmentalism, feminism, workers' rights etc) should merge at a certain point. Does he not himself refer to the moment when there rises a 'total revolution against all forms of oppression'? Is this not one of the meanings of a 'revolution on a human scale'?[13] There is great value in coming back to the idea of political regime in order to explain what goes on. Constituent power means the process by which society changes itself yet cannot do so directly, as 'society has no essence'[14] and does not exist outside a diversity of operative discourses; it takes founding fathers, movement-parties and later constitutional courts. But in any case, as Ackerman rightly points out, 'the transformative target is the political regime itself'. Ackerman's lesson here is that, whatever our political agenda, we should all benefit by returning to the classical language of political regime when we analyse constitutional change.

At the same time, civil society keeps on influencing constitutional change. There is a Montesquieu-like quality in Ackerman's narratives of the interactions between society and high politics. He insists on the role of civil societies in fighting and toppling authoritarian regimes (as communist Poland or the Shah's pre-1979 government in Iran) and later in struggling against existing ones. This is a fascinating theme which goes a long way towards justifying Ackerman's idea that constitutionalism exists in non-Western regimes, be they parliamentarian and pluralistic (India) or inclining much more towards new forms of authoritarianism (Iran). Sometimes, tyrants or at least very *authoritarian* figures (Khomeini or today Erdogan) are able to speak *authoritatively* in the name of society, because they better understand its cogs and wheels. At least for some time, they speak the language of society. Sometimes too, in more 'advanced' democracies, other institutions such as constitutional courts seem to do a good job of speaking for society and catering for its needs. The paradox here is that political autonomy can be furthered – for a time – by confiscating the ability to speak for society by certain institutions or certain leaders. Yet democracies should be wary of philosopher kings, even those in in judicial robes. This ability

[12] *Id.* at 30.
[13] *Id.*
[14] Ernesto Laclau & Chantal Mouffe, Hegemony and Socialist Strategy (2001).

to be the voice of society is also the path to dictatorship or, in the case of constitutional courts, of a propensity to step beyond their proper sphere. Democratic autonomy is a hard-won trophy and it can also be lost. Failure in that matter means different forms of social breakdown, for which *Revolutionary Constitutions* does not lack examples. The case of Poland, and the very shaky history of Solidarity, or South Africa and the sorry developments of the ANC under Zuma, should suffice to provide examples of this state of affairs. We should be grateful to *Revolutionary Constitutions* for showing us why it is important to tell such stories and why they also belong to the province of constitutional law in their own right.

Yet society is not a 'thing'. It is not an organised, inherently self-conscious and active entity. For all the exaggerations of post-structuralism and the 'linguistic turn', it is an important lesson of the theory of radical democracy that society has no essence and is made up of various discourses and practices – indeed, a lesson that constitutional lawyers should not lose sight of. This is the case when we make use of the categories of 'majorities' and 'minorities' in our own scholarship, as when we discuss ad nauseam of the 'countermajoritarian difficulty' and so on. Majorities and minorities are not readily identifiable and stable entities. We must constantly ask ourselves of what stuff they are made, how they appear, how they evolve and sometimes morph into other entities. The South African case is a beautiful example of the difficulty of pinpointing what a 'majority' is and giving it constitutional recognition. The same would be true of 'minorities'. What goes on in Australia today regarding the difficult recognition of aboriginal rights goes some way towards making that very same point. As a matter of fact, Western democracies are, more often than not, less imaginative and more clumsy than other types of regime in doing so. We are, it seems, more fearful of breaking the democratic homogeneity of 'the people' and – as in France – of acknowledging its inherent heterogeneity. The role of the constitutional principle of equality, as in France or the US, has had a similarly inhibiting effect. Non-Western regimes are less fearful and more pragmatic in this regard.

Revolutions occur because societies retain a certain capacity to exist beyond the way in which they have been institutionalised. This is the force of the Hegelian conceptual structure in which 'civil society' pre-dates the 'state'. And the lesson I would draw from *Revolutionary Constitutions* is that 'good' constituent power is the one that maintains a link with society (South Africa), while 'failed' constitutional experiments can more often than not be blamed on legislators who – in pure Montesquieu style – have failed to maintain the link with civil society and the 'national character' (Poland). 'Society' is the name of the constant and fluid process in which human communities make and unmake themselves. In fact, this is an underlying theme of most of the case studies in *Revolutionary Constitutions*: societies rebelling against empires (India) and against totalitarianism (Poland), civil societies building themselves up against inhuman oppression under the influence of well-organised, yet by no means Leninist, 'movement-parties' (South Africa). *Revolutionary Constitutions* gives pride of place to various forms of social activism such as trade unions (Solidarity) or general strikes (as in the case of South Africa). A 'good' movement-party is one which is able to unite various social groups and 'bracket their diversity', as the ANC managed to do with its 'broad range' of constituent groups. Conversely, a movement-party plummets when it becomes unable to unite those diverse social groups, as became the case for Solidarity after its initial successes against the communist system. This is evidence that one should not, as many European liberals – or indeed socialists – tend to do, exclusively identify the Arendtian 'social question' with the economic sphere. The 'social question' is inherently political and it is no less a constitutional question.

There are some less dramatic, but no less meaningful, examples, such as the role Ackerman attributes to the events of May 1968 in France. The French political right has a propensity to dismiss *Mai 68* as a farce, a mock-revolution conducted by a generation of young spoiled bourgeois from the Latin quarter. At the same time, ideologues from the same quarters tend to claim that the events of 1968 are the cause of the decadence of mores in the West. How can it be both at the same time? The reason is that *Mai 68* – in Paris as well as Berkeley or Berlin – was more than a farce; it was the moment at which Tocqueville's democratic 'providence' – the perceived historical inevitability of democracy – moved beyond the state and the political sphere to hit society itself. *Mai 68* was the moment of the 'democratisation of society', or at least its (partly farcical, as the ways and means of achieving this purpose were unknown to the actors themselves) historical inception. Ackerman explains very well how this democratisation of society has had a deep effect on French political institutions and why 1968 also marks the beginning of a revolution in the political constitution.[15] Even the Gaullist landslide at the elections of June 1968 and the General's ability to eventually salvage his own position after a very shaky start have paved the way for the rising role of the French constitutional court in the early 1970s. The Conseil constitutionnel did a lot to undo what was done in 1958 (the enactment of de Gaulle's Constitution) and this is one of the long-term effects of the events of 1968. Beyond political and historical contingencies, there was indeed a kind of sociological necessity that made this course of events, if not inevitable, at least very likely.

If the concept of society has mattered so much to constitutional law, it is because constitutions have always – at least since antiquity – been envisaged as solutions to the problem of social diversity and potential (or actual) social antagonisms. For a long time, during the pre-democratic era, this is what caused the success of mixed government. Society was split between several 'estates' or 'classes' and political institutions were supposed to reflect either their diversity (as in the case of the British two houses, one representing the 'people' and the other, the House of Lords, *being* one of the estates) or to being an image of social unity (the monarch). 'Bourgeois' constitutions – a formula frequently used in the nineteenth century and pre-Second World War Europe – were also solutions to the 'social question' that

[15] See *id.* at 135 f.

had appeared after the eighteenth-century revolutions and the Industrial Revolution. Ackerman's national models and ideal types show how deeply the structures of political representation have been challenged by the 'revolutions' that he depicts. Ultimately, this is all about the main purpose of modern constitutions: individual as well as collective autonomy. Constitutional law is the law of self-government. A constitution in the modern sense is an instrument of self-government. It is a legal *instrumentum* which aims at establishing self-government in the sense of individual and collective autonomy. Yet, in contemporary circumstances, this ability of written constitutions – and the legal apparatus evolved to protect and enhance the values they contain – to act as instruments of self-government has been put to the test, if not already eroded to a large extent. I will come back to this in my concluding remarks. But first, a word needs to be said on Ackerman's contribution to the theory of comparative government.

III. Systems of Government

A. The Plasticity of the Westminster Model

Ackerman's volume is a timely reminder that our theory of systems of government is outdated and that an overhaul is long overdue. *Revolutionary Constitutions* is not afraid to emphasise that European models – rather than the US Constitution – have been able to spread over the world, even in non-Western (or even anti-Western) polities. An interesting question is how and why they have been able to do so? Is this due to their inherent flexibility or, as Bentham and a large number of the eighteenth-century thinkers thought, thanks to the Enlightenment's ability to capture universal political values? A thread of the present chapter is to suggest that this has to do with the relationship between constitutional law and the idea of society. A given constitution – and indeed constitutional law as such – only works if it is able to generate stable and operative social forms. This is probably what Ackerman has in mind when he speaks of a constitution's 'constitutive features'.[16] In my view, this is an acknowledgement of the fact that constitutions constitute societies. They are not so much the byproduct of a pre-existing society that – in a Lockean fashion – decides to 'go political'. They generate social reality. A good instance of this in *Revolutionary Constitutions* is the fascinating case of South Africa. For Mandela, presenting the provisional constitution as legally binding, despite the evident flaw in constitutional theory, made it possible to establish the ANC as 'a movement party which could credibly speak for the people'.[17]

In this regard, the plasticity of Western constitutional models is simply remarkable, as is evidenced by their success outside the perimeter of Western countries,

[16] *Id.* at 80.
[17] *Id.* at 99.

and even in polities directly and openly aiming at creating a political system that rejects Western values. A great example of this is Pakistan. Pakistan has taken on board parliamentary government in same the way as it has adhered to cricket: as a means to reject the West rather than as a path towards becoming a Western country. The plasticity of the Westminster model is simply staggering. Ackerman provides us with a key reason for this plasticity and this is, in my view, one of the books' key legacies. The flexibility of parliamentary government is not so much due to the values of constitutionalism as to the power structures that it establishes. This is extremely well laid out in the chapter in *Revolutionary Constitutions* devoted to the Iranian case. As a matter of fact, I would beg to differ with Ackerman when he states that a key difference between India and France is that: 'The Indian system is parliamentary; the French, presidential.'[18] The Fifth Republic is very much a parliamentary government in its own right.[19] The cabinet is accountable to Parliament and can be dismissed by a vote of no confidence in the National Assembly (Articles 49 and 50 of the 1958 Constitution). The large powers and personal authority of the president are only grafted upon that machinery of parliamentary government. As a result, therefore, the French model is just another instance of the plasticity of the Westminster model. This is relevant to my next point.

B. De Gaulle Gone Global?

One of the book's main themes appears to be that de Gaulle's 1958 scheme of government was influential well outside France. In fact, Ackerman tells us, it has influenced Poland, Iran and even Israel in the short-lived experiment of electing the prime minister directly by the people. In a country like Walesa's Poland, we are told that adoption of the so-called 'superpresidential' French model has caused nothing less than a constitutional 'tragedy'.[20] But, conversely, in Khomeini's Iran, the French model has proved successful. One is tempted to wonder whether the Gaullist model has been as influential as is suggested in *Revolutionary Constitutions*. It would be helpful to see more historical evidence of this being adduced, especially in the Polish and Iranian cases. The differences are perhaps too important for us to bring together the Gaullist model – which after all was loyally republican and secular – and the Iranian case, for instance. And in the case of Poland or Turkey, one should not underestimate the role of several centuries of political cultures that made those countries diverge from the path of Western liberal democracy. No one should underestimate the fact that Poland or Hungary do not have the same culture of liberty as France or Germany. This goes a long way towards explaining the present predicament of the European Union (EU). In those cases,

[18] *Id.* at 48.

[19] This is a minor quibble since, as a matter of fact, Ackerman is not unaware of this state of affairs; he frequently (and rightly) refers to the French 1958 model as 'semi-presidential'.

[20] Ackerman, *supra* at 254.

these political cultures have diverged from that of France and have not converged in such a way as would make the reference to France an enlightening one. This may be why, as Ackerman readily acknowledges, 'the negative Polish experience with the French model cannot be generalized into a hard-and-fast rule. Sometimes semi-presidentialism promotes revolutionary constitutionalism; sometimes, it supports it', as in Iran. It may be the case then that the reference to France is not important as such and is instead there just as an example of a label for a larger phenomenon that Ackerman identifies and that has little to do with France's influence: 'the perils of superpresidentialism'.[21] Take the short-lived attempt to have the Israeli prime minister elected directly by universal suffrage from 1996 to 2001. Ackerman sees this episode as an attempt to build a 'quasi-gaullist elected presidency'.[22] Others have sometimes mentioned the American influence in this regard. In any case, the reference to the French model may not be the most helpful in this context; rather, it would seem that the reasons for the 1996–2001 experiment were for the most part internal to the Israeli case and, more largely, to the difficulties of managing a 'classical' Westminster-style model of parliamentary government. In most parliamentary governments around the world, the problem of governmental stability is a central one. Many a reformer has been itching to bring in 'more democracy', although how to do so exactly was obviously tricky. Israel has attempted to put down in writing what many thought was already implicitly in place in the UK, the mother of all such classical parliamentary governments: namely, that every voter decides, with her individual ballot, not only what majority should run the country but also, more effectively, the name of the future prime minister. In this regard, Israel has just been bolder than other fellow members of the Westminster club for reasons that would be too long to spell out here, but are quite well known (especially the ultra-democratic culture of the country since its founding, but also the remarkable instability brought about by full proportional representation and the party system). In this context, the reference to France may not be the most enlightening. A similar remark would be true, I think, about Iran or South Africa. In South Africa, probably because of the fraught history of the move to a democratic post-apartheid constitution, the regime cannot, in my view, be safely put in the category of either pure 'parliamentary' or pure 'presidential' government. It is both, or maybe neither, as the ousting of President Zuma has recently shown. The Constitution incorporates both a mechanism of impeachment in the US style and a set of clauses which enable the National Assembly to remove either the cabinet alone or the cabinet *and* the president. The role of the Constitutional Court (as shown in the recent landmark case of *Freedom Fighters Party* in 2017) is more central to the functioning of this *sui generis* regime than is generally the case in Europe, where courts have to take for granted the political system as it stands.[23]

[21] *Id.* at 257.
[22] *Id.* at 368.
[23] The same could be said of Kenya, as is evidenced by the last two presidential elections and the Supreme Court's role in their management.

IV. A Darker Future?

A. Uncharismatic Constitutionalism

Constitutional charisma can mean two interrelated things: the charisma of great founders being 'constitutionalised' (de Gaulle as a role model for the *Président de la République*, a constitutional role to be taken up by others after him); or the 'charisma' of the constitution itself, as an instrument of self-government hammered out in heroic times and bearing the marks of this founding era. However, both these forms of constitutional magic tend to wear off in ordinary times, when the exceptional circumstances of the founding period have disappeared. This is what has happened in France, for better or for worse, after de Gaulle's death. Nobody, not even Mitterrand, has been able to wear de Gaulle's clothes and become a 'larger than life' president, as the job description requires.

Charisma should never be taken for granted. It is a result of what Weber called 'the politics of genius', which is by definition not replicable and notoriously difficult to constitutionalise. In fact, uncharismatic 'legal' constitutionalism quite easily prevails under modern circumstances. The constraints of space mean that is it not possible to spell out the reasons for this here. Yet the main characteristics of 'uncharismatic constitutionalism' are easy to identify. The management of the welfare state by large administrative machineries and the rise of a greater concern for fundamental rights have become the order of the day. They supersede political autonomy – which is supposed to have been gained once and for all in 'time one' of the constitutional revolution – as the dominant political purposes of the state. Welfarist policies necessitate an expansion of the administrative sphere and its legal apparatus. At the same time, concern for equality, human dignity and human rights justifies a greater concern for the rule of law. As a result, uncharismatic judicial and bureaucratic elites take over. Constitutions lose a great deal of their force as symbols of political autonomy and beacons of democratic self-government. They become a 'normalised' legal instrument amongst others, which can be freely interpreted by courts and, in countries like France or Germany, frequently amended by bureaucrats (albeit with the adequate democratic stamp, of course). If – and when – international treaties do a better job of furthering welfarist policies or better protecting human rights, they prevail over domestic law and the constitution matters less than the country's international commitments. All these developments happen for a reason. As such, they are not worthy of blame; on the contrary, their goals are highly commendable. Yet their cost in constitutional terms is blatant: the benefits of 'revolutionary constitutionalism' are progressively brushed away. If revolutionary constitutionalism means the intention to 'give "the masses themselves" a sense of "direct participation … [in] shap[ing] their own destiny"',[24] the more the modern state and its welfarist and humanitarian policies

[24] Ackerman, *supra* at 284.

develop, the harder this becomes to achieve. 'Uncharismatic' constitutionalism has in many regards won the day. Yet there are certain clues that the tide is turning.

B. Counter-revolutions (at a Human Scale?)

I would be tempted to be less optimistic than Ackerman when he says, for instance, that France has been moving towards greater 'constitutionalisation of charisma' and greater 'checks and balances'.[25] One should not be overly impressed by some accounts of the role of the French constitutional courts in the English language that have depicted it as an overall success for the idea of the 'rule of law' and the recognition of civil liberties.[26] The picture is far less rosy than that. If there is a country where there is massive bureaucratisation of the constitution and little overall concern for 'revolutionary constitutionalism', this is certainly contemporary France. De Gaulle's towering figure has not been replaced and probably cannot be. What the French constitutional court has done is not to constitutionalise charisma, but to bureaucratise the Constitution. It did not reinforce the checks and balances in the Constitution; rather, it has increased the centralisation of power. In many regards, it has weakened parliament and other counterbalancing forces. Contemporary France should therefore not be looked at as a model of 'revolutionary constitutionalism'. The EU is another outstanding example of this type of 'uncharismatic constitutionalism'. What took place on a large scale in the constitutional law of many countries – including the pre-Brexit UK – was in fact sheer bureaucratisation, juridification and the oblivion of the lessons of classical constitutionalism about the perils of raw political power.[27]

As much as I admire Ackerman's ability to put in context judicial activism in post-war Germany, France in the 1970s or Israel in the early 1990s, it seems to me that constitutional courts have therefore gone well beyond their 'time four' (in the step-by-step pattern given in *Revolutionary Constitutions*) role of consolidating the achievements of the heroic era of revolutionary movement-parties and founding fathers. In France at least, the constitutional court has been busy consolidating bureaucratic control over society at the expense of the French 'revolutionary' (or simply democratic) aspiration towards collective autonomy. Under the aegis of the top French courts, the constitution has to a large extent lost its ability to remain an instrument of self-government. The same has more or less happened in Britain in a context of 'weak judicial review' and an unwritten constitution. This I would take to be one of the underlying reasons for Brexit. It could also be shown

[25] *Id.* at 250 f.

[26] See especially A. Stone Sweet, The birth of Judicial Politics in France (1992), whom I think has taken too seriously the triumphal accounts of the rise of the French constitutional court that were prevalent in French scholarship in the 1990s.

[27] On both Brexit and the EU, I take the liberty of referring to D. Baranger, *Brexit as a Constitutional Decision: An Interpretation*, Jus Politicum 20–21 (July 2018), available at: http://juspoliticum.com/article/Brexit-as-a-Constitutional-Decision-An-Interpretation-1241.html.

that a parallel phenomenon has taken place in the very 'juristocratic'[28] model of 'European Union constitutionalism' in which the popular will expressed in national referendums has repeatedly been disregarded (as in the case of the Lisbon Treaty). This rise of 'uncharismatic constitutionalism' has come at a high cost, one which we only begin to pay with the emergence of populist governments and their anti-liberal agenda of breaking up transnational institutions in the name of national sovereignty and curtailing the power and independence of courts at the expense of the rule of law. The values of constitutionalism are receding on an international basis. What happens in Poland, Hungary or with the Brexiteers' all-out war on the European Court of Human Rights and the Court of Justice of the European Union is ample evidence of this. In other words, now may unfortunately be the time of 'counter-revolutions at a human scale'. I would be tempted to think that the rise of nationalism and the growing disdain for the rule of law thrusts its roots in the not-so-successful 'intergenerational' connection between the founding moment and the rise of judicial supremacy.

However, in no way should the pessimistic account of ongoing transformations that I have just tried to sketch out detract from the magnificent accomplishment of *Revolutionary Constitutions*. The book is an admirable account of an extremely complex set of changes across the world. Our understanding of constitutionalism and its contemporary changes is very much enriched by it. One cannot think of a better plea for 'political constitutionalism'.

[28] In the sense made popular by Ran Hirschl, Towards Juristocracy: The Origins and Consequences of the New Constitutionalism (2004).

4

Bruce Ackerman's Theory of History

ROBERTO GARGARELLA

I. Introduction

Bruce Ackerman's new book has many of the virtues that were already present in his previous books, and it is important to take note of them.[1] Let me begin by referring to some of the enduring virtues of Ackerman's work. First, Ackerman taught us to look at the law differently, by paying attention to the existing connections between the law and 'We the People'. Against those who merely study the law as a 'top-down' phenomenon, he has always insisted on paying attention to 'bottom-up' processes of law-making. Similarly, and also similarly important, he has called our attention to the fact that the law emerges not only from formal procedures, such as a Constitutional Convention or a formal National Assembly, but also from more informal and (extended in time) processes of mass mobilisation – let us call them 'constitutional moments'. This renewed perspective has also allowed Ackerman to improve our thinking about the law in numerous fundamental respects, including crucial topics such as judicial review and constitutional interpretation. Extremely serious theoretical problems – like those relating to the tension between constitutionalism and democracy or those relating to the origins and force of rights, to mention just two of them – seem to find plausible and new responses when we look at them through the lenses of Ackerman's analytical apparatus. I want to celebrate the publication of Ackerman's new book and his efforts to study and learn from foreign authors and foreign legal experiences.[2] The product of this effort is a great book, full of brilliant ideas and insights.

Among the number of thoughts and insights that distinguish his new book, I would highlight Ackerman's remarks about the rule of law;[3] his critical dialogue with legal positivism and the 'rule of recognition';[4] the way in which he challenges

[1] Bruce Ackerman, Revolutionary Constitutions: Charismatic Leadership and the Rule of Law (2019).

[2] See, for example, Bruce Ackerman, The Future of the Liberal Revolution (1994).

[3] Ackerman, *supra* note 1 at 2, 5.

[4] *Id.* at 36.

the civil law–common law distinction;[5] his polemic against rational-choice analysts, like Tom Ginsburg[6] or Jon Elster[7] and his critique of the approach that reads judicial review merely through the lens of a 'rational actor';[8] or the way in which he relates and distinguishes his work from the writings of other fundamental legal and social thinkers of our time, including Max Weber,[9] Hannah Arendt[10] and Carl Schmitt.[11] In particular, I would like to express my admiration for the amount of detailed knowledge he acquired of foreign constitutional experiences. Both the purpose of his enterprise –to learn from foreign legal practices – and his actual achievements seem admirable. In other words, his contribution to the development of a rather novel discipline, namely comparative constitutionalism, results outstanding.[12]

In what follows, and trying to continue some of the conversations that Ackerman has opened up in his book, I will critically examine some problems that I find in this new work. In most cases, these are problems that Ackerman has properly recognised (sometimes by denial, sometimes through an explanation), in this or in previous works. I will be referring to problems such as those of legal formalism; the problem of relying on 'We the Judges' instead of 'We the People'; that of assuming that 'one-size-fits-all'; that of failing 'to integrate the voices of movement activists'; and that of presenting what is actually a normative position as if it were a fundamentally descriptive view.

II. Constitutionalism's Different Pathways

A. Three Pathways

In the Introduction of his book, Ackerman presents 'three different pathways through which constitutions have won legitimacy over the past century'. Each pathway, he adds, 'generates a distinctive ideal-type – with its own set of attractions and problems'.[13]

According to Ackerman's description, the first path or scenario appears when 'a revolutionary movement makes a sustained effort to mobilise the masses against

[5] *Id.* at 37.
[6] *Id.* at 39.
[7] *Id.* at 40.
[8] *Id.* at 39.
[9] *Id.* at 8.
[10] *Id.* at 41.
[11] *Id.* at 42.
[12] This book, together with some other previous work, would put Ackerman in the pantheon of great comparative scholars in the area of constitutionalism, together with Mauro Cappelletti, Tom Ginsburg, Rosalind Dixon and Mark Tushnet, who seem to be similarly open to studying and learning from foreign constitutional practices.
[13] Ackerman, *supra* note 1 at 1.

the existing regime', which sometimes leads to bloody repression and sometimes results in success stories, on which he focuses his attention.[14] India, South Africa, Italy and France would be examples of this first route.

In the 'second ideal-type', he claims, 'the political order is built by pragmatic insiders, not revolutionary outsiders'. In these cases, when 'confronting popular movements for fundamental change', the insider-establishment would respond with 'strategic concessions' that would split the outsiders into 'moderate and radical camps'.[15] At this stage, the insider-establishment would invite the 'moderate outsiders' to join the political establishment in governing the country in a 'co-optation strategy' that would culminate in 'landmark reform legislation'.[16] Great Britain would be his paradigmatic example of the second ideal-type.

The third path through which constitutionalism would have won legitimacy concerns the case Ackerman calls 'elite construction'. Under this scenario, he writes, 'the old system of government begins to unravel but the general population stays relatively passive on the side-lines'. This 'emerging power vacuum', then, would be exploited by previously 'excluded political and social elites', who serve as the principal force in the creation of a new constitutional order.[17] Spain after the death of Franco would be his main example of this third route.

B. A Four-Stage Dynamic

Ackerman dedicates most of his book to analysing the kind of revolutionary constitutionalism that took place in countries such as India, South Africa, France, Italy, Poland, Israel and Iran. Writing about these cases, he claims that 'despite their obvious differences from one another, the constitutions of all these nations are rooted in a common experience – in which revolutionary insurgents manage to sustain a struggle against the old order for years or decades before finally gaining political ascendancy'.[18] This revolutionary moment – 'typically a time of high-energy politics, in which leaders and followers are bound together by long years of common sacrifice' –he calls *Time One*. We would recognise, instead, that we are in *Time Two*, when the initial period of high-energy politics is translated into a constitution 'that seeks to prevent a relapse into the abuses of the past, and commits the republic to the new principles proclaimed during the long hard struggle of Time one'.[19] Ackerman characterises this period as the time of *constitutionalisation of revolutionary charisma*.

The first initial references to *Time Three* appear only on page 12, where Ackerman refers to the time when 'the revolutionary regime confronts a legitimacy vacuum'.

[14] *Id.* at 3.
[15] *Id.* at 4.
[16] *Id.*
[17] *Id.* at 6.
[18] *Id.* at 3, 4.
[19] *Id.* at 4.

This is the time when 'the revolutionary party serves as a pathway to power', thus attracting 'countless opportunists who care little about the old ideals' of the founding moment. Similarly, he claims, 'millions of ordinary people who lived through the revolution' now play 'minimal attention to current politics in the distant capital'.[20] Political authority now moves towards *the normalisation of revolutionary politics*. This period would be marked by a series of succession crises, 'in which an increasingly confident judiciary will confront an increasingly normalized political class in an intensive struggle to occupy the "legitimacy vacuum" left by the preceding generation'.[21]

For Ackerman, Time Three is a period when 'in many cases, the judiciary successfully manages to gain the grudging recognition of its claims from the political branches'.[22] The 'ultimate fate' of this period 'depends on the success of the next generation or two of professionals in consolidating their position, through a variety of techniques' – this is *Time Four*. At this time, Ackerman proclaims later on, 'an increasingly self-confident legal profession engages in an ongoing process which consolidates the judiciary's claim to supremacy'.[23]

III. Descriptive Problems

Ackerman's description of the three paths of constitutionalisation and the four periods of revolutionary constitutionalism resembles the kind of periodisation that he presented, for example and more recently, in his book *The Civil Rights Revolution*. In his previous work, in fact, he described the six phases that would distinguish the formation and development of a 'constitutional moment' –the 'dynamic process of popular sovereignty', as he called it.[24] The phases included those of 'signaling', 'proposition', 'elections', 'elaboration for mobilization', 'electoral ratification' and 'consolidation'. Now, in my view, both schemas – the one that he introduces in his new book and the one that was present in his previous book – are descriptively implausible, and finally unnecessary, even though this problem would not affect, in any case, the importance and attraction of his works. Let me briefly refer in what follows to some of the problems I have in mind that are related to his recent book.

To begin with, all the classificatory efforts he makes (particularly those summarised in his 'four-stage dynamic') sound somehow odd coming from an author who, reasonably and from the very beginning of his new book (actually

[20] *Id.* at 8.
[21] *Id.* at 10.
[22] *Id.*
[23] *Id.* at 159.
[24] Bruce Ackerman, We the People, Volume 3: The Civil Rights Revolution 43–47 (2014). See also Bruce Ackerman, We the People, Volume 1: Foundations (1993); Bruce Ackerman, *The New Separation of Powers*, 113 Harv. L. Rev. 633 (2000).

from the second paragraph of *The Rise of World Constitutionalism*), denounces the pretention of studying constitutionalism as 'a 'one-size-fits-all' ideal that animates a common project throughout the world'.[25] Why, then, does he insist on those paths and periods when, as we shall see, the exceptions and deviated cases are so many?

Also, and in spite of what Ackerman says at different points in his book, it is not clear that his work has the merely descriptive character he claims it to have. At the very beginning of his book, he states: 'I want to understand the different historical and cultural dynamics that have transformed each of [the ideal-types] into powerful engines of legitimation over the course of the twentieth century'.[26] Later on, he persists with this idea by mentioning that he wants to 'bracket' his 'own philosophical commitments to make a different point', namely that 'regardless of whether they are "right" or "wrong" revolutionary movement-parties confront the same series of legitimation problems in constitutionalizing their charisma over time'.[27] Now, in spite of all these warnings and clarifications, his work looks fundamentally 'normative'. He does seem to be primarily interested in making critical judgements about the legal evolution of different countries. At almost every point of the book, he is ready to make critical judgements about the evolution of constitutionalism and also ready to show that he has in mind very specific ideas about what a proper constitutional evolution should look like.

IV. A *Procrustean* Approach?

What about the actual cases Ackerman describes? In my view, many of his descriptive histories look fragile. To be sure, most countries have gone through processes of mass mobilisation; almost all have constitutions, which among other things have created a system of judicial review; and all have fallen – at one moment or other – into profound political and social crises. But it is a different thing to affirm that those facts concatenate in a certain specific way, to state that these moments always or frequently follow one after the other, or to claim that they appear in a somehow predictable sequence. To maintain those claims, I believe, would require underlining or highlighting certain historical facts, while neglecting others of similar or greater importance. In fact, the exceptions and variations that Ackerman himself recognises in relation to his classifications are so numerous that his schema ends up becoming somehow useless.

One initial reply would be this: Ackerman's book does not need such classifications. He is only trying to make his explanation clearer. He is simply attempting to organise the comparative data that he has collected in the best way.

[25] Ackerman, *supra* note 1 at 5.
[26] *Id.* at 1.
[27] *Id.* at 36.

Another possible reply would be this: Ackerman is presenting some 'ideal types' that are not supposed to describe actual reality, but only serve as ideal models to organise and think about actual facts. I understand those claims and I sympathise with those ambitions. However, I am afraid that a more significant problem is involved here. This would be so because, in my view, his analytical schema – his 'common framework for comparing some of the greatest revolutions of the twentieth century' – tends to appear, on occasions, like a kind of *Procrustean bed*, where historical facts are selected in order to make them conform to the announced schema. In some occasions, he appears to be choosing certain facts, underlining certain events or ignoring the importance of other factors, mainly in order to make history fit into his classification.

Let us now pay attention to some of Ackerman's more detailed descriptions relating to cases such as India, South Africa, France, Italy, Poland, Israel and Iran. From this list, the cases of Italy and India seem to provide the best examples of the dynamics that he describes, particularly if we pay attention to the way in which, in both countries, the revolutionary principles evolved and became finally consolidated through judicial supremacy. Now, Ackerman himself recognises that South Africa offers an important variation to the model, while France's Fourth Republic would constitute the 'big exception', given that the judiciary 'made no similar claims to supremacy during the regime's brief existence'.[28] So here we have two cases that, in his own opinion, are somehow deviated from the general rule. But what about the other cases, such that of India, which seems to be one of the 'good' cases? Does this case really confirm or favour Ackerman's approach? I doubt it, particularly if we pay attention to the way in which India has evolved in recent decades and the way in which its highest court worked in relation to the ideal of consolidating the old revolutionary principles incorporated into the Constitution. In my view – and I will explore this this case in more detail below – the Indian Supreme Court has been systematically failing to fulfil its expected or desired role as a tribunal that worked for the sake of the disadvantaged. One could in fact claim that its decisions over the last decade or so have been either socially irrelevant or contrary to the expectations the tribunal itself had contributed to developing (see below).

In addition, take the case of Italy, which also seems to offer a 'good' example concerning Ackerman's general approach. My understanding of this case, and particularly about the working of the Italian Constitutional Court in recent decades, differs from the more optimistic view about it that appears in *The Rise of World Constitutionalism*. But let me put my own opinions on the subject into brackets and stick to Ackerman's own words about it. The fact is that Ackerman dedicates less than one page to the description of Italy's Time Four, which is curious given that this case seemed promising in terms of supporting his approach. What is more concerning about his description here is that, among the few things

[28] *Id.* at 160.

he says about the 'good' Italian case, he openly admits that his initial assumptions on the matter showed 'limits'. This is so, he claims, because while justices decisively displaced traditional centres of legal authority, they acted with great restraint on the political front. 'Justices', he claims, 'played no role' in the main political struggles of the time, and in the first 15 years after fascism 'only struck down laws passed during the Fascist, or earlier, eras'.[29] The point is that even the 'good' Italian case seems, in the end, to be a rather anomalous one in terms of what concerns Ackerman's analytical schema. I am leaving aside the analysis of the unpredictable, irregular cases of Iran or Poland, which seem very difficult to understand and classify, from whatever theoretical or historical perspective we have assumed. In conclusion, and considering all these difficulties, one wonders whether Ackerman's classification of four periods is descriptively interesting, accurate or useful at all.

Now, my previous comments referred to the cases that Ackerman presented in his book. However, before concluding this section, I would like to say a few words about cases coming from Latin America, which I know best – cases that, I believe, Ackerman is reserving for his following volume on comparative constitutionalism. First (and this initial difference might be the source of all the following disagreements), I would tend to classify the Latin American cases as instances of revolutionary constitutionalism. Contemporary Latin American constitutionalism is clearly rooted in the region's nineteenth-century revolutions. More to the point, it seems clear to me that the basic structure of most contemporary Latin American constitutions (particularly in terms of the organisation of powers) is intimately related to the constitutional structure that was developed in the region during the 1850s.[30] From that perspective, if I had to find something like Ackerman's four periods in Latin America, it would be very difficult for me to determine where to look. For instance, in the search of Time One, it would be difficult for me to recognise what revolution should be taken into account (the independence revolutions that took place during the 1810s, social revolutions like the Mexican 1910 revolution, legal revolutions such as the one that took place in Colombia in 1991?). In the search for Time Two, I would find it difficult to decide which among the numerous constitutions that were adopted in the region over the last two centuries should be given relevance (there were more than 100 constitutions written during the nineteenth century and more than 100 constitutions during the twentieth century). In the search for Time Three, I would not know which of the numerous crises or periods of crises that regularly exploded in the area deserved special attention. Worse still, and in the search for Time Four, I would tend to underline the political dependence of the judiciary rather than their (independent) work on the consolidation of the founding principles. In fact, and in relation to the judiciary,

[29] *Id.* at 155.

[30] This is one of the main points that I defended in my book THE LEGAL FOUNDATIONS OF INEQUALITY (2010) and also in LATIN AMERICAN CONSTITUTIONALISM 1810-2010 (2013).

we would find some exceptional cases of active constitutional courts in the absence (or in place) of high-energy politics (high-energy politics that was sometimes prevented by a high level of political violence, like in Colombia), but, most commonly, cases of high-energy politics followed by non-autonomous or politically dependent courts (eg, in Venezuela, Ecuador, Bolivia, Nicaragua and many other countries).

Let me conclude this section by saying something that I hope can be valid both for this new book and for previous books like *The Civil Rights Revolution* too. My uneasiness with Ackerman's 'six-phase' dynamic of 'constitutional moments' or his present 'four-stage' phase of 'revolutionary constitutionalism' does not affect what I understand is the core of his project(s). I do believe that the distinction he proposed between 'normal politics' and 'constitutional moments' has provoked a paradigm shift in the study of constitutionalism, and I think that this highly ambitious new book will make a definite contribution to the novel discipline of comparative constitutionalism; his approach to the cases is so rich, full of details and novel insights that his contribution will be lasting. But these enormous achievements do not need the 'six-phase' dynamic or the 'four-stage' phase. Ackerman's great academic contributions in these recent books are independent of those schemas. In other words, we do not need to assert the accuracy of those phases in order to recognise the high value of Ackerman's renewed insights to constitutionalism.

V. Which Theory of History?

Ackerman's characterisation of the four periods (Time One to Time Four) that would distinguish revolutionary constitutionalism is extremely brief. The summary that I presented at the beginning of this chapter covers, I believe, the essence of what he says in the book about those moments. Then, in the remaining chapters, Ackerman offers illustrations of those moments, related to specific case studies, which sometimes help him to provide a more detailed account of his view about history.

Now, given the importance of the sequence, which in the different chapters organises the presentation of the different cases, a fuller or more complete foundation of Ackerman's theory of history would have been useful. Readers may reasonably ask him to provide more arguments in support of his fundamental claims about the 'dynamics of history'. They may pose questions like the following: what would explain which countries tend to follow those paths? Why would many countries follow those ways and not alternative ones? Why would revolutionaries and their followers tend to privilege their commitments to the revolution rather than their purely egoistic self-interest? Why would constitution-makers try to honour the will of the 'founding fathers' rather than serve their own interests? Why would judges feel constrained to defend the legacy of the founders rather than protect their own privileges? Which political and social alliances would support and explicate these developments? What would motivate the different actors in such different countries and moments of history to act in similar ways? What would be the micro-foundations –the 'nuts and bolts' – of those movements?[31] How and why – out of what motivations – would the main actors of history move from here (Time One) to there (Time Four)?

Let me be clear about this: to elaborate a full theory of history seems an extraordinary difficult project to complete. But the fact is that Ackerman suggests to have such an understanding about how constitutional history evolves – his 'four-phase dynamic of revolutionary constitutionalism' suggests so.[32] In fact, in every chapter, he insists on giving this 'dynamic' a central place in his explanations about how each of the selected countries evolves. The problem that is present here, I believe, is bigger than suggested. It is not only that Ackerman refers to a theory of history that he does not fully expose and explain, but also that the theory that he seems to be suggesting seems wrong. If his theory of history seems wrong, this is because his account of history is –in my view – overlegalistic and insufficiently informed by social and economic elements.

Now, even though developing a theory of history (or, more precisely, of legal history) is not an easy task, we still find cases of some authors who have tried to build it and have offered elaborate attempts to understand and explain the progression of history. I want to refer to some of these attempts because of what they can teach us concerning how to approach the dynamics of history. Take, for instance, Karl Marx's dialectic approach to history. Marx's view on the subject was complex and somehow ambiguous, but still powerful. In one of the best studies of Marx's views on this subject, Jon Elster explored two candidates for the 'fundamental motive force in [Marx's view of] history'. The first of these explanations would say that all history is the history of the relationship between productive forces and relations of production: 'The relations of production that distinguish modes of production from one another rise and fall according to their tendency to promote or hinder the growth of the productive forces.'[33] This view would be derived from Marx's book on *The German Ideology* and also from his Preface to *A Contribution to the Critique of Political Economy*. Meanwhile, the second explanation would be derived from Marx's famous dictum in *The Communist Manifesto*, according to which: 'The history of all hitherto existing society is the history of class struggle.'[34]

[31] See Jon Elster, Explaining Social Behavior (2015).

[32] Ackerman, *supra* note 1 at 43.

[33] See Jon Elster, Making Sense of Marx (1987).

[34] Both of these explanations have some plausibility, but the problem is that they are not clearly interconnected, so we do not know which one to choose and for what reason, or why to abandon the other. Elster also analyses at least one possible way of relating one explanation to the other. For this more complex, interrelated explanation, 'history would be the succession of ever more powerful institutions for extracting the surplus from the immediate producers'. This alternative view would serve to connect the development of productive forces with class struggle. Thus, classes would 'confront one another over surplus extraction'; see Elster, *supra* note 33 at 304. The problem with this more plausible view would be that Marx never exposed it openly, although it would be implicit in his account of the transition from feudalism to capitalism.

Another interesting, and more recent, theory of history is the one offered by Professor Barrington Moore in his book *Social Origins of Dictatorship and Democracy*.[35] Moore's approach is particularly interesting for our purposes because revolutionary moments play a crucial role in his account and also because his selection of country case studies is, surprisingly or not, quite similar to Ackerman's case studies. In fact, Moore examines 'Lord and Peasant in the Making of the Modern World' (this is the subtitle of his book) through eight main examples, namely those of England, France, the US, Germany, Russia, China, Japan and India. In addition, Moore's view seems attractive because of the way in which it focuses on human decisions, motivations and rationality in order to understand the progress of history (in this aspect, his approach seems more complete than the one offered by Marx).

In his book, which was first published in 1966, Moore explains the state's path from feudalism to modernity in ways that have many things in common with the Marxist explanation, including the centrality he gives to class relations and the attention he gives to social and economic factors. *Social Origins* in particular focuses on great landowners and rural peasants, the class alliances that they constitute, and their confrontation with the growing interests of urban business and central government. It shows how different class-based responses to similar economic developments generated three main political outcomes in different contexts, namely democracy, fascism and communism.[36]

My interest in referring to Marx and Moore's theories of history has been twofold. I wanted to show, first, that we have some initially plausible theories of history that can help us reconstruct and explain the evolution of our countries. In addition, I was interested in showing that theories like those offered by Marx and Moore properly stressed the importance of social and economic factors in the explanation of history – factors that, unfortunately, do not occupy a central role in Ackerman's reconstruction of history.

Of course, I understand that Ackerman is not interested in describing or explaining the history of the world, but rather the evolution of constitutionalism. This reason would adequately explain why his approach is centred on constitutions and had constitution-makers or judges as the main actors. However, still in this

[35] See Barrington Moore, Social Origins of Dictatorship and Democracy (4th ed., 1993).

[36] According to Moore's typology, in 'bourgeois revolutions' such as those that took place in England, France and the US, the new commercial interests absorb the rich landowners and the peasants, and the capitalist and democratic state emerges. In other cases, a 'revolution from above' occurs and the traditional upper classes manage to keep their privileges through repression – this would be the case in the emergence of fascism or Nazism, like in Germany and Japan. Finally, in some cases, a 'peasant revolution' takes place, leading to communism, such as in China and Russia. Moore's view about the development of modern history has been the object of significant criticisms (ie, concerning the role of the bourgeoisie in the development of democracy), but his theory still represents a crucial contribution to our understanding of modern history. See Gregory Luebbert, *Social Foundations of Political Order in Interwar Europe*, 39 World Politics 452 (1987); Dietrich Rueschmeyer, Evelyne Huber & John Stephens, Capitalist Development and Democracy (1992).

case, for an author who has taught us – lawyers and jurists – to pay special attention to 'We the People', this over-emphasis on the role of constitution-makers or judges (frequently, a few outstanding judges rather than the judiciary as a group or class) seems exaggerated (I will return to this point later). Frequently, judicial decisions that, from the perspective of progressive lawyers, look glorious have only a minor impact on the actual life of an entire society. If this were frequently the case (as I assume it is), then to insist in presenting the legal history of our countries as intimately related to some spectacular judgments courts or justices seems inappropriate.

VI. From 'We the People' to 'We the Judges'

At the end of *The Civil Rights Revolution*, Ackerman refers to some problems that legal scholars attributed to his work. In this book, he recognised the force and importance of some of those criticisms. Here, I want to refer to some of those comments because I think these are also relevant for understanding some difficulties that I also find present in his new book. Let me begin by mentioning two of the problems that he himself recognised in his previous volume. First, in *The Civil Rights Revolution*, he concedes that his book failed to 'do justice to social justice movements' for groups such as women and the poor.[37] In addition, he recognises that in his work he was too focused on 'top-down' decisions by those in power (he admits that his is a 'Washington-centered book', which failed 'to integrate the voices of movement activists'). I believe that the kinds of problems that were present in his previous book (a view from the standpoint of 'We the Judges') continue to be present in *The Rise of World Constitutionalism*. This seems curious, given that, from the beginning of his new book, Ackerman shows that he is aware of these risks. Moreover, he openly objects to traditional approaches to comparative constitutionalism adopting a court-centred approach. In spite of all this, his analysis in *The Rise of World Constitutionalism* still seems to be excessively legalistic –a tribute to juristocracy and 'We the Judges'. His books gives disproportionate attention to certain courts and decisions, focusing excessively on how judges decide and what they say in their decisions, and – in the most extreme cases – on certain 'heroic' judges (thus, for instance, in his considerations about Aharon Barak). In this way, one could claim that his analysis pays insufficient attention to how 'We the People' receive, process and reshape legal and judicial decisions. This is, I believe, a serious problem for someone like him, who was well aware of the risk of legalism. This seems particularly concerning in the work of someone who taught us how to look at the law from below and also about the importance of adopting the perspective of social movements.

[37] Ackerman, We the People, Volume 3, *supra* note 23 at 314.

Let me use the case of the Indian Supreme Court to illustrate what would be, in my view, an improperly biased legal analysis – an analysis that is improperly biased towards 'We the Judges'. Because of some really spectacular decisions made by this Court – particularly, but not only, when it was led by Justice Bhagwati (1985–86) – the main Indian tribunal became the focus of great international admiration. Legal doctrinaires from every part of the world came to study and write about this case.[38] Ackerman seems to subscribe the glorious version of the Indian Supreme Court. In fact, he summarises the experience of the Indian Court as 'a vivid example of the 'consolidation' dynamic described', where it 'became an increasingly confident guardian of the constitutional legacy',[39] and he also claims that 'the court's case-law has often emphasized the enduring relevance of the founding era's constitutional commitments'.[40]

I find many problems in Ackerman's approach to the work of the Indian Supreme Court (problems that, I want to insist, illustrate his approach to high courts in general). First, his description is, in my view, not only incomplete but also incorrectly focused on a very particular (and rather short) period of the history of the Indian Court. This presentation neglects, in my view, what has been a consistent and worrisome evolution of its jurisprudence in recent years. In fact, some authors have presented the Indian Court as an isolated, elite institution, which has been working not for the consolidation, but rather for the actual demolition of the principles of social justice embodied into the Indian Constitution.[41] The general point is that Ackerman's view about courts seems descriptively objectionable, but – let me say – objectionable in a particular way: he seems inclined to consider Supreme Court Justices as the main (and positive) characters of the political story of our time.

[38] See Uprenda Baxi, *Taking Suffering Seriously: Social Action Litigation in the Supreme Court of India*, 4 Third World Studies 107 (1985); P. Craig & S.L. Deshpande, *Rights, Autonomy and Process: Public Interest Litigation in India*, 9 Oxford Journal of Legal Studies 356 (1989); Mark Galanter & Jayanth Krishnan, *Bread for the Poor: Access to Justice and the Rights of the Needy in India*, 55 Hastings Law Journal 789 (2003); Varun Gauri, *Fundamental Rights and Public Interest Litigation in India*, 1 Indian Journal of Law and Economics 71 (2011).

[39] Ackerman, *supra* note 1 at 72.

[40] *Id.*

[41] It has been claimed, in fact, that 'the multiplicity of court-appointed bodies, the lack of clarity about their terms of reference and procedures, the extent of their investigative or executive powers and the non-availability of their records or minutes together made the entire adjudicatory process of PIL impenetrable and almost impossible to challenge'. See Anuj Bhuwania, Courting the People: Public Interest Litigation in Post-Emergency India (2017) 9. In recent years, it has been said that 'the PIL procedure enabled it to function as a highly effective slum demolition machine. Almost a million people were made homeless by the wonders of PIL in the first decade of the twenty-first century in Delhi. This ferocious campaign utilized the undemocratic potential of PIL to the fullest.' For these critics, the PIL has infected Indian legal culture more generally … [becoming in this way notorious for] the challenge it poses to democracy in India' (*id.* at 13). Again, we may disagree about the extent and deepness of the crisis of the Indian Supreme Court, but we should not minimise the importance of such a crisis. See also, for instance, the journal *Verfassubg ybd Recht in Ubersee. Law and Politics in Africa, Asia and Latin America*, which dedicated one of its 2018 issues to the crisis of the Indian Court.

Similarly, Ackerman's analysis seems too focused on the role of high courts, but in ways that obscure or neglect the actual life of Indian civil society. In this way, his analysis would disregard the impact of the Supreme Court's decisions in the actual life of 'We the People'. His description, one could say, would be 'relying on We the Judges instead of We the People'.[42] In this way, his new book would (again) be too concerned with 'top-down' decisions by those in power, thus failing 'to integrate the voices of movement activists'. These were, as we know, the kinds of problems that he himself identified as difficulties that were present in his previous book.[43]

In sum, it is not by chance that I have been comparing Ackerman's *The Rise of World Constitutionalism* with his previous work on *We the People* or *The Civil Rights Revolution*. The problem is that, in spite of himself, he tends to take the example of the US – with the independence revolution, the 'founding fathers', the role of courts, the life of Supreme Court Justices etc – as a model, and thus as the parameter from which to examine, understand and evaluate the working of foreign constitutional systems.

VII. The Normalisation of Domination

Let me conclude this chapter by proposing, in an extremely tentative way, an alternative approach to legal history, which would try to take into consideration the social and economic factors that seem to be mostly absent from Ackerman's book. This alternative approach, I submit, would refer us to conclusions that would significantly differ from Ackerman's conclusions. In particular, I believe that we

[42] See Ackerman, We the People, Volume 3, *supra* note 23 at 290, 330, 322.

[43] Let me offer some data in support to my previous claims. Most scholars agree on the fact that the Indian Court has become much more active on socio-economic affairs since the late 1970s; see, for instance, Sanjay Ruparelia, A Progressive Juristocracy? The Unexpected Social Activism of India's Supreme Court (Kellogg Institute, 2013) https://kellogg.nd.edu/sites/default/files/old_files/documents/391_0.pdf). Now consider the following statistics. According to a recent paper by Chancel and Piketty, 'over the 1951–1980 period, the bottom 50% group, in India, captured 28% of total growth and incomes of this group grew faster than the average, while top 0.1% incomes decreased. Over the 1980–2014 period, the situation was reversed; the top 0.1% of earners captured a higher share of total growth than the bottom 50% (12% vs. 11%), while the top 1% received a higher share of total growth than the middle 40% (29% vs. 23%)'; Lucas Chancel & Thomas Piketty, Indian Income Inequality, 1922–2014: From British Raj to Billionaire Raj?, Wid. World Working Paper Series (2017), http://wid.world/wp-content/uploads/2017/12/ChancelPiketty2017WIDworld.pdf. In other words, the years of hyper-activism on the part of the Indian Supreme Court on socio-economic affairs was not accompanied by a gradual moderation or reversal of the country's profound social and economic inequalities. By contrast, these were precisely the years when the gradual equalisation ended and the levels of inequality became much bigger. Of course, I do not mean to say that the Court was responsible for these horrendous social figures, but I do want to stress that we scholars need to take such economic and social figures more seriously in our analysis of judicial decisions. If we do not pay attention to these figures, we run the risk of ascribing a merely formal and legalistic approach to constitutionalism. We may then assume that the law is working for social equality when it is not, or we may come to believe that some progressive judicial decisions are changing social history when social history is running in the opposite direction and moving according to other, independent causes.

would thus come to understand the working of politicians and judges differently – we would thus recognise that in many contemporary societies, judges and politicians do not tend to work primarily for the consolidation of revolutionary principles of any kind. My suggestion would be that these top public officers tend to work for the *normalisation of domination*, so to speak.[44] Let me add a few and tentative comments in order to support these claims.

A. Politicians

To begin with, an alternative view that emphasised the existing connections between social inequality, class and the law would be more sceptical about Ackerman's ideas about revolutionary leaders and politicians in general. For Ackerman, political leaders recognise an obligation to constitutionalise the principles that motivated the great struggles of the past.[45] He advances such a claim in the midst of his polemic against authors who have adopted a rational-choice approach. While the latter tend to reduce constitutional moments to rational calculations and self-interest, Ackerman maintains that the revolutionary constitution 'emerges from a period of passionate insurgency against the old regime'. In a similar vein, he claims that 'in the revolutionary scenario', the 'movement-leadership enters the constituent assembly with pride in the great sacrifices that their followers have made for the common good; they do not view passionate commitment with fear and trembling'.[46] In particular, he distinguishes his conclusions about constitutional conventions from Jon Elster's early conclusions on the matter: 'to put it mildly, this is not the mind-set captured by Elster's invocation of Ulysses and the Sirens … [T]he revolutionary pathway has in fact generated constitutional arrangements that have imposed powerful constraints on would-be autocrats. The challenge is to see understand how and why this has happened repeatedly over the course of the twentieth century'.[47]

Now, it seems clear that Elster's original view on Ulysses and the Sirens was both attractive and misleading. Elster, in fact, did not take into consideration all the reasons and passions that characterise constitutional moments. But it is a little unfair not to recognise that the same Elster became the main critic of his earlier approach to Ulysses and thus came to argue that 'constitution-makers are *more* likely to be vulnerable to impulsive passions than those whose behavior they are trying to regulate'.[48] Elster admits that he changed his initial views on Ulysses after

[44] By this, I mean that in the context of unequal societies, politicians and judges tend to reinforce rather than challenge the existing (or new) status quo, which usually implies the preservation of the main social and economic inequalities prevailing in society.

[45] Ackerman, *supra* note 1 at 40, 46.

[46] *Id.*

[47] *Id.*

[48] Jon Elster, Ulysses Unbound (2000) 173; Jon Elster, Roberto Gargarella et al., Constitutional Conventions (2018).

his conversations with historians, who taught him that, usually, 'in politics, people never try to bind themselves, only to bind others'.[49] For him, this statement was too stark, but still 'closer to the truth than the view that self-binding is the essence of constitution-making'.[50] I fully share his new conclusions, particularly if they are applied to the context of unequal societies. This new conclusion, I submit, tends to match what common sense would suggest and would at the same time be open (naturally) to thousands of additional, occasional and unpredicted variations. Ackerman's more idealistic approach seems, by contrast, distanced from truth and common sense, and also distant from what a class-oriented approach to history would predict.

B. Judges

There are numerous elements to consider in order to explain judicial behaviour. These elements include references to the way in which judges are appointed, the way in which they socialize with other judges, the conditions of their stability, their tenure, their degree of independence from politics, the existing levels of popular mobilisation etc.[51] My impression is that in the context of unequal societies – and particularly in profoundly unequal societies, such as those of India, South Africa, Colombia and Brazil – one should expect judges to work for what I called the 'normalization of domination'. In other words, in those contexts of inequality, one should not expect judges – who usually tend to be selected from the upper sectors of society – to challenge the social elite to which they belong or in other ways contribute to undermining the economic structures from which they emerged.

This sceptical view about judicial behaviour and judicial decisions would help us understand certain outcomes that otherwise would be difficult to comprehend. To begin with, in unequal societies, the presence of independent courts, the presence of 'activist' courts and the presence of 'socially activist' courts (for example, courts that are concerned with the 'social question') does not seem to be correlated with a reduction in the existing levels of social and economic inequalities.[52] To state this does not imply saying that Courts play an 'oppressive' institutional role, but is consistent instead with the idea that Courts tend to work for the 'normalisation

[49] Elster, Ulysses Unbound, *supra* note 48 at ix.

[50] He states: 'In *Ulysses and the Sirens* I came close to claiming both that constitutions *are precommitment* devices (in the intentional sense), and that societies *ought to* bind themselves by constitutional precommitment devices. As I have been saying in various places earlier, these claims are eminently contestable, on conceptual, causal, and normative grounds'; *id.* at 167.

[51] Among many others, see, for instance, Gretchen Helmke, Courts under Constraints: Judges, Generals and Presidents in Argentina (2005); Lee Epstein & Stephanie Lindquist, eds., The Oxford Handbook of US Judicial Behavior (2017).

[52] I tried to support this claim by offering some data related to the case of India (see above). There are other works on other socially activist courts, such as the Colombian Constitutional Court, which go in the same direction.

of domination'. In fact, in a series of empirical studies on courts that I co-directed, we found that in the context of unequal societies, courts acted in many different ways: there were courts that tended to honour, say, the principles of the founding period, but also courts that tended to do the contrary; we found socially activist courts and non-activist courts; we found courts that seemed to be committed to the cause of the disadvantaged and courts that were not.[53] These variations are again consistent with the idea that courts work for the 'normalization of domination', but do not match well with Ackerman's suggestions about the work of courts in the 'consolidation period' or Time Four.

In sum, the counter-intuitive character of many of Ackerman's central claims about, say, the role of revolutionary politicians and Supreme Court judges put the burden of proof on his side. I believe it is his task to convince us about what seem to be, in principle, controversial claims about what passionate revolutionaries, committed constitution-makers and heroic judges would tend to do with the extraordinary powers they enjoy in the context of unequal societies.

[53] Roberto Gargarella, Pilar Domingo & Theunis Roux, Courts and Social Transformation in New Democracies (2006).

5

Constitutionalism and the Predicament of Postcolonial Independence

AZIZ RANA

I. Introduction

Perhaps no other political and legal technology is more closely identified today with the modern nation-state than the written constitution. When the US, France and Poland adopted their constitutions in the late eighteenth century, they were historical anomalies. Very few existing states had such formally implemented documents and, indeed, of the states that existed before 1789 (the year the US Federal Constitution went into effect), half would go over 300 years before eventually writing their own texts.[1] But by the mid-nineteenth century, constitution writing had become an almost automatic political act for new states. As Zachary Elkins, Tom Ginsburg and James Melton write, 'by the second year of life a full 85 percent of post-1789 states had adopted their first constitution, and by five years, almost 95 percent of them had such instruments'.[2] Even more tellingly, 220 states have appeared on the global stage since 1789 and between them they have produced a remarkable 900 written constitutions.[3]

If constitution writing has become such a prerequisite of modern statecraft, this raises a set of foundational questions, ones that scholars have explored for decades: what challenges do new constitutions face when taking root in a particular state? What conclusions can be drawn about when constitutions are likely to succeed or fail? And, more generally, why have written constitutions so endured as a technology of governance? Bruce Ackerman's first volume in a planned trilogy, *Revolutionary Constitutions: Charismatic Leadership and the Rule of Law*, is a landmark engagement with these issues and an essential contribution to the field of

[1] Zachary Elkins et. al., The Endurance of National Constitutions 42 (2009).
[2] *Id.*
[3] Tom Ginsburg, *Written Constitutions around the World*, 15 Insights on Law & Soc. (2015).

comparative constitutional development. In it, Ackerman argues that the answer rests on more than just the contingent experiences of specific countries. Rather, the constitutional projects of modern states have generally followed one of three distinct pathways grounded in how they were initially constructed: revolutionary, establishmentarian and elite. Although all constitutional projects confront problems of institutional and ideological legitimacy, these legitimacy struggles have taken different forms depending on the particular pathway. And according to Ackerman, only by understanding these pathways can we make sense of today's ongoing constitutional crises, since not all crises are alike. Instead, to the extent that particular cases fit one or another of the pathways, they are likely to face distinctive issues of legitimation and entrenchment.

For starters, revolutionary constitutions are the product of successful revolts in which 'revolutionary outsiders' are able to overthrow 'establishment insiders' and then institutionalise their rule through new founding instruments.[4] In these revolutionary settings, the central challenge is how to avoid the problem of permanent upheaval. To endure over time such constitutional projects must somehow 'translate … high-energy politics'[5] into a durable governing model. This is especially urgent once the founding generation begins to exit the political stage and new leaders emerge who do not have the same personal revolutionary authority. Ackerman refers to this predicament as a matter of 'constitutionaliz[ing] … revolutionary charisma'.[6]

By contrast, establishmentarian constitutionalism develops when 'pragmatic insiders'[7] are able to diffuse popular movements for fundamental change. These insiders succeed in dividing 'revolutionary outsiders'[8] into moderate and radical camps, and then convince the former to join them in new governing arrangements marked by landmark reform legislation. Under such projects, legitimacy emerges through the repeated success of political leaders in being able to reach common ground across divisions and to 'muddle their way through'[9] in the face of crises. But what happens when such muddling fails and the short-term calculations of responsible insiders generate deadlock? For these regimes, reverting to popular referenda or other invocations of 'We the People' is inherently hazardous, since it risks subverting establishment legitimacy and generating cycles of '[d]isestablishment'.[10]

Finally, the third pathway of constitutional development is elitist, emerging without any backdrop of 'massive popular uprising'.[11] A combination of previously

[4] Bruce Ackerman, Revolutionary Constitutions: Charismatic Leadership and the Rule of Law 3 (2019).

[5] *Id.* at 4.

[6] *Id.*

[7] *Id.*

[8] *Id.*

[9] *Id.* at 21.

[10] *Id.* at 10.

[11] *Id.* at 6.

excluded and old elites constructs a new political order that is not a 'revolutionary creation'.[12] But unlike the establishment model, old elites have limited control of these developments. Rather than holding on to power by making 'strategic concessions', old elites only retain some 'share of power' by giving up meaningful control and accepting 'elaborate compact[s] with outside elites'.[13] For such arrangements, the basic challenge is that of 'authenticity'.[14] These projects face serious difficulties in gaining buy-in from the broader population, a population that was essentially excluded in constitutional genesis and maintenance.

What makes Ackerman's analysis so compelling is its ability to tease out the shared dilemmas of seemingly divergent societies, highlighting, for instance, how from the US and France to India and South Africa, the issue of how best to constitutionalise revolutionary charisma has proceeded through clear iterative steps. One of the most significant contributions of the book is to unsettle the tendency to engage in comparison across familiar regional or ideological examples. By contrast, Ackerman suggests provocatively that the US experience may have more in common with revolutionary histories in places like Iran or South Africa than with elite projects in Europe. Ackerman thus helps us see beyond the conventional terms by which readers have been trained to divide up the world: between liberal democracies and authoritarian regimes and, especially, between the 'West' and the rest of the globe.

Moreover, Ackerman's reassessment of the US project in volume one's final pages presents a beautiful critique of American constitutional exceptionalism. Focusing on Franklin Delano Roosevelt's choice to pursue constitutional change during the New Deal era through court-packing rather than formal amendment, he underscores the similarity of this dilemma with equivalent challenges for constitutionalising revolutionary charisma in India and Israel. He also uses these comparative cases to tease out the tragic consequences for the New Deal of Roosevelt's decision to avoid the Article V path. By emphasising court appointments and eschewing formal change, Roosevelt not only lost the fight over court-packing, but also left the era's constitutional reforms far more open to reversal by future Supreme Courts. In this way, Ackerman's global lens provides an organising structure to a wide plethora of constitutional experiences. It also allows the American reader to see with fresh eyes their own familiar case – a real achievement.

However, for the remainder of this chapter, I would like to focus on something that Ackerman's approach tends to avoid. This is the broader international context for the vast majority of modern constitutional projects: the breakdown of the imperial global order and how that breakdown shaped the terms of postcolonial

[12] *Id.*
[13] *Id.*
[14] *Id.* at 18.

constitutional development in a manner that cannot be reduced to Ackermanian pathway. If statehood and constitution writing have proceeded together in lockstep since the mid-1800s and have both proliferated exponentially in the twentieth century, why has this been the case? The answer is relatively straightforward. The spread of constitutions was the product of the collapse of the great European empires and the emergence of newly independent nation-states, especially during particular 'global waves'[15] that punctuated modern history: the revolutionary upheavals of 1848, the two world wars, the Cold War and the fall of the Soviet Union. At the heart of new projects of statehood was the desire of nationalist elites to establish both independence from past imperial rulers and to assert the equal and sovereign status of their polities vis-a-vis previous great powers and state formations. Constitutions emerged as a key institutional and symbolic mechanism for establishing legitimate sovereign statehood internationally and for codifying for domestic audiences both political rupture and the principles of the new polity. In this way, the global rise of constitutions is inextricably bound to the long historical narrative of decolonisation, beginning with the eighteenth-century fracture of European imperialism in places like the US and continuing all way to the post-Second World War anti-colonial struggles and political foundings across Asia and Africa.

Yet from the start, constitutional legitimacy faced two profound challenges rooted in the historical predicament of the postcolonial state. The first challenge concerned what Ghanaian President Kwame Nkrumah famously called 'neo-colonialism':[16] how can one ensure that a formally independent state actually enjoys meaningful control over its internal economic and political decision-making? This struggle often facilitated the constitutionalisation of centralised and expansive executive power, aimed at overcoming perceived internal divisions and ensuring political unity in the face of global pressures. As section II will explore, by highlighting the surprising links between the American and Kenyan post-independence experience, postcolonial states often found themselves facing common dilemmas and resorting to similar constitutional responses regardless of the initial Ackermanian pathway.

Section III then turns briefly to the second challenge, which also has bedeviled the constitutional politics of postcolonial states in ways that cannot be straightforwardly linked to revolutionary, establishment or elite genesis. The issue here is that twentieth-century American and European ideas of what a post-imperial global order should look like emphasised transforming multi-communal and plural imperial polities into distinct nation-states, each built around a single ethno-cultural or religious 'people'. However, the problem was that all such states necessarily had a majority ethnic community and a minority that found itself on the outside looking in. The result were constitutional orders that over time generated

[15] Ginsberg, *supra* note 3.
[16] Kwame Nkrumah, Neo-colonialism: The Last Stage of Imperialism (1969).

mutually reinforcing projects of majoritarian nation-building and minority exclusion and even secession. By way of a conclusion, I draw out the value of combining Ackerman's account with an emphasis on decolonisation in order to understand more fully the twentieth-century history of constitutional crisis. I further note that to the extent that domestic predicaments are bound to features of the international system, reforms must similarly move beyond a focus on internal legal or political alterations alone and also address the structural dynamics of that system.

II. The Spectre of Neo-colonialism and the Turn to Centralised Authority

In 1965, Nkrumah published his seminal book *Neo-colonialism: The Last Stage of Imperialism*, in which he argued that decolonisation may have altered the juridical status of African countries, but it had not produced substantive independence. In place of direct political control, postcolonial societies now faced a variety of economic, financial and trade restrictions imposed by former imperial masters. These restrictions reduced nominally sovereign states to the level of dependent satellites, with limited capacity to dictate the terms of their own collective future. Describing this condition as neo-colonialism, Nkrumah wrote: 'The essence of neo-colonialism is that the State which is subject to it is, in theory, independent and has all the outward trappings of international sovereignty. In reality its economic system and thus its political policy is directed from outside.'[17]

For Nkrumah, economic dependence went hand in hand with two other common experiences. First, neo colonialism, like direct political control, inevitably exported those 'social conflicts'[18] that marked the aggressor state. To the extent that government decisions were dictated from abroad, the inequities embedded in foreign social systems took root locally as well. Thus, foreign states continued to perpetuate forms of corruption and unfreedom in nominally independent societies. Second, unlike the relatively exclusive control exercised in direct imperial relations, postcolonial governments now found themselves in a global arena of competing powers; juridical independence simply meant the capacity to 'change masters'[19] rather than to escape domination once and for all and to 'exist without a neo-colonial master'.[20] Subject to external authority, African states found themselves the economic and political prey of global powers scrambling once more to divide the spoils of the continent.

We usually do not think of the US as a state that faced its own fears of neo-colonialism, and even more rarely do we highlight the continuities between

[17] *Id.* at ix.
[18] *Id.* at xii.
[19] *Id.* at xiv.
[20] *Id.* at 5.

early American constitutional development and that of decolonising African societies. But as a comparison of 1787 America and 1963 Kenya indicates, the structural similarities are nonetheless extensive and had profound effects on shaping early constitutional choices. In particular, independence leaders in both settings were deeply concerned about internal division and the potential for external powers to use disorder to reclaim control. To a remarkable extent, founding constitutional debate was framed around the perceived need for greater legal and political centralisation in the face of external and internal centrifugal tendencies. This means that one can tell a story of shared American and Kenyan constitutional crisis and legitimacy that owes far less to initial pathway and far more to the issue of postcolonial independence in a world of global powers.

A. Postcolonial Weakness and the Articles of Confederation

Ackerman highlights how the US was an early modern experiment in revolutionary constitutionalism. But it was also the first significant postcolonial society. Of course, the latter point must be made with a major caveat. As I have argued elsewhere, in the American context, independence and constitutional founding did not entail the end of colonisation. Rather, political rupture constitutionalised a new imperial project that explicitly empowered local Anglo-European settler populations and thus spurred a second phase of both expansion and political control over indigenous, enslaved and outsider groups. This meant that instead of simply one history of empire, the US was marked by a double history of English and then locally led expropriation.[21]

Nonetheless, the break from England placed the new settler polity in a position that Nkrumah would have found familiar and, indeed, his neo-colonial spectre was an intense preoccupation for revolutionary-era leaders.[22] North American colonies developed as mercantile appendages of the British Crown, which dictated – although not always successfully – economic development and settler migration around the material goals of England's mercantile community. Although the revolution produced a formal end of such control, as historian Walter Licht writes: 'The fortunes of the now former colonialists remained in the grips of British commercial interests; the ups and downs of economic activity during and after the 1780s reflected the abilities of British merchants to flood the American market with good or block American exports.'[23] For the founding generation, the difficulties of breaking from imperial dependence were compounded by the general political weakness of the colonies and the seeming fragility of independence in a world

[21] See Aziz Rana, *Colonialism and Constitutional Memory*, 5 U.C. Irv. L. Rev. 263, 283 (2015).

[22] The arguments in this section draw from Aziz Rana, The Two Faces of American Freedom 131–42 (2010), which develops more fully the competing American settler responses to the danger of neo-colonialism.

[23] Walter Licht, Industrializing America: The Nineteenth Century 18–19 (1995).

of predatory European states. While the colonies may have been able to extract themselves from British control, would such extraction simply replace one master with another that was perhaps even more oppressive? Robert Wiebe comments of revolutionary-era leaders:

> Since 1783 they had pictured their nation as a prisoner on parole, protecting its precarious freedom against international forces that it might elude but never control. Even the best leaders and the most ingenious measures, they believed, could not stop the great powers from swaying America's citizens, corrupting its officials, or infiltrating its governments, scheming against the nation, allying against, or warring against it … Partition, absorption: here were the apt analogies for America's jeopardy.[24]

For those who gathered in Philadelphia, events such as the Shays' Rebellion crystallised the potential threats of dissolution and European subjection that confronted the independent colonies. It underscored the vulnerability facing semi-sovereign polities organized under the Articles of Confederation of 1781, a thoroughly decentralised constitutional system marked by limited national powers of purse and sword, congressional voting tallied by state, no clearly separated national judicial branch, and rotating presidents appointed by Congress. The result was effectively a parliamentary system without an energetic prime minister and with extensive substantive power consciously left to the states.

For defenders of increased centralisation, such as George Washington, the revolt in Massachusetts brought home the extent to which 'the want of energy in our government'[25] left the new polity subject to a combination of popular revolt and external domination. The rebellion itself was initially precipitated by the decision of British merchants to close their doors to American business. The ability of a foreign power to produce internal social strife simply by changing economic policy illustrated the extent to which although formally independent, the colonies remained under external sway.[26] Moreover, the popular unrest that resulted not only imperilled effective government, according to some elites, but also threatened the very permanence of the union. Throughout the 1780s and 1790s, frontier settlers repeatedly contemplated independence from the US under the aegis of one or another European power. Perhaps the most famous of these was the Franklin secession movement, in which the three western counties of North Carolina declared their independence in 1784 and sought a Spanish alliance throughout the 1780s so as to wrest local power away from North Carolina and the Continental Congress.[27]

[24] Robert Wiebe, The Opening of American Society: From the Adoption of the Constitution to the Eve of Disunion 68 (1984).

[25] Quoted in David Szatmary, Shays' Rebellion: The Making of an Agrarian Insurrection 123 (1980).

[26] See generally *id.* at 19–36; and Rana, *supra* note 22 at 100–02.

[27] See Thomas Slaughter, The Whiskey Rebellion: Frontier Epilogue to the American Revolution 51–53 (1986).

Given these worries, for those participating in Philadelphia, behind closed doors and in secret (it should be noted), the possibility of substantive independence rested on creating a central structure that could both limit external control and suppress the potential for future internal disorder – especially that generated by popular economic anxieties. In fact, both Alexander Hamilton and James Madison invoked a postcolonial predicament in arguing for greater executive, legislative and judicial power organised at the federal level. Fearing the possibility that the separate colonies might become ensnared in competing European alliances, Hamilton warned in the *Federalist Papers*:

> America, if not connected at all, or only by the feeble tie of a simple league, offensive and defensive, would, by operation of such jarring alliances, be gradually entangled in all the pernicious labyrinths of European politics and wars; and by the destructive contentions of the parts into which she was divided, would be likely to become a prey to artifices and machinations of powers equally the enemies of them all. *Divide et impera* must be the motto of every nation that either hates us or fears us.[28]

Echoing the same sentiments, Madison argued that without a stronger federal government, the US would remain a weak and dependent satellite, unable to check powerful European states in their pursuit of North American fiefdoms:

> The fortunes of disunited America will be even more disastrous than those of Europe. The sources of evil in the latter are confined to her own limits. No superior powers of another quarter of the global intrigue among her rival nations, inflame their mutual animosities, and render them the instruments of foreign ambitions, jealousy, and revenge. In America the miseries springing from her internal jealousies, contentions, and wars would form a party only of her lot. A plentiful addition of evils would have their source in that relation in which Europe stands to this quarter of the earth, and which no quarter of the earth bears to Europe.[29]

In quoting Hamilton, Madison and Washington, I am not assuming that their dim assessment of the Articles of Confederation was necessarily accurate. In many ways, the decentralised system worked just fine, especially for small farmers on the ground who were able to assert greater control over local decision-making. Thus, I also do not accept Hamilton and company's essentially elitist suspicion of poor settlers or their wariness of direct popular self-rule and opposition to systematic debt relief. But what I do find noteworthy is the extent to which all three figures mimicked precisely the concerns about potential European dependency that became bedrock nationalist fears in post-Second World War African polities. Moreover, while scholars tend to think of the 1787 Constitution as marked by significant constraints on executive and legislative authority, it is useful to appreciate the extent to which (within the context of 1780s post-independence settler politics) the new structure was a significant move towards enhancing just these

[28] Federalist No. 7 (Alexander Hamilton).
[29] Federalist No. 41 (James Madison).

centralising powers. And even the genesis of an independent national judiciary was far less about checking the federal government and far more about employing the courts to legitimate new governing arrangements vis-a-vis recalcitrant states.

But ultimately, the development that critically shifted American concerns away from that of many postcolonial constitutional projects was the practical disappearance of neo-colonialism as a fear in the early nineteenth century. With Europe engulfed in its own internecine struggles – from the Napoleonic Wars to the revolutions of 1848 – and England retreating from direct confrontation with the US after the War of 1812, American development was able to proceed relatively free of external imperial meddling. The types of dismemberment worries that plagued the initial years of the republic became increasingly less relevant for institutional life. As the Kenyan contrast will highlight, this likely played a key role in limiting, during the first half of the nineteenth century, a continual ideological and political resort to greater executive power as a way of safeguarding the polity. As Hamilton recognised, if the new constitution offered much-needed centralised authority, this authority posed the danger of becoming limitless, at worst collapsing into military despotism, if the country remained subject to continuous imperial intervention. Thus, what he called an 'insulated situation'[30] – enhanced by the oceans, but also by European disinterest – operated, at least until the issue of slavery became irreconcilable, to preserve much of the basic institutional framework forged in 1787.

B. Kenya, Executive Despotism and the Demise of the Lancaster Constitution

Very little about the Kenyan example follows the American Ackermanian pathway. If anything, the emergence of the 1963 Constitution at independence most approximated an elite model, with elements also of the establishmentarian model. The end of British rule in Kenya had witnessed a mass anti-colonial uprising known as the Mau Mau Rebellion and led by dispossessed squatters contesting imperial land policy. The revolt highlighted to the British the untenability of permanent colonial authority in Kenya and pressed those in London to accept, albeit haltingly, local independence. But by the time that the British gathered various nationalist, settler and colonial administrative constituencies together in 1960 for extensive constitutional talks at London's Lancaster House, the popular uprising had been brutally suppressed.[31] As with the elite pathway, the British had come to accept that they would be relinquishing effective governance over the country. But they still hoped

[30] Federalist No. 8 (Alexander Hamilton).

[31] For more on the extreme tactics of the British in defeating the Mau Mau, including the use of concentration camps to imprison 'over a million' Kenyans of 'Kikuyu, Embu, Meru and Kamba' origin, see MAKAU MUTUA, KENYA'S QUEST FOR DEMOCRACY: TAMING LEVIATHAN 55–58 (2008); and generally CAROLINE ELKINS, IMPERIAL RECKONING: THE UNTOLD STORY OF BRITAIN'S GULAG IN KENYA (2005).

that the Lancaster talks would generate a constitutional system that safeguarded their key interests.

In particular, the British wanted assurances that the property rights of white settlers on the ground – precisely what had been a central flashpoint in the Mau Mau movement – would be protected and were wary of any constitutional order that might allow the national government to radically redistribute land. These positions were backed at the talks by conservative elements among the nationalists, as well as by representatives of smaller ethnic communities who sought a more decentralised system – given fears that Kikuyus and Luos in particular (the two largest groups) would dominate political power. Although leading independence figures, like Jomo Kenyatta and especially the more radical Oginga Odinga, remained unhappy with the document, they ultimately accepted the new constitution as a condition of speeding the process towards actual independence.[32] In the end, the Lancaster Constitution that went into effect in 1963 was marked by a strong bill of rights, with extensive property protections, a bicameral parliament and a decentralised system of 'autonomous regional governments'.[33] Parliament's upper house, the Senate, was also the meant as a representative institution for the autonomous local regions and thus aimed to preserve this decentralised system of internal regionalism popularly known as 'Majimboism'.

Superficially, the Lancaster Constitution looked most like the 1787 US Constitution, given the degree to which it mirrored American language and had a bill of rights, a Senate aimed at preserving regional interests, a House of Representatives and an independent judiciary. Indeed, Thurgood Marshall himself played a notable role in pressing for these elements. Marshall was a friend of the more conservative Kenyan leader Tom Mboya and a key advisor during the Lancaster negotiations to the most significant African party – of which Kenyatta and Odinga at the time were also both members – the Kenyan African National Union (KANU). Marshall strongly backed Majimboism as well as the importance of ensuring minority and property protections, seeing them together as offering the same 'double security' from majority tyranny that Madison saw in federalism and the separation of powers. If in the US, such tyranny was visited upon black citizens, in Kenya Marshall viewed the relevant threats as towards white settlers and the local Asian population.[34]

But if one peers beyond these similarities, in many ways the Lancaster arrangement more closely embodied for many Kenyan nationalists precisely those worries generated by the Articles of Confederation. From the outset, Odinga saw the document as ill-equipped for confronting Kenya's most immediate challenge – avoiding

[32] See Mutua, *supra* note 31 at 59.

[33] *Id.* at 60.

[34] For more on Marshall's role in constructing the Lancaster Constitution, see Mary Dudziak, *Working Toward Democracy: Thurgood Marshall and the Constitution of Kenya*, 56 Duke L. J. 721–80 (2006).

neo-colonialism and with it both external economic control and internal fracture. As he wrote in 1967:

> The stage following on independence is the most dangerous. This is the point after which many national revolutions in Africa have suffered a setback, for … national governments have left too much in their countries unchanged, have not built for effective independence by transferring power and control to the authentic forces … and have forgotten that internal elements of exploitation are closely related to reactionary external pressures.[35]

In his view, if the problem of land access and a proper distribution of material wealth stood at the heart of anti-colonial resistance, including the Mau Mau Rebellion, this would have to be addressed systematically by the new government or Kenya would remain subject to the same conflicts that had wracked the colonial era. What stood in the way was the long arm of the British and their ability to use 'the temptations of office and property'[36] to maintain control over a subset of nationalist leaders. Even worse, the Lancaster system's constraints on effective central authority meant that even well-meaning leaders were limited in their pursuit of significant change. In his mind, the constitution was a cumbersome behemoth ('one of the most involved constitutions ever devised for Africa')[37] and although 'it ha[d] been called a constitution of checks and balances … I would say there were more checks than anything else'.[38] For Odinga, all of this meant that the neo-colonial spectre was real, as '[e]verything [had been] done to ensure that the accredited heirs of colonial interests capture power'.[39]

As for others in KANU, many came to agree with this sentiment even if they were less committed to Odinga's redistributive goals. Part of the reason was that the early years of independence saw serious secessionist struggles, especially among Somalis in the country's Northern Frontier District. This was a region that had been subject to brutal suppression by the British and where the local community remained wary of the newly independent state, many seeking instead to become part of Somalia.[40] But as with Franklin and other similar movements in the US in the 1780s, such disorder led Kenyan nationalists to question the viability of regionalism at all and to see decentralised politics as a recipe for internal dissolution and external domination.

Consistent with Ackerman's elite pathway, a clear issue for the Lancaster Constitution was its lack of authenticity – the sense among numerous Kenyan independence voices was that it was a patchwork document that no significant

[35] Oginga Odinga, Not Yet Uhuru 255–56 (1967).
[36] *Id.* at 256.
[37] *Id.* at 233.
[38] *Id.*
[39] *Id.* at 256.
[40] Mutua, *supra* note 31 at 62.

African constituency claimed as its own. Most nationalists treated it as an imposed condition in order for England to formally leave. For Odinga, even Marshall's presence was not something that enhanced its legitimacy. He wrote of the African American advisor to KANU: 'This gave United States' circles a foot in the door of the conference and I was not happy about it.'[41] In the minds of the more radical anti-colonial figures, Marshall and his focus on settler property rights spoke to a key predicament of many newly independent states. They would no longer be subject exclusively to the old imperial ruler, but now found themselves navigating the competing ideologies and rivalries of various global powers – in this case the Cold War stratagems of the pro-business and capitalist US and its communist Soviet adversary.

But as Odinga's scepticism of Marshall underscores, the issue of authenticity – while real – was clearly reflected through the basic concern over neo-colonialism. And it was a concern that generated a very similar process of constitutional rupture in Kenya to that which pushed American elites away from the Articles of Confederation. Even if the quasi-federalist and highly constrained Lancaster Constitution had been more directly and exclusively the product of nationalist deliberation, any arrangement would still have faced the difficulty of Kenya's structural context: a small state experiencing internal instability as well as external imperial and global interveners. For both Kenyatta and Odinga, the only way of ensuring substantive independence was to have a constitutional order grounded in a strong unitary state. With Odinga's backing, the first significant move Kenyatta made as Prime Minister was to undo the Lancaster Constitution through widespread legislative constitutional reform. There was no formal convention, but the result nonetheless was a thoroughly rewritten text. As Makau Mutua narrates the events in 1964, a new constitutional amendment 'declared Kenya a republic in which an executive president would be head of state and government as well as commander in chief of the armed forces. It abolished the office of the prime minister and took back many of the powers reserved for the regional governments.'[42] The effect was to establish a robust and centralised presidential system – Kenyatta became the first President and Odinga the first Vice President – and to do away with Majimboism.

Yet for Kenya, unlike the early American case, the move towards centralisation did not stop there. Odinga supported the initial changes as a necessary condition for land reform and for economic redistribution. But what happened instead was that Kenyatta repeatedly foiled these efforts, while using his legislative backing to transform the presidency into an instrument of personalised despotism. Between 1964 and 1969, Mutua describes how Kenyatta's supporters:

> [P]assed a raft of amendments to make it easier to amend the constitution; declare a state of emergency; abolish the right of appeal to the Privy Council, the last court of appeal for the extant and former British colonies; require members of Parliament to seek

[41] Odinga, *supra* note 35 at 177.
[42] Mutua, *supra* note 31 at 61.

> reelection if they defected from the party on which they were elected; grant presidential power to detain individuals without judicial review; abolish the bicameral Parliament; completely abolish regionalism; and provide that presidential elections would be direct, but that the candidate had to be nominated by a political party.[43]

In pressing for these moves, Kenyatta took advantage of economic anxieties and of secessionist politics in places like the Northern Frontier District. Addressing both, according to Kenyatta, required extreme centralised power – including engaging in widespread military abuses against Somalis in the border region and using the discriminatory targeting of Kenyan Asians as a way to scapegoat the community and to alleviate rising tensions over property and wealth. The ultimate result was the consolidation of a one-party state and the elimination of Kenyatta's political opponents, with Mboya assassinated and Odinga imprisoned by the end of the decade.

For Odinga, the tragedy of Kenyan constitutionalism under Kenyatta was that some consolidation of power was necessary to ensure both an adequate distribution of the state's resources to the various ethnic communities and to solve the long-running problem of land access. But once Kenyatta claimed control over the direction of that consolidation, it was very difficult to disrupt his growing despotism. And, moreover, Kenyatta was able to employ the very same postcolonial crises over resources and national cohesion to cement his authority. The Lancaster Constitution may have been constitutively unable to address the country's basic postcolonial predicament, but heightened centralisation also paved the way for authoritarian entrenchment. In fact, to this day, the country continues to struggle with questions of distribution and land rights, with the central political figures representing the competing sides none other than the sons of Kenyatta and Odinga.

Kenya's constitutional path towards one-party authoritarianism may well have been overdetermined. However, for our purposes, I want to highlight the significance of the neo colonial spectre in pressing a variety of nationalist constituencies to look favourably on a unitary state and to allow constitutional development to proceed initially down a particular track. The American and Kenyan stories clearly diverged for various reasons, not least of which was US isolation and growing geostrategic strength in contrast with the latter country's relative political weakness and the permanence of imperial and Cold War involvement in Africa. But both cases nonetheless illustrate how the aim of substantive independence – a key goal of many constitutional projects – generated specific dynamics around centralisation and the need for effective control that carried with them real authoritarian risks. These dynamics were part of a postcolonial predicament facing new states. While the Ackermanian pathway – revolutionary, establishmentarian or elite – was not irrelevant to the outcome for each state, developments were hardly driven by those pathways alone.

[43] *Id.* at 62.

III. Who are the 'People' of the Postcolonial State?

Part of the tragedy of the Kenyan story in the 1960s concerned the question of how to think of ethnic minorities, whether Asians in the cities or Somalis in the border region. Were they truly Kenyans or outsider populations embodying economic and security threats to the new state? This question of membership was not unique to Kenya and was itself a direct product of the collapse of the old imperial orders. Those orders had been ethnically plural and multi-confessional polities, and their disintegration raised a basic dilemma over the ethnic and religious organisation of independent nation-states. For postcolonial societies, a significant feature of constitutional development therefore had to do with addressing this dilemma. And state responses – often to their detriment – occurred against the backdrop of past colonial policies as well as the new international legal order promoted by emerging powers such as the US.

To make sense of just how vexing the matter of peoplehood became for many constitutional projects, one must begin by exploring the role of 'tribe' or ethnicity in earlier imperial models like the British one. The British Empire was famous for being structured around a system of indirect rule, in which empowered indigenous elites served essentially as the bottom rung of the colonial administrative authority. These elites was organised according to 'tribe' and then given the right to frame traditional institutions – the customary law of each tribe – as they saw fit. Mahmood Mamdani famously describes this approach as 'decentralised despotism', with imperial overseers unleashing preferred local chiefs to determine and enforce what counted as 'indigenous' practices. Very little of this was 'indirect' and instead proceeded despotically with a mixtures of local elites and colonial administrators imposing often brutal authority.[44] Crucially, while African subjects were clearly racialised and faced legal discrimination vis-a-vis whites, customary law and indirect rule understood peoplehood as far more variegated than simple racial category. As Mamdani writes: 'The notion of the ethnically defined customary was both deeper and more differentiated than the racially defined native … The natives denied civil freedoms on racial grounds were thereby sorted into different identities and incorporated into the domain of so many ethnically defined Native Authorities.'[45] For a place like colonial Kenya, along with a foundational and racial inequality structuring the rights of Africans with respect to white settlers, this meant that the African population was also then divided politically into a number of ethno-cultural and religious identities.

As these imperial orders began breaking down, initially during the First World War I, for those in Europe and the US, the essential question became why? According to US President Woodrow Wilson, who would play a critical role in the

[44] See generally MAHMOOD MAMDANI, CITIZEN AND SUBJECT: CONTEMPORARY AFRICA AND THE LEGACY OF LATE COLONIALISM 37–61 (1996).

[45] *Id.* at 112.

construction of the twentieth-century international order, the answer was obvious: the very plural nature of those disintegrating empires. Wilson and others did not challenge the imperial focus on ethnic category as the basic unit of political organisation; rather, Wilson took these units as given and simply argued that each one ideally should have its own nation-state. In doing so, he was partly informed by the ideas of ethno-racial conflict and hierarchy that had come to shape the American settler project – the country's own history of colonisation, which had been spurred on by formal independence from England.

Wilson, the son of a Virginia slave owner, had been deeply traumatised by the experience of Reconstruction, which he saw as the denial by a tyrannical North of political liberties to Southern whites. In his view, the world – not unlike how British administrators conceived their colonial possessions – was best understood as divided into distinct ethno-cultural and religious 'peoples' at different stages in the process of political evolution. White Americans, especially of Anglo-Saxon descent, stood at the forefront of this evolution, due to their long-standing acculturation in the practices of republican freedom. African Americans, by contrast, supposedly remained in their political infancy. Thus, what made Reconstruction so problematic was how it inverted this developmental account; it prematurely provided political rights to an ethno-cultural people ill-equipped for them, while at the same time removing those rights from a group long habituated to self-rule. As he declared in a 1907 lecture at Columbia University:

> Self-government is not a mere form of institutions, to be had when desired ... It is a form of character. It follows upon the long discipline which gives a people self-possession, self-mastery, the habit of order and peace and common counsel, and a reverence for law which will not fail when they themselves become the makers of law: the steadiness and self-control of political maturity.[46]

For Wilson, by ignoring these facts, Reconstruction had amounted to both political and racial chaos. It had also produced real victimisation and oppression, as an effectively foreign power (the Northern army) trampled on the ability of a local white people to govern themselves.

As Wilson turned to international matters, he projected these views onto debates about anti-colonial resistance to the great empires. Especially given the backdrop of the Southern white experience, if the US stood for anything, it had to stand for the value of self-government – a value that was basic and universal. But this did not mean that all foreign, especially non-white, peoples could live according to the principle in the here and now, since to do so required a process of political maturation. 'Only a long apprenticeship of obedience can secure' less developed peoples 'the precious possession' of real self-government, Wilson stated, 'a thing no more to be bought than given'.[47] This suggested that the US, ideally through the

[46] Woodrow Wilson, *The Place of the United States in Constitutional Development*, *in* The Philippine Islands, 511–12, at 511 (W. Cameron Forbes ed., 1928).

[47] *Id.* at 512.

League of Nations' mandate system, had a key role to play on the global stage: its primary purpose was to shepherd less developed peoples on the path to freedom and thus create a world of self-governing ethno-national republics.

For our purposes, alongside Wilson's ideas of racial and ethnic hierarchy, what is critical was his ideal vision of a fully reconstructed global order. For him, especially in the aftermath of the First World War, global violence had in large part been the product of the imperial refusal to accept the centrality of ethno-national identity to popular attachment. It had also been generated by the related and false imperial belief – from the Ottomans to the English – that plural orders, combining within one polity countless peoples and nations, could enjoy permanent political stability. Within the US, this was a central reason why Wilson defended both a harsh brand of 'Americanisation' for new European immigrants and viewed whiteness as so foundational to the republic. He believed that in order for a political order to survive, it required a governing majority population organised around a cohesive racial and ethnic identity. The problem internationally was that while the world was made up of distinct peoples, these peoples were distributed across various empires in ways that undermined the ability of any specific ethno-cultural community to enjoy explicit self-determination. In thwarting nationalist ambitions, the great empires thus created the conditions for inter-communal conflict and set the stage for the First World War.

Therefore, the goal of a postcolonial world was to remake the plural imperial orders into self-determining democratic nation-states organised around a single people. As Wilson declared to Congress in outlining his Fourteen Points, after enough guided maturation, '[a]ll peoples and nationalities' would ultimately 'live on equal terms of liberty and safety with one another, whether they be strong or weak'.[48] He and others recognised that such a vision could never be perfectly achieved; states would necessarily have a majority ethno-cultural community along with a minority population. But, as theorist and historian Robert Meister has explored, the underlying hope was that minority rights would be respected through two features. The first was an international system of status protections framed through mutually agreed-upon treaties and enforced by institutions like the League of Nations and later the United Nations. The second feature was bound to the fact that a minority in one state would be a self-determining democratic majority in another. This reality would ensure an international framework of mutual co-national support across political boundaries.[49]

But as the Kenyan example highlights, the implementation of this was far easier said than done. This was because if the new order was a break from the old imperial pluralism, it nonetheless took the previous model's ethnic political unit as its basic building block. As a result, it allowed Kenyatta to take advantage

[48] Woodrow Wilson, *The Fourteen Points, in* THE POLITICAL THOUGHT OF WOODROW WILSON (Edmund Cronon ed., 1965).

[49] See generally ROBERT MEISTER, AFTER EVIL: A POLITICS OF HUMAN RIGHTS 365–66 n.112–13 (2011).

of the idea that Asians and Somalis were both communities 'out of place' – not truly Kenyan and so rightly subject, if they remained, to discrimination and, in the latter case, extreme violence. In this way, the Kenyan story was a small-scale replication of how the Wilsonian postcolonial vision often operated more generally. Indeed, one might argue that the segregationist Wilson simply promoted abroad the racial imaginary and suspicion of meaningful inclusion that so bedevilled the long history of American nation-building. Thus, unsurprisingly, throughout the twentieth century, the notion of democratic self-determination through majoritarian 'peoples' with minority ethnic populations proved to be catastrophic in its effects. As simply one example, take inter-war Europe, which witnessed mass transfers of populations and even genocide.

And in decolonising Asia and Africa after the Second World War, such violence and exclusion was also marked by a second tendency, again illustrated by the Kenyan example. Many new nation-states did not simply have one majority and one minority. Given the nature of colonial organisation, they often stitched together numerous ethic communities that had previously enjoyed legal rights, political autonomy and material resources on the basis of their ethno-cultural or religious identity. After independence, this created understandable and clear built-in pressures, including from empowered local elites, for policies that maintained such structures (hence the real sentiment among some Kenyans for Majimboism or internal regionalism). But just as centrally, it also led to powerful electoral dynamics that facilitated the move to authoritarianism.

One can appreciate this last point by reflecting on how in theory democracy and majoritarianism are meant to be joined together. Ideally, democratic legitimacy is bound to the notion that electoral majorities and minorities are temporary, grounded in the particular question at hand and shifting with each political decision. But leaders like Kenyatta quickly saw that, given the centrality of the ethnic unit to the colonial state, such units could be employed post-independence to create permanent and ethnically defined voting majorities. By maintaining the focus on ethnic identity for political organisation and resource provision and by creating a powerful coalition of insider communities (who would have access to these resources), Kenyatta was able in the 1960s to repeatedly secure large majorities in Parliament. In a sense, he took advantage of how democratic categories of majority and minority were also marked critically as *demographic* categories. He understood that by creating majority ethno-cultural coalitions, he could overcome the threat of political removal, a threat that was central to the functioning of the democratic ideal. Once so empowered, he then used permanent majorities to suppress political dissent, criminalise opposition parties and impose authoritarian rule. These developments also shaped the terms of how political conflict came to be understood in Kenya. This was because much of state oppression focused on ethnically organised local resistance centred in communities – like Mboya's and Odinga's Luo population – that had been excluded from ethnic bargains.

All of this speaks to the importance of the post-imperial and ethno-national model of state formation in making sense of twentieth-century constitutional development. New projects, again irrespective of an initial Ackerman pathway, found themselves navigating a postcolonial predicament structured around the nature of nation-state independence in a world of global inequality and rivalry. On the one hand, the neo-colonial spectre highlighted the need for greater centralised control in order to direct local economic decision-making and avoid external interference. On the other hand, such centralised control opened up the potential for elites to use ethno-cultural politics to impose their authority, in the process exacerbating minority vulnerabilities and feeding secessionist impulses. If new states and their elites saw constitution writing as an essential prerequisite for claiming legitimate and equal sovereign power on the international stage, such postcolonial challenges often dictated what their documents looked like as well as how institutional development proceeded.

IV. Conclusion

Bruce Ackerman's *Revolutionary Constitutions* offers crucial insights for the study of global constitutional development. One of its greatest strengths is how the focus on initial pathway re-imagines the classic cases in constitutional analysis, allowing us to appreciate continuities between examples from the Global North and South that are often placed in different categories. But, in a sense, the focus on the internal dynamics of the cases themselves can have the unwitting effect of abstracting away from the context within which these projects were situated. And the most profound context – during precisely the periods that witnessed the explosion of new states and new constitutional enterprises – was the breakdown of the great European empires.

As I have argued, this imperial collapse, as well as the nation-state vision of post-imperial order that took root in its wake, critically informed the constitutional politics of emerging polities. It left many such states prey to a combination of authoritarian intensification and internal ethno-religious violence that in the long run undermined the legitimacy of existing institutional structures. These features of the global order may not have affected all states in the same way, as the divergences between the early US and decolonising Kenya underscore. But they nonetheless created remarkably common challenges – over substantive independence, demography and majoritarianism, and the nation-state vision of 'peoplehood' – that were especially thorny for postcolonial constitutions to navigate.

This means that in order to make sense of today's ongoing constitutional crises, one has to incorporate into any analysis both international power dynamics (the effects of structural inequalities between the former empires and their independent colonies) and the hard-baked implications of the nation-state model itself. Indeed, whether revolutionary, establishmentarian or elite, these features of the global system provided common sources of crisis over legitimacy and effective governance that reappeared time and again. This suggests the need not only to foreground the story of decolonisation when assessing the global rise of constitutionalism and development, but also emphasises the value of combining Ackerman's essential discussion of country-specific pathways with an account of international order and political structure. Such a framework would highlight the overall shift from the era of European imperialism to that of formally equal nation-states. It would make evident how a shared postcolonial predicament has differentially affected constitutional development along Ackerman's three pathways.

Just as critical, this foregrounding would cut against the related presumption that the exclusive or primary way to address legal and political crises is through internal domestic reforms. To the extent that the structural forces generating nation-state instability and authoritarian entrenchment are global in nature, responses similarly have to move beyond constitutional alterations alone to confront defining features of regional and international order. And, indeed, this was precisely the perspective of independence figures, like Oginga Odinga, when imagining truly postcolonial conditions. Odinga and others saw genuine self-determination – in place of neo-colonialism and continuing ethno-cultural conflict – as requiring new forms of regional federation as well as transformed global economic arrangements. On gaining its formal independence in 1960, Nkrumah pressed for language in Ghana's new constitution that gave parliament 'the power to provide for the surrender of the whole or any part of the sovereignty of Ghana'[50] to a hoped-for federation of African states. At the same time, those like Tanzania's President Julius Nyerere called for a New International Economic Order (NIEO) to refashion the international system into one that ensured domestic economic control and mutual global interdependence. For supporters of the NIEO, this would entail, among other policies, international arrangements that gave states greater authority to regulate the activities of multinational corporations, domestic nationalisation powers, protections for commodity associations among poorer polities and legal support for technology transfers to the Global South.

As political theorist Adom Getachew writes, many independence figures understood that internal nation-building and substantive – rather than merely formal – independence would only be achieved if it were grounded in 'anticolonial worldmaking',[51] expressed concretely through federation and mechanisms like the NIEO. These levers created the possibility for postcolonial states to operate in a refashioned world environment, one that ensured that no individual state remained a neo-colonial pawn, subject to the old imperial rivalries. Moreover, the Pan-Africanist and Third Worldist ideals of federation and economic solidarity cut against the focus on an individual's specific ethno-cultural group as the central locus of political identity. This was because both frameworks de-emphasised the need of particular groups to assert dominance over the state as the *only* basis for

[50] Quoted in Adom Getachew, Worldmaking after Empire: The Rise and Fall of Self-Determination 182 (2018).

[51] *Id.*

enjoying material benefits. Since global wealth would be equitably distributed through regional and international economic arrangements, the local sense of zero-sum conflict over state resources would be mitigated – and, relatedly, the space for more plural and overlapping political identities expanded.

The story of the political retreat in recent decades of both Pan-Africanism and alternative international economic visions is beyond the scope of this chapter.[52] But what that earlier moment no doubt highlights is the contemporary need to see our present constitutional crises with the same capaciousness and intellectual imagination. This means appreciating that in order to navigate seemingly internal domestic crises, local constitutional change has to be bound to structural shifts in global economic and political relations. If the dynamics of the international order replicate social problems across the postcolonial world – often irrespective of initial constitutional pathway – then only a legal and political analysis that connects the domestic predicament to the realities of that order offers a necessary vision of reform.

[52] Along with Getachew's excellent work, I would also recommend Antony Anghie, *Whose Utopia? Human Rights, Development, and the Third World*, 22 Qui Parle 63 (2013); and Samuel Moyn's recent book for powerful analyses of the NIEO and its international political fate, Not Enough: Human Rights in an Unequal World (2018).

6

Revolution on a Human Scale

Liberal Values, Populist Theory?[1]

ANDREW ARATO

Unglücklich das *Land*, das Helden nötig hat
[Unhappy the country that needs heroes], Bertolt Brecht, *Galileo*, 1943

I. Introduction

For me, the most important clue to Ackerman's whole orientation to constitutional politics is still a point repeatedly made in volume one of *We the People*.[2] There, he first explains that the American doctrine of popular as against governmental sovereignty entails that no governmental instance in normal politics has the right to claim to be the embodiment of the supreme democratic power. Yet, he goes on to argue (on good textual bases in the *Federalist Papers*) that in an extraordinary constitution-making moment, this very thing can and should be done, but only in a way that allows a body to *legitimately* claim the name of 'the People'. I myself have described this as the antinomy in the original American model of constitutional politics between sovereign and non-sovereign, populist and constitutionalist, political theological and democratic conceptions.[3] However, Ackerman has consistently remained faithful to his original stress on embodied popular sovereignty as the most likely (if never fully secure) source of modern constitutionalism.

Unlike Ackerman,[4] I do believe that varieties of right and left populism represent the greatest threat to constitutional democracy today.[5] This leads me to ask

[1] The following is a heavily cut version of the original submitted. The full version is available from arato@newschool.edu on request.

[2] Bruce Ackerman, We the People, Volume 1: Foundations 184 ff. and passim (1991); Bruce Ackerman, We the People, Volume 2: Transformations (1998).

[3] Andrew Arato, Adventures of the Constituent Power (2017).

[4] Bruce Ackerman, World Constitutionalism 5 (forthcoming, 2019). I relied on the manuscript version.

[5] Andrew Arato, Post Sovereign Constitution Making: Learning and Legitimacy 269–98 (2016).

whether a combination of constitutionalist values and what I take to be a stress on mythological (or 'fictional') versions of popular sovereignty helps or hurts us in the fight against the old/new foe. Let me stress that Ackerman and I share a high regard for the norms of constitutionalism as expressed above all in the defence of the integrity and basic structure of the higher law by an apex court against the ordinary acts of government constituted by that law. Where we fundamentally differ is whether revolutionary appeals to popular sovereignty in themselves represent a threat to or a promise from the same normative point of view.

We approach the matter with partially different sets of ideal types, constructed differently,[6] that lead to the subsumption of some cases under different types. It is true that we both classify India under the category I took from him, namely revolutionary reform. But for Ackerman, Poland and South Africa had revolutions in the 1990s, while for me they had negotiated changes of regime, in common with Spain, Hungary and Bulgaria. However, ideal types are to be used, not turned into bedrock realities. They are useful if they serve legitimate purposes, whether theoretical or political. I strongly believe that my ideal types serve our common purpose of constitutional legitimacy and constitutionalism better than Ackerman's.

II. Defining Revolution

Ackerman defines revolution as a process when revolutionary insurgents backed by a social movement manage to challenge and replace political incumbents, and establish the foundations of a new regime. This idea resembles my own (and I believe clearer) recent stress, following Trotsky and Charles Tilly, that revolution on the political level always entails the 'dual power' of forces with sovereign claims and, when successful, the replacement of the old sovereign with a new one.[7] Like my definition, on the legal level, Ackerman assumes a crisis and break in legitimacy in revolution, but, unlike me, he no longer insists on a break in legality so that he can subsume cases of legal continuity. Most importantly, he says (in a weaker version than Arendt's, for whom the link was normatively definitional) that constitutionalisation is an option for the new revolutionary regime, not an imperative.[8] Undoubtedly, he assumes (as did Arendt) that revolution in permanence and/or dictatorship are also possible outcomes. But these follow from the wrong type of revolution, the total one, aiming to radically transform all the subsystems of society. The alternative is non-total 'revolution on a human scale'

[6] For my scheme, using the dimensions of legality/legitimacy and continuity/break leading to four main types (by adding the variables of external/internal, we would get eight), see ANDREW ARATO, CONSTITUTION MAKING UNDER OCCUPATION: THE POLITICS OF IMPOSED REVOLUTION IN IRAQ (2009).

[7] *Id.*; and S. ARJOMAND, THE TURBAN FOR THE CROWN: THE ISLAMIC REVOLUTION IN IRAN 134–36 (1989).

[8] ACKERMAN, *supra* note 4 at 6–7.

and is also occasionally called 'constitutional revolution', which certainly has the implication that the norm of a constitutional outcome is likely to be realised. The category is derived from Arendt's notion of political as against social revolution, with the new proviso that dealing with the 'social question' in a reformist or 'social democratic' manner need not deform the revolutionary process.

The seven cases Ackerman subsumes under the new concept are emphatically contrasted with total revolutions, even as they are now only 'constitutional' rather than also 'liberal'. As against Arendt's views concerning the American exception, Ackerman certainly believes that revolutions on a human scale are potentially strong foundations (perhaps even the strongest) for democratic constitution-making, and constitutionalism as a result. This potential has to do with the (I agree) all-important problem of legitimacy. As against evolutionary-reformist and elitist constitution-making, revolutions on a human scale can rely on the strong combination of legitimacy derived from plausible claims of embodying the people ('popular sovereignty') and charismatic legitimacy inherent in popular leadership usually by a single, identifiable person (Nehru, Mandela, De Gasperi, de Gaulle, Walesa, Khomenei and Ben-Gurion in *World Constitutionalism*, along with Washington, as against *The Future of Liberal Revolution*,[9] where Yeltsin too was still included).

I do see why strong charismatic legitimacy of revolutionary founders (Time One) could legitimate strong constitutional defence by an apex court at some point down the line (Time Four). What is left out in any case are Times Two and Three, namely why the possessor of such super-legitimacy along with the political power would establish constitutionalist protections in the first place. The contrasting Przeworski/Ginsburg insurance model that I defend but Ackerman rejects has, of course, an explanation for such an outcome.

III. Subsuming Cases: Israel and Iran

Ackerman likes to be provocative. Including Israel and Iran as cases of revolutions on a human scale producing constitutionalism could seem like a provocation to the anti-Zionist left on the one hand and the Islam-hating right on the other. I do not belong to either of these categories and can see instead that his point remains consistent with his soft spot for revolutions in the name of popular sovereignty, as long as they can somehow be distinguished from the ideal-type total revolutions. Thus, I attribute the inclusion of these two cases to theoretical affinity to the charismatic dimension of populism, and his attempt to show that the type of revolution he prefers, in the name of popular sovereignty, has at least a strong elective affinity with constitutionalism.

[9] Bruce Ackerman, The Future of Liberal Revolution (1994).

In the process of making this attempt, Ackerman faces empirical counter-evidence, in part provided by himself, that throws serious doubt on his whole typology and thus his thesis. To begin with, are Israel's founding and Iran's Islamic Revolution rightly included under the category of 'revolutions on a human scale'? That they are correctly said to be other than total revolutions proves little, since we have known since the time of Tocqueville that no revolutions are genuinely total. At the same time, as Theda Skocpol demonstrated long ago,[10] the Islamic Revolution belongs to the relatively small set of great revolutions, involving as much change and in as many spheres as most of the others.[11] Most assuredly, one cannot limit the radical and rapid transformation this entailed merely to the political sphere.

But total or partial is not really the main issue. What really matters is instead the logic of revolution entailed, in Ackerman's own model, by a charismatic leadership focused around one man who has no competitors and is bound by no previous law, making claims in the name of 'the People' with a capital p. This logic in my admittedly somewhat conventional view is not conducive to constitutionalism, but to old and new forms of authoritarian rule. Most authoritarian forms have constitutions in the material Kelsen sense, but rather than constitutionalist, they are forms of the 'dual state' as thematised in Ernst Fraenkel's crucial but neglected work.[12] The idea of the dual state[13] is that even under an authoritarian but modern regime, there are spheres of a normative state (the bureaucracy, economy, family life etc) ordinarily regulated by legal institutions. There is also a prerogative state where discretion and political will are free of all legal limits. Most importantly, at issue is not only dualism, but also the priority and superiority of the *prerogative* that can always trump the normative even in its own spheres.

Notice that I (perhaps also provocatively) am bringing Israel and Iran under the same ideal-type structure. While I would not myself simply call Israel (except for the occupied territories) 'a functioning democracy with a strong supreme court',[14] I of course recognise the fundamental differences. The similarity of structure is disguised by the location of the prerogative in a theocracy in one case and a majoritarian democracy in the other, and by the very different *ordinary or normal* operation of the two systems permitting free elections and competitive media in one case, and controlled elections and strong censorship in the other. Of course, these regimes, like all others, face political and many other (eg. natural) limitations, but neither system should be described as 'constitutionalist'.

[10] Theda Skocpol *Rentier State and Shi'a Islam in the Iranian Revolution*, 11(3) *Theory and Society* 265 (1982).

[11] See Arjomand, *supra* note 7 regarding education, media, family life and even originally the economy.

[12] E. Fraenkel, The Dual State (1941). The thesis was developed to deal with the maintenance of the capitalist economy in National Socialist Germany and had a strong influence on Arendt, whose concept of totalitarianism has unfortunately eclipsed it.

[13] Not to be confused with dual power or dual sovereignty, part of the definition of the revolutionary situation that ended with the replacement of sovereignty.

[14] Ackerman, *supra* note 4 at 343.

In Israel's case, a logic incompatible with the establishment of constitutionalism is very much evident in Ackerman's treatment of the origins of the independent state. And while the matter cannot be reduced to the failure to enact a formal constitution, this set of events very much symbolises what was going wrong. The reader is struck by Ackerman's use of the term 'betrayal' for Ben-Gurion, who is otherwise depicted as a true revolutionary hero on a par with Nehru and Mandela, but also Khomeini. This term and the charge are extremely common in the history of revolutions.[15] In Ben-Gurion's case, it was a betrayal in two steps, though Ackerman uses the term only for the first. Accordingly, this step involved the violation of the supposedly explicit text of the Proclamation (or Declaration) of Independence, by fusing, via a Transition Law, the constituent with ordinary political and legislative functions, renaming the Constituent Assembly the First Knesset. Ackerman claims that the Declaration[16] provided for differentiated political bodies, the People's Council and the Assembly, that exercised these functions.[17]

Yet the second step in betrayal did not follow automatically. The Constituent Assembly (now no longer a 'convention') or rather the First Knesset did generate a constitution-making committee and, via the latter, several interesting drafts presented by Ackerman as great achievements having strong tables of rights and, more importantly, a powerful apex court along with a high level of entrenchment.[18] Ackerman shows that the old charge that all of these drafts failed because of religious opposition cannot be sustained.[19] It was the framer, Leo Kohn, who made concessions to religious symbolism, and it was the Prime Minister who objected to these, even though he had previously been willing to concede the famous status quo of religious jurisdictions to the Orthodox parties.[20] So why did he object and bring the project down? Ackerman notes the power interest involved, along with Ben-Gurion's supposedly sincere admiration for the Westminster model as currently the conventional interpretation, which he concedes but rightly considers insufficient.

In short, was Ben-Gurion merely a betrayer of constitutionalism or was he also a 'revolutionary hero'? In Ackerman's treatment he was both, and in my view the two are consistent with one another. Indeed, other revolutionary heroes, such as

[15] See most famously L. Trotsky, Revolution Betrayed (1997 [1937]). Ackerman would repeat the charge, at least speaking for Kaczynski, in the case of Walesa.

[16] See Ackerman, *supra* note 4 at 351, 373 fn. 39. As much as I like this line of thought, the text does not clearly sustain the interpretation.

[17] In this rare context, Ackerman does make the difference between 'doubly differentiated' models of constitution-making (conventions) and sovereign constituent assemblies. Previously, he also made the distinction in *The Future of Liberal Revolution*, before calling it unimportant (Ackerman, *supra* note 9 at. 51, 55 vs. 59). On this important distinction, see Arato, Post Sovereign Constitution Making, *supra* note 5, ch. 3.

[18] Two-thirds being high in a country now with proportional representation, where the leading party, Mapai, was receiving slightly over a third of the votes.

[19] *cf* H. Lerner, Making Constitutions in Deeply Divided Societies (2011), who still makes this argument.

[20] The Status Quo letter was written 1947; the objection to the status of religion in the Kohn draft by Ben-Gurion came in 1948.

Robespierre and Lenin, made analogous moves with respect to constitutionalism, the former suspending the popularly ratified Constitution of 1793 and the latter going a step further and dissolving the All Russian Constituent Assembly altogether in 1918.[21] Thus, next to the material interests of greater power and the pragmatic interest of identification with the Westminster model of parliamentary sovereignty, Ackerman rightly adds the logic of revolution, rooted in revolutionary charismatic legitimacy that I would describe as generically populist.[22] Ben-Gurion was accordingly not willing to share the glory as the 'great Founding Father of the Republic' with Menachem Begin, who was more classically a revolutionary and who was at that time a constitutionalist liberal and a defender of the original project and status of the Constituent Assembly. Such was hardly the attitude of Washington (only one of several 'founding fathers'), or Nehru, though always in the shadow of Gandhi, who was willing to share glory with Ambedkar as well as his Congress colleagues, or Mandela, who consented to share the Nobel Prize with de Klerk, and who had many peers on the ANC side as well.

How is such founding and such leadership supposed to lead to constitutionalism? Like everyone else, Ackerman mentions the compromise of the Harari Resolution of 1950, with its provision of the stepwise enactment of basic laws with the eventual goal of a full, documentary constitution. According to him, Ben-Gurion was forced into this opportunistic compromise, very slightly violating the Westminster logic, because of a fear of defections in his own party. However that may be, I am not convinced that any genuine concession to even a future constitutionalism was involved. The first basic laws, which had to wait until 1958, provided for no court that was capable of review, and clarification of the status of the judiciary had to wait until 1984. Nor were they seriously entrenched, except with reference to states of emergency. Even later entrenchment was weak, amounting to only absolute majority, ie, 61 votes that coalitions already possess, as we have seen in the case of the last Basic Law, the infamous Nation State Law of 2018.[23]

Ackerman's hypothesis is saved by his differentiation of the process in terms of temporal stages, and the epicycle of 'the constitutional revolution' of the 1990s. This type of argument works well for India, placing Nehru's leadership in Times One and Two, and the evolution of the Basic Structure doctrine of the Constitutional Court in Time Four, after the succession crisis and during the dominance of Indira Gandhi. But unlike Ben-Gurion, Nehru, whatever his own inclination towards the Westminster model with regard to the amendment rule and the problem of entrenchment, was willing to operate in a pluralist constitution-making framework and accept strong basic constitutional rights, constitutional review

[21] See ARATO, *supra* note 3, *Epilogue*.

[22] For my definition of populism, derived from Ernesto Laclau's ON POPULIST REASON (2005), see also ARATO, POST SOVEREIGN CONSTITUTION MAKING, *supra* note 5, ch. 6.

[23] There was one exception with respect to entrenchment, relating to the limits of emergency regulations, an admittedly important matter since Roman precedents.

and, in the end, innovative solutions of the entrenchment problems at several levels.[24] Thus, the Indian Supreme Court in the 1970s not only had good reason but also legal bases to defend the founding act against later political repudiation.

The case is very different in Israel, as Ackerman occasionally notes. Here his idea that the heritage of a founder (one strongly linked to majoritarian democracy!) is preserved by a court acting in the name of the Basic Laws, all but the first two having been passed after Ben-Gurion was definitively out of power, is very unconvincing to say the least. To Ackerman, what happened in Time One, despite the betrayal of constitutionalism in Time Two, became its very foundation in Time Four. This should mean that now at least constitutionalism is established. But can it be really established where the primacy of the prerogative exercised by a governmental majority is maintained? The history of Israel after Barak's 'revolution' seems to confirm a pessimistic judgement. Some 20 or more years later, can we still assume that constitutionalism triumphed and that the Supreme Court, constantly under the threat of being packed or replaced or shorn of part of its jurisdiction, can still preserve it? Even Ackerman fears that we no longer can do so.[25]

The situation is seemingly better in the case of Iran, where a constitution was enacted in 1979 and where efforts parallel to those of Barak to redress or reverse the balance within the dual state, led by President Khatami after 1997 and now by President Rouhani, had at least constitutional text among its supports. Yet Ackerman begins his presentation with the words: 'it may seem odd to consider Iran in a book dealing with revolutions on the human scale'. I agree. And so does Ackerman, since the term 'human scale' and the problem of subsumption under it appears only once, without any explanation, in the subsequent historical analysis. For good reason. Iran's revolution came to be of the relatively total genre as confirmed by Ackerman at least implicitly, radicalising not just the state, but also culture, family life, the arts, criminal law and military organisation to mention only the most obvious. Initially there were even projects for an Islamic economy, as Ackerman passingly admits. Equally seriously, the terms 'constitutional' and 'constitutionalist' are systematically conflated in his analysis. Iran is said to have constitutionalised the revolution in Time Two, here meaning having established a written, documentary constitution. This is indeed undeniable. But Ackerman also implies (without daring to say so) that the constitution is constitutionalist, in the sense of having formally established fundamental rights, separation of powers, checks and balances, elections and even a Council of Guardians modeled on the Gaullist Conseil constitutionnel that since 1971 has been able to exercise judicial review.

[24] See G. Austin, The Indian Constitution: Cornerstone of a Nation (1966). The same model works a lot less well in the case of France, where two revolutionary breaks, one in 1946 and the other in 1958, were not followed by strong constitutionalism until de Gaulle stepped down from power in 1969. Was a strengthening of the Court under Mitterrand a way of defending the General's founding act or a way of contesting it?

[25] Ackerman, *supra* note 4 at 367.

Unfortunately, since the time of Benjamin Constant (if not Caesar Augustus, the Frenchman's classical model), we know that dictatorship can very well function while formally preserving many institutions of electoral and even constitutionalist regimes. There is admittedly a crucial difference between Soviet-type constitutions and many in authoritarian states that was first pointed out by Karl Loewenstein[26] and was further refined by Said Arjomand, the best constitutional expert on Iran.[27] The constitutions of the Soviet type were and are paper constitutions; Loewenstein included them under the loose category of 'semantic' and the real operation of power does not appear in them. For example, the politburo and the central committee are never mentioned in these documents, and the ruling party makes an appearance typically only under a very bashful article postulating its highly unclear 'leading role'. From this type, Arjomand distinguished ideological constitutions,[28] where the real powers and authoritarian ruling structures and their high level discretionary power do appear in the codification and where they are justified by an elaborate ideology. Both semantic and ideological constitutions are options after revolutions. They both establish dual states, as understood here, one on the level of the material constitution and the other on the formal level as well. Clearly, in spite of the conflicts it gave rise to from the beginning, Iran's Constitution incorporated a deeply personalistic, 'anti-constitutionalist vision'.[29]

According to Arjomand – and this converges with Ackerman's analysis – during Bazargan's 10-month Prime Ministership in 1979, a constitution was drafted that would have been constitutionalist and was indeed modelled on that of the Fifth Republic.[30] Both analyses indicate that it was emphatically under Khomeini's charismatic authority that the constitutional text was radically transformed.[31] Here we can precisely follow the construction and 'constitutionalisation' of the authoritarian (rather than constitutional) dual state. Elements of the Fifth Republic Constitution remained, to constitute the normal state, while the Islamic additions represented the superior prerogative state focused around the Mandate of the Jurist and the person of Khomeini very explicitly. Importantly, the Council of Guardians was transformed from a constitutional control judicial body with only judicial functions into a super-executive body in charge of exclusionary gatekeeping.[32]

[26] Who, however, tended to conflate paper constitutions with openly authoritarian ones. See K. Loewenstein, *Reflections on the Value of Constitutions in Our Revolutionary Age*, *in* Constitutions and Constitutional Trends since World War II (2nd ed., A.J. Zurcher ed., 1955).

[27] In this section I mostly rely on his work, as well as my student, Bahareh Ebne Alian's, not yet published work.

[28] For example, S. Arjomand, After Khomeini: Iran under His Successors 29 (2009).

[29] See N. Brown, Constitutions in a Nonconstitutional World (2012) 188, 190 etc. Brown tries hard to save even the Mandate of the Jurist from his own charge, but manages to do so only in terms of theorists outside of Iran. Of course, it was also the revolutionary scenario and not only theology that led to the authoritarian interpretation of Khomeini and the subsequent practice of the dual state.

[30] Arjomand, *supra* note 28 at 27 ff.

[31] I leave aside the astonishing claim that the Ayatollah Khomeini and Nelson Mandela faced 'a similar problem' of leadership and 'resolved it in a similar fashion' (Ackerman, *supra* note 4 at 390–91).

[32] Arjomand, *supra* note 28 at 43–45; Brown, *supra* note 29 at 186.

Even more crucial was the introduction of the highest authority of the Supreme Leader of the Islamic Revolution, an institution unknown to the Fifth Republic, but postulated by Khomeini's heretical Shiite theory of the Mandate of the Jurist many years earlier.[33] The changes were anticipated by the transformation of the original plan of a constituent assembly into a clerically dominant and manipulated Assembly of Experts.[34] With these three changes alone (and there were many others),[35] it is futile to talk about the Constitution of the Islamic Republic as being of French inspiration. To be sure, it is the operation of the material constitution that matters rather than the formal document, which Ackerman does not analyse and I cannot so do here. The actual operation of the Islamic Republic under Khomeini, to be sure only Time Three in Ackerman's scheme, yields a full demonstration of the dual state and the primacy of authoritarian prerogative. Just to stay with his history, the banning of parties other than the governmental party, the manipulation of elections (Ackerman does not seem to be unduly disturbed by support for the regime being as high as 95 per cent),[36] the exclusion of most candidacies, the obvious violations of the constitutional structure in regulating the succession, not to speak of the extra-legal persecution, prosecution and indeed execution of enemies all testify to the operation of a classical dual state. The point is best confirmed by the location of Kompetenz-kompetenz in the Constitution in the hands of the Supreme Leader,[37] whether or not he is capable of exercising it in all political moments.[38]

Yes, a dual state, and thus the documentary Constitution of Iran that established one, permits contestation over the primacy of the prerogative or the normative. This is true not only because of the built-in conflicts of the parts of the French model carried over into the Iranian context, eg, between the executive and parliament, and the president and the prime minister, but, more importantly, when an authoritarian regime survives long enough, necessary liberalisation attempts may follow that involve either an institution or a movement plausibly representing the rule of law, whether in the name of parts of the constitution or other principles. The evolution of such states very often involves a reduction of the dual state to its essence, to the Kompetenz-kompetenz ultimately in the hands of the highest power, while more and more spheres of life (the economy, family life, the arts etc) becoming substantively normalised.[39] And it is true that both reform attempts

[33] Arjomand, *supra* note 28, *passim*.

[34] *Id.* at 28 ff.; Brown (n 28) 185. Both explicitly deny what Ackerman seems to readily accept: that this was the revolutionary Constituent Assembly originally planned.

[35] See his discussion in both books about the bewildering construction of new bodies, most clerically dominated in and beyond the constitution.

[36] Indeed, art 1 of the Constitution speaks of ratification by 98.2 per cent.

[37] Article 110.

[38] According to Bahareh Ebne Alian (in a personal note to me), the following provisions, among others, establish the leader's prerogative and a theocratic rather than a popular form of sovereignty: arts 5, 56 and 57.

[39] Ackerman does this regarding the economy; Bahareh Ebne Alian will make the full argument re different domains of civil law on civil law.

from above or challenges from below in the name of the normal state can lead to cracks and even a crisis in the dual system. But to describe recent Iranian history involving the economic reform attempts of Rafsanjani, the failed challenge of Khatami, the Green movement and the currently ambiguous position of Rouhani's measures as some kind of oscillation between theocracy and French-style presidentialism is a serious error.

IV. Intermediate Theoretical Reflections

Fortunately for Ackerman (as well as my own work), an ideal-type theoretical model can be evaluated on the bases of its link to theoretical tradition first and interpretive strengths second, rather than probably unavoidable weaknesses of either excluding or including too much on their borders. However, I find Ackerman's new book wanting in both these respects. Regarding theoretical traditions, only the work of Arendt and Schmitt really come into play.[40] As to the first, I think that Ackerman is right to be enthusiastic about Arendt's linking of revolution and constitution, right to reject the thesis of American exceptionalism (on which more below) and also right in suggesting that the puzzle of the social question could be and has often been solved in reformist or 'social democratic' ways. However, he is wrong not to follow her example of providing and insisting on a clear, normative meaning of 'constitutionalism' and at times conflating this term with having a constitution.

Yet it is more with respect to the second theorist, Carl Schmitt, where Ackerman gets into a lot of trouble. He refutes Schmitt on a point where to my mind it has not been necessary for a long time, namely the link of his earlier plebiscitary conception to the Nazi regime that the theorist eventually became an apologist for. It is likely that this exercise is carried out because of the presence in Schmitt of a version of the charismatic-plebiscitary conception that is important for Ackerman's own theory. Thus, he must distinguish himself, and does so on the rather weak foundation of a few examples, such as the self-limiting norms guiding a Nehru and a Mandela that so obviously failed in the case of Walesa, de Gaulle and Khomeini, as he shows.

In spite of this serious weakness, which is political as well as theoretical, I see the problem even more with Ackerman's affinity to another Schmitt, the theorist of the sovereign dictatorship, that at least initially implied the preference for sovereign constituent assemblies among the examples of forms of constitution-making. Ackerman too very much seems to prefer this model, though, strangely for a jurist, no longer seems very interested in the actual legal or procedural forms of constitution-making. Thus, with the brief exception of the first 'betrayal' in Israel,

[40] Of course, Max Weber does this as well with the concepts of ideal type and charisma. However, Ackerman does not reflect on the methodological problems of the first of these.

he does not follow the example of Schmitt (as well as Böckenförde and Grimm, and even his earlier work) in making distinctions between regular parliaments, American-type non-sovereign and 'doubly differentiated' conventions, sovereign constituent assemblies and executive commissions, a list to which I would add non-sovereign constitutional assemblies of the South African type (where the name was deliberately chosen). Thus, he does not notice either Schmitt's preference among these types for the sovereign version, unlimited by prior law and also exercising governmental functions, or the structural (and not necessarily empirical) link of this to political dictatorship. Nor does he notice the attempts in India, Poland and South Africa to avoid this model in different non-sovereign or post-sovereign versions. And while he does not openly adopt the model of sovereign dictatorship, he seems to at times fall into it as the critical standard by which cases are evaluated. In summary, as a result, he neither criticises the sovereign dictatorships of the constitution-making moments in Israel and Iran, nor does he notice the determined efforts to get away from this paradigm in Poland and South Africa.

V. Poland and South Africa

This brings me to the second set of theoretical objections that have to do with the weakness of the argument even where he has reconstructed the political history in interesting and at times compelling ways. Ackerman's emphatic and rather polemical move of the cases of Poland and South Africa from the negotiated transition column to the revolutionary column undoubtedly has something to do with his need for more cases to illustrate his implicit argument about the plausibility of 'constitutional revolutions'. In spite of this suspicion, I do agree with him that the problem of legitimacy is the Achilles' heel of the negotiated cases, which in my view can be solved through the democratic multi-stage process, while for Ackerman, this can happen only if there is a revolutionary turn or acceleration. I would also agree with him stressing the element of time (Poland) and non-completion (Israel and Hungary), that along with the generation of new legitimacy was effectively dealt with in the case of South Africa.

However, where we fundamentally differ is at the point where Ackerman seems to repeatedly put the blame on negotiated solutions of the problem of transition and does not recognise the national-populist danger present in that argument for all the cases from the very beginning.[41] Indeed, he criticises attempts at negotiation, compromise and self-limitation on the part of new forces from perspectives that come uncomfortably close to the positions of the populists themselves, who complain about betrayed and stolen revolutions in all these settings. On the deepest level, he simply does not see the normative gain in negotiations by a plurality

[41] For my early critique, see ANDREW ARATO, CIVIL SOCIETY, CONSTITUTION AND LEGITIMACY (2000) ch. 3.

of different forces, where each side must settle for a second best (for example, constitutionalism in South Africa) in preference to majoritarian democracy and consociationalism both.[42] He simply has no problem with majoritarian imposition by a politically victorious single force, and one indeed should not be surprised by his ambivalence with respect to the 'populist' Kaczynski's recent efforts aside from their content.

The assumptions lead to serious interpretive problems that admittedly arise in cases that in my conception too are close to the boundary among ideal types, between revolution and regime change.[43] The first of these is Poland, which is treated as an example of a 'revolution on a human scale', even as its constitution-making effort is said to exemplify 'the death of revolutionary constitutionalism'. Thus, the social movement driving the process is said to be a revolutionary organisation and many of its leaders are identified as 'revolutionary heroes'. This goes against self-identification or 'self-reflection' that Ackerman otherwise considers important. With the exception of marginal right radical offshoots, the term 'revolutionary' was not used[44] and the process was defined as 'radical reform', 'new evolutionism' and 'self-limiting revolution' that all involved a conscious rejection not only of the revolutionary tradition but also of logic.[45] Ackerman seems to be ambivalent on this issue as well as the outcome, and indeed he sometimes refers to his 'revolutionary heroes' as sober statesmen adhering to the principle of *pacta sunt servanda*. The Polish Round Table negotiations are also at times referred to as revolutionary, even as its process and results are depicted as being anything but. Indeed, Ackerman strongly criticises both process and its 'heroes' for repeatedly halting or decelerating the revolutionary process and the latter also for honouring previous agreements. While he seems to be aware of the danger of authoritarian populism (citing Michnik) when Walesa, for example, tried to act as a classical revolutionary leader, in general he faults him for not doing soon and decisively enough.

Of course, we now all see that the Polish process went wrong eventually from our common normative perspective. Ackerman faults the adoption of a French-type regime he calls 'super' rather than 'semi'-presidentialism, and this is a welcome and well argued change over his earlier own presidentialist conception of the desirable model of transition.[46] Even now, when he changed his opinion on both Walesa and Yeltsin, it is not yet clear why, following Walesa's election as President, he would have expected anything other than a presidentialist outcome.

[42] Thus he does not see that two out of his seven cases involve the important correction of the logic of revolution by negotiations among former enemies.

[43] In my conception, neither should be treated as a revolution, not only because of the legal continuity that is more important than Ackerman implies, but also because of the absence of true dual power where the new force could have taken power without any negotiations and self-limitations.

[44] See A. Touraine et al., Solidarity (1983), as well as A. Arato, From Neo-Marxism to Democratic Theory: Essays on the Critical Theory of Soviet-Type Societies (1993) chs. 8–10.

[45] See A. Michnik, Letters from Prison (1986) on the destruction and construction of Bastilles.

[46] See Ackerman, *supra* note 4 at 54–63.

We know that all the constitutional drafts Walesa supported contained this feature. More importantly, Poland's specific version of presidentialism adopted in 1989 is chalked up to the famous Round Table negotiations of that year. This is historically correct, but is explainable along with the electoral compromise having to do with Poland being the first domino in the chain of Round Table transitions when Soviet tolerance still had to be experimentally tested. While Ackerman seems to imply that all round tables adopted the French model, in fact Poland is at best the only case that did so (with the Hungarian, Bulgarian, Czechoslovak and German Democratic Republic negotiations opting for parliamentary regimes).

Yet Poland did go wrong, constitutional democracy is under severe challenge today and it is worth asking whether the bargain between old and new forces is responsible. This is what Kaczynski twins and their Law and Justice Party claimed when they spoke about a stolen or betrayed revolution, justifying their project of a new revolution and a new republic. Ackerman at times comes uncomfortably close to their diagnosis, if certainly not their specific constitutional proposals. It is too bad that at a time of attacks on the Round Table agreements, as well as the constitution-making of 1997, he joins these attacks, even if in the name of a liberal vision that the new right rejects.

Yes, it is the analyst's responsibility to ascertain what went wrong. Ackerman fortunately hints at two alternatives in addition to blaming the negotiated transition that was pioneering for the region. One of these is the collapse of Solidarity and the resulting political infighting that made constitution-making first impossible and then dominated by the ex-Communist successor party. The other is shock therapy and austerity, on which he does not pass economic judgement, but considers it responsible for the collapse of Solidarity.[47] I would add to this the identification of the ex-Communist left with this very policy that eventually gave its victims no other alternative than the radical right, which was the only force to renounce austerity and argue for the reconstruction of social welfare at least for 'deserving' citizens. That this was the case is hinted at by Ackerman, but his own outline of an imaginary alternative does not touch on the question. According to him, what could and should have happened is that Walesa and his advisors should have rejected both the super-presidentialism and the only partially free electoral formula that the negotiations eventually converged upon. They should have held out for immediately free elections in a parliamentary system that would have allowed Solidarity to maintain its unity, as the ANC would do five years later. Then the organisation could have completely dominated the process of constitution-making, the result supposedly being a more legitimate constitution than the one approved in the referendum with an admittedly fateful seven-year delay.

Ackerman considers his alternative scenario of what should have happened in Poland to be the imaginary anticipation of the South African process of the 1990s.

[47] See D. Ost, The Defeat of Solidarity: Anger and Politics in Postcommunist Europe (2005).

He is partly right: the South African scenario did represent a significant improvement over the Polish scenario that began earlier and actually ended later – I would even say within the same model, even if a post-revolutionary one. But he is wrong on two points. First, even if in hindsight following the end of communism, such a radical alternative is now imaginable, it was not seen as such by anyone at the time, whether Polish protagonists or foreign politicians (see Ackerman's own reference to George Bush) It took partial Polish success and its Soviet tolerance for the Hungarian Round Table and the referenda that followed it to be able to reject all partially democratic solutions. And, second, the imaginary alternative model outlined is not the South African model.

Of course, Ackerman rather desperately tries to have us accept the idea that South Africa was not a culmination of negotiated transitions, as I and many others claim,[48] but a revolutionary one. Indeed, South Africa had many revolutionaries who considered themselves as such. It is only a question, but hardly the main one, as to whether they were the main force behind the process and whether its logic was anything like what they would have wanted. The idea that Mandela threatened de Klerk with a revolutionary destruction of the Republic and the construction of 'a revolutionary order bottom up' claimed by Ackerman, is fanciful and undocumented.[49] Much more important is Ackerman's constant downplaying of negotiations and their compromise results for both the process and the outcome. Thus, he calls the importance of the famous 'talks about talks' exaggerated,[50] reduces CODESA to the opening hostile statements by de Klerk and Mandela misunderstanding how much had already been accomplished at this venue, and calls the pluralism of the subsequent Kempton Park negotiations window-dressing. At issue is thus not only a different evaluation of the overall process from mine, but, more particularly, an interpretation of the main events that is contrary to all the experts on the subject, as well as the most important participants. The significance of legal continuity too is downplayed, and thus the main feature of the process tying it to all the round tables, but distinguishing it from all great revolutions.

Finally, the role of compromise is also poorly evaluated, even as Ackerman's description confirms its importance both in relation to process and result. As to the former, it was compromise in which both sides made serious concessions that led to the famous two-stage process Ackerman mentions. One side wanted a constitution negotiated by experts, while the other wanted one enacted by the majority of a freely elected assembly. But the choice between 'experts' and 'the people' or 'democracy' was not a binary one; it was possible to have both. Thus, the two-stage process allowed the creation of two constitutions: a negotiated

[48] In my case most recently in ARATO, *supra* note 3, ch. 3; see also H. EBRAHIM, THE SOUL OF A NATION: CONSTITUTION-MAKING IN SOUTH AFRICA (1998); and S. FRIEDMANN, ed., THE SMALL MIRACLE: SOUTH AFRICA'S NEGOTIATED SETTLEMENT (1992); P. ANDREWS & S. ELLMAN, eds., THE POST-APARTHEID CONSTITUTIONS: PERSPECTIVES ON SOUTH AFRICA'S BASIC LAW (2001).

[49] ACKERMAN, *supra* note 4 at 93.

[50] *Id.* at 99.

interim constitution and a final constitution in which democratic elections and public involvement played central roles. However, this was not going to be a case of *lex posterior*, since the principles agreed upon at the first stage would bind the Constituent Assembly, which would emphatically not be a sovereign body. Interestingly, Ackerman recognises that this scheme allowed de Klerk to control and pacify 'counter-revolutionaries' on his side. He should have said the same concerning Mandela and the revolutionaries on his side.

As to results, one side wanted a consociationalist outcome, as Ackerman stresses, while the other side wanted a majoritarian outcome. While elements of consociationalism were included in the interim constitution, the final constitution could remove those that were not included among the principles. Yet the result was not a majoritarian democracy, as Ackerman claims,[51] but a constitutional one, and that is quite a different matter. One (but only one) of the main differences was a very strong constitutional court that unusually (although perhaps inspired by the Indian example) was even given the power of amendment review. Ackerman recognises the unusual power of the new court, but in his conception, this is grounded in the revolutionary legitimacy of the process and the result. This argument does make sense, even if it reveals only a possible logical connection and not an empirical regularity. The court itself in any case interpreted its own legitimacy in terms of the 'solemn promise' the sides made to one another and, on one famous occasion that Ackerman cites, Mandela agreed.

More importantly, however, the revolutionary legitimacy would not apply to the court when it was operating only under the interim (ie, contractual) constitution and when no transfer of sovereignty had then occurred. Yet it was precisely this court that was given the most dramatic task of controlling the adherence of the final constitution to the principles of the interim constitution. Ackerman has a lot of trouble with this provision. First, he states that no 'serious jurists' inside or outside the country could accept such a final say by judges using old rules to control the new constitution. This is right at least for lawyers, serious or unserious, who share the still-dominant traditional idea of Sieyès and Schmitt that the constituent power is in the state of nature limited by no law or norms of any kind. Yet, he goes on to immediately admit that 'current scholarly consensus' confirms exactly such a role for a new form of constitution-making. What happened between the supposed old and obvious new juristic consensus was of course South Africa doing something new. Not only were the judges given a portion of the constituent power, but they actually used this power. It is doubly wrong, as Ackerman claims, that the judges restricted their role in constitutional certification to minor issues. Federalism and the entrenchment of the Bill of Rights are major, not minor points.[52] Moreover, the prospect of challenge in front of the

[51] *Id.* at 116.

[52] See the fine pieces by C. Murray, *Negotiating beyond Deadlock* and C. Rickard, *The Certification of the Constitution of South Africa, in* POST-APARTHEID CONSTITUTIONS (P. Andrews & S. Ellmann eds., 2001).

court put the constitution-makers under the shadow of review, as much as they elsewhere operated under the shadow of the referendum. Given the high total vote for the ANC, it was indeed the court's prospective role that most emphatically distinguished the constitutional assembly it was called from the constituent assemblies of the revolutionary tradition.

VI. The Exception Revisited

It is only in the last chapter entitled 'American Exceptionalism?' that we discover Ackerman's motives for writing such an ambitious work and including some very questionable cases within his concept. He clearly wishes to battle the idea that the American paradigm of constitution-making, to which he has committed so much energy and learning, is not applicable to most such efforts around the world. To be sure, he explicitly attacks exceptionalism in the name of the opposite idea, a modest one, namely that Americans themselves have something to learn from analogous, popular sovereignty-based efforts either because they went well or because they have failed in some essential respects. But in any case, this last chapter is based on the conclusion that India, France, South Africa and Poland, though this time fortunately not Israel or Iran, 'are travelling down the very same path that the United States has been following since the Founding'. If the US was once unique, this is no longer the case.

Again, astonishingly for a jurist, Ackerman's case is not made in relation to actual processes of constitution-making, but the supposedly four-stage temporal sequence of revolutions on a human scale. But, in fact, even more than a stage model, it is the comparison of personalities and their choices that dominate the analysis. Thus, Nehru, de Gaulle, Mandela and Ben-Gurion are compared to Washington and FD Roosevelt, and admittedly some episodic analogies are discovered. Yet, after striking similarities are claimed between the two totally different personalities Generals Washington and de Gaulle, Ackerman is forced into the admission that there were two fundamental differences between them. These were the highly important matters of Washington's reluctance to threaten force or even illegality against domestic competitors and his relative lack of interest in constitutional questions. All that remains of the parallel is charisma that Washington, unlike de Gaulle, refused to exploit, as would all populists. Here the parallel is with Mandela, who left office after one term, and thus we are told that Washington was a cross between de Gaulle and Mandela. This idea does not help much in making the case.

To isolate a main issue, the Nehru/Ben-Gurion contrast works better for their contemporary Franklin Roosevelt. Ackerman is on solid ground with Nehru, but rather than comparing the two men, he finally brings in a dimension that was greatly and inexplicably neglected in this earlier chapter on India, namely colonial constitutional development.[53] This India and the US indeed shared, and especially, as he says, the building up of representative institutions on a provincial level was common to both colonies before independence. This is the old point made by Arendt (contra Sieyès and Schmitt) about the importance of the constituent power not being 'in the state of nature', but possessed and exercised by organised bodies that will then federate rather than create a sovereign nation-state whose paradoxes she explored. To Arendt, this was the way in which the American Revolution was exceptional with respect to the progeny of the French. Its constitution-making paradigm involved non-sovereign conventions differentiated from legislative bodies that remained in place. Assuming it we would have to notice that the same logic was followed first by Canada in a hesitant way in the 1850s,[54] then by Australia in a quite remarkable and advanced form in around 1900,[55] and then by South Africa in a racist and exclusionary form in 1910 that uniquely produced a unitary state in spite of earlier British advice.[56] Finally, India during the very last days of colonial rule followed the same logic. Arguably even Germany under the post World War II allied occupation did so with the prior reconstruction of the governments of the Länder on which the process subsequently rested. Whether the fiction of popular sovereignty was appealed to (as in Australia and India) or not (as in Canada and Germany) is not the main issue at all.

In the second volume of *We the People*, Ackerman used the term 'revolutionary reform' for the American case instead of the term 'revolution' for a moment associated with the French. I much prefer this term and to have it applied to whole processes such as that of India, and not just reform within revolutions as Ackerman now seems to. His earlier point was reliance on some important inherited institutions, not just leaving them intact as in the idea of human scale, but mobilising them in new constitution-making efforts. I accepted this idea and coupled it with the continuation of some inherited forms of legitimacy around a key institution even in the midst of legal breaks that are always ambiguous and contestable in such cases as the US and India.[57] However, I believe that there are many more such cases, many successfully establishing constitutionalism, although there are some, like Yeltsin's version, that culminated in dual power and constitutional failure. Focusing on Israel again, where there was a revolutionary-type

[53] Until the very last chapter (Ackerman, *supra* note 4 at 423–24), Ackerman tends to de-emphasise or even entirely neglect important stages of the colonial and even decolonising process: the Government of India Acts well before the 1930s, the Simon Commission and its response, the Nehru Report, the Round Tables in London in the 1930s and the Cabinet Mission.

[54] See P. Russell's two books Constitutional Odyssey (2006) and Canada's Odyssey (2017).

[55] Remarkable because Australians even realised the anti-federalist demand of a democratically elected second convention! See Nicholas Aroney, The Constitution of a Federal Commonwealth: The Making and Meaning of the Australian Constitution (2009); and John Andrew La Nauze, The Making of the Australian Constitution (1972).

[56] L.M. Thompson, The Unification of South Africa: 1902–1910 (1960).

[57] Ackerman, We the People, Volume 1, *supra* note 2, argues for a break; We the People, Volume 2, *supra* note 2, argues for legal secession. For India, see Arato, *supra* note 3, ch. 4.

legal break, there too it would have been possible to rely on inherited institutions and especially universalist norms of legitimacy to create a constitutional state, as the Declaration demanded. This was subverted by Ben-Gurion primarily. It is hard to avoid the impression that charismatic personalities are a problem rather than an advantage from the point of view of this model. Yeltsin and Ben-Gurion cannot prove this negative point, but make it plausible. Washington and Nehru speak for a more positive interpretation; however, the former refused to constitutionalise his charisma, despite calls for this by the officers of the Society of the Cincinnati. But who even knows the names of their countries' constitutional founders outside of Canada and Australia?

VII. Constitution-Making under Occupation

But what about revolution that we cannot simply banish by fiat or turn into revolutionary reform where a plurality of independent republican institutions are not available, as was the case in revolutionary France in 1789? How can it be saved from its destructive logic so clearly indicated by the French and Russian prototypes, and even the great revolution in Iran? This was the question addressed by Condorcet to his countrymen, fearing the authoritarian answer that led to his death. I have tried to show that Ackerman's answer to this question is based on three types of cases. First among these are changes of regime that are not revolutions according not only to my definition stressing a legal break among other characteristics, but all others that take negotiated transition seriously as well as the self-understanding of the main actors (Poland and South Africa). Second, there is a case that he uses – India – that is better understood as one of revolutionary reform. Third, there are Israel and Iran, where the clearly present revolutionary logic blocks the way to constitutionalism. What then is left from Ackerman's series of case studies are the 'revolutions' of France and Italy in 1944–45. These satisfy not only his concept of revolution, but also the human scale concept, as they have left many traditional spheres of social life – above all, the capitalist economy and religion – intact or at most susceptible to later reforms. They also satisfy my definition in terms of breaks in legality and legitimacy, as well as conflicts around the duality (or plurality) of sovereignty claims.

There will of course be critics who will wish to deny the term 'revolution' where the doubling of sovereign power as well as the overthrow of the old regime relied on external military force. I am not and cannot be one of them for the obvious reason that I have treated Iraq after 2003 as a case of externally imposed revolution[58] and have always regarded the people's democracies as revolutionary regimes, even if and when their establishment was externally imposed. Moreover,

[58] See Andrew Arato, Constitution Making under Occupation: The Politics of Imposed Revolution in Iraq (2009).

in the two cases treated here by Ackerman, as in Iraq later, there were significant internal resistance forces that admittedly could not liberate their countries as the guerrilla army of Yugoslavia did, but could challenge sovereignty as soon as the previous occupier's hold on the country was broken by external military invasions. Indeed, these forces played crucial roles in both the liberation of parts of national territories and the formation of provisional governments. So how is it that they were not able to impose the logic of revolution and revolutionary dictatorships after liberation?

Ackerman answers this in terms of the ideology and organisation of plurality of resistant forces. This comes very close to the insurance argument around choosing the second best that he explicitly rejects, though he secretly makes use of this when he describes how communists and socialists in Italy belatedly came to support strong constitutional review that they have previously rejected for ideological reasons. Yet during the provisional governments in the very beginning, something else was also involved: the presence of American and English occupying forces, which in the two chapters discussed here Ackerman mentions only once, and only to indicate their non-interference with the process.

Though I have not seriously investigated the matter, I accept the claim that the occupying forces intervened in constitutional negotiations and drafting less in France and Italy than even in Germany and far less than in Japan. But with serious and powerful revolutionary forces on the terrain, unlike in Germany and Japan, the role of the occupiers was different. I ask the obvious question. Why were France and Italy so different from Czechoslovakia with its coup by the Communist Party or Greece with its long and destructive civil war? The communist forces were hardly much stronger in Czechoslovakia[59] and Greece than their French and Italian counterparts, and all these parties at that time were emphatically revolutionary. In each country, they had the best-organised and best armed forces of the internal resistance (here Poland was the big exception). We know the answer to this. Already at Yalta, Stalin conceded dominance in Western Europe to Britain and the US and, as in Greece, he kept his end of the bargain (except in the case of Hungary and partially in Poland).[60]

Thus, Togliatti's famous Svolta di Salerno was based at the very least on emphatic Soviet advice if not outright decisions much more than on the recognition of plurality of oppositions, or anticipations of Eurocommunism, or constitutional values. We should note that he had by far the largest partisan forces during the late stages of the war, while the forces which de Gasperi, Ackerman's main 'revolutionary hero', in reality a determined centrist, could rely on were very modest in reality. Togliatti nevertheless disarmed many of his partisans, joined the provisional government and during the Constituent Assembly acted like an even more effective Socialist Party fighting for elements of a social welfare state.

[59] The vote of the combined Communist Parties was about 38 per cent, which is not of a different magnitude compared to the French or Italian results.

[60] E. Agarossi & V. Zaslavsky, Stalin and Togliatti (2011).

All this was beneficial, but, even more so, it was wise. The American and British forces present, as Stalin was in the best position to know, would never have allowed a communist-led taking of power or even a communist-socialist coalition to dominate the proceedings. Thus, de Gasperi was to be a guarantee that under his leadership, the parties of the left could retain some undetermined portion of their influence on many features of the Constitution (the fact that he was to betray them all does not take anything away from the original reason why he was there). The Constituent Assembly elections that he won against the communists, but lost against the combined left, only confirmed the power position he gained with his incumbency, and the undetermined extent of the American and British (not to mention clerical) support that he received.

The situation in France was somewhat similar, because here too the temporary occupiers were not going to let the Communist Party and the socialists, who originally controlled the main forces of the *internal resistance* and who dominated the first Constituent Assembly elections, establish a regime they dominated. Yet external forces were not the ones who defeated in a referendum the constitution that this assembly enacted, one that had many very progressive features, including the transformation of the empire into a voluntary federation that Ackerman strangely disregards.[61] In France, as Ackerman rightly stresses throughout, the danger came not from Thorez, a very uncharismatic personality, but from the right: from de Gaulle. The Allies, whose leaders did not like de Gaulle, had little trouble in accepting him as the formal head of the first Liberation Government. But de Gaulle was no de Gasperi. Even if he did not see himself as a revolutionary, he did believe that he was indeed a hero. While in the presence of the Allies and the organised communist and socialist forces, he could not even dream of pushing through a right-wing authoritarian form of government, he could and did make a determined effort, to use Ackerman's words, to constitutionalise his charisma in a regime of strong presidentialism. However, in 1946, as compared to 1958, the conditions were not there for him to be accepted as the nation's saviour. So he did the third best thing and urged as many supporters to bring down the first assembly's draft in a referendum, although this only led to a second assembly and a second draft that was more defensive of an empire dominated by the French metropole, though it was no more presidentialist than its predecessors.

To draw the balance sheet: the Allies could block a regime enacted by the left. The left could block any solution de Gaulle tried to impose. De Gaulle could block one constitution agreed to by the parties. Everyone was supposed to live with the third- or fourth-best option, something that de Gaulle was constitutionally unable to do. Such an arrangement does not produce constitutional patriotism or even loyalty. The fact that de Gaulle was to have another chance to impose his second if not his first preference was due to the Constitution's concessions to the inherited

[61] F. Cooper, Citizenship between Empire and Nation (2016).

empire and the subsequent government 's attempts to consolidate this tottering structure in Vietnam and Algeria. But this story, which is included among Ackerman's chapters, is not part of the history of the revolutionary assemblies.

Let me sum up my contention regarding the two cases involving external occupation. As in India, Poland and South Africa, here too in France and Italy, it was not the logic of revolution that produced constitutionalism. Here that logic was controlled or subverted not merely by internal forces, such as when making a federation or coming to an agreement, but in significant part by the external occupier for geopolitical reasons.

PART II

Constitutional Evolutions and Transformations

7

Charismatic Fictions and Constitutional Politics

TOM GINSBURG

Pushpa Kamal Dahal, known as Prachanda, is a charismatic fellow. A Hindu Brahmin turned communist revolutionary, he emerged as the major figure in the armed wing of the Communist Party of Nepal (Maoist) (CPN-M), which led a violent insurgency against the Nepalese government from 1996 to 2006. Faced with an entrenched and corrupt monarchy, which cohabited with a set of elitist parliamentary parties, the CPN-M demanded an end to the feudal monarchical system, the termination of the Indo-Nepal friendship treaty and the creation of a 'people's government'. The target monarch, King Gyanendra, had ascended to the throne in 2001, after the murder of his older brother and much of the royal family by the Crown Prince, who then killed himself. Gyanendra was from central casting. A dour-faced and distant man, he faced a major challenge when the traditional political parties in the parliament, who had been willing to live with the monarchy for decades, turned against him and mass protests engulfed the capital in 2005.

In such circumstances, monarchs face two choices: they can capitulate and survive as constitutional monarchs; or they can crack down, in which case they either survive as absolute monarchs or lose the throne entirely.[1] Gyanendra made the choice to crack down, instituting direct rule in 2005. This turned out to be the wrong decision, as it spurred a new alliance between the Maoist revolutionaries and the traditional political parties, galvanising republican sentiment. By 2006, these players had signed a Comprehensive Peace Agreement with a plan to create a new constitution. Prachanda appeared in public in Kathmandu for the first time in 25 years, proclaiming the victory of the people's revolution. Within two years, the new Constituent Assembly, in its very first session, abolished the 240 year-old monarchy.

Of course, the hard part came next. Elections for the Constituent Assembly rewarded the CPN-M and its allies, and Prachanda was named Prime Minister

[1] See Adam Przeworski, Tamar Asadurian & Anjali Thomas Bohlken, *The Origins of Parliamentary Responsibility*, *in* Comparative Constitutional Design 101–36 (2012).

during the initial period of constitution-making. But hard bargaining ensued, as the CPN-M did not have the majority needed to make constitutional decisions on its own. Political gridlock followed and the Assembly's timetable was repeatedly extended before the Supreme Court declared that it had finally run out in 2012. A second election for a constituent assembly was held and it produced a new political configuration, with the traditional parties back in charge (these were the Nepali Congress and the United Marxist-Leninists, which led me to observe on one visit to the country that only in Nepal and my hometown of Berkeley could the Marxist-Leninists be a centrist party). Eventually, after a devastating earthquake, a new constitution was produced, emphasising rights, a new federal structure, and the long-suppressed ethnic identities of minorities. Prachanda was elected the first prime minister and a new era for Nepal had begun.

Nepal's was a revolution on a human scale. The social and economic structure remained intact, even as the political system was radically restructured. How can we best understand the process encompassing eight years of the constitutional negotiations? What lens will provide the most insight? The lens of routinising charisma? Or the more conventional lens of analysing constitutional politics as the product of conflicting interests, negotiated under conditions of incomplete information and subject to random events that change the calculus down the road? This is, roughly speaking, the challenge I want to take up in this chapter.

Before proceeding, let me say that I am genuinely honoured to comment on Professor Ackerman's book, which reflects his great ambition, boundless learning and global reach.[2] As a committed Weberian in my private life, I find his approach persuasive and quite illuminating in places, but not in others, and will use the occasion to make a brief defence of my own scholarly approach to these issues, since Ackerman uses this approach as a foil in places. I will start with laying out some of the strengths of his approach and the major contributions of the book. Then I will say a little about the overall framework of the three volumes, before turning to the role of charisma and its proper deployment in social analysis, critiquing Ackerman's use in places. Next, I will argue that a more conventional frame is more illuminating of the problems covered in his book. I conclude by returning to Prachanda and Nepal to close the discussion.

I. Three Paths?

Revolutionary Constitutions illustrates many of the themes of Ackerman's decades of groundbreaking scholarship: his focus on the people as a major force in constitutional change; his engagement with revolution; and his insistence on

[2] Bruce Ackerman, Revolutionary Constitutions: Charismatic Leadership and the Rule of Law (2019).

a rigorous framework for understanding how constitutional orders unfold over time. This generational approach introduced in this volume is exciting, and Ackerman deploys it to generate novel comparative insights across time and space. It becomes easier to understand Mandela in light of Nehru, Mitterrand in light of Indira Gandhi, and de Gaulle in light of Washington. These contributions are creative and breathtaking, and there is likely no other scholar who could have pulled this off.

Ackerman distinguishes three models of constitutional legitimation, which will correspond to the three volumes in his project. The revolutionary model is discussed in his first volume. There is the insider model, in which elites co-opt pressures for change. This is the model of British-style parliamentarism, in which a rising set of social forces confronts an old (usually monarchical) order and manages to extract concessions that lead ultimately to democratic constitutionalism. The third model is that of elite construction, in which the old order experiences a crisis that is resolved by pact.

This first volume, *Revolutionary Constitutions*, focuses on what sociologists have called the 'routinization of charisma' over time. Initially, a charismatic revolutionary movement succeeds in taking power (Time One), and the common sacrifice and shared experience helps legitimate their efforts to consolidate their movement into a written constitution (Time Two). However, as the revolutionary generation fades, opportunists replace the charismatics in running the revolutionary movement and a legitimacy vacuum ensues (Time Three). This framework sheds new light on the role of courts in constitution-building, emphasising that their role can potentially grow with temporal distance from the founding. In Ackerman's account, judicial supremacy in the revolutionary type of constitutional order emerges from struggles for authority in Time Three. The revolutionary generation is dying, but the new order is not yet born. This generational model has a specific prediction about the timing of judicial empowerment, which contrasts somewhat with my own insurance theory that Ackerman is kind enough to mention.[3] Note the difference: Ackerman says that in revolutionary constitutionalism, judicial supremacy emerges late, after the founders are gone; I say that in pacted constitutionalism, it emerges early. The mechanisms are different: I think that any delay in establishing judicial supremacy is a result of the need to accumulate judicial power, while he implies that it comes when courts internalise their proper role as agents of the founding vision. These differences are something to explore in later volumes of his project.

Along the way in this volume, we gain new insights into the foundering of the European Union (EU), whose major countries experienced very different and possibly incompatible constitutional trajectories. The current British situation, in which the source of authority seems completely muddled, is illuminated by

[3] Tom Ginsburg, Judicial Review in New Democracies (2003); see also Ackerman, *supra* note 2 at 39–40.

Ackerman's insights into responsible government.[4] We learn a good deal about revolutionary Iran, and a sustained exploration of the French semi-presidential model at home and aboard. And we have new concepts to deploy: the idea of 'Human Scale' revolutions is itself tremendously illuminating, as it recognises the partial nature of goals and ambitions of a social movement.[5] For constitutionalists, this idea allows us to isolate our variable of interest and categorise degrees of change. I could go on about all the good things in the book, but in short, this is a very valuable project that no one else could have pulled off, and it will become a must-read classic alongside the *We the People* trilogy.

Because we do not have the complete three-volume study, it is impossible to know yet whether Ackerman's categorisation of different pathways will have any correspondence to normatively desirable outcomes. Ackerman's outcome of interest is *legitimated* constitutional projects, that is, those constitutional orders that have a modicum of public acceptance. It is not restricted to liberal orders, as the inclusion of Iran illustrates, and this broadening is a welcome extension of his earlier work.[6] Authoritarians, it turns out, have constitutions too. It is easy to be critical of a government that shoots its own citizens, but it is also the case that Iran has a genuine constitutional order that is complex and fits Ackerman's framework of constitutionalised charisma.

I am still uncertain about the framework for the other two volumes, as the distinction between elite pacts and establishmentarianism is not fully clear to me.[7] Into which box will contemporary South Korea fall, I wonder? The military regime of Chun Doo Hwan followed that of the charismatic dictator Park Chung-hee, but in the late 1980s faced a paralysing set of public demonstrations. Analysts point to the key role of these demonstrations, which broadened from organized labour to the middle class, in tumbling Chun. This led to a pacted transition, refounding the country as the Sixth Republic, in which the military-backed candidate won the first election, but the Constitutional Court developed as a major force fairly early on. This looks like an elite bargain, *à la* Spain, but also had a mass movement that pushed the process over the edge. Unlike Ackerman's reading of the Spanish case, though, South Korea seems to have had little problem 'authenticating' its constitutional order, which has witnessed two impeachments, multiple changes in power and a vigorous constitutional jurisprudence.

[4] Note that Ackerman's second ideal type, of insiders creating a responsible government, does not in his view support much of the emergence of constitutional review. As he puts it, 'claims to judicial supremacy have no proper role in this ideal type'; Ackerman, *supra* note 2 at 11. This account provides a nice framework for understanding the 'New Commonwealth model of constitutionalism' and why appeals to 'the people' fit so badly within that system. See Stephen Gardbaum, The New Commonwealth Model of Constitutionalism (2013); Ackerman, *supra* note 2 at 11–12.

[5] Ackerman, *supra* note 2 at 28–29.

[6] *cf* Bruce Ackerman, The Future of Liberal Revolution (1992).

[7] But there is, of course, virtue in recognising the various paths by which constitutional orders come about.

Legitimacy is a relatively loose concept, which is why many social scientists eschew it as empirically intractable.[8] This has significance for Ackerman's broader project: revolutions need not lead to legitimate constitutional orders, and legitimate constitutional orders do not require revolutions. Take the Japanese case, which Ackerman refers to briefly in his discussion of elite constructions.[9] Ackerman suggests in passing that Prime Minister Abe's efforts to reform the constitution indicate deep legitimacy problems with the founding text, presumably because of its foreign origins. In fact, the situation is completely the opposite.[10] In 1946, General Douglas MacArthur jotted a brief note of four points to be included in the Constitution, which he then handed to his staff to draw up. This note, it turns out, intuitively captured a bargain in Japanese society between left and right, with the Emperor system retained but war renounced.[11] Each side has things it likes about the current text. It is true that among nationalist conservatives, in whose lineage Abe squarely falls by both birth and inclination, the origins of the Constitution have prompted demands for revision since virtually the minute the occupation ended in 1952. But these have not succeeded despite multiple attempts; Abe himself has tried twice and has not succeeded. Even today, Article 9 is intact and in safe hands, despite the fact that Abe and his coalition partners control a majority sufficient to amend the Constitution. The reason they do not proceed is very simple. Revision of Article 9 is deeply unpopular. There is a genuine sense among the Japanese public that the constitutional identity should remain in place. Meanwhile, as Professor Yasuo Hasebe has recently shown, the Supreme Court is showing signs of increasing activism.[12] Japan has some significant social and political problems, but constitutional legitimation is not one of them.[13]

If there is any suggestion that elite constructions or even occupation constitutions can never be legitimated, or not as well as revolutionary projects, I simply disagree. The cases I know best in which liberalism has become deeply entrenched and sustained have often involved iterated rounds of negotiation and accommodation. Revolutions have a real risk of regression, perhaps illustrated by Ackerman's Iranian case, whereas a pattern of sustained and iterated inclusive reform can generate a more rooted liberal regime. But perhaps Ackerman's claim is narrower

[8] See generally Peter G. Stillman, *The Concept of Legitimacy*, 7 Polity 32 (1974).

[9] Ackerman, *supra* note 2 at 19.

[10] Hajime Yamamoto, *Interpretation of the Constitutional by the Bureau of Cabinet Legislation: A New Source of Constitutional Law*, 26 Washington International Law Journal 99 (2017); Yasuo Hasebe, *The End of Constitutional Pacifism?*, 26 Washington International Law Journal 125 (2017); Shigenori Matsui, The Constitution of Japan: A Contextual Analysis (2010).

[11] Zachary Elkins et al., *Baghdad, Tokyo, Kabul: Constitution-making in Occupied States*, 49 William & Mary Law Review 1139–78 (2011).

[12] *Yasuo Hasebe, The Supreme Court of Japan: One Step Forward, But Only Discreetly*, 16 International Journal of Constitutional Law 672 (2018).

[13] Note the internal problem with asserting that a constitution is not legitimate because of a proposal to change it several decades later. By this standard, we might want to say that Modi's attack on India's founding project demonstrates that it was never legitimate.

and restricted to constitutions drafted under occupation. In passing, he refers to the 'collapse' of the Iraqi and Afghan constitutions.[14] Without making light of the grave situations in both places, I think this statement is too glib. Tough as it is for us opponents of the 2003 war to recognise, the Iraqi Constitution is entering a period of consolidation and even effectiveness, despite its poor design at the outset.[15] The central government has recently faced down a poorly conceived secession attempt by the Kurdistan region, consolidating its territorial authority. Sunnis who held out at the formation of the Constitution have been brought into government. The country has had a peaceful turnover in power and now a modicum of stability. It is not Denmark, but to assert that the constitutional order has collapsed is far too strong. And as Aziz Huq and I have argued, the Afghan Constitution has done a decent job in very difficult conditions by the standard of legitimacy, if not the securing of public order.[16] A legal system is under construction.[17] Participation in elections is high where they are safe; constitutional institutions have been used to constrain executive power, and opinion data suggests that the parliament of Afghanistan is a good deal more popular than the US Congress. I suspect one could find many other elite bargains that ended up performing solid constitutional work.

But all these are preliminary comments on the preliminary part of the book. Let us turn to the main discussion.

II. On Charisma and Constitutions

Weber's classic typology of legitimation seeks to answer the question of why people obey. Like other theorists of modernity, he starts with the distinction between traditional and modern (rational-legal) authority. But he goes further to introduce the idea of charisma, borrowed from the German scholar Rudolph Sohm.[18] 'Charisma', wrote Weber, 'is a certain quality of an individual personality by virtue of which he is set apart from ordinary men and treated as endowed with supernatural, superhuman, or at least specifically exceptional powers or qualities. These as such are not accessible to the ordinary person, but are regarded as of divine origin or as exemplary, and on the basis of them the individual concerned is treated as a leader.'[19] Charisma, his framework suggests, is specifically unpredictable and

[14] Ackerman, *supra* note 2 at 18.

[15] *cf* Zaid al-Ali, The Struggle for Iraq's Future (2015).

[16] Tom Ginsburg & Aziz Huq, *What can Constitutions Do? The Afghan Case*, Journal of Democracy (2014).

[17] Siavash Rahbari, *From Normative Pluralism to a Unified Legal System in Afghanistan?* 5 Asian Journal of Law and Society 289 (2018).

[18] See David Norman, *Faith, Reason and Charisma: Max Weber, Rudolph Sohm and the Theology of Grace*, 68 Sociological Inquiry 32–60 (1998).

[19] Max Weber, The Theory of Social and Economic Organization (Talcott Parsons, ed., 1947).

essentially revolutionary.[20] Born out of suffering or conflict, charisma may 'result in a radical alteration of the central system of attitudes and directions of action with a completely new orientation … toward the different problems and structures of the "world"'.[21] One cannot know when it will emerge *ex ante*, as it relies on emotional appeals and personal qualities. But once it emerges, it recedes like a wave, and its ongoing effects depend on the phenomenon of routinisation or instantiation in institutions. This description has much in common with political revolutions, which are not *ex ante* predictable or amenable to the kind of calculus of interests, costs and benefits that my own favoured line of analysis usually pursues.

Since Ackerman uses me as a foil at times, I should make my position clear. The big things in human history, I submit, cannot be explained as a matter of rational calculus, negotiated interests or institutional logics. Charismatics like Gandhi, Hitler and Jesus changed the world far more than any run-of-the-mill pursuit of material or political interests. Charismatics do so by inspiring their followers to create new forms of membership, fusing elements of old and new ideas into new forms of meaning, and creating political and social forces that change the world. In this act of fusion, charismatic projects have something in common with successful constitution-making episodes in that they involve elements of *both* transformation and preservation, and can create a new form of being and identity, in the form of a demos.[22] It is this cobbling together of disparate elements in different ways that really changes the world, and it is exciting to draw on the framework in thinking about constitutions.

But charismatic figures and projects are unpredictable and rare, or at least rarely successful. If charisma can explain the really big things, it cannot explain ordinary politics, which fall into Weber's other category of rational-legal authority. Most people most of the time act in ends-means relationships with the world, even if they do so imperfectly and clumsily. And most constitutional politics are ordinary politics – the stuff of interests, passions and reasons, in which negotiators work on the basis of assumptions, and institutions then operate.[23] Bargainers have assets and liabilities that they bring to the table, and face particular challenges that resist easy solutions. Incentives and information are the stuff of institutional analysis, which in my humble opinion can help to clarify the underlying logics in these situations. More controversially, institutional analysis also allows us to generate falsifiable propositions or predictions about the world. The analysis of charisma analysis can only serve as a lens to explain what happens, but does not allow us to even gesture at a social science to specify mechanisms and causes.

[20] *Id.* at 363.

[21] *Id.* See generally E. San Juan, Jr., *Orientation of Max Weber's Concept of Charisma*, 11 Centennial Review 270–85 (1967).

[22] Ginsburg & Huq, *supra* note 16.

[23] Jon Elster, *Forces and Mechanisms in the Constitution-Making Process*, 45 Duke L.J. 364 (1995).

To be sure, the claims of positivist analysis are frequently overstated. In the real world, it is difficult to know with confidence what ought to be done in constitutional design.[24] But the difficulty does not mean that we should just throw up our hands in frustration, and wait for a charismatic to come along and fix things. Such an approach ultimately implies setting aside the normative aspirations of law as a discipline, in which we connect various sources of knowledge to say what should be done. The best we can do is normative analysis grounded in positivist guesses about what will happen on the basis of incentives; this is not easy, but it is worth a try.

Returning to Ackerman's book, the question becomes which cases are best explained by which approach. Of cases included in the volume, the India-South Africa pair is the paradigm, introducing the concept of charismatic foundings. In each case, a broad inclusive movement with a paramount leader helps to overturn the old order and institutionalises the project into a constitution that creates a nation. Poland too fits nicely as an illustration of the failure of the charismatic movement to stay together. Ackerman's reading of these cases broadens our understanding immensely, supplementing existing accounts based on interests and bargains.[25]

However, the account does less well in some of the other cases. In his account of the Italian founding, Ackerman stretches his own framework quite far and, despite his best efforts, actually provides an account that supports the insurance theory of judicial review. In the Myanmar case, he allows himself a detour to describe liberal aspirations which are not present. And some of the illuminating material on France is compatible with an interest-based account rather than a charismatic account. In short, I assert that an interest-based account explains more than one grounded in charisma.

III. Italy

Let us start with Italy.[26] At first glance, the lack of a single leader of the Italian democratic movement poses challenges to the analysis. Yet, being committed to the framework of charismatic authority, Ackerman attributes a kind of collective charisma to the several parties in the postwar bargain. In other places, the charisma is De Gasperi's alone. But either way, the details that are recounted in the story are those of bargaining, elections and negotiations – precisely the kind of data that the institution-based framework is better at explaining.

[24] Tom Ginsburg, *Constitutional Knowledge*, 2 Know: A Journal of the Formation of Knowledge 15 (2018).

[25] On South Africa, see Jens Meierhenrich, The Legacies of Law (2008). See also Rosalind Dixon, *Constitutional Drafting and Distrust*, 13 International Journal of Constitutional Law 819 (2015).

[26] Ackerman, *supra* note 2 at 131.

The fact that De Gasperi's allies were denied, by a bare margin, the majority needed to form a government in 1953, which would have allowed them to obtain the supermajority control entrenching their power through the 'Fraud Law', is hardly attributable to charisma, though it was an enormously consequential moment in the unfolding of the Italian constitutional order.[27] Can we really say that another 100,000 votes would have demonstrated a vindication of De Gasperi's charisma? Hardly. Instead, the framework in which constitutions are bargains, subject to shocks, that forms the core of the institutional account is far better equipped to understand the issues in Italy. How else can we understand the design of the Italian Constitutional Court, allowing each of three institutions to appoint five seats? How else can we understand the timing of setting up the Court and the delay? To quote Ackerman: 'With the Marxists controlling 40% of the assembly, the Christian Democrats could not be confident that they would control the government after the next election.'[28] He goes on to quote Calamadrei's analogy to painting: 'put the frame upside down, and put yourselves for a moment, forgetting your solid majority, in the conditions of the minority. Would you propose the amendments you are defending today were you in the opposition?' Is there a clearer statement of the political configuration behind the insurance theory?[29]

In his narrative on Italy, Ackerman is not only agreeing with me, but with the most distinguished American commentator on these issues, Mary Volcansek.[30] In her article on the Italian constitutional founding, she argues that the insurance model provides the best account of the decision of the Italian Christian Democrats to support creation of a constitutional court at the point of constitutional design, but also to delay implementation once in power. The left-wing parties had the opposite set of preferences, opposing the establishment of the court at the Constituent Assembly, but championing judicial review once out of power. This seems to me to be a pretty concise account of what happened and is in fact Ackerman's story.[31]

IV. Myanmar

One of the interesting things about this Ackerman as opposed to the early Ackerman is his new emphasis on text. To illustrate the point, consider his treatment of

[27] Mary L. Volcansek, *Bargaining Constitutional Design in Italy: Judicial Review as Political Insurance*, 33 West European Politics 280, 283 (2010); see also Mary Volcansek *Political Power and Judicial Review in Italy*, 26 Comp. Political Studies 492 (1994).

[28] Ackerman, *supra* note 2 at 147.

[29] In the version of the manuscript I commented on, Ackerman refers to this as a Rawlsian veil of ignorance, but in the published version of the book, he amends his account slightly to emphasise the deferral of the decision through vagueness. Either way, his account is quite consistent with the insurance perspective.

[30] Volcansek, *Bargaining Constitutional Design*, *supra* note 27.

[31] Ackerman, *supra* note 2 at 148–50.

Aung San Suu Kyi, the housewife turned political prisoner turned national leader, whose National League for Democracy (NLD) dominates the civilian side of the government of Myanmar. The qualification of 'civilian side' is important, in that the military is run autonomously and retains the right to take over power under Article 40(c) of the Constitution of Myanmar should it find there to be a national emergency.[32] Dan Slater insightfully characterises the situation in Myanmar as being one of cohabitation between the NLD and the military.

When the NLD swept into power in national elections in 2015, Aung San Suu Kyi was prevented from taking the presidency by Article 59.f, which bars the office to those with close family members who have foreign nationality.[33] Instead, the NLD produced a constitutional workaround, naming Suu Kyi a state counsellor, with her long-time associate Htin Kyaw taking power.[34] Ackerman takes the view that this was a key juncture that temporarily derailed the completion of the revolution. Instead of maintaining the cohabitation, he thinks 'the Lady' (as Aung San Suu Kyi is known locally) could have and should have insisted on taking the presidency, daring the military to oppose her.[35] This would have created a 'constitutional moment' allowing the completion of the transition.

I have two problems with this analysis. First of all, it is oddly formalist, to use one of Ackerman's favourite scholarly epithets. Indeed, both here and in the discussion of the New Deal in the book's last chapter, we see Ackerman adopt a new emphasis on text, implying that instantiating the revolutionary arrangements into formal constitutional language can be consequential. I do not disagree – texts sometimes help movements and elites coordinate their understandings and behaviours – but it is a noteworthy and new argument in light of the earlier approach of *We the People*.

Second, and more importantly, Myanmar does not seem like a context in which formal alignment between power and position was really necessary. The Lady commands absolute respect within her party, and her position has in fact been instantiated into law – in this case, a statute. What difference would it have made had she confronted the military over her personal title? A cost-benefit analysis suggests that the risks would have been grave indeed and the benefits slight. But don't take my word for it; this was the calculation on the ground.

[32] The article reads: 'If there arises a state of emergency that could cause disintegration of the Union, disintegration of national solidarity and loss of sovereign power or attempts therefore by wrongful forcible means such as insurgency or violence, the Commander-in-Chief of the Defence Services has the right to take over and exercise State sovereign power in accord with the provisions of this Constitution.'

[33] In listing qualifications for the presidency, the article says 'shall he himself, one of the parents, the spouse, one of the legitimate children or their spouses not owe allegiance to a foreign power, not be subject of a foreign power or citizen of a foreign country'. While this on its face seems to target Aung San Suu Kyi, it is hardly an unreasonable requirement for a constitution.

[34] See generally Mark Tushnet, *Constitutional Workarounds*, 87 Tex. L. Rev. 1499 (2009).

[35] Ackerman, *supra* note 2 at 289–94.

It is not as if the NLD has not tried to modify the constitution in its early years.[36] In 2013, the parliament convened a Constitutional Review Committee, still dominated by the military and its aligned party, the Union Solidarity Development Party. The Committee also included seven NLD members who had been elected in a 2012 by-election. The NLD proposed many of the reforms suggested by Ackerman, but these were rejected by the Amendment Committee. In 2015, two relatively minor amendments did pass parliament, but these did not address the core institutional arrangements. And as I write, a parliamentary committee to propose amendments has been created, suggesting that formal change may indeed be imminent.

Ackerman reads Myanmar through a fairly standard Western lens, which is incomplete in important ways. The standard view is one of democratisation and liberal reform. It sees Suu Kyi as a Mandela-like figure who is unable to get a handle on the military and thus shares blame for its brutal repression of the Rohingya minority which she is powerless to stop. I think a fuller account would emphasise her own goals – that is, her perception of interests. Suu Kyi, who never knew her father, sees her role as completing Aung San's charismatic mission. Aung San, it will be recalled, was the man who convinced most of the various tribal peoples to remain in Myanmar during the famous meeting at Panglong in 1947. He was *also* the founder of the Burmese military. Completing Aung San's mission would require ending the seven decades of civil war that have followed his premature death by assassination. This means bringing together the lowland Burman people with the hill tribes, under a civilian government that integrates the military. This is a nationalist goal, which is far more complex than simply proclaiming a set of liberal guarantees.

Indeed, it is arguable that Aung San's vision cannot be achieved by liberal means, for a stable government integrating the nation would be dominated by the majority ethnic group. Many of the tribes run their own states, some with quite lucrative resources. The most recalcitrant tribal group may be the Wa, who occupy a territory rich in precious gems bordering on Yunnan in China.[37] Well-armed, and increasingly wealthy, what possible interest could they have in submitting to a government dominated by lowland Burmans, whose language and culture they do not share? Why would they even join a constitutional order on the basis of a promise made decades before to Suu Kyi's father?

Within this framework, the Rohingya, who were a focus of Ackerman's analysis, are simply irrelevant. The Muslim Rohingya are universally perceived by Buddhist Burmans as late arrivals, essentially as Bangladeshi migrants. They are not citizens,

[36] Melissa Crouch, *Authoritarian Straightjacket or Vehicle for Democratic Transition? The Struggle to Change Myanmar's Constitution and its Risks*, *in* From Parchment to Practice: Implementing New Constitutions (Tom Ginsburg & Aziz Huq eds., forthcoming 2020).

[37] This leads me to mention another key factor ignored by the emphasis on charisma: the international environment.

were not a party to the original bargain and have no status in the main game of territorial negotiations with the hill tribes. One feels for Suu Kyi, as she is being blamed for the military's genocidal campaign, but it has little to do with the main drama of Myanmar, except that the tactics in evidence in Rakhine state have been deployed in many other parts of the country for the past seven decades. Suu Kyi's inability to navigate the situation may be in some small part attributable to her personality – unlike Mandela, she is a notorious micromanager and a less skilled politician.[38] But a large part of the problem is simply structural. The configuration of interests is thorny and it is not likely to end in a liberal democracy or even a revolution.

To summarise my critique of the analysis of Myanmar: it is not clear that it belongs in the revolutionary category. The actual Constitution, adopted unilaterally by the military in 2008, was a top-down affair, not even an elite pact. But the political transition that has occurred to date *was* an elite pact, in which two of the three major forces negotiated a modus vivendi that included some constitutional workarounds. It is also clearly *not* a case of a *liberal* revolution. The Rohingya crisis illustrates that liberalism is not deeply embedded in the society – and how could it be after decades of isolation and underdevelopment?[39]

This brings us finally turn to the Constitutional Tribunal, which is a central part of Ackerman's generational model. Perhaps we shall one day reach a Time Four in Myanmar, in which this young court gives voice to a founding vision. So far, it has struggled to find a role. The first constitutional tribunal set up by the new Constitution was impeached by parliament after deciding a case in which it sided with the President on the question of which bodies could submit legislative proposals.[40] In a later incarnation, the Constitutional Tribunal held *unconstitutional* an administrative action that would have granted voting status to the Rohingya, who as I mentioned are not citizens, but hold temporary identification documents.[41] Arguably this decision *upheld* the founding vision for majoritarian

[38] South Africa too involved intense and serious negotiations, in which a charismatic leader was a critical asset in the negotiations. In this sense, the better analogy for George Washington than de Gaulle is Mandela. After all, both the American and South African negotiations proceeded with a clear understanding of who would be the first president. And though present in the constitutional negotiations, Mandela – like Washington – was largely silent. He understood charisma and how to deploy it sparingly in order to preserve its power.

[39] In general, there is a risk of reading others to share our preferences. Bruce rereads Aharon Barak as giving voice to Israel's founding values, but he commits the rather common sin of selecting the founding values that he likes. It is true that Barak, on one account, is fulfilling Ben-Gurion's vision. But the better account of the Israeli founding is one of an incompletely theorised agreement, in which the founding values of a Jewish democracy are put into play in a kind of (sometimes) productive tension. It would be equally accurate to say that the founding values of the Jewish state are being advanced by the ethno-nationalist project of the current coalition. That is also a revolutionary vision, instantiating diasporic Judaism into the form and structure of a modern nation state. But it is a different and ultimately illiberal one.

[40] Melissa Crouch, *Dictators, Democrats and Constitutional Dialogue: The Constitutional Tribunal of Myanmar*, 16 International Journal of Constitutional Law 421–46 (2017).

[41] *Id.*

unity, though at great cost to the Rohingya. Now that the NLD is in control, the Tribunal is seeing a new set of petitions from the military members of parliament, who are in the minority. Providing access to these minority actors fits an insurance account, but is hard to square with a view that the Tribunal is advancing the cause of revolutionary charismatic transformation. Perhaps, though, we shall look back in a generation and see that the Tribunal has navigated itself into a position so that, like the French Conseil and the Israeli Supreme Court, it is in a position of giving full force to the forces of the revolution.

V. Gaullism

Ackerman's account of the development of the Fourth and Fifth Republics in France is one of the strengths of his book. My only comment comes again from the account of the development of constitutional review. This occurred in three major steps: the 1971 decision of the Conseil Constitutionnel to incorporate the Declaration of the Rights and Duties of Man into the Constitution from the Fourth Republic; the expansion of access to the Conseil, initiated by President Giscard d'Estaing in 1974; and the 2008 incorporation of *ex post* review. These fit nicely into the generational account of constitutional review. The head of the Conseil in 1971 had been de Gaulle's right-hand man, who had helped lead the referendum for popular election of the presidency and so had a flexible view of the Constitution initially. But in 1971, the General was gone, and so the Conseil's incorporation of the Declaration constrained Pompidou instead.

The 1974 expansion of standing to legislative minorities, which Ackerman asserts is problematic from a rationalist point of view, is actually easy to explain.[42] Giscard, after all, headed a small party, with short time horizons, and unlikely to govern long into the future; indeed, his government was dependent on the Gaullists for majority support. Small and weak parties are precisely those that we would predict would prefer a greater scope of constitutional review, and when a window is opened to achieve it, why not? It is also worth considering that Giscard was a technocrat, without a large party movement behind him and without a transformative programme. Constraint on majorities was desirable from this point of view, as it proved to be after Mitterrand's election in 1991. At least at this stage, charisma did not provide much help in understanding developments.

There might be a competing account of the third step in the French expansion, grounded in the diffusion of ideas from abroad. *Ex post* review, after all, had spread throughout Europe by the first decade of the twenty-first century, with only the UK as a major holdout. The transnational regime of the European Convention

[42] Ackerman, *supra* note 2 at 206.

on Human Rights meant that French legislative decisions were routinely being reviewed by judges outside France. It would be hard to maintain a sustained objection to such review by the French Conseil. In addition, the number of countries exercising constitutional review expanded continuously in the period from 1971 to 2008, so *ex post* review was 'in the air'. I do not know the inside workings of the Balladur Commission well enough to guess whether there was any role for the transnational in their deliberations. But surely the spread of the Gaullist model *outside* France has relied on the dynamics of diffusion, being mainly confined to former French colonies and the single wave of post-Cold War constitutions. These countries nearly uniformly adopted the system of a two-headed government at a time when it had just proved effective at constraining a French socialist who sought to nationalise major portions of the economy. It was not a crazy choice for that context, but is slipping slightly in popularity now.

More generally, international forces are underplayed in Ackerman's account, as he emphasises the internal dynamics of countries and their charismatics. I am sure he would agree that outside forces can play a role at the margins in providing the conditions for charismatic emergence and consolidation. The South African apartheid regime might have killed Mandela, but did not; it might have held off on releasing him in the 1990s, but succumbed to the threat by the rest of the world of what Hathaway and Shapiro call 'Outcasting'.[43] The 1980s boycotts of South Africa helped facilitate the preconditions for the struggle for supremacy. This was in part because the apartheid regime lacked what the Burmese generals had, which was a powerful neighbour (China) that was able to insulate them from the international boycotts that ensued once the military ignored the results of the 1990 election. Here, the role of charisma *is* relevant, but power is the final determinant of whether charismatic revolution can actually unfold. The 1990 election elevated Suu Kyi into the role of a charismatic leader of a movement. But she lacked the backing to fully convert this symbolic role into effective power.

One of the great contributions of Ackerman's book is a sustained conversation with the semi-presidential model in which a directly elected president co-exists with a government responsible to parliament.[44] This model served the charismatic leader who designed it, de Gaulle, and was blessed by multiple direct appeals to the people. But Ackerman insightfully notes that it fragmented politics in Poland, preventing the revolutionary Solidarity movement from consolidating its authority. Now that Poland faces a challenge from a unified anti-liberal government, semi-presidentialism may not be having the restraining effects that its proponents assert. One might speculate that semi-presidentialism is asymmetric in its effects on revolution: it prevents the consolidation of a democratic revolution, but poses no barrier to authoritarian backsliding.

[43] Oona Hathaway & Scott Shapiro, The Internationalists (2017).
[44] Robert Elgie, Semi-presidentialism: Subtypes and Democratic Performance (2011).

VI. Quibbles and Bits

Since the occasion is one of comments on Ackerman's book, I want to point to some missing cases that might better fit the framework. I chafed at a description on page 54 which says that the three leading cases of constitutionalism in Asia are India, Japan and Australia/New Zealand, since the latter is not in Asia. And what of the Philippines, whose People Power revolution overturned the Marcos regime? Surely it ought to qualify. People Power quickly became constitutionalised and its leader, Corazon Aquino, became the first President. I would argue that the Philippines still counts as a constitutional democracy, if an extremely messy one. Its system has survived two presidential impeachments, multiple failed attempts to change term limits and an attempted coup. The current holder of the presidency, Rodrigo Duterte, may brag of extra-judicial killings, but his ambitions take infra-constitutional form. At the time of writing, the country is debating whether to switch to a federal system of government and a semi-presidential system of government. I think asking why the Philippines does or does not count would help us understand the case selection in the volume. But it might not fit Ackerman's model so easily: now that the founding generation is mostly gone, the Supreme Court has not risen to the fore to defend constitutional values; instead, it seems to be going along with Duterte.

The Philippines, like Poland, may be an example of backsliding. When anti-democratic forces mobilise, they sometimes move fast, but, increasingly in our era, cause slow, step-by-step erosion.[45] The risk of a series of small attacks on the liberal order, that together serve to undermine it completely, calls for new thinking, both on the constitutional toolkit and also on the forces that sustain and extend revolutionary transformation in the first place. Examining instances of constitutional failure, or anti-liberal revolution, is valuable in order to gain a complete picture of the phenomenon. We should remember that charisma is sometimes more of a danger to democracy than a force to sustain it; hence, in the end, I recognise that it has the power that Ackerman ascribes to it, but also believe that it is not advisable to count on it.

VII. Conclusion

Let us return to Prachanda, with whom we started. His CPN-(M) Maoist movement surely meets Ackerman's test of revolutionary constitutionalism, seeking a complete transformation of the society. It had what Ackerman calls self-consciousness and bold aspirations.[46] At a critical moment, after some 19,000 deaths, its leaders decided to come in from the cold mountains. They then worked

[45] Tom Ginsburg & Aziz Z. Huq, How to Save a Constitutional Democracy (2018).
[46] Ackerman, *supra* note 2 at 32–33.

with other parties, in De Gasperi-like fashion, to articulate a vision for a new Nepal. Does it fit the case for a charismatic party? Was it a revolution on a human scale?

In some senses yes. But I submit that the case is a bit more like Italy, which I have argued does not fit the charismatic framework very well, and less like India or South Africa. India had a genuine integrative movement party encompassing all the social forces and enjoying overwhelming popularity. The CPN-(M) was a more discrete social force, one among many. It turned out to be the critical driver of the republican turn, which would not have been possible without the military pressure brought by the Maoist insurgents (again a bit like Mandela, who leveraged the Spear of the Nation). But there were many other players and actors that led to the ultimate outcome. And the intense politics of eight years of constitutional negotiations led to a somewhat muddled constitutional scheme.

Nepal did succeed in constitutionalising a new set of arrangements. But early returns suggest that the conflict is not over. The challenges of setting up a new federal system without the benefit of prior boundaries are severe. The country remains poor and divided. Southerners who form the plurality of the country's population continue to feel excluded and it is not clear that the new document has broad legitimacy.

In understanding how this story unfolded, should we focus on charisma or interests? Przeworski analyses such situations with simple game theory: constitutional bargains succeed when the hardliners on both sides are marginalised by the moderates, who come together to create a new constitutional order.[47] This was his story in Eastern Europe in 1991 and it seems to fit Nepal in the 2000s as well. The hardline King and some members of the military sought to retain the old arrangements, and the moderates, the traditional political parties, had put up with this for a time. Prachanda represented the military wing of the leftist forces, but in an act of statesmanship traded the life of a guerilla for a seat at the prime minister's table. He jumped into the moderate camp and completed the quite-partial revolution.

An interest-based perspective on this history would consider assets and liabilities at the time of constitutional design. One important factor was that in Nepal, as in South Africa, there was a legacy of some legalism. Unlike France, with its long tradition of judicial subordination, or Poland or many of the other cases discussed in *Revolutionary Constitutions*, Nepal had a functioning and prominent Supreme Court that was an asset for negotiations. This makes the case parallel to South Africa, where the legacy of law facilitated the use of a Constitutional Court to oversee the political transition by having it sign off on the interim draft.[48] The Court became a commitment device, without which the interim constitution may not have been concluded in the first place. Where the courts did not exist as an earlier resource, as in Myanmar, France and Poland, it may be more difficult to shepherd

[47] Adam Przeworski, Democracy and the Market (1991).
[48] Meierhenrich, *supra* note 25.

the constitutional transition, and so charisma becomes much more necessary if the project is to succeed. In other words, courts may be helpful at Time One, and, if so, Time Three may never arise.

To conclude with a summary of my views: one cannot understand history without understanding charisma. One cannot understand institutions without understanding incentives. Constitutions create institutions by mobilising political energy, for which charisma is helpful when it is available as a resource. Are these accounts so incompatible? It is perhaps unfair to treat the two approaches in the fashion of a horse race. They share certain premises: the rejection of legal positivism in favour of a sociological realism; the rejection of 'critical' structuralism; and the suspension of normative analysis in favour of trying to understand what actually occurred.

One way to unify the accounts is to return to an idea developed in Ackerman's earlier work, namely dualism. Famously, Ackerman argued for a distinction between ordinary politics and constitutional politics, occasional episodes when 'We the People' rise to demand major changes in the constitutional order through sustained political action.[49] These episodes are rare and require sustained mass social mobilisation. Similarly, the ordinary politics of institutions – involving voter ignorance, self-interested politicians and bargaining – dominate in most places most of the time. Occasionally, however, the perception of higher stakes arises, as a result of social entrepreneurs acting within a particular opportunity set. On such occasions, which are mysterious in origin, passions dominate and there is a possibility of true revolution. Sometimes, but not always, this leads to constitution-making. But most episodes of constitution-making are best viewed as the result of bargaining under constraints, with a set of assets and liabilities in hand.

[49] Bruce Ackerman, We the People, Volume 1: Foundations (1991).

8

Uncharismatic Revolutionary Constitutionalism

STEPHEN GARDBAUM*

In his magisterial opening volume of *The Rise of World Constitutionalism*, Bruce Ackerman distinguishes between two broad types of modern revolutions – 'totalizing' and 'revolutions on a human scale' – and then focuses on revolutionary constitutionalism as an important instance of the latter.[1] He insightfully and persuasively identifies the multi-stage dynamics of revolutionary constitutionalism and diagnoses its characteristic legitimacy problem through detailed study of some of its major examples (India, South Africa, France and Italy immediately following the Second World War, Poland, Israel and Iran) in the twentieth century. This common legitimacy problem is the succession crisis faced by the regime when the charismatic revolutionary party leadership and generation that had engineered the revolution eventually passes from the scene at the third of the four developmental stages, to be replaced by a 'normalised' or routinised party elite, typically a decade or more after its founding and constitution.[2]

This chapter first identifies a distinct, but no less common, type of revolutionary constitutionalism that Ackerman does not consider in his analysis; namely, the spontaneous, leaderless or movementless constitutionalist revolution. Prominent examples of such successful 'uncharismatic' revolutions over the past century include the Mexican (1910–20), the Philippine (1986), the Romanian (1989) and the Tunisian (2011) revolutions. It then argues that this subtype of revolutionary constitutionalism typically faces a different legitimacy crisis and at a much earlier stage in its history: during the initial founding of the new regime and constitution that replaces the ousted one.[3] Lacking the initial source of legitimacy

* Thanks to Bruce Ackerman and Richard Albert for inviting me to participate in the symposium, and to panel chair Daniel Markovits and fellow participants for very helpful questions and comments on the previous draft presented.

[1] Bruce Ackerman, Revolutionary Constitutions: Charismatic Leadership and the Rule of Law (2019).

[2] *Id.* at ch. 1.

[3] This part of my chapter develops a theme in an earlier article of mine. See Stephen Gardbaum, *Revolutionary Constitutionalism*, 15 Int'l J. Const. L. 173 (2017).

that comes from having a Nehru, Mandela, Walesa, de Gaulle, Ben-Gurion or Ayatollah Khomeini at the head of the revolutionary movement-party that (more than nominally) represents 'the people' and then the new regime, uncharismatic revolutionary constitutionalism must find an alternative source from the outset.

One such source of legitimacy, as the different outcomes of the Tunisian and Egyptian revolutions of 2011 suggest, is the constitution-making process itself. While in Tunisia this involved engagement and investment on the part of many differing and competing groups, both religious and secular, in Egypt the process of drafting the new constitution was dominated by the Muslim Brotherhood, the partisan beneficiary of 'organizational asymmetries'[4] among rival political groupings, resulting in alienation and ultimately a sense of delegitimation on the part of other factions.[5] This failure to fill the initial legitimacy vacuum enabled the eventual military coup. A second source of such founding legitimacy where there is no movement party that singly or in cooperation with others has a plausible claim to represent the people as a whole may be the military victory of one faction over another, bringing about long-sought-for peace and relative stability ('the war of the victors' in Mexico).[6] A third may be the cross-cutting support for a newly emerged, post-revolutionary leader reflected in a broad and sweeping electoral victory, as perhaps in Romania.[7] In short, Ackerman's volume masterfully analyses an important type of revolutionary constitutionalism, but not the entire phenomenon per se.

In addition to the point that not all revolutionary constitutionalism is charismatic and movement-party led, Ackerman's account derives so much of its heft from the implications of charisma that it is useful to remind ourselves of the converse: not all charismatic revolutionary regimes are constitutionalist. By focusing on the problem that is distinctive to them, Ackerman's account arguably turns more on the charismatic rather than the constitutionalist nature of the revolutionary movement – a feature common to other movement-led political revolutions of the twentieth century.[8] In other words, succession crises are a distinct legitimacy problem of charismatic revolutionary regimes of all stripes, including totalising ones, with 'constitutionalism' doing little independent work. Recent/current examples are the post-Chávez and post-Castro succession and legitimacy issues in Venezuela and Cuba respectively.

A final consequence of the partial nature of Ackerman's account is a slightly myopic approach to judicial supremacy that arguably both overstates its importance to revolutionary constitutionalism as a whole and understates its role in non-revolutionary pathways to constitutionalism. For if judicial supremacy is a common response to the problem of fading revolutionary charisma, as Ackerman

[4] David Landau, *Constitution-Making Gone Wrong*, 64 Al. L. Rev. 923, 975 (2013).
[5] See *infra*, text accompanying notes 52–53.
[6] See *infra*, text accompanying note 17.
[7] See *infra*, text accompanying notes 37–38.
[8] See *infra*, text accompanying notes 58–59.

argues, it seems to follow that it would be less important or likely in the case of uncharismatic revolutions. And, indeed, this is what we find. None of the successful leaderless revolutions discussed below has obviously consolidated its power by ceding to the courts supremacy as the distinctive guardians of the revolution. On the other hand, Ackerman's account appears to overlook the more general reasons that judicial supremacy might be appealing to constitutionalist regimes *of all types*, revolutionary or otherwise, and that help to explain the overall trend in this direction. It also overlooks the more general political circumstances that make judicial supremacy more or less likely in practice.[9] These are less the fading of revolutionary charisma than the existence and longevity of a dominant political party within *all* pathways to constitutionalism.

These three related critiques are set out in the three sections of this chapter. Section I identifies the uncharismatic, non-movement-party-led variety as a second major, but overlooked, type of revolutionary constitutionalism with its own characteristic and different legitimacy crisis. Section II calls into question Ackerman's distinction between totalising revolutions and revolutions on a human scale, as well as the role that 'constitutionalism' plays in his analysis, insofar as the succession crisis he posits as a characteristic of revolutionary constitutionalism appears to be a common feature of charismatic revolutionary regimes of all stripes, including those of Lenin and Mao, and not generally of uncharismatic constitutionalist revolutions. Section III addresses Ackerman's treatment of judicial supremacy.

I. Two Types of Revolutionary Constitutionalism

The common theme behind all of Ackerman's case studies is the revolutionary movement-party and leader whose legitimacy, forged during the long period of struggle and sacrifice on behalf of the people (Time One), is unquestioned and extends seamlessly to the new regime it founds at the moment of victory (Time Two). This 'constitutionalization of charisma'[10] that defines the revolutionary hero's task at this point delays the characteristic legitimation problem until the 'succession crisis' at Time Three, usually decades later, when the revolutionary leader and generation have passed from the scene. Now a more ordinary, routinised or 'normalised' political leadership faces an increasingly emboldened judiciary that claims legitimacy for itself as the distinctive guardian of the framers' revolutionary constitution. Frequently, this claim is successful as the regime reconsolidates its popular legitimacy at Time Four in the form of judicial supremacy.[11]

[9] See Stephen Gardbaum, *What Makes for More or Less Powerful Constitutional Courts?*, 29 Duke J. Int'l & Comp. L. 1 (2018); and *infra*, text accompanying notes 63–65.

[10] See Ackerman, *supra* note 1 at 8.

[11] *Id.* at chs. 1–2.

As successful and persuasive as Ackerman's induction of the general pattern from the individual histories undoubtedly is, it remains a partial account of the developmental stages and legitimacy problems faced by revolutionary constitutionalism because it does not consider an equally prominent subtype of the species: the spontaneous or leaderless revolution. Here, without the guidance, preparation and organisation of the revolutionary movement-party, the vacuum in legitimate authority that is both the cause and consequence of the fall of the old regime at Time Two is not immediately and seamlessly filled by the 'constitutionalization of charisma' and the rise to power of its leader. Rather, the direction and political leadership of the revolution are deeply contested and any successful claim to legitimacy must be earned in the here and now, it has not already accrued or vested. Accordingly, the acquiring of legitimacy in the first place, *during* the revolutionary turmoil rather than potentially losing it a generation hence, is the characteristic problem of spontaneous, leaderless revolutions, and the key factor in their success or failure. This would not matter, or would matter far less, if such episodes of revolutionary constitutionalism were either rare or almost always unsuccessful by comparison with the movement-party-led, charismatic ones on which Ackerman focuses. But this does not seem to be the case.[12] Indeed, the two types arguably go all the way back to the late eighteenth century and the birth of modern revolutions: the American (at least partly charismatic, via George Washington) and the French (leaderless). Famous (full or partial) failures of uncharismatic revolutionary constitutionalism include such paradigms as the latter and both the 1905 and February 1917 Russian Revolutions. But alongside these, if somewhat less well-known and studied, are the numerous successful examples of the phenomenon, right up to the present: exactly 100 years separate the outbreaks of the Mexican and Tunisian revolutions, with several others in between.

A. The Mexican Revolution

The Mexican Revolution, usually dated from 1910 to 1920, which replaced the autocratic regime of Porfirio Díaz, the Porfiriato, with the new revolutionary constitutionalist one after several years of civil war, is a clear instance of a successful spontaneous, movement-party-less revolution lacking charismatic political leadership.[13] As one of the leading historians of the revolution puts it, 'the

[12] Identifying the frequency of spontaneous, unorganised, leaderless revolutions, Hannah Arendt nonetheless attributes to 'professional revolutionists' (of which Lenin and his party are the prototype) a typically major role in how they turn out after their initial outbreak. Although this first part is accurate with respect to the modern revolutions on which I focus, the second is less so. See Hannah Arendt, On Revolution, 259–61 (1963).

[13] To be sure, the charismatic regional guerilla leaders Francisco ('Pancho') Villa and Emiliano Zapata played important roles in the armed revolution, but they were never interested in being, or deemed qualified to become, national political leaders of the revolution.

revolutionary creed was cobbled together over time and *ex post facto*'.[14] Indeed, an official revolutionary party, the Partido Nacional Revolucionario (PNR), was not created until 1929, so that it was very much a 'product not progenitor'[15] of the revolution. The revolution was spurred not by one or more movement-parties, but by a large and growing number of opposition factions reflecting and representing a host of different 'outsider' interests and positions excluded from the Díaz regime: wealthy northern landowners; landless central and southern peasants; middle-class urban professionals and intellectuals; and working-class trade unionists.[16] Among these disparate groups divided by geography, ethnicity and class, there was no single opposition platform, party or leader. The first post-Díaz President, the liberal, landowning, bookish and ill-fated Francisco Madero, was really only the nominal leader of the revolution[17] and, following the revolutionaries' defeat of the Huerta military dictatorship in 1914 and intra-faction civil war, he was succeeded by a series of more worldly and ruthless, but no more charismatic, revolutionary presidents in Venustiano Carranza (1917–20), Alvaro Obregón (1920–24) and Plutarco Elías Calles (1924–28). Nonetheless, following the period of civil war among the various revolutionary factions ('the war of the victors'), in terms of growing power, stability and legitimacy, the new revolutionary regime was undoubtedly successful. From its creation by Calles in 1929, the PNR became the overwhelmingly dominant party in Mexico's democracy until its successor party lost the presidency for the first time in 2000.

Does Ackerman's four-step developmental stage apply? What we see, I believe, is that Mexico's spontaneous, leaderless revolution followed a path that is similar in some respects, but different in others, to that of his movement-party revolutions. In particular, although mobilised insurgency (Time One), constitutional founding (Time Two) and revolutionary consolidation (Time Four) are each present, albeit in a different variation from his cases, crucially there is no Time Three of faded charisma and inter-generational succession crises representing the characteristic and existential legitimacy problem. This is emphatically not to say that succession was always smooth and easy – it was not – but rather that the key legitimacy problem is a different one and arises far earlier, during Time Two.

In Mexico, Time One plays out between 1900 and 1911 in the shape of the crisis in, and growing opposition to, the Porfiriato, leading to Díaz's resignation from office and exile in May 1911. Resulting from a combination of economic depression and crisis starting in 1907 – which wiped out many established middle-class entrepreneurs, triggered the rise of strong working-class opposition, created

[14] Alan Knight, The Mexican Revolution: A Very Short Introduction 62 (2016).

[15] *Id.* at 76.

[16] The historical material and description here draws on Knight, *supra* note 14; Alan Knight, The Mexican Revolution (1986); John Womack, *The Mexican Revolution, 1910–1920*, in Mexico since Independence (Leslie Bethell ed., 1991); Anita Brenner, The Wind that Swept Mexico: The History of the Mexican Revolution of 1910–1942 (1943).

[17] Knight, *supra* note 14 at 30.

frustration among the young, educated middle class and threw many peasants off the land – and a near-inexplicable loosening of political repression that enabled the growth of several liberal opposition parties (such as Madero's Anti-Reelectionist Party) for the first time,[18] Díaz's fraudulent re-election in June 1910 was the immediate spark for revolution. To the surprise not only of Díaz but also Madero, whose call for armed revolt in response had gone largely unheeded in his home state of Coahuila, a serious uprising broke out in the mountains of western Chihuahua, led by popular regional guerilla leaders Pascual Orozco and Pancho Villa.[19] Returning from the US, where he had fled, to assume the leadership of the Chihuahuan revolutionaries, Madero saw local revolts spread across Mexico so that most of the countryside was in the hands of revolutionaries by April 1911, at which point Díaz agreed to Madero's Treaty of Ciudad Juarez, left office and ceded power to a provisional government. Under the terms of the agreement, the provisional government, with Madero's increasingly active support, attempted to disband the various revolutionary armies and guerilla bands. When Madero was elected President in October after the freest and fairest election in the country's history, as far as he was concerned, the revolution, having achieved its goal, was essentially over.[20]

Time Two, from revolution to constitution, occupies the years from 1911 to 1920. It is characterised by: (1) Madero's increasing isolation as a moderate liberal caught in between the two rising forces of counter-revolution and a broader, more popular revolution centred on land reform, ending in a military coup and his assassination in February 1913; (2) two additional periods of civil war – the war of the revolutionary 'Constitutionalists' together with the Villa and Zapata armies against Huerta's military dictatorship (1913–14), followed by 'the war of the victors' among the rival revolutionary forces (1914–15); and (3) the establishment of the revolutionary constitution by the winner, Carranza, in 1917. This period constitutes the legitimacy crisis of the revolution, as each faction – Madero, Carranza, Villa and others – struggled to establish their revolutionary legitimacy in the absence of a movement party and leader that had previously earned the mantle. The crisis was not one of subsequent succession, but of initial and immediate possession. It was mostly resolved by success on the battlefield, as the last faction standing, but was supplemented by the revolutionary Constitution of February 1917 that also helped to legitimise the administration of Carranza and the 'Sonoran dynasty' which he founded. Drafted and approved after long and heated debate by an all-Carrancista constituent assembly, albeit one split between 'conservatives' and 'radicals', the latter mostly prevailed despite Carranza's support of a more modest

[18] The standard explanation derives from a 1908 interview that Díaz gave to the American journalist James Creelman, meant presumably for the American public, in which he claimed that he would welcome real opposition in the 1910 presidential election. See, eg, Brenner, *supra* note 16 at 19–20.

[19] See Womack, *supra* note 16 at 131–32.

[20] Knight, *supra* note 14 at 32.

replacement of the 1857 'liberal' Constitution.[21] The new revolutionary Constitution that emerged after Carranza's first draft was rejected barred the church from politics and primary education,[22] contained several social and economic rights in Article 123,[23] and declared the social function of property permitting the state to regulate foreign investment and pursue land reform.[24] Under this first modern revolutionary charter, Carranza was soon afterwards elected constitutional President.

Time Three, the period of regime consolidation and institutionalisation under the Sonoran dynasty, begins after the last violent change of government in 1920. This occurred when Carranza's lieutenant and tactical mastermind of the 1914–15 civil war against the Villaistas, Alvaro Obregón, was elected President after Carranza himself fled and was killed as a result of attempting to impose his chosen but unpopular civilian successor over widespread military opposition within his Sonoran faction.[25] Under Obregón and his successor as president, Calles, who dominated politics until 1934, political stability gradually returned after a decade, although not easily or smoothly. Through a combination of thinning out the revolutionary military to prevent a repeat of the 1920 revolt, populist politics and land reform to retain popular support, and the 1920s economic boom, the revolutionary regime not only survived but also consolidated its power. When President-elect Obregón was assassinated by a Catholic militant in 1928, Calles was legally prohibited from extending his own term, but mostly retained power for the next six years by governing through a series of hand-picked non-entities, known as the *Maximato*.[26] In 1929, Calles established an official revolutionary party, the PNR, for the first time, which began by absorbing the multiple small, pro-regime parties as an umbrella organisation, but gradually became the hegemonic political force in Mexico under its various incarnations.[27] The consolidation and popularity of the regime reached its height under Lázaro Cárdenas, President from 1934 to 1940, with his unique combination of nationalism, corporatism, folksy populism, anti-fascism and social reform.[28] Despite growing corruption and cronyism in the decades following Cárdenas, the PNR, from 1946 the Partido Revolucionario Institucional (PRI), remained in power continuously until 2000 and returned in 2012, although whether, following the political liberalisation of the 1990s, the

[21] See generally E.V. Niemeyer, Revolution at Querétaro: The Mexican Constitutional Convention of 1916–1917 (1974).

[22] Mexican Constitution 1917, arts. 3, 130.

[23] Including the right of workers to an eight-hour day, to strike, to one day of rest a week, and against unjust termination.

[24] Mexican Constitution 1917, art. 27.

[25] Womack, *supra* note 16 at 192–95.

[26] See Jean Meyer, *Revolution and Reconstruction in the 1920s in* Bethell, *supra* note 16 at 215–18.

[27] Knight, *supra* note 14 at 76.

[28] When Cárdenas nationalised the foreign-owned oil companies during the Depression, millions of ordinary Mexicans brought in their jewellery to government offices to help pay off the debt incurred by the compensation paid.

revolutionary regime can be said to have survived is perhaps a more difficult question to answer.[29]

B. The People Power Revolution in the Philippines

The successful non-violent revolution through mass popular uprising and protests that ousted dictator Ferdinand Marcos in February 1986 served as the model for many in Central and Eastern Europe three years later. It was also, in many ways, quite similar to the first stage of the Mexican Revolution that resulted in Madero's presidency, apart from the armed versus peaceful uprising. In both cases, electoral fraud by the incumbent dictator that procured their 'victory' in the presidential election over the opposition candidate was the immediate spark for the revolution, leading to the dictator leaving office and fleeing abroad, and the succession of the 'defeated' candidate as the new president at the head of a revolutionary government. Both Madero and Corazon Aquino, the widow of assassinated senator Ninoy Aquino, emerged as the symbolic or nominal leaders of broad and diverse political opposition to the old regime, but neither was the charismatic head of a movement party that, singly or in combination with others, earned the right to represent 'the people' after long years of mobilisation, struggle and sacrifice. Neither had much political experience at the time they were catapulted into power by the popular uprising. Both were from wealthy, upper-class backgrounds, which arguably played a role in their resistance to the more radical demands for land reform coming from below and limited the trust in which they were held by the masses.

In the Filipino case, the revolution that ousted the dictator was brought about not through armed revolt by local guerilla leaders (as in the Mexican case), but significantly by calls for mass popular demonstrations soon after the disputed election on the part of high-up defectors from the armed forces (notably Defence Minister Juan Ponce Enrile and General Fidel V Ramos) and the Catholic Church hierarchy, in particular Cardinal Sin, the Archbishop of Manila.[30] Responding to these calls, despite the threat of violence from the initially still mostly loyal military, up to two million ordinary citizens filled Epifanio de los Santos Avenue (EDSA) in protest against Marcos over the four days from 22 to 25 February, culminating in his fleeing to exile in Hawaii and the installation of Aquino as President.

[29] Arguably made a little easier by the PRI's candidate finishing a poor third, with only 16 per cent of the vote, in the presidential election of 2018.

[30] This section draws on Amado Mendoza, *'People Power' in the Philippines, 1983–1986, in* Civil Resistance and Power Politics: The Experience of Non-violent Action from Gandhi to the Present (Adam Roberts and Timothy Garton Ash eds., 2008); Brian Johnson, The Four Days of Courage: The Untold Story of the People Who Brought Marcos Down (1987); Kurt Schock, *People Power Unleashed: South Africa and the Philippines, in* Unarmed Insurrections: People Power Movements in Nondemocracies (2005).

Although, unlike Madero, Aquino did not face or win a new presidential election after the revolution, her revolutionary government was able to acquire the more or less uncontested legitimacy that eluded Madero in Time Two. Despite both some disappointment and sense of betrayal on the left due to the moderate nature of her land reform policies and a series of attempted coups and counter-revolutions on the right, Aquino survived and never found herself on a rapidly disappearing middle ground in the way that befell Madero. The decision of the newly re-organised and independent Supreme Court in October 1986 that the Aquino government was 'in fact and law a de jure government'[31] was highly influential, as was the swift and near-universal international recognition of the new government as legitimate. Finally, the urgency that Aquino brought to having a new constitution drafted to replace Marcos' 1973 instrument, along with its content matching the revolutionary demands for re-establishing democracy, civil liberties and social justice, and its overwhelming approval by referendum in February 1987, all helped to cement the popular legitimacy of the regime. This was manifested by the absence of a succession crisis when Aquino made the decision not to seek re-election in 1992 in order to set an example to the people and politicians,[32] even though she could have pushed the argument that the one-term rule under the 1987 Constitution did not apply to her as it had not been in effect in 1986. Instead, she supported General Ramos as her party's candidate, who narrowly defeated populist candidate Miriam Defensor Santiago of the People's Reform Party.[33]

C. The Romanian Revolution

The Romanian Revolution of 16–22 December 1989, the last of that tumultuous year's successful anti-communist revolutions in Central and Eastern Europe, was unlike the others in two respects. It was the only bloody revolution, ending with approximately 1,000 dead and an executed dictator, and it was the only wholly spontaneous, unorganised and leaderless one.[34] There were no round table talks between government and opposition as in Hungary, nor the Romanian equivalent of a Lech Walesa or Vaclav Havel. Instead, mass demonstrations started in Timisoara, spread to Bucharest and were met with violent suppression ordered by Ceauşescu and carried out initially by the most repressive secret police force in the Soviet Bloc before the scale of operations required the military.[35] After many of the

[31] In re: Saturnino v. Bermudez, G.R. No. 76180 October 24, 1986.

[32] See KeriLynn Engel, Corazon Aquino, Revolutionary Leader of the Philippines, December 29, 2011, www.amazingwomeninhistory.com/corazon-aquino-revolutionary-president-philippines/.

[33] *Ramos is Declared New President 6 Weeks after Philippine Election*, New York Times, June 23, 1992, https://www.nytimes.com/1992/06/23/world/ramos-is-declared-new-president-6-weeks-after-philippine-election.html.

[34] See generally George Galloway & Bob Wylie, Downfall: The Ceausescus and the Romanian Revolution (1991); Stephen D. Roper, Romania: The Unfinished Revolution (2000).

[35] See Galloway & Wylie, *supra* note 34 at 10–15.

latter switched sides and Ceauşescu was ousted, a newly formed political entity, the National Salvation Front (NSF), led by a triumvirate of former Communist Party insiders who had broken with Ceauşescu, rapidly emerged and took over power as the provisional national unity government.[36]

The extent to which the NSF, its leading figure Ion Iliescu or the new regime that it headed had or acquired revolutionary legitimacy in the several years following the revolution is unclear. Although institutionally, the Romanian Communist Party essentially disappeared and did not transform itself into a post-revolutionary democratic opposition party challenging the pace or principle of market reforms as elsewhere in the region, Romania is unique in terms of the extent to which, as individuals, former Communist Party officials dominated the new regime.[37] Moreover, they also employed some of the tried-and-tested party tactics. For example, first as acting and then as elected provisional President, Iliescu on several occasions called in the miners to violently break up anti-communist and anti-NSF demonstrations (the so-called Mineriads) and permitted only a brief period of public discussion before the referendum on the new Constitution, drafted by a committee of legislators and constitutional lawyers appointed by the NSF-dominated parliament, was held in December 1991.[38] Parliamentary and presidential elections called by provisional government decree in May 1990, and then under the new Constitution in September 1992, were marred by a degree of intimidation and violence that was noted at the time.[39] And more broadly, many of the servants of the Communist-era 'deep state' appeared to have survived in the military, bureaucracy and police.

On the other hand, in these first two sets of elections, Iliescu and his party (initially the NSF until he and many others split from it in April 1992 to form what would become the current Social Democratic Party) easily won what were still contested elections, and 77.3 per cent of voters approved the new Constitution in the referendum.[40] When Emil Constantinescu, a former academic, running with the support of the center-right Romanian Democratic Convention, defeated Iliescu in the presidential run-off in 1996 for the first peaceful transfer of power after the revolution, there was a general sense that democratic forces had prevailed. And yet Iliescu returned to power in 2000, and his party, sometimes in coalition with its Liberal Democratic Party rival (which also had its origins in the NSF), has mostly governed ever since.

[36] *Id.* at 21–24.

[37] See Emma Graham-Harrison, *Twenty-Five Years after Nicolae Ceausescu was Executed, Romanians Seek a 'Revolution Reborn'*, The Guardian, December 6, 2014, https://www.theguardian.com/world/2014/dec/07/romanians-seek-a-reborn-revolution-25-years-after-ceausescu.

[38] Galloway & Wylie, *supra* note 34 at 85–87.

[39] See International Republican Institute and the National Democratic Institute for International Affairs, *Report on Romania's Democratic Transition*, www.iri.org/sites/default/files/Romania%27s%201992%20Presidential%20and%20Parliamentary%20Elections.pdf.

[40] See Dieter Nohlen & Philip Stover, Elections in Europe: A Data Handbook 1598–91 (2010).

D. The Tunisian Revolution

The Tunisian Revolution, sometimes referred to as the Jasmine Revolution (only) in the West, was the first domino to fall and the spark for other revolutions of the so-called Arab Spring of 2011, as well as thus far the only successful one.[41] It was also, like the others in the region that followed, a leaderless, spontaneous uprising of the people against an authoritarian dictatorship, unorganised by any revolutionary movement party. Once Ben Ali resigned and fled to Saudi Arabia in mid-January 2011, a month after vegetable seller Mohamed Bouazizi's self-immolation and three weeks after the nationwide mass demonstrations began, the initial continuance in power of his Prime Minister Mahomed Ghannounchi as head of the first provisional national unity government was deemed illegitimate and he was replaced after six weeks.[42] But, in the absence of a clear movement party and charismatic leader that had fought for decades to bring about the revolution, the broader legitimacy of the new regime very much depended on the contingencies of the arrangements for its establishment and the transition to democracy, including the Constitution. Once again, this legitimacy had to be earned in the moment, it was not something that had already been allocated or acquired. Following the election of the constituent assembly in October 2011, the approval of the new Constitution in January 2014, and elections for the new legislature and president under its provisions in October and November 2014, for reasons that will be briefly explored, the new democratic regime acquired sufficient political legitimacy for it (thus far) to withstand a very difficult set of economic challenges. Yet the success of the revolution continues to be balanced on a knife edge in the face of these challenges, which pose a serious threat to its perceived economic legitimacy. Survival rather than consolidation remains the urgent priority.

Here, Time One is constituted not by the decades and accreted layers of sacrifice by the movement party leadership on behalf of the people, but by the decades and accreted layers of sacrifice by the people themselves – in terms of poverty, unemployment and political repression – under the authoritarian rule of Presidents Bourguiba (1959–87) and Ben Ali (1987–2011), and their corrupt one-party state regime. The already bad situation worsened after the global financial crisis, with unemployment, and particularly youth unemployment, increasing still further and the state reducing its subsidisation of many goods and services, thereby increasing the cost of living.[43] Publication by major newspapers around the world in November 2010 of leaked documents detailing corruption and repression by the regime also

[41] See *Revolution and Constitution in the Arab World, 2011–12*, in Beyond the Arab Spring: The Evolving Ruling Bargain in the Middle East (Mehran Kamrava ed., 2014); Nouri Gana, ed., The Making of the Tunisian Revolution: Contexts, Architects, Prospects (2013), Laryssa Chomiak, *The Making of a Revolution in Tunisia*, 3 Middle East L. & Governance 68 (2011).

[42] Chomiak, *supra* note 41 at 70–71.

[43] Gana, *supra* note 41 at 20.

contributed to the context in which the desperate act of protest by the beaten and humiliated vegetable seller on 17 December took place.[44] Local demonstrations in Sidi Bouzid, the scene of the self-immolation, were met with harsh responses by the police, and the protests against high unemployment and the cost of living, as well as in support of Bouazizi, quickly spread across the country, some of which were hurriedly organised by trade unions, students and lawyers.[45] The government called in the military to quell the protests, which resulted in a downward spiral of violence and increasingly repressive measures, but no end to the crowds, culminating in Ben Ali's fleeing the country for Saudi Arabia on 14 January 2011. A state of emergency was declared, the Army Commander pledged to 'protect the revolution' and Prime Minister Ghannouchi briefly assumed the interim presidency before the head of the Ben Ali-created Constitutional Council confirmed the speaker of the legislature as the lawful successor, who in turn announced the formation of a temporary national unity government.[46]

Time Two, from the 2010–11 revolution to the 2014 Constitution, is where not only the shape and survival but also the legitimacy of the revolutionary process and resulting regime was crucially at stake. Unlike in Mexico, where the creation of the Constitution in 1917 in a sense partially institutionalised the victory and supplemented, but did not create, the revolutionary legitimacy of the winning faction, in Tunisia the legitimacy of the new regime very substantially turned on the constitution-making process and result.[47] All the hopes of the revolution were focused on the work of the constituent assembly.

Crucially, the national unity government that formed the day following Ben Ali's departure was under civilian control, with the armed forces not driving events, but taking orders. After Ghannouchi's resignation as Prime Minister at the end of February, the former pre-Ben Ali Prime Minister Beji Caid Essebsi took over until the constituent assembly election in October. At that election, the moderate Islamist and pro-democracy party Ennahda, led by returned exile Rached Ghannouchi (no relation) and which had been largely non-existent inside the country before the revolution, won 37 per cent of the votes and 89 of the 217 seats under the party-list PR system.[48] The constituent assembly overwhelmingly elected human rights activist and physician Moncef Marzouki as interim President, who in turn appointed Ennahda politician Hamadi Jebali as Prime Minister of the provisional government in coalition with the then two leading (although far smaller in terms of seats, at 55 combined) secular centrist parties. Having adopted a provisional constitution in December, the assembly, which doubled as an interim

[44] Chomiak, *supra* note 41, at 72.
[45] *Id.*
[46] GANA, *supra* note 41 at 25–26.
[47] See Gardbaum, *supra* note 3.
[48] *Tunisia's Islamist Party Claims Electoral Victory*, DAILY TELEGRAPH, October 25, 2011, https://www.telegraph.co.uk/news/worldnews/africaandindianocean/tunisia/8847315/Tunisias-Islamist-party-claims-election-victory.html.

legislature and to which the government was politically accountable, set to work on drafting the permanent new constitution, although it was not given a specific deadline. The Ennhada-led 'troika' eventually disbanded in January 2014 in favour of a technocratic government.

Accordingly, the balance of party politics (absent a dominant revolutionary movement) and political sentiment in Tunisia – the absence of a clear Islamist majority party and ineradicable cross-party suspicion and hostility, itself partly a result of the experience of power sharing during the interim regime and constitution-making process – created an experience of relatively inclusive government and fierce debates, but ultimately not a winner-takes-all approach towards the process of drafting the constitution on the part of the leading parties. The eventual result, after a little more than two years, was the approval of a document that reasonably accommodated, and compromised between, all pro-revolutionary sides and factions. The role of Islam and Sharia in the new Tunisia was expressed in deliberately ambiguous terms in Article 1,[49] an artfully drawn semi-presidential form of government was designed to avoid the twin pitfalls on an overly strong executive and the instability of a parliamentary system with relatively weakly institutionalised parties lacking experience in government,[50] and a fairly extensive set of civil, political and economic rights, certainly by regional standards.[51] The outcome of a constitution-making process that was widely perceived as fair and inclusive and resulted in a constitution that most could bring themselves to support was the gradual bestowing of revolutionary legitimacy on the new regime during Time Two. It could be, and was, plausibly understood as what the revolution had been fought for.

A comparison with the failed revolution in neighbouring Egypt is instructive.[52] There, following the ousting of Mubarak, the army seized firm control of the revolution. In order in large part to escape this domination at the earliest opportunity, pro-revolutionary groups and factions agreed to regular presidential and parliamentary elections before drafting a new constitution. Given the unequal condition of the various political groupings in terms of institutionalisation and preparedness, and the electoral returns that almost inevitably followed from them, this enabled the Muslim Brotherhood, which had played almost no role in the revolution, to take advantage of 'organisational asymmetries' to gain full, undivided control of it and the levers of power before, during and after the constitution-making process.

[49] 'Tunisia is a free, independent, sovereign state; its religion is Islam, its language Arabic, and its system is republican. This Article might not be amended.' CONST. OF TUNISIA, art. 1.

[50] See Sujit Choudhry & Richard Stacey, Semi-presidentialism as a Form of Government: Lessons for Tunisia, International IDEA & Center for Constitutional Transitions at NYU Law Working Papers: Consolidating the Arab Spring – Constitutional Transition in Egypt and Tunisia, 2013, https://ssrn.com/abstract=3025975.

[51] *Tunisia Signs New Constitution*, THE GUARDIAN, January 27, 2014, https://www.theguardian.com/world/2014/jan/27/tunisia-signs-new-constitution-progressive.

[52] This section draws on Sahar Aziz, *Bringing Down an Uprising: Egypt's Stillborn Revolution*, 30 CONN. J. INT'L. L. 1 (2014); Mohammed Fadel, *What Killed Egyptian Democracy?*, BOSTON REV., January 24, 2014; Gardbaum, *supra* note 3 at 197–99.

The non-competitiveness of the multiple small and divided liberal-secular parties compared to the two Islamist parties in the legislative elections of November 2011–January 2012, compounded by the mixed majoritarian and PR electoral system in place, meant that despite the narrowest of presidential election victories, as head of a unified or consolidated majority government of the Muslim Brotherhood, President Morsi was not required to – and did not – engage in any form of power sharing. This premature 'winner-takes-all' system was responsible for the perceived partisanship and failure to reach out to opponents that rapidly detracted from any cross-party sense of engagement in a common enterprise. The constitution that emerged from the government-appointed and Brotherhood-dominated constituent assembly was tainted with claims of self-dealing from the outset and lost all claims to general legitimacy after the secular opposition walked out in protest. In addition, the inherent inflexibility of the permanent presidential office meant that Morsi was legally and politically unchallengeable for the full four-year term, despite mounting opposition and dwindling popularity, which increased the likelihood of the ultimate military coup.

In Tunisia, Time Three's attempt to stabilise and consolidate the democratic regime began with the first parliamentary and presidential elections under the new Constitution in October and November 2014 respectively. The newly formed main secular party bloc Nidaa Tones ('Call of Tunisia') won 86 of the 217 seats to become the leading party, with Ennahda second with 69 seats.[53] This resulted in the formation of a new unity government, but one that involved a significant inter-party transfer compared to the first provisional one. Nidaa Tounes' candidate, Essebsi, then won the subsequent presidential election with a 55/45 run-off victory against incumbent interim President Marzouki, with Ennhada declining to run a candidate. Since then, the democratic regime that emerged from the revolution has been faced with a series of major economic and security challenges. The already deeply troubled economic situation was significantly worsened by several ISIS-organised terrorist attacks on tourists deliberately designed to cripple the country's leading industry. The dire employment outlook, especially for the young, and the still-rising cost of living means that the ongoing success of the revolution, the only one in the region, hangs by a thread, as demonstrators have returned to the streets. The continued political legitimacy of the revolution likely depends on the economic.

II. Charisma and Constitutionalism

The previous section argued that, contrary at least to the strong impression created by Ackerman's account, the characteristic and distinctive legitimacy problem of

[53] *Tunisia Election Results: Nida Tunis Wins Most Seats, Sidelining Islamists*, The Guardian, October 30, 2014, https://www.theguardian.com/world/2014/oct/30/tunisia-election-results-nida-tunis-wins-most-seats-sidelining-islamists.

revolutionary constitutionalism is not always or necessarily the succession crisis at Time Three. This is because not all episodes of revolutionary constitutionalism involve the type of charismatic leadership and role of the movement party that is the common feature of Ackerman's case studies. In the face of numerous key counter-examples of leaderless revolutions that faced a different and earlier legitimacy crisis, his thesis turns out to address an important subtype of revolutionary constitutionalism, but not the whole phenomenon; that is, not all revolutionary constitutionalism is of the charismatic variety. In this brief section, I will additionally argue that not all charismatic revolutionary movements are constitutionalist and that charisma rather than constitutionalism may be doing most of the work in generating the characteristic legitimacy problem that Ackerman identifies and analyses. Many successful non or anti constitutionalist ('totalising') revolutionary movement parties with charismatic leaders faced the same or similar characteristic succession crises that threatened the legitimacy of the regimes they had forged. In other words, among successful revolutionary parties, succession crises may be more a consequence of charisma than constitutionalism.

Take the two paradigmatic totalising revolutions of the twentieth century: the Bolshevik Revolution of October 1917 and the Chinese Revolution of 1949. Each was, of course, engineered by the respective communist revolutionary movement parties and by as charismatic a leader as you could conceive in Lenin and Mao. In both cases, Ackerman's general four-stage developmental history seems a good fit: (1) organised mobilisation against the existing regime and huge sacrifice on behalf of 'the people', eventually leading to revolutionary overthrow; (2) the founding of the new regime; (3) succession/legitimacy crisis; and (4) consolidation after the passing of the charismatic leader. Lenin's series of strokes from 1922 and death in 1924, while earlier in relation to Time Two than in Ackerman's case studies, created a regime succession crisis for several years until the wholly uncharismatic party insider Stalin had eliminated all of his rivals,[54] and a legitimacy crisis that arguably lasted until Hitler's invasion of the Motherland in April 1941. Following Mao's death in 1976, the People's Republic of China (PRC) regime also suffered both a succession and legitimacy crisis, as the 'cult of personality' that had sustained Mao died with him. The eventual new leader, Deng Xio Ping, was forced to abandon Chinese Communist Party shibboleths and instigate radical economic reform by the depth of public hostility towards communism as it had been put in practice by the party, especially during the Cultural Revolution.[55]

Currently, two totalising revolutions are experiencing major legitimacy crises as a result of the passing of the charismatic leader and/or revolutionary generation. In Cuba, the end of the Castro brothers' combined 59 years in power have raised serious legitimation questions for the regime. Fearing to appoint another next-generation family member to succeed him, Raúl Castro's choice of the distinctly

[54] See, eg, STEFAN T. POSSONY, LENIN: THE COMPULSIVE REVOLUTIONARY (1964).

[55] Gregory C. Chow, *Economic Reform and Growth in China*, 5 ANNALS OF ECONOMICS AND FINANCE 127, 128 (2004).

uncharismatic Miguel Díaz-Canel, born one year after the revolution, has provoked serious questions about whether his leadership will be accepted by the rest of the party and, more importantly, the citizens of Cuba.[56] In Venezuela, the 'Bolivarian revolution' of the charismatic Hugo Chávez has been in legitimacy crisis ever since his death in 2013 and succession by the uninspiring Nicolas Maduro,[57] even before the dive in world oil prices and Maduro's increasingly desperate and unambiguously authoritarian steps to remain in power appear to have made the regime's eventual fall a matter of when rather than if.

In short, the legitimacy crisis posed by the passing of a charismatic leader and/or revolutionary generation appears to be a general problem faced by charismatic revolutionary regimes of all stripes, and not only constitutionalist ones. The 'constitutionalization of charisma' may be the distinctive task of the latter at Time Two, but it is far from clear that this plays much of a role in either the generation or solution of the particular problem at Time Three. The problem has been a common one for all revolutionary regimes whose legitimacy is significantly based on charismatic leadership, and the solution in almost all cases has been a combination of choice of successor by either the old leader alone or by the other members of the revolutionary party elite (India, South Africa, Soviet Union, China and Cuba) and acknowledgement/accommodation of enough of the contemporary policy concerns underlying the crisis to permit at least the partial renewal of legitimacy. In India, judicial supremacy may be seen as the necessary accommodation of the concerns raised by and during the Emergency,[58] just as Deng Xiao Ping's market reforms in post-Mao China were aimed at blunting public hostility towards the party resulting from the excesses of the Cultural Revolution.[59]

III. Judicial Supremacy?

In Ackerman's account, the succession crisis of revolutionary constitutionalism at Time Three is frequently (although not always or necessarily) resolved by consolidation of the regime at Time Four in the form of 'judicial supremacy'. India and Israel are prime examples, perhaps France and Italy too. The reason is that as the revolutionary charisma and legitimacy of the movement party fades with the passing of the leadership that toppled the old and established the new regime, leading to the succession crisis, the claim of the judges to greater revolutionary legitimacy

[56] See Azham Ahmed, *Raúl Castro Prepares to Resign as Cuba's President, Closing a Dynasty*, New York Times, April 18, 2018, https://www.nytimes.com/2018/04/18/world/americas/raul-castro-resigns-cuba-president.html?action=click&module=RelatedCoverage&pgtype=Article&region=Footer.

[57] See, eg, Susan Grainger, Hugo Chavez and Venezuela Confront His Succession, December 11, 2012, https://www.bbc.com/news/world-latin-america-20678634.

[58] See Ackerman, *supra* note 1, ch. 2; see also S.P. Sathe, Judicial Activism in India: Transgressing Borders and Enforcing Limits (2002).

[59] See *supra*, note 55 above.

as a result of their task of interpreting and applying the founding document grows in comparison to the new generation of 'normalised', uncharismatic party politicians. This greater connection to, and relationship with, the revolution comes to be viewed as a stronger source of legitimacy by Time Four.[60] Thus, for example, it was only after Nehru's death and the succession crises of the Congress Party that followed, during which its legitimacy drastically fades to the extent of losing an election and power for the first time in 1977, that the Supreme Court of India was emboldened to emerge as the leading constitutional actor it has since become.[61] The Israeli 'constitutional revolution' of 1992 is another example.

Putting to one side the question of what exactly Ackerman means by 'judicial supremacy', which he never really defines,[62] he may here be overlooking the extent to which judicial empowerment and supremacy is a *general* tendency within contemporary constitutionalism, ie, within all three pathways and not only the revolutionary one. In other words, the broad trend towards increased judicial power and supremacy may be explicable independently of the growing relative revolutionary legitimacy of courts at Time Four. The very general (even minimal) conception of constitutionalism that Ackerman identifies and uses to distinguish among types of modern revolutions, as involving legal constraints on the exercise of political power,[63] certainly suggests a potentially significant role for courts, regardless of which of the three pathways to it is taken. Thus, the importance of the rule of law and, especially within contemporary constitutionalism, of institutional checks and balances on power rather than unchecked, majoritarian democracy seem to account for the general transfer of power to courts that has corresponded to 'the rise of world constitutionalism'.[64] To be sure, some of the 'usual suspects' for the most powerful constitutional court in the world stem from the revolutionary tradition – India and the US – but so too do courts in countries that followed a non-revolutionary pathway, such as Germany and Colombia since 1992.[65] In short, it is far from clear that judicial supremacy is limited to, or especially connected with, the revolutionary strand of constitutionalism.

So, judicial supremacy may not be distinctive to revolutionary constitutionalism. However, at the same time, not all revolutionary constitutionalism results in the problem to which judicial supremacy is the frequent answer. Indeed, it is

[60] Ackerman, *supra* note 1, ch. 1.

[61] *Id.* at ch. 2.

[62] Or rather perhaps, which among the term's various meanings he is employing. See Stephen Gardbaum, *What is Judicial Supremacy?*, *in* Comparative Constitutional Theory (Gary Jacobsohn and Miguel Schor eds., 2017).

[63] Ackerman, *supra* note 1 at 5.

[64] Public choice explanations for the rise of constitutional courts and judicial power, such as Tom Ginsburg's 'insurance' and Ran Hirschl's 'hegemonic preservation' theses, also appear to cut across the various pathways to constitutionalism. See Tom Ginsburg, Judicial Review in New Democracies: Constitutional Courts in Asian Cases (2003); Ran Hirschl, Towards Juristocracy: The Origins and Consequences of the New Constitutionalism (2004).

[65] See, eg, Gardbaum, *supra* note 9 at 1–2.

far from clear that the route to, and rationale for, judicial supremacy applies to revolutionary constitutionalism as a whole rather than the subpart of it on which Ackerman focuses. Where a legitimacy vacuum is not caused by, or first encountered at, the fading of revolutionary charisma at Time Three, then the greater claim to legitimacy of the judges than the new generation of normalised party politicians may well not apply. In other words, successful leaderless revolutions – ie, ones that survive the earlier legitimacy crisis at Time Two – may be less likely to consolidate under judicial supremacy.

This is certainly what we find in the case of Mexico. The increasingly hegemonic position of the PNR after its establishment in 1929 (from 1946 the Partido Revolucionario Institucional (PRI)) meant that although constitutional discourse and legal form were important components of the revolutionary regime from the outset and much time was spent debating judicial institutions at the constituent assembly,[66] consolidation occurred without anything remotely resembling judicial supremacy. The newly created Supreme Court of Justice of the Nation may have helped to bestow legitimacy on the revolutionary regime, but from 1917 until the end of PRI dominance and the 1994 constitutional reforms, it was deeply subordinated to the executive branch. As one legal scholar puts it: 'The Mexican Supreme Court has been characterized by its passive political role, and its submission to the will of the executive.'[67] Granted from the outset only the limited scope of judicial review constituted by the *amparo* jurisdiction, which has no legally binding effect beyond the plaintiff unless confirmed by five similar judgments, the institutional independence of the court was reduced by one constitutional amendment switching from congressional appointment to presidential nomination in 1928 and another by replacing life tenure with six-year terms in 1934.[68] But institutional details aside, the very success and longevity of the revolutionary regime and party as the dominant political force in Mexico rendered judicial supremacy an unlikely political outcome.

In Tunisia, of course, we are still only eight years into the revolution, if its fragile legitimacy survives perhaps at the very beginning of the consolidation phase. However, despite the Constitution calling for the creation of an independent constitutional court for the first time in the country's history and the enactment of an organic statute for it in 2015, no judges have been appointed and the court has yet to be established.[69] Incumbent politicians are perhaps more reluctant to cede power to it than the initial constitutional drafters were. If the regime survives, there is no way to tell at this stage whether it will end up with judicial supremacy. As we have seen, by no means is this always the case with revolutionary

[66] Niemeyer, *supra* note 21.

[67] Pilar Domingo, *Judicial Independence: The Politics of the Supreme Court in Mexico*, 32 J. Lat. Am. St. 705, 706 (2000).

[68] *Id.* at 710–12.

[69] Sharan Grewal, Tunisia Needs a Constitutional Court, Brookings, November 20, 2018, https://www.brookings.edu/blog/order-from-chaos/2018/11/20/tunisia-needs-a-constitutional-court.

constitutionalism as a whole. But if it does, this may well be the result of more general factors than a succession/legitimacy crisis.

Among these, judicial supremacy appears to be significantly a function of the existence or absence of a dominant political party in constitutionalist regimes *of all pedigrees* rather than either a distinctive feature of revolutionary constitutionalism in general or the result of fading revolutionary charisma and succession crises in particular.[70] Among revolutionary regimes, it seems to be the existence and longevity of the revolutionary party's political dominance that matters and not so much whether it is charismatic or the original bearer of revolutionary legitimacy. Thus, the major difference between the movement-led and charismatic revolutionary regime in India that consolidates under judicial supremacy and the non-charismatic one in Mexico that does not is the ability of the PNR/PRI to maintain its political dominance for several more decades than the Congress Party. This is, of course, despite its non-charismatic origins as the inheritor rather than the creator of legitimacy.[71] Only once this dominance is seriously challenged for the first time in the 1990s is there political space for a more robust and independent constitutional judiciary. The US has never had a dominant political party or faction along the lines of these two.

Similarly, with respect to the elite pact pathway to constitutionalism, the Federal Republic of Germany is an example of such a non-revolutionary regime without (at least since 1969) a dominant political party that has a very powerful constitutional court as 'guardian of the constitution'.[72] By contrast, Japan is an example of the elite pact pathway in which a single party, the Liberal Democratic Party (LDP), has long been dominant and the Supreme Court is universally perceived as one of the weakest among constitutionalist democracies.[73] And this is despite the twin facts that its formal powers were modelled on, and are largely similar to, those of the US Supreme Court, and that, since the 1946 Constitution has never been amended, it faces less threat of being overruled by constitutional amendment than the US, German or Indian courts.[74]

The South African Constitutional Court may appear to be a partial exception, as it has operated within a dominant party democracy. But despite its undoubted influence, judicial supremacy does not seem to be an accurate characterisation of the regime as a whole during the period of ANC dominance, which may now be

[70] See Gardbaum, *supra* note 9 at 25–30.

[71] See *supra* note 15.

[72] See, eg, *The Most Extraordinarily Powerful Court of Law the World has Ever Known? – Judicial Review in the United States and Germany*, 65 Md. L. Rev. 152, 153 (2006) (arguing that the German Constitutional Court has surpassed the US Supreme Court to become the most powerful in the world).

[73] See, eg, David Law, *The Anatomy of a Conservative Court: Judicial Review in Japan*, in Public Law in East Asia (Albert H.Y. Chen & Tom Ginsburg eds., 2013); Shigenori Matsui, *Why is the Japanese Supreme Court So Conservative?*, 88 Wash. U. L. Rev. 1375 (2011). See also Gardbaum, *supra* note 9 at 36–39 (explaining why the Japanese court is weak, including the role of the dominant LDP).

[74] See Gardbaum, *supra* note 9 at 37.

coming to an end.[75] Moreover, as Ackerman charts, its influence was built in at the outset when the newly established Constitutional Court was given a highly unusual and unusually prominent role in the constitutional founding: of ruling on the consistency of the final constitution with the 34 'constitutional principles' contained in the interim one.[76]

IV. Conclusion

As a pioneering volume identifying the existence and implications of three distinct pathways to constitutionalism and developing an in-depth history of the revolutionary tradition in the twentieth century, Ackerman's *Revolutionary Constitutions: Charismatic Leadership and the Rule of Law* is an immensely ambitious and impressive work. Its global coverage and detailed case studies provide rigorous and persuasive support for his overarching thesis about the common developmental stages and challenges of the revolutionary pathway to constitutionalism.

And yet, as extensive as his case studies are, this chapter has argued that the volume provides a partial account of the phenomenon of revolutionary constitutionalism and not the whole. For it deals exclusively with only one of its two major subtypes: the constitutionalist revolution engineered and led by a charismatic hero and movement party that has earned its legitimacy through long years of struggle and sacrifice on behalf of the people against the old regime. It overlooks what has been an equally common and globally dispersed type of revolutionary constitutionalism over the same time period, with a not obviously dissimilar rate of success and failure – what I have referred to as the 'uncharismatic' variety. This is the spontaneous, leaderless or movementless constitutionalist revolution, exemplified by the Mexican, Filipino, Romanian and Tunisian Revolutions discussed.

The existence and history of this second common type of revolutionary constitutionalism problematises much of Ackerman's analysis as inherent to, or characteristic of, this pathway to constitutionalism as a whole. For it has tended to face a quite different key legitimacy crisis and at a different time: an initial one during the revolutionary turmoil rather than a succession crisis a generation later. Indeed, such succession crises appear not to be distinctive to revolutionary constitutionalism per se, but rather to charismatic revolutionary regimes of all stripes, including the more notorious 'totalising' ones of the twentieth century. Similarly, experience of the uncharismatic strand strongly suggests that judicial supremacy is not, contrary to Ackerman, specially connected to revolutionary constitutionalism. None of the uncharismatic case studies has obviously resulted

[75] In the 2016 municipal elections, the ANC lost control of three metropolitan municipalities, including the city of Johannesburg, to opposition parties for the first time.

[76] Ackerman, *supra* note 1, ch. 3.

in judicial supremacy and several countries that took the non-revolutionary path to constitutionalism have. The key variable here is arguably the presence or absence of a dominant political party.

This chapter introduces an additional layer to the topic of revolutionary constitutionalism. The hope is that scholars will be inspired, rather than intimidated, by the scale and ambition of Ackerman's book to bring similar depth to bear on the uncharismatic strand (and any others that might be found to exist) and build on his outstanding foundation to further our understanding of the revolutionary mode *tout court* and its inter-connections with the other pathways to constitutionalism.

9

Unconventional Adaptation and the Authenticity of the Constitution

ALESSANDRO FERRARA

The dualist paradigm for constitutional democracy – initially formulated by Bruce Ackerman, incorporated by John Rawls into his 'principle of liberal legitimacy' and recently dubbed 'legitimation by constitution' by Frank Michelman[1] – rests on the assumption, more general than the opposition of 'constitutive' and 'constituted' power,[2] that a distinction ought to separate the constitutive rules[3] of a game and each specific instance of the game. While different hands, sets and instances of a game can be played according to the same rules, rules are not supposed to change in the midst of a game. Likewise, since Thomas Kuhn's groundbreaking philosophy of science, we understand a paradigm as a core idea underlying theories that are falsifiable through methods different from the reflective judgement concerning the overall promise of the paradigm. Similarly, twentieth-century linguistics, from Ferdinand de Saussure to Noam Chomsky and beyond, stipulates that *langue* is a form, conceptualised as a grammar, that can be actualised in infinite instances of *parole*, or a generative competence that can produce infinite grammatical sentences.

In all these cases, the superordinate framework 'legitimates' each token instance. In the absence of consensus on its merits, being within the bounds of the constitution legitimates a statute for a liberal-democratic public; consistency with a paradigm reassures us about the worth of theories in spite of moderate anomalies; and the 'rules of grammar' are often invoked to justify linguistic usage.

[1] Bruce Ackerman, We the People, Volume 1: Foundations 3–33 (1991); John Rawls, Political Liberalism 137, 231–33 (expanded ed., 2005); Frank Michelman, *Political Liberalism's Constitutional Horizon: Some Further Thoughts*, 4 Riv. Int. Fil. Dir. 599 (2017).

[2] See Emmanuel Joseph Sieyès, *What is the Third Estate?* (1789), *in* Political Writings 134–35 (2003). See also John Locke, Two Treatises of Government (1690), a critical edition and with an introduction and apparatus criticus by Peter Laslett (1965), § 243, 477.

[3] On 'constitutive rules', see John Searle, Speech Acts: An Essay in the Philosophy of Language 33–42 (1969).

However, superordinate frameworks relate to the token instances of their actualisation in different ways. The rules of chess are rigid. One cannot move the castle diagonally and claim to still be playing chess. Grammatical rules are looser: over time, *parole* changes *langue*, if slippage in language use follows a consistent pattern. Language use thus shapes grammar to an extent unequalled in the cases of chess or football. No number of fouls can reconfigure the rules of the game unless a separate agreement to that effect is reached, but different ways of playing a social role end up reconfiguring the script. The script regulates its own execution, but convergent and incremental slippage in execution reconfigures the script, as has happened with highly gendered roles over the past decades.

How do constitutions relate to the statutes, executive orders, decrees, ordinances and sentences comprised within their regulatory scope: rigidly (as in the case of the rules of chess) or more flexibly (as in the case of language use and grammar)?[4] The originality of Ackerman's approach can be measured against the polarity which opposes Rawls's, Dworkin's and Michelman's constitutionalism as based on a 'chess-like' separation of higher law from the rest of the legal and institutional order,[5] and the so-called 'political constitutionalism' championed by Jeremy Waldron, Richard Bellamy and Mark Tushnet, who question the merit of judicial review and understand the constitution as co-extensive with the democratic process; in the words of Bellamy, 'the democratic process *is* the constitution'.[6]

Ackerman's constitutional theory ingeniously cuts across this binary through his notion of 'unconventional adaptation'. While Rawlsian constitutionalism would have constitutional change proceed strictly within the tracks established by the Constitution (Article Five, in the case of the US Constitution) and on the basis of public reason deliberation in the public forum,[7] and while Bellamy's or Waldron's 'political constitutionalism' would have constitutional change emerge from open contestation in the legislative forum and in the public sphere, Ackerman's theory fits neither of these alternatives.

[4] For a reconstruction of three models of the relation of the Constitution to its amendments – (a) the *textual model*, ie, legitimate amendments proceed *solely* from strict observance of the constitutional provisions for amendment (Canada); b) the *political model*, ie, legitimate amendments may *also* originate from the political process, beyond the formal procedures for amendment, and need not necessarily be encoded formally in the Constitution (the US); c) the *substantivist model*, ie, legitimate amendments must substantively conform with the core of the Constitution as interpreted by a Constitutional Court (India, South Africa and Germany) – see Richard Albert, *Nonconstitutional Amendments*, 22 Can. J. L. & Juris 5 (2009).

[5] Rawls appears to waver between a rejection of 'judicial supremacy', typical of the *political model* ('The constitution is not what the Court says it is. Rather, it is what the people acting constitutionally through the other branches eventually allow the Court to say it is'; Rawls, *supra* note 1 at 237) and advocacy of a *substantivist model* (eg, an amendment to repeal the First Amendment, even if enacted by the procedure of Article Five, should not be accepted as valid higher law by the Supreme Court; Rawls, *supra* note 1 at 238–39).

[6] See Richard Bellamy, Political Constitutionalism: A Republican Defence of the Constitutionality of Democracy (2007); Jeremy Waldron, Law and Disagreement (1999) and The Dignity of Legislation (1999); Mark Tushnet, Taking the Constitution away from the Courts (1999).

[7] See Rawls, *supra* note 1 at ch. 6.

The 'unconventionality' of unconventional adaptation is attested by the fact that major constitutional change – in the American context the Founding, Reconstruction, New Deal and Civil Rights eras – never followed exactly the tracks of Article Five without significant input coming from political contestation and its results: landmark statutes, exemplary cases and appointments to the Supreme Court. On the one hand, for Ackerman, constitutional transformations of historical significance always occupy an intermediate point between the extremes of 'legality as usual' and total revolution from *tabula rasa*. On the other hand, the 'adaptive' moment in 'unconventional *adaptation*' signals that, unlike the paradigm of 'political constitutionalism', Ackerman's view remains anchored to a normative core of the constitution (Rawls' 'constitutional essentials'), consisting not so much of legal details, but of the evolving vision of a proper way of living together politically, capable of reverberating *constitutional authenticity* down the generational line. While his reconstruction of the New Deal and the Civil Rights era acknowledges the extra-constitutional avenues for constitutional reform operative in the twentieth and twenty-first centuries, Ackerman propounds bringing the 'political' ways of amending the Constitution 'back' into a solidly legal framework through his 'popular sovereignty initiative'.[8]

I. Varieties of Unconventional Adaptation

Revolutionary Constitutions enriches the paradigm of dualistic constitutionalism. Constitutional moments other than those experienced by the US, and representative of one among three distinct pathways to constitution-making, are explored.

Considering India, South Africa, France, Italy, Poland, Burma, Israel and Iran, Ackerman shows that the 'revolutionary' as opposed to the 'establishmentarian' or 'elitist' pathway typically manifests a four-stage sequence of: (a) regime change under the guidance of charismatic-democratic leadership; (b) a race against time to constitutionalise revolutionary charisma; (c) succession crises; and (d) the intervention of previously less decisive constitutional courts through judicial review.

In a sense, *Revolutionary Constitutions* casts light on the *prologue*, as it were, to democratic dualism. Before conformity with the constitution can render contentious statutes, decrees and sentences legitimate, the constitution itself must be regarded as legitimate. And when its legitimacy derives from a revolutionary 'new beginning', 'unconventional adaptation' becomes crucial.

In this section I will highlight variations of the meaning and intensity of 'unconventional adaptation'. Because revolutionary constitutionalism, more than other pathways, revolves around unconventional adaptation, it becomes crucial to focus on the common denominator and the variants of this notion. The common denominator is discontinuity or rupture in an established legal, political or social

[8] Bruce Ackerman, We the People, Volume 2: Transformations 415 (1998).

pattern. The variants relate to the dimensions of *authorisation*, *interpretation*, *representation*, *political intimidation or pressure* and *formal innovation*. Within some of these dimensions, we can also observe different *gradients* of unconventionality.

A. Shortfall of Authorisation

Lack of authorisation is among the most common kinds of unconventional rupture of legality. The convening of the Constitutional Convention in Philadelphia by the Continental Congress in February 1787 authorised the delegates to deliberate 'for the sole and express purpose' of revising the 1781 Articles of Confederation. The subversion of the Articles in the direction of a federal scheme of government was beyond such a mandate. Within this general lack of authorisation, the gravest breach consisted in subverting the rule for amending the Articles – from the unanimity of the state *legislatures* to a majority of three-quarters of the states as represented by *conventions* akin to the Philadelphia Convention. In the Reconstruction era, shortfalls of *authorisation* intertwined with problems of *representation*. These two aspects of unconventionality are combined in the proclamation of the Thirteenth Amendment on 18 December 1865 by Secretary William H Seward, including eight states of the former Confederation among the 27 approving states in spite of the decision by Congress, 14 days earlier, that 'no legal state governments', and thus no legislatures, existed in 10 Southern states.[9]

During France's two-act transition from the Third to the Fifth Republic, we observe the extra-legal appointment of a provisional government on 3 June 1944, based on the idea that *neither* the Vichy constitutional order *nor* the overturned Third Republic could be recognised as legitimate.[10] However, the status of such government, established as a *fait accompli* in the course of armed conflict, and the ensuing 'legitimation vacuum',[11] was rectified later by de Gaulle's call on 21 October 1945 for a referendum that gave the choice between reviving the Third Republic or starting a new constitutional order directly to the electorate.

A second rupture, again in relation to authorisation, occurred in 1958, when the crisis-ridden Fourth Republic, whose coalition governments lasted on average less than a year, faced the Algerian crisis. Humiliated by the 1954 Dien Bien Phu defeat in Vietnam, conservative constituencies, right-wing French settlers in Algeria and the high ranks of the military stationed in Algeria firmly opposed the independence there. Unstable Fourth Republic governments were accused of betraying French interests and historical role in North Africa, and of undermining the heroic efforts of local settlers to withstand the pressure of anti-French

[9] *Id.* at 101.
[10] See Bruce Ackerman, Revolutionary Constitutions: Charismatic Leadership and the Rule of Law 122 (2019).
[11] *Id.*

independentists. De Gaulle somehow kindled these resentful forces. In May 1958, the alleged 'appeasement' policy of the newly appointed Pflimlin government led to protests in Algiers escalating, with crowds of French settlers proclaiming a 'Committee of Public Safety' headed by General Massu, the strongman of anti-FLN repression during the Battle of Algiers. De Gaulle re-entered the arena. When golpista forces launched 'Operation Resurrection', established a bridgehead in Corsica and were reportedly ready to march on to Paris, de Gaulle obtained from President Coty the nomination to the position of prime minister, six months of exceptional powers and the mandate to draft a new constitution premised on the idea of a president with the mandate to appoint a prime minister and chair the sessions of the Council of Ministers. Upon taking office, in May 1958, de Gaulle asked Minister of Justice Michel Debré to produce a draft, later presented to the Council of Ministers and President Coty on 3 September, which was submitted to a referendum and approved with a resounding 80 per cent majority on 28 September. The unconventionality of this way of proceeding is attested by Mitterand's calling the new constitution a *coup d'etat*, in spite of the 80 per cent consent, because of the lack of proper authorisation for a prime minister – as formally De Gaulle was – to change the rules of the constitutional game in stride, in a plebiscitary way, aided by the threat of a *coup d'etat* and by his own revolutionary charisma.

Unconventionality as a shortfall of authorisation comes in a variety of *gradients*. India and Italy are examples of the *least discontinuous* constitution-framing processes. The Indian Constituent Assembly, which was elected in 1946 to prepare India (and the later separated Pakistan and Bangladesh) for independence, represented *no breach* of the existing order, at least from the perspective of formal authorisation. The unconventional aspects of the Indian constitutional process concern dimensions other than authorisation.

In the Italian revolutionary path to constitutionalism, like the French case, the political forces in favour of regime change were divided into three ideological traditions (but with no non-partisan charismatic figure) and, like in India, unconventional ruptures initially were minimal. The Constitutional Assembly entrusted to write the post-war, anti-fascist constitution was convened by a decree of the De Gasperi government, countersigned by King Umberto I, the last of the lame-duck Savoy monarchy: on 2 June 1946 a referendum offering a choice between a monarchical or republican regime and elections for the Assembly took place. The process unfolded within the context of the 'national unity' governments appointed by the king pursuant to the (still formally valid) 1848 Statuto Albertino.[12] Within the Italian constitutional process, unconventionality resided not so much in the formal making of the new Constitution as in its substantive discontinuity from the Statuto in matters of religious freedom, rights and democratic participation. The 'sobriety'

[12] Only after the final approval of the Constitution by the Assembly in December 1947 and its enactment on 1 January 1948 did the new republican Constitution that is still in force today become operative.

and 'statesmanship' of the Italian Constitutional Assembly[13] are due to the willingness, on the part of the moderate and conservative forces, to accept progressive provisions advocated by the Marxist left in recognition of its final renunciation, since the 'Svolta di Salerno', of revolutionary aims, and due to a contingent veil of ignorance, which prevented the major players of Italian politics from knowing who would govern the country once the Constitution became operative.

A higher but still *moderate* shortfall of authorisation characterises the early stages of the Polish case. After a decade of mobilisation, in 1989 the confrontation of Lech Walesa's Solidarity movement with General Jaruzelski's regime entered a new stage. The movement's successes induced the regime to renounce repression and undertake negotiations. During the so-called 'Round Table' negotiations, the parties pursued diverse agendas: 'legal recognition of its legitimacy' for Solidarity, confining Solidarity 'to a strictly subordinate role within the existing regime' for the representatives of the regime.[14] After a stalemate over the prerogatives of the president and of other institutions, both sides agreed on a compromise that included: (a) a partition of the Sejm (the lower Chamber), with 65 per cent of the seats reserved for the Communists and their allies, and 35 per cent remaining open to competition and thus potentially to Solidarity; (b) a new elected Senate; and (c) a president endowed with enhanced powers.[15] However, after finalising the agreement, the representatives of the regime insisted on a Gaullist super-presidency endowed with the authority to call a state of emergency (and with the prerogative to use military force against insurgents) and also to veto legislation approved by the Sejm.[16] Considered a success by Walesa in the sense that the elected Senate would allow the movement to claim direct investiture by popular sovereignty, the compromise reached at the Round Table negotiations needed to be turned into valid law. To that effect, the party used its overwhelming majority in the Sejm to enact the necessary constitutional amendments with the required supermajority. This process made it tangible 'that it was the revolutionary Round Table, not the Sejm, which had become the *legitimate* constitutional authority in revolutionary Poland'[17] – an inversion of planes whereby the legal authority (ie, the Sejm) became a rubber stamp for legitimating constitutional transformations wrought at an extra-legal venue (ie, the Round Table). The moderate shortfall of authorisation consisted of enlisting legally legitimate institutions for transferring legitimacy onto informal deliberation perceived as *substantively legitimate*.

Focusing back on Italy, one major difference compared to France is the fact that the expressions 'First Republic' and 'Second Republic', commonly used to designate respectively the political system operating from 1948 to 1992, with six to seven distinct parties, and the tendentially bipolar (not really two-party) system

[13] See ACKERMAN, *supra* note 10 at 147.
[14] *Id.* at 239.
[15] *Id.* at 240–41.
[16] This veto power was also shared by a two-thirds majority of the Senate; see *id.* at 241.
[17] *Id.* at 245.

of the Berlusconi 1994–2011 era, describe different political configurations that operated within one *basically unchanged* constitutional framework. In France instead, the Fourth and Fifth Republics designate distinct constitutional arrangements of a parliamentary and presidential nature respectively. But the apparent durability of the Italian constitutional framework, which as late as 2016 withstood a concerted attempt at reform instigated by the governmental coalition, should not mislead us into underestimating the problem of 'governability' that Italy shared with France's Fourth Republic. Instability of government leads to inconclusiveness in governmental policy. Absent a charismatic figure capable of catalysing presidentialist reform, in Italy all attempts at creating more stability have focused on the electoral law as a tool. Thus, although the 'scam' law, passed in 1953 by a De Gasperi government, was an ordinary statute that would grant 15 per cent additional seats to the party or coalition obtaining more than 50 per cent of votes, it should be treated (as the leftist opposition did) as the first of several attempts to alter the Italian 'parliamentary' regime through a *landmark statute* designed to ensure stability by granting 65 per cent of the seats to a majority. Note that pursuant to Article 138, the putatively 'rigid' Constitution of 1948 allows a qualified parliamentary majority of two-thirds, voting twice at an interval of at least three months, to change the Constitution without even allowing for a referendum. Thus, the 'scam' law would have in practice put the Constitution – which entrenches only the so-called 'republican form' (Article 139) – in the hands of an electoral majority. Indeed, 1953 was a moment of rupture ignited by a 'landmark statute'. Just by a fraction of a percentage point, the coalition led by Demo-Christians and other parties missed the 50 per cent mark, so the 'scam' law was buried for a whole political era, but its underlying aim – to alter the strictly parliamentary inspiration of the 1948 Constitution by weakening the checks and balances imposed on governmental action – would surface again in the following decades in the form of repeated attempts to make the prime minister elective ('to vote for the "Mayor of Italy"' was the slogan in the 1990s), to strengthen the presidency, to overcome bicameralism, and time and again to create bonus seats for majorities.[18]

[18] In 1979, future socialist Prime Minister Bettino Craxi opened up the discussion of a 'Great Reform', aimed at attaining 'governability' through presidentialism, in a climate marked by communist leaders like Terracini and Berlinguer calling for the abolition of the Senate in order to streamline the legislative process, characterised by a shuttling of bill drafts back and forth between the two Houses. In 1983, a bicameral committee, presided by Aldo Bozzi, worked for two years on a new election law and on differentiating the functions of the two Houses, but failed to create a proposal that all could agree on. Then in the 1990s, Mario Segni, a Demo-Christian, led a referendum campaign for directly electing the prime minister. The Constitutional Court did not authorise the referendum on this point, but only on the secondary issue of the abolition of 'preference votes' in the ballot. It was a triumph of the Yes vote (95.6 per cent) in a referendum with a turnout of 62 per cent of the electorate, despite the campaign for abstention conducted by the main parties. This result led, in the wake of the *Mani Pulite* scandal on corruption, to a new referendum for the introduction of a 'first past the post' electoral mechanism for the Senate aiming to achieve stability, which was approved by 82.5 per cent of voters (with a 77 per cent turnout) in 1993. See Giorgio Crainz & Carlo Fusaro, Aggiornare la Costituzione. Storia e ragioni di una riforma 30–31 (2016). Then in 2005, Northern League representative

At the same time, the episode exemplifies a moderately 'unconventional' use of statutes to alter matters of constitutional significance without going through the provision of Article 138 for revising the Constitution.

Finally, a *more severe* example of a shortfall of authorisation can be observed in France in 1962. De Gaulle, aware that once his personal charisma would no longer be available, a president elected by an Electoral College would be at a disadvantage in confronting a prime minister who, although designated by the president, would obtain a confidence vote from a National Assembly elected directly by the voters,[19] planned to remedy this flaw by also having the president elected directly. Assisted by special circumstances, he chose an 'unconventional' solution. When 'on August 22, bitter-enders in the Secret Army almost succeeded in assassinating him and his family in retaliation for his "betrayal" in Algeria', he announced 'while parliament was in recess, that he would *unilaterally proceed with a referendum on the popular-election amendment*' (emphasis added).[20] His initiative was condemned as 'unconstitutional' by the Constitutional Council and by the Council of State. However, the referendum took place on 28 October 1962 in a climate in which the National Assembly toppled Prime Minister Pompidou following a no-confidence vote and 'censured the president for "violating the Constitution"'.[21] De Gaulle, in response, dissolved the National Assembly, called for new elections and stepped up his campaign by 'equating his opponents in the democratically elected parliament to the seditious conspirators who had tried to kill him'.[22] Although his reform passed by 62 per cent to 38 per cent in the referendum, his conduct certainly counts as a rupture of the constitutional order on the authorisation side. Today his initiative would fall under the rubric of *populism*, the illiberal antagonist of constitutionalism – a *populist* kind of unconventional adaptation summarised in the formula 'Popular Sovereignty = personal revolutionary charisma + media appeals + popular referenda'.[23] De Gaulle had a fascination for referendums as 'the most direct, frankest and democratic form of political consultation that exists'.[24]

Roberto Calderoli, at Berlusconi's instigation, managed to have a new election law approved. This was another statute of constitutional importance: it provided for a bonus for the majority party or coalition, regardless of a minimum threshold of votes, and abolished the possibility for voters to indicate a preference for an individual candidate within the voted party-slate. This landmark statute, which regulated elections in the later phases of the Italian Second Republic in 2006, 2008 and 2013, was eventually declared unconstitutional by the Court in 2014 for those two characteristics, which were deemed to violate the constitutional principle of the equality of voting citizens. This event led to a new election law, returning to a proportional scheme, and to the Renzi government's unsuccessful attempt to amend the Constitution in 2016 in order to abolish bicameralism, reduce the number of representatives and exclude the Senate from voting confidence in the government.

[19] See Ackerman, *supra* note 10 at 187–88.

[20] *Id.* at 189.

[21] *Id.* at 190.

[22] *Id.* at 191.

[23] *Id.* at 193.

[24] Quoted in R Brizzi, Charles de Gaulle and the Media: Leadership, TV and the Birth of the Fifth Republic (2010), 152 (2018); for a discussion of de Gaulle's use of TV appearances, see 137–59 and for an analysis of his populist use of TV to bypass party leaders and directly reach

However, what followed in the aftermath of the referendum exemplifies not just a shortfall of authorisation, but also a *different kind* of unconventional adaptation, which will be discussed below.

The Iranian Revolution offers an even more radical example of an authorisation gap, eventually bridged by a plebiscitary referendum. The ailing health of Ayatollah Khomeini in 1989 highlighted the need to choose a successor to the role of Supreme Leader. After the Ayatollah had pressed his formerly designated successor Montazeri to resign, the remaining candidates were Ali Khamenei, the President who for two mandates had successfully led the Iranian counter-offensive against Saddam Hussein's aggression; Hashemi Rafsanjani, the President of the Iranian Parliament between 1980 and 1989 and also a military leader in the war against Iraq; and Mohammad Reza Golpayegani, who of the three was the only religiously qualified *marja* or Grand Ayatollah, but was virtually unknown to the wider public. A choice urgently needed to be made. In order to avoid future discord, Rafsanjani and Khamenei would need to somehow bridge the gap between the positions of Supreme Leader, vested of unmatched authority, and of President, which the French-inspired Constitution had combined with a prime minister elected by Parliament. The solution was to abolish the office of prime minister and equalise the influence of the other two offices – a reform to be formally proposed by Parliament and accepted in a referendum. At this juncture, an unconventional rupture occurred. Based on a letter written by Khomeini on 24 April 1989, an 'Assembly for the Revision of the Constitution' was established, composed of 20 officials named by the Ayatollah and five additional members named by the Majlis. As Ackerman notes:

> [I]t is impossible to determine whether Khomeini was sufficiently alert to make these appointments during the final weeks of his life … and it is quite possible that Khamenei and Rafsanjani played a key role in the selection of the ad hoc group.[25]

The Assembly claimed that Khomeini had himself recommended the proposed solution and the convergence of the two leaders discouraged all challenges. Despite his lack of full clerical credentials, Khamenei was appointed '*temporary* Supreme Leader' by the Council of Experts at the suggestion of Rafsanjani, and a referendum on the constitutional reform was convened. The creation of an enhanced presidential office, to which Rafsanjani was elected for two mandates until 1997, the abolition of the premiership and the abolition of the requirement of being a *marja* for acceding to the office of Supreme Leader, to which Khamenei was elected in 1989 and which he has held up to the present day, were sanctioned by a majority of 98 per cent on 29 July 1989.[26]

out to the voters, see 193–214. On the grandiose ceremony of the 'presentation of the draft of the [1958] Constitution to the people of France', see J Gaffney, Political Leadership in France: From Charles de Gaulle to Nicolas Sarkozy 31–33 (2010).

[25] Ackerman, *supra* note 10 at 350.

[26] *Id.* at 352.

B. Unconventional Interpretations

Not all unconventional ruptures take the form of (more or less severe) shortfalls of authorisation. Sometimes the breach of the rule of law materialises as an instance of dubious, counter-intuitive or blatantly flawed adjudication by a formally appointed judicial body.

When the constitutionality of the 1962 referendum through which the President of France was made to be elected by popular vote was challenged, the Constitutional Council decided not to decide, claiming that its mandate could not possibly include reviewing the constitutionality of measures 'adopted by the people following a referendum, which constitutes the direct expression of national sovereignty'.[27] Underlying this pronouncement was the notion that a referendum has a *self-validating nature*, regardless of the conditions under which it has been convened.[28] Two aspects of this doctrine seem dubious. First, the core of the illiberal 'sovereigntist' populism of the 2010s revolves precisely around the conflation of 'the People' and the present electorate. 'The People' spans over generations, sometimes centuries, and the presently voting citizens do not 'own' the Constitution, while of course they are entitled to leave their mark on it. There is a difference between *pro tempore* 'owning' the Constitution, with the attached prerogative of bending it in whichever direction, and being entitled to inscribe one's sensibility onto it in a way that does not disfigure its spirit and preserves it for future generations of citizens. Paying this difference its dues requires an act of judgement on the constitutionality of amendments that the Constitutional Council abdicated. Second, if one imagines that every generation of voters will bend the Constitution to its dominant sensibility, it is hard to see in what sense the Constitution would maintain any transtemporal relevance. Paraphrasing Aristotle, where the will of the voters constantly, and without reflective filters, reshapes the Constitution, there is no Constitution at all, only ordinary law.[29]

In other cases, legal breaches based on questionable interpretations appealed to counter-intuitive legal notions. For example, the agreements reached at Kempton Park between Mandela's ANC and the de Klerk government established a legally counter-intuitive relation between the Kempton Park 'provisional' Constitution that 'the newly elected parliament could radically revise … in the process of proposing a permanent Constitution', and the new Constitutional Court's 'unprecedented power to invalidate provisions in the "final" charter that violated the fundamental principles of their "interim" text'.[30] At stake was the

[27] *Id.* at 192.

[28] The Constitutional Council has consistently adopted the doctrine that when a constitutional referendum takes place, the French people exert sovereignty and thus their will cannot be overruled by a constituted power such as the judiciary. For an accurate reconstruction of this doctrine, see Richard Albert, Malkhaz Nakashidze and Tarik Olcay, The Formalist Resistance to Unconstitutional Constitutional Amendments, 70 Hastings L.J. 22 (2019).

[29] Aristotle, The Politics 1292a31, 251, translated by T.A. Sinclair (1992).

[30] Ackerman, *supra* note 10 at 97.

preoccupation that the Constitutional Court could use judicial review to strike down redistributive measures in favour of victims of past white oppression. The idea that a 'provisional' constitutional court could protect white property rights against legislation passed by an elected constitutional assembly – in other words, that *provisional* constitutional arrangements could trump the *final* constitutional arrangements – was certainly very unconventional and indeed a 'remarkable inversion of conventional legal wisdom'.[31]

Another example of unconventionality as dubious interpretation comes from Poland. In the early 1990s, the Communist Party's decision to dissolve itself undermined whatever legitimacy the constitutional order derived from the Round Table negotiations still had. Recognising this fact, Jaruzelski resigned. Constitutional debate started again on whether, following the model of the French Fifth Republic, the presidency was to be assigned by popular election. Walesa eventually won the presidency and used his constitutional powers to attack the government expressed by the Sejm. However, in 1995, he lost the presidency to his rival Marian Krzaklewski. The new President, from the Left Alliance (the reformed successor of the Communist Party), redefined the agenda as the completion of the constitutional project. A 'constitutional commission' was created, which pursued a compromise between orientations to classical liberal rights and social rights, secular and Catholic bioethical views. In 1997, a referendum was called but only 43 per cent of the electorate voted, of which 53 per cent approved the new Constitution: this raised the question whether approval by less than 50 per cent of the total voters counted as legitimate approval. The Constitutional Tribunal found that, based on a provision of the 1989 Constitution, a majority of voters was unnecessary – a conclusion at the edge of unconventionality, with the formality of the rule of law being respected, but a questionable substantive judgement being passed.

Another case of constitutionalism premised on an unconventional legal interpretation concerns Israel. The Declaration of Independence referred to a constitution 'to be drawn up by a Constituent Assembly not later than the first day of October, 1948'. Elections would then be convened for the first legislative assembly due to operate under the new constitution. The attacks by neighbouring Arab countries made it impossible to complete the drafting of the constitution within the deadline: elections were held on 25 January 1949, but one peculiar constitutional rupture occurred. Under a *Transition Ordinance*, issued 12 days before the election, the Provisional Council changed the mandate of the new legislative body from framing a constitution to acting as a full-fledged government. When the new Assembly met, Ben-Gurion proposed a Transition Law that renamed the Assembly a 'Knesset' and requalified it as a regular parliament, which needed no new constitutional framework. This move provoked fierce opposition. Menahem Begin moved for an amendment to the Transition Law, reaffirming that the primary task of the Assembly was to frame a constitution and then to call for new elections.

[31] *Id.* at 98.

With no debate allowed, 'the Transition Law was pushed through the Assembly by a margin of 77 to 0, with 11 abstentions – although 42 members chose to absent themselves from the chamber'.[32]

Prime Minister Ben-Gurion had sunk the possibility of an Israeli-written constitution. A breakthrough occurred in 1950 with the Harari Resolution. On 13 June 1950, Representative Harari successfully proposed that the Knesset give up on a comprehensive constitution and instead launched a Basic Law piecemeal project: 'The constitution will be built chapter by chapter, in such a way that each will constitute a separate Basic Law … all the chapters together shall comprise the Constitution of the State.'[33] The approval of the Resolution proved problematic: out of 113 votes, 50 were in favour, with 39 against. The remaining 24 included 13 abstentions and 11 people who abandoned the voting. Since 63 out of 113 did not vote in favour, it remained doubtful whether this resolution, formally an amendment to the Transition Law, should count as valid. In the case of Israel, we see a *dual* unconventional adaptation at work: first, the shift from a written constitution to the Harari Compromise had a dubious status, then the validity of the vote on the Harari Compromise was dubious.

However, we also observe an unprecedented innovation: no one had ever seen a *gradually enacted Constitution* before. The project, after its inception, never came to a declared completion. At the time of writing, there are 14 Basic Laws, but the unconventional aspect is that it is hard to tell the exact meaning of each provision if the set of all the constitutional provisions is not complete.[34] Furthermore, the Basic Law on Human Dignity and Liberty contains a 'validity of laws' provision that protects all previously enacted legislation from having to conform with the Basic Law, which then really has constitutional status *only relative to future legislation*.[35]

Finally, India offers an example of unconventionality that goes beyond dubious or merely counter-intuitive legal interpretations and instead involves a *straight violation* of legal principles. In violation of the principle of non-retroactivity of the law, the Nehru-inspired 1951 First Amendment to the Constitution entrenched (and deprived the judiciary of all possibility of intervention in) the legal cases raised by legislation that redistributed land and property in the previous years. By *fiat*, legal challenges to contentious measures were retroactively put beyond the reach of courts by this Amendment.[36]

[32] *Id.* at 305.

[33] Center for Israel Education, Harari Proposal Passes, Ending Prospects for an Israeli Constitution, https://israeled.org/harari-proposal-constitution.

[34] On this point, see Aharon Barak, Human Dignity: The Constitutional Value and the Constitutional Right 285 (2015).

[35] For a critique of the 'Validity of Laws Clause' as disturbing 'the harmony and unity' of the constitutional legal system by way of insulating previous legislation from constitutionality screening, see *id.* at 306.

[36] Concerning land redistribution, see art. 31A inserted into the Constitution of India, pursuant to its First Amendment, 18 June 1951.

C. Defective Representation

A third kind of unconventional adaptation concerns problems of *representation*. During the Founding, Rhode Island was absent from the Philadelphia Convention and the State of New York was not counted as present either, despite the individual presence of Alexander Hamilton. The unconventionality of these aspects of the 'revolutionary Constitution' hammered out by the Philadelphia Convention was mitigated, as Ackerman points out, by the English tradition of convening a Convention as a 'legitimate higher-lawmaking body' whenever a legally flawless meeting of Westminster was not possible – for example, when King James II abandoned the country in 1688, his throwing the Great Seal into the Thames was to be construed as an act of abdication. The House of Commons and the House of Lords issued their call to William and Mary jointly in a 'Convention', given the absence of the king. Furthermore, 'conventions' was the usual name adopted by self-convened colonial assemblies, in the tradition of pre-independence local rule, when they petitioned or protested against imperial fiscal impositions.

D. Political Pressure and Intimidation

Finally, revolutionary constitutionalism is often fraught with unconventional breaches of legality falling under the heading of sheer political pressure and intimidation.

For example, the final ratification of the Philadelphia Constitution by Rhode Island in 1790 took place under the threat 'of a devastating economic boycott' in the event that Rhode Island continued 'to withhold its consent'.[37] Unconventional political pressure also occurred in 1867, when the ratification of the Fourteenth Amendment was potentially blocked by 10 Southern states. Congress grouped these states into five military districts and authorised the commanders of these districts 'to call new constitutional "conventions", but only after they had compiled new voting registers' designed to favour the election of pro-ratification delegates.[38] In sum, through the Reconstruction Acts, Congress 'rather than allowing the republican governments of the South to accept *or* reject the Fourteenth Amendment … was telling them, loud and clear, that their decision to reject deprived them of all political power in the councils of the nation'.[39]

Relative to these examples, the court-packing threatened by Roosevelt in 1937, when his legislation was blocked by the Supreme Court, seems a milder sort of breach. It falls into the category of political pressure; it was only a stretching of legality, not an all-out infringement of it. Similarly, during the Civil Rights

[37] Ackerman, *supra* note 10 at 370.
[38] Ackerman, *supra* note 8 at 110.
[39] *Id.* at 111.

revolution, there was certainly heated confrontation and instances of police brutality, but such episodes fall under the headings of criminal law and political tension rather than those of higher law and constitutional reform.

In the Indian constitutional process, the moment of sharpest discontinuity occurred when Indira Gandhi declared a state of emergency in response to the Allahabad High Court's indictment of her for electoral irregularities during the 1971 elections. During the night of 25–26 June 1975, on the basis of an alleged 'imminent danger to the security of India being threatened by internal disturbance'[40] and pursuant to Article 352 of the Constitution, she called for a state of emergency. Opposition leaders and public dissenters of stature were arrested and the electric power lines to major newspapers were cut. Subsequently, emergency legislation was passed and entrenched against a possible adverse judgment on its constitutionality by the Supreme Court.[41] Indira Gandhi's state of emergency is one of the clearest cases of unconventional adaptation taking the form of *political intimidation* of opponents. However, unlike in the cases of the American Founding or Reconstruction, political intimidation of opponents was rebuked by the standard political process. When in 1977 Indira Gandhi lost control of parliament in favour of the Janata opposition alliance, she then voted to repeal her own emergency legislation.

II. Authenticity and the Constitution

This survey of varieties of unconventional adaptation suggests that the quality and degree of intensity of breaches of legality that accompany constitutional transformations do not significantly affect the public's perception of the 'authenticity of the constitution' or the growth of 'constitutional patriotism'. France, between the Fourth and the Fifth Republics, underwent ruptures instigated by a single charismatic leader and vindicated in a plebiscitary manner,[42] not too unlike what has occurred in Erdogan's Turkey in the twenty-first century. Yet, Gaullist presidentialism is perceived by French citizens as more legitimate than Italian constituencies perceive their hyper-constrained parliamentary prime ministers, who are perhaps more in line with the spirit of their Constitution.[43] India's lack of a revolutionary

[40] Quoted in Pranab Mukherjee, The Dramatic Decade: The Indira Gandhi Years 4 (2015).

[41] See Ackerman, *supra* note 10 at 68.

[42] See Gaetano Quagliariello, De Gaulle e il gollismo 556–65 (2003).

[43] During the so-called First Republic (1948–92), Italian cabinets lasted 11 months on average and during the so-called Second Republic (1994–2013) about 21 months. Still, the public perception of a need to correct the Westminster-type arrangement grew, mostly in the direction of support for a landmark statute changing the electoral rules. However, if cabinets lasted only for a short time, the coalition of parties that guaranteed confidence votes for Christian-Democrat-led cabinets was much more stable. 'Centrism' (Christian-Democrats plus other moderate to conservative parties, excluding the left) lasted from 1947 to 1963, 'Centrosinistra' (the same as the above, but with the Socialists in place of the laissez-faire Liberal Party) lasted from 1963 to 1976 and the so-called 'Pentapartito'

rupture does not make its citizens perceive the Constitution as less authentically theirs than the authorisation breaches undergirding the Philadelphia Convention make the US Constitution appear to American citizens. Ben-Gurion's betrayal of his previous commitment to the constitutional effort invoked by the Declaration of Independence did not make Israeli citizens identify less with the constitutional order emerging from the Basic Laws.

Second, the key to a constitution's success in being recognised for 'reasons of principle' as the focal point of a dualist scheme of democratic governance, and in integrating society,[44] appears to be related not to the unconventional aspects of the constitution-making process, but to the *authentic* connection of the substance of the constitution with the will of the citizens. This connection could be successfully evoked by the relevant actors in the cases of India, South Africa, Italy, France, Israel and Iran. It has instead experienced substantial enfeeblement in the case of Poland and has ultimately been aborted in the case of Burma. The analysis of varieties of unconventional adaptation has thus introduced us to the object of this section: the nexus – solid or tenuous, authentic or less authentic – of the constitution with the political will of the authors to which it is imputed.

At over a dozen junctures of Ackerman's argument, the terms 'authenticity' and 'authentic' are used in relation to constitutional texts and actors' moves within a struggle over constitutional meanings. Conceptual fine-tuning of this notion is urgent both at this stage of Ackerman's project and in view of the announced salience of 'the authenticity problem' for the elite constitutions.

A. Two Meanings of the Authenticity of a Constitution

Let me start with some of Ackerman's points. The Indian and South African experiences of revolutionary constitutionalism shared in common (a) outsider-initiated social movements which gave rise to (b) an organised political party, which in turn (c) played a central role in the transformation of the old regime and within which

(the same as the above, but with both the Liberal Party and the Socialists) lasted from 1980 to 1992. See Luca Tentoni, Fasi politiche e durata dei governi, October 15, 2016, https://www.mentepolitica.it/articolo/fasi-politiche-e-durata-dei-governi/1002. Prime ministers (and ministers) changed, but the political substance remained pretty much unchanged. In the Second Republic instead, the fall of longer-lasting cabinets coincided with the alternation between centre-left (post-Communist-led) and centre-right (Berlusconi-led) coalitions or 'poles'. The 10 longer-lasting cabinets are equally distributed across the First Republic (Craxi I, 1983–86; Moro III, 1966–68; De Gasperi VII, 1951–53; Segni I, 1955–57; and Andreotti VI, 1989–91) and the Second Republic (Berlusconi II, 2001–05; Berlusconi IV, 2008–11; Renzi I, 2014–16; Prodi I, 1996–98; and Prodi II, 2006–08). Yet the perceived inconclusiveness of governmental action across the two 'Republics' has generated a powerful political demand for correction in the direction of strengthening the executive.

[44] As Dieter Grimm puts it, 'a constitution is subject to expectations that extend far beyond its normative regulatory function. People expect the constitution to unify their society as a polity, thereby transcending the differences of opinion and conflicting interests that exist in all societies'; in Dieter Grimm, *Integration by Constitution*, 3(2) I-CON 194 (2005).

(d) a small circle of leaders gained *symbolic centrality*.[45] These conditions enabled Nehru and Ambedkar in India, and Mandela in South Africa to gain recognition for their countries' constitutions 'as *authentic* expressions of the principles that had inspired a generation to sacrifice greatly in support of the INC/ANC liberation struggles'.[46]

This claim to authenticity becomes less convincing when the unity of the four factors is fragmented, because the social roots of the political organisation are less capillary,[47] because factionalism arises[48] or because rival personalities vie viciously with each other (as in Poland). But Italy and France show that even in these non-ideal circumstances, the 'Constitution's claim to authenticity' can be vindicated.

An initially dubious, risky, but ultimately successful claim of authenticity is connected with the French transition from the Fourth Republic to the Fifth Republic. At the height of an unprecedented crisis, through a mix of charisma, savvy use of the media and the concurrence of favourable circumstance, de Gaulle managed to convince his fellow citizens that the new presidential republic should be understood as 'an authentic effort by We the People of France to revolutionize the foundations of their government'.[49] Half a century later, this presidentialist constitution is still perceived by French citizens as their own. The Italian case is different. In spite of common journalistic references to a Second Republic, Italy never experienced substantial alteration of the basic structure of its 1948 Constitution. The Renzi government in 2016 pursued a major reform, but the failure of this attempt has strengthened the perception of the 1948 Constitution as a bulwark against all 'post-liberal' temptations.

Instead, Walesa's inability to vindicate the Constitution, in the eyes of his fellow citizens, 'as an authentic expression of Solidarity's decade-long struggle against Communist authoritarianism',[50] has resulted in a vulnerability of Polish democracy to all sorts of illiberal attacks. Israel offers another significant example in the area of authenticity. The Kohn draft for the Constitution, which was never enacted as such, mentioned 'the dignity of man' as a fundamental constitutional value. Aside from the Irish Constitution of 1937 and the German *Grundgesetz* and the UDHR of 1948, no other constitutional document at that time mentioned this normative notion.[51] In the Israeli context, Ackerman argues that the constitutional

[45] Ackerman, *supra* note 10 at 116.

[46] *Id.*

[47] This is the difference that separates the Gandhi-Nehru experience from the Mandela experience.

[48] This is what sets the Italian and the French experiences apart from the Indian and South African experiences.

[49] Ackerman, *supra* note 10 at 170.

[50] *Id.* at 227.

[51] At a subsequent time, an impressive number of Constitutions embedded some reference to human dignity: Afghanistan (Articles 6 and 24); Albania (preamble), Andorra (Articles 4 and 29); Angola (preamble and Articles 7, 31, 32, 89); Armenia (Article 23); Azerbaijan (Articles 13, 18, 24, 46); Bahrain (Article 18); Bangladesh (Schedule 7); Belgium (Article 23); Belize (Article 3); Bolivia (Article 73); Bosnia and Herzegovina (Preamble): Brazil (Articles 1 and 226); Burundi (Articles 14, 21 and 27); Colombia (Articles 1 and 53); Congo (Article 36); Costa Rica (Article 33); Cote d'Ivoire

value of 'human dignity', especially when linked to the preservation of 'the sanctity of human life', 'would have gained worldwide significance in the light of the Holocaust'.[52] This is a point about authenticity. A dignity-centred constitution would have acquired a profound quality of authenticity by virtue of the experience of the Holocaust. No other constitution, though mentioning human dignity, could have anchored the principle of human dignity in a tragic historical experience of unique significance for humanity in its entirety.

To complete the picture, the whole pathway of elite constitutionalism is argued to be negatively affected by the 'authenticity problem',[53] with very different manifestations in today's Spain, Germany and Japan. Only the 'establishmentarian' pathway seems to be relatively free of the 'authenticity problem'.

But what does it mean for a constitution to be 'authentic'? A constitution's authenticity apparently resides in its capacity to be expressive of the will of the people. However, many institutional acts can be imputed to a 'demos' in a contingent, non-defining, less-than-authentic way. The 'demos', then, might as well *not* have performed such acts and still represent itself as the same political subject. Thus, in order for an act to count as an *authentic* expression of the people's will, some special relationship must connect the subject and its act.

As regards persons, we understand this special relationship as an exemplary, disinterested alignment of the subject's inner states and outer conduct, which generates a sense that, to use Bernard William's phrase, 'some things are in some real sense really you, or express what you are, and others aren't'.[54] In other words, such alignment amounts not only to full autonomy, but also to shaping one's life

(Preamble, Article 2); Cuba (Article 42, 43); Czech Republic (Preamble, Article 10); Dominican Republic (Preamble, Articles 5, 7), Egypt (Preamble, Article 78); Equatorial Guinea (Article 14); Eritrea (Preamble); Estonia (Article 10), Ethiopia (Articles 21, 24, 29, 30, 91); Fiji (Preamble, Chapter 1, 1); Finland (Chapter 1, 2); Gambia (Article 31); Greece (Article 7, 106); Guinea-Bissau (Article 17); Haiti (Article 44); Honduras (Article 60); Hungary (Preamble, Articles 2, 9, 37); Indonesia (Article 34); Italy (Article 41); Jordan (Article 8); Kazakhstan (Article 17); Kenya (Articles 10, 20, 24); Korea (Article 32); Kosovo (Article 23); Kuwait (Article 29); Kyrgyzstan (Articles 20, 22); Latvia (Preamble); Liechtenstein (Article 27 bis); Madagascar (Article 29); Malawi (Articles 19, 42); Maldives (Article 68); Mexico (Articles 1, 3); Moldova (Preamble, Articles 1, 3); Morocco (Article 22); Mozambique (Article 119); Myanmar (Article 44); Namibia (Articles 8, 98); Nicaragua (Article 82); Niger (Article 50); Nigeria (Articles 17, 21); Oman (Article 31); Pakistan (Article 11); Panama (Preamble); Paraguay (Preamble, Articles 1, 68); Philippines (Article 13); Portugal (Article 26); Romania (Article 1); Russian Federation (Article 1); Sao Tome and Principe (Preamble); Serbia (Article 19, 23, 69); Sierra Leone (Article 8); the Solomon Islands (Preamble); Somalia (Article 10); South Africa (Chapters 1, 7); South Sudan (Preamble, Part one); St Lucia (Preamble); St Vincent and the Grenadines (Preamble); Sudan (Preamble, Chapter 1, Part Two, Article 45); Suriname (Article 16); Swaziland (Chapter 3, 5); Switzerland (Articles 7, 119, 119A), Syrian Arab Republic (Article 19); Tanzania (Chapter 1); Thailand (Chapters 1, 3); Tunisia (Article 23); Turkey (Article 17); Tuvalu (Preamble, Part 2); Uganda (Articles 16, 24, 35); Venezuela (Articles 47, 55, 80, 81, 332); Zimbabwe (Articles 46, 50, 51, 56, 62, 86).

[52] ACKERMAN, *supra* note 10 at 314.

[53] *Id.* at 18.

[54] See Bernard Williams, quoted in Steven Jeffries, *The Quest for Truth*, THE GUARDIAN, November 30, 2002, https://www.theguardian.com/books/2002/nov/30/academicexperts.highereducation.

after a model not imported, even if willingly, from without, but 'found within'.[55] Rousseau's implicit ethics of authenticity equates full human flourishing with 'being true to my own originality, which is something only I can articulate and *discover*'.[56] For Herder, the same applies to a people *qua* ethnic entity, a *Volk*; also, a *Volk* should be true to its unique cultural identity.[57] Today, the idea of authenticity has come a long way from these formulations. It can be disentangled altogether from the dubious notion of a 'true self' and can be equated with reflective alignment between, on the one hand, core self-definitional commitments and, on the other hand, significant, non-trivial segments of the subject's life.[58]

Yet, how should the authenticity of constitutions be understood? In a similar fashion to individual subjects, peoples, in their capacity as putative collective authors of a legal charter that regulates political life, also define themselves through their actions and self-descriptions. A difficulty is posed by the simultaneous presence of three kinds of provisions in a constitution. First, constitutions include general, non-individuating provisions, usually but not exclusively consisting of the enumeration of rights and values necessary in order to give the polity a liberal-democratic shape: *A-type* provisions.

Second, constitutions include 'functional' provisions that outline the basic structure of legislative, judicial and governmental institutions and regulate their interaction: *B-type* provisions.

Third, constitutions often include provisions reflective of deep-seated normative intuitions that the framers consider to be uniquely distinctive features of the people. Through such *C-type* provisions, the framers of revolutionary constitutions convey their 'message to the world' and claim the unique place that 'the People' deserve to take, and be recognised for, in the 'space of constitutions'.

Does the authenticity of a constitution and its effects down the line (the empowerment of courts to defend it, the availability of a reservoir of constitutional patriotism and bulwarks against populist or authoritarian degenerations) depend just on the perception that the *A*- and *B-type* provisions result from the political will of the people, free from the influence of external powers ('Authenticity in the first sense'), or does it also require that certain recognisable *C-type* provisions be in place ('Authenticity in the second sense')? Two examples will clarify this question.

[55] Charles Taylor, *The Politics of Recognition*, *in* MULTICULTURALISM AND 'THE POLITICS OF RECOGNITION' 30–31 (1992).

[56] See CHARLES TAYLOR, THE ETHICS OF AUTHENTICITY (1992). On Rousseau's view of the authentic self not as an essence discovered, but as something of our own making and yet not entirely at our disposal, see ALESSANDRO FERRARA, ROUSSEAU AND CRITICAL THEORY 34 (2017).

[57] Taylor, *supra* note 55 at 31.

[58] See Alessandro Ferrara, *Authenticity without a True Self*, *in* AUTHENTICITY IN CULTURE, SELF, AND SOCIETY 32–33 (Philip Vannini & J. Patrick Williams eds., 2009).

B. The Authenticity of the Italian Constitution

For Italians, the perception of the 1948 Constitution as 'authentic' rests not simply on its originating from an elected Constitutional Assembly or on an appreciation of the framers' ability to somehow reconcile the Catholic, Marxist and liberal political cultures of the country, but first and foremost on the perception that new ground was broken. Generations of Italians, across political divisions, have always identified the qualification of Italy, in Article 1, as a democratic republic 'founded on labour' (*fondata sul lavoro*) as distinctively their own. This peculiar expression was coined by Fanfani, the Demo-Christian framer and future leader, as a compromise between the 'republic of workers', advocated by Togliatti, and the absence of any specific qualifier, advocated by the liberals. The clause has come to be understood not restrictively, as though 'working' designated an extra requirement, beyond citizenship, for participating as free and equal in the life of the republic, but as gesturing to the full inclusion and participation of citizens from all classes. Giuseppe Saragat, Constituent Assembly member and President between 1964 and 1971, famously commented that Article 1 calls attention to the priority of labour over property. Property being a product of labour, as Locke suggested, in order for property to exist and require protection, there must be labour. The expression 'founded on labour', Fanfani continues, implicitly denies that the republic might be premised on privilege, hereditary lineage or someone else's toil. It also implies that citizens have a duty to contribute to the country's flourishing and that the well-being of the national community presupposes that everyone is in a position to offer his or her best contribution to the 'common prosperity'. 'Founded on labour', Fanfani concludes, counts as a basic commitment of the Italian Constitution.[59]

In Article 3, various facets of authenticity can be observed. The first clause is a standard equality provision that is similar to analogous provisions found in many constitutions and autonomously adopted by the framers – it manifests 'authenticity in the first sense'. However, the second clause is perceived as perhaps the most important locus of the 'authenticity in the second sense' of the Italian Constitution:

> All citizens shall have equal social dignity and shall be equal before the law, without distinction of gender, race, language, religion, political opinion, personal and social conditions.
>
> It shall be the duty of the Republic to remove those obstacles of an economic or social nature which constrain the freedom and equality of citizens, thereby impeding the full development of the human person and the effective participation of all workers in the political, economic and social organisation of the country.

[59] Italian Chamber of Deputies, Digitalized Record of the Constituent Assembly. Session of 22 March 1947, http://legislature.camera.it/frameset.asp?content=%2Faltre%5Fsezionism%2F304%2F8964%2Fdocumentotesto%2Easp%3F.

The second clause, in which the liberal value of equality is combined with the Republic's 'concern' for the flourishing of 'the person', is perceived as so authentically distinctive of the Italian political identity that even after two decades of Berlusconian neoliberal individualism, followed by populism, no one has ever dared to publicly question it. The clause states that the *flourishing* of each citizen – not just his or her equality before the law – is such a paramount constitutional value that it is incumbent on *all the citizens*, and on the Republic, to remove the (mainly socio-economic) obstacles that by limiting their freedom and equality end up also limiting their potential to flourish. The second part of the second clause, which reflects the views of the communists and the socialists, is equally unique, but is perceived as dated and is not pervaded by the same aura of authenticity.

Article 3 was meant to detail what being 'founded on labour' implied for the new Republic. The framers had a clear preoccupation, nourished by historical experience, that the principle of equality of the 1789 French Revolution could remain inoperative, reduced to a merely *formal* 'equality before the law' or 'equal protection of the law', unless the powerful socio-economic impediments to the inclusion of workers within the democratic life of the country were removed. Lelio Basso, a socialist Assembly member and co-author of Article 3, connected Articles 3 and 1 in the following way:

> We do not wish to have a republic of abstract individuals, a republic of citizens who only share a legal bond, we strive to create a republic, a State in which each participates proactively through his work, in the life of all.[60]

Aldo Moro, the future Demo-Christian leader kidnapped and assassinated by the Red Brigades in 1978, understood the point of Article 3 as being a:

> [C]ommitment, on the part of the newly formed Italian State, to solve as best as possible … the problem of integrating ever more closely within the social, economic and political life of the country those working classes that, for a number of reasons, had been longer excluded from the State and from the economic and social life.[61]

These elucidations, coming from such diverse quarters, signal that Articles 1 and 3 exert not just a normative, regulatory function, but also constitute the *expressive pivot* on which the authenticity of the Italian Constitution revolves. This expressive function seems to be a precondition for perceiving the whole document as unique and distinctive.[62]

[60] *Id.* at (6.3.1947) 1824.
[61] *Id.* at (6.3.1947) 2014.
[62] On the expressive moment of higher law-making, see Cass R. Sunstein, *On the Expressive Function of Law*, 144(5). Penn. L. Rev., 1996, 144, 5, 2021 (1996); Mark Tushnet, Weak Courts, Strong Rights: Judicial Review and Social Welfare Rights in Comparative Constitutional Law 12–14 (2008): Richard Albert, The Expressive Function of Constitutional Amendment Rules, 59 McGill U. Law Journal 226 (2013).

C. Constitutional Authenticity and the EU

Let us now consider the opposite case: the implicit 'Constitution' of the EU. As an exemplar of 'supranational' constitutions – for which no basis for comparison yet exists – it is an 'implicit', very 'establishmentarian' constitution, sunk by two referenda years ago, even though the oxymoronic expression 'constitutional *treaty*' was prudently used, and yet resurrected at the heart of the subsequent Lisbon Treaty. It is a constitution associated in three out of four meanings with the word 'constitution'.

First, the *acquis communautaire* functions as a constitution for Europe in the sense of articulating what Plato and Aristotle meant by *politeia*, ie, a specification of what the main institutions of a polity are and how they relate to one another. Second, the *acquis communautaire* is a constitution in the sense, inaugurated by Magna Carta, of having provisions for the protection of the rights of individuals against the authorities. This crucial aspect resides in the Lisbon Treaty's incorporation of the Charter of Fundamental Rights, which was previously part of the Treaty of Nice, and also included in the 'Constitutional Treaty'. Third, Europe has a constitution in the sense of sharing a standard for assessing the legitimacy of the exercise of political power. The *acquis communautaire* of the EU polity functions in that sense, in combination with the practice of voluntary yielding to the will of other *demoi* on the part of each *demos*, or Weiler's Principle of Constitutional Tolerance.[63] This implicit yet effective Constitution of the EU is certainly *authentic in the first sense*. No external powers have imposed it on the Member States. However, in spite of the good reasons for treating the EU's current primary law as constitutional law,[64] the European 'Constitution' lacks appeal and any grip on the heart of the Europeans – not just of Brexiteers, but also of the continental non-Eurosceptics that Macron has tried to mobilize. The European functional 'Constitution' generates no *constitutional patriotism*. Although its provisions satisfy the requirement for authenticity in the first sense, they fail to generate a perception of the authenticity of the *acquis communataire* in the second sense: as a reflection of what the citizens of the EU stand for and of the distinctive values that they jointly affirm.

This neglect of the 'authenticity-as-uniqueness' side of the constitution-like *acquis communataire* is all the more baffling if one considers that several provisions offer ample potential for that purpose: the explicit prohibition against including the death penalty in penal law (an obvious point of contrast with current US and Chinese legislation);[65] the explicit prohibition, within medical science and

[63] Joseph Weiler, The European 'Constitution': Requiescat in Pace, 121–22, www.fundacionfaes.org/file_upload/publication/pdf/00052-11_-_the_european_constitution.pdf.

[64] Armin von Bogdandy & Jürgen Bast, eds., Principles of European Constitutional Law (2006).

[65] Lisbon Treaty version of the Charter of Fundamental Rights of the European Union, art 2.2.

biology, of 'making the human body and its parts as such a source of financial gain';[66] the constitutionalisation of the right to privacy;[67] the new right to 'freedom of information' (alongside the more traditional right to 'freedom of expression' or 'free speech') as an obligation to respect 'the freedom and pluralism' of the media, where the 'pluralism' of the media calls for legislation targeting the concentration of media property;[68] the constitutionalisation of gender equality 'in all areas';[69] 'a high level of consumer protection' in order to bridge the influence gap between big market players and single consumers without indulging in the regressive utopia of the abolition of the market;[70] and, finally, the 'right of the elderly to lead a life of dignity and independence and to participate in social and cultural life'.[71] Perhaps the neglect of these 'constitutional essentials' originates from the lack of influence of the revolutionary pathway among EU elites – only Giscard d'Estaing and Prodi, both from political cultures steeped in revolutionary constitutionalism, emphasised the word 'constitution' in 2004.

III. Conclusion

These examples illustrate how the perception of the authenticity of a constitution need not just be anchored in political autonomy – namely, in the constitution's *A*- and *B-type* provisions being 'of our own making' – but may additionally require (a) a perception that a reflection of the unique historical experience of the people is bound up with it, and b) that through the *C-type* provisions, the people contribute something to humankind's 'conversation of constitutions' – 'human dignity' in the Israeli Basic Laws, a republic 'founded on labour' and committed to remove what stands in the way of the 'full development of the human person' for the Italian people, 'government of the people, by the people, for the people' for France (as earlier for Lincoln). In the first sense, the authenticity of a constitution is linked to the *autonomy* exercised in its framing and in the second sense to the *exemplarity* of its agent-specific, people-specific contents.

Let me conclude with urging, against the backdrop of a point made by Ackerman in his discussion of Iran, that this distinction should be explored further. Noting that 'the Iranian constitution gives the Guardian Jurist far greater power to repel the advances of his democratic adversaries',[72] but at the same time

[66] *Id.* at art. 3.2c.
[67] *Id.* at art. 7.
[68] *Id.* at art. 11.2.
[69] *Id.* at art. 23. It is worth noting that the second clause of the article goes so far as to provide for the admissibility of affirmative action based on gender quotas.
[70] *Id.* at art. 38.
[71] *Id.* at art. 25.
[72] Ackerman, *supra* note 10 at 360.

obliges the Supreme Leader to *earn* that authority through the recognition of his fellow clerics and political officials, Ackerman argues that such non-monocentric structure of legitimate authority defines the difference between constitutionalism and despotism: 'Dictators also encounter resistance to their commands, but they refuse to recognize that such shows of opposition are legitimate. Constitutional regimes, in contrast, require the most powerful officials to engage in ongoing competition with institutional rivals for the final say over the future course of political development.'[73] Such is the case with Iran, in spite of the theocratic bent of its constitutional culture.

The broader implication is that constitutionalism represents a principle even more fundamental than those expressed by the liberal Enlightenment. While all forms of liberalism – including Rawls' 'political liberalism' – are premised on the equality of citizens and of their rights, constitutions are responsive to the more basic principle that power cannot emanate from one centre alone. Legitimately, it can only be exercised by institutionally serious rivals who engage in an ongoing contestation over the country's future. While liberalism is the standard for building a polity of *free and equals* who pursue their visions of happiness, constitutionalism, in whatever variant, is larger than liberalism and has a worldwide reach, which liberalism cannot match. Constitutionalism provides the grammar of *political decency*. That such a baseline standard of decency mandates not just uniformity with a *passe-partout* model, but makes it possible to express the uniqueness of each people's historical experience, is the teaching that *Revolutionary Constitutions* affirms.

[73] *Id.*

10

Constitutional Revolution, Legal Positivism and Constituent Power

YASUO HASEBE*

Ackerman's *Revolutionary Constitutions* dynamically describes ideal types and concrete cases of constitutional revolution. His theory is gripping and overwhelming. To avoid becoming mesmerised, I will focus on just two issues: the difference between Ackermanian constitutional revolution and positivist conceptions of revolution (section I); and the similarity between Jean-Jacque Rousseau's 'Lawgiver' and Ackermanian charismatic leaders of constitutional revolution, closely related to the difference between totalising revolution and revolution on a human scale (section II).

I. Constitutional Revolution and Legal Positivism

A. Constitutional Revolution in Light of Hartian Theory

In Chapter 1 of *Revolutionary Constitutions*,[1] Ackerman expressly distinguishes his conception of constitutional revolution from positivist conceptions of revolution:

> If, for example, the state is suddenly dominated by lawmakers who transform basic principles in a big way, the positivist doesn't count this change as 'revolutionary' if it is enacted in conformity with the pre-existing constitution. It's only when these foundational rules are broken that the positivist recognizes that something 'revolutionary' is going on.
>
> It is here we part company. The positivist definition is both over-inclusive and under-inclusive for my purposes. It is too broad since a decisive break with the established 'rule of recognition' may be achieved down all three pathways. Suppose, for example, that the

* The author wishes to thank Richard Albert, Alessandro Ferrara, Stephen Gardbaum and, above all, Bruce Ackerman for their illuminating and encouraging comments on earlier drafts of this chapter.

[1] Bruce Ackerman, Revolutionary Constitutions: Charismatic Leadership and the Rule of Law 36–37 (2019).

> new constitutional order is an elite construction which has been imposed in violation of the old rule of recognition. This is enough to make it revolutionary for the positivist, but it fails my test, since the new regime is not the product of a mobilized movement that has self-consciously repudiated the status quo to demand a 'new beginning' in the name of the People.
>
> Positivism is also under-inclusive. Some insurgent movements at Time One manage to constitutionalize their revolutions at Time Two *without* breaking any of the old regime's rules for formal amendment. Although a revolutionary regime's legalistic link to the past may play a secondary role in gaining political legitimacy, the relationship between its experience at Time One and Time Two is far more important. As we shall see, its success in constitutionalizing its charisma at Time Two will set up a distinctive set of legitimation problems at later stages of development.

These paragraphs are a little confusing. Ackerman rightly asserts that 'a decisive break with the established "rule of recognition" may be achieved … without breaking any of the old regime's rules for formal amendment'. However, he cannot then conclude that the positivist does not count a significant change in basic principles as 'revolutionary' if 'enacted in conformity with the pre-existing constitution'.

The rule of recognition forms the cornerstone of HLA Hart's legal theory.[2] As Ackerman apparently suggests, it would not be unreasonable to suppose that, for Hart, a revolution occurs when the ultimate rule of recognition changes, entailing the end of one legal system and/or the emergence of a new one.[3] It is quite sensible to call such phenomena 'revolutions' from the legal point of view. In this understanding, even when changes to a constitution's basic principles follow its amendment procedure, acceptance by judges and officials that the ultimate rule of recognition has changed would confirm the occurrence of a revolution in the Hartian sense.

Consequently, this Hartian conception of revolution is obviously over-inclusive in Ackerman's analysis of constitutional revolution. Countries which took the establishmentarian pathway, such as Australia, Canada and New Zealand, should be eliminated from the 'constitutional revolution' club[4] because their ultimate rules of recognition are not 'the product of a mobilized movement that has self-consciously repudiated the status quo to demand a "new beginning" in the name of the People'. The same conclusion applies to countries which took the elite-construction pathway, such as Germany and Japan, where judges and public

[2] Some scholars argue that there may be various ultimate rules of recognition in a legal system. See Joseph Raz, The Concept of a Legal System 200 (2nd ed. 1980). For an opposite view, see Matthew Kramer &, H.L.A. Hart, The Nature of Law 84–88 (2018). Since this issue is unimportant in this chapter, I will use the singular expression 'the ultimate rule of recognition'.

[3] I regard this as congruent with Hart's considered view, although he also suggests that 'revolution' only denotes a situation where 'rival claims to govern are made from within the group' of people (H.L.A. Hart, The Concept of Law 118 (3rd ed. 2012)). Some may argue that this should be termed 'disruption of the continuity of a legal system' instead of 'revolution', but the choice of wording is unimportant for the present purposes.

[4] Ackerman, *supra* note 1 at 5.

officials of the new regimes would obviously accept that the rules of recognition have changed without any popular movement.[5] But is the Hartian conception under-inclusive? I am inclined to disagree.

Let us consider the case of India, which apparently corroborates Ackerman's under-inclusive thesis.[6] The Indian Independence Act 1947 was enacted by the UK Parliament in Westminster. It accorded independence to India and gave the Indian legislature full law-making power, no longer subordinated to the UK Parliament's authority.[7] The 'positivist' imagined by Ackerman would say that since India's independence and law-making power were granted by the Westminster Parliament, its constituent power was also accorded by the same parliament. Ackerman observes that the constituent assembly was not 'summoned in a fashion which marked a decisive break with the "rules of recognition" established by the previous regime'.[8] Therefore, the Constitution of India adopted in 1949 and effective from 1950 was not established in violation of the former rule of recognition; rather, the new Constitution was premised on the idea that laws established in accordance with UK parliamentary decisions were valid in India. Such a way of thinking is obviously under-inclusive for Ackerman's purposes.

However, Hart would not agree with Ackerman's interpretation of 'the positivist': he would contend that after the establishment of the Constitution of India, judges and public officials accepted a new ultimate rule of recognition, directing them to implement laws which are valid because they ultimately accord with that constitution – which now has a 'local root' – rather than with directions from the UK Parliament. Regarding the 'well-behaved dominions' of Australia, Canada and New Zealand, whose constitutions were originally enacted by the UK Parliament, Hart contends that their ultimate rules of recognition have now shifted and new legal systems have emerged, such that the UK Parliament's legal competence to legislate for these former colonies is no longer recognised.[9] The argument he develops on Australia, Canada and New Zealand would also apply to India. Following Hart, just as post-independence Canadian judges embrace the ultimate rule of recognition which has now a 'local root', Indian judges similarly embrace the 'local root' of the new rule of recognition. Were the UK Parliament to purportedly retract India's independence and declare that it can still make laws for India, Indian judges would dismiss such action as nonsensical.

[5] *Id.* at 6–7.

[6] *Id.* at 59–61.

[7] Article 1, clause 1 of the Indian Independence Act of 1947 stipulates that: 'as from the fifteenth day of August, nineteen hundred and forty-seven, two independent Dominions shall be set up in India, to be known respectively as India and Pakistan'. Its art. 6, clause 1 stipulates that 'The Legislature of each of the new Dominions shall have full power to make laws for that Dominion' and clause 2 stipulates that: 'No law and no provision of any law made by the Legislature of either of the new Dominions shall be void or inoperative on the ground that it is repugnant to the law of England, or to the provisions of this or any existing or future Act of Parliament of the United Kingdom.'

[8] Ackerman, *supra* note 1 at 59. The processes of making the constitution are summarily described in Arun K. Thiruvengadam, The Constitution of India 26–34 (2017).

[9] Hart, *supra* note 3 at 120.

Hart admits that judges may accept the ultimate rule of recognition for various reasons; for instance, in accepting that public officials, including judges, should obey a constitution and the laws enacted in accordance therewith, they might not sincerely accept the contents to be morally justified.[10] But this does not mean that judges would revolt against a constitution established in an Ackermanian constitutional revolution or deny its supremacy independent of the UK Parliament. While they remain judges, they cannot but claim, or at least pretend, that the constitution is morally justified, thereby implying that the constitutional revolution leading to its establishment was also morally justified. Therefore, the Indian case does not ultimately corroborate Ackerman's under-inclusive thesis as to Hartian theory.[11]

The same conclusion applies to the French Fifth Republic.[12] General de Gaulle demanded that the Fourth Republic Constitution be revised and changed into a new constitution to reflect his idea that the country should be led by the strong president, since parliament was immobilised by quarrelling political parties. To accomplish the required change, the amending clause of the 1946 Constitution (Article 90) was first changed, and the new Constitution was then drafted and adopted in accordance with the changed amending process,[13] that is, 'without breaking any of the old regime's rules for formal amendment'. The Ackermanian 'positivist' may assert that, since the new Constitution's validity can be traced to the former Constitution of 1946, there is no revolution in the legal sense.

However, for the same reason as for India, Hart would disagree with this conclusion. He would argue that judges and public officials have accepted a new ultimate rule of recognition that directs them to implement statutes enacted in accordance with the 1958 Constitution and not that of 1946. Since the ultimate rule of recognition has changed, he would say that a revolution occurred. While statutes which contravene the Declaration of the Rights of Man and of the Citizen of 1789 and the preamble to the 1946 Constitution are declared unconstitutional and void, this is because the preamble to the 1958 Constitution directs the Conseil constitutionnel to regard these instruments as standards of constitutional review rather than foundations to the current Constitution's validity.[14]

[10] H.L.A. Hart, Essays on Bentham 265–68 (1982); H.L.A. Hart, Essays on Jurisprudence and Philosophy 9–10 (1983). It should be noted that, as Joseph Raz points out, such a view is incompatible with judges performing their professional duties; therefore, judges with such views must 'pretend' to fully endorse the moral justifiability of laws they apply. See Joseph Raz, The Authority of Law 155 note 13 (2nd ed., 2009). It seems that Hart misinterprets Raz's view as holding that judges should at least pretend that *every* positive law in a legal system is morally justified.

[11] Ackerman is right to suggest that positivist theories do not explain why the Indian people accept the Constitution as legitimate (Ackerman, *supra* note 1 at 60), but this is irrelevant to the pertinence of the under-inclusive thesis.

[12] *Id.* at ch. 8.

[13] See Francis Hamon and Michel Troper, Droit Constitutionnel, 446 (37th ed., 2016). Ackerman rightly points out that both Mendès-France and Mitterrand, who opposed de Gaulle's constitutional change as a coup d'etat, 'could point to no technical violation of the constitutional rules of the Fourth Republic'; Ackerman, *supra* note 1 at 177.

[14] I think that Hart would say so because he was an inclusive (or soft) positivist. He thinks that the rule of recognition may recognise these instruments expressing political morality as positive laws. See Hart, *supra* note 3 at 250–54.

I do not find any of the other cases discussed in Ackerman's book, including South Africa,[15] to better corroborate his under-inclusive thesis. Neither the 'peace treaty' character of the Constitution of South Africa nor the step-by-step transformation of the political regime makes it any less likely that Hart would recognise a change in the rule of recognition, as the Kempton Park settlement has become accepted by the entire populace. As explained below, since the Hartian revolution is a change of legal practice, we should not expect an abrupt change in the legal system's foundation; judges and public officials would only gradually change their attitudes and way of thinking.

It is important not to conflate the ultimate rule of recognition with the constitution.[16] Very simplistically, a state's ultimate rule of recognition requires public officials (as well as citizens) to treat the constitution as the standard to judge whether a given rule is a valid law in that state. Obviously, the rule of recognition should be distinguished from the constitution in this case. If the rule of recognition is included in the constitutional text, this entails an extremely vicious self-reference. We cannot take a constitutional text seriously which asserts: 'You should obey me because I tell you so.' Besides, the ultimate rule of recognition is a duty-imposing rule, whereas constitutional provisions confer powers on and regulate constitutional organs.[17] Their functions thus differ.

While a constitution can be changed in accordance with its amendment process, it is difficult to find a case in which the ultimate rule of recognition is changed in accordance with any formal process. The ultimate rule of recognition is a customary practice shared among judges, public officials and private persons, in charge of applying rules recognised as valid in the legal system. 'Its existence is a matter of fact'[18] and it 'is seldom expressly formulated as a rule … its existence is shown in the way in which particular rules are identified, either by courts or other officials or private persons or their advisers.'[19]

The ultimate rule of recognition emerges, consolidates and gradually declines. It is sometimes violently attacked and destroyed, but would not be changed in accordance with a formal process because it cannot be enacted. The ultimate rule of recognition can only be customary: in order for a legislature to enact it, there must be another superior rule which accords that authority to the legislature, which is a manifest contradiction.[20] Thus, the ultimate rule of recognition is not immediately changed by any legislative fiat. Its change needs time, and whether and how such change occurs depends on various contingent factors, such as political situations, the society's history and protagonists' personalities.

[15] See Ackerman, *supra* note 1, ch. 3, particularly at 96–100.

[16] See John Gardner, Law as a Leap of Faith 102–16 (2012).

[17] Raz, *supra* note 2 at 198–99; Gardner, *supra* note 16 at 103. It may be said that officials who should recognise certain norms as positive laws are also conferred the powers to do so. However, such a way of saying is without substance. Should we say that a citizen who should pay a tax is also conferred a power to pay it?

[18] Hart, *supra* note 3 at 110.

[19] *Id.* at 101.

[20] See the clear explanation on this point by Gardner, *supra* note 16 at 102.

Regarding the Israeli example, Ackerman's 'positivist' may say that the Transition Law, which violated the express terms of the Declaration of Independence by transforming the Constituent Assembly into a British-style parliament, also violated the rule of recognition.[21] However, Hart would retort that, during such tremendous post-independence turmoil, there was not yet any ultimate rule of recognition commonly shared among judges, public officials and ordinary citizens. As Hart reasons,[22] it is not rare for uncertainty in the rule of recognition to be detected, particularly in cases of revolution, foreign occupation or independence.

I think that studies of Ackermanian constitutional revolution should not lightly disregard the ultimate rule of recognition. In order to accomplish a constitutional revolution, public officials and ordinary citizens must accept that the current laws' validity should be judged, at least partly, by whether they are established in accordance with the new constitution entrenching the revolutionary charisma. Without this professional acceptance, robust constitutional review would not emerge at Time Four. It is thus an indispensable component of a successful constitutional revolution.[23]

At the same time, many revolutionary ideas formulated in a written constitution should be refined through judicial interpretations, rendering them effective criteria for public officials and ordinary citizens to judge whether a given norm is a positive law in their society. Without such judicial endeavours, revolutionary ideas, which are typically vague principles, could not guide people's conduct.

B. Constitutional Revolution in Light of Kelsenian Theory

Ackerman also repeatedly refers to Hans Kelsen.[24] Does Kelsen's idea of revolution correspond to Ackerman's 'positivist' view? Hart may think so.

In criticising Kelsen's theory, Hart suggests a 'wild hypothetical example' where the UK Parliament passes 'an Act which purports to validate the law of the Soviet Union by providing that the laws currently effective in Soviet territory … shall be valid'.[25] Under this 'Soviet Laws Validity Act', the validity of every effective Soviet law could apparently be traced to this fictitious statute, on the basis of which Kelsen cannot but admit that the Soviet and British legal systems actually form one legal system: a weird conclusion. Conversely, from Hart's perspective, Soviet judges and public officials would not recognise the British legislature's operations as criteria for identifying the law they must enforce, and so would disregard this absurd statute. If applied to the examples of constitution-building in the 'well-behaved

[21] *cf* ACKERMAN, *supra* note at 1303–05. Ackerman does not say so expressly.

[22] HART, *supra* note 3, ch. VI, s. 3 and ch. VII, s. 4.

[23] What I said here seems broadly congruent with Ackerman's analysis of legal professionals' attitudes during a constitutional revolution; ACKERMAN, *supra* note 1 at 9–10. I wonder whether Ackerman has to repudiate the rule of recognition.

[24] *Id.* at 60, 143 and 245.

[25] HART, ESSAYS ON JURISPRUDENCE AND PHILOSOPHY, *supra* note 10 at 319.

dominions', Hart thinks Kelsen must conclude that these countries remain under the authority of the UK Parliament which originally enacted their constitutions; Hart's own view, by contrast, is that the ultimate rules of recognition have already shifted and new legal systems have emerged in these countries. Therefore, his idea of the rule of recognition is more common-sensical than Kelsen's basic norm.[26]

Kelsen may disagree with Hart. In his *Pure Theory of Law*, Kelsen states:

> By regulating its own creation and application, the legal order determines the beginning and the end of the validity of the legal norms. Written constitutions usually contain special rules concerning the method by which they can be changed. The principle that a norm of a legal order is valid until its validity is terminated in a way determined by this legal order or replaced by the validity of another norm of this order, is called the principle of legitimacy ... [However,] this principle does not apply in case of a revolution. A revolution in the broader sense of the word is every not legitimate change of this constitution or its replacement by an other constitution ... Decisive is only that the valid constitution has been changed or replaced in a manner not prescribed by the constitution valid until then.[27]

Kelsen seems to assert that, as far as a constitution is intact or changed according to its own rules concerning the *method* for change, it remains the same and identical constitution.[28]

However, the above paragraph allows another interpretation, which I consider more congenial to Kelsen's legal theory as a whole. His above explanation is situated in the context of trying to elucidate the concept of the basic norm. What he intends to make clear is that, when a revolution occurs and a new constitution becomes valid, 'so simultaneously changes the basic norm'.[29]

A typical case is where the old constitution underpinned an absolute monarchy and the new one a parliamentary democracy. Kelsen summarises this situation as follows

> [T]he new basic norm no longer reads: coercive acts ought to be carried out under the conditions and manners as determined by general and individual norms posited by the absolute monarch or the organs authorized by him; instead, the basic norm reads: coercive acts ought to be carried out under the conditions and manners as determined by the new constitution and general and individual norms posited by the parliament elected in accordance with the new constitution or the organs authorized by the parliament.[30]

[26] Raz shares this view. See Raz, *supra* note 10 at 127–28.

[27] Hans Kelsen, Pure Theory of Law, Max Knight, trans., 209 (1967). A similar explanation appears in Hans Kelsen, General Theory of Law and State, Anders Wedberg, trans., 117 (1945).

[28] This is the understanding that Raz endorses: 'according to his [Kelsen's] theory, two momentary systems A and B belong to the same legal system if, and only if, the creation of all the laws of B which are not identical with laws of A was authorized by the laws of A'; Raz, *supra* note 2 at 188.

[29] Kelsen, Pure Theory of Law, *supra* note 27 at 210; *cf* Kelsen, General Theory of Law and State, *supra* note 27 at 118.

[30] Kelsen, Pure Theory of Law, *supra* note 27 at 210. Here, I do not strictly follow Max Knight's translation.

Thus, a factor that is decisive for the occurrence of a revolution is whether the basic norm has changed. If a regime changes from an absolute monarchy into a parliamentary democracy, the basic norm thereby changes, constituting a revolution. While the former is based on the sovereignty of an absolute monarch, the latter is based on the principle of popular sovereignty. If the change were authorised and continued to be authorised by the sovereign monarch ordering the populace to take command of democratic government from time X_1, the monarch at a later time X_2 could retrieve governmental power, which is manifestly absurd.

Kelsen's above-cited explanation states that the principle of legitimacy – whereby the validity of a legal order norm can only be terminated as determined by that order – 'does not apply in case of a revolution'. Even when the change from absolute monarchy to parliamentary democracy is executed in conformity with the former constitution's amendment clause, a revolution is still a revolution: 'From the point of legal science it is irrelevant whether this change of legal situation has been brought about … by the member of the [legitimate] government or by a mass movement of the population.'[31] A manner of change 'not prescribed by the constitution valid until then' should be read broadly; it does not denote merely the amendment process prescribed by the former constitution.

Is the Kelsenian theory so understood over- or under-inclusive for Ackerman's purposes? I think that we cannot reach a decisive conclusion on this question, since unlike Hart's rule of recognition, Kelsen's basic norm is a transcendental presupposition and not a matter of fact.

One possible way to explain Kelsen's basic norm is as follows: Kelsen starts from the specific image of a somewhat eccentric person living in a given legal system,[32] who thinks that he must obey every positive law in the society. How is such a way of thinking possible? He cannot justify his view by appealing to some objective moral idea, because each person has his own idea of morality; each form of morality is subjective. Therefore, he must rely on the idea that a given law is posited by an authoritative organ, whose authority is granted by its superior law. Yet this chain of legitimation ultimately leads to the historically first constitution, which might be created after a revolution or the state achieving independence. At this stage, the only explanation is that the person presupposes the basic norm stating that we must obey this historically first constitution.[33]

[31] *Id.* at 209. Relying on this point, many Japanese constitutional scholars argue that the validity of Japan's current Constitution, despite its establishment conforming with the preceding Meiji Constitution's amendment process, presupposes the occurrence of a revolution in the legal sense in August 1945. See, for example, Yasuo Hasebe, *The August Revolution Thesis and the Making of the Constitution of Japan*, 17 Rechtstheorie, Beiheft 335 (1997).

[32] Raz calls him 'the legal man'. See Raz, *supra* note 10 at 141–42.

[33] Kelsen, Pure Theory of Law, *supra* note 27 at 198–205. According to Kelsen's restatement in his later years, 'the basic norm says: we ought to obey the constitution and, consequently, the legal norms established in conformity with the constitution'; Hans Kelsen, *On the Pure Theory of Law*, 1 Isr. L. Rev. 1, 6 (1966).

This hypothetical man may not be conscious of his own presupposition, but as in Kant's categorical imperative, the validity of the explanation relying on this presupposition does not depend on such consciousness.

According to Kelsen's explanation, a revolution occurs when the imagined man changes his presupposition for why he must obey every positive law in the society. However, it is very difficult to tell whether and when a revolution occurs. Since the basic norm is a transcendental presupposition, *pace* Hart, we cannot definitely say that the constitution-building in Canada, for example, did not constitute a revolution in the Kelsenian sense. We may say that, after independence, the hypothetical man purporting to represent Canadian people changed his basic norm and now thinks he must obey the Canadian Constitution, not the UK Parliament.

However, we could also assume that the hypothetical man did not change his basic norm and continues to presuppose one demanding obedience of the UK Parliament and, consequently, all legal norms established in conformity with its orders. Both conclusions are valid as coherent explanations of why the person thinks every Canadian law should be obeyed and are broadly congruent with the social facts in contemporary Canadian society. Likewise, for India and France, we cannot be sure whether these societies' basic norms have changed because they are not matters of fact.

In conclusion, we cannot definitely say whether the Kelsenian theory is over- or under-inclusive for Ackerman's purposes.

II. Rousseau's Lawgiver and Constitutional Revolution

A. Rousseau's Lawgiver

Readers of Ackerman's narrative on various charismatic leaders of constitutional revolutions may be inclined to associate them with the 'Lawgiver' (*le législateur*) described by Jean-Jacques Rousseau in his *Of the Social Contract*.[34] Charismatic leaders not only radically transform the basic framework and principles of social life but also entrench the framework and principles in the form of constitutional law. They establish new nations and new states.

Rousseau's Lawgiver 'dares to institute a people'. He is 'in every respect an extraordinary man' and 'must feel capable of, so to speak, changing human nature; of transforming each individual who by himself is a perfect and solitary whole into

[34] Jean-Jacques Rousseau, Of the Social Contract (1762); hereinafter, I refer to pages of Jean-Jacques Rousseau, The Social Contract and Other Later Political Writings, Victor Gourevitch, ed. and trans. (1997). Recent analyses of Rousseau's Lawgiver include Alessandro Ferrara, Rousseau and Critical Theory 46–50 (2017) (pointing out the significance of the chapter entitled 'Of the People' (Book II, ch. 8) of Of the Social Contract in understanding Rousseau's Lawgiver).

part of a larger whole from which that individual would as it were receive his life and being'.[35] A Lawgiver drafts the laws of the society, but has no legislative power. Only the people, who establish laws through free suffrage, can decide whether the Lawgiver's draft conforms with the general will.[36]

Rousseau cites Lycurgus, Moses, Muhammad and Calvin as examples of Lawgivers. They intend to make the people obey the laws they draft in the similar way as the people obey the laws of nature. Since their reason is so sublime that the people cannot understand it, Lawgivers draw on divine authority to secure public belief in the merits of their laws.[37] At the origin of nations, religion serves as the instrument of politics.[38]

It should be noted that the 'laws' (*loix*) Rousseau discusses here are not ordinary laws, like present-day parliamentary statutes;[39] rather, they are fundamental laws of the society – in other words, constitutions. In this regard, Rousseau clearly distinguishes between sovereignty and government: the former is the people's power to make (constitutional) laws, while the latter is the function of dealing with the day-to-day business of the state. Enacting various present-day statutes, such as those regulating specific industries or setting tariffs to be imposed on specific goods, fall into the latter category. These statutes have specific subjects; therefore, they are products of particular rather than general will. The people's sovereign power should only make laws on general subjects.

Constitutional scholars tend to regard Rousseau's 'laws' as the equivalent of today's parliamentary statutes. Therefore, they tend to think that people in the Rousseauian polity should be endowed with the power to instruct their parliamentary representatives on how to speak and vote on specific issues (*mandat impératif*). However, this is quite contrary to Rousseau's idea. The polity in which people instruct their representatives on specific issues every day should be characterised as a direct democracy. Rousseau famously rejects the regime in which people are directly in charge of government: 'in the strict sense of the term, a genuine democracy never has existed, and never will exist … If there were a people of Gods, they would govern themselves democratically. So perfect a government is not suited to men'.[40] Behind this rejection of direct democracy lurks Rousseau's pessimistic view of modern citizens. To defend his *Of the Social Contract* against attacks from Geneva, he contends:

> Ancient people are no longer a model for modern ones; they are too alien to them in every respect. You [Genevans] are neither Romans, nor Spartans; you are not even Athenians. Leave aside these great names that do not suit you. You are Merchants, Artisans, Bourgeois, always occupied with their private interests, with their works,

[35] Of the Social Contract, *supra* note 34 at 69 (Book II, ch. 7).
[36] *Id.* at 70 (Book II, ch. 7).
[37] *Id.* at 71 (Book II, ch. 7).
[38] *Id.* at 72 (Book II, ch. 7). The Iranian constitutional revolution may provide a prominent example.
[39] Here, I follow Richard Tuck's analysis in The Sleeping Sovereign: The Invention of Modern Democracy ch. 3 (2015).
[40] Of the Social Contract, *supra* note 34 at 91–92 (Book III, ch. 4).

> with their trafficking, with their gain; people for whom even liberty is only a means for acquiring without obstacle and for possessing in safety ... not being idle as ancient peoples were, you cannot ceaselessly occupy yourselves with the Government as they did: but by that very fact that you can less constantly keep watch over it, it should be instituted in such a way that it might be easier for you to see its intrigues and provide for abuses. Every public effort that your interest demands ought to be made easier for you to fulfil since it is an effort that costs you and that you do not make willingly.[41]

The default position of modern citizens is that they seek and struggle to achieve their short-term private interests. They suffer from collective action problems that prevent them from instituting a genuine republic. If they are fortunate, a Lawgiver appears and induces an Ackermanian constitutional moment, radically transforming their spirits and enabling them to achieve genuine general will. However, the Lawgiver's magic works merely for constitution-building. Following this, people's general interests are secured by the constitutional mechanism rather than their daily participation in politics. As Richard Tuck observes: 'Rousseauian democracy was not an idyll of an ancient city-state transported to the present day, but a serious attempt at working out how a modern commercial state might genuinely deserve the title of a democracy.'[42]

This understanding of Rousseau might be challenged. In *Of the Social Contract*, he criticised the constitution of England:

> Sovereignty cannot be represented for the same reason that it cannot be alienated; it consists essentially in the general will, and the will does not admit of being represented: either it is the same or it is different; there is no middle ground. The deputies of the people therefore are not and cannot be its representatives, they are merely its agents; they cannot conclude anything definitely. Any law which the people has not ratified in person is null; it is not a law. The English people thinks it is free; it is greatly mistaken, it is free only during the election of members of Parliament; as soon as they are elected, it is enslaved, it is nothing.[43]

Does Rousseau not advocate, here, a system in which the people instruct their deputies on specific issues? On the contrary, this paragraph is perfectly congruent with the above understanding: 'law' is a constitutional provision and 'sovereignty' a constituent power. Rousseau asserts that constituent power cannot be represented. We must recognise that, since England has no entrenched constitutional code, the UK Parliament can, at any time, transform the constitutional framework.[44] Rousseau's statement that 'upon close examination, very few Nations would be found to have laws'[45] corroborates this understanding. In the age of Rousseau, very few nations had rigid constitutional codes.

[41] Jean-Jacques Rousseau, *Lettres écrites de la montagne, neuvième letter, in* Oeuvres Complètes, vol III, 881 (1964). Here, I follow Tuck's translation; see Tuck, *supra* note 39 at 141–42.

[42] Tuck, *supra* note 39 at 142.

[43] Of the Social Contract, *supra* note 34 at 114 (Book III, ch. 15).

[44] See Tuck, *supra* note 39 at 138.

[45] Of the Social Contract, *supra* note 34 at 115 (Book III, ch. 15).

B. Totalising Revolution and Revolution on a Human Scale

This image of the British Parliament triggers associations with two of the constituent assemblies described by Ackerman that have also exercised ordinary legislative powers: the Israeli Knesset and the French National Convention. The former was convened as a constituent assembly, but following the initiative of David Ben-Gurion, it transformed itself into a British-style parliament, possessing both constituent power and ordinary legislative power.[46] The Lawgiver retracted his promise to accord a 'law'. On the other hand, in France the Lawgiver suspended the 'law' it had accorded to the people.

Ackerman indirectly refers to the National Convention led by the Montagnards as the 'totalizing variant' of modern revolution, where 'the mobilized movement of the People aims for a root-and-branch reconstruction of all aspects of social and political life. This aspiration legitimates the worst pathologies of the twentieth century', reaching its peak with Stalin and Mao.[47]

By contrast, revolutions on a human scale do not attempt to totally transform the society: 'They focus on *particular sphere(s) of social and political life*, and mobilize participants to repudiate currently dominant beliefs and practices within *the target of revolutionary concern* while leaving intact the prevailing mores in other spheres.'[48] The constitutional revolutions Ackerman analyses in this book are revolutions on a human scale.

From a purely legal point of view, it is apparently difficult to distinguish the Israeli Knesset from the National Convention. Both were convened as constituent assemblies. In the latter case, its name was borrowed from conventions of the US which deliberated and adopted constitutions of states or the Union.[49] The National Convention was convened in September 1792, after the suspension of the 1791 Constitution, to deliberate and adopt a new constitution. It successfully enacted the Constitution of 1793, which was approved by referendum in August that year. At least from its outset to the establishment of the 1793 Constitution, the Convention aimed to constitutionalise a revolution on a human scale.

However, confronted by foreign invasions and internal disturbances, the Convention suspended the implementation of the new Constitution and declared on 10 October 1793 that: 'The government of France is revolutionary until the peace.'[50]

Robespierre clarified the distinction between revolutionary and constitutional government in his speech on 25 December 1793:

> The object of constitutional government is to preserve a republic. The object of revolutionary government is to create it. A revolution is a war by freedom against its enemies,

[46] Ackerman, *supra* note 1 at 303–05. It is not unusual for a constituent assembly to function as the ordinary legislature until its dissolution on the adoption of a new constitution.

[47] *Id.* at 27–28.

[48] *Id.* at 28.

[49] *cf* Gordon Wood, The Creation of the American Republic 1776–1787, 306–10 (1998).

[50] Moniteur, Number 21 of the Republican Year II, 86.

> and a constitution is the regime of freedom winning a victory and peace … revolutionary government is sustained by the most sacred law, *salut public*, and also by most irrefutable title, the necessity.[51]

Manifestly, the Convention exceeded its authority. Once the Constitution was approved by the populace, the Convention had accomplished its mission and should have dissolved itself.

Yet Carl Schmitt asserts that this move by the Convention was justified, since it was exercising none other than constituent power.[52] He challenges as nonsensical the assertion that the holder of constituent power is the people, not the Convention. As Emmanuel Sieyès contends in his *Qu'est-ce que le Tiers-Etat?*, constituent power always remains in the state of nature and is not bound by any norm or form.[53] Therefore, it can also take the form of a convention. Since constituent power is *plenitudo potestatis* – that is, sovereign power – it is not bound by anything and, naturally, can also exercise legislative power.[54]

Moreover, the Convention was armed with the above-described revolutionary ideology. The Convention represented the sovereign people through identifying with them. To represent the people through the identification with them, the identity and homogenisation of the people had to first be accomplished. Thus, the people had to be purified by excluding and purging enemies of the revolution.[55] The principle of Article 16 of the Declaration of the Rights of Man and of the Citizen of 1789 – every society in which rights are not guaranteed and the separation of powers is not established does not have a constitution – seems to bring about its inverse conclusion (though the inference is fallacious): where constituent power is in motion, there is not yet a constitution; therefore, no rights are guaranteed and no separation of powers is established. No rights are guaranteed for enemies of the revolution; all violent powers should be concentrated and used to exclude the enemies of freedom and to create a virtuous people deserving of a new constitution. All spheres of social life become the concern of revolutionary politics and, as Sieyès points out, the 'ré-public' degenerated into the 'ré-totale'.[56] Similar lines of reasoning sustained totalising revolutionary movements in twentieth-century Russia and China.

Apparently, the same logic may apply to the Knesset, as a constituent assembly equipped with the whole state power. Since it did not even enact any constitutional code, it might have induced a ferocious revolutionary government to realise the identity and homogeneity of the Jewish nation. However, it only prosecuted

[51] Moniteur, Number 97 of the Republican Year II, 390.

[52] Carl Schmitt, Dictatorship, Michael Hoelzl & Graham Ward, trans., 127–31 (Polity Press, 2014 [1921]); Olivier Jouanjan, *La suspension de la constitution de 1793*, 17 Droits 125, 132 (1993).

[53] Emmanuel Sieyès, Qu'est-ce que le Tiers-Etat? 132 (1988 [1789]).

[54] Schmitt, *supra* note 52 at 123–24, 130–31.

[55] Jouanjan, *supra* note 52 at 134; Lucien Jaume, Le Discours Jacobin et la Démocratie 134–39 (1989).

[56] Emmanuel Sieyès, speech on July 20, 1795, in Moniteur, Number 307 of the Republican Year III, 1236.

revolution on a human scale. The Israeli revolution followed the trajectory of the ideal type of constitutional revolution, and at Time Four, robust constitutional review practices emerged, while in the case of the National Convention, it lacked judicial review in any meaningful sense.

It is risky to try to summarise the difference between the National Convention and the Israeli Knesset. It would be extremely difficult to analyse causality.[57] Background factors are diverse and numerous, and the two assemblies differ tremendously from each other, including in terms of their duration. The prospect of periodical elections in Israel might give politicians the incentive to frame a system of checks and balances in order to protect their long-term interests; Tom Ginsburg's 'insurance rationale' might have worked.[58] Conversely, for politicians in the Convention, who faced the threat of being sent to scaffolds without due process, their instrument for urgently protecting personal interests was to initiate counter-terror and summarily execute leaders of the terror government.

One difference between their end states is that the Knesset, despite being equipped with the whole power of the state, saw the emergence of a kind of common-sense morality shared and enforced by jurists,[59] the creation and consolidation of which was led by Justice Aharon Barak.[60] That morality is symbolised by the term 'human dignity' and was presumed to correspond to the founding ideal of the Israeli revolution. Correspondence with the founding idea does not itself distinguish the National Convention from the Knesset: the French Revolution started from a not significantly different idea, which was purported to be universally valid.[61]

Certainly, the enactment of the Basic Law on Human Dignity and Liberty helped to consolidate the judicially enforced common-sense morality.[62] However, constitutional interpretations by the judiciary are typically not logical deductions from canonical texts, but, rather, accord appropriate meanings to such texts in each context, often appealing to the common-sense morality shared among

[57] It may even be said that in the Ackemanian context, to inquire causality is off the mark because his theory does not intend to analyse causality in the first place.

[58] Tom Ginsburg, Judicial Review in New Democracies: Constitutional Courts in Asian Cases 25 (2003); *cf* Ackerman, *supra* note 1 at 39–40, 98 and 132.

[59] Ackerman uses the term 'professional narrative'; see Ackerman, *supra* note 1 at 217.

[60] Ackerman takes notice of Barak's leading role of creating a 'pure case of *common-law constitutionalism*', which transformed 'the abstract dignitarian principle into a set of hard-edges doctrines that could serve as a legally rigorous framework for the protection of fundamental rights'. See *id.* at 314.

[61] Ran Hirschl argues that the enactment of the Basic Law on Human Dignity and Liberty as well as the rise of judicial activism of the Supreme Court of Israel were promoted by those who have better access to the legal arena and who, faced with serious threats to their political and cultural hegemony, wished to protect their worldviews and policy preferences. See Ran Hirschl, Towards Juristocracy: The Origins and Consequences of the New Constitutionalism 50–74 (2004); *cf* Ackerman, *supra* note 1 at 318–19.

[62] Ackerman points out that the support for the Basic Law at the Knesset was quite feeble: 'only a quarter of the 120 members' said 'Yes to Human Dignity' (Ackerman, *supra* note 1 at 321).

professional jurists. This is the morality that sustains social cooperation in a society composed of people embracing various incompatible values.[63]

Aharon Barak's interpretation of the phrase 'a Jewish state' in the Basic Law exemplifies such a doctrinal exercise. He states that 'this phrase should be understood at a high level of abstraction – which would unite all members of the society'. His conclusion is that 'a Jewish state' means a state which embraces the foundational values of Judaism, namely, 'the love of mankind, the sanctity of life, social justice, equity, protecting human dignity, the rule of law over the legislatures, etc.'.[64] As Raz observes, in the same sense, 'France too can be a Jewish state'.[65] Barak's interpretation almost erased the phrase's contents.[66]

In my opinion, whether this common-sense morality emerges is decisive on whether a revolution stays within a human scale rather than degenerating into a totalising version. Focused on '*particular sphere(s) of social and political life*',[67] revolution on a human scale presumes the division between the public sphere, which is the concern of revolutionary politics, and the private sphere, where citizens lead their lives in accordance with their own lifestyles and/or worldviews. This is congruent with the modern idea of constitutionalism.[68] In this regard, the recent enactment in July 2018 of the Basic Law: Nation State, which defines Israel as the nation-state of the Jewish people, seems to be a disturbing omen for the future of constitutionalism in Israel.[69]

This common-sense morality should not be conflated with the rule of recognition, which is the standard by which to judge whether a given rule is a positive law in that society. Why? Because constitutional review is particularly necessary when applying a positive law to a concrete case seems to produce a conclusion contrary to common-sense morality. They are both, in essence, customary standards. Common-sense morality may be partially enacted into canonical texts, for

[63] Such judicial activities may not be essential components for other pathways of constructing constitutionalism. For instance, Nordic countries and Japan are not well known for active constitutional review. In Japan, the judiciary has focused its energies on the social question, such as gender equality in private workplaces. See Frank Upham, Law and Social Change in Postwar Japan (1987) especially ch. 4. This is one way to consolidate the reformist legacies of the American occupying forces without coming into conflict with the political branch.

[64] Aharon Barak, *The Constitutional Revolution: Protected Basic Rights*, in The Jewish Political Tradition 502–03(Michael Walzer, Menachem Lorberbaum & Noam Zohar eds., 2000).

[65] Joseph Raz, Value, Respect and Attachment 37 (2001).

[66] Ran Hirschl points out that the Supreme Court of Israel has functioned as a 'bastion of 'reason' and 'sanity' for Israel's '"enlightened public"'; Ran Hirschl, Comparative Matters: The Renaissance of Comparative Constitutional Law 63 (2014). In his view, 'in present-day Israel, as they are located on the edge of the East, its judges seem to express a yearning to belong to … the West' (at 60).

[67] Ackerman, *supra* note 1 at 28.

[68] See Yasuo Hasebe & Cesare Pinelli, *Constitutions*, in Routledge Handbook of Constitutional Law 9, 12–14 (Mark Tushnet, Thomas Fleiner & Cheryl Saunders eds., 2013).

[69] *cf* Ackerman, *supra* note 1 at 321. Barak says that the Knesset's power to amend the Basic Laws is limited – that is, a new Basic Law containing provisions, 'which reject the character of Israel as a Jewish or democratic state is unconstitutional'. See Aharon Barak, Human Dignity: The Constitutional Value and the Constitutional Right 284 (2015).

example, as basic right clauses of a constitution, but the ultimate rule of recognition (as explained in section I.A above) cannot be enacted.

III. Conclusion

While constitutional scholars tend to regard constitutional principles as timeless and universally applicable, Ackerman rejects this static idea. Constitutional principles can be revolutionised; they can be newly constitutionalised and developed by various parties in changing political situations. Particular contingencies and personalities play a big role in these processes.

Besides, Ackerman's idea of constitutionalism is broader than 'Western constitutionalism'.[70] As far as an effective checks-and-balances system is constructed, which prevents it from collapsing into a top-down system of autocratic rule, the system is 'constitutional' and not despotic.[71] Therefore, Iran provides another case of constitutional revolution. This broad conception of constitutionalism would also provoke intense debate.[72] I think that, in the modern world, constitutionalism starts from the idea that public powers should ensure the fair social cooperation of people embracing mutually incompatible, even incommensurable, worldviews. From such a view, the Iranian regime, which purports to realise 'an Islamic society', might not be classified as constitutionalist, though President Rouhani's reforms may lead Iran to a more pluralist society in the future.[73]

[70] Ackerman, *supra* note 1 at 324.

[71] *Id.* at 325 and 360.

[72] I suspect that the Japanese political system before the Second World War would be characterised as a constitutionalist regime in this broad sense, though the military forces as well as public prosecutors exerted immense political influence there. Instead of the judiciary, the Cabinet Legislation Bureau and the Privy Council functioned as de facto constitutional review organs.

[73] However, Ran Hirschl points out that Iran has a long legacy of constitutionalism from the early twentieth century and Khomeini invented a constitutional mechanism to resolve disputes between traditional clerical voice expressed by the Guardian Council and progressive egalitarian views represented by the Majlis (the parliament). See Ran Hirschl, Constitutional Theocracy 24–25, 57–59 (2010).

11

The Traditions of Constitutional Change

RICHARD ALBERT*

I. Introduction: Constitutionalism and Constitutional Change

In *Revolutionary Constitutions: Charismatic Leadership and the Rule of Law*, Bruce Ackerman identifies three paths to constitutionalism.[1] The revolutionary, establishmentarian and elite paths to constitutionalism reveal patterns that distinguish one from the other, each raising distinct challenges of governance and renewal, as Ackerman so ably shows. But a crucial distinction among these paths remains unspecified: each of the three paths to constitutionalism corresponds to different traditions of constitutional change. We see recurring resort to the exercise of unbounded constituent power in the revolutionary tradition while the establishmentarian and elite traditions both try to manage the use of constituent power through constituted powers. To put it succinctly, the three paths of constitutionalism separately seek to unleash, moderate and control the exercise of constituent power.

Each of the three traditions of constitutional change reveals its own peculiar problems and pathologies. The revolutionary tradition in France confronts the problem of illegality when it recognises the validity of stark departures from the codified rules of amendment. The establishmentarian tradition in Britain risks the problem of incongruity in law and politics when it seeks to moderate constitutional change by neutralising or alternatively co-opting the forces of popular mobilisation. And in the elite tradition in Japan, the Constitution tries to control the way in which the Constitution changes, but the problem of imposition looms over the question how to legitimate constitutional change. These three problems – illegality, incongruity, and imposition – are compounded in

* For helpful comments and criticisms, I am grateful to the participants at the conference on 'Revolutionary Constitutionalism', held at the Yale Law School on 24–25 August 2018, where I presented an earlier draft of this chapter.

[1] Bruce Ackerman, Revolutionary Constitutions: Charismatic Leadership and the Rule of Law (2019).

countries that do not fit comfortably within a single constitutional tradition of constitutional change, such as Canada, whose modern constitutional experiences expose traces of each. In this chapter, I develop this simultaneously complimentary and complicating critique of Ackerman's groundbreaking study of *Revolutionary Constitutions.*

II. The Revolutionary Tradition in France

Constituent power does not express itself in the same way across time and place, or even among countries from the same constitutional tradition. Among the countries Ackerman classifies in the revolutionary tradition – France, India, Iran, Israel, Italy, Poland and South Africa – only France treats the result of a referendum as an unassailable expression of constituent power. Not even India, the most similar French comparator according to Ackerman, who describes the country as France's 'sister republic',[2] gives the referendum the same use and status. This hints at a point of some significance: constituent power is a sociological concept that takes on a form specific to a people's self-understanding of its history, law and politics. Yet there may be a basic similarity in constitutional change among countries in the revolutionary tradition: legally discontinuous but nonetheless legitimate constitutional transformations can occur outside of the codified rules of amendment where they spring from expressions of popular will that are recognised as valid.[3]

A. Here the People Rule

For Ackerman, the constitutionalisation of Charles de Gaulle's charisma is reflected in an 'entrenched system of checks-and-balances'.[4] With entrenchment ordinarily comes a powerful court, and Ackerman casts the French Constitutional Council in the leading role. He looks into the future to imagine that 'if and when a revolutionary movement-party does gain control of the presidency and parliament … it will confront a Constitutional Council whose authority to defend the fundamental principles of the Fifth Republic is broadly recognized and institutionally entrenched'.[5] Ackerman therefore concludes that the French revolutionary model features a strong court guarding the values of the Constitution and the heritage of the founding moment.

[2] *Id.* at 165.

[3] I discuss this point at greater length in Richard Albert, Constitutional Amendments: Making, Breaking, and Changing Constitutions (2019).

[4] Ackerman, *supra* note 1 at 223.

[5] *Id.*

But modern French political history suggests a counter-narrative: the result of the constitutionalisation of de Gaulle's charisma is the supremacy of the referendum. As much as Ackerman stresses the centrality of the referendum in the French experience, he gives insufficient attention to its use in the period after de Gaulle's departure. Since then, the referendum has remained integral to the self-definition of the Fifth Republic and it has retained the revolutionary meaning it achieved in de Gaulle's extraordinary referendum on direct presidential elections in 1962. On this view, the key moment of constitutionalisation was not 1958, at the birth of the Fifth Republic, but later in 1962, when the effect of de Gaulle's unconventional referendum changed the rule of recognition for constitutional amendment. Since then, the Constitutional Council has acquiesced to the constitutionality of amendments passed both in conformity with the Constitution's codified rules of change and in conformity with the 1962 precedent of extraordinary change by referendum. In these cases, the Council has not asserted the broad authority Ackerman projects onto it. It has instead resorted to the same strategy it used in 1962: dismissing the matter for lack of jurisdiction. This is not the portrait of a court that will enter a showdown with the president and Parliament in order to defend the fundamental principles of the Republic.[6]

The essential teaching from the Council's judgment in 1962 is that the court will not review a change to the Constitution made in a referendum. Referendums are 'direct expressions of national sovereignty' that rest on a higher plane than the 'activities of public authorities' and, according to the Council, neither the Constitution nor the Organic Law gives the Council the power to review the constitutionality of a 'bill adopted by the French people by way of referendum'.[7]

Later in 2003, the Council confirmed that no popular act is more authoritative than a referendum. Senators had challenged the Constitutional Law on Decentralized Organization of the Republic, adopted as an amendment in a joint meeting of the National Assembly and the Senate under the procedure codified in the Constitution.[8] The senators argued that decentralising local government was a violation of the Constitution's unamendable rule protecting the republican character of the state from any alteration.[9] The Council's response echoed its holding 40 years earlier in its judgment on the referendum on direct presidential election: the Council held that it lacked jurisdiction even to hear the matter because it involved a referendum to change the Constitution, and here the Council was powerless to evaluate a choice of constituent power.[10]

[6] See Richard Albert, Malkhaz Nakashidze & Tarik Olcay, *The Formalist Resistance to Unconstitutional Constitutional Amendment*, 70 Hastings L.J. 101, 123–28 (2019) (illustrating and explaining the French Constitutional Council's resistance to reviewing constitutional amendments).

[7] CC décision no. 62-20DC, Nov. 6, 1962, Rec. 27 ¶ 5.

[8] *Id.*

[9] France Const., art. 89.

[10] CC décision no. 2003-469DC, Mar. 26, 2003, Rec. 293.

B. The Problem of Illegality

The codified French Constitution creates more than one route for amendment.[11] Where an amendment bill is adopted in both Houses of Parliament, the president can either submit the bill to Parliament for approval or put it to a referendum. If it is submitted to Parliament, both houses convene together as a Congress and the bill becomes official if approved by at least three-fifths of all votes cast. The president may alternatively put the bill to a referendum, where a simple majority vote is required.

Ackerman explains that the 1962 referendum did not follow any of these procedures, passing instead through Article 11 of the Constitution, which was not definitively intended for amendment.

But Ackerman might have found a deeper meaning to the 1962 referendum had he also looked to 1992, when the Council approved the ratification of the Maastricht Treaty.[12]

The Council in 1992 showed how it interprets the amendment power: the amendment power doubles as the constituent power. When the French people speak through a referendum, they are at the height of their power to make and remake their constitution without judicial oversight. Contrary to the conventional understanding of the amendment power as an inferior constituted power, the Council equates constitutional amendment with constitution-making, the consequence being that there are no restrictions on the amendment power, just as there would be no restrictions on the constitution-making power. The referendum power possessed by the people in France is therefore not unlike the continuing constituent power of the Knesset in Israel.[13] There is no distinction between amendment and constitution in France when the referendum is the chosen vehicle for change.

This points to a central problem in the revolutionary tradition: the problem of illegality. The 1962 referendum was illegal – it defied the codified rules of amendment – but it was not illegitimate since the choice to depart from the rules of amendment was retrospectively legitimated by the people in the referendum. Like the US Constitution, adopted in breach of the unanimity rule in the Articles of Confederation, the direct presidential election amendment was similarly approved in a manner contrary to the amendment rules in the French Constitution. This parallel between France and the US should come as no surprise, since both are rooted in the revolutionary path to constitutionalism and both place primacy on popular mobilisations that are recognised as the valid expression of constituent power. The formation of the popular consensus required to reflect constituent power of course differs in France and the US: the latter does not recognise the referendum tradition of the former. But in both countries, codified

[11] France Const., art. 89.

[12] CC décision no. 92-312DC, Sept. 2, 1992, Rec. 76.

[13] Claude Klein, *Basic Laws, Constituent Power and Judicial Review of Statutes in Israel: Bank Hamizrahi United v. Kfar Chitufi Migdal and Others*, 2 Eur. Pub. L. 225, 230–33 (1996.

rules and strict legality are susceptible to defiance by legitimate expressions of popular will.

III. The Establishmentarian Tradition in Great Britain

For Ackerman, Great Britain is 'a paradigmatic example' of the establishmentarian tradition. Here, pragmatic incumbents, locked in a battle with challengers, make 'strategic concessions that split the outsiders into moderate and radical camps'.[14] The incumbents 'then invite the moderate outsiders to desert their radical brethren and join the political establishment in governing the country'.[15] What results are landmark statutes that formalise some reforms yet maintain continuity in the establishment.[16] According to Ackerman, other countries in this tradition include Australia, Canada, New Zealand and certain countries in Asia, Scandinavia, and Latin America.[17] One of the pathologies in the establishment tradition arises from the incongruity between law and politics where referendums are held in countries whose organising logic is parliamentary sovereignty.

A. Evolutionary Change and Continuity

Codified constitutions are commonly amended according to special procedures and approval thresholds – a contrast with the procedures required for ordinary law-making.[18] Constitutional change does not occur the same way in Great Britain, where there is no formal distinction between higher and ordinary law. Formal constitution-level change occurs just like ordinary law-making: Parliament may make and unmake any law.[19] Constitutional change occurs also in the evolution of unwritten constitutional norms that reflect changing political norms and morality.[20]

Constitutional practice in Great Britain has revealed the emergence of a hierarchy in law, an important parallel with codified constitutions that distinguish between constitutional and ordinary law in both form and function. The difference rests in how higher law acquires its special status in Great Britain. Codified master-text regimes identify constitution-level law in the way it is made – special

[14] Ackerman, *supra* note 1 at 4.
[15] *Id.*
[16] *Id.*
[17] *Id.* at 5.
[18] See, eg, Arend Lijphart, Patterns of Democracy 204–07 (2nd ed. 2010); Edward Schneier, Crafting Constitutional Democracies: The Politics of Institutional design 224–25 (2006).
[19] A.V. Dicey, Introduction to the Study of the Law of the Constitution 39 (8th ed., 1982).
[20] Ivor Jennings, The Law and the Constitution 134–36 (1967). Of course, codified constitutions are also changeable by unwritten constitutional norms. See Hans Kelsen, General Theory of Law and State 259 (1945).

amendment procedures – while in Great Britain, constitution-level law is recognised in its treatment by political actors. A given statute may be treated as 'constitutional' because it concerns 'state institutions and … substantially influences, directly or indirectly, what those institutions can and may do'[21] – hence the difference, as Ian Cram has observed, between the Fixed-Term Parliaments Act 2011 and the Scrap Metal Dealers Act 2013.[22] In Great Britain, these constitutional statutes are a close analogue to formal amendment, though important differences nonetheless remain that have compelled some scholars to speak of 'constitutional reform' or 'constitutional change' and to avoid the term 'constitutional amendment', which is susceptible to a strictly formalist understanding of constitutional alteration.[23]

The European Communities Act 1972,[24] a constitutional statute yet formally an ordinary Act of Parliament, has had a transformative effect on Great Britain. It brought the country into the European Economic Community and required Parliament to agree to the Community's obligations, including to the legal supremacy of the Community.[25] The result was significant for a regime whose cardinal law is that Parliament is sovereign: a new rule of the Community would be automatically incorporated into the law of Great Britain without needing to pass discrete legislation in Parliament. This Act therefore changes the very nature of parliamentary sovereignty.[26]

Years later, the deep integration of the country into the European Union (EU) is now being undone. The Brexit referendum has catapulted Great Britain into a period of major constitutional change that is intended to culminate in a withdrawal from the EU and to end the legal supremacy of the EU in Great Britain. This change would not occur by constitutional amendment in the conventional sense; it would occur in Parliament with a formally ordinary law. But the function of the law – the Great Repeal Bill – would be extraordinary.

B. The Problem of Incongruity

Referendums have not been uncommon in Great Britain. Nor indeed have they been unused in the other countries Ackerman classifies in the establishmentarian tradition. As pressure mounts around the world for greater popular involvement in governance, referendums may well become increasingly deployed in countries of

[21] Adam Perry & Farrah Ahmed, *Constitutional Statutes*, 37 Oxford J. Leg. Stud. 461, 471 (2017).

[22] Ian Cram, *Amending the Constitution*, 36 Leg. Stud. 75, 76 (2016).

[23] See Robert Blackburn, *Constitutional Amendment in the United Kingdom*, *in* Engineering Constitutional Change: A Comparative Perspective on Europe, Canada and the USA 359, 361 (Xenophon Contiades ed., 2013).

[24] European Communities Act 1972, II Elizabeth, c. 68.

[25] *Id.* at s. 2(1).

[26] Dawn Oliver, *The United Kingdom*, *in* How Constitutions Change: A Comparative Study 329, 342 (Dawn Oliver & Carlo Fusaro eds., 2011).

the establishmentarian tradition, perhaps ultimately displacing their fundamental rules, like the rule of parliamentary sovereignty in Great Britain. Ackerman sees a risk ahead: the referendum is a serious threat in Great Britain.[27] It is a threat because 'rather than allowing the time-tested parliamentary leadership the chance to hammer out sensible solutions to pressing problems, referenda open the way for demagogic appeals to ordinary citizens who lack the time and knowledge required for such fateful choices'.[28]

Referendums have been used with binding effect in New Zealand (as opposed to purely advisory effect, as was at least nominally the case with Brexit), a country in the establishmentarian tradition where parliamentary sovereignty remains the rule. In reforming its electoral system from first past the post to proportional representation,[29] New Zealand voters went to the polls for two separate referendums over the course of two years, the first being advisory and the second binding. The result in the second referendum on the electoral system that voters would choose for themselves required Parliament to pass the Electoral Act 1993,[30] a nearly 400-page law that has transformed the nature of representative democracy in New Zealand. In a master-text constitutional regime, a change on this scale would almost certainly be made by constitutional amendment using special rules requiring heightened thresholds of agreement. But in New Zealand, where Parliament is supreme, the change was made by a simple law – a law compelled by a binding vote of the people.

The legal and political agreement on the effect of the binding referendum in New Zealand highlights the problem of incongruity in Great Britain as it confronts the question Ackerman raises: 'Which has priority in determining Britain's constitutional future – the 2016 vote in the referendum or the 2017 vote for Parliament?'[31] In *Miller*, the UK Supreme Court considered whether the Brexit referendum was legally inoperative and specifically whether the choice to remain or leave the EU belongs to Parliament alone.[32] The precise question before the Court was whether notice of the intention to withdraw from the EU – as required by Article 50 of the Treaty on European Union – could be made by a governmental declaration informed by the political result in the referendum, or whether the government needed the legal validation of statutory authorisation. The Court held that the government needed parliamentary approval to give notice of its intention to withdraw.[33] The effect of the judgment was effectively to render the Brexit referendum legally invalid despite its high political salience.

[27] Ackerman, *supra* note 1 at 12.
[28] *Id.*
[29] See Jack Vowles, *The Politics of Electoral Reform in New Zealand*, 16 Int'l Pol. Sci. Rev. 95, 113 (1995).
[30] Electoral Act 1993, Pub. Act. 1993, No. 87 (NZ).
[31] Ackerman, *supra* note 1 at 17.
[32] R. (Miller) *v.* Secretary of State for Exiting the European Union, [2017] U.K.S.C. 5.
[33] *Id.*

The Brexit referendum reveals the incongruity between the legal and political treatment of its result. The referendum had been neither required by law nor made binding under law. It was instead a discretionary choice of the Prime Minister of the day, David Cameron, who felt compelled to promise what amounted to a politically binding referendum meant to placate the strong anti-EU forces in his party and also to keep at bay the rival UK Independence Party, which was at the time growing in strength at the expense of his Conservative Party.[34] The Conservative Party had pledged earlier in its 2015 election manifesto to hold what later became the Brexit referendum and moreover vowed to 'honour the result of the referendum, whatever the outcome'.[35]

The incongruity became clear when the Brexit process was challenged in court. As a political matter, the government of the day believed the result was on its own sufficient to legitimate the withdrawal from the EU. Legitimacy on this view came from the referendum itself, not only its success but in the very act of the popular choice it reflected. Yet for the UK Supreme Court, legitimacy could come only from the legal machinery of parliamentary decision-making. It was not direct democracy that mattered for the Court, but rather a mediated form of representative democracy exercised in and by Parliament. While the government anchored its argument in the sociological legitimacy of the referendum, what mattered for the Court was legal legitimacy.

This problem of incongruity between legal validity and political effect is not unique to the establishmentarian tradition – indeed, we have encountered it in our discussion of the French referendum on direct presidential elections where the legal effect of the referendum differed from its political consequences. The difference between the British and French cases resides in the response to the incongruity. In the French revolutionary tradition, the sociological force of the referendum trumps the strictly legal requirements for constitutional change. In the British establishmentarian tradition, the legal requirements that attend its incrementalist and conservative approach to law-making and law-changing deny legal effect to the revolutionary referendum. And this is a serious challenge not only for Great Britain but also other establishmentarian jurisdictions that have yet to accept the referendum as a legitimacy-conferring device under law.

IV. The Elite Tradition in Japan

Ackerman calls his third ideal type of constitutionalism an elite construction. This category includes the 1949 German Basic Law, the 1947 Japan

[34] See Steven Erlanger & Stephen Castle, *In 'Brexit' Vote, David Cameron Faces Problem of His Own Making*, N.Y. Times, June 21, 2016, https://www.nytimes.com/2016/06/22/world/europe/david-cameron-brexit-european-union.html.

[35] Conservative Party Manifesto 2015: Strong Leadership; A Clear Economic Plan; A Brighter, More Secure Future 73 (2015) (copy on file with the author).

Constitution, the 1997 Polish Constitution and the 1978 Spanish Constitution.[36] Elite constructions do not arise out of a popular movement. They are instead generated by political elites, both traditional insiders and outsiders, who negotiate a solution to a crisis in the regime.[37] That crisis may be, for instance, a leadership succession in the transition to democracy, as in Spain. Alternatively, it may be a post-war conquest leading to the writing of new rules that restructure the defeated regime, as the world witnessed in Germany and Japan. The construction of the rules of constitutional change in the elite tradition reveals an interest in controlling the course of future change, whether by creating a complex structure of escalating amendment rules (as in Spain), by assigning to courts the power to review the constitutionality of amendments (as in Germany) or by making amendment extraordinarily onerous (as in Japan).

A. Bargain-Formation and Bargain-Maintenance

The principal challenge in the revolutionary tradition is to mount and sustain a successful popular movement, but the central task in the elite tradition is the formation and maintenance of the bargain reflected in the new constitution. Elite constructions are all in some way imposed constitutions, whether they are imposed in the midst of a purely domestic crisis or in the aftermath of a military defeat. The new Japanese Constitution, known as 'MacArthur's Constitution' in reference to the American general who directed its drafting, illustrates the latter.

It is necessary to stress the word 'constitution' because political actors formalised the legal reconstruction of post-war Japan as an *amendment* to the existing 1889 Meiji Constitution. Concerns about illegality and the uncertainty of an interregnum suggested this strategy as a prudent course of action.[38] The ordinary rules of change served as a bridge in this extraordinary moment.

The Meiji Constitution required a valid amendment to be adopted by a two-thirds supermajority in each house of the legislature, with a two-thirds quorum requirement as well.[39] The final step was promulgation by the Emperor.[40] On 3 November 1946, the Emperor made this constitutional overhaul official and announced in a remarkable statement that the choice to reconstruct the constitution had been made internally 'according to the will of the Japanese people' by their representatives in the Diet, fully consistent with Japan's constitutional laws:

> I rejoice that the foundation for the construction of a new Japan has been laid according to the will of the Japanese people, and hereby sanction and promulgate the amendments

[36] ACKERMAN, *supra* note 1 at 6, 7, 49.

[37] *Id.* at 6.

[38] Robert E. Ward, *The Origins of the Present Japanese Constitution*, 50 AM. POL. SCI. REV. 980, 1004 n.59 (1956).

[39] MEIJI CONST., art. 73 (Japan).

[40] *Id.* at art. 6.

> of the imperial Japanese constitution effected following the consultation with the Privy Council and the decision of the Imperial Diet made in accordance with Article 73 of the said constitution.[41]

The preamble in the revised Constitution keeps up appearances that it is written by 'We, the Japanese people, acting through our duly elected representatives in the National Diet' and that it was the result of a self-determined choice to 'secure for ourselves and our posterity the fruits of peaceful cooperation with all nations and the blessings of liberty throughout this land', a choice expressed by the collective will of the people 'that never again shall we be visited with the horrors of war through the action of government'. Of course, it is not unusual for constitutions to invoke the people as the central source of legitimacy in the regime, even where reality belies this claim.[42]

The three most important changes to the Meiji Constitution involved human rights, peace and future constitutional alteration. In relation to the first, the renovated constitution protects 'fundamental human rights',[43] elevating them to constitutional status and removing them from the purview of the Emperor's grace, as had been true of the Meiji Constitution.[44] The second, to which I return below, is the new commitment to pacifism. A permanent reminder of the consequences of military defeat,[45] the Peace Clause commits Japan 'to an international peace based on justice and order' and cements into law the Japanese people's vow to 'forever renounce war as a sovereign right of the nation and the threat or use of force as a means of settling international disputes'.[46] The revised Constitution also creates a new amendment procedure, which is today more onerous than under the Meiji Constitution: amendments now require two-thirds support of all members in each of two houses of the Diet, followed by a national referendum and finally promulgation by the Emperor.[47]

B. The Problem of Imposition

The challenge of constitutionalising what counts as a sufficient aggregation of popular will reflecting the considered judgement of the people is evident in the design of Japan's new amendment rules. On the one hand, there is today a higher threshold for constitutional amendment in Japan than was used (at least

[41] Harold S. Quigley, *Japan's Constitutions: 1890 and 1947*, 41 Am. Pol. Sci. Rev. 865, 866 (1947) (quoting *Official Gazette*, extra, Nov. 3, 1946, p. 1).

[42] Wim Voermans et al., Constitutional Preambles: A Comparative Perspective 26–30 (2017).

[43] Japan Const., ch. III.

[44] Shigenori Matsui, The Constitution of Japan: A Contextual Analysis 30 (2011).

[45] George P. Fletcher, *The Storrs Lectures: Liberals and Romantics at War: The Problem of Collective Guilt*, 111 Yale L.J. 1499, 1537 (2002).

[46] Japan Const., art. 9.

[47] *Id.* at art. 96.

nominally) for constitution-making. Yet, on the other hand, some in Japan suggest that the new amendment rules in Article 96 are insufficiently onerous to legitimate the change the incumbent prime minister is hoping to achieve: to repeal or rewrite the Peace Clause.

Long before he first became Prime Minister in 2006, Shinzo Abe set his sights on changing this clause. Indeed, rewriting it was one of his Liberal Democratic Party's primary objectives as early as 1955, and later Abe saw himself as the one who might fulfil that objective. When he finally entered the high office, he declared his intention to move quickly to amend the clause and even managed to pass through the national legislature a referendum law that would govern what he believed would be an eventual popular vote on the amendment, as required by the amendment rules themselves. His plan hit a roadblock when he resigned following his party's historic losses in parliamentary elections, but amending the Peace Clause has been on his agenda since his return to power in 2012.

Abe's efforts to amend the Peace Clause raise a question that plays out uniquely in the context of an imposed constitution: how should actors legitimate a transformative constitutional change? Is it adequate to follow the rules laid out in the militarily imposed constitution or are those rules tainted by their origin? For now, Abe and his side believe that these rules are sufficient, but part of their earlier plans involved amending the amendment rules to lower their supermajority thresholds. What motivated their twin aims of amending Articles 9 and 96 was to give Japan a homegrown, autochthonous constitution to replace the foreign one that has governed them since 1947.

But something quite fascinating happened in the intervening decades since McArthur imposed the Constitution on Japan: the Peace Clause grew roots deep into Japanese society, gaining strong popular support at first grudgingly, but today largely enthusiastically, such that it has become something of a supra-constitutional norm. The Peace Clause is not formally entrenched against amendment or repeal, and indeed it has been interpreted and re-interpreted by an executive agency, the Cabinet Legislation Bureau.[48] Yet the force of its expressive commitment has made the Peace Clause the core of the Constitution's modern identity and 'the heart and soul of the people'.[49]

Returning to the problem of imposition: how should a change to the Peace Clause be legitimated? Those who disagree with Abe that the current amendment rules are sufficient have two options, both suboptimal, although for different reasons. One option is a non-starter because it entails repudiating the consequences of Japan's military defeat: to claim that Japan's modern Constitution is an

[48] See Craig Martin, *The Legitimacy of Informal Constitutional Amendment and the "Reinterpretation" of Japan's War Powers*, 40 Fordham Int'l L.J. 427, 462–89 (2017).

[49] See Chaihark Hahm & Sung Ho Kim, Making We the People: Democratic Constitutional Founding in Postwar Japan and South Korea 96 (2015); Chaihark Hahm & Sung Ho Kim, *To Make 'We the People': Constitutional Founding in Postwar Japan and South Korea*, 8 Int'l J. Const. L. 800, 814 (2010).

illegitimate imposition and that it is proper to revert to the pre-war amendment rules in the Meiji Constitution. The second option is problematic because it either freezes the Constitution or it invites instability: to claim that a change to the Peace Clause would be so transformative that it would amount to creating a new constitution – and that this can be achieved only through a much more involved constitution-making process than that contemplated by the current amendment rules. The consequence of this latter view is either to render the Peace Clause formally immutable or to write an altogether new constitution that would visit both turmoil and change in the country. Neither option seems palatable or wise. The source of these problems resides in the imposed beginnings of the modern Japanese Constitution: today there is disagreement about whether the right formula was anticipated in 1947 in specifying the quantity and configuration of political consent that would later be recognised as valid to legitimate the making of transformative constitutional changes.[50]

V. A Hybrid Tradition in Canada?

We have so far discussed the problems of illegality, incongruity and imposition as they surface in the revolutionary, establishmentarian and elite traditions. But these problems are not mutually exclusive. Consider Canada, which Ackerman classifies in the establishmentarian tradition.[51] There is much in the Canadian constitutional experience suggesting that Ackerman is correct. The country's founding constitution makes it clear that the provinces joined together in confederation 'with a Constitution similar in Principle to that of the United Kingdom',[52] and the culture of constitutional politics leans towards constitutional change by gradual evolution rather than big-bang moments of wholesale renovation just as we would expect of a country in the establishmentarian tradition. And yet there exists much in the country's experience that complicates Ackerman's classification of Canada.

A. Incongruity, Imposition, and Illegality

Turn to the amendment rules in the Canadian Constitution. When Confederation came to be in 1867 in a statute passed by the Imperial Parliament, the power of formal amendment remained in London, with only a few exceptions.[53]

[50] I explore this fundamental problem of constitutional legitimation in Richard Albert, *Constitutional Amendment and Dismemberment*, 43 Yale Int'l L.J. 1 (2018).

[51] Ackerman, *supra* note 1 at 5.

[52] Constitution Act 1867, 30 & 31 Victoria, c. 3 (UK), preamble.

[53] See *id.* at s. 92(1) (authorising provincial legislatures to amend their own provincial constitution) and s. 101 (authorising Parliament of Canada to amend the Constitution as to certain judicial matters).

It took over a century for Canadian political actors to finally acquire the power to amend their own constitution without permission from abroad. Canada acquired this basic power in 1982, choosing to create an intricate escalating framework of amendment that seeks to structure an orderly, predictable and disciplined process of change.

The Constitution codifies five amendment procedures, each one specially designated for amending specific provisions and principles.[54] The degree of difficulty of these five procedures rises according to the importance of the provisions and principles entrenched under each of them: for instance, amending constitutional matters of parliamentary procedure requires only the agreement of both Houses of Parliament,[55] but amendments to Canada's links to the monarchy, to the composition of the Supreme Court of Canada and to the amendment procedures themselves require unanimous agreement among the Houses of Parliament and all 10 provincial assemblies.[56]

We see in the design, use and interpretation of these rules traces of each of the three distinct problems confronting the three traditions of constitutionalism: the problem of illegality is evident in recent efforts to update the Canadian Constitution through quasi-constitutional legislation; the problem of incongruity between law and politics has arisen in connection with recent referendums, one national and the others provincial; and the problem of imposition remains ever-present in the foreground of the country's constitutional politics – a politics defined by many different peoples in search of reconciliation with themselves and with the country's own lived history.

As we would expect from a constitution in the establishmentarian tradition, there is a problem of incongruity in Canada, specifically in the status of the referendum in law and politics. Ten years after the patriation of the Constitution, political actors found themselves in the heart of a constitutional crisis of self-definition and self-understanding. They had failed dramatically, from 1987 to 1990, to ratify the Meech Lake Accord, a major package of constitutional changes designed to assuage Quebec's concerns over its place and powers in Confederation. And so in 1992 they tried again, though this time in an even bigger package known as the Charlottetown Accord designed to address concerns not only from Quebec but also from the West, Indigenous Peoples and others.[57] Because the Meech Lake process had been negotiated in backrooms that were closed to the public, political actors felt compelled in the Charlottetown process to bring

[54] See Constitution Act 1982, being sched. B to the Canada Act 1982, ss 38–48 (UK).

[55] *Id.* at s. 44.

[56] *Id.* at s. 41. What results from this design of escalating thresholds is a hierarchy of constitutional importance. See Richard Albert, *The Expressive Function of Constitutional Amendment Rules*, 59 McGill L.J. 225, 244–57 (2013).

[57] For more on the Accords, see Meeting of the First Ministers on the Constitution, The 1987 Constitutional Accord (Ottawa, June 3, 1987); Coordinating Committee, Consensus Report of the Constitution: Final Text, Doc CP22-45/1992E (Charlottetown, August 27–28, 1992).

the people more squarely into discussions on building a new constitutional consensus.[58] This involved public consultations around the country and also putting the entire package to the people in a countrywide referendum.

The choice to put the Charlottetown Accord to the test of a referendum is the same one David Cameron would make 25 years later on Brexit. Neither choice was required by the constitution; both were felt to be political imperatives necessitated by forces internal to the governing party exerting significant pressure in favour of a referendum. The Brexit referendum succeeded, but the *Miller* Court held the referendal ratification legally inoperative, instead requiring Parliament to make the determination under law whether to remain in or leave the EU. In contrast, the Charlottetown referendum failed and therefore did not raise the question of its propriety in court. But even without a constitutional challenge, the question arose as to whether the Charlottetown referendum was valid. On the one hand, Canada's formal amendment rules present themselves as a complete code for constitutional change and they make no mention of a referendum as a lawful part of any amendment process. On the other hand, there is no prohibition in Canada on organising a referendum as an advice-seeking tool to inform political actors of public preferences on matters of governance, including on questions of constitutional amendment.

The following question therefore presents itself: would the Canadian Supreme Court have evaluated the propriety of the referendum in the same way as the *Miller* Court? The Court would have been hard-pressed to give any other answer than the one the *Miller* Court did. It would have had to declare the legal invalidity of the referendum itself, whether it had been used as a supplement to the Constitution's formal amendment rules or fully instead of them. Yet the Court would also have had to recognise the high political salience of a public expression of popular preference registered in a countrywide referendum on a subject so crucial to the future of the state. This duality of views on the referendum – that it is valid in constitutional politics, but not in constitutional law – emerges from the Court's own acknowledgement of the sociological force but legal insufficiency of the referendum when used in connection with a province's declared wish to secede from the country.[59]

We have also seen in the judicial interpretation of Canada's formal amendment rules what we would expect from political actors rooted in the elite tradition. The elite tradition channels change – whether large or small – through orderly procedures intended to keep legal continuity in the regime. Legally discontinuous periods invite disorder and uncertainty, and this threatens to undermine the carefully constructed legal-political settlement that has been negotiated by competing factions. It is therefore not unusual for constitutions in the elite tradition to codify

[58] See Mary Dawson, *From the Backroom to the Front Line: Making Constitutional History or Encounters with the Constitution: Patriation, Meech Lake, and Charlottetown*, 57 McGill L.J. 955, 983 (2012); Peter H. Russell, *Can the Canadians Be a Sovereign People?*, 24 Can. J. Pol. Sci. 691, 705–06 (1991).

[59] See Reference re Secession of Quebec, [1998] 2 S.C.R. 217, at paras. 87–88.

rules of amendment that authorise changes across the entire spectrum, from small-scale changes to revolutionary changes. For instance, in Spain – Ackerman's paradigmatic example of an elite construction – the Constitution's formal amendment rules codify the distinction between amendment and reconstitution, with some procedures authorising minor adjustments to the Constitution and others contemplating the possibility of transformative changes, both achieved with legally continuity.[60] The elite tradition therefore raises something of a paradox: its amendment rules contemplate changes that would otherwise be legally discontinuous, but because a constitution in the elite tradition authorises these transformative changes, they can be made while retaining legal continuity.

Along these lines, the Supreme Court of Canada has interpreted the Constitution's amendment rules as creating a legally continuous procedure for making an otherwise legally discontinuous change. In the *Secession Reference*, the Court acknowledged that a change as significant as a provincial secession would of course 'be profound' and would be 'undoubtedly … inconsistent with our current constitutional arrangements', but ultimately it was 'not persuaded' that secession could be lawful only if it were authorised by something *more* than an amendment:

> Some commentators have suggested that secession could be a change of such a magnitude that it could not be considered to be merely an amendment to the Constitution. We are not persuaded by this contention. It is of course true that the Constitution is silent as to the ability of a province to secede from Confederation but, although the Constitution neither expressly authorizes nor prohibits secession, an act of secession would purport to alter the governance of Canadian territory in a manner which undoubtedly is inconsistent with our current constitutional arrangements. The fact that those changes would be profound, or that they would purport to have a significance with respect to international law, does not negate their nature as amendments to the Constitution of Canada.[61]

A close reading of this passage yields two critical observations. The first is the Court's recognition that even 'radical and extensive' constitutional changes can be achieved using the formal amendment rules codified in the Constitution Act 1982. Formal amendment can therefore be used to transform some significant part or feature of the Constitution, presumably provided it conforms to the exacting thresholds entrenched in the Constitution's default multilateral or unanimity procedures,[62] the two most difficult formal amendment thresholds in the Constitution.

The second exposes the problem of imposition common to the elite tradition. The Court held that Quebec's secession may proceed by formal amendment, but it did not specify which of Canada's five amendment procedures must apply to a

[60] SPAIN CONST., arts. 166–68.
[61] Reference re Secession of Quebec, *supra* note 59, at para. 84.
[62] Constitution Act 1982, ss. 38, 41, 42.

constitutional amendment on secession. This is surprising in light of the Court's traditional emphasis on the primacy of the codified parts of the Constitution. The reason why it chose not to specify which of the five amendment procedures applies to Quebec's secession may well be that it would have been inappropriate to appeal to the rules of formal amendment because these rules lack legitimacy for many in Quebec.[63] The Quebec provincial government rejected the Constitution Act 1982 when it was proposed and has yet to formally accept it to this day. To require the peoples of Quebec to play by the rules of what many of them regard as an imposed constitution would undermine the Court's careful construction of the legal rules for secession.

The problem of illegality has also surfaced in Canada in connection with constitutional change. Because of the difficulty of constitutional amendment on matters of great importance – difficult because they require a higher degree of consent from political actors with competing priorities[64] – political actors have innovated constitutional workarounds in order to achieve constitution-level changes with recourse only to subconstitutional procedures. These 'quasi-constitutional amendments' possess constitution-level status and effect, but they have been made in the course of the ordinary legislative process, using the same institutions and rules to pass an ordinary statute.

For instance, the Regional Veto Law is formally an ordinary statute passed by Parliament.[65] The law does for Quebec the same thing it does for the other regions of Canada, with the exception of the North:[66] it gives to each a veto in constitutional amendment. The veto may be exercised by Ontario, Quebec, British Columbia and at least two provinces from each of the Atlantic and Prairie regions where the two represent at least half of the regional population. The Law gives the veto to these regions indirectly through the federal government: it requires a Cabinet minister to first obtain the consent of each of the five major regions as well as a majority of all provinces *before* introducing a major amendment proposal under the multilateral default amendment procedure.[67] The Law therefore confers a functional veto, not a formal one.

The Regional Veto Law was prompted by the 1995 Quebec referendum. The Law fulfilled the federal government's promise to give Quebec a veto over future

[63] Sujit Choudhry & Robert Howse, *Constitutional Theory and the* Quebec Secession Reference, 13 Can. J. L. & Juris. 143, 150 (2000).

[64] The Constitution of Canada may in fact be the most difficult to amend in the world. See Richard Albert, *The Difficulty of Constitutional Amendment in Canada*, 53 Alberta L. Rev. 85 (2015).

[65] An Act Respecting Constitutional Amendments, S.C. 1996, c. C-1 (Regional Veto Law).

[66] *Id.* at s. 1(1).

[67] Canada's Constitution entrenches five amendment procedures. Three of them already give each of the affected provinces a veto over an amendment: the unilateral provincial procedure, the regional amendment procedure and the unanimity procedure. The fourth – the unilateral federal procedure – authorises Parliament to amend its own internal constitution and therefore makes no provision for provincial involvement. It is the fifth procedure – the multilateral default amendment procedure – that the Regional Veto Law was intended to address.

constitutional amendments, a pledge made as an inducement to encourage Quebec voters to reject secession,[68] which they did.

Just like the French referendum on direct presidential election, the Law is at least arguably formally illegal. It imposes a prior restraint on the power of Cabinet ministers to propose an amendment, something not contemplated by the constitutional amendment rules themselves. It also complicates amendment under the multilateral default procedure by changing the sequence for a successful Parliament-initiated amendment: the Constitution requires federal proposal, then provincial ratification, but the Law now requires provincial consent, then federal proposal and finally provincial ratification. More crucially, the Law effectively amends the country's amendment rules, though without having navigated the Constitution's procedures for amending the rules of amendment, which require unanimous agreement among the Houses of Parliament and each of the provincial assemblies.[69] This constitution-level change was made by Parliament alone.

B. Competing Sources of Legitimation

Much like Europe confronts the problem of competing sources of legitimacy, Canada is composed likewise of many nations, each with its own distinct legitimating vocabulary. These competing sources of legitimation in Canada reveal themselves in the country's most trying times of constitutional change and also in clashing self-understandings of how the people may speak.

The revolutionary impulses in Canada, located exclusively for now in the provinces, largely in Quebec but also in the West, portray Canada as a confederation – the way it was first constructed – with the provinces and the centre on an equal footing, each with equal sovereignty. The main modality of legitimation here is the referendum, which Quebec has deployed as a forum for self-definition, as a vehicle to drive home to the federal government how seriously it means what it says and as a self-reinforcing justification to stress that the people are entitled to have what they say they want. The referendum has grown in popularity across the country as a check on elected representatives, perhaps signalling the expansion of the revolutionary tradition beyond Quebec and the West. We observe the rise of referendums most notably in connection with constitutional amendment: in many provinces, statutory law requires either binding or advisory referendums before provincial assemblies vote to ratify a constitutional amendment, whether the amendment concerns

[68] See Robert A Young, *Jean Chretien's Quebec Legacy: Coasting Then Stickhandling Hard*, 9 Rev. Const. Stud. 31, 38–39 (2004).

[69] Constitution Act 1982, s. 41.

provincial, regional or national matters.[70] This is significant because the Constitution's formal amendment rules do not require a referendum at any stage of the process, nor do they even recognise its use.[71]

The inclination towards the elite tradition is felt in the management of conflict and contestation, which since patriation occurs largely in the courts through the federal reference procedure.[72] Indeed, the tradition of elaborating constitutional meaning through courts by way of the reference procedure began well before patriation, but it was in the heat of this patriation controversy – over whether Canada was a union of two linguistic and cultural solitudes or a federalist state with all provinces standing on equal footing – that the Court proved itself capable of mitigating quite serious national tensions in moments of impasse amounting to constitutional crisis. The Court's capacity to defuse conflicts derives from the culture of legalism that constitutes a competing foundation of constitutional legitimacy. The judiciary has relied on a particular legal vocabulary to manage internal crises, including the living tree doctrine,[73] the concept of proportionality[74] and the idea of purposive interpretation.[75] Antagonistic to the popular foundations of referendums, this legalistic culture of constitutionalism is evidence of the influence of the elite tradition in Canada. The non-use of the federal legislative override – which authorises political actors to shield a law from judicial review or to suspend

[70] Constitutional Referendum Act, RSA 2000, c. C-25, ss. 2(1), 4; Constitutional Amendment Approval Act, RSBC 1996, c. 67, s. 1; Referendum Act, RSBC 1996, c. 400, s. 4; Referendum Act, SNB 2011, c. 23, ss. 12–13; The Referendum and Plebiscite Act, SS 1990–91, c. R-8.01, s. 4; Public Government Act, SY 1992, c-10, s. 7; Consolidation of Plebiscite Act, RSNWT 19888, c. P-8, s. 5; Elections and Plebiscites Act, SNWT 2006, c. 15, s. 48; La Loi sur la consultation populaire, LRQ 2000, c. C-64.1, s. 7; Plebiscites Act, RSPEI 1988, c. P-10, s. 1; Elections Act, SNL 1992, c. E-3.1, s. 218.

[71] For more on this phenomenon, see Richard Albert, *The Conventions of Constitutional Amendment in Canada*, 53 Osgoode Hall L.J. 399, 419–36 (2016).

[72] The reference procedure authorises the federal government to request an advisory opinion from the Supreme Court of Canada on questions of law and fact concerning any constitution act, federal or provincial statute and among other questions the distribution of federal-provincial powers; Supreme Court Act, R.S.C., 1985, c. S-26, s. 53. The federal government has redirected many of the most contentious questions of constitutional politics to the Supreme Court for resolution under its special reference procedure. These have included the rules of provincial secession (Reference re Secession of Quebec, *supra* note 59), how to reform the Senate (*Reference re Senate Reform*, [2014] 1 SCR 704), the legality of marriage equality (Reference re Same-Sex Marriage, [2004] 3 S.C.R. 698), the status of English and French as national languages (Reference re Manitoba Language Rights, [1992] 1 S.C.R. 212) and the constitutional status of the Supreme Court itself (Reference re Supreme Court Act, ss 5 and 6, [2014] 1 S.C.R. 433). The Supreme Court has also answered reference questions on appeal from provincial courts. The Court's advisory opinions have addressed some of the country's most important constitutional controversies, including whether the patriation process was lawful (Reference re Resolution to Amend the Constitution, [1981] 1 S.C.R.753), whether Quebec was entitled to a veto in patriation by virtue of its status as a founding partner in Confederation (Reference re Objection by Quebec to a Resolution to Amend the Constitution, [1982] 2 S.C.R. 793), how properly to design electoral boundaries (Reference re Provincial Electoral Boundaries (Sask), [1991] 2 S.C.R. 158), what judicial independence requires (Reference re Provincial Court Judges, [1997] 3 S.C.R. 3) and whether the federal government can create a national firearms registry (Reference re Firearms Act, [2000] 1 S.C.R. 783).

[73] Edwards v. Canada (Attorney-General), [1930] A.C. 124.

[74] R v. Oakes, [1986] 1 S.C.R. 103.

[75] R v. Big M Drug Mart Ltd., [1985] 1 S.C.R. 295.

the application of a court judgment[76] – reinforces the supremacy of the Supreme Court in matters of constitutional meaning.[77]

And yet the legacy of Great Britain's establishmentarian influence continues to predominate in Canada. Constitutional changes occur gradually over time, often taking longer than they should, and rare are those constitutional transformations driven by expressions of popular preference. Even big changes that should be made at the level of constitutional law are often made at the level of statutory law or executive decree, both because it offers the path of least resistance to success and because it is easier to deal with the question as a single subject rather than as an omnibus package of amendment proposals that history has shown is fated to defeat. The new Senate appointments process offers a recent example of a constitution-level change made instead by subconstitutional means.[78] An earlier example is the 1960 Canadian Bill of Rights.[79] Where political actors do not rely on the reference procedure to resolve disputes, they handle them on their own in negotiation in Parliament or in provincial assemblies, preferring the path of moderation and collaboration over one that invites escalation to the level of large-scale popular mobilisation.

VI. Conclusion: A Constructive Complication

How may the people speak and what can they say? The three paths to constitutionalism Ackerman identifies in *Revolutionary Constitutions* suggests different answers to both questions. The revolutionary tradition in France tolerates some measure of illegality when the people speak in ways that defy the Constitution's formal amendment rules, clothing with legitimacy both the process and outcome of a referendum vote, whatever the people may choose to say. The establishmentarian tradition in Great Britain directs the people to speak through their representatives in Parliament, which today remains the locus of sovereignty, though referendums have underscored the problem of incongruity in law and politics. And the elite tradition in Japan makes it difficult for the people to change their Constitution – a process that requires supermajority agreement in the Diet as well as a referendum – both because the Constitution was deliberately made hard to amend and also because the conservative culture of elite-managed

[76] Constitution Act 1982, s. 33.

[77] I have explored the reasons for the non-use of this federal power in Richard Albert, *Constitutional Amendment by Constitutional Desuetude*, 62 Am. J. Comp. L. 641, 669–73 (2014).

[78] See Government Announces Immediate Senate Reform, Government of Canada, December 3, 2015, www.democraticinstitutions.gc.ca/eng/content/government-announces-immediate-senate-reform; Minister of Democratic Institutions Announces Launch of the Permanent Phase of the Independent Senate Appointments Process, Government of Canada, July 7, 2016, http://news.gc.ca/web/article-en.do?nid=1095799&tp=1&_ga=1.62793134.328809842.1468471660.

[79] S.C. 160, c. 44.

constitutional change prioritises executive-led interpretive evolution through the Cabinet Legislation Bureau.

The Canadian Constitution, which Ackerman classifies in the establishmentarian tradition, offers many different answers to these questions. The establishmentarian tradition may well prevail in Canada, but there are strong traces of the revolutionary and elite traditions of constitutionalism. These are evident in the design of the country's constitutional amendment rules and in how constitutional actors have understood, interpreted and deployed them. The result is that sometimes the people may speak directly with constructive legal effect through popular mobilisations like referendums, sometimes the people may speak only through Parliament and sometimes the people may not speak in either way. The Canadian case complicates Ackerman's account in a constructive way: it suggests that there may be a tradition of hybridity that emerges both from deep historical conflict internal to a regime and from modern influences of external constitutional practice.

PART III

The Future of Europe

12

Constitutional Crossroads

A View from Europe

NEIL WALKER

I. Introduction: Temporal and Conceptual Crossroads

The area of greatest interest in any thesis – especially a large and original thesis – is often also its area of greatest vulnerability and controversy. Bruce Ackerman's large and original thesis in *Revolutionary Constitutions*, which extends and refines through an ambitious exercise in global comparison a methodology and explanatory approach well known from earlier works,[1] provides a good example of this. Ackerman draws a fundamental distinction between three ideal typical constitutional pathways; the 'revolutionary' type; the 'pragmatic adaptation' type; and the 'elite construction' type. In so doing, he wants to make a number of claims, two of which stand out. First, when we set out to analyse how and to what effect constitutional institutions and mechanisms work in any particular time or place – for example, apex courts, executive organs or referendums – Ackerman insists that we should look beyond the bare normative design and immediate operative context of these institutions and mechanisms, just as we should look beyond universalistic assumptions about how actors might think and act in their rational self-interest.[2] We should reckon instead that a good part of the explanation turns upon which of the three ideal typical pathways is being (more or less) followed. Second, the development of this new taxonomy provides a platform from which Ackerman seeks to argue, against a certain scepticism in contemporary literature, that the revolutionary type – and more particularly the 'revolutionary on a human scale' type – remains a live and normatively defensible option in recent and prospective constitutional development.

Yet if, as Ackerman invites us so to do, we are to take the revolutionary type seriously as a distinctive and still viable avenue of constitutional development,

[1] See, amongst many, Bruce Ackerman, The Future of Liberal Revolution (1992).

[2] Bruce Ackerman, Revolutionary Constitutions: Charismatic Leadership and the Rule of Law 36–40 (2019).

we must evaluate his thesis both in the round and at its point(s) of application. We must ask just how and to what extent the overall three-way, path-dependent scheme that he develops actually helps us to explain when, why, how and with what prospects of success the revolutionary route might have been taken or might yet come to be taken. Ackerman seeks to answer this explanatory challenge by providing us with a systematic account of a stepwise trajectory peculiar to the revolutionary type and by illustrating the operation of that stepwise trajectory over a wide range of recent or contemporary constitutional case studies across four continents. Within the revolutionary trajectory, a route is traced from revolutionary insurgency, through the constitutionalisation of charisma (in and following the constitution-making event itself) to the legitimation challenges involved in the gradual normalisation of the political settlement.

Yet this can only take us so far. It is an approach that is good at telling us how we make progress along the revolutionary path. It also demonstrates how, in the course of our journey, we might lose momentum, veer off track or even come to a dead end, as and when the revolutionary generation dies off, absent an effective process of constitutional consolidation. But the Ackermanian scheme is arguably less adept at explaining the ways and means by which we get on to the revolutionary path in the first place.

How so? After all, Ackerman is far from ignoring origins. Rather, he suggests that the clearing of the revolutionary pathway begins with the mobilisation of a revolutionary movement against the existing regime during what he calls 'Time One' – the first stage in his stepwise trajectory. Often this movement will fail, sometimes defeated by means of 'violent repression'.[3] The revolutionary path, then, frequently becomes blocked and the new constitutional moment never arrives. But where, exceptionally, popular mobilisation does succeed in delegitimising the old regime, it is followed at Time Two by a new constitutional founding. In Ackerman's causal sequencing, therefore, the flow from Time One to Time Two and then beyond to Times Three and Four[4] (a sequencing adopted in the 'pragmatic adaptation' and 'elite construction' models as well as in the 'revolutionary' model) describes a movement from a pre- or extra-constitutional context, namely the configuration of forces in the wider environment of politics and civil society, to a post- or intra-constitutional context. In other words, while the explanatory trajectory at Time One focuses on non-constitutional factors alone, from Time Two onwards, it is concerned with developments within and closely conditioned by the emergent constitutional framework.

The progression from extra- to intra-constitutional might seem perfectly rational and, indeed, to offer a judiciously balanced approach. In line with a sociological realism and particularism that has not always been sufficiently acknowledged in constitutional analysis, especially amongst constitutional lawyers, constitutional beginnings in Ackerman's model are understood to be

[3] *Id.* at 8.
[4] *Id.* at 4–10.

non-constitutional in nature, while in subsequent developments within the relevant constitutional regime, legal texts and institutions, in appreciation of their genuine structuring effects, become an important part of the *explanans* rather than the mere *explanandum*. Yet this still leaves the matter of revolutionary origins under-explored, for simply to state that the revolutionary model requires the catalyst of revolutionary mobilisation against the existing regime begs the prior question of the necessary or sufficient preconditions of the impulse towards such a successful revolutionary mobilisation. The answer to the question of revolutionary preconditions may, of course, be so richly various that little beyond bland generalisation are available by way of general explanatory overview. For while revolutionary mobilisation often takes place in the very broad context of a post-imperial or other national independence movement, or in the equally broad context of a post-war or other post-conflict reconstruction where the existing regime – which may itself have had deep revolutionary origins – has been defeated or significantly weakened, the real explanatory devil lies in the detail of every individual case. And Ackerman is very good at depicting just that rich variety of detail across a wide range of cases in which origins are marked by a sharp and final break from an earlier regime or polity, and in offering up his general explanatory sketch of such 'discontinuous' beginnings with a suitably light touch.

But the problem of revolutionary origins – and of the adequacy of our account of these origins – stubbornly persists. For in some contemporary cases, we may come to the revolutionary path *not* through a rejection of the imperial yoke or an imposed transnational ideology – as in the Indian, South African and Polish cases that he considers at length[5] – or the carving of a new territorial space – as in the original (and also, of course, post-imperial) US case[6] or that of modern Israel,[7] or from a context in which a previous regime with deep revolutionary origins collapses due to the ravages or legacy of international war – as in his similarly closely examined French and Italian cases.[8] Rather, we might arrive at the threshold of the revolutionary road from another type of constitutional pathway – either the 'pragmatic adaptation' or the 'elite construction' track. As already indicated, Ackerman want to argue that these other pathways, just like the revolutionary pathway, also have their own internal 'path-dependent' explanatory logic. But if that is so, the point where the paths are recognised as crossing, and a new path comes to be followed, is the point where Ackerman's main explanatory framework may begin to lose traction, or at least to become awkwardly aligned with the facts. On the one hand, origins, as we have seen, are basically accounted for in the revolutionary model, as in all the Ackermanian types, in extra-constitutional terms, by reference to the play of wider political and social forces.

[5] *Id.* at chs. 2 (India), 3 (South Africa), and 9 and 10 (Poland).
[6] *Id.* at ch. 13.
[7] *Id.* at ch. 11.
[8] *Id.* at chs. 4, 7 and 8 (France), and 5 (Italy).

On the other hand, if this originary context is one that happens to lead from and emerge out of a pragmatic adaptation or elite construction pathway, it is one that will also be conditioned by these quite distinct constitutional milieux, and so also subject to explanation in the later Time-Two-and-after, path-dependent explanatory dynamics internal to these constitutional types. So in constitutional crossroads of this sort, it seems that we must somehow accommodate and reconcile two distinct modes of explanation – the pre-constitutional phase within one ideal type alongside the post-constitutional phase within another ideal type.

Ackerman is, of course, aware of such complexities, and some of the more detailed case studies in later volumes of his comparative project will deal with just these types of crossroads and new thresholds. In this chapter I want to anticipate some part of that examination, and in so doing take the opportunity to scrutinise some of the assumptions that Ackerman may bring to that examination, by looking at two cases that Ackerman refers to and discusses briefly, but defers close analysis of until these later volumes. These are the British 'pragmatic adaptation' case[9] and the EU 'elite construction' case.[10] In both examples, there are incipient movements towards political revolution and resettlement (or something that at least bears a family resemblance to this) that nevertheless remain conditioned by the extensive legacy of pragmatic adaptation in one case and elite construction in the other. Here the circumstances under which political revolution and resettlement is likely to take place repay close examination, offering an interesting test (and one close to my European heart!) of the capacity of the Ackermanian approach to make sense of the switch between constitutional types in two of the most consequential – and also interconnected – dramas on the contemporary global constitutional stage.

In looking at these two cases, the present inquiry probes the more specific normative and analytical claims that accompany the Ackermanian thesis. Normatively, it tests the outer limits of our sense of what is possible by way of the kind of collectively self-conscious political revolution on a human scale for whose continued relevance Ackerman wants to argue. Where the polity is made *ex nihilo*, or remade from war or violent struggle, the political revolution becomes a kind of imperative – a necessary filling of the vacuum. Where instead the political revolution is sought at a constitutional crossroads, succeeding a previously establishment-based or elite constitution, a different quality of reflexive reconstruction is in play, and the question of the success conditions of any such distinctive process demands close inquiry. And such inquiry also requires that we re-engage with the question of the analytical credentials of the Ackermanian scheme. For when confronted by what we might provisionally call a *managed revolution* from an establishmentarian or elite baseline, where and how do we locate this kind of development in terms of his basic and presumptively important conceptual distinction between a

[9] *Id.* at 4–5, 12–18.
[10] *Id.* at 21–23.

political revolution and a mere further phase in the pragmatic or elite narrative? Ackerman himself seems relaxed about such blurring and the prospect of hybrid cases[11] – what we might call instances of *conceptual crossroads* alongside (and, indeed, flowing from) various *temporal crossroads*. But if the original ideal types no longer fit key cases, then this may bring into question the continuing explanatory purchase or plausibility as normative models of the basic tripartite scheme and suggest the need for new distinctions appropriate to a new age.

II. The UK and the Limits of Pragmatic Adaptation

According to Ackerman, the UK supplies the paradigm case of pragmatic adaptation, and one that has influenced many parts of the Commonwealth, as well as finding echoes in parts of Scandinavia, South America and Asia.[12] The basic contours of the argument are familiar to those with even a passing interest in the history of the British constitution.[13] These concern the development of a relationship between a distinctively evolutionary political dynamic[14] and a particular doctrine – the sovereignty of Parliament. The latter was famously canonised by Dicey in the late nineteenth century[15] as the keystone of the British constitution, but, in fact, dates from the seventeenth century and the resolution of the critical struggle for sovereignty between Crown and Parliament in favour of Parliament. The basic fit between evolutionary constitutionalism and the sovereignty of Parliament is clear, indeed symbiotic. The resilience of the doctrine that Parliament can make or unmake any law and that no other entity can override or set aside parliamentary legislation – since it solidified as the pre-eminent norm of the constitution over the course of the seventeenth century – has been at one and the same time expression, consequence and reinforcing cause of an evolutionary constitutional order that, unlike the more programmatic designs associated with revolutionary settlements or elite constructions, is not tied to any specific collective *telos*.

The sovereignty of Parliament is, first, a clear expression and vehicle of an evolutionary constitutional logic. In holding that the Crown-in-Parliament always retains the last (or, rather, latest) legislative word both against its own previous authority and against any and all other sources of law and claims to legal authority, the doctrine treats any and all laws as subject to change by ordinary legislative process and so facilitates an incremental approach to the reform of the content

[11] He contemplates just such a 'hybrid' in the British case (*id.* at 17) and a 'creative synthesis' in the EU case (*id.* at 23).

[12] *Id.* at 5.

[13] See, eg, Neil Walker, *Our Constitutional Unsettlement*, Public Law 529 [2014]; Martin Loughlin & Stephen Tierney, *The Shibboleth of Sovereignty*, 81 Modern Law Review 989 (2018); Vernon Bogdanor, The New British Constitution (2009).

[14] Vividly portrayed by Walter Bagehot in The English Constitution (2009 [1867]).

[15] A.V. Dicey, Lectures Introductory to the Study of the Law of the Constitution (1885).

of the constitution. Parliament is competent at any time, unfettered by decisive external legal constraint, to amend the rules concerning the entire range of constitutional matters, from the composition, role and overall pattern of the institutions of government to the relations between government and citizens. Second, the persistence of parliamentary sovereignty is also a consequence of an evolutionary constitutional order. The deep continuities of modern British political history – the relative absence of the ruptures of conquest, of political revolution, or of territorial fracture or re-alignment directly affecting the metropolitan centre[16] – has meant that, once established against the courts and the executive, there has been little occasion (neither clear opportunity not irresistible political pressure) to depart from the doctrine of the legislative supremacy of the central institutional complex of the British state.

Third, parliamentary sovereignty provides reinforcement for the evolutionary constitution. It does so in two senses: symbolic and instrumental. Symbolically, parliamentary sovereignty long supplied an object of continued affirmation and embedded identification within our political culture. It helped to dignify the very notion of evolution – of constitutional gradualism – treating this as the dividend of a flexible and responsive centralism based upon a proud and venerable institution rather than as a matter of cumulative historical accident and rudderless drift. In addition, parliamentary sovereignty supplied the anchor for the broader notion of an unwritten British constitution, allowing this to be portrayed as superior to the practice of documentary constitutionalism rather than an apologetic second best. Indeed, from the 1780s onwards, in response to events unfolding across the Channel and the Atlantic, 'Paper constitution' emerged as a term of ridicule, and precisely the UK's 'lack of a written constitution [came] to serve a distinguishing and celebratory function'[17] for many generations of defenders of the national constitutional faith.[18]

Instrumentally, not only was parliamentary sovereignty a vehicle for the gradual adaptation of the content of the constitution, but it was itself also a gradually adaptable and adapted vehicle. No extraordinary or plainly discontinuous assertion of constitutional authority was required to adjust the constitution to new times and circumstances, but merely the latest and so normatively continuous assertion of a supple legislative sovereignty doctrine. Through procedures and conventions that adjusted the composition of Parliament and the manner and form of its law-making from time to time, the doctrine of parliamentary sovereignty proved pliable enough to allow continuity and adaptation, or at least the appearance of

[16] On the history of relative inattention at the English centre of British constitutional thought and practice to the lessons of constitutional flux and the examples of constitutional difference at the Celtic edges and in the colonial beyond, see, eg, Christine Bell, *Constitutional Transitions: The Peculiarities of the British Constitution and the Politics of Comparison*, Public Law 446 [2014]; see also Christopher McCrudden, *Northern Ireland and the British Constitution since the Belfast Agreement*, in The Changing Constitution 227 (6th ed., Jeffrey Jowell & Dawn Oliver eds., 2007).

[17] Linda Colley, Acts of Union and Disunion 140 (2014).

[18] Including, famously, both Bagehot, *supra* note 14 and Dicey, *supra* note 15.

continuity and adaptation, in situations where the structure, role or reach of the very institution – Parliament – to which the doctrine referred was at stake and where a more rigid doctrine would have provoked rupture.

In the case of Union with Scotland in 1707, for example, according to the dominant constitutional understanding, though with intermittent protests from Scottish political culture and constitutional thought,[19] the sovereignty of the Westminster Parliament merely continued and the new was 'incorporated into' and absorbed by the old.[20] Similarly, the initiation of the great democratic revolution of Parliament in the Reform Act of 1832 or, towards the end of that journey, the move to limit the competence of the undemocratic Lords to frustrate the will of the democratic house in the Parliament Acts (1911 and 1949) promised structural reform of Parliament and its internal relations without disturbing the basic concept and status of parliamentary sovereignty.

Ackerman's ideal type of establishment-centred pragmatic adaptation captures well enough this long-running constitutional narrative. He points to the strategic efforts of the British governing classes to secure the avoidance of the revolutionary route taken by France at the time of the Napoleonic Wars as one important landmark in the consolidation of a tradition in which pragmatic insiders repeatedly make concessions to moderate outsiders, thereby absorbing them into the political establishment and separating them from their more radical brethren.[21] He appreciates the self-reinforcing quality of this constitutional orientation, the way in which, just as much as in the case of the more legible heritage of a revolutionary constitutional document, both the basic material structure of the unwritten British constitution – the institutions and supporting doctrine of parliamentary sovereignty – and the ambient constitutional culture facilitate continuation in the same incrementalist vein and militate against any radical departure.

Yet Ackerman also points to the ways in which this conservative logic has begun to erode. His particular focus is on the continuing saga of the UK's turbulent relationship to the EU, and in particular on the drawn-out endgame – if that is what it turns out to be – of Brexit.[22] He makes much of the anomalous quality of the referendum within the UK's evolutionary tradition of pragmatic adaptation – of how the plebiscite's direct democratic appeal to the people as the fount of constitutional authority sits uncomfortably with the more establishmentarian basis of legitimacy implicit in the idea of the sovereignty of

[19] Growing louder and more insistent in the twentieth century, and supplying an important bridging resource for the sovereigntist claims that underpin contemporary arguments for Scottish independence; see, eg, Neil Walker, *Beyond the Unitary Conception of the United Kingdom Constitution*, Public Law 384 [2000].

[20] See in particular A.V. Dicey and Robert Rait, Thoughts on the Union between England and Scotland (1920) especially ch. 4; for discussion, see Neil MacCormick, Questioning Sovereignty: Law, State, and Nation in the European Commonwealth (1999) ch. 4; Colin Kidd, Union and Unionisms: Political Thought in Scotland, 15002000: Political Thought in Scotland, 1500–2000 (2008).

[21] Ackerman, supra note 2 at 4–5.

[22] *Id.* at 12–18.

the Crown-in-Parliament. The opportunistic introduction of the referendum mechanism by the Labour government in 1975 may have worked as a means to affirm and solidify the UK's new membership of the European Union (EU), but it also set a precedent for the undoing of that result through a second vote 41 years later. Not only has the Brexit vote created profound tension between Parliament and the people as competing sources of legitimacy, with a significant post-referendum majority in Parliament remaining opposed to or ambivalent about withdrawal and with ongoing controversy about the extent to which the sovereign legislature can or should guide or otherwise interfere with the withdrawal process, but this novel assertion of constitutional voice has also upsets other features of the constitutional orthodoxy within the pragmatic tradition. In particular, as the landmark *Miller* case[23] has demonstrated, it places the apex court in the position of constitutional umpire between the traditional constitutional source of Parliament and the new stream of popular authority. This is an elevated role with which the senior British judiciary is hardly familiar and to which, in the absence of a canonical textual framework to authorise and direct its interventions, it has dubious title.

In offering only a snapshot, Ackerman cannot, of course, tell the whole story of the erosion of the UK tradition of pragmatic adaptation. He could have said more, as he has done at some length elsewhere,[24] about the pressures towards greater autonomy and even independence in the Celtic nations. He could have discussed how the referendum mechanism has also had a destabilising effect in this context – notably in the only narrow failure of the 'Yes' vote in the Scottish independence referendum of 2014 – and also how the classical solution of a symmetrical organisation of state governments in accordance with a governing federal law is hardly available in the UK, with its lop-sided regions (with England accounting for over 85 per cent of the population) and with no constitutional provision for legislative hierarchy. He could also have spoken of other pressures within an increasingly multi-polar legal environment, such as those occasioned by membership of the human rights regime of the Council of Europe. More generally, he could have talked of how a repetitive pattern of resistance to the various challenges to the absoluteness of the doctrine of parliamentary sovereignty has underlined the resilience of the politico-cultural 'shibboleth'[25] that a unitary

[23] R (Miller) v. Secretary of State for Exiting the European Union (2017) U.K.S.C. 5.

[24] Bruce Ackerman, *Why Britain Needs a Written Constitution – and Can't Wait for Parliament to Write One*, 89 Political Quarterly 584 (2018); and see further in the same journal issue Stuart White & Anthony Barnett, *Towards Popular Sovereignty: A Response to Bruce Ackerman's 'Dis-united Kingdom': Constitutional Choices after Brexit* (at 590); Felicity Matthews, *Fully Symmetrical Federalism: A Bold Idea But One That's Not Demanded* (at 594); Michael Kenny, *Why Symmetry May Not Be the Answer to the UK's Constitutional Unsettlement: A Response to Bruce Ackerman* (at 600); Graham Allen, *Democracy: Defend Yourself or Die: A Response to Bruce Ackerman' (604); Bruce Ackerman, 'Is Britain Ready for a Constitutional Convention?' A Rejoinder* (at 608).

[25] As Loughlin & Tierney, *supra* note 13, argue, for all that the doctrine of parliamentary sovereignty is closely linked to the idea of an evolutionary constitutional order, the scope for such evolutionary change has long been constrained by the deep cultural conviction that ultimate political authority should be concentrated at the centre

and highly centralised framework of constitutional authority should remain the doctrine's institutional accompaniment, and in so doing has also exposed the limits to the flexibility of the evolutionary model. And, relatedly, he could have referred to the cumulative effect of the experience of the various recent challenges, and of the political friction generated by these challenges, upon the UK's 'high' judicial and legal-intellectual culture, undermining elite confidence in the efficacy of the constitutional inheritance (an effect exacerbated by increasing domestic awareness of the anomalous position of the UK in a global environment where the template of a written constitution of higher law is the norm and sovereignty is concentrated on no single institution).[26]

Against this wider backdrop, too much might be made of the Brexit moment, and the undoubtedly disruptive re-introduction of the referendum virus. For this is only one of a number of potential triggers of constitutional stress in an environment where the default source of any solution to the problem of constitutional legitimacy is also the source of the problem itself; namely, the very institutional arrangement in whose favour the writ of parliamentary sovereignty still runs, delivering the power of constitutional renewal and reform itself, and, just as importantly, the power of denial of renewal and reform, into the narrow hands of the political party and executive able to command a legislative majority in the House of Commons in any particular electoral cycle rather than in some more broadly inclusive and more widely legitimated constituency. Therefore, we should not focus narrowly on the contingencies of the Brexit scenario, including the series of political miscalculations by the Conservative government that brought the 2016 referendum about and helped galvanise the Leave vote, as the catalyst for constitutional turmoil. Arguably, as the Scottish independence referendum of 2014 also revealed and as is further demonstrated by the tensions stoked by the stubborn failure of the Brexit negotiations to safeguard the open border between the Northern Irish part of the UK and the Irish Republic on which the continuing adhesion of Northern Ireland to the UK may depend,[27] the lack of an agreed, diversity-sensitive mechanism of constitutional reform to counter the centripetal tendencies within the constitutional order has threatened and continues to threaten profound constitutional difficulties on a number of fronts.

In sum, the UK appears to be encountering a 'paradox of initiative'[28] in its constitutional politics. While some political voices have called for root and branch reform, and perhaps even a written settlement,[29] the very factors which make

[26] See, eg, the collection of critical constitutional writings by the most influential English Court of Appeal judge of his generation: Stephen Sedley, Ashes and Sparks: Essays on Law and Justice (2011).

[27] See, eg, John Doyle & Eileen Connolly, *Brexit and the Northern Ireland Question, in* The Law and Politics of Brexit 139 (Federico Fabbrini ed., 2017).

[28] Walker, *supra* note 13 at 542; see also Ackerman, *Why Britain Needs a Written Constitution, supra* at note 24.

[29] See, eg, Christine Palau, The Politics of a Written Constitution for Britain (February 12, 2015), https://blog.politics.ox.ac.uk/politics-written-constitution-britain; Tom Clark, *Crisis: Why it is Time to Rewire British Politics*, Prospect 19 (2019).

renewal urgent also conspire against its happening. In Ackermanian terms, we might say that while the pragmatic adaptation model is in trouble, there is neither the widely endorsed revolutionary momentum to overturn it, nor are political forces so aligned as to encourage the formation or facilitate access to the constitutional levers of the state of the kind of elite coalition that could trigger reconstruction. What this means for the future of the British constitution in a changing European setting, and what it implies for Ackerman's scheme as a way of making sense of the British constitution, we will return to after we have considered the case of the EU.

III. The EU and the Limits of Elite Construction

In his preliminary discussion of the ideal type of elite construction, Ackerman does not place the EU top of his list; rather, he looks to post-Franco Spain and to post-war Germany and Japan as clearer examples of where and how a power vacuum is filled by previously excluded or unformed elites. Unlike the revolutionary model, here 'the general population remains relatively passive on the sidelines',[30] whereas unlike the pragmatic-adaptive model, the existing political establishment does not remain in control of the situation, but must defer to (and, at best, participate in) a new elaborate compact produced by outside (though not necessarily foreign) elites. As Ackerman recognises, many constitutional pathways forged through elite construction, as much as those led by revolutionary movements, begin from a point of political collapse, a circumstance which provides favourably pliant conditions for resourceful elites just as it does – in the revolutionary model – for mass-party movements. Therefore, at least as interesting and challenging as the question of how elite constructions are constructed is the question of how they retain their legitimacy once the vacuum has been filled, the initial urgency has receded and the regime has become routinised. This Ackerman dubs the problem of 'authenticity'.[31] Representing neither a revolutionary movement engaged in a sustained struggle to honour the revolutionary principles nor a deeply entrenched establishment with a long track record of stable government, the second-generation elite regime encounters a distinct set of difficulties in sustaining its title to constitutional authority.

In certain respects, the EU hardly fits this model of elite construction. Most fundamentally, unlike every other example considered by Ackerman, it is not a state and, as Ackerman asserts and as I would agree, it cannot be treated as equivalent to a state just because it shares some of the power-distributive features of a federal union.[32] Rather, it is unique in its successful assertion of some of the areas

[30] Ackerman, *supra* note 2 at 6.
[31] *Id.* at 18.
[32] *Id.* at 21.

of final authority we associate with a state without making the monopolistic claim to comprehensive and only *self*-limiting external-regarding sovereign authority peculiar to a state. Therefore, the EU's relationship with its own Member States – a relationship that also changes the character of these members – is not one of the mutual exclusivity of monopolistic sovereign authority, as in the classical pattern of inter-state relations of high political modernity. Instead, it involves the disaggregation, mutual distribution and reconciliation of the various aspect of sovereign power between the 'centre' and the 'parts', with neither source ceding to the other as an overall authority in the final instance.[33]

In other more particular respects too, the EU differs from the paradigm case of elite construction. Even though we cannot make sense of its origins other than by reference to the broader project of state *re*construction in post-war Europe, the EU did not itself replace any failed or war-ravaged state, or seek to carve out a new sovereign territory within the wider disorderly space left by conflict. It supplemented rather than substituted, providing a supranational context to add to and in some ways reshape and connect the various nation-states within its purview; however, these very nation-states both provided its generative force and survived its generation. For the EU was born *not* of previously excluded elites seeking to usurp existing power complexes within the nation-state, as in Ackerman's typical case. Rather, it was an initiative of senior political representatives of these various member states seeking to provide a new stabilising framework of continental relations based upon a degree of transnational policy integration – particularly in economic matters – that was unprecedented in the history of the modern state.

Yet it is undoubtedly the case today that the EU suffers from many of the same second-generation 'authenticity' problems associated with Ackerman's numerous statist examples of elite construction. To repeat, supra-national Europe may not have been constructed by elites external to existing state power structures, though there was a notable common thread of cosmopolitan commitment joining key national 'founding fathers' such as Schuman, Monnet, Adenauer and De Gasperi.[34] However, its basic architecture, with the European Commission as the key policy-making body, placed an elite administrative corps at the centre of its political machinery from the very outset. And, with the Commission and its presidents often in the vanguard as the remit of the EU has expanded far beyond the original mandate of the EEC in the over 60-year-old Treaty of Rome to cover a wide range of policy areas beyond the micro-economic core, and from its initial Western European club of six to today's 28 states, the initial justificatory context has become increasingly remote from contemporary concerns. In particular, since the 1992 Treaty of Maastricht's innovative designs in monetary, social, justice and foreign policy, Europe had undergone a period of rapid expansion of competences and regulatory infrastructure as well as of territory. It is an expansion that has

[33] See, eg, Neil Walker, *Constitutional Pluralism Revisited*, 23 European Law Journal 333 (2016).

[34] See, eg, Joseph Weiler, *The Political and Legal Culture of European Integration: An Exploratory Essay*, 9 International Journal of Constitutional Law 678 (2011).

taken the European project well beyond its early comfort zone of an elite-driven 'permissive consensus'[35] on market-making and the consolidation of continental peace.

In these circumstances, as Ackerman claims, the failed documentary constitutional initiative of the previous decade might be seen as a missed opportunity to reboot the EU's legitimacy.[36] In the summer of 2007, the European Council announced its decision to 'abandon' the 'constitutional concept' it had endorsed so optimistically only four years previously on receiving the draft of a first Constitutional Treaty for the European Union from the Convention on the Future of Europe. Established by the European Council (of national government leaders) under the presidency of Giscard d'Estaing following the failure of the Treaty of Nice (2001) to deliver significant reform to the EU's machinery of government,[37] the Convention had developed significant early momentum and delivered a draft within two years. But after 'a period of reflection'[38] following the pivotal 'no' votes in the 2005 French and Dutch referendums to the (duly promulgated) Constitutional Treaty, and recognising the document's uncertain popularity and unratified status in various other Member States, Europe's leaders opted to jettison the brave new world of a supranational constitution and return to the more familiar international law vehicle of a reform treaty.[39]

Yet we should be careful just how we read the historical implications of the failed constitutional initiative. One the one hand, we should not be too quick to view the failed Constitutional Treaty, counterfactually, as a solution to the EU's problems. On the other hand, we should also acknowledge that the very fact of its having been tried and failed might have had significant and lasting – and perhaps negative – consequences for the legitimacy of the EU.[40]

If we examine the second matter first, we find conflicting views. Certainly, the abruptness with which the 'Big-C'[41] word was dropped by the European Council and consigned to the dustbin of unmentionables in 2007 speaks of a determination to put behind them what many of the Constitutional Treaty's erstwhile sponsors had come to view as an ill-starred adventure. According to this revised understanding, such an ambitious project had been doomed from the start, although it required the salutary lesson of its failure for the political classes of Europe to appreciate this and to return to pre-constitutional business as usual.

[35] Ian Down & Carole Wilson, *From 'Permissive Consensus' to 'Constraining Dissensus': A Polarizing Union?*, 43 Acta Politica 26 (2008).

[36] Ackerman, *supra* note 2 at 22–23.

[37] German Presidency Conclusions, European Council, Brussels, June 21–22, 2007.

[38] Belgian Presidency Conclusions, European Council, Brussels, June 16–17, 2005.

[39] Treaty of Lisbon amending the Treaty on European Union and the Treaty establishing the European Community, Dec. 13, 2007, 2007 O. J. (C 306) 01.

[40] For an extended treatment of these questions, see Neil Walker, *Europe's Constitutional Overture, in* The Rise and Fall of the European Constitution 177 (Nick Barber, Maria Cahill & Richard Ekins eds., 2018).

[41] Neil Walker, *Big "C" or Small "c"?*, 12 European Law Journal 12 (2006).

But perhaps the failed constitutional project was no mere legacy-free historical blip. Perhaps it was not just a failed solution, but itself part of the problem. In this more sceptical reading, the Constitutional Treaty provides a forewarning of later difficulties and, more concretely, may even supply an early link in the causal chain that has led the EU to its current state of political vulnerability and increasing uncertainty over its future. From this perspective, the abortive constitutional initiative marked and in some measure contributed to a downturn in the health of the supranational body politic. The trend in the 20 years preceding the constitutional project had been towards ever-deeper integration in an ever-widening EU, with each new treaty – the Single European Act, and the Treaties of Maastricht, Amsterdam and Nice – a fresh chapter in a cumulative success story. However, after the failure of the constitution, and notwithstanding the repairs achieved at Lisbon, the EU encountered a series of fundamental challenges. These began with the sovereign debt crisis and the pressure this placed on the single currency and the framework of Economic and Monetary Union, and have continued through unprecedented problems of mass migration and security to the more remote but real contemporary threat – headlined by Brexit but also present in the rise of nativist Euroscepticism across Europe[42] – to the very sustainability of the EU as a political settlement. In this more pessimistic vision, the failed constitution can be viewed as indicative of a pattern of institutional overreach – and associated political hubris – which risked and has found a severe reaction in subsequent events.

If we now return to the counterfactual question – would a successful Constitutional Treaty have made a positive difference – we see that the answer is a complicated one, and also one that throws into doubt any strong claims about the actual effects of the Constitutional Treaty's failure. We can begin this inquiry by drawing on Ackerman's own well-expressed scepticism about the significance of positive law as a marker of constitutional change. Ackerman claims that the distinctions he draws between the three ideal types of constitutional trajectory – revolutionary, elitist and insider-pragmatic – are far from mapping neatly onto different levels of formal constitutional (dis)continuity.[43] Elite constitutional constructions often manage a decisive break – a Kelsenian revolution – from the past in terms of legal form and, indeed, Ackerman notes it to be a feature, and a conscious strategy, of many such elite constitutions to mimic the more radical moods and gestures of revolutionary constitutions.[44] Conversely, some genuinely insurgent movements, such as South Africa at Time One, manage to gain constitutional traction without departing from any of the formal amendment rules of the old constitution.

The key point to take from this sceptical insight is that constitutional form only tells us so much about the real significance of constitutions and of the

[42] See, eg, Jan-Werner Muller, What is Populism? (2016).
[43] Ackerman, *supra* note 2 at 36–37.
[44] *Id.* at 6–7.

changes they may bring about. And that, I would contend, is both because constitutions are multi-functional instruments and because one of their key functions involves making claims that are performative rather than descriptive, aspirational rather than evidential, persuasive rather than disinterested. To briefly explain, we may understand constitutional functions as operating across two broad dimensions. In the legal-institutional dimension, the documentary constitution has a normative design function, supplying both an 'operating manual' for the system of governmental authority and a 'blueprint'[45] of how and to what purposes the polity should develop. In the socio-political dimension, by contrast, the documentary constitution has an expressive function,[46] and it is here that the broader performative meaning of the constitutional act and process is nurtured. Through various devices – the mobilisation of support in the constitution-making phase, the investment in the constitutional agreement itself as both token and achievement of a common way of political being, the continuous assertion and refinement of key communal norms and aspirations and the valorisation of key constitutional institutions, and the collective memorialisation over time of a litany common events, experiences and accomplishments as part of the constitutional record – the constitution operates as a cultural vector concerned with the process and terms of socio-political integration. In other words, the constitution nurtures and (through various constitutionally interested actors) conveys a set of meanings about its particular object – the polity (and typically statal) entity which has been constituted or is being (re)constituted – that encourages the audience of those addressed and affected to develop an image of that entity *qua* polity; an image in terms of which that audience comes to see itself and sustain an understanding of itself as a community of attachment engaged in a particular form of common political life.

If we return to the draft Constitution of 2003–07, we can see that it was in fact a magnet for number of different types of project that combined normative design and expressive functions in different ways. In other words, the unprecedented idea of a written constitution for a supranational object came to be supported in sponsorship of quite different conceptions of the European polity.[47] On one view, a written constitutional settlement was primarily a symbolic measure – a way of charting and commemorating a new and higher stage of common achievement in the gradual progression of the European project, or even, and more conservatively, as a way of according 'finality'[48] to the distinct cumulative accomplishment

[45] Tom Ginsberg & Alberto Simpser, *Introduction, in* Constitutions in Authoritarian Regimes 1 (Tom Ginsberg and Alberto Simpser eds., 2015).

[46] Mark Tushnet, *The Possibilities of Comparative Constitutional Law*, 108 Yale L.J. 1225 (1999).

[47] For fuller discussion, see Neil Walker, Europe's Constitutional Momentum and the Search for Polity Legitimacy, 3 International Journal of Constitutional Law 211, 225–31 (2005).

[48] In the well-known formulation of Joschka Fischer, Foreign Minister of the Federal Republic of Germany, From Confederacy to Federation – Thoughts on the Finality of European Integration (speech at the Humboldt University, Berlin, 12 May 2000), https://federalunion.org.uk/joschka-fischer-from-confederacy-to-federation-thoughts-on-the-finality-of-european-integration. This speech is widely credited as a key moment in the mobilisation of political opinion in favour of a 'Big C' constitutional process.

of the supranational form and supplying a token of the successful attainment of a minimal threshold of transnational political community. For others, more ambitiously, and combining both instrumental and expressive functions, it was seen as a platform from which to build on the unwritten constitutional *acquis* towards a fuller political entity with more state-like tendencies, including a still wider and deeper jurisdiction and a more ample framework of democratic representation.[49] However, in marked contrast to all these views, some positions wary of further supranational expansion also came to endorse the idea of attributing constitutional weight and significance to a new settlement as a way of reining in and containing the process of integration. The (short-lived) conversion of the traditionally Eurosceptic *The Economist* magazine to the case for a written constitution, for instance, was contingent upon such a limiting approach.[50] So too, to take another example, was the support of the German Länder, wary of the internal competence creep of national federal government over an expanding set of matters deemed to fall within its 'foreign affairs' European jurisdiction. In these and other cases, a constitutional settlement was affirmed for its capacity, through mechanisms such as the EU Charter of Rights and the competence catalogue, to condition and restrict as much as to constitute supranational governmental authority. Importantly, however, this too involved endorsing not only certain aspects of normative design, but also the symbolic power and cultural force of the constitutional idea in expressing a particular – if more restrictive – vision of the Europolity.

That in the final analysis the constitutional project, despite being ratified by 17 out of 27 Member States, was, of course, *not* successfully concluded speaks to the difficulties for any such symbolic capital-building endeavour to 'get going' in the face of substantial internal differences over specific normative content, general integrative aspiration and legal form, and over their optimal combination. For we have observed how the particular polity visions favoured by different constituencies – evolutional, conservative, transformative and truncated – were quite distinctive, involving contrasting understandings of the scope and trajectory of the EU polity and of its appropriate relationship to the existing Member State polities. But in addition to these differences of vision – and their different associated cognitive understandings and practical orientations – not to mention the possible differences, separately noted by Ackerman, caused by different national constituencies tending to favour the supranational model most closely aligned to their own national constitutional ideal type,[51] the constitutional project also had to overcome the opposition of those firmly set against the constitutional form itself,

[49] See, eg, Jurgen Habermas, *Why Europe Needs a Constitution*, 11 New Left Review 5 (2001).
[50] See The Economist, November 4, 2000.
[51] Ackerman, *supra* note 2 at 24–26. I remain unsure just how significant this kind of cultural-aesthetic affinity was (or might become) in explaining differences of approach to the EU constitution, as opposed to the strategic preference for models in terms of their likelihood to produce differing levels of integration that I have focused upon here. But this additional and under-researched question of legal culture certainly deserves closer study.

and so against the very idea of the EU as an entity capable of developing its own reflexive conception of the common good rather than a dependent product of its Member States.[52] Popular rejection in France and the Netherlands was, arguably, as much if not more about political-cultural opposition from those who believed that *no* form of autonomous constitutional identity for the EU (and so no version of 'we' feeling) could do other than 'steal the clothes' of the Member States and diminish their constitutional standing as it was about distinctions and disagreement amongst the different constitutional polity visions for the EU.[53]

Therefore, just because it was itself capable of bearing so many meanings and carrying such diverse aspirations, it would be wrong to read too much about the *general* potential of constitutionalism in the European setting into the failure of this initial Big 'C' constitutional project. Its demise, then, should not be seen as the demise of any particular constitutional perspective, but speaks to the failure to find sufficiently secure common ground amongst all the contending visions of Europe's constitutional future. Certainly, however, to return to the matter of historical causality, in the short term the failure of 2001–07 *did* have a chilling effect. There was little explicit talk of a documentary constitution for a number of years afterwards. Yet at the same time, one of the consequences of the whole process was that constitutional discourse became more familiar and so continued, and even intensified, in a lower political key. Constitutional debate kept going through discussion in judicial, political and academic circles of the 'many' aspects of EU's supposedly unwritten constitution – not just the 'juridical constitution' but also the 'political constitution', the 'economic constitution', the 'security constitution' and the 'social constitution'[54] – and if not a written constitution, then at least norms of 'supra-constitutional'[55] standing, a 'constitutional compromise' or an informal 'constitutional settlement'.[56] While much of this talk remained ostensibly within a legal-institutional register, the inseparability of this

[52] The academic expression of this deeper form of Big 'C' constitutional scepticism comes in various forms. On one view, which is actually quite close to the approval of a written constitution as a mark of evolutionary achievement, the EU is seen as possessing an unprecedentedly organic development and complex richness which cannot be appropriately reduced to and frozen in a single self-contained documentary Constitution; see, eg, Joseph Weiler, *In Defence of the Status Quo: Europe's Constitutional* Sonderweg, *in* European Constitutionalism beyond the State 7 (Joseph Weiler & Marlene Wind eds., 2003). Or, in a more uncompromising variation of the sceptical theme, resort to constitutional language by an entity so lacking in the properties of comprehensive political self-authorisation associated with the state tradition is deemed of such incongruence that for it to develop a fully fledged written constitution would be a 'category error' – an exercise in misconceived and wilful self-aggrandisement; see, eg, Andrew Moravcsik, *A Category Error*, Prospect 22 (2005).

[53] See, eg, Stephen Tierney, Constitutional Referendums 156–61 (2012); Min Shu, *Referendums and the Political Constitutionalisation of the EU*, 14 European Law Journal 423 (2008).

[54] See, eg, the discussion of the many faces of European constitutionalism in Kaarlo Tuori, European Constitutionalism (2015) especially ch. 1.

[55] See, eg, Yaniv Roznai, Unconstitutional Constitutional Amendments (2017) ch. 3.

[56] See, eg, Andrew Moravcsik, *The European Constitutional Compromise and the Neo-functionalist Legacy*, 12 Journal of European Public Policy 349 (2005); Andrew Moravcsik, *The European Constitutional Settlement*, 31 The World Economy 158 (2008).

normative dimension from the expressive dimension and its socio-political register meant that the cultural suggestion of larger constitutional possibilities never disappeared.

Today, faced with the more fundamental set of challenges to the sustenance of the EU discussed earlier, we can detect the stirrings of renewed contemplation of a Big 'C' constitutional initiative, not just in civil society and academic settings but increasingly in high political circles.[57] These build upon and feed into a wider re-engagement with the possibility of route and branch reform of the EU, exemplified by the Commission's recent 'White Paper on the Future of Europe'.[58]

But what prospects are there at this constitutional crossroads for a successful new initiative succeeding the long phase of elite constructivism? And how, if at all, might any such initiative be understood in terms of Ackerman's revolutionary paradigm? Let us now consider that question alongside that of the similar prospects of the UK.

IV. At the Crossroads: Towards Managed Revolution?

Earlier I provisionally introduced the term 'managed revolution' in trying to imagine what might happen at the crossroads between an establishmentarian constitution in the British tradition or an elitist constitution in the EU tradition, and a more open-ended constitutional process that draws upon at least some of the features of Ackerman's more widely inclusive conception of political revolution. 'Managed revolution' is obviously oxymoronic, and intentionally so. But the point is not to celebrate paradox or to indicate the impossibility of combining apparently opposite features; rather, it is to understand what might be both familiar and well-trodden, and at the same time novel and distinctive, about constitutional movement at these particular crossroads.

In setting out his general scheme, Ackerman, as already noted, wants to guard against the view that the revolutionary paradigm has had its day and is now giving

[57] See, eg, the Sorbonne speech of French President Emmanuel Macron of 26 September 2017, http://international.blogs.ouest-france.fr/archive/2017/09/29/macron-sorbonne-verbatim-europe-18583.html (English version). See also the Ljubljana Initiative, launched by Slovenian President, Borut Pahor: www.up-rs.si/up-rs/uprs-eng.nsf/pages/5D15E0B0A4878677C12580E20041A7E7?OpenDocument; and the Rome Manifesto, https://www.united-europe.eu/uncategorized/the-rome-manifestoproposals-by-the-next-generation. See also the DiEM 25 Initiative, launched by former Greek Minister Yanis Varoufakis in 2015, A Manifesto for Democratizing Europe, https://diem25.org/manifesto-lange-version. For general discussion of the state of constitutional ripeness in the EU today, see, eg, Matej Avbelj, Transformation of EU Constitutionalism (June 22, 2016), http://dx.doi.org/10.17176/20160622-161220; see also Markus Patberg, *Challenging the Masters of the Treaties: Emerging Narratives of Constituent Power in the European Union*, 7 Global Constitutionalism 263 (2018).

[58] European Commission, White Paper on the Future of Europe, https://ec.europa.eu/commission/white-paper-future-europe-reflections-and-scenarios-eu27_en, discussed at length in Matej Avbelj, What Future for the European Union?, WZB Discussion Paper 2017–802, July 2017, https://bibliothek.wzb.eu/pdf/2017/iv17-802.pdf.

way to other models. In particular, he stresses the distinction between the revolutionary paradigm and what he calls recent 'Third Wave' approaches,[59] which, broadly speaking, focus upon the operation of elites and upon 'pacted transitions' negotiated by elites as the key motor of change and which, for Ackerman, would presumptively belong within his quite separate elite construction paradigm. Against the view that the Third Wave is becoming the new norm, he insists on the continued relevance and clear distinctiveness of a form in which 'a mass-movement of citizen-activists [have] struggled in the People's name'[60] and where the bargaining process at the constitutional table 'is profoundly shaped by the high-energy politics in the larger society'.[61]

Yet, as again previously indicated, Ackerman is also prepared to contemplate hybridity in both British[62] and EU[63] cases. And, certainly, there are features of his broader constitutional theory which incline in that direction. In particular, his well-established work on Deliberative Polls and on the notion of a Deliberation Day[64] point towards a conception of constitutional process which is both closely planned and 'managed' in advance and broadly transformative, even 'revolutionary' in intent. Whereas in the classic revolutionary model, the constitutional process is galvanised by the broader political movement, in the deliberative model, the constitutional process is intended to be *galvanising*. The aim, executed through a multi-stage process of constitutional learning and involvement,[65] is to engage the two main constitutional functions at a high level – both to refine the normative design of the constitution and to deepen its expressive potential as a way of mobilising a new consensus on the nature and direction of the political society. What is more, Ackerman has explicitly set out proposals in both the British[66] and the EU[67] context which would involve intervention along these lines.

However, the following question remains: just how feasible is it to construct and pursue this kind of hybrid approach? A Procrustean scepticism might hold that any such managed revolution is bound to collapse back into either of two more conventional (and Ackerman-familiar) options. On the one hand, given

[59] Ackerman, *supra* note 2 at 38–40 and see the references therein to a range of key authors, from Juan Linz to Tom Ginsberg.

[60] *Id.* at 6.

[61] *Id.* at 39.

[62] *Id.* at 17.

[63] *Id.* at 23.

[64] See especially Bruce Ackerman & James Kishkin, Deliberation Day (2004).

[65] For a recent approach which overlaps considerably with the Ackermanian turn to hybridity, see the 'Round Table' thesis of Andrew Arato, Post-sovereign Constitution Making: Learning and Legitimacy (2016).

[66] Ackerman, *Why Britain Needs a Written Constitution*, *supra* at note 24; Ackerman, *Is Britain Ready for a Constitutional Convention?*, *supra* at note 24.

[67] Bruce Ackerman and Miguel Maduro, How to Make a European Constitution for the 21st Century (October 8, 2012), https://globernance.org/ackerman-maduro-how-to-make-a-european-constitution-for-the-21st-century-4/?lang=en.

Ackerman's own caution concerning the tendency of elitist constitutions to wear revolutionary clothes, it might well be that the broader revolutionary claims of any new British or EU constitutional initiative that happened to succeed would be largely a matter of window-dressing – a 'managed' outcome of a 'managed' process with limited broader participation and limited penetration of the broader reaches of civil society. On the other hand, to the extent that the process was genuinely revolutionary in intent, we are faced again with the paradox of initiative and its attendant viciously circular logic. *How is it possible to persuade a broad constituency – majorities in all the constituent nations in the UK case and in all Member States in the EU case – that they have a common interest, the better service or even the preservation of which depends upon their embarking on a new and inclusive process leading to a fresh and deep constitutional commitment to common cause, when there is presently the kind of disagreement within that broad constituency about the direction, and for some the very principle of such common cause, whose prospects of successful resolution would seem to depend on just that kind of process of engagement already having taken place?* In other words, as the contemporary politics of the UK and the EU suggest, the very conditions that fuel the call for a new and genuinely transformative settlement also militate against its serious attempt.

Yet if we relax our Procrustean severity, we might, in conclusion, glimpse another possibility. The unsettled nature of the European constitutional scene today is throwing up a large number of urgent problems, ranging from Brexit to the fragmentary pressure of the Celtic nations in the UK, and of the autonomous regions – especially Catalonia[68] – in Spain, and to the very future of the EU itself, faced with new Eurosceptic challenges in many states, including Italy, Austria, Hungary and Poland.[69] At the heart of these problems lies the very question of the continuing adequacy of the modern sovereigntist framework of constitutional possibilities. Europe under the aegis of the EU, as we have seen, has hosted a constitutional experiment over 60 years in which the traditional prerogatives of sovereignty are increasingly split across different levels of government. This has led to two sharply opposing tendencies.

On the one hand, it has meant that many constitutional disputes and projects have lost their either/or quality. In 2014, for example, the Scottish bid for independence from the rest of the UK was predicated upon and indeed encouraged by the prospect of continuing membership, alongside the rest of the UK, in the EU post-independence, while the thwarted Catalan process was, at least from the Catalan side, predicated upon the same sense of the separating and recombination

[68] Jose Luis Marti, Catalonia in Deadlock: And Why That is a European Problem' (January 2, 2018), https://verfassungsblog.de/author/jose-luis-marti.

[69] See, eg, Nicholas Pawley, *Mainstreaming Euroscepticism? An Analysis of the Effects of the Politicisation of Europe in Domestic Elections on the Framing Strategies of the Centre-Right in Britain, France and Germany*, Les cahiers européens de sciences Po 3 (2017), https://www.sciencespo.fr/centre-etudes-europeennes/sites/sciencespo.fr.centre-etudes-europeennes/files/03_2017%20Pawley.pdf.

of sovereign authority across different levels.[70] When outcomes are no longer zero-sum for all interested parties in terms of the presence or absence of sovereign authority or of recognition of a singular (as opposed to a plural) constitutional identity and citizenship claim, it is easier to conceive of processes which are both somehow widely agreed or acquiesced and closely managed in their initial design – as, for example, in the hybrid quasi-international 'Edinburgh Agreement' between the sovereign UK government and the devolved Scottish government setting out the terms of the 2014 referendum,[71] yet potentially revolutionary in terms of depth of engagement and impact. By the same token, it is also easier in these less fraught circumstances to envisage the kind of planned deliberative transformation that Ackerman and others contemplate.

On the other hand, however, we find in the same European culture of constitutional politics a strong reaction against this very multi-level sensibility. The Spanish government's rejection of any kind of legal plebiscite for Catalan independence and its reiteration of the indivisibility if the Spanish nation is one example; the uncompromising attitudes of many of the Leave camp in the Brexit vote and in the subsequent pursuit by many of a so-called 'Hard Brexit' is a second example; and the re-assertion of strong forms of autonomous constitutional nationalism from inside the EU by the Hungarian and Polish leadership is a third.

Europe today, it seems, is host to a debate not just about various particular constitutional futures, but at a second-order level, about the very nature and stakes of constitutional debate. On one side, we can see movement towards the kind of hybrid approach of managed revolution in a context of the promotion of multi-level positive-sum constitutional solutions not as an occasional anomaly, but perhaps as a new trend, and one in which Europe is a leading player, if by no means the sole one.[72] On the other side of the debate, we see a reassertion of an older zero-sum sovereigntist constitutional politics – often presented in a populist and exclusionary vein.[73] It is a politics which, like that of its opponents, increasingly has to argue its case not only in the particular, but also in terms of the merits of that kind of approach in general, and, indeed, which gains additional traction

[70] For a comparison of the treatment of the Scottish and Catalan clams to national autonomy within Europe's multi-level constitutional space, see Neil Walker, *Teleological and Reflexive Nationalism in the New Europe, in* Changing Borders in Europe: Exploring the Dynamics of Integration, Differentiation and Self-Determination in the European Union 163 (Jacint Jordana, Michael Keating, Axel Marx and Jan Wouters eds., 2019).

[71] Agreement between the United Kingdom Government and the Scottish Government on a Referendum on Independence for Scotland (Edinburgh, October 15, 2012), https://www.webarchive.org.uk/wayback/archive/20170701045319/www.gov.scot/About/Government/concordats/Referendum-on-independence.

[72] See, eg, Michael Keating, Plurinational Democracy: Stateless Nations in a Post-sovereignty Era (2001).

[73] For discussion, see Neil Walker, *Populism and Constitutional Tension*, 17(2) International Journal of Constitutional Law 515 (2019).

from arguing its case in general, as part of a second order, transnationally shared, sovereign-nationalist constitutional imaginary.[74]

And in that unstable matrix of new types of constitutional contestation, we can begin to discern certain developments which, though outside the strict terms of Ackerman's three-way scheme, can be seen as emerging from their remixing. Revolution, we may concur with the author of *Revolutionary Constitutionalism*, still has a part to play in the evolving drama of global constitutionalism, even if shifts in the background scenery mean that, in some cases at least, its internal dynamic will be much changed.

[74] See, eg, Paul Blokker, Populist Constitutionalism (May 4, 2017), www.iconnectblog.com/2017/05/populist-constitutionalism. See also Paul Blokker, *The Imaginary Constitution of Constitutions*, 3 Social Imaginaries 1 (2017).

13

How Europe Brought Judicial Review to France

A Response to Bruce Ackerman

DANIEL HALBERSTAM*

I. Introduction

The European Union (EU) is often presented as an external challenge to the constitutional democracies of the Member States. On this view, the EU threatens to intrude upon the hard-won structures of constitutionalism developed in each Member State on its own, ie, independently of joining the EU. Sometimes, the EU's claim of authority is met with resistance and rejection on this account, as in the UK, Poland and Hungary. At other times, the EU's claim of authority is met far more positively, as in France, Germany and Ireland. Even here, however, the assumption often seems to be that the EU is an external threat to the fully formed constitutionalism of the Member States. In other words, even if we recognise that the EU does some good, we are warned that the EU's supranational governance threatens the 'achievement of constitutionalism' of the Member States themselves.[1]

Bruce Ackerman echoes this theme in his tour de force, *Revolutionary Constitutions*, which takes us on an ambitious tour through modern France, India, Iran, Israel, Italy, Poland, South Africa and the US.[2] Building on Max Weber, Ackerman argues that constitutional law in these systems serves to embody the 'charisma' of revolutionary politics, especially after the charismatic revolutionary leaders are gone or their special virtue has subsided. The revolutions Ackerman singles

* Thanks to Raphaël Beauregard-Lacroix for research assistance. Unless otherwise noted, all translations are mine.

[1] Dieter Grimm, *The Achievement of Constitutionalism and its Prospects in a Changed World*, *in* The Twilight of Constitutionalism? (P. Dobner & M. Loughlin eds., 2010).

[2] Bruce Ackerman, Revolutionary Constitutions: Charismatic Leadership and the Rule of Law (2019).

out change prior legal understandings and practices, but they do not completely remake society in totalitarian fashion. Instead, they preserve the rule of law and embed their revolutionary achievements in a constitution, which everyday actors will enforce for the foreseeable future – or at least until the next revolutionary constitutionalists come along with fresh charisma all of their own.

Returning to Europe, one of the stated goals of Ackerman's enterprise is to show that the EU is uniquely problematic among federations, in that its constituent states come from different constitutional moulds. While the constitutions of some Member States (such as France and Italy) are based on revolutionary constitutionalism, those of others (such as the UK) are the product of pragmatic bargaining by insiders to stave off insurgent outsiders, and those of yet others (such as Germany and Spain) were exclusively constructed by elites in a power vacuum while the general population looked on. One of the important lessons Ackerman wants to draw from all this, both in the book and elsewhere[3] – a meta-narrative, if you will – is that the different traditions of constitutionalism within the various nation-states of Europe are profoundly incompatible with one another, and therefore present deep problems for the EU as a whole.

This chapter responds to the persistent myth of Member States' independent constitutionalism, as well as to Ackerman's European story, with a case study that turns the constitutional inquiry around. It shows how the constitutional traditions of the EU's Member States are not pre-existing conditions confronting Europe, but how Europe profoundly shaped important domestic constitutional developments within the Member States themselves.

This is not the usual story of how Member States compromised their existing constitutions to make way for Europe. Instead, my claim goes beyond that well-known story to demonstrate how Europe shaped and strengthened the underlying development of domestic constitutionalism as such. In particular, focusing on a key Member State that is also a prominent case study in Ackerman's book, I aim to show how Europe was central to the basic development of judicial review in France.

While the French Constitutional Council (Conseil constitutionnel) may have expanded its *ex ante* review of legislative proposals at the behest of privileged officials, it was the regular French judiciary engaged in the implementation of European law that developed *judicial review*, ie, *ex post* constitutional review of enacted legislation in everyday court cases.[4] While the first of these developments,

[3] See *id.* at 21–23; Bruce Ackerman, *Three Paths to Constitutionalism – and the Crisis of the European Union*, 45(4) Brit. J. Pol. Sci. 705 (2015).

[4] What Americans call 'judicial review', ie, a court reviewing the constitutionality of legislation, is considered a certain form of 'constitutional review' in France. In French, when and where such constitutional review takes place becomes clear by additional description or context. While generally using the American term, the text will sometimes use a combination, eg, 'judicial (constitutional) review', or more elaborate phrases,. eg, '*ex post* constitutional review in court' for the sake of clarity.

which Ackerman discusses at length, was authorised by the revolutionary 1958 Constitution, the second development, which Ackerman ignores,[5] was not.

What we find in France, then, is not (only) revolutionary constitutionalism in which heirs to revolutionary movements look back to vindicate prior revolutionary achievements or forge their own. Instead, a central component of modern constitutionalism in France emerges from a rather gradual development of rational construction over time. What is more, this development, which had begun in similar fashion in earlier constitutional eras yet repeatedly stalled, was re-ignited by France's membership in the European Community and finally completed under the decisive influence of the EU and the European Convention on Human Rights (ECHR).

In terms of any meta-narrative, then, Europe and France may not be a constitutional mismatch after all. And France's constitutionalism as we know it today is not solely a domestic achievement. Instead, in a constitutional symbiosis transcending the state, Europe was pivotal in helping France adopt what many consider to be the bedrock of modern constitutional governance – judicial review.

II. The Fourth Republic's Stalemate: International Treaties, Domestic Law and Judicial Review

To understand the significance of European law to the development of French constitutionalism, we must first recall where things stood before France joined the European Community. After the Revolution of 1789, France sat uncomfortably between embracing rights as a normative matter, while institutionally committed to banning judges from any kind of judicial review. While on the one hand placing natural rights at the foundation of all societies and every constitutional enterprise, the Declaration of the Rights of Man and of the Citizen insisted, on the other hand, that any Constitution must also guarantee 'the separation of powers'.[6] The revolutionaries' dislike for the courts of the *ancien régime* had led to an abiding commitment to keep judges out of the business of the legislature. Accordingly, even with its *rights foundationalist* normative theory, France's institutional arrangements since the Revolution had affirmed the pre-eminence of legislation and rejected the idea of judicial review.

Despite efforts of judges and scholars over time to advocate for judicial (constitutional) review,[7] when the 1946 Constitution, marking the creation of the Fourth Republic, was passed, the normative commitment to rights foundationalism was

[5] The chapters on French constitutionalism do not discuss France's membership of the EU or the ECHR.

[6] *Déclaration des droits de l'homme et du citoyen* (1789), art. 16.

[7] See Alec Stone, The Birth of Judicial Politics in France 33–40 (1992).

carried over into the preamble, while the institution of judicial review was rejected yet again.

However, with the Constitution of 1946, debates about judicial review were joined by a seemingly different question: the domestic application of international treaties. The preamble to the Fourth Republic's founding document declared that France, 'faithful to its traditions, abides by the rules of public international law'. Furthermore, the new Article 26 provided that duly ratified diplomatic treaties shall 'have the force of law even if they are contrary to French laws'. And Article 28 emphasised that unless formally abrogated by proper withdrawal, such treaties 'have an authority superior to that of internal laws'. Although these provisions might casually be read as ending the long-standing debate on whether courts should give priority to treaties over contrary domestic legislation, the provisions instead fused this question with the more general one about (domestic) judicial review.

It had long seemed uncontroversial to enforce a treaty in the face of previously passed, contrary legislation.[8] Indeed, the requirement of Article 27 requiring that all treaties 'which modify domestic French laws' must be ratified by a law of Parliament meant that this kind of conflict – ie, between a law and a *later* treaty – was easy. Because the law and the treaty were both passed by Parliament, the conflict between a statute and a *later* treaty could be resolved by simply following the latest expression of Parliament's will.

Yet, the more difficult question arose where a law conflicted with a *prior* treaty. Here, ordinarily, the last-in-time rule dictated disregarding the treaty in favour of the later law. To be sure, even on this rule, a simple interpretive move could often save the earlier treaty. Courts could presume that all laws intend to preserve the force of existing treaties. That is, indeed, what the *Matter* doctrine, named after the principal prosecutor at the French Cour de cassation, the highest court in the regular French judiciary, had held since the 1930s.[9] But what if the later law clearly intended to contradict an earlier treaty? In such a case, the *Matter* doctrine firmly held that the most recent parliamentary act governs and that judges must obey the later law as they 'do not and cannot know any other will than that of the law'.[10]

The burning question, then, was whether the new Articles 26 and 28 changed this rule. Should French courts in the Fourth Republic give force to a treaty even in the face of a later law that explicitly contradicted that earlier treaty? In other words, should courts recognise the 'superior authority' of treaties spelled out in the new Constitution?

The ensuing debate among judges and scholars quickly identified the issue as being, at heart, about judicial review. After all, if a court were to give priority to

[8] See generally Les grands arrêts de la jurisprudence civile 36–37 (Henri Capitant et al. eds., 13th ed., 2015.

[9] See Conclusions de M. le procureur général Paul Matter, Cass. Civ. 22 Dec. 1931, 1 Dalloz (1932) 131.

[10] *Id.* at 140. See also Jens Plötner, *Report on France, in* The European Court and National Courts, 41, 44–45 (Anne-Marie Slaughter et al. eds., 1998).

a treaty over a clearly contrary later law, it would seem to be reviewing, at least indirectly, the constitutionality of that later law.[11] Giving priority to the treaty over the later law would seem to require striking down, setting aside or, at a minimum, ignoring for purposes of a particular case an Act of Parliament because that act was in conflict with the constitutional rule on the priority of treaties.

However, the 1946 Constitution failed, on its terms, to grant judges the power of constitutional review. What is more, the drafters of the 1946 Constitution had repeatedly considered proposals to provide for judicial (constitutional) review, consistently rejecting any such idea. In keeping with France's constitutional history, at least three successive discussions in the drafting of the 1946 Constitution failed to generate support for expanding the traditional role of courts. Indeed, the last debate ended in an explicit vote to reject 'constitutional review'.[12] Even international law enthusiasts, such as Professor Niboyet, longtime editor of a leading French journal on the conflict of laws, thought that this rejection of judicial review precluded courts from enforcing the constitutional supremacy of treaties:

> What would happen if the national assembly passed a law that was contrary to the primacy of treaties, and what would be, in such a case, the approach of the courts? We must recognize that the latter have not received any new powers, and this somewhat tempers Article 28. Even though such a law would indisputably contravene a treaty, and if this were clearly [the law's] meaning, the courts will be disarmed tomorrow as they were yesterday.[13]

Nonetheless, decisions from some first instance and appellate tribunals sought to draw on the constitutional supremacy of treaties over domestic legislation to enforce international treaties. Leading the charge was the Court of Appeals of Paris, which already in 1948, in perhaps the first such judgment, had granted rights under an international treaty to a foreign national in a civil suit on the grounds that the treaty prevailed over contrary, subsequent domestic legislation.[14]

Yet, these lower court advances were rebuffed by the Fourth Republic's Cour de cassation. The rejection was packed into an intricate set of avoidance doctrines, including, most prominently, that of deference to the government on matters of treaty interpretation. But the rejection was nonetheless clear.

A 1950 Cour de cassation decision, for example, firmly established that courts applying treaty-derived norms must rely on the government's interpretation

[11] Tribunal correctionnel [T.corr.] [First-instance tribunal in penal matters] Paris, 17e ch., May 9, 1952. REVUE CRITIQUE DE DROIT INTERNATIONAL PRIVÉ [R.C.D.I.P] 1952, 473–74 ('Mayol'), at Note Freyria, 480.

[12] STONE, *supra* note 7 at 28 (quoting JEANNE LEMASURIER, LA CONSTITUTION DE 1946 ET LE CONTRÔLE JURIDICTIONNEL DU LÉGISLATEUR 28 (1954)).

[13] Jean-Paulin Niboyet, *La Constitution nouvelle et certaines dispositions de Droit international*, 23 RECUEIL DALLOZ DE DOCTRINE DE JURISPRUDENCE ET DE LÉGISLATION [D. Jur.] 89, 91 (1946).

[14] Cour d'appel [CA] Paris, 6e ch., Jan. 30, 1948, R.C.D.I.P 1948, 493 at 495 ('Lambert c/ Jourdan'), *translated in* 44 AM. J. INT. L. 206, 207 (1950). *C.f.* Lawrence Preuss, *The Relation of International Law to Internal Law in the French Constitutional System*. 44 AM. J. INT. L. 641, 665–66 (1950).

whenever the question was one of public, as opposed to private, law.[15] And in a consolidated set of appeals in 1953, *Bruni*,[16] the criminal division of the Cour de cassation extended this principle of deference to the government for all treaty-derived norms:

> [I]nternational treaties are acts of high administration that can only be interpreted … by the powers among whom they were concluded … The court seized of the dispute is [therefore] necessarily compelled either to conform to the official interpretation or to stay its ruling if such an interpretation has not been made.[17]

Under *Bruni*'s rule of deference, a litigant could win only if the government, in effect, confessed error. In the words of a respected contemporary study on the relationship of international and domestic law in France:

> [R]ather than set aside an enacted law, as the Constitution commands, the [French judge] has the tendency either to deny the conflict, often against better evidence, or to defer to other authorities the responsibility of choosing [which norm to apply].[18]

In so holding, the Cour de cassation aligned its jurisprudence with the long-standing practice of France's high administrative tribunal, the Conseil d'État,[19] which had consistently shown the same approach of avoidance, denial and, ultimately, deference to the government. As another scholar surveying both tribunals wryly concluded: 'One may hope that by granting treaties authority superior to law, and above all by giving them a constitutional basis, Articles 26 to 28 of the Constitution prefer a certain simplification of jurisprudential rules. One must not nourish too many illusions.'[20]

Lower courts in the regular French judiciary pushed back again after *Bruni*, but without success.[21] As a result, when the Treaty of Rome was signed in 1957, a knowledgeable observer could sum up the existing position of the Fourth Republic's French courts thus:

> Although [treaties] formally prevail over municipal law, whether antecedent or subsequent, in practice the French judge is in most instances averse to declare the supremacy of treaties over French law.[22]

[15] Cass. ch. réuns., Apr. 27, 1950, D. Jur. 1950, 379 ('Consorts Friedman c/ Ministère public'), discussed in Louis C. Bial, *Some Recent French Decisions on the Relationship between Treaties and Municipal Law*, 49 Am. J. Int. L. 349, 351 (1955). *cf.* Pierre Lardy, La Force Obligatoire Du Droit International En Droit Interne 147 (1966).

[16] See Cour de cassation [Cass.] crim., Mar. 24, 1953, D. Jur. 1953, 425. See generally Bial, *supra* note 15 at 350–53.

[17] D. Jur. 1953, *supra*, note 16 at 425. See also Bial, *supra* note 15 at 351.

[18] Lardy, *supra* note 15 at 141.

[19] Michel Virally, *Le Conseil d 'Etat et les traites internationaux*, La semaine juridique [Juridical Weekly] I 1098 (1953). See also Bial, *supra* note 15 at 350–55.

[20] *Id.*

[21] See, eg, CA Paris, 13e ch., Apr. 1, 1954, D. Jur. 1954, 280 ('*Vallès*'); CA Paris, 13e ch., Apr. 1, 1954, Gaz. Pal. 1954, 1, 337 ('*Hurtado*' and '*Sastella*'). See also Bial, *supra* note 15 at 352–53.

[22] Gerhard Bebr, *The Relation of the European Coal and Steel Community Law to the Law of the Member States*, 58 Colum. L. Rev. 767, 778 (1958). See also Léontin-Jean Constantinesco, *Anmerkung zu Conseil d'Etat vom 1. März 1968 (Semoules)*, 3 Europarecht 318, 323–25 (1968).

III. The Fifth Republic Meets the European Community

When the revolutionary General de Gaulle came to power the following year and promptly passed his 1958 Constitution inaugurating the Fifth Republic, the constitutional text did not change much on treaties. The new Article 55 proclaimed in familiar fashion: 'Upon their publication, properly ratified or approved treaties or agreements have authority superior to that of laws, subject for each agreement or treaty, to its application by the other party.' This mostly consolidated Articles 26 and 28 of the previous Constitution while also codifying an established proviso on reciprocity.

And yet the world had changed. With the signing of the Treaty of Rome during de Gaulle's absence the year before, France had committed itself to an institutional architecture for Europe that would effectively bring constitutional review into French courtrooms. To be sure, the European Community was geared towards serving France's political interests, especially those in agriculture. In that sense, the Community was not a political fluke or mistake; indeed, it was a basic pact de Gaulle would have pursued as well. But had the charismatic nationalist de Gaulle been at the helm when the Treaty of Rome was made, Europe would have been more 'intergovernmental', ie, with more legal flexibility for its Member States.[23]

When de Gaulle took office in 1958, the legal implications of the existing Treaty on European Economic Community were far from clear. But they were sufficiently worrisome for his constitutional scrivener, Michel Debré, to craft safeguards against the creation of further supranational treaties. The 1958 Constitution would grant the President's newly minted Constitutional Council (Conseil constitutionnel) jurisdiction to review not just proposed legislation but also proposed treaties for their constitutional compatibility. The Constitutional Council was thus to serve the freshly strengthened French presidency in two ways: first, to protect the executive against parliamentary encroachment into matters of presidential regulation; and, second, to protect both the executive and the French Republic as a whole from implicit constitutional modifications via international treaty. Along with the power conferred by Articles 61 and 62 to review proposed acts of parliament for their constitutionality, the 1958 Constitution therefore provided in Article 54: 'If the Constitutional Council, called upon by the President of the Republic, the Prime Minister, or the President of one or the other of the Assemblies, has declared that an international commitment contains a provision that is contrary to the Constitution, authorization to ratify or approve such commitment cannot obtain until after revising the Constitution.'

But in a crucial sense, the provision preventing treaties from changing France's domestic constitution came too late. The safeguards against future changes did not stop the unfolding of the judicial architecture already embedded in the

[23] See Andrew Moravcsik, The Choice for Europe 137 (1998).

1957 Treaty of Rome. In particular, Article 177 of that treaty – the preliminary reference procedure – proved to be the EEC's nose under the tent of the Member States' legal systems.[24] By inviting lower courts, and requiring courts of last resort, to send questions concerning the interpretation of Community law to the European Court of Justice (ECJ), this provision ultimately brought the full force of EU law into domestic legal systems.

French Advocate General Maurice Lagrange, who had helped draft the predecessor Treaty Establishing the European Coal and Steel Community, was well aware of the power packed into this innovative provision. When the very first preliminary reference arrived at the Court in 1961, Lagrange began his opinion with a prescient observation:

> [Article 177] is apparently designed to play a central part in the application of the Treaty. The progressive integration of the Treaty into the legal, social and economic life of the Member States must involve more and more frequently the application and, when the occasion arises, the interpretation of the Treaty in municipal (i.e. member state) litigation, whether public or private … Applied judiciously, one is tempted to say loyally – the provisions of Article 177 must lead to a real and fruitful collaboration between the municipal courts and the Court of Justice of the Communities with mutual regard for their respective jurisdictions.[25]

In the second preliminary reference action, the ECJ issued its watershed *Van Gend en Loos* judgment, holding that the Treaty of Rome created 'individual rights which national courts must protect' even when those rights conflict with a Member State's obligations under a subsequent treaty.[26] And in the following year, the ECJ held that the Treaty of Rome trumped a Member State's subsequent domestic laws as well.[27] Put simply, the ECJ demanded Member State courts do for Europe just what the French high courts had up to this point declined to do for any treaty.

IV. The French Tribunals React to European Law

Parts of the following story have been well told by now, but with a focus on the supremacy of EU law that has obscured its significance for the development of domestic judicial review.[28] We shall therefore limit ourselves only to the great

[24] See generally J.H.H. Weiler, *The Transformation of Europe*, 100 Yale L.J. 2403 (1991); Eric Stein, *Lawyers, Judges and the Making of a Transnational Constitution*, 47(1) Am. J. Int'l L. 1 (1981). On art. 177 in particular, see Daniel Halberstam, *Constitutionalism and Pluralism in Marbury and Van Gend*, *in* The Past and the Future of EU Law 26 (Miguel Maduro & Loic Azoulai eds., 2011).

[25] Case 13/61, Bosch v. de Geus, 1962 E.C.R. 47, at 55–56.

[26] Case 26/62, Van Gend en Loos v. Nederlandse Administratie der Belastingen, 1963 E.C.R 2, at 13.

[27] Case 6/64, Costa v. ENEL, 1964 E.C.R 587.

[28] See generally Marie-France Buffet-Tchakaloff, La France devant la Cour de justice des communautés européennes (1985); Monica Claes, The National Courts' Mandate in the European Constitution 214–65 (2006); Karen Alter, Establishing the Supremacy of European Law 124–81 (2001); Plötner, *supra* note 10 at 41–75.

outlines of the EU story, while digging deeper where necessary to expose the particular importance of European law to the creation of judicial review, ie, review of the constitutionality and determination of the enforceability of enacted legislation in the course of actual litigation.

A. The ECJ's Counterparts in France

To understand the reaction of the various French tribunals, let us briefly recall the differences among the various addressees of the ECJ's call for cooperation. First, we have the courts of the regular judiciary, divided into subject matter tribunals (Tribunaux), with Courts of Appeals (Cours d'appel) and, as a final instance, the Supreme Court (Cour de cassation). Next, we have the administrative courts, with regional tribunals (Tribunaux administratifs), administrative courts of appeal (Cours administratives d'appel) (albeit only after 1989), and the Council of State (Conseil d'État) on top. Finally, we have the freshly minted Constitutional Council.

The history and power dynamics among these various bodies are critical to how the story unfolds. Let us recall that the courts of the regular French judiciary had emerged out of a revolutionary tradition that viewed judges with great scepticism, as potential enemies of the people and of the 'general will' as pronounced by parliament. Since 1790, for instance, French law made it a crime for judges to 'take part directly or indirectly in the exercise of legislative power or hindering or suspending the execution of legislative decrees'.[29] To help ensure judges would stick to their mandate of being 'the mouthpiece of the law' ('la bouche de la loi'),[30] the national assembly in the same year created the Cour de cassation (originally termed the Tribunal de cassation) to review and control the decisions of the judicial tribunals. While first operating in the legislative branch with judges elected every four years,[31] and even later after Napoleon Bonaparte had changed their election to presidential appointment,[32] the Cour de cassation doggedly stuck to its job and rejected ambitions to review the constitutionality of legislative or administrative acts.[33]

Administrative acts could be challenged only by appeal to the Head of State, and to help with this function, Bonaparte in 1799 created the Conseil d'État. This council would serve two distinct functions: first, to advise the executive on draft

[29] Loi des 16 et 24 août 1790 sur l'organisation judiciaire [Law on the Organization of the Judiciary of August 16 and 24, 1790] title II, art. 10, Archives nationales [National Archives] AE II 3075, quoted in Michel Troper, *Constitutional Law, in* Introduction to French Law 9 (George Bermann & Etienne Picard, eds. 2008).

[30] Montesquieu, De l'esprit des lois 327 (Garnier, 1777).

[31] See Pierre Bennet, *France. La Cour de cassation*, 30 Revue internationale de droit comparé [R.I.D.C] 193, 215 (1978).

[32] See James W. Garner, *The French Judiciary*, 26 Yale L. J. 349, 387 (1917).

[33] See Cass. crim., May 11, 1833, S. Jur. 1833, 357–60; Stone, *supra* note 7 at 26 (discussing the same).

bills and regulatory decrees; and, second, to adjudicate claims challenging the government's administrative actions.[34] In the Third Republic, after Napoleon III had fallen from power, the Conseil d'État was granted formal independence from the executive branch, adjudicating in the name of 'the state' and advising 'the state', as opposed to the Head of State.[35] Nevertheless, to this day, the Conseil d'État is widely viewed as sympathetic to the government due to its dual function, close government contact and professional culture derived from the École Nationale d'Administration (an elite academy that trains high-level government bureaucrats, including those who wind up as the Council of State's members and staff).[36]

The Constitutional Council was launched into this landscape by the 1958 Constitution as the only institution that could review the constitutionality of a law. However, as originally designed, the Constitutional Council could only review a bill at the behest of specified government and parliament officials, and only *before* its enactment into law. And even though the president of either of the assemblies, as well as the President of the Republic, could call upon the Council for an opinion, the Constitutional Council was widely viewed as the President's tool – a 'cannon aimed at Parliament'[37] – to protect the President's authority to pass regulations. The Constitutional Council was not conceived of, and did not function, as a court – let alone an independent court. The Council's first president, for example, remained a personal advisor to de Gaulle while serving on the Constitutional Council, and its second president openly admitted to his own lack of power to disagree with the President of the Republic:

> I must plead guilty. In fact, it seemed to me absurd to explain to the author of the Constitution how that text should be applied. When I tried to do so, expressing the most timid of reservations, the General would simply explain to me the precise reasons that had led him to adopt such and such an article – and I could not turn the Constitution against its own author! Had I tried, his Socratic dialectic would have very soon stopped me cold.[38]

As might be expected based on their institutional roles, these different adjudicative bodies reacted quite differently to the challenges and opportunities the European Community and its Court of Justice presented.

B. Rejecting Europe and Judicial Review

As France's most powerful domestic adjudicative body and the one most closely connected to the government, the Conseil d'État kept Community law and

[34] See Troper, *supra* note 29 at 10.
[35] *Id.*
[36] Alter, *supra* note 28.
[37] François Luchaire, le Conseil Constitutionnel 31 (1980), quoted in Stone, *supra* note 7 at 60–61.
[38] *Id.*

the ECJ at a distance for a long time. The Council early on refused to send requests for preliminary rulings to the ECJ[39] and, as is well known, in a landmark case involving the importation of semolina ('semoules') in 1968 squarely rejected the application of Community law over a contrary, later law.[40]

However – and important for our story – the argument in that landmark case centred on the Conseil d'État's inability to engage in judicial review. As the Commissaire du gouvernement[41] Nicole Questiaux observed, the case should be dismissed, and no reference to the ECJ made, because domestic law rejecting the application of Community law was clear. 'To be sure, under Article 55 of the Constitution, a treaty which has been duly ratified has … an authority superior to that of statutes', she allowed.[42] Nevertheless, she concluded that 'the administrative court cannot make the effort which is asked of it without altering, by its mere will, its institutional position'.[43] Questiaux read the Constitution as having 'specifically dealt with the judicial review of legislation by adopting a restrictive view and conferring such review upon the Constitutional Council'.[44] As a result, judges, including members of the Conseil d'État, are 'not qualified to implement a hierarchy between laws' and must not 'rely on the obligation to apply a text of a so-called higher validity in order to disregard … a subsequent statute'.[45] Although a judge may attempt to reconcile an international treaty with a statute, 'if the legislator has manifested a precise will … no provision of the Constitution, [not even] Article 55 in particular, excuses the judge from respecting that will'.[46]

The present case, Questiaux concluded, should be dismissed without reference to the ECJ because the domestic legislator's will was clear in that it 'forbade the Government to subject the importation in question to the application of the Community levies or to the [Community] system of import certificates'.[47] The Conseil d'État followed Questiaux, inaugurating what became known as the 'Semoules doctrine'. Squarely at odds with the ECJ's foundational judgments, the doctrine remained in effect at the Conseil d'État for another 20 years.

[39] See, eg, Buffet-Tchakaloff, *supra* note 28 at 94–105; Alter, *supra* note 28 at 135–45; Claes, *supra* note 28 at 214–65.

[40] See C CE Sect., Mar 1, 1968, Actualité Juridique Droit Administratif [A.J.D.A.] 1968, 235; 1970 Common Mkt. L. Rep. 395 (English).

[41] Commissaires du gouvernement are civil servants of the French executive dispatched to the Conseil d'État in cases implicating their department. They participate in the case, but do not vote. See Code de la justice administrative [Administrative Judiciary Code] art. R123-24. *cf.* George A. Bermann & Etienne Picard, Introduction to French Law 58, 100 (2008).

[42] 1970 Common Mkt. L. Rep. 395, 403.

[43] *Id.*

[44] *Id.*

[45] *Id.*

[46] *Id.* at 404–05.

[47] *Id.* at 406.

C. Embracing Europe: *Marbury* Comes to France

The regular French judiciary, by contrast, quickly embraced the supremacy of Community law and the role of the ECJ. Article 177 of the EC Treaty was really tailor made for effecting change in the regular judiciary. Recall that lower courts and courts of appeals had chafed under their traditionally limited powers and had long agitated in favour of enforcing the supremacy of treaties. To be sure, the Cour de cassation had deflected the lower courts' attempts to change the *Matter* doctrine, but the top judiciary court too had much to gain relative to the Conseil d'État in terms of power, prestige and the judicial enforcement of rights by granting supremacy to the European treaties.[48]

In the ECJ, the regular French judiciary now had an ally who made enforcing the supremacy of treaties, in this case Community law, seem far less fanciful. Moreover, French courts willing to engage would become part of a pan-European judicial community, drawing inspiration and support from, and perhaps even gaining prestige by contributing to, the larger judicial conversation beyond France.

The regular French judiciary took to Community law, almost immediately endorsing the reference procedure and the ECJ's decisions as part of the supremacy of Community law. By 1965, an eager Cour de cassation held lower courts to their duty to file preliminary reference actions to Luxembourg.[49] By 1967, the regional Cour d'appel in Colmar held that the supremacy of Community law is 'imposed on national jurisdictions [ie, French judges]' and that 'respect for the interpretation given by the ECJ is directly and intimately bound up with that of the Treaty itself, whose primacy is not up for discussion and results, at least in France, from Article 55 of the Constitution'.[50] By March of the following year, the Cour de cassation agreed that interpretations of the Court of Justice are themselves 'binding on national courts'.[51]

And, so it happened: in 1970 the Cour de cassation issued a decision, *Ramel*, casually contradicting the *Matter* doctrine and enforcing the constitutionally

[48] On the 'judicial empowerment thesis', see Weiler, *supra* note 24, at 2426; R. Daniel Kelemen & Alec Stone Sweet, *Assessing the Transformation of Europe*, *in* The Transformation of Europe (M. Wind & M. Poiares Maduro eds., 2017); Anne-Marie Burley & Walter Mattli, *Europe before the Court*, 47(1) International Organization 41 (1993); Alter, *supra* note 28. *cf.* Tommaso Pavone, *Revisiting Judicial Empowerment in the European Union*, 6(2) J. of L. and Courts 303 (2018). On considerations beyond institutional self-interest, see Daniel Halberstam, *The Bride of Messina: Constitutionalism and Democracy in Europe*, 30 Eur. L. Rev. 775 (2005).

[49] See Cass. civ., 2e ch., Dec. 1, 1965, Gaz. Pal. 1966, 1, 97, translated in R.H. Lauwaars, *Caisse d'assurance régionale v. Torrekens*, 4 Common Mkt. L. Rev. 237, 237–38 (1966).

[50] Alexandre Charles Kiss, *Jurisprudence française concernant le droit international – Année 1967*, 14 Annuaire Français de Droit International 802, 867 (1968) (reporting on CA Colmar, Nov. 15 1967, R.G.D.I.P.1968, 860).

[51] Cass. 2e civ., Mar. 21, 1968, Gaz. Pal., 1968, 2, 83, reported in Dennis Tallon & Robert Kovar, *The Application of Community Law in France in 1968*, 6 Common Mkt. L. Rev. 419, 420 (1969).

required supremacy of Community law in ordinary litigation in an ordinary French court.[52]

This decision tends to be neglected in conventional accounts about the emergence of constitutional review in France, and it is neglected in Ackerman's account as well. Conventional accounts focus instead on the Constitutional Council's landmark decision, *Liberté d'association* of the following year.[53] This 1971 decision grew out of a headline-grabbing controversy involving the attempts of Jean-Paul Sartre and Simone de Beauvoir to revive a judicially dissolved leftist political movement. When the government attempted to strengthen its own hand with a proposed law,[54] its draft bill was put before the Constitutional Council for review. In a historic ruling, the Council declared the proposed law unconstitutional, holding that '[i]n view of the Constitution and notably its preamble', the bill violated the fundamental principle of freedom of association.[55] The terse reference to the preamble of the 1958 Constitution,[56] effectively incorporating a broad set of fundamental rights going back to the Declaration of 1789, was seen as nothing short of a 'revolution … made in four words'.[57] The parliamentary opposition quickly seized upon this newfound tool, which, especially with the 1974 expansion of the right to refer bills to the Constitutional Council,[58] became an institutional fixture of French constitutional politics ever since.

But however great the Constitutional Council's expansion of its own scope of review, the *Liberté d'association* decision was no *Marbury v Madison* moment. The Constitutional Council was still not a court engaged in judicial review.[59] As Alec Stone Sweet rightly explains, the Council functioned more like a third chamber, a special legislative veto chamber on constitutional grounds before a law was passed.[60] The Constitutional Council was not a constitutional court: it did not have adversary proceedings; it was not accessible to ordinary individuals; and it did not hear challenges to enacted laws.

[52] Cass. crim., Oct. 22, 1970, Bull. crim., No. 276, at 657; 1 THE RELATIONSHIP BETWEEN EUROPEAN COMMUNITY LAW AND NATIONAL LAW: THE CASES 279 (Andrew Oppenheimer ed., 1994) (English).

[53] Conseil Constitutionnel [CC] decision No 71-44DC, July 16, 1971 ('*Freedom of association*'). See also ACKERMAN, *supra* note 2 at 199–226; STONE, *supra* note 7 at 66–69. *cf.* LES GRANDES DÉCISIONS DU CONSEIL CONSTITUTIONNEL 413–14 (Patrick Gaïa et al. eds., 18th ed. 2016).

[54] See Jacques Robert, *Propos sur le sauvetage d'une liberté*, 87 REV. DU DROIT PUBLIC 1171, 1175 (1971).

[55] CC. No. 71-44DC, *supra* note 53).

[56] 'The French people solemnly proclaim their attachment to the rights of man and to the principles of the national sovereignty as they were defined in the Declaration of 1789, confirmed and completed by the preamble of Constitution of 1946'; 1958 CONSTITUTION, Preamble.

[57] Jean Rivero, *Rapport de Synthèse*, *in* COURS CONSTITUTIONNELLES EUROPÉENNES ET DROITS FONDAMENTAUX 520 (1982), quoted in STONE, *supra* note 7 at 68.

[58] Article 61 of the 1958 Constitution originally allowed referrals only from the President of either chamber, the Prime Minister or the President of the Republic. A 1974 amendment authorised 60 members of the National Assembly or of the Senate to refer proposed legislation to the Constitutional Council as well.

[59] But see George D. Haimbaugh, Jr., *Was it France's Marbury v. Madison?*, 35 OHIO STATE L. REV. 910 (1974).

[60] See STONE, *supra* note 7 at 97 and 209–21.

Real judicial review was being developed elsewhere: in the regular judiciary and as a result of European law. To be sure, the political stakes in the Cour de cassation's 1970 *Ramel* decision were low. The government chose not to appeal the case.[61] But low stakes in an individual case or lack of government involvement should not lead one to underestimate the significance of a decision. After all, *Costa v ENEL* involved a challenge to a $3 electric bill before a justice of the peace,[62] and James Madison declined to show up in court or even send counsel to argue on his behalf in the famous case that bears his name.[63]

The *Ramel* case of 1970 involved the importation into France of 923 hectolitres of white wine from Italy in accordance with an EEC decision, allowing such importation as long as the wine satisfied the rules of the country of origin. The trouble was that the imported wine failed inspection by French authorities, who found added sugar in contravention of the French Wine Code. As a result, France prosecuted Ramel for fraud and for violating the tax code by importing improperly described products. After the lower courts dismissed the charges on the basis that the imports were allowed under Community law, the decision was appealed to the Cour de cassation.[64]

The Cour de cassation's reasoning in *Ramel* was as subtle as it was momentous. The court first solemnly rehearsed that 'according to the terms of Article 55 of the 1958 Constitution', properly ratified and published treaties and agreements have 'superior authority to that of [domestic] laws'.[65] Next, it noted that based on the combined terms of the French General Code on Imports and a 1963 presidential decree, imported alcohols and wines are 'subject to all the provisions made by internal legislation and must therefore conform to French rules'.[66] Under the *Matter* doctrine, this would mean granting the appeal, reversing the lower court, ignoring Community law, and reinstating the prosecution against Ramel for violating French laws.

Instead, however, the Cour de cassation affirmed the decision of the lower court, explaining it was 'by the accurate application of Article 55 of the Constitution' that the judges below found they 'could not apply' the French Wine Code and that the tax penalties were inapplicable because 'the principle of territoriality of taxation laws was unable to overrule international law whose authority must prevail by virtue of constitutional law'.[67] In so holding, the French Supreme Court had, for the first time, set aside a clear national law because it contravened the constitution.

[61] *cf* ALTER, *supra* note 28 at 147 (noting that *Ramel* was politically uncontroversial).

[62] Case C-64, Costa v. E.N.E.L., 1964 E.C.R. 585 (Opinion of Advocate General Lagrange).

[63] See William W. van Alstyne, *A Critical Guide to Marbury* v. *Madison*, 18 DUKE L. J. 1, 5 (1969).

[64] The government, which lost, did not appeal, but other parties to the case did. See OPPENHEIMER, *supra* note 52 at 281.

[65] Ramel, *supra* note 52 at 660.

[66] *Id.*

[67] *Id.* The French formulation 'par l'exacte application' has become a term of art indicating the approval of the lower courts' reasoning.

Ramel was France's *Marbury v Madison*. Perhaps the names of the tribunals have led so many to focus their attention on the Constitutional Council. Perhaps the subtle reasoning, the context of treaties, the relative lack of prominence of early Community law or the government's lack of interest in the underlying case obscured *Ramel*'s significance for judicial power. Nevertheless, the decision of the Cour de cassation applying Community law to a merchant importing cheap white wine from Italy,[68] not the Constitutional Council in a later ruling involving philosophers and the freedom of association, should be recognised as the real, judicial revolution. It was the Cour de cassation following Community law that first established judicial review in France.

V. *Conventionnalite* versus *Constitutionnalité*: A Rose by Any Other Name …

Labels obscured what had happened and drove what followed. The Constitutional Council stubbornly avoided drawing on Community law for its own review of draft legislation, despite the superior authority of treaties over domestic laws under Article 55. Recall the debates in the Fourth Republic that equated the vindication of the supremacy of international law with constitutional review. As the only institution expressly authorised to engage in constitutional review of proposed legislation, it would seem only proper for the Constitutional Council to review whether a proposed law violated the provisions of an existing treaty. What is more, in the *Semoules* case, the Conseil d'État had punted questions on the supremacy of Community law to the Constitutional Council on exactly these grounds. And yet the Constitutional Council refused to play ball.

In a subsequent landmark decision on abortion, the Constitutional Council held that due to the reciprocity requirement of Article 55, the supremacy of international treaties was only 'contingent'.[69] The Constitutional Council used this to distinguish between controlling the constitutionality ('contrôle de constitutionnalité') and conventionality ('contrôle de conventionnalité') of a proposed law, and held that only the former fell within its powers.

The Cour de cassation was quick to seize this opening created by the Constitutional Council. Only a few months after the abortion decision, it issued a holding that expressly, and by explicit reasoning parroting the ECJ, vindicated the supremacy of the EEC Treaty over a subsequent law passed by the French Parliament.[70] In the *Jacques Vabre* decision (after the name of the coffee

[68] On Pierre Ramel, see Frank J. Piral, *Donnybrook in the Midi*, New York Times Magazine, Aug. 29, 1979, at 50.

[69] See Conseil Constitutionnel [CC] decision No. 74-54DC, Jan. 15, 1975 ('IVG').

[70] See Cass. ch. mixte, May 6, 1975, Bull. Mixte IV, at 6 ('*Jacques Vabre*'), translated in Oppenheimer, *supra* note 52 at 296.

company involved), the arguments of the Procureur général[71] Adolphe Tuffait were breathtakingly broad. An international and EU law enthusiast (and former professional soccer player), Touffait had previously presided over the Court of Appeals in Paris that had issued so many of the pro-European decisions in the past. Several of his arguments as Procureur général in *Jacques Vabre* are well beyond what we shall consider here, but two are of particular importance for our purposes.

Touffait's first argument downplayed the significance of setting aside an act of parliament. He cleverly suggested that granting supremacy to Community law did not involve constitutional review at all. Contrary to the Conseil d'État's ruling in *Semoules*, Touffait said that giving precedence to Community law 'is in no way a question of a confrontation of the internal statute with the Constitution but, on the contrary, of a comparison, by virtue of that Constitution, of that provision with the treaty'.[72] As the lower court concluded, he added, '[i]t is thus not a matter of judging the constitutionality of a statute'.[73] To be sure, the government in the lower court had derided this argument as one of 'mental self-restraint',[74] but Touffait maintained that the lower court's circuitous reasoning could now find a stamp of approval in the reasoning of the Constitutional Council.[75] Granting supremacy to the treaty was just applying one legal provision over another, not striking down any law. Granting supremacy to Community law over national law was merely reviewing *conventionnalité*, not *constitutionnalité.*

Second, Touffait tapped into the constitutional discourse in other Member States (as his counterpart in the court below had also done).[76] France, we must remember, was the last of the six founding Member States of the Community whose courts were not enforcing the supremacy of Community law at this time. Touffait warned the French judges that the other Member States would be watching them, and expecting France to respect Community law too. He concluded: 'It is in this context that the judgement you are to deliver will be read and commented upon; its audience will extend beyond the frontiers of our country and spread over the whole of the member-States of the Community'.[77] In its characteristically terse form of decision, the Cour de cassation responded largely favourably:

> [T]he Treaty [of Rome] of 25 March 1957, which by virtue of … Article of the Constitution [Article 55] has an authority greater than that of statutes, institutes a separate legal order integrated with that of the member-States. Because of that separateness, the legal

[71] The main role of the Procureur général près la Cour de cassation is to 'render advice' to that court 'in the interest of the law and the common good'. See https://www.courdecassation.fr/institution_1/parquet_general_9077/presentation_9078/general_cour_40896.html.

[72] Submission of Procureur général Touffait in Cass. May 6, 1975, translated in Oppenheimer, *supra* note 52 at 296.

[73] *Id.*

[74] *Id.*

[75] *Id.* at 299.

[76] See *id.* at 304–07; see also CA Paris, 1e ch., Jul. 7, 1973, D. 1974, 159.

[77] See Touffait, *supra* note 72 at 307.

order which it has created is directly applicable to the nationals of those States and is binding on their courts. Therefore, the Cour d'appel was correct and did not exceed its powers in deciding that … the Treaty was to be applied in the instant case, and not section 265 of the [French] Customs Code, even though the latter was later in date.[78]

From that point on, the vindication of the supremacy of Community law in the regular French judiciary became routine.

The Conseil d'État, by contrast, still fought the enforcement of Community law for another dozen years. Initially, the Conseil d'État had the backing of Parliament, where Gaullists attacked the Cour de cassation as being an 'accomplice' of the ECJ.[79] But with the rising importance of European integration to French economic interests, the government, first through Valéry Giscard d'Estaing's moderate conservatives and then Mitterand's socialists, blocked Parliament's most severe attacks on the Court and made European integration a political priority.[80]

Shortly after Mitterand took office, French socialists under Justice Minister Robert Badinter, a foe of the death penalty and human rights champion, added a second European pressure point. Badinter passed a decree allowing individual litigants to petition yet another European court: the European Court of Human Rights. France had been a founding signatory of the European Convention on Human Rights in 1950, but the new decree would greatly boost the Strasbourg human rights tribunal's influence. French laws, even those the Constitutional Council waved through with a domestic stamp of approval, could now be challenged in Europe.

The Constitutional Council changed its position soon thereafter. In part, the Constitutional Council became concerned that a judgment in Strasbourg against France would be embarrassing.[81] Also, with the socialists in power, membership of the Constitutional Council came to include distinctly pro-Europeans as well.[82] When Badinter became President of the Constitutional Council in 1986, it finally reversed course to include international treaties in the scope of its review.[83] Thereafter, and in short order, the Constitutional Council embraced the Cour de cassation's jurisprudence, enforcing the supremacy of international treaties over domestic legislation in its own review, and urged the Conseil d'État to do the same.[84] The Constitutional Council even modelled such review for the Conseil d'État in a case in which the Constitutional Council acted as an administrative

[78] Cass. ch. mixte, May 6, 1975, translated in Oppenheimer, *supra* note 52 at 309. The Court rejected claims based on lack of reciprocity given that Member States could sue each other for failure to abide by the Treaty (at 310).

[79] See Buffet Buffet-Tchakaloff, *supra* note 28 at 346.

[80] See Alter, *supra* note 28 at 157–58; Moravcsik, supra note 23 at 238–313.

[81] See Alter, *supra* note 28 at 159 fn. 82.

[82] *Id.*

[83] See CC decision No. 86-216DC, Sep. 3, 1986.

[84] See CC decision No. 88-1082/1117AN, Oct. 21, 1988 ('Val d'Oise 5e circ'). See generally Alter, *supra* note 28 at 159.

election court.[85] To be sure, the Constitutional Council stuck to the formal distinction between *conventionnalité* and *constitutionnalité*. But it had become a distinction without a practical difference.

Soon thereafter, the Conseil d'État caved in as well. As EU scholars have explained,[86] by 1988 the Conseil d'État had lost any reasonable justification or institutional motive for its rejection of Community law. In general, Parliament and the executive had embraced European integration. Also, in a specific blow to the Conseil d'État, French lawyers had succeeded in transferring jurisdiction over competition law – increasingly determined in Brussels, not Paris – from the Conseil d'État to the Cour de cassation. Here and elsewhere, the Conseil d'État found itself left out of the increasingly important developments of European law. In addition, both the Constitutional Council and the government were openly urging the Conseil d'État to change its position. Separately, a Constitutional Council decision had acknowledged the constitutional status of the Conseil d'État,[87] which meant that the Conseil d'État could now afford to speak out against a law of Parliament with less fear of retribution. And finally, the personnel of the Conseil d'État had changed over the years: in 1987, the government appointed pro-European Marceau Long as the new Vice President,[88] and in 1988 Yves Galmot returned to the Conseil d'État from a six-year stint as judge at the ECJ, intent on reforming the jurisprudence of the top French administrative court.[89]

The switch at the Conseil d'État came in *Nicolo*, a 1989 challenge to a French election law (regarding the European Parliament) as incompatible with the Treaty of Rome.[90] In an extensive submission, the Commissaire du Gouvernement Frydman urged the Conseil d'État to abandon its old *Semoules* jurisprudence, arguing that even though there was nothing formally wrong with that old decision, 'a different reading of Article 55 is certainly equally conceivable in law and is infinitely preferable from the point of view of expediency'.[91]

Frydman directly attacked the still-prevailing distinction between review for compatibility of a law with an international treaty and constitutional review. Noting that these labels should not be of concern to any real court,[92] he argued that the former was only a narrower form of constitutional review that was specifically provided for in Article 55 of the Constitution.[93] To be sure, in terms of French constitutional history, his reading of Article 55 as authorising courts to ignore or

[85] See CC No. 88-1082/1117AN, *supra*note 84.

[86] See generally Alter, *supra* note 28 at 157–66; Plötner, *supra* note 10 at 66–71; John Bell, *French Administrative Law and the Supremacy of European Laws*, 11 Eur. Pub. L. 487 (2005.

[87] See CC decision No. 86-224DC, Jan. 23, 1987, para. 15. *cf.* Alter, *supra* note 28 at 161; Plötner, *supra* note 10 at 66–67.

[88] See Alter, *supra* note 28 at 162.

[89] See Plötner, *supra* note 10 at 68–69.

[90] CE Ass., Oct. 20 1989, Rec. Lebon 190 ('*Nicolo*').

[91] Submission of *Commissaire du gouvernement* Frydman *in* CE Ass., Oct. 20, 1989, JCP 1989 II 21371, as reported and translated in Oppenheimer, *supra* note 52 at 341.

[92] *Id.*

[93] See *id.* at 343–44.

strike down laws was pure fiction.[94] But as a matter of normative constitutional theory, his argument that vindicating the supremacy of treaties suggested engaging in judicial review was dead on.

Frydman further argued that the divergence between the French administrative tribunals and regular judiciary made no sense. It also violated notions of equality when looking across the European Community. It was, for instance, 'quite shocking … that citizens cannot rely, before French administrative courts on a [European] regulation which they would be allowed to rely on in other countries of the Community solely on the ground that in our country, the regulation has been set aside by a contrary statute'.[95] Frydman saw this as 'a difference in treatment which is difficult to reconcile with the very principles of Community law'.[96] Looking beyond France much as Touffait had done, Frydman emphasised 'that your Court is now the last which formally refuses to apply Community measures which are contradicted by their laws'.[97]

The Conseil d'État was finally convinced. In a characteristically terse judgment, it dismissed the case, noting simply that the contested French law was 'not incompatible with the clear stipulations of the … Treaty of Rome'.[98] The decision came without any statement or reasoning as to the relationship between treaties and domestic law. The decision did not even say why the judgment had considered Community law at all. But the short reference to the Treaty of Rome was enough. Everyone knew what had happened.

VI. What's Sauce for Europe …

With all tribunals reviewing the validity of domestic legislation in light of European law, the judicial landscape in France had profoundly changed. Judicial review – reviewing the compatibility of enacted laws at the behest of ordinary individuals in actual litigation in court – had been roundly rejected by revolutionaries since the beginning of the first French Republic. But it had nonetheless been established in the context of European law.

Focusing on the ECHR, Olivier Dutheillet de Lamothe, member of the Conseil d'État and previous member of the Constitutional Council, explained that the situation presented a 'double paradox'.[99] It seemed like a 'judicial paradox' to enforce the rights of the ECHR and not those contained in the Constitution. And it seemed like a 'political paradox' because checking domestic laws against the ECHR but

94 See section II above.
95 Frydman, *supra* note 91 at 346.
96 *Id.*
97 *Id.*
98 *Nicolo*, *supra* note 90.
99 See Olivier Dutheillet de Lamothe in Conseil d'État, Le Droit Européen des Droits de l'Homme 124–25 (2012) [Droit Européen]. *cf.* Ben Goldin, The Integration of European Law by the French High Courts 28–29 (unpublished draft) (discussing de Lamothe).

not the Constitution would seem to 'place the European Convention on Human Rights – instead of our Constitution – at the top of our legal order'.[100]

The same, of course, held true with regard to EU law. French courts had effectively brought about judicial review to vindicate the constitutionally mandated superiority of both EU and ECHR law over ordinary French laws. But if courts were vindicating the French Constitution's provisions on Europe, why not do the same for the rest of the Constitution? Three aspects of the European development, in particular, brought about a consensus in favour of judicial review.

A. Overcoming a Taboo

Labels aside, judges and counsellors had become comfortable with the power to set aside legislation in favour of constitutionally mandated higher law. As the former President of the Cour de cassation put it in 2003, 'a half century of applying community law liberated the judge of the French judiciary of two centuries of absolute submission to domestic law',[101] adding that European law had led to a '"cultural" opening of judges, the consequences of which have not yet been fully assessed'.[102] European law engendered 'a different attitude toward domestic legislation, which was no longer a unique and incontestable source [of law], but a relative one that was malleable and, depending on the situation, open for discussion'.[103] As Jean-Louis Debré, President of the Constitutional Council and son of the draftsman of the 1958 Constitution, would later put it, 'the judges had tasted the forbidden fruit'.[104]

In the public's eye too, this functional equivalent of judicial review broke the taboo that had existed for two centuries prohibiting the questioning of domestic legislation by citizens in court. Indeed, it would seem increasingly difficult to explain why rights that were unrelated to European law, but also guaranteed in the French Constitution, could not be similarly protected. After all, as the Balladur Commission reported, the European principles that ordinary judges and administrative tribunals used to set aside French laws were 'often neighbors of those [principles] one ought to have considered if these courts and tribunals or the Constitutional Council would have been empowered to address the constitutionality of the enacted law'.[105]

[100] See Dutheillet de Lamothe, *supra* note 99 at 125–26.

[101] Guy Canivet, *Le droit communautaire et le juge national*, *in* Le droit communautaire et les métamorphoses du droit 81 (Denys Simon ed., 2003).

[102] *Id.* at 84.

[103] *Id.*

[104] Jean-Louis Debré, President, Constitutional Council, Contrôle de constitutionnalité et contrôle de conventionnalité (June 6, 2008), https://www.conseil-constitutionnel.fr/sites/default/files/as/root/bank_mm/discours_interventions/2008/pdt_debre_afdc_06062008.pdf.

[105] Comité de réflexion et de proposition sur la modernisation et le rééquilibrage des institutions de la Ve République, Une Ve République plus démocratique 89 (Édouard Balladur et al. eds., 2007).

B. Protecting Rights

With constitutional review limited to privileged legislators challenging draft laws in the Constitutional Council, the only proper judicial protection of fundamental rights for ordinary citizens came via Europe. Overall, this meant less judicial protection of rights in France than elsewhere in the EU.

If individuals suffered a rights violation outside the scope of EU law or if they could not make it to Strasbourg to claim a violation of the ECHR, they were largely out of luck. To be sure, there were some workarounds, such as suits against the executive for exceeding statutorily defined powers, or limiting interpretations of a statute based on general principles of law.[106] And, of course, proposed laws violating fundamental rights could be stopped by the Constitutional Council. But as long as Parliament's intent was clear, and the law was passed, no court could prevent the application of an unconstitutional statute – except, again, in the context of European law.

To add insult to injury, the situation led to France being more frequently condemned by the Court of Human Rights in Strasbourg than its sister states of the EU. As Marc Guillaume, Secretary General of the Constitutional Council, noted, France was found to have violated the ECHR eight times as often as Germany, with nearly five times as many cases pending in Strasbourg against France as compared to those brought against Germany or Spain.[107] These discrepancies were not caused by any substantive difference in laws or policies between France and the other Member States, but simply by the 'insufficient internal legal avenues' to remedy the violation of constitutional rights in France.[108]

C. Vindicating 'Sovereignty'

The final straw was the 'supremacy' of the French Constitution. If French courts invalidate domestic laws based on conflicts with European law, but do not review conflicts of domestic laws with the French Constitution, does that not render European law supreme over domestic constitutional law? In theory, the answer could be 'no', but it was a somewhat complicated answer that escaped the public.

In theory, all three tribunals adhered to the supremacy of France's constitution – at least as far as French authorities were concerned. The Constitutional Council, for instance, would review whether a proposed French law implementing European law was compatible with the French Constitution.[109]

[106] See, eg, Jean Rivero, *The Constitutional Protection of Human Rights in French Law*, 12 Irish Jurist 1 (1977).

[107] See Marc Guillaume in Droit Européen, *supra* note 99 at 126, 127.

[108] *Id.*

[109] See, eg, CC decision No. 77-89DC, Dec. 30, 1977. See generally, Constitutional Courts and European Integration 73–74 (Eur. Comm. for Democracy through L., 2005) (compiling cases).

The Cour de cassation had specifically based the enforcement of EU law on Article 55, suggesting that the French Constitution controlled the force of EU law in France.[110] And when the Conseil d'État finally enforced the supremacy of Community Treaties over domestic statutes and regulations, it grounded all this in the French Constitution as well.

As the EU evolved, the fundamental positions of the three tribunals on the supremacy of the French Constitution remained unchanged. For example, the Constitutional Council struck down the proposed implementation of a Community Directive as violating French constitutional protections of equality.[111] The Council also made good on the supremacy of the French Constitution when reviewing proposed treaty revisions, such as the 1992 Maastricht Treaty, for their compatibility with the French Constitution.[112] Complying with that ruling, Mitterand's socialists promptly passed the necessary amendments and granted the EU a privileged place in Article 88 of the French Constitution.[113] Following the letter of that article, both the Constitutional Council[114] and the Conseil d'État[115] henceforth grounded the force of EU law in France in the French Constitution yet again.

But these finer points of law were lost on politicians and the public. The issue came to a head in February 2007, when the Conseil d'État considered a constitutional challenge to a government decree implementing a European emissions trading directive. Arcelor, along with other French steelmakers, complained that the French decree violated the constitutional principle of equality by not regulating other industries that likewise produced harmful emissions. But instead of checking whether the French decree complied with the French Constitution, the Conseil d'État thought it necessary to check, first, whether the EU's principle of equality provided 'equivalent' protection to French constitutional equality norms and whether the decree violated those EU principles of equality. Because EU law on that point was not clear, the Conseil d'État referred the question to the ECJ.[116]

The referral caused an uproar in France. To be sure, the Conseil d'État had reserved for itself the final power to consider whether EU law provided

[110] See Capitant et al., *supra* note 8 at 8.

[111] CC decision No. 94-348DC, Aug. 3, 1994.

[112] See CC decision No. 92-308DC, Apr. 9, 1992 (ratification law – Treaty on the European Union); see also CC decision No. 91-294DC, Jul. 25, 1991 (ratification law – Schengen Agreement).

[113] See Chloé Charpy, *The Status of (Secondary) Community Law in the French Internal Order*, 3 European Const. L. Rev. 450 (2007). By eliminating reciprocity, art. 88 increased the powers of the Constitutional Council, which now considered EU law implementation a specific constitutional mandate. *cf.* CC decision No. 2006-540DC, Jul. 27, 2006 (considering whether the proposed implementing law was faithful to the European Directive).

[114] See, eg, CC decision No. 04-496DC, Jun. 10, 2004 ('LCEN'); and CC decision No. 04-497DC, Jul. 1, 2004 ('*Loi communications électroniques*').

[115] See CE Ass. Feb. 8, 2007, Rec. Lebon 55.

[116] See *id.* (French case); Case 127/07, Arcelor Atlantique and Lorraine and Others v. Premier Ministre, 2008 E.C.R. I-9895 (preliminary reference).

fundamental rights protection 'equivalent' to the French Constitution, suggesting it would vindicate the French Constitution if the latter were threatened.[117] But the media did not see the case that way. Instead, the press read the reference 'as implying Community law's absolute precedence over national law, even national law of a constitutional nature'.[118] *Le Monde* charged the Council with 'disappearing behind the European Court of Justice' in 'a new transfer of French sovereignty to the European level'.[119] The paper dismissed the Conseil d'État's promise to judge the constitutional violation for itself after the case returned from Luxembourg, as that would require trusting the French court to wage a 'war among judges'.[120] (As it happened, the ECJ found no violation of equality, and when the answer came back from Luxembourg, the French court agreed.) In an editorial, the paper predicted that Eurosceptics would seize the decision as a '"Waterloo" of French sovereignty'.[121] That phrase, in turn, 'became a self-fulfilling prophecy as sovereigntists were eager to stress that even *Le Monde* called the ruling a "Waterloo"'.[122]

The decision also came during heated French sovereignty debates in the aftermath of the referendum rejecting the proposed Constitutional Treaty on Europe. To be sure, that treaty had been drafted under the leadership of former President Valery Giscard d'Estaing, and originally championed by then-President Jacques Chirac. But this did not save the Constitutional Treaty from rejection by the French public. However, despite the referendum, mainstream politicians thought the Constitutional Treaty's substance was necessary to preserve the EU. As Nicolas Sarkozy succeeded Chirac in May 2007 from within the same centre-right Gaullist party, Sarkozy therefore walked a fine line. In his election campaign, he had promised not to revisit the rejection of the Constitutional Treaty while at the same time championing the subsequent Lisbon Treaty, which, as everyone knew, took over the Constitutional Treaty's substance without the EU fanfare.[123] Key to moving forward productively, then, was preserving Europe, on the one hand, while prominently promoting the image of French 'sovereignty', on the other.

[117] The Conseil d'État and the Constitutional Council had developed doctrines whereby each, within the bounds of its powers, would ensure that implementation of EU law provided protection 'equivalent' to the French Constitution (Conseil d'État) and preserved the 'constitutional identity' of the French Constitution (Conseil Constitutionnel). See Charpy, *supra* note 113.

[118] *Id.* at 458.

[119] Christophe Jakubyszyn, *Le Conseil d'Etat s'efface derrière la justice européenne*, LE MONDE (Feb. 8, 2007), https://www.lemonde.fr/europe/article/2007/02/08/le-conseil-d-etat-consacre-le-primat-du-droit-europeen_865076_3214.html.

[120] *Id.*

[121] *Loi européenne: L'Europe va mal, entend-on de tous côtés*, LE MONDE (Feb. 8, 2007), https://www.lemonde.fr/idees/article/2007/02/08/loi-europeenne_865047_3232.html.

[122] Mark Beunderman, *French Sovereignty Passions Clash with EU Legal Primacy*, EU OBSERVER (Feb. 20, 2007), https://euobserver.com/institutional/23538.

[123] DAVID MARRANI, DYNAMICS IN THE FRENCH CONSTITUTION 84–85 (2013).

D. The Deed is Done

And so, when in 2008 the French Parliament passed the constitutional amendment providing for formal *ex post* (constitutional) judicial review, the change was as much symbolic as it was functional. Introducing the amendment, Prime Minister François Fillon decried the fact that French judges could set aside a French law that violated an international treaty and 'not address the conformity of that law with the Constitution, which had been placed into doubt'.[124] The amendment would thus do for the French Constitution in general what all French tribunals had been doing for Europe.

The evidence shows that Fillon did not have to push hard – adopting judicial review had become a matter of broad political consensus.[125] The left had long wanted the kind of fundamental rights protection that Europe demanded from, and modelled within, the French legal system. And the right wanted to assert that the French Constitution was supreme. *Ex post* judicial (constitutional) review became everyone's preferred solution. The implementing legislation passed the next year accordingly created the 'question prioritaire de constitutionnalité' (QPC), spelling out the reference procedure for individual constitutional complaints to the Constitutional Council, while emphasising both procedurally and in name the 'priority' of the French Constitution. The deed was done.

VII. Conclusion

The EU is often presented as a foreign intrusion onto home-grown constitutionalism. Following this trend, Bruce Ackerman argues that the constitutional claims of the EU stand in fundamental tension with France's 'revolutionary' brand of constitutionalism. However, in cleaning up France's story by focusing on revolutionary struggles, Ackerman neglects other important developments in France.

As we have seen, the movement towards judicial review in France is far less concerned with harking back to charismatic revolutionary achievements than it is propelled by a gradually growing commitment to the institutional protection of rights by independent courts. The movement in favour of judicial review in France gained its force not so much from revolutionary charisma as from

[124] Session ordinaire de 2007–2008, 161e séance, 3e séance du mardi 20 mai 2008 [Ordinary session of 2007–2008, 161st session, 3rd meeting of Tuesday May 20th], JOURNAL OFFICIEL DE LA RÉPUBLIQUE FRANÇAISE [J.O.] [OFFICIAL GAZETTE OF FRANCE], 2008, p. 2221.

[125] Unlike the many contested provisions, judicial review sailed through the amendment process virtually unchanged. See Michel Verpeaux, *La révision constitutionnelle à l'arrachée*, JCP 2009 1 170, at 18. *cf.* ASSEMBLÉE NATIONALE, Projet de loi constitutionelle, No. 820, Apr. 23, 2008; SÉNAT, Projet de loi constitutionnelle, No. 365, Jun. 3, 2008; ASSEMBLÉE NATIONALE, Projet de loi constitutionelle, No. 993, Jun. 25, 2008; SÉNAT, Projet de loi constitutionnelle, No. 459, Jul. 10, 2008; CONGRÈS DU PARLEMENT, Projet de loi constitutionnelle, Jul. 21, 2008. *cf.* Dutheillet de Lamothe, *supra* note 99, at 125–26 (noting that QPC was adopted 'de façon très consensuelle').

engagement with Europe, from jockeying among domestic courts, as well as from the internal substantive justification of constitutionalism, which has come to include the protection of rights in court.

In terms of the meta-narrative of Europe, then, it seems a mistake to see the EU as seeking to impose its foreign constitutional logic on Member State constitutions that were fully baked at home. It is time that the EU and the ECHR are recognised not just as a threat, but also as a boon, to *domestic* constitutionalism. The supranational governance structure in Europe, from the EU's constitutional demands regarding direct application of EU law to the ECHR's direct review of Member State protection of human rights, has served as a useful irritant profoundly shaping domestic constitutionalism as such. Europe has served to demand, model and promote key elements of *domestic* constitutionalism in the Member States, as it did in bringing judicial review to France.

14

Constituting the Judiciary, Constituting Europe

MITCHEL LASSER

I. Introduction

Over the last 25 years, the European Union (EU) and the Council of Europe have engaged in sustained efforts to reconstruct the profile of the European Court of Justice (ECJ) and the European Court of Human Rights (ECtHR). These efforts yielded their most visible results in 2009–10: vetting panels of judicial experts were now going to pass judgement on the fitness of the candidates put forward by Member State governments to sit on both the ECJ and the ECtHR.

Taking its cue from Bruce Ackerman's *Revolutionary Constitutions*,[1] this chapter examines these judicial appointments reforms as efforts at constitutional (re)construction. The ECJ and the ECtHR have played utterly central roles in the constitution of Europe as it exists today. Any targeted attempt to alter the processes and outcomes of the European judicial appointments process therefore represents an important constitutional intervention.

This chapter offers three interlocking readings of the European judicial reforms that demonstrate the constitutional import of these procedural, institutional and conceptual developments. Viewed from an intergovernmentalist perspective, the reforms represent an attempt by the established Western European Member States to protect the European constitutional status quo against potential disruptions resulting from the accession of new Member States from the East, who would now appoint nearly half the judges who would sit on the ECJ and the ECtHR. The reforms effectively stripped these new Member States of the traditional governmental capacity to select European judges more or less at will.

However, viewed from a neo-institutionalist perspective, the reforms represent 'separation of powers' struggles. Judicial actors, constituted as the new European judicial vetting panels, have developed their own agendas and have gone their

[1] Bruce Ackerman, Revolutionary Constitutions: Charismatic Leadership and the Rule of Law (2019).

own way. Enlisting the help of specialised civil servants working in European executive bodies, they have pushed to strip *all* Member State governments of their traditional powers over the European and domestic judiciaries.

Viewed from a constructivist perspective, these governmental motives and institutional agendas gradually triggered a new and increasingly shared professional perspective. Prioritising the authority and legitimacy of the European courts, key judicial, academic and civil service actors came to elaborate a new constitutional vision, in which domestic executives would be hemmed in by an increasingly professional, powerful and self-controlling national and supranational judiciary.

The full import of the European judicial reforms can therefore only be grasped if we think of them in constitutional terms. Not only do they impact directly upon the distribution and separation of powers, but they are also an integral part of a conceptual project to enhance the constitutional legitimacy of Europe by boosting the authority and legitimacy of its judiciary. Though framed in the seemingly self-evident terms of the separation of powers, this new constitutional construct reflects neither the pre-existing European constitutional structure nor the existing constitutional consensus of Europe's Member States.

Ackerman's *Revolutionary Constitutions* is not only useful for describing the European judicial reforms as attempts to construct and legitimise a new European constitutional order; it also helps for critiquing these developments. As Ackerman explains, the nations of Europe display a wide range of different constitutional traditions. This suggests not only that Europe possesses its own constitutional identity, but also that this identity must perpetually be squared with the varied constitutional identities of its Member States. To the extent that the European judicial reforms do not demonstrate sensitivity to this constitutional diversity, they are unlikely either to resonate broadly or to generate widespread allegiance.

This chapter argues that the constitutional diversity of Europe and its Member States may be even larger and more complex than Ackerman suggests. The constitutional tradition of any given political entity is by no means a given, waiting patiently to be properly described. It is a site of ongoing struggle where different players seek to offer compelling constitutional descriptions in order to advance and legitimate their preferred institutional, political and constitutional prescriptions. Similarly, constitutional traditions may not be limited to political entities such as Europe and its Member States: the European judicial debates and reforms suggest that professional and other social groups may well evince conflicting constitutional understandings and projects of their own.

II. The European Judicial Appointment Reforms

Only months apart in 2009–10, the EU and the Council of Europe instituted dramatic reforms to the judicial appointments processes to the ECJ and the

ECtHR. For the EU judiciary, Article 255 of the Treaty of Lisbon established a vetting panel 'to give an opinion on candidates' suitability to perform the duties of Judge and Advocate-General of the Court of Justice and the General Court'.[2] The Council of Europe followed suit in a Resolution of its Committee of Ministers, which established 'a Panel of Experts' to advise 'whether candidates for election as judges of the European Court of Human Rights meet the criteria' for judicial office.[3] After more than 50 years of existence, the two great European courts had suddenly been endowed with similar judicial screening devices.

These nearly simultaneous reforms look dramatic. After all, from the very inception of the two European courts, the Member States of the EU and the Council of Europe had adopted judicial appointment procedures that – appearances notwithstanding – had effectively ensured that they could appoint European judges more or less of their own choosing. The 1957 Treaty of Rome declared that appointment to the ECJ was to be made 'by common accord of the Governments of the Member States for a term of six years'.[4] In practice, this unanimity/veto process ('common accord') actually meant that each government could freely appoint its own judge, lest it play tit-for-tat with any other inclined to challenge the appointment. Appointment (formally 'election') to the ECtHR was distinctly more procedurally complicated: it called for the Parliamentary Assembly of the Council of Europe (PACE) to elect the judge from a list of three candidates put forward by the Member State. But the reality was much more straightforward. National governments made their preferences known; and because the PACE was composed of representatives of national parliaments, its membership had little inclination to override the revealed governmental preferences of neighbouring parliamentary democracies. In both instances, therefore, the reforms would necessarily impinge on the pre-existing governmental powers to select their preferred European judges.

Although these reforms appear quite sudden, one should not be misled by the 2009–10 dates. The debates over reforming the appointments processes actually date back to the mid-1990s; and over the intervening 15 years, both the EU and the Council of Europe had already debated and/or instituted a rather broad array of associated judicial reforms.

This section therefore places the 2009–10 reforms in both chronological and substantive context. First, the chronology. Although the EU's Treaty of Lisbon instituted the 'Article 255 Panel' in 2009, the idea of such a vetting panel was first

[2] Article 255 of the Consolidated versions of the Treaty on European Union and the Treaty on the Functioning of the European Union (Treaty of Lisbon).

[3] Committee of Ministers, Resolution CM/Res(2010)26 on the Establishment of an Advisory Panel of Experts on Candidates for Election as Judge to the European Court of Human Rights (10 November 2010).

[4] Treaty of Rome, art. 167.

formally proposed in 2000,[5] and the debates over reforming the ECJ appointments process date back at least to 1995, when the ECJ raised the possibility of moving to a longer, non-renewable judicial term of office.[6] The ECtHR debates date from roughly the same mid-1990s, when the Committee of Ministers was signing on to Protocol 11 to the European Convention on Human Rights (ECHR) (which finally established a 'new', permanent, full-time and single Court with compulsory jurisdiction over individual complaints).[7]

Second, the substance. The debates and reforms have by no means been limited to the establishment of the vetting panels. This is particularly clear in the ECtHR context, in which the Strasbourg institutions have been promoting a broad array of reform measures regarding the judiciary in general and judicial appointments in particular. These measures began most visibly in 1994, when the Committee of Ministers passed its Recommendation 'On the Independence, Efficiency and Role of Judges'.[8] Targeting domestic judicial appointment processes, it stated:

> All decisions concerning the professional career of judges should be based on objective criteria, and the selection and career of judges should be based on merit, having regard to qualifications, integrity, ability and efficiency. The authority taking the decision on the selection and career of judges should be independent of the government and the administration. In order to safeguard its independence, rules should ensure that, for instance, its members are selected by the judiciary and that the authority decides itself on its procedural rules.[9]

The institutions of the Council of Europe then put forward increasingly precise measures that not only directed national governments to adopt this approach for appointments to national judicial office, but also extended it to the national process used to select candidates for European judicial appointment.[10] These new measures, such as the 2001 'Standards Concerning the Independence of the Judiciary and the Irremovability of Judges', not only called for the establishment of formal norms to govern all aspects of the judicial profession (from hiring to promotion to discipline), but also for these norms to be applied via 'formal

[5] *Report by the Working Party on the Future of the European Communities' Court System ('The Group of Wise Persons' or 'The Due Report'), in* The Future of the Judicial System of the European Union 145, 201 (Alan Dashwood & Angus Johnston eds., 2001).

[6] *Report of the Court of Justice on Certain Aspects of the Application of the Treaty on European Union, in* Court of Justice, 1995 Annual Report (1996), paras. 17–21.

[7] See Council of Europe, Explanatory Report to Protocol No 11 to the Convention for the Protection of Human Rights and Fundamental Freedoms, Restructuring the Control Machinery Established Thereby, https://rm.coe.int/CoERMPublicCommonSearchServices/DisplayDCTMContent?documentId=09000016800cb5e9.

[8] Committee of Ministers, Recommendation Rec R (94) 12 on independence, efficiency and role of judges (October 13, 1994) 6 (hereinafter '1994 Recommendation').

[9] *Id.*

[10] See, eg, PACE Committee on Legal Affairs and Human Rights (Rapporteur: Lord Kirkhill), Report on the Procedure for Examining Candidatures for the Election of Judges to the European Court of Human Rights 1, Doc. 7439, 1403-15/12/95-1-E (1995) (hereinafter '1995 PACE Report'); European Charter on the Statute for Judges, DAJ/DOC (98) 23 (1998), https://rm.coe.int/16807473ef.

procedures' by a formally established 'independent authority with substantial judicial representation'.[11] Further measures aimed to shape the processes used at the national level to select candidates proposed for election in Strasbourg: the domestic authorities would now have to issue a formal call for candidates in the specialised press, establish and apply formal and transparent procedures for the selection of candidates, include at least one woman in their slate of three nominated candidates and so on.[12]

These institutional demands for reform also migrated to the processes used at the European level for the appointment/election of judicial candidates put forward by the national governments to sit in Strasbourg. These candidates would now be made 'to fill in a model curriculum vitae, so that the Assembly will have comparable information at its disposal' when selecting among the three candidates for election. Member State governments would have to transmit these three CVs in alphabetical order rather than in order of governmental preference.[13] Then the candidates would 'be interviewed by a sub-committee of the Assembly, for their qualities to be assessed', which would then lead to a recommendation to the Assembly.[14] These procedural reforms would 'improve [the PACE's] own procedure for examining the candidatures and for the selection of candidates, for more efficiency and professionalism'.[15]

In short, the creation in 2009–10 of vetting panels to the European courts was not a sudden or isolated incident. It was but the next in a long line of reforms dating back to the mid-1990s, some of which were framed explicitly in terms of European judicial appointments, but others of which were couched in terms of adjacent issues, such as judicial independence, judicial councils and judicial quality. Taken as a package, these reforms represent a rather concerted and long-term effort at judicial reform.

III. Why Think of these Reforms as Constitutional Interventions?

Although this package of judicial reforms appears at first blush to be focused primarily on procedural and institutional matters, they should really be understood as constitutional in nature. The first and most obvious reason is because of

[11] Consultative Council of European Judges, 'Opinion No 1 on Standards Concerning the Independence of the Judiciary and the Irremovability of Judges', CCJE (2001) OP N° 1 (hereinafter 'CCJE Opinion 1').

[12] PACE Recommendation 1429 (1999); PACE Recommendation 1649 (2004); PACE Resolution 1646 (2009) on the Nomination of Candidates and Election of Judges to the European Court of Human Rights.

[13] See *id.*

[14] 1995 PACE Report, *supra* note 10.

[15] *Id.*

the sheer importance of the constitutional roles played by the ECJ and the ECtHR. But these reforms also profoundly affect the constitutional relations between the Member States, alter the vertical and horizontal distribution of powers between domestic and supranational authorities, and reconstruct the conceptual underpinnings of European political power and judicial legitimacy.

A. The Sheer Importance of the ECJ and the ECtHR as Constitutional Actors

Given the existing literature, there is little need at this point to re-emphasise the hugely important role that the Luxembourg and Strasbourg Courts have played in the constitution of Europe.[16] This story is most often told in the context of the EU, in which the ECJ quickly established itself as a major – and, at times, *the* major – institutional protagonist in European constitutional developments. Indeed, it was the ECJ that authored the seminal constitutional doctrines of the supremacy and direct effect of European law, recruited the domestic courts and individual litigants in the construction of a legalised and judicialised Europe, established state liability for violations of EU law, constructed EU fundamental rights jurisprudence out of thin air and so on. It is simply impossible to talk about the constitution of Europe as it currently exists without placing the ECJ somewhere near the centre of the story.

The rise of the ECtHR as a major constitutional player is somewhat more recent, but no one could fail to see the importance of its jurisprudence. True, its impact tends to be somewhat more substantive than structural in orientation; its remit, after all, is to enforce a human rights treaty whose provisions tend to protect substantive and procedural rights, such as the right to free speech, freedom of religion, property rights and so on. This has led to a growing – and often controversial – jurisprudence over such politically charged issues as policing practices, LGBT rights, prisoner voting rights, Iraqi detentions, immigration/asylum treatment etc.[17] But such substantive rights issues are often difficult to disentangle from their structural constitutional implications. To limit certain police and immigration practices is to restrict certain kinds of governmental decision-making, which obviously re-arranges the horizontal distribution of powers between the executive and the judiciary. The ECtHR thus impacts heavily upon both the substantive and the structural constitution of governmental authority.

Given the patently constitutional effects of the European courts' jurisprudence, one clearly ought to think of efforts to restructure the appointments processes for,

[16] For the canonical reference, see Joseph Weiler, *The Transformation of Europe*, 100 Yale L.J. 2403 (1991).

[17] See, eg, Ireland v. UK, Application (5310/71) [1978] E.C.H.R. 1; Dudgeon v. UK, 45 Eur. Ct. H.R. (ser. A) at 14 (1981); Hirst v. UK (No. 2), [2005] E.C.H.R. 681; Al-Jedda v. UK (27021/08) [2011] E.C.H.R. 1092; Khlaifia and Others v. Italy, [2016] E.C.H.R. 406.

and membership of, those courts in constitutional terms. Simply put, the reform efforts seek to reconstitute a key constitutional actor.

B. An Intergovernmentalist Perspective

Although the judicial appointments reforms seek to influence the constitution of the European courts, their primary target may well lie elsewhere. The key to understanding this is to push against the judicial independence and judicial quality language that dominates the judicial appointments debates concerning the European courts.

To do so, we must make two important distinctions. The first concerns the beneficiaries of judicial independence. It is not the European courts per se that are in need of such independence. As we have seen, these courts have been immensely powerful actors, aggressively expanding their jurisdiction and boldly imposing their jurisprudence, profoundly affecting the fundamental constitutional architecture of Europe. Despite periodic attempts such as the Maastricht Treaty's 'three pillar' structure,[18] the Member States have ultimately had little success in containing the influence of the two courts.

It is instead the judges themselves who have needed protection. For all of the power of the ECJ and the ECtHR as major constitutional actors, the individual judges have traditionally been very much at the mercy of their own national governments. These governments held almost unfettered power to appoint whomever they chose to sit in Luxembourg and Strasbourg. Furthermore, the renewable six-year judicial terms initially established in the 1950s meant that the governments could effectively recall any judge who had incurred their displeasure. Finally, these governments would be the power-brokers when ECJ and ECtHR judges would return home in need of re-insertion into the national judicial, ministerial or academic fields from which they had come.

The second distinction, which follows directly from the first, is that the target of such European judicial independence measures has not in fact been European political institutions. It has instead been the Member State governments. At their core, the European judicial appointments, judicial independence and judicial quality reforms are primarily directed at the relationship between individual judges and their own national governments. The underlying institutional problem is that the very same judges who can exert massive constitutional power when acting as a judicial college at the European level are – as individuals – terribly professionally dependent on their own national governments.

[18] Martin Shapiro severely criticised the jurisdictional limitations imposed by that (now defunct) structure. See Martin Shapiro, *The European Court of Justice*, *in* JUDICIAL INDEPENDENCE IN THE AGE OF DEMOCRACY: CRITICAL PERSPECTIVES FROM AROUND THE WORLD 273, 297 (Peter Russell & David O'Brien eds., 2001).

This toxic combination of institutional power and personal vulnerability, which had been an unchallenged feature of the ECJ and ECHR systems since their very inception, had now became intolerable, eventually leading to the establishment of the two vetting panels in 2009–10. Why? This is where our reconstruction of the historical timeline is so useful: the key date is not 2009–10, as the birth of the panels would suggest, but the mid-1990s, when the European judicial reforms began in earnest. In other words, the triggering historical event was the fall of the Berlin Wall and the impending mass accession of former Eastern Bloc countries into the EU and the Council of Europe.

This historical perspective allows us to grasp the truly constitutional nature of the judicial appointments reforms. Faced with an almost overnight doubling of the number of European Member States and thus with a doubling of the judges sitting on the powerful Luxembourg and Strasbourg courts, the existing Member States sought to minimise the potential disruption that these Eastern parvenus might provoke via their appointment of judicial flunkies. Viewed from this historically informed intergovernmentalist perspective, we can therefore see that the broad array of European judicial reforms actually functioned as a means for the established Member State governments to exercise a degree of control over the governments of the newly acceded Member State governments, thereby limiting their ability to leverage their judicial appointments as a means to alter the European constitutional landscape.

Finally, the price that the established Member States had to pay to defang Central and Eastern European judicial appointments has been somewhat lower than one might imagine. The vetting panels, ie, the gatekeepers, have usually been stacked with high-ranking Western European judges.[19] Furthermore, the judicial quality standards that have been deployed are far less constraining for the established Member States for the simple reason that they have many more experienced European jurists to choose from: they are far more populous and their legal systems have been intertwined with Europe for several generations. Finally, these established Member States have expressly been cut slack by the European authorities.[20]

In short, the mass accession of new European Member States from the East yielded a new constitutional arrangement: national governments would no longer be able to dominate their judicial appointments to the high European courts. These governments, and especially those from east of Berlin, would have a much harder time using their judicial appointment powers to influence judicial outcomes of constitutional magnitude.

[19] For example, of the seven figures who sit on the 255 Panel at a given time, only *one* – Justice Peter Paczolay of Hungary or Mirosław Wyrzykowski of Poland – has come from Eastern Europe.

[20] See, eg, 1994 Recommendation, *supra* note 8 at 3 (creating an exception based on 'constitutional or legal provisions and traditions').

C. A Neo-institutionalist Perspective

Although the judicial reforms should thus be thought of as restructuring the constitutional relationship between the old and new Member States of Europe, it would be a mistake to limit the analysis to a purely state-centred perspective. Both the substance and the process of these reforms have largely escaped state control.

Perhaps the best way to grasp the independent momentum of the reforms is to look quickly at the institutional form of the vetting panels. Such panels, composed overwhelmingly of prominent judges, were not invented out of whole cloth in 2009–10. On the contrary, the panels represent the transplantation at the European level of national judicial councils tasked with overseeing a wide panoply of judicial matters, ranging from appointments to training to discipline. Such judicial councils have exploded worldwide, to such an extent that 'the World Bank and other multilateral donor agencies have made judicial councils part of the standard package of institutions associated with judicial reform and rule of law programming'.[21] Indeed, the Council of Europe institutions actively promoted their adoption in the midst of the great wave of Eastern enlargement in the mid-1990s.[22]

The next step was to propose that *national* judicial councils also be used by Member States to select judicial candidates to the European and international courts.[23] The institutional form of the judicial council then migrated to the *European* level in the form of the vetting panels. Once established, these panels then began to pursue agendas that the national governments would likely not have foreseen or desired. Thus, the EU's 255 Panel came not only to speak of itself as a proto-judicial council that vetted judicial candidates,[24] but also to propose that their powers be expanded, for example, to take on the task of evaluating and ranking candidates for the EU's General Court and for the EU's eventual judicial seat on the ECtHR.[25] It also the decided to publish a periodic 'activity report', which then spelled out in detail the substantive and procedural standards that the Panel would use to assess the fitness of ECJ judicial candidates. In other words, the 255 Panel quickly came to dictate not only what sorts of candidates it would accept, but also what sorts of procedures the Member States should use to select the candidates it would propose. For its part, the Council of Europe's Advisory Panel of

[21] Nuno Garoupa & Tom Ginsberg, *Guarding the Guardians: Judicial Councils and Judicial Independence*, 57 Am. J. Comp. L. 103, 109 (2009).

[22] See, eg, 1994 Recommendation, *supra* note 8 at 2.

[23] See, eg, CCJE Opinion 1, *supra* note 11 at para. 56.

[24] See, eg, Jean-Marc Sauvé, *Selecting the European Union's Judges: The Practice of the Article 255 Panel*, *in* Selecting Europe's Judges: A Critical Review of the Appointment Procedures to the European Courts 78, 84 (Michal Bobek ed., 2015).

[25] Jean-Marc Sauvé, 'Le rôle du comité 255 dans la séparation des pouvoirs au sein de l'Union européenne' 9, intervention lors du colloque pour le 130ème anniversaire du Conseil supérieur de la magistrature le 24 octobre 2013, https://www.conseil-etat.fr/actualites/discours-et-interventions/la-separation-des-pouvoirs-l-union-europeenne-et-le-comite-255.

Experts worked quickly to garner the power to veto proposed judicial candidates (a gambit that was vehemently opposed by the Member States and the PACE).[26] Once established as independent institutions, the vetting panels thus pressed their own independent agendas, seeking to place significant limits on the governmental capacity to dictate judicial appointments and judicial policy.

This institutional perspective can and should be thought of as a separation of powers struggle. Judges had played a central role in calling for the establishment of such vetting panels;[27] they had then populated them almost exclusively; and they eventually acted to wrest away from national governments a good deal of their traditional power to dominate judicial appointments. One might of course applaud the establishment of such judicial counterbalances to national executive authority, which has expanded at the European level at the expense of national parliamentary power. However, what matters for our purposes is simply that we recognise that judicial institutions have taken their own paths, acting in high-handed ways that national governments have often come to regret and oppose.[28]

That said, one should not reduce the institutionalist analysis to a straightforward separation of powers between the national executives and judicial institutions. The judicial panels are not the only important institutional actors in play. Take the Committee of Ministers of the Council of Europe. It is nominally the intergovernmental arm of the Council of Europe, as it is formally composed of the national foreign ministers. But most of the time, it is run by ambassadorial Permanent Representatives and other staff who live in Strasbourg and meet weekly in thematically organised formations and sub-formations. The Committee of Ministers therefore consists of a large institution of high-grade civil servant professionals with significant legal expertise and a commitment to the European human rights project and its institutions. It is not (as classic intergovernmentalist theory might suggest) composed of national politicians who reside in their

[26] See Advisory Panel of Experts on Candidates for Election as Judge to the European Court of Human Rights, Proposals made by the Panel in its Submission to the CDDH in May 2013, in Final Activity Report for the Committee of Ministers at Appendix 2; Steering Committee for Human Rights, CDDH Report on the Review of the Functioning of the Advisory Panel of Experts on Candidates for Election as Judge to the European Court of Human Rights, CDDH(2013)R79 Addendum II (November 29, 2013) at para. 28.

[27] See, eg, Jean-Paul Costa, Letter from the President of the European Court of Human Rights, addressed to member states' Permanent Representatives (Ambassadors) on 9 June 2010, in PACE Committee on Legal Affairs and Human Rights (Rapporteur: Wohlwend), Report on National procedures for the selection of candidates for the European Court of Human Rights, PACE document 12391 (October 6, 2010) Appendix, http://assembly.coe.int/nw/xml/XRef/X2H-Xref-ViewPDF.asp?FileID=12764&lang=en.

[28] A distressing number of governments came to thumb their noses at the Advisory Panel of Experts, either by failing to present it their lists of proposed judges prior to submitting them to the PACE for election or by outright refusing to heed their (negative) judgements. See, eg, Steering Committee for Human Rights, Ministers' Deputies Exchange of Views with Mr. Luzius Wildhaber, Chairman of the on Candidates for Election to the European Court of Human Rights (January 30, 2013), in DH-GDR (2013)005, February 5, 2013.

national capitals and engage in arm's-length bargaining in their country's pre-determined self-interest.

Viewed from an institutional perspective, a great deal of the judicial appointments reforms has actually been produced by an institutional sub-formation of the Member State governments themselves. Operating at some remove in Strasbourg, it was this Committee of Ministers that, responding to the call of ECtHR President JP Costa, actually established the Advisory Panel of Experts, whose own institutional manoeuvres would soon exasperate assorted Member State governments to the point of revolt. The constitutional redistribution of appointment powers was therefore the product of unanticipated (and often undesired) projects undertaken in part by institutions that had escaped the control of the very national governments to which they nominally belong.

D. A Constructivist Perspective

The judicial appointments reforms that resulted in the establishment of the Advisory Panel and of the 255 Panel in 2009–10 should therefore be understood simultaneously as: (1) a clever mechanism for long-standing Western European Member States to protect their interests in the European *acquis* by controlling the governments of new accession States from the East; and (2) the unplanned consequences of domestic and international actors leveraging the opportunities afforded by European institutional structures. But one should not lose sight of the fact that these debates and reforms also constitute bold constitutional reconstructions of the European legal, political, institutional and ideological fields by well-placed judges, academics and executive actors.

In short, the European judicial debates and reforms need to be understood in constructivist as well as intergovernmental and neo-institutional terms. They have been gradually elaborated through the interaction of a broad set of different actors operating in varied and shifting institutional contexts. These actors' ideas, alignments, identities and interests co-evolved to arrive at an increasingly common professional perspective that has been voiced increasingly clearly by leading judicial academic figures, supported by national and European civil servants working largely in European venues.

Section IV will examine the resulting conceptual, professional and institutional construction in greater detail and will do so in Ackerman's constitutional terms. For now, it is enough to underline that this constitutional reconstruction has hinged on two key features, neither of which pre-dated the European judicial appointments debates. First, judicial appointment on the basis of professional quality has supplanted appointment on the basis of governmental political will. This transformation, exemplified by the transplantation of the judicial council form, reproduces the ethos and procedures governing the 'ordinary' judiciaries of most civilian jurisdictions, but it does so at the expense of the Kelsenian notion of political representation that traditionally underlies the selection of constitutional and international judges.[29]

Second, this professionalising trend has gone hand in hand with an ambitious constitutional reconstruction of the separation of powers. The appointments literature has increasingly argued that liberal democracy demands that the judicial branch be a co-equal, independent and largely self-governing branch of government, free of executive branch interference. Neither of these positions reflects a pre-existing European consensus regarding the judicial role at either the national or the European/international level. Yet the European literature insists that without them, the legitimacy and authority of the ECJ and the ECtHR are doomed.[30]

IV. Ackerman's Constitutional Perspective

In *Revolutionary Constitutions*, Ackerman offers a compelling account of the variety of constitutional paradigms that have succeeded in constructing legitimacy and garnering adherence in the contemporary world. Although not directly applicable to the European judicial reforms we have been discussing, his analysis does offer a persuasive perspective that can be fruitfully brought to bear on the European judicial debates. His analysis is useful first for descriptive purposes. It suggests that the European judicial reforms really should be thought of in constitutional terms. They affect the limits of governmental powers in a manner that impacts directly upon the separation of powers. They are an integral part of a project to enhance the constitutional legitimacy of Europe in general and the European judiciary in particular. And they reflect an ongoing project to internalise and institutionalise a new understanding of the European judicial and constitutional order.

At the same time, Ackerman's framework is immensely useful for the purposes of critiquing these European debates and reforms. As he explains, there exist not one, but several different models of constitutional construction. If this is so, then the construction of European constitutional legitimacy represents a two-tiered project: not only must Europe fashion its own constitutional identity, but that identity must also be squared with the divergent constitutional identities of its Member States.[31] Unfortunately, the European judicial debates and reforms show little sign of possessing the requisite sensitivity to succeed in such a delicate project.

[29] See Alec Stone Sweet, *Constitutional Courts, in* COMPARATIVE CONSTITUTIONAL LAW 816, 824 (Michel Rosenfeld & Andras Sájo eds., 2012).

[30] See, eg, Jutta Limbach et al., Judicial Independence: Law and Practice of Appointments to the European Court of Human Rights (2003), www.interights.org/jud-ind-en/index.html ('While paying tribute to the [ECtHR], this report notes that its credibility and authority risk being undermined by the ad hoc and often politicized processes currently adopted in the appointment of its judges').

[31] For the classic statement of two-level international relations analysis, see Robert Putnam, *Diplomacy and Domestic Politics: The Logic of Two-Level Games*, 42(3) INT'L ORGS. 427 (1988).

A. Description

Ackerman's analysis is quite useful for descriptive purposes. As section III explained, the European judicial reforms really should be thought of in constitutional terms. Whether one analyses those reforms in intergovernmentalist, neo-institutionalist or constructivist terms – or, as I prefer, in all three – the underlying point is inescapable: these reforms limit the exercise of governmental powers in a manner that impacts directly upon the separation of powers.

From an intergovernmentalist perspective, the reforms are above all intended to manage the uncertainty generated by the mass European accession of former Eastern Bloc countries in the post-1989 period. The means chosen were to limit the capacity of those new Member State's governments to appoint judicial flunkies and thereby to control European judicial decisions and policy. The solution was to create a certain firewall between national executives and judicial institutions at both the national and European levels. This represents quite plainly a constitutional project.

From a neo-institutionalist perspective, the reforms demonstrate the tendency of institutions to develop their own agendas, to enlist support and eventually to go their own way. Once established and unleashed, those institutions routinely come to develop interests and projects that their creators would not have anticipated or desired. And indeed, regardless of whether one focuses on nominally executive branch institutions (such as the Committee of Ministers of the Council of Europe) or on judicial ones (such as the European judicial vetting panels), the trajectory is the same: these institutions, though established by (and, in the former case, actually representing) the Member States, developed constitutional projects that sought to rein in the capacity of the Member State governments to dominate European judicial affairs.

From a constructivist perspective, Ackerman's analysis really shines. The key point is that the judicial debates and reforms clearly represent an effort to construct a constitutional identity for Europe. This project involves the construction of a proper European system of separation of powers that would thereby enhance the authority and legitimacy of the European judiciary, which would in turn enhance the overall legitimacy of Europe in general. Starting from these grand constitutional premises, the European reforms work hard to concretise them into specific institutional structures and procedures. The reforms therefore represent a surprisingly bold attempt to formulate a European constitutional order from first principles and to work out its specific institutional and procedural entailments.

Ackerman's analysis therefore prompts us to appreciate what is really at stake in the European judicial debates and reforms. Although these debates appear a first blush to be about relatively technical issues (ie, the details of judicial appointments) and although they appear to offer rather trite additions to well-trodden debates about judicial independence, they are actually rather bold interventions aimed at constructing and legitimising a European constitutional identity. What is really at stake is the place of the European judiciary and, with it, the very legitimacy of the European constitutional order.

Once we understand these debates as interventions directed towards the European constitutional plane, Ackerman's descriptive framework comes into play once again. Although *Revolutionary Constitutions* discusses the EU only relatively obliquely, one can infer what Ackerman's analysis might look like when he will address it more directly in volume II. For now, he states:

> My three ideal types will also enable a more discriminating form of trans-national learning. If, as I suggest, the leading countries of Europe emerge from different constitutional pathways, these differences should be treated with respect if the European Union is to sustain itself as a vital force in the coming generation.[32]

From lines such as these, we can infer that Ackerman understands the problem of European constitutional legitimacy as a two-tiered inquiry. On one level, there is the question of the constitutional identity of Europe itself. To speak in Ackermanian terms, should we think of the EU as evincing a revolutionary, establishmentarian or elite constitutional tradition?

However intriguing this first question may be, Ackerman suggests that it addresses only part of the constitutional conundrum. The second involves the relationship between the constitutional identities of Europe and of its constituent Member States. And this is where things get dicey. As Ackerman explains, the constitutional traditions of France, Britain and Germany are quite different, and given that Europe and its constitutional tradition interact with – and often veritably impinge upon – the constitutional orders of its Member States, Europe would be wise to attend to these different constitutional relationships and to their inherent tensions.

On this Ackermanian understanding, Europe does not exist in a vacuum. Its constitutional legitimacy rests not only on itself, but also on its relation to the varied constitutional identities of its Member States. Consequently, the EU's legitimacy challenge is likely to be quite different in Warsaw, London and Madrid, regardless of which constitutional tradition best describes the EU itself. Countries with revolutionary constitutional traditions such as France and Poland, for example, are likely to experience the EU quite differently from those with establishmentarian (British) or elite (German and Spanish) ones.

As a result, European constitutional actors should strive to account for the constitutional traditions and proclivities of the Member States when making policy judgements with constitutional consequences. Such comparative constitutional awareness should of course focus on pragmatic structural issues. What, for example, might a particular policy judgement do to the distribution of constitutional authority within the EU, between the EU and the Member States, and within each of the Member States?

But that is not all. The authority and legitimacy of European governmental, political and legal structures is largely an ideological affair. For Europe to succeed

[32] Ackerman, *supra* note 1 at 2.

therefore requires a good deal of conceptual and pedagogical work: the legitimacy of Europe and of its policy decisions must be constructed, translated and conveyed in a manner that bridges the different constitutional traditions of Europe's Member States.

B. Critique

Having suggested these descriptive paths, Ackerman's analysis can be leveraged to critique the ongoing European judicial reform efforts and their constitutional consequences. Above all, the European debates have made little effort to recognise or come to terms with the constitutional diversity of its Member States. They have tended instead to put forward simplistically monolithic constitutional understandings. As a result, they have done almost nothing to try to square European constitutional efforts with the diverse constitutional traditions of the European Member States. This categorical, and ultimately dismissive, conceptual posture severely limits the constitutional legitimacy that Europe might eventually attain.

This failing permeates the judicial appointments debates and reforms. Not only do they propound a rather specific notion of what the European judiciary should be, they do so on the basis of categorical statements about the nature of the judiciary in any proper liberal democracy. Take, for example, Opinion No 1 of the Consultative Council of European Judges (CCJE) on 'Standards Concerning the Independence of the Judiciary and the Irremovability of Judges'. Promoting a cut-and-dried vision of the nature and power of the judiciary in a 'modern democratic state', the CCJE – chaired by Lord Mance, who would soon be appointed to the 255 Panel – declares:

> *The rationales of judicial independence*
>
> 10. Judicial independence is a prerequisite to the rule of law and a fundamental guarantee of a fair trial …
>
> 11. This independence must exist in relation to society generally and in relation to the particular parties to any dispute on which judges have to adjudicate. The judiciary is one of three basic and equal pillars in the modern democratic state. It has an important role and functions in relation to the other two pillars. It ensures that governments and the administration can be held to account for their actions, and, with regard to the legislature, it is involved in ensuring that duly enacted laws are enforced, and, to a greater or lesser extent, in ensuring that they comply with any relevant constitution or higher law (such as that of the European Union). To fulfil its role in these respects, the judiciary must be independent of these bodies, which involves freedom from inappropriate connections with and influence by these bodies. Independence thus serves as the guarantee of impartiality. This has implications, necessarily, for almost every aspect of a judge's career: from training to appointment and promotion and to disciplining.[33]

[33] CCJE Opinion 1, *supra* note 11 at paras. 10–11.

Whatever its normative merits, this confident pronouncement about the co-equal and independent nature of the judiciary relative to the political branches is demonstrably historically inaccurate. Europeans have by no means universally accepted that a democratic state requires a 'judicial power' that sits on an equal footing with the political branches of government, never mind one that ensures that they 'comply with any relevant constitution or higher law'.

Indeed, the French tradition – arguably Europe's most influential – refuses to this day to grant the judiciary such elevated status, or checks-and-balances role, or higher law powers. Title VIII of the 1958 French Constitution explicitly reduces the judiciary to a mere 'autorité judiciaire', thereby denying it co-equal status with the political branches.[34] The 1790 Judiciary Act explicitly denies the judiciary the power to interfere with legislative or administrative decisions;[35] administrative review is therefore performed by an entirely separate set of administrative tribunals housed in the executive branch. And far from entrusting its judiciary with the task of ensuring constitutional compliance by the political branches, the French Constitution (like so many others) establishes a separate Constitutional Court (named 'Constitutional Council' precisely to distinguish it from the ordinary courts) that, furthermore, does not sit in the judiciary at all. Nor is such discomfort with judicial power limited to French or civilian jurisdictions, as the fractious British debates regarding the Human Rights Act 1998 and the Constitutional Reform Act 2005 (establishing the Supreme Court of the UK) clearly demonstrate.

Yet this universalising tendency has long dominated the European judicial debates and reforms, which walk a fine line between dubious description and categorical prescription. And such sweeping declarations are hardly limited to first principles regarding the role of the judiciary in a proper separation of powers; they have spelled out in increasing detail the norms, procedures and institutions that should govern all aspects of the judicial profession, ranging from selection to training, to promotion and to discipline, whether at the national or the European level. In 1994, for example, the Council of Ministers passed a Recommendation that: 'All decisions concerning the professional career of judges should be based on objective criteria, and the selection and career of judges should be based on merit, having regard to qualifications, integrity, ability and efficiency.'[36] In 1998, the 'European Charter on the Statute for Judges' called for an 'independent authority' (in effect, a judge-dominated judicial council) to govern all aspects of the judicial profession, ranging from selection, to training, to promotion and to discipline.[37] The judicial council form was then transplanted to the European level, eventually leading to the establishment of the two vetting panels.

[34] Titre 8, Constitution du 4 octobre 1958. Indeed, the Swedish Constitution did not even list the judiciary as a separate governmental power until 2011! See Constitution of Sweden: The Fundamental Laws and the Riksdag Act (with an Introduction by Magnus Isberg) (2016), https://www.riksdagen.se/globalassets/07.-dokument--lagar/the-constitution-of-sweden-160628.pdf, 21, 90.

[35] Code de l'orgnisation judiciaire tit II, arts 10 and 13, August 16–24, 1790.

[36] Committee of Ministers Rec R (94) 12 (October 13, 1994) at 2.

[37] European Charter on the Statute for Judges, *supra* note 10 at para. 1.3.

But this was hardly the end of it. Arguing that the criteria for assessing judicial candidates 'could be more clearly and precisely explained', the EU's 255 Panel, for example, generated its own standardised list:

> The panel's assessment ... is therefore made on the basis of six considerations: the candidate's legal expertise, professional experience, ability to perform the duties of a Judge, assurance of independence and impartiality, language skills and aptitude for working as part of a team in an international environment in which several legal systems are represented.[38]

The Panel then spent the next two and a half pages working methodically through these six criteria, producing, inter alia, detailed linguistic requirements and seniority benchmarks.[39] The end result of these ever more precise standards was to dictate the broad outlines of a successful ECJ candidate: a 50 to 55-year-old judge, academic or high-level civil servant with 'twenty years' experience of high level duties' and significant experience in European legal issues, very good language skills (especially in French and English) and comparative legal training (likely gained through some combination of legal education and international legal work). And to put teeth into these selection criteria and procedures, the 255 Panel interviews each candidate for a full hour according to a procedure that is painfully reminiscent of advanced university exams, doctoral defences or professorial accreditations.[40]

The net effect has therefore not only been to impose a dubiously universal understanding of the place of the judiciary in a liberal democratic order, but also to define ever more precisely the portrait of a proper European judge and the processes by which he or she must be selected. The point here is not to debate the merits of these selection procedures and criteria, but to recognise that they represent an act of constitutional construction: they aim to bolster the legitimacy of the European judiciary by reframing the bases of its authority.

These new judicial selection norms and processes point in a very specific direction. In particular, they work to normalise the European judiciary as 'ordinary' (ie, civil, commercial and criminal) judges along the model favoured by European civilian jurisdictions. Judges are trained in national judicial schools or centres,[41] which rely on demanding entrance examinations ('concours'), testing and ranking of assorted kinds. They are then subject to judicial quality control through national judicial councils, which enforce standards and dominate promotions. The European judicial reforms thus run ostentatiously in the direction of 'ordinary' national judiciaries, complete with their conception of a professionalised, career, civil service judiciary.

[38] Article 255 Panel, Activity report of the panel provided for by Article 255 of the Treaty on the Functioning of the European Union, First Report of 17 February 2011 (No 6509/11) 8–9.

[39] See *id.* at 9–11.

[40] *Id.*

[41] The French Ecole Nationale de la Magistrature, the Escuela Judicial Española, the Italian Scuola Superiore della Magistratura and the Portuguese Centro de Estudios Judiciários offer good examples. See https://e-justice.europa.eu/content_national_training_structures_for_the_judiciary-406-en.do.

But this represents a major change. The institutions, processes and ethos governing international and constitutional judges do not traditionally reflect this professionalised conception. As we have seen, the European status quo ante demonstrated this clearly: judicial appointments to the ECJ and the ECtHR traditionally operated on the basis of political discretion, not professional and institutional qualification. The same continues to hold true for the appointment of constitutional judges in most of Europe. Typically working in a neo-Kelsenian vein, appointment to these national courts is primarily governed by political means.[42] The whole point is to reserve delicate separation of powers issues and fundamental rights matters to politically sensitive – rather than professionally oriented – institutions.

The European judicial reforms therefore represent a marked shift in the symbolic identity of the European judiciary, and this shift in turn marks an attempt to normalise and legitimise European legal, political and constitutional structures. This legitimation strategy works off of an a priori idea of the nature and place of the judiciary in a proper liberal democracy that simultaneously calls upon stock features of 'ordinary' national judiciaries (ie, the institutional form of the judicial council and the professional ethic of a properly trained and vetted corps of judicial actors) and renounces the defining logic for distinctive constitutional and international courts. The high European judiciary and its institutional allies have thus sought to bootstrap legitimacy from the recognisable trappings of the 'ordinary' judiciary in the domestic setting. These stock forms and conceptions have been leveraged to yield meaningful institutional and procedural reforms, including most importantly the limitation of governmental authority over judicial appointments, the concomitant empowerment of high-ranking domestic and European judicial figures, and the technical professionalisation of judicial profiles.[43]

However, it is not at all clear why these reforms would actually work to boost the authority and legitimacy of the European judiciary to any significant degree. First, this unitary vision of the judiciary and of its place in the European constitutional order, for all that it offers a reasonable and eminently defensible vision of the separation of powers, simply does not square with the constitutional traditions of many of Europe's Member States, which, as Ackerman accurately stresses, are deeply varied. Its resonance is therefore inherently limited. Second, although the reforms do evoke the particular institutional forms (eg, judicial councils), procedural features (eg, oral examination of candidates) and conceptual traits (eg, the valorisation of professional quality) of some national systems, this guarantees little

[42] In France, the President and the Presidents of the two houses of the legislature each unilaterally select one judge of the Constitutional Council every three years. These judges are subject to no political or professional vetting process and require no formal educational or professional qualifications. Though more legally professionalised than its French counterpart, the German constitutional bench is nonetheless appointed by explicitly political means (two-thirds majorities of the Bundestag and the Bundersat).

[43] For more on this shift in profiles, see Mikael Rask Madsen, *The Legitimization Strategies of International Judges: The Case of the European Court of Human Rights*, *in* Bobek, *supra* note 24 at 259.

in the way of increased European judicial legitimacy, never mind increased European legitimacy *tout court*. To think that it would is to mistake form for substance or perhaps cause for effect.

Although this is not the place to offer a detailed examination of the fonts of judicial or political legitimacy, a quick example will suffice to make the point. As the reader may have surmised, many of the European judicial reforms mesh particularly well with the highly influential French judicial tradition: the French system, for example, offers rigorous *concours*-based admission into the judiciary, advancement via a combination of seniority and quality-based rankings, and so on. But these characteristic institutional traits do not represent the core of French judicial legitimacy; they merely contribute to it. The core lies instead in the republican ethos of the French state, according to which a corps of elite and quality-tested civil servants, representative of the best of French citizenry and inculcated in the cherished values of the state, are put in an institutional position to advance the French 'general welfare'. The key therefore lies in the representative nature of the state and of its agents: high-grade civil servants are recruited from, and educated for years in, the public education system, leading to ever greater policy-making authority as these public servants move towards the top of an ostensibly inclusive – if rigorously elite – state-centred hierarchy.

Viewed in the proper context, the procedural and institutional features of the French system – such as the examination of professional qualities by judicial councils – are not what drive its legitimacy. They are but mechanisms to get at something deeper: the representative nature of that system. The idea is to identify the most talented future agents of the state and to give them a proper inculcation (the telling French term is 'formation') in the state's republican values so that, when the time comes and their training justifies it, these agents will be in a position to act legitimately in the name of the public welfare. Indeed, it is precisely the gradual – and depressingly justified – erosion of faith in the representative nature of these state institutions and actors that has increasingly bled the French state of its perceived legitimacy.[44]

Given these realities, it should come as no surprise that the mere adoption of some new institutional forms and procedural features would hold so little promise for increasing the overall legitimacy of the European courts, never mind of the European constitutional order. Without a meaningful representative link between the European citizenry and the European institutions that act on their behalf, these institutional forms and procedural features are but empty signifiers. They are locally recognisable symbols of proper governmental representation; but without

[44] The 'gilets jaunes' demonstrations of late 2018 are but the latest manifestation of this representational deficiency. Furthermore, the erosion has become so severe that Emmanuel Macron – the very prototype of the French administrative elite – has proposed the closing of his alma mater, the Ecole Nationale d'Administration (ENA). See Benoît Floc'h, Macron confirme la disparition de l'ENA et des grands corps, https://www.lemonde.fr/politique/article/2019/04/26/macron-confirme-la-disparition-de-l-ena-et-des-grands-corps_5455235_823448.html.

more, there is little perceived substance behind them. To write in Ackermanian terms, there is as yet no specific, recognised and valued European constitutional tradition; and the diversity of constitutional traditions within the Member States of Europe continues to pose severe challenges to constructing one that might speak to each. To pretend that taking on the procedural and institutional trappings of one particular type of national constitutional order will ipso facto create a viable European constitutional tradition is to engage in wishful thinking.

V. Value Added

The Ackermanian perspective demonstrates something very important about the nature of the European judicial appointments debates and reforms. Those debates offer implicit, and sometimes explicit, understandings of the nature of European constitutional legitimacy. They present a logical argument: in a liberal democracy, the rule of law and the separation of powers require the adoption of a recognisable institutional architecture, procedural organisation and conceptual framework. To the extent that Europe adopts these essential features, not only will its judiciary ground its authority and increase its legitimacy, but so too will the resulting European constitutional order.

Stressing the constitutional diversity of Europe's Member States, Ackerman's analysis gives us good reasons to question this logic. If, as is undoubtedly empirically true, these diverse European states actually demonstrate a wide variety of institutional architectures, procedural organisations and conceptual frameworks, then there is no particular reason to believe that the adoption of the model favoured in the current European judicial and academic debates would actually resonate with European citizens from London to Tallinn to Athens, leading to a marked upsurge in European judicial and constitutional legitimacy. Indeed, the European approach probably has things backwards: it represents an attempt to bootstrap constitutional legitimacy from certain institutional, procedural and conceptual forms, instead of recognising that such forms may at most reinforce a particular constitutional tradition.

By way of conclusion, I would like to touch briefly on two questions triggered by Ackerman's analytic prism. First, how does one identify the constitutional tradition of a legal/political order? And second, what is the connection between such a tradition and particular institutional, procedural and conceptual forms?

The European judicial reforms speak to both questions. On the one hand, these reforms certainly look like a concerted attempt to reconstruct the European judiciary – and with it, the European constitutional order – as an appropriately elite system, with qualified professionals taking control at the expense of national political figures. This approach conforms to the elite nature of the European constitutional order, whether this order is viewed as a historical artifact (ie, a creation of French, German and Italian governmental notables) or as a style of governance (ie, an opaque approach dominated by knowledgeable executive branch professionals).

On the other hand, this elite model also describes the French ordinary judiciary and administrative tribunals. But what are we to make of this? Under Ackermanian analysis, the Fifth Republic is one of the archetypes of a revolutionary constitutional tradition. How, then, can seemingly *elite* institutional forms (eg, judicial councils), procedural features (eg, oral examination of candidates) and conceptual traits (eg, the valorisation of professional quality) not only be leveraged to promote the legitimacy of an *elite* constitutional order such as the European one, but also sustain the judiciary of a *revolutionary* constitutional tradition such as the French one?

There are at least two ways to approach this question. The first is to make use of the distinction first advanced by Mirjan Damaška in his seminal book *The Faces of Justice and State Authority*.[45] As Damaška explains, the procedural and institutional organization of a given state's legal order need not reflect or match its governing ideological framework.[46] This suggests that the French system can be structured in an elite (Damaška would say 'hierarchical') manner despite the revolutionary ethos of its constitutional tradition.

The second approach is to question how one should go about classifying a given tradition as 'revolutionary', 'establishmentarian' or 'elite' in the first place. I use quotation marks to stress that the taxonomic exercise of (a) defining these categories and (b) assigning particular constitutional examples to those categories is not merely a straightforward and post hoc descriptive enterprise. Ackerman's constitutional traditions do not simply exist as objective descriptions of the ontological nature of particular constitutional orders. On the contrary, legal and political actors make tactical use of such categories and classifications in real time as a means to advance their particular procedural, institutional, political and constitutional projects; in other words, they *use* their descriptions as the means to generate prescriptions.

If we recognise such discursive and tactical use of constitutional traditions and combine it with Damaška's warning about the relative autonomy of a legal system's procedural/institutional forms from its governing ideas about the state's proper nature and purpose, we can arrive at an important double insight. Constitutional traditions are contested constructions that are used to justify procedural and institutional projects; and contested procedural and institutional constructions are used to justify constitutional projects.

This conclusion both amplifies and confounds Ackerman's insight that different countries possess different constitutional traditions. It suggests, first, that different constitutional traditions and different procedural/institutional regimes can legitimately coexist within a given country; and, second, that contrary to what tactically inclined reformers may claim, there is no necessary connection between

[45] Mirjan Damaška, The Faces of Justice and State Authority: A Comparative Approach to the Legal Process (1991).

[46] See *id.* at 13–15.

any of these traditions and specific procedural and/or institutional regimes. At the very same time, in the very same systems, different claims are made about the nature of the system in question. Different players offer different configurations of the available materials to generate different descriptions of the existing state of affairs, which then puts them in a better position to support their prescriptive claims about what ought to be done moving forward. Damaška is very likely correct that a legal system's procedural and institutional structures need not reflect its governing ideological justifications (eg, elite structures are routinely used in revolutionary systems); but experience shows that legal and political actors nonetheless make a point of supporting their procedural and institutional projects with ideologically based constitutional claims (and vice versa).

The European judicial reform debates demonstrate this perfectly. The elite judicial model is being used to justify important constitutional reforms even as a new constitutional vision is being used to justify important judicial reforms. But these categorical claims and their dubiously circular entailments cannot generate the increased authority and legitimacy that reformers hope will accrue to the European judiciary and, as a result, to Europe in general. They are but monolithic and doctrinaire articles of judicial faith that fly in the face of the long-standing procedural, institutional, conceptual and constitutional diversity that exists not only *between* the different countries of Europe, but also *within* each of them.

A few concluding thoughts. First, to say that constitutional traditions are not merely *ex post* empirical descriptions, but also contemporaneous normative claims that are leveraged for prescriptive purposes, is not to say that some descriptions and some claims do not function better than others; it simply means that these descriptions and their claimed entailments represent interventions in fundamentally and perpetually contested debates. Different players must convince their audiences that they have compiled the best description and drawn the best prescriptive conclusions. This is largely a constructive exercise, highly dependent on context and audience.

Second, the deeply conflicted – and sometimes outright acrimonious – nature of the European judicial debates should perhaps prompt us to consider whether we should not take Ackerman's variegated and contextual understanding of constitutional traditions one step further. In particular, why should we assume that Britain or France, never mind Europe, is sufficiently internally homogeneous to possess a single constitutional tradition? One might instead understand the European judicial debates as demonstrating that competing constitutional traditions co-exist within any given constitutional order.

The European judicial reforms deploy institutional forms (eg, judicial councils), procedural features (eg, standardised examination of candidates) and conceptual traits (eg, judicial independence and expertise, and the separation of powers) that reflect a constitutional vision that is currently held by most of the European judiciary and its institutional allies in the high national courts, in specialised European executive bodies, in high academic circles and so on. For this identifiable social and professional tranche, this has become *their* constitutional tradition, regardless of whether they hail from the European courts, the French Conseil d'Etat, the Hungarian Constitutional Court, the British civil service, the Spanish Ministry of Justice or the Law Faculties of the Universidade Católica in Lisbon or Charles University in Prague.

This professional constitutional tradition cuts across national boundaries with remarkable ease. While this common ground offers important opportunities for (elite?) constitutional construction, one should not fool oneself into believing that this construction speaks to, or will resonate with, the constitutional constructions of other social groupings in their particular local contexts. The vehement diatribes that Brexiteers launch against the European courts make this all too plain.[47] For European constitutional renovation to occur successfully will require self-consciously constructive work that seeks to overcome not only, as Ackerman suggests, the kinds of constitutional divides that separate national traditions, but also the ones that separate social and professional traditions within and across those national boundaries.

[47] See, eg, the tirades of the rebellious (and vehemently Eurosceptic) Tory MP Philip Davies gleefully reported in the Daily Mail: www.dailymail.co.uk/news/article-2449256/Human-right-make-killing-Damning-dossier-reveals-taxpayers-European-court-payouts-murderers-terrorists-traitors.html#ixzz570KcIxit.

PART IV

The Law and Politics of Revolution

15

Sustaining Revolutionary Constitutions

From Movement Party to Movement Court

MENAKA GURUSWAMY

I. Introduction

Revolutionary Constitutions is a real tour de force. With this book, Bruce Ackerman demonstrates his enormous learning across varied constitutional jurisdictions including India, South Africa, France, Italy, Poland, Burma, Israel, Iran and America. The book deftly introduces the reader to the rich constitutional and political histories of these countries. Ackerman presents an analysis of these varied jurisdictions. And this is a significant feat, for the countries in question do not necessarily have common origins, nor are interconnected as being part of a common empire. They are a fair mix from both the Global North and the Global South.

As if this were not enough, Ackerman provides us with a methodological lens to appreciate constitutionalism around the world. He aims high, wanting to 'organise the bewildering complexity of global experience into a compelling comparative framework'.[1] And he opts to delve deep into the political, social and constitutional histories of these various jurisdictions. Not for him the more conventional 'big n' or 'small n case' studies that delve into the comparison of one institution, for instance, the judiciary or the military or even a constituent assembly. Neither does he opt for a 'large n study' that focuses on textual provisions of the galaxy of various constitutions.

Instead, Ackerman dives deep into the political, social and constitution-making journeys that create constitutionalism. In doing so, he engages the founding of nations, the revolutionary movements that led to the new constitutions, the personalities that led the revolutions and subsequently successors who either consolidated or debilitated these constitutional foundings. He is equally at ease discussing charismatic constitutionalists like Iran's Ayatollah Khomeni, South Africa's Nelson Mandela or India's Jawaharlal Nehru.

[1] Bruce Ackerman, Revolutionary Constitutions: Charismatic Leadership and the Rule of Law 37 (2019) 37.

And Ackerman is adroit in familiarising readers with the intricacies of organisations with charisma, like Poland's Solidarity or India's National Congress. He has had over 60 years of teaching, writing and practising constitutional law to finally arrive at this book, which will push the boundaries of the comparative method and will force all of us comparatists to up our game. Yet', Ackerman's thesis and work must be engaged with further, to build on its methodological and substantive contributions, and also to critique its conclusions.

II. Aims and Structure of the Chapter

Section III of this chapter briefly discusses Ackerman's methodology, including its strengths and possible weaknesses. Its rich political and historical depth and detail make it a method that demands expertise and knowledge of multiple jurisdictions. It exposes the reader to larger political assessments and inter-institutional power play that few other comparatists attempt. Could this methodology have any weaknesses? When the method is premised on interpretations of political power play and charismatic personalities, could there be many alternate readings of an event or motive?

Section IV contests his thesis that hegemonic parties, owing to their domination, and having spearheaded national revolutions make successful constitutions. In responding to the case study on India, I argue that it is not hegemony, but acquiring the skills necessary to craft a radical enough constitution that would be seen to be continuing the revolutionary values of the movement that is definitive. India's movement party committed to reparative constitutionalism as a core value, during the colonial era, and its party organisation acquired the skills to make a successful constitution. It also enjoyed political legitimacy and goodwill, which ensured that the revolutionary constitutional values could be implemented through legislation and diffused into the social fabric – both made possible by the steady grip of the rule of the party that lead the revolution.

Section V argues that the contest between India's Supreme Court and its elected representatives (in the executive and the legislature) is shaped by the institutional design of the court and not by Ackerman's description of the Indian judiciary's enlightenment shaped secular values. The Court has been able to arrogate enormous power, often at odds with constitution design due to its early inroads into regulating the powers of parliament and its institutional design that facilitates wide access and the constitutionalisation of all state business. Much of this state business is typically outside of a judiciary's purview.

III. What is the Ackermanian Method?

This book is not just a glamorous overview of world constitutions. It is the first volume (as Ackerman has already commenced work on the second volume) of a three-volume compendium on 'Revolutionary Constitutions'. Not all constitutions qualify as 'revolutionary'. To sum up in Ackerman's words, the new constitution must be the product of a mobilised movement that has self-consciously repudiated an old regime to demand a new beginning.[2]

But surely this a rather wide net to cast? After all, even dictators and totalitarians have constitutions that consolidate their power. Therefore, Ackerman is also clear that not all revolutionary constitutions lead to constitutional regimes. But what sets apart dictatorships from constitutional regimes is that when a dictator encounters resistance to her commands, she refuses to recognise such shows of opposition as legitimate. Constitutional regimes by contrast require the most powerful officials to engage in ongoing competition with institutional rivals for the final say over the future course of political development.[3]

An example that Ackerman provides of the succession battles is the political jostling and quest for power in Iran between Khameni (the Guardian Jurist) and Rouhani (the elected President), both constitution office-holders. Both occupied powerful positions provided for by the Constitution, must jostle for influence, and each must win a mandate from their constitutionally envisaged constituencies of voting clerics (Guardian Jurist) and the voting public (President).

If the Ackerman methodology were superimposed onto a graph, the horizontal axis would have variables like revolutions and new beginnings. The vertical axis would have a separate set of variable that described 'time'. What do I mean by this? The book relies on a method of following national journeys through 'time'. Each 'time' is spread across zones. Time One is that of the founding, when there is a mobilised insurgency or organised movement that has specific larger goals in mind. For instance, Time One is a 'new beginning' commenced by the removal of colonial and apartheid regimes in India and South Africa. Alternatively, the same 'time' could be that of 'resistance movements' that existed in opposition to the Nazis in France and the fascists in Italy in the Second World War era.

In Time Two, constitutions are debated, contested and finally attempted to be formalised. For instance, in Time Two, stewarded along by the Indian National Congress, which dominated the Constituent Assembly, the country's new Constitution was drafted between 1946 and 1949 and was adopted in 1950. 'Succession crisis' defines Time Three, as founders die during this period. The death of founding Prime Minister Nehru and subsequent contests to success him indicates this time.

The constitutional founding is either consolidated or crushed by successors in Time Four. 'Times One to Four' span events and generations through each of the case studies. In turn, the case studies are also categorised as pairings.

[2] *Id.* at 37.
[3] *Id.* at 360.

For instance, Part 1 of *Revolutionary Constitutions* pairs India and South Africa, with their obvious similarities of the founding 'movement parties', the Indian National Congress and the African National Congress. I particularly appreciate the richness of Ackerman's method, the appreciation of a multiplicity of events, institutions and personalities that the use of time makes possible. It enables a holistic appreciation of power dynamics, founding moments and key personalities. The use of time enables a demarcation of specific conduct after the removal of the old regime by the organised movement: the drafting of the constitution (Time Two), the death of the founders and succession crisis (Time Three) and the consolidation (Time Four) of constitutional values by the successors.

I also really like Ackerman's choice of case studies. His is not a methodology that compares a so-called more established country of the Global North with a newer democracy from the Global South[4] – for instance, a comparison of India with the US. It also does not restrict itself to liberal constitutional democracies. One of the most dazzling chapters is the study of Iran and its semi-presidential system, with fascinating little links between the French-inspired Iranian Constitution of 1979, which draws on the semi-presidential French system, that is replaced by a Guardian Jurist (supreme religious leader) and a popularly elected President, who are competing seats of power, envisaged by the Iranian Constitution.

This leads the conversation to the US–Iran nuclear deal as one instance of conflict between the Guardian Jurist Khamenei and the elected President Rouhani, with the former opposing the deal and the latter supporting it. This is an apt illustration of the how the Iranian Constitution envisages the separation of powers. I particularly relished having the chance to read about Iran in this book, a country whose constitutionalism is rarely discussed. So it is particularly important to have this chapter in Part II of this book, as belonging to the club of semi-presidential countries that included France and Poland, both of which are studied in detail in this book. It is extremely clever to see this rather unusual grouping of France, Poland and Iran as being in conversation with each other.

Ackerman's method is richly intricate, like the weave of a high-quality Persian carpet. Here is an example of what how he compares the cross-generational succession battles of India and South Africa, using the:

> Recall the scenario that followed Nehru's death. Three competitors emerged to claim the top spot. One was his trusted aide (Shastri), who lacked charisma but was skilled in organisational politics. Another was a politically dynamic up-and comer (Desai) who promise to put new energy into the movement party. Finally there was Nehru's daughter (Indira Gandhi), who tried to inherit the charisma her father earned through decades of sacrifice.

[4] Daniel B Maldonado ed., Constitutionalism of the Global South: The Activist Tribunals of India, South Africa and Colombia 1–38 (2013).

> The same choices presented themselves in South Africa. Mandela's Shastri was Thabo Mbeki, who had effectively handled the business of government as deputy president during the preceding five years but was aloof and distant in dealing with the public. His Desai was Cyril Ramaphosa, whose charismatic leadership style provided a strong contrast to the technocratic Mbeki. Finally the South African equivalent to Nehru's daughter was Winnie – who like Indira sought to revitalise the Congress Party's revolutionary commitments to social democracy and economic redistribution.[5]

This method of comparison at once exposes the reader to commonalities between succession battles for the control of the movement parties. I cite the above paragraphs since it gives the reader a sense of the intricate nature of the comparative methodology across two jurisdictions. It does mean that as one progresses through the book, what comes alive are the familiar patterns of succession crisis triggered by charismatic personalities that are sometimes solved by the emergence of charismatic constitutionalist. And that is what sets apart a nation that continues its revolutionary constitutionalism across Times One to Four, as compared to others whose constitutional trajectory is rudely interrupted by collapse.

The magnitude of Ackerman's knowledge of the intricacies of political dynamics such as succession battles of different nations across historical periods is impressive. However, it is also a high-risk methodology, as it presumes a great degree of knowledge of the intricacies of larger political processes, which not all comparatists may possess or agree with. The Ackermanian methodology also opens itself up to competing assessments of how to understand the functioning of a movement party, or how to interpret a succession battle, or even whether a movement qualifies as an organised movement that inspires a regime change and new beginnings. Is the separation of powers really practised in Iran? Or in reality is the Supreme Leader far more powerful than the elected President? Does the removal of a colonial power, but the retaining of the framework of the old in a new constitution, qualify as a new beginning? When does colonisation truly cease? And how much reform qualifies as a new beginning? In the next section of this chapter, I will illustrate my thoughts with a deeper engagement of my own country, India, through Times One to Four.

Finally, what I also would have liked to see Ackerman do is to apply his methodology and gaze to an appreciation of the rise of populism in established and new constitutional democracies. I would imagine that his method lends itself well to an assessment of whether certain conduct by key actors in the earlier Times One, Two and Three leads to or has dodged the advent of populism. The threat that populism poses to democratic constitutionalism is far too enormous not to be dealt with in an ambitious book such as this. And if anyone has the skills to assess the growth populism through multiple jurisdictions, it is Ackerman.

[5] Ackerman, *supra* note 1 at 77–115.

IV. India's Movement Party

A. Is Hegemony Enough?

Revolutionary Constitutions commences with its first two case studies being two success stories from the Global South: India and South Africa. Both have much in common, well-known movement parties and charismatic leaders. Ackerman's comparison of the Indian National Congress (INC) and the African National Congress (ANC) make for fascinating reading. He also points to the differences between the two, owing the nature of the opposition they confronted.

Ackerman correctly captures that while the INC had decades of organising and electoral experience under the British, the ANC did not. Its organisation was brutalised by the apartheid regime. This lack of organisational hierarchy hampered the ANC as it came to power and Mandela provided the legitimacy that was needed. And while Mandela had to contend with the military wing of the ANC, the Spear of the Nation, Nehru's INC had no such armed wings to negotiate with. But, apart from this, it is unclear that being a dominant movement party with a majority in constituent assembly with charismatic leadership is enough to ensure a successful constitution-making project and a constitution that enjoys enduring legitimacy.

For instance, Pakistan, created after the partition of India, had the Muslim League, a movement party that enjoyed an overwhelming majority in the Constituent Assembly (CA). The party had a charismatic leader, Mohammad Ali Jinnah, considered to be the founder of Pakistan. Yet, unlike India, Pakistan did not adopt a new constitution and instead contended with years of military rule and successive military coups throughout Times One to Four. In fact, India and Pakistan at partition had a common military, common Federal Court and even the same interim constitution, the Government of India Act 1935.

The INC, India's movement party, was integral to the drafting and adoption of her Constitution. Ackerman explains part of its success largely as being a 'hegemonic movement party' with little opposition both within the CA and outside, given a post-partition Muslim population of 11 per cent. Hence the INC dominates the assembly proceedings. Yet, this only partially explains the INC's success in drafting and adopting an enduring constitution. While India's constitution was being drafted by its 'hegemonic movement party' Pakistan also commenced its crafting project. Like in India, the post-partition minority population of Hindus and Christians in Pakistan was approximately 11 per cent.

Yet, the Muslim League was not able to draft an enduring constitution and was only able to pass a draft in 1954, seven years after independence. In fact, in the post-partition Pakistan Constituent Assembly, Hindu members from the Pakistan National Congress were steadily leaving the country after being unable to convince their fellow members within the Assembly of a move against the creation of an Islamic Republic to the apparent detriment of religious minorities. Therefore, clearly it is not simply about hegemonic majorities of religious communities or a lack of any meaningful opposition within the CA. The Muslim League, Pakistan's founding party, enjoyed a similar majority within the CA much like the INC, and chose a different path and destination towards a constitutional identity of the nation. What set the INC apart from other movement parties like the Muslim League? What accounts for the successful constitutional foundation of India's movement party as compared to Pakistan? How can we account for varying institutional cultures within movement parties? And what are the consequences of this on Times Two, Three and Four?

Ackerman recognises that the bigger question of why India succeeded and Pakistan failed to generate a 'credible' constitution is a question that merits thought.[6] Yet, since he does not weigh in on the quality or nature of constitutional values, he offers no analysis of their differences in impact. In India, land reform and constitutional amendments to enable 'reservation' for scheduled castes, tribes and other backward classes in public employment, education institutions like colleges and reserved political constituencies enables an expansion of the numbers and kinds of groupings that bought into the constitution. The nature of the INC early support base, which included the landless and the landed, rural and urban, minorities and majorities of different hues, was very important. Contrast this with the Muslim League in Pakistan, which was a party of landlords and elites.

Ackerman poses an important question as to what explains 'India's constitutional order sustaining broad based legitimacy under such uncongenial circumstances'. He explains its success as being intimately connected to the INC, the 'movement party' that successfully 'constitutionalized its high energy politics during the Nehru era'. This constitutionalisation provided a foundation for the Supreme Court to emerge and evolve into its current role of muscular defender of India's constitutional order.

I am in agreement with much of Ackerman's analysis of the INC being the foundational glue within and outside the Indian CA that drafted the constitutional text from 1946 to 1949. The Constitution was adopted on 26 January 1950 and has endured. However, I would like to add a few extra layers to its role in constitution-crafting. Much of this is related to the INC's political strategy of marrying a reformist constitutionalism with popular mobilisation against the British Raj. And this is important, since, unlike Ackerman, I see this as an influence that began even before Time One. This poses a more fundamental question about movement parties: is the commitment to new constitutionalism something that is built from an earlier time during the old regime? My argument is that the India case study shows that it is not only that revolutionary constitutionalism is sustained by a movement party and its successors, but that the movement party should have invested in new constitutionalism as a goal in the pre-Time One period.

[6] *Id.* at 157–66.

B. Creating Legitimacy for a Revolutionary Constitution

In this section, I will discuss the context for the constitution-crafting project that was dominated by the INC. It will also discuss the four features that emerge following the analysis of the role of this movement party. These features are more akin to strategies adopted by the INC. First, a narrative was created by nationalist leaders like Nehru within the CA that enabled an imagination of indigenous ownership of the project. Second, the fact remains that India's constituent body was relatively homogeneous, dominated by the INC, the founding political party of the country. Its founding political party could have bulldozed its values and pushed through a constitution. Yet, it adopted a more refined role.

Third, the constitution-making project was tightly run and reflected the hierarchy and streamlined nature of decision-making within the party. Finally, past organising and resistance to previous colonial constitutions gave the party institutional knowledge of constitutionalism and this was a top priority, since a constituent body crafting a constitution for a free country was an age-old INC demand. While Ackerman elegantly makes the first two points as well, the third and fourth phenomena also require discussion in any chapter on India. These last two points in fact deepen our appreciation of what is a movement party and what its relationship must be to constitution-making and constitutionalism, for the terms of this relationship which are set in the pre-Time One era continue across Times One to Four.

Let us examine the making of India's Constitution in Time Two and how it was shaped by the institutional culture and party hierarchy of the dominant movement party. Granville Austin argues that 'consensus' was the aim of the decision-making processes adopted by India's CA and was the reason for the effectiveness of the body itself.[7] He explains that 'consensus and the decision-making process in general were made possible largely by the atmosphere of unity, idealism and of national purpose that pervaded the Assembly'.

Other scholars disagree with this somewhat simplistic approach.[8] Conversely, Upendra Baxi meticulously shows that the simple consensus-oriented decision-making process that Austin postulates is not accurate. Baxi breaks down the decision-making in the CA into three layers: (1) the decision-making structures; (2) the ways of decision handling; and (3) special situational features.[9] Within each

[7] Granville Austin, The Indian Constitution: Cornerstone of a Nation 311(1999).

[8] See Aditya Nigam, *A Text without Author: Locating the Constituent Assembly as an Event*, 39 Eco. & Pol. Weekly 2107 (2004).

[9] Upendra Baxi, *The Little Done, the Vast Undone: Reflection on Reading Granville Austin's* The Indian Constitution, 9 J. of Ind. Law Inst. 323, 422 (1967) (explaining that in the first layer, the decision-making structure has five sub-categories: (a) the large and fluid 'assembly party' of the INC that includes non-INC members; (b) the 'Canning Lane Group' consisting of certain members of the Assembly who made more or less constant contributions to the formulation of the Constitution; (c) the oligarchy and the experts, from whom most basic decisions emanated, the Oligarchy providing

of these categories, Baxi describes more complex decision-making structures. The first categorisation of decision-making structures had stratifications of influential decision-makers based on their position within the INC and other parties. The second grouping was based on methodologies adopted to arrive at decisions, including more fluid and informal processes like bargaining or politicking, and more formal procedural options like whips and amendments. Finally, the third category was the 'special situation' that was independence, constitution-making and the culmination of the nationalist movement led by charismatic personalities. Baxi's essential point is that Austin's simplification does not reflect the reality of decision-making that involved a variety of factors:

> [N]ear unanimity was the outcome of problem-solving, persuasion, bargaining, politicking as well as numerous constraints arising out of previous ideological commitments, world historical factors and then prevalent situation of imminent disorder, crying out for quick and effective action based on unity on fundamental policies.[10]

Baxi's analysis is also located in the disciplined leadership, organisational strength and conflict resolving mechanisms within the INC. Therefore, while this explanation feeds into Ackerman's assessment of the strength of the movement party, it reflects the foundation that was laid in the pre-Time One era.

C. Contested and Resistance Constitution-Making from the Time One Era

Perhaps what defines the Time One foundation best is the movement method of 'resistance constitution-making'. Here constitution-making by the British colonial Raj was met with resistance, leading to agitation that resulted in reform. This constitutionalism is a multi-layered phenomenon characterised by agitation and reform. The creation of a more familiar rights-oriented counter-majoritarian, elite or coloniser-busting constitution is created in waves that might often take many decades. The moment is replaced by founding processes that span long period of time and many generations of leaders who possess varying ideologies.

'political power and experience in government, and the experts providing the knowledge of the law. (d)The Oligarchy constituting the focus of power; (e) the dyarchy within the oligarchy – the core of the oligarchy, consisting of Nehru and Patel mutually depending on each other. In the second layer of the ways of decision handling are informal ways of handling decisions that covered categories (b)–(e) above and involved 'problem solving, persuasion, bargaining and politicking'. The second subset of this was the formal ways of decision handling that at the Assembly level involved whips, amendments and counter-amendments. Finally, Baxi has a third layer of decision-making called 'Special Situational Features'. This in turn involved five features: first, the constitution-making situation itself; second, a spontaneous sense of national purpose arising from the freedom struggle against the British; third, the unifying power and influence of the oligarchy; fourth, preparatory technical work done by the experts; and, finally, the undeniable charisma of Jawaharlal Nehru.

[10] *Id.* at 423.

Dietmar Rothmund highlights the unique evolution of Indian constitutionalism; that each set of reforms introduced by the British coloniser while being designed to fulfil certain demands leads to inspiring new agitations.[11] Rothmund alludes to an important phenomenon of the production of Indian constitutionalism, through the process of resistance to the colonial edicts, legislation and colonial constitutional enactments.[12] This creation of constitutionalism is multi-layered and complex. It resists neat explanations of the origins of Indian constitutionalism, being simply the adoption of the 1950 Constitution or that the framework for the Indian Constitution is the Government of India Act 1935.

One should go further back in time, to an earlier pre-Time One era, for an accurate appreciation of the origins of contemporary Indian constitutionalism. From 1858 onwards, when Queen Victoria was proclaimed Empress of India, a dynamic was established between 'popular agitation and constitutional reform'.[13] Similarly, Rohit De points out that the method is that one constitutional enactment leads to popular uprisings that leads to a newer enactment, which leads to dialogue that in turn opens up some space for reforms or further agitation.[14]

De gives us an example of this phenomenon. The British passed the Government of India Act 1935, which the INC denounced as a 'slave constitution that attempted to strengthen and perpetuate the political and economic bondage of India'.[15] Soon thereafter, the INC won a cross-section of provincial and central legislative assembly elections and passed resolutions asserting that the 1935 Act did not represent the will of Indians and was designed to oppress them.[16] Hence, the INC demanded a repeal of the Act and its replacement by a constitution for a free India framed by a CA elected by universal adult franchise.[17]

[11] Dietmar Rothmund, *Constitutional reform versus Nationalist Agitation in India: 1900–1950*, 21 J. Asian Studies 505 (1962).

[12] Arvind Elangovan, *The Making of the Indian Constitution: A Case for a Non-nationalist Approach*, 12 Hist. Compass 1, 2 (2014) (arguing that it is necessary to shift attention from viewing the Constitution as a product of consensus underwritten by nationalism to viewing the documents as a product of resolved and unresolved conflicts, including ones that challenge any imposition of nationalism).

[13] Rothmun, *supra* note 11 at 505.

[14] Rohit De, *Constitutional Antecedents, in* The Oxford Handbook on the Indian Constitution 25 (Sujit Choudhry et al. eds., 2016), illustrating this phenomenon with numerous examples such as the Government of India Act 1919, which was taken to be the Constitution of British India. This Act, which introduced elections for a diarchy system of representation, was boycotted by the INC and sparked popular agitation against the other enactments as well. This led in turn to the 1929 Report of the Simon Commission, which was a review of the 1919 Act, and to three Round Table Conferences where a variety of Indian leaders and princely states were invited to discuss constitutional reforms with the British political leadership.

[15] *Id.* at 28, citing Z.A. Ahmed, A Brief Analysis of the New Constitution: Congress Political and Economic Studies No. 3 (1937).

[16] *Id.* at 29.

[17] *Id.*, citing B. Shiva Rao, *Resolution in Provincial Assemblies Regarding the Constituent Assembly, in* 1 Framing of India's Constitution 94 (2015), giving a list of examples to illustrate this creation of constitutionalism as a contested site of struggle – Rammohan Roy, who was not educated in the West, speaking of liberal constitutionalism in the early nineteenth century – and is meant to be product of new Indian elites of Calcutta along with non-official Europeans and mixed blood Euroasians asserting freedoms against arbitrary power. Tanika Sarkar writes of women's rights emerging through

Another instance of this sort of constitutional development is drawn from the Resolution of Fundamental Rights and Economic Changes at the Karachi Session of the Congress in 1931. This Resolution argued that in order to 'end exploitation of the masses, political freedom must include economic freedom'. Along with fundamental rights, it provided for the ending of bonded and child labour, free primary education, expansion of labour welfare, regime protection labour unions, women workers, providing for the redistribution of resources through state control over key industries and national resources, recognising the communal problem and outlining protection of minority rights.[18] Apparently, almost all the rights found in 1931 Resolution found their way into Parts III and IV of the Constitution.[19]

What this analysis shows is that resistance constitutionalism was a political strategy adopted by the INC, the movement party from the colonial era. And this is important, since it was long in the making, and hence came naturally while drafting free India's Constitution. But this has less to do with enjoying a majority in the CA and more to do with the colonial-era technique of engaging British statutes, elections and governance through mobilising for law reform. Such efforts to push for reform came with the persuasive clout of an increasingly popular and well-organised political party. This was a strategy that easily complemented Gandhian techniques of non-violence and non-cooperation.

All scholarly explanations of India's crafting project make it clear that there was a concerted effort to accommodate religious, ethnic and linguistic differences, and amalgamate them into the political mainstream and constitution project that would be India. Such accommodation is critical in the context of a post-partition, post-conflict country in order to ensure that fears of alienation and exclusion were mitigated. But it was the learnt colonial era mobilisation for a reformist constitutionalism that was key in ensuring that the INC had both the commitment and expertise within the party to deploy within the CA and then eventually to create a narrative of a people's ownership and a text's legitimacy.

Ackerman's methodology does not interrogate the nature of the constitutional values that are consolidated from Times One to Four. He makes it clear that he is not dealing with the values of the revolution. Therefore, we are unable assess whether certain kinds of revolutionary constitutional values are more amenable to consolidation as compared to others. For instance, is religious freedom more amenable to consolidation over recognition of only one religion in a multireligious society?

In Ackerman's pairing of India and South Africa, the question of whether a specific constitutional value lends itself better to consolidation is not posed,

'messy encounters' between scriptural law and the Anglo-American legal system, and not through some form of systematic thinking. De also writes of the Congress agitations asking for fundamental rights, or rather rights of procedure, appeal and review granted under the Criminal and Civil Procedure Codes. Elite Indians began to claim rights of citizenship within the Empire rather than against it.

[18] *Id.* at 34.

[19] *Id.*

whereas, given India's poverty, illiteracy, conflict, inequality and divisions caused apparently by religion and caste, the question of why democratic constitutionalism and its sole Constitution of 1950 has endured is often posed. Was it just the quality of the movement party? Instead, it is constitutional values from Time One that were consolidated across Times Two, Three and Four. This ensured that the revolutionary Constitution persisted.

I would argue that what distinguishes India's revolutionary Constitution and has enabled it to be consolidated in Time Four is that it has lent itself well to expanding the constituencies that believed in it for their own different interests and reasons. Making reparations is a quintessential Indian revolutionary constitutional value. It is unique to India, for the Constitution and the movement that preceded it made it clear that reparation in the form of reservations of political constituencies, public employment and education would be set aside for scheduled castes and scheduled tribes. This expanded the constituencies that believed in the Constitution and that were became deeply invested in its success and consolidation.

Reparations create new constituencies that invest their faith in the constitution, since they see their interests being reflected for the first time ever in policy-making. This reparative constitutionalism is unique to India and it is not a path that was followed by South Africa or other countries that began Time One or Two with a history of deep discrimination.

Through its provisions of equality before the law,[20] prohibition of discrimination on grounds of caste[21] and the abolition of untouchability, the Constitution of India clearly outlaws the practice of caste.[22] Through constitutional amendments, such methods of challenging social morality also include provisions for reparations for the discrimination and disadvantage that 'other backward castes' (lower castes), 'scheduled castes' (Dalits or untouchables) and 'scheduled tribes' (Adivasis or indigenous people) have suffered due to the historical practices of caste-based traditions.

Such reparations, constitutionally termed 'special provisions',[23] often take the form of reservations of seats in public employment and educational institutions.[24] Such a constitutional understanding stems from an appreciation that caste-based discrimination has been practised for centuries in India.[25] This despite their being

[20] India Const., art. 14.
[21] *Id.* at art. 15, §1.
[22] *Id.* at art. 17.
[23] *Id.* at art. 15, §5.
[24] *Id.* at art. 15, §4.
[25] India's caste system is a system of social stratification, estimated to be over 3,000 years old, practised predominantly within Hinduism. It divides caste Hindus into four main subgroups of Brahmins, Kshatriyas, Vaishyas and Shudras. A fifth caste – that of untouchables or Dalits – were considered to be below these four castes and were to clean the waste of the four groupings above. One is born into a caste and this controlled the occupations, life opportunities and access to resources that each person had. The Constitution of India 1950 strictly prohibits untouchability (art 17), which is also a caste practice, and recognises that historical discrimination suffered by lower castes must be redressed through reparations like reservation in public employment, education and political constituencies.

societal support for the practice of caste for it is a core part of Hinduism, which is the religion practised by a majority of Indians.[26] So the Constitution clearly establishes its morality as distinct from that of societal and majoritarian morality. Therefore, India may have a social morality that accepts and perpetuates the practice of caste, but it also has a constitutional mandate that demands the court move against such social norms.

This has enabled members of the scheduled castes and scheduled tribes to gain political power, be represented and access educational and employment opportunities all by means of the constitution-making provisions for such entitlements. It has also enabled the Supreme Court to get on with the job of becoming deeply investing in regulating this reparations project. The Supreme Court decides the upper limit of reservations (whether it can exceed 50 per cent of seats in education in a state) or whether reservations include promotion in government employment. Therefore, perhaps a question that remains for volumes 2 and 3 of *Revolutionary Constitutions* is are there certain constitutional values that better enable consolidation? What also sets India apart from other countries is the evolution of what was a colonial-era Federal Court that practised judicial restraint on many issues of executive action in Time One into the politically charged Supreme Court that in Times Three and Four has steadily expanded its power. This court has played a dramatically important and constitutionally non-envisaged role in consolidating the revolutionary Constitution in Time Four.

V. The Movement Court and the Consolidation of Constitutionalism

The Supreme Court of India has played an extraordinary role in the endurance of constitutionalism in the country. However, while doing so, it has also created constitutional challenges for the executive and the legislature in relation to the manner in which it has expanded its own powers and has waded into political and policy questions. The institutional design of the Supreme Court has contributed enormously to the confidence with which the judges perform this avidly politicised role.

Much has been written about the rise of the Supreme Court as a bid to salvage the beating its reputation took in the aftermath of its conduct during the Emergency. There have also been more contemporary-era critiques of the court. Yet there has been an ever-spreading process of constitutionalism in India. This has also been a result of the institutional design of the Court along with its use of specific jurisprudential techniques to accumulate an enormous amount of power.

The Supreme Court has used a series of jurisprudential techniques to expand its power. It has created the unamendable 'basic structure' of the Constitution and

[26] Trina Vithayathil and Gayatri Singh, *Spaces of Discrimination*, 47 Eco. & Pol. Weekly 60 (2012).

has used its ability to carry out 'complete justice' and act under writ jurisdiction in order to tremendously expand its power. Through a series of cases, the court created the 'collegium' (of the Chief Justice and four senior most judges) system to appoint judges. This process has been critical in insulating the Supreme Court from every other branch of the state and from any external oversight.[27]

Therefore, it was entirely unsurprising that recently, the Supreme Court struck down the Modi government's National Judicial Appointments Commission (NJAC), which had been created by a constitutional amendment that passed with bipartisan political support. The NJAC envisaged an appointment process where the government, the political opposition and the judges would all have a say in judicial appointments.

Ackerman describes this as a moment 'between Hindu nationalists in the government and enlightenment secularists on the Court'.[28] I disagree with this characterisation, for it presumes that only the ruling Modi government wanted to change the system of judicial appointments. This is clearly not true; the NJAC constitutional amendment is one of the few legislative initiatives that had bipartisan support across the political spectrum. Furthermore, like any institution, the Court and the judges who comprise it consist of an assortment of individuals, many with secular values and others who believed in Hindutva.

The battle between the executive and the Supreme Court has been one long in the making, but it is not as simple as one between Hindu nationalists in government and enlightenment secularists on the court. This tussle is part of a long-running larger process and is a result of both institutional design of the Court and the jurisprudence of supervision of the executive and the legislature that it has created. And this supervision commences with the creation of norms for parliament to function in the absence of parliamentary practice, unlike the British Westminster model. Let us examine both of these points briefly.

A. The Institutional Design of the Supreme Court

Tom Ginsburg has written that the character of judicial review in new democracies is shaped by the institutional design of the court and citizens' access to it, and that the court's decisions relating to jurisdiction and standing play a major role in the articulation of its political role.[29] By enabling free-flowing access, by hearing the widest possible range of cases and by virtually doing away with the requirements of standing, the Indian Supreme Court has ensured for itself a deeply political and structurally crucial role in this relatively constitutional democracy.

[27] S.P. Gupta v. Union of India, 1981 Supp S.C.C. 87 (India); Advocates-on-Record Association v. Union of India, (1993) 4 S.C.C. 441 (India); In Re Presidential Reference, A.I.R. 1999 S.C. 1 (India). The Court used its judgments in these three cases to systematically expand its own power at the expense of the executive in terms of appointing judges to the Supreme and High Courts.

[28] Ackerman, *supra* note 1 at 75.

[29] Tom Ginsburg, Judicial Review in New Democracies 34 (2009).

The institutional design of the Supreme Court is such that it functions as panels of judges. It does not sit en banc. On any given day, the Court, with a sanctioned strength of 30 judges, has up to 13 court rooms in operation, hearing and disposing of an astonishing number of cases.[30] For instance, in the three-month period from 1 January to 31 March 2017, it heard 20,666 new cases. In the same three-month period, it disposed (decided or adjudicated to completion) of 21,892 cases. If you examine the numbers, it is clear that each of the justices disposed of 781.86 cases in this three-month period. Appendix A below makes clear the scale of the enterprise that is the Supreme Court, mapping the number of cases heard and disposed by the Supreme Court from 2014 to 2017.

Let us locate the number of cases which the Supreme Court hears in a comparative perspective. The American Supreme Court typically hears about 75–80 cases in any one year.[31] The South African Constitutional Court decided about 30 cases between 1 April 2010 and 31 March 2011, and 115 new cases were filed during this period.[32] Meanwhile, the House of Lords hears around 80–90 appeals a year.[33]

What are the consequences of the startling number of cases that the Supreme Court of India hears? These cases cover an extraordinary range of causes of action, including property, family, criminal, constitutional and administrative, and intellectual property. Every known area of law is litigated before the apex court. They would include fresh cases instituted or those that were on appeal, since the Supreme Court has both original and appellate jurisdictions. In 70 per cent of cases, the government is a litigant.

Therefore, each judge and the Supreme Court as a collective institution feels very familiar and capable of understanding and holding the state – whether the legislature or the executive – to account. The judges feel they have the expertise to check these other institutions. And this large number of cases, across every conceivable area of law, goes a long way towards creating an institutional culture

[30] NUMBER OF CASES DISPOSED OF PER JUDGE FROM 1 JANUARY 2017 TO 31 MARCH 2017: 781.86. *Institution, Disposal and Pendency of Cases in the Supreme Court*, 12 Court News 1 (Supreme Court of India, New Delhi), Apr. 2017, at 6, https://www.sci.gov.in/pdf/CourtNews/COURT_NEWS_Vol_XII_No_1_JANUARY_TO_MARCH_2017.pdf; NUMBER OF CASES DISPOSED OF PER JUDGE FROM 1 JANUARY 2014 TO 30 JUNE 2014 (6 MONTHS): 1,632.4. *Institution, Disposal and Pendency of Cases in the Supreme Court*, 9 Court News 2 (Supreme Court of India, New Delhi), Jul. 2014, at 6, https://www.sci.gov.in/pdf/CourtNews/2014_issue_2.pdf; NUMBER OF CASES DISPOSED OF PER JUDGE FROM 1 JULY 2014 TO 30 JUNE 2015 (1 YEAR): 3,137.36. *Institution, Disposal and Pendency of Cases in the Supreme Court*, 9 Court News 3 (Supreme Court of India, New Delhi), Jul. 2015, at 16, https://www.sci.gov.in/pdf/CourtNews/2014_issue_3_July,%202014 June,%202015.pdf; NUMBER OF CASES DISPOSED OF PER JUDGE FROM 1 JULY 2015 TO 30 JUNE 2016 (1 YEAR): 2,920.55; NUMBER OF CASES DISPOSED OF PER JUDGE FROM 1 JULY 2016 TO 31 MARCH 2017 (9 MONTHS): 2,423.7.

[31] Supreme Court of the United States, Frequently Asked Questions, www.supremecourt.gov/faq.aspx.

[32] Constitutional Court of South Africa, Annual Performance Report: 2010/2011, www.constitutionalcourt.org.za/site/Admin/constitutional-court-annual-report-2010-11.

[33] The House of Lords, House of Lords Briefing: Judicial Work, www.parliament.uk/documents/lords-information-office/hoflbpjudicial.pdf.

of consistently monitoring the executive and the legislature. While the virtually unimpeded access to the Supreme Court and the large number of litigants and wide array of cases contribute to each of the 30 judges feeling capable to adjudicate on any issue, it is not the only reason to explain this establishment of what I refer to as a 'movement court'; it is also the specific kind of role that was thrust upon the Court shortly after the Constitution was adopted. For instance, in the first decade of the Constitution's existence, the Court was asked to shape the contours of the powers of Parliament. How so? It has to do so in the absence of parliamentary precedent or convention with regard to its powers. The Indian Parliament, unlike that of the UK, from which it drew its inspiration, has no parliamentary conventions that were established to shape the contours of its powers and practices.

Therefore, fairly early in the life of the new republic in 1951, Justice Kania distinguished the British and Indian Parliaments:

> [T]he principal point of distinction between the British Parliament and the Indian Parliament remains and that the Indian Parliament is the creature of the Constitution of India and its powers, rights, privileges and obligations have to be found in the relevant articles of the Constitution of India. It is not a sovereign body, uncontrolled with unlimited powers. The Constitution of India has conferred on the Indian Parliament powers to make laws in respect of matters specified in the appropriate places and Schedules, and curtailed its rights and powers under certain other articles and in particular by the articles found in Chapter III dealing with fundamental rights.[34]

This would be the first step with which the Supreme Court commenced its role of limiting and interpreting parliamentary powers and shaping parliamentary practice. But this would not be restricted to merely subjecting Parliament to the Constitution.

A decade later, the Court would wade into a conflict between the state legislature of Uttar Pradesh (India's biggest state) and the High Court of the State.[35] The Speaker of the state legislature had sentenced a member to a term of imprisonment for breaching privilege. The High Court directed the member's release. The Supreme Court was approached for advice and was asked to resolve the situation. While ruling in favour of the High Court, the Supreme Court concluded that the supremacy of the Constitution is protected by the authority of an independent judicial body to act as the interpreter of a scheme of distribution of powers.[36] Hence, the Supreme Court made it clear that even in relation to processes within the legislature, including that of conflict between the High Court of a state and the state legislature, it would interpret the extent of power and functions of each. These early cases are but two examples of the multiple occasions on which the Supreme Court was called upon to decide the extent of powers of elected representative bodies.

[34] In Re Delhi Laws Act 1912, (1951) S.C.R. 747 (India).
[35] UP Assembly Case (Special Reference No. 1 of 1964), A.I.R. 1965 SC. 745 (India).
[36] *Id.*

B. Jurisprudential Techniques to Become a Movement Court

The Supreme Court uses its powers of writ jurisdiction[37] and power to carry out 'complete justice' to wade deep into supervising and even curtailing the powers of the executive. What are writ petitions? Article 32 of the Constitution, which provides the Court with the power to issue writs, was to enable the protection and the enforcement of fundamental rights by the Court.[38] However, in its contemporary use, this provision enables easy access to the Court and allows it to engage with a variety of political, legal and policy questions. For instance, the Court gives detailed instructions on waste management,[39] initiates *suo motu* proceedings on police crackdowns on demonstrators sleeping in a public space,[40] and even orders quick trials for those who have been languishing in prison for years.[41]

The Supreme Court also used Article 142 of the Constitution, which empowers it to carry out 'complete justice' to expand its powers.[42] It has found that the power to carry out complete justice includes the authority to quash criminal charges and direct the framing of new ones,[43] to reduce a sentence to below the statutory minimum,[44] to reduce the interest rate provided for in an award,[45] to direct investigation by the Central Bureau of Investigation against the police of a state[46] and to direct the state to provide for compensation in a case of custodial violence leading to death.[47]

It is clear that between the massive numbers of cases heard and its steady foray deep into executive areas of functioning like governance, development and even the monitoring of criminal trials, the Supreme Court has made it a point to become the regulator and supervisor of executive power and functions. And it is this enthusiastic embrace of this role of a supervisor has further enabled it to become the movement court.

In conclusion, Ackerman's methodology enables the telling of the successes and failures of revolutionary constitutions by providing a complex picture of the political, historical and legal journey that a nation takes. His method is invaluable because it enables a multi-dimensional appreciation of why some revolutionary constitutions succeed while others fail. When it comes to India, the revolutionary constitutionalism of its movement party has been sustained by a power-desirous, movement-oriented Supreme Court, whose institutional design and ambition have enabled it to play this role.

[37] India Const. art. 14; Lok Sabha Secretariat, Official Report of the Constituent Assembly Debates: 9 December 1948 953 (5th reprint, 2014).
[38] A.K. Gopalan v. State of Madras, A.I.R. 1950 S.C. 27 (India).
[39] Almira H Patel v. Union of India, (2000) 2 S.C.C. 166 (India).
[40] In Re Ramlila Maidan Incident, (2012) 5 S.C.C. 125 (India).
[41] Kadra Pahadiya and Others v. State of Bihar, (1983) 2 S.C.C. 104 (India).
[42] India Const. art. 142.
[43] Keshub Mahindra v. State of Madhya Pradesh, (1996) 6 S.C.C. 129 (India).
[44] Datla Krishnam Raju v. Excise Inspector, 2000 (10) S.C.C. 370 (India).
[45] Marshall Sons & Co. Ltd. v. Sahi Oretrans (P) Ltd., (1999) 2 S.C.C. 325 (India).
[46] Pure Helium India Pvt Ltd v. Oil & Natural Gas Commission, (2003) 8 S.C.C. 593 (India).
[47] C. Chenga Reddy v. State of Andhra Pradesh, (1996) 10 S.C.C. 193 (India).

Appendix A: Movement Party to Movement Court

30 judges in the Supreme Court on 31 March 2014[48]

Institution, disposal and pendency of cases in the Supreme Court from 1 January 2014 to 31 March 2014[49]								
Institution			**Disposal**			**Pendency**		
Admission matters	**Regular matters**	**Total matters**	**Admission matters**	**Regular matters**	**Total matters**	**Admission matters**	**Regular matters**	**Total matters**
19,210	2,843	22,053	20,818	3,254	24,072	34,144	30,186	64,330

Number of cases disposed of per judge from 1 January 2014 to 31 March 2014: 802.4

25 judges in the Supreme Court of India on 30 June 2014[50]

Institution, disposal and pendency of cases in the Supreme Court from 1 April 2014 to 30 June 2014[51]								
Institution			**Disposal**			**Pendency**		
Admission matters	**Regular matters**	**Total matters**	**Admission matters**	**Regular matters**	**Total matters**	**Admission matters**	**Regular matters**	**Total matters**
20,201	2,258	22,459	17,845	2,974	20,819	36,500	29,470	65,970

Number of cases disposed of per judge from 1 April 2014 to 30 June 2014: 832.76

28 judges in the Supreme Court on 30 June 2015[52]

Institution, disposal and pendency of cases in the Supreme Court from 1 July 2014 to 30 June 2015[53]								
Institution			**Disposal**			**Pendency**		
Admission matters	**Regular matters**	**Total matters**	**Admission matters**	**Regular matters**	**Total matters**	**Admission matters**	**Regular matters**	**Total matters**
70,628	13,529	84,157	71,849	15,997	87,846	35,279	27,002	62,281

Number of cases disposed of per judge from 1 July 2014 to 30 June 2015: 3137.36

[48] Court News, Supreme Court of India, Vol. IX, Issue No. 1, p. 5, https://www.sci.gov.in/pdf/CourtNews/2014_issue_1.pdf.

[49] *Id.* at 7.

[50] Court News, Supreme Court of India, Vol. IX, Issue No. 2, p. 4, https://www.sci.gov.in/pdf/CourtNews/2014_issue_2.pdf.

[51] *Id.* at 6.

[52] Court News, Supreme Court of India, Vol. IX, Issue Nos. 3 & 4 and Vol. X, Issue Nos. 1 & 2, p. 9, https://www.sci.gov.in/pdf/CourtNews/2014_issue_3_July,%202014-June,%202015.pdf.

[53] *Id.* at 16.

28 judges in the Supreme Court on 30 September 2015[54]

Institution, disposal and pendency of cases in the Supreme Court from 1 July 2015 to 30 September 2015[55]								
Institution			**Disposal**			**Pendency**		
Admission matters	**Regular matters**	**Total matters**	**Admission matters**	**Regular matters**	**Total matters**	**Admission matters**	**Regular matters**	**Total matters**
20,573	2,742	23,315	22,346	3,340	25,686	33,506	26,404	59,910

Number of cases disposed of per judge from 1 July 2015 to 30 September 2015: 917.36

26 judges in the Supreme Court on 1 January 2016[56]

Institution, disposal and pendency of cases in the Supreme Court from 1 October 2015 to 31 December 2015[57]								
Institution			**Disposal**			**Pendency**		
Admission matters	**Regular matters**	**Total matters**	**Admission matters**	**Regular matters**	**Total matters**	**Admission matters**	**Regular matters**	**Total matters**
16,821	2,470	19,291	17,064	2,865	19,929	33,263	26,009	59,272

Number of cases disposed of per judge from 1 October 2015 to 31 December 2015: 766.5

25 judges in the Supreme Court on 31 March 2016[58]

Institution, disposal and pendency of cases in the Supreme Court from 1 January 2016 to 31 March 2016[59]								
Institution			**Disposal**			**Pendency**		
Admission matters	**Regular matters**	**Total matters**	**Admission matters**	**Regular matters**	**Total matters**	**Admission matters**	**Regular matters**	**Total matters**
17,903	2,333	20,236	17,790	2,123	19,913	33,376	26,219	59,595

Number of cases disposed of per judge from 1 January 2016 to 31 March 2016: 796.52

[54] Court News, Supreme Court of India, Vol. X, Issue No. 3, p. 2, https://www.sci.gov.in/pdf/CourtNews/July,%202015-sept-2015.pdf.

[55] *Id.* at 4.

[56] Court News, Supreme Court of India, Vol. X, Issue No. 4, p. 3, https://www.sci.gov.in/pdf/CourtNews/Supreme%20Court%20News%20Oct-Dec%202016.pdf.

[57] *Id.* at 7.

[58] Court News, Supreme Court of India, Vol. XI, Issue No. 1, p. 5, https://www.sci.gov.in/pdf/CourtNews/2016_issue_1.pdf.

[59] *Id.* at 7.

29 judges in the Supreme Court on 30 June 2016[60]

Institution, disposal and pendency of cases in the Supreme Court from 1 April 2016 to 30 June 2016[61]								
Institution			**Disposal**			**Pendency**		
Admission matters	**Regular matters**	**Total matters**	**Admission matters**	**Regular matters**	**Total matters**	**Admission matters**	**Regular matters**	**Total matters**
15,080	1,298	16,378	12,194	1,133	13,327	36,262	26,384	62,646

Number of cases disposed of per judge from 1 April 2016 to 30 June 2016: 459.55

28 judges in the Supreme Court on 30 September 2016[62]

Institution, disposal and pendency of cases in the Supreme Court from 1 July 2016 to 30 September 2016[63]								
Institution			**Disposal**			**Pendency**		
Admission matters	**Regular matters**	**Total matters**	**Admission matters**	**Regular matters**	**Total matters**	**Admission matters**	**Regular matters**	**Total matters**
20,270	2,502	22,772	22,536	1,944	24,480	33,996	26,942	60,938

Number of cases disposed of per judge from 1 July 2016 to 30 September 2016: 874.28

24 judges in the Supreme Court on 31 December 2016[64]

Institution, disposal and pendency of cases in the Supreme Court from 1 October 2016 to 31 December 2016[65]								
Institution			**Disposal**			**Pendency**		
Admission matters	**Regular matters**	**Total matters**	**Admission matters**	**Regular matters**	**Total matters**	**Admission matters**	**Regular matters**	**Total matters**
18,208	1,651	19,859	16,099	2,161	18,260	36,105	26,432	62,537

Number of cases disposed of per judge from 1 October 2016 to 31 December 2016: 760.83

[60] Court News, Supreme Court of India, Vol. XI, Issue No. 2, p. 6, https://www.sci.gov.in/pdf/CourtNews/2016_issue_2.pdf.

[61] *Id.* at 8.

[62] Court News, Supreme Court of India, Vol. XI, Issue No. 3, p. 5, https://www.sci.gov.in/pdf/CourtNews/2016_issue_3.pdf.

[63] *Id.* at7.

[64] Court News, Supreme Court of India, Vol. XI, Issue No. 4, p. 6, https://www.sci.gov.in/pdf/CourtNews/COURT_NEWS_Vol_XI_Issue_No4_October_to_December_2016.pdf.

[65] *Id.* at 8.

28 judges in the Supreme Court on 31 March 2017[66]

Institution, disposal and pendency of cases in the Supreme Court from 1 January 2017 to 31 March 2017[67]								
Institution			**Disposal**			**Pendency**		
Admission matters	**Regular matters**	**Total matters**	**Admission matters**	**Regular matters**	**Total matters**	**Admission matters**	**Regular matters**	**Total matters**
17,744	2,955	20,699	19,542	2,350	21,892	34,307	27,037	61,344

Number of cases disposed of per judge from 1 January 2017 to 31 March 2017: 781.86

1. Number of cases disposed of per judge from 1 January 2014 to 30 June 2014 (6 months): 1,632.4
2. Number of cases disposed of per judge from 1 July 2014 to 30 June 2015 (1 year): 3,137.36
3. Number of cases disposed of per judge from 1 July 2015 to 30 June 2016 (1 year): 2,920.55
4. Number of cases disposed of per judge from 1 July 2016 to 31 March 2017 (9 months): 2,423.7

[66] Court News, Supreme Court of India, Vol. XII, Issue No. 1, p. 4, https://www.sci.gov.in/pdf/CourtNews/COURT_NEWS_Vol_XII_No_1_JANUARY_TO_MARCH_2017.pdf.

[67] *Id.* at 6.

16

The Italian Constitution as a Revolutionary Agreement

MARTA CARTABIA*

[P]er compensare le forze di sinistra di una rivoluzione *mancata*, le forze di destra non si opposero ad accogliere nella Costituzione una rivoluzione *promessa*.[1]

I. Introduction

Italy is one of the paradigmatic examples of Bruce Ackerman's *Revolutionary Constitutions*, the first ideal type of the three different pathways by which constitutions have won legitimacy in the past century. It is considered one of the success stories, which – along with France, India, South Africa, Poland, Israel and Iran – went through the 'four-time' development and was able to overcome times of crisis, establishing a fairly solid constitutional regime that has endured to the present day.

Following Ackerman's account, in the Italian case, Time One – where, according to his theory, 'revolutionary movements' 'mobilize the masses' and 'manage to oust establishment-insiders', denouncing the existing regime as 'illegitimate'[2] – was marked by the guerrilla fighters of the Resistance movement, who managed to create grassroots revolutionary governments in key areas of the north of Italy and finally succeeded in seizing and killing Mussolini during the closing days of the war.

* I would like to thank Dr Alessandro Baro for his thorough editing, his integration of footnotes and cited references, and his insightful observations on style and content; his help allowed me to enlighten and expand on my idea. Many thanks to Sabino Cassese, who introduced me to Bruce and was the first to read the draft of this chapter in its early stages; his remarks and observations gave further depth to my reflections. Moreover, I benefited of the conversation at the Yale Law School with all the participants to the Conference on 'Revolutionary Constitutionalism' held on August 24–25, 2018. I take full responsibility for the contents presented here.

[1] 'To give compensation to the left parties for a *missed* revolution, the right parties did not resist to admit in the Constitution a *promised* revolution.' Piero Calamandrei, La Costituzione e le leggi per attuarla 7–8 (2000 [1955]).

[2] Bruce Ackerman, Revolutionary Constitutions: Charismatic Leadership and the Rule of Law 6–7 (2019).

In Time Two – the time for the construction of a new regime based on the translation of 'high-energy politics into a Constitution that seeks to prevent a relapse into the abuses of the past, and commits the republic to the new principles proclaimed during the long hard struggle of Time one', ie, 'the constitutionalization of the revolutionary charisma'[3] – the polls of 2 June 1946 are given an important place in Italian history. A majority of the Italian people[4] chose the Republic and rejected the monarchy, and also elected the Constituent Assembly, which was vested with the power to draft a new republican constitution.

Time Three – a time of crisis, which takes place when the founding generation dies off, the political authority moves towards the 'normalization of revolutionary politics' and the regime confronts a 'legitimacy vacuum', which is occupied by an increasingly confident judiciary[5] – is identified in Italian history with the end of the first legislature (1948–53), when De Gasperi's leadership of the Christian Democrats was 'defeated'[6] and he fell from power and was stripped of his formal position as the head of the Christian Democratic Party. He died a few months later. At this time, the new Constitutional Court was established and began operating taking a vigorous stance among the other republican institutions.[7]

Time Four is the time of consolidation[8] of the new constitutional regime, thanks, if I am not mistaken, to the undisputed authority of the judicial bodies.

All things considered, Italy roughly fits in the ideal type of revolutionary constitutionalism. However, in Italy the role and the nature of the Italian 'revolution' in the transition from fascism to the Republic has some peculiarities that deserve attention in order to understand revolutionary constitutionalism as such.

In reality, the protagonists of the birth of the Republic hesitated to qualify the transition from the fascist state to the Republic as a revolution. The revolutionary approach was debated and rejected by the main political forces involved and, in the Constitution itself, a revolution was announced more than codified. As Ackerman acknowledges, the Italian experience can be described by the famous words of one of the most popular protagonists of the epoch, Piero Calamandrei: 'to compensate the forces of the left for a circumvented revolution, the forces of the right showed no opposition to a promised revolution in the Constitution'.[9] In the Italian case, the Constitution, rather than translating the chief tenets of a political revolution into higher legal principles, provides a legal framework that leaves room for a revolution yet to come. The question of whether this promise was later maintained is another matter.

In other words, Italy is a successful example of path one, precisely because (and not despite the fact that) the revolutionary side had only a limited role,

[3] *Id.* at 4.
[4] *Id.* at 141.
[5] *Id.* at 8–9.
[6] *Id.* at 150–52.
[7] *Id.* at 152.
[8] *Id.* at 155–56.
[9] *Id.* at 143.

extending only to Time One, in the transition from fascism to the Republic. As for its relationship with the past, the Italian Constitution is undeniably a 'never again' constitution: one that rejects the previous regime. Nevertheless, as to the future of the polity, the features of the new Republic were, in a way, 'undecided'. It is true that there is a revolutionary side in the Italian transition, which marks a clean break with the fascist regime. The Constitution is imbued with anti-fascist principles. Yet, the construction of the new polity was successful because of its inclusive, dialogical and incremental approach to constitutional change.

This character had some consequences for the 'consolidation' of the new regime. First, the implementation of the new constitutional architecture was neither immediate nor swift, and even less complete. Moreover, the delayed implementation included some institutions that were intended to play a crucial role in the constitutional system. The first of these was the Constitutional Court. Second, the new constitutional order, in the 1970s and 1980s, very soon went through recurrent periods of crisis, and broad calls for constitutional reform began when the process of implementation of the Republican Constitution was not yet complete.

I would like to revisit here some of the historical steps of the founding period that show the importance of the capacity to bridge divergent forces and design converging avenues in Time Two as elements of the success of Italian constitutional revolutionary history. More generally, I ask whether this capacity for 'building bridges' is a necessary component of 'Time Two' in all constitutional experiences at the time of the construction of a new polity after the dismantling of a previous regime.

Stephen Gardbaum's chapter[10] points out that among the Arab Spring revolutions, the Tunisian example is the only one that was successful. Its success can hardly be credited to a single charismatic personality or a single revolutionary party. The productive contribution of the Tunisian National Dialogue Quartet to the building of a pluralistic democracy in the wake of the Jasmine Revolution of 2011 was in no way a secondary element. The Quartet was established in the summer of 2013 when the democratisation process was in danger of collapsing as a result of political assassinations and widespread social unrest. Then in 2015, it was awarded the Nobel Prize for Peace. It should be noted that the prize was a tribute to the Quartet as such, not to the four individual organisations, representing different sectors and values in Tunisian society, that contributed to completing the constitutional process.

Another success story is South Africa, where much credit was given to the charismatic personality of Nelson Mandela and to his party. However, his personal charisma was not imposed *ex cathedra* on the people. His leadership was able to connect opposed factions, so much so that nobody doubts that the most relevant role was played by the Truth and Reconciliation Commission in the successful constitutional transition of South Africa.

[10] See Gardbaum, ch. 8 in this volume.

In these examples, and certainly in the Italian case, the building of the new order was not the 'codification' of a single 'charisma'; rather, it was the result of difficult agreements, an inclusive pact which opened a new process, an open-ended and incremental enterprise.

I consider it very important to learn this kind of lesson from history, particularly for the present stage of constitutionalism around the world. To me and to many Europeans, 'revolution has a destructive logic' (as Andrew Arato pointed out),[11] after the French and Russian prototypes. European experience shows that a revolutionary action is unable, as such, to have a generative effect. Conflict brings about more conflict. As to the origins of the Italian Republic, the context cannot be overlooked: after two World Wars and 20 years of fascism, the priority for the Italian leaders was the reconstruction and re-unification of a devastated country.

II. Revolution and Constitution: A Multi-faceted Relationship

The Italian Republican Constitution was indeed a *new beginning* in the history of the country, and the state was reconstructed on new founding principles. Remarkable differences distinguish the Republic from the fascist and the prior liberal state.

At the same time, the debate on the continuity and discontinuity of the state since its origins in 1871 is still open and has never been settled, with some legal and political historians maintaining that the evolution from the liberal to the fascist to the republican phases took place without any clear-cut interruption,[12] and others heralding the new republican era as a veritable new world.[13]

In reality, the great majority of scholars maintain the first thesis. One of the most representative supporters of this position was Piero Calamandrei, who had originally championed the need for a revolutionary reaction against the fascist regime and, after the approval of the Constitution, wrote:

> It was a *popular* constitution, approved when any hindrance from the former king had been barred by the institutional June 2, 1946 referendum … But *it wasn't a revolutionary constitution* in the sense of consecrating, in juridical forms, a *politically accomplished revolution*.[14]

[11] See Arato, ch. 6 in this volume.

[12] See, eg, at least Guido Quazza, La Resistenza italiana: appunti e documenti (1976); Claudio Pavone, Alle origini della Repubblica. Scritti su fascismo, antifascismo e continuità dello Stato (1995); Sabino Cassese, Lo stato fascista (2010).

[13] See Valerio Onida, *La transizione costituzionale*, 2 Diritto pubblico 571 (1996).

[14] My translation from Calamandrei, *supra* note 1 at 5: '[F]u una costituzione *popolare*, deliberata, quando ormai ogni ingerenza dell'ex sovrano era stata esclusa dal referendum istituzionale del 2 giugno 1946 … Ma *non fu una costituzione rivoluzionaria*, nel senso che consacrasse in forme giuridiche una rivoluzione politicamente *già compiuta*.'

For those who expected a 'total makeover' or, at least, a radical renovation, the new Constitution was disappointing.

I would like to continue this discussion by dividing my reasoning into two threads: first, I will move on to the *legal* plane (section II.A) and show some elements of continuity and discontinuity between the fascist regime and the Italian democratic Republic; then, I will conduct a similar analysis on the *political* plane (section II.B).

A. Continuity and Discontinuity in the New Legal Order

If a revolution is meant to reset a legal order from scratch, Italy can be hardly considered a good example of path one. Yet, since Ackerman's revolution 'on a human scale' does not aim at a totalising break with the past, and includes old and new elements, the conclusion is more nuanced.

i. Departures from the Past in the Basic Legal Structure of the State

Indeed, the Republican Constitution has introduced a relevant number of *legal innovations*, and almost all of them were responses to the legal tenets of fascism.

First and foremost, according to the results of the institutional referendum, the Constitution established a *republican* regime and rejected the *monarchy*, which had been tainted by fascism.

Moreover, the Constitution set in motion a paradigm shift in the legal order, because of its *normative* and *rigid character* as opposed to the *political* and *flexible* attributes of the Statuto Albertino.[15] This was a major and essential innovation that the Italian Republican Constitution shares with other twentieth-century European constitutions, following the US model. This move was a true breaking point; in fact, the normative supremacy of the Constitution washed away the traditional idea of the sovereignty of parliamentary legislation and framed a new balance between Parliament and the judiciary.

The superior value of the Constitution paved the way for judicial review of legislation to be carried out by a new special body, the Constitutional Court. Over time, this new institution would renovate the constitutional mindset that had informed the legal culture prior to the dawn of the Republic.

Under these and many other respects, the new constitutional principles contrasted with the main features of the fascist state and went far beyond the basic ideas of the liberal state, which had left too much leeway to the manoeuvres of the fascist regime.[16] Let us mention just a few of them.

[15] The Statuto Albertino (Albertine Statute) was the predecessor of the current Italian Constitution; it was released by King Carlo Alberto in 1848.

[16] Cassese, *supra* note 12 at 47 ff.

The protection of fundamental rights increased sharply. Whereas the liberal ideas of individual rights were influenced by the theory of the *Reflexrechte* (elaborated by Gerber in Germany and imported to Italy by Rocco),[17] under the Republican Constitution human rights are the first limit on the power of the state. To highlight this point, Article 2 of the Constitution states that the inviolable rights of each person are *recognised*, and not conferred, by the Republic, thus implying that they belong to each person and not to the state. Therefore, they are *inviolable*: nobody can be stripped of his or her rights, the state has no power to repeal them and even constitutional amendments that infringe upon the core of those individual rights are considered unconstitutional (eternity clauses).

Special attention was given to freedom of speech (Article 21), which was utterly repressed under fascist *propaganda*.

As opposed to fascist corporativism, freedom of association (Article 18) and freedom of other intermediate bodies (Article 2), including political parties (Article 49) and trade unions (Article 39), was released from state control.

Alongside social pluralism, veritable political pluralism was re-established, after many years of a single political party – *partito unico* – which had deprived the right to vote and electoral competition of any effective meaning.

The long-standing tradition of local self-government was restored (Articles 5 and 114 of the Constitution), whereas the fascist state had imposed strict governmental control by means of the *prefetti* (prefects) and *podestà* (the town mayors under the fascist regime), according to its centralised character. In the same vein, a new regional architecture was envisaged (Articles 114 ff of the Constitution), with five Regions endowed with enhanced autonomy at the legislative, administrative and financial levels, and another 15 with ordinary autonomy.

The Constitution carefully countered the concentration of power that was one of the main features of the fascist state, under which the role of Parliament was pre-empted by the government. It aimed at curbing such a powerful government and any other form of concentration of power. 'The specter of totalitarian dictatorship'[18] suggested that the Parliament be returned to a central position (Article 70). The Chambers were vested with the legislative function (Article 72), whereas the normative power of the government was strictly regulated (Articles 76 and 77). The political structure was centred on the confidence relationship (Article 94) between the Parliament and the government in order to maintain strict parliamentary control over the political choices of the government.

This analysis could go on, but these examples suffice to conclude that the Republican Constitution has indeed deeply transformed the constitutional principles on which the Italian state was based.

[17] See Antonio Baldassarre, *Le ideologie costituzionali dei diritti delle libertà, in* Diritti della persona e valori costituzionali (2007).

[18] Giuliano Amato terms this weakness of the Italian politics as 'the complex of the tyrant', in *Dal caso italiano al capitalismo ingovernabile, in* Una repubblica da riformare 37 ff. (1980).

ii. An Undecided New Polity

Yet, such innovations were not organised into a coherent new idea of a state. The Italian Republic was not founded on a single political idea; it was the result of different ideologies – Christian democrat, communist, socialist and liberal – that were bound together by a common *anti-fascist* commitment, but which did not share a common vision of the future. The unity and the innovations came from a common *reaction against the past* rather than from a shared new plan for the future. The Constitution was intended to prevent a relapse into the abuses of the totalitarian regime and was firmly grounded on an anti-fascist commitment. If any revolutionary charisma can be detected in the Constitution, it was the anti-fascist one:

> In those years, the break with the past assumed a more negative connotation, rather than showing the traits of a definite and constructive project. In other, more precise, words, they wanted to prevent the restoration of fascism at any cost, even in disguise; yet, the common will to adopt an anti-fascist Constitution was not enough when it came to determining the features of the new forms of the State and the Government.[19]

iii. The Legacy of the Past: Legal Rules and Public Officials

The Italian Republic after the Second World War shows some legal continuities with the past that one would not expect from a constitutional revolution. This does not diminish the importance of the discontinuities highlighted above; however, it does demand a more complex reading of the Italian constitutional experience.

Whereas the king was ousted and a new constitution replaced the old 'Statute', the underlying legal system was wholly transplanted from the fascist state into the Republic. The Criminal Code of 1930 and the Civil Code of 1942, both drafted and approved by the fascist government, were and still are in force. The same is true of the procedural codes and all the basic administrative laws, the law on the judiciary, military legislation and even the infamous law on public order[20] – not one of them was repealed.[21]

The sub-constitutional legal framework of the new republic was imbued with fascist culture. The responsibility to wipe away all the legal dross of the fascist epoch would later be taken on by the Constitutional Court. Instead of resetting the legal system from scratch, the Republic was reconstructed within the legal

[19] My translation from Livio Paladin, Per una storia costituzionale dell'Italia repubblicana 35 (2004): '[L]a rottura con il passato in quegli anni assunse connotazioni negative, piuttosto che presentare i tratti di un definito e costruttivo progetto. In altre e più chiare parole, ciò che si volle evitare ad ogni costo fu la restaurazione del fascismo, quand'anche mutato nelle sue vesti; ma la comune volontà di adottare una Costituzione antifascista non fu sufficiente a fissare le caratteristiche delle nuove forme di Stato e di Governo.' See also Massimo Luciani, *Antifascismo e nascita della Costituzione*, 2 Politica del diritto 183 ff. (1991).

[20] Royal Decree of 18 June 1931, n. 773 (Testo unico delle leggi di pubblica sicurezza).

[21] For a more detailed analysis, see Cassese, *supra* note 12 at 47 ff.

framework of the fascist state. Step by step, norm by norm, the legislation in place was eventually brought into line with constitutional principles by the judiciary: both the Constitutional Court and the ordinary courts. This incremental renovation took decades and the business is still unfinished. At the outset, the old and the new lived together in the new republican constitutional legal system. Later on, some of the old elements underwent a process of *unconventional adaptation* (to recall Ackerman's wording), whereas many others had to be struck down because they were utterly incompatible with the new Constitution.

The alignment of the old legislation with the new constitutional principles was slow and difficult because the civil servants working in the public administration and the judiciary, who had been educated under the fascist culture, were still in office: 'The administrative personnel of the state were mostly still the fascist ones, and the continuity was not only in the people themselves, but also in their mindset.'[22] The bureaucratic bodies had not been renovated and the employees were still the same 'conservative, authoritarian, and bureaucratic' people.[23]

After all, the tentative 'epuration' – that was supposed to purge all the public institutions from those who had been entangled with the authoritarian regime – was faltering and uncertain. For many commentators, it was, by and large, disappointing.

After a severe beginning with the first two decrees of December 1943 and July 1944,[24] the legislation on epuration was softened by numerous acts handed down starting in the final months of 1945.[25] Similarly, the enforcement of this legislation was strict and severe in the first months, but later became more tolerant and indulgent. All things considered, the epuration machinery produced a massive number of files, but resulted in very few convictions.

Long after the entry into force of the new Constitution, the top-level agents of the public administration were still people trained and educated under fascism.[26] The members of the judiciary remained almost untouched: after examining some 100 cases, only a few units of judges were dismissed, even most of the judicial body under fascism had been connected with the regime and had operated under the direction of the government.[27]

[22] My translation from Aurelio Lepre, Storia della prima Repubblica. L'Italia dal 1942 al 1992 56 (1993): 'Il personale nell'amministrazione statale era ancora, in gran parte, quello fascista e la continuità non era solo nelle persone ma anche negli atteggiamenti mentali.'

[23] These are the words of MP Zuccarini at the Constituent Assembly (March 7, 1947), quoted in Paladin, *supra* note 19 at 38; on this point, see also Onida, *supra* note 13 at 571 and many others.

[24] They were the Royal Law Decree 28 December 1943, no. 29/B and the Royal Regency Legislative Decree 27 July 1944, no. 159.

[25] Guido Melis, *Note sull'epurazione dei ministeri, 1944–46*, 4 Ventunesimo secolo 17 (2003); see also Achille Battaglia, *Giustizia e politica nella giurisprudenza, in* Dieci anni dopo 21 ff. (Achille Battaglia et al. eds.,1955).

[26] Sabino Cassese, La formazione dello stato amministrativo 5 (1974).

[27] Antonella Meniconi, Storia della magistratura italiana 250 ff. (2012). See also Pietro Saraceno, *Le 'epurazioni' della magistratura in Italia. Dal Regno di Sardegna alla repubblica: 1848–1951*, 39 Clio 521 ff. (1993).

The drive towards the national pacification of a divided, destitute and dejected country exceeded the urge to punish and vindicate, to the point that, right after the referendum for the Republic, on 22 June 1946 Palmiro Togliatti, the historical leader of the Communist Party acting in his capacity as Minister of Justice in the government, signed a general amnesty for common and political crimes.

B. Political Continuity and Discontinuity in the Transitional Phase

The same ambivalence between continuity and innovation can be found in the *political process* that took place in the crossover phase between the old illegitimate regime and the new constitutional era.

From a historical point of view, two major facts give a revolutionary flavour to the founding of the Italian Republic: the role of the National Liberation Committees, the institutional offspring of the Resistance movements; and the institutional referendum of 2 June 1946, when the Italian people chose the Republic rather than the monarchy.

i. A Constitution Born Out of the 'Resistance'?

It is often said that the Italian Constitution was 'born out of the Resistance'. This statement wishes to recognise the value and the importance of popular participation in the final stage of the dismantlement of the fascist regime. This importance is undisputable. However, the very same statement can be misleading if it is read as suggesting that the Italian Constitution is solely the result of the violent uprising of a group of people who were able to take power, replacing the fascist regime.

As a matter of fact, the 'resistance guerrillas' were present in only some areas of Italy, namely in the north and centre of the country, whereas in the south, the king still governed, and it was the Allies who began the liberation of the country. Moreover, the nature and functions of the National Liberation Committees was not entirely clear. Certainly, they aimed at a double target: to set Italy free from both the external and the internal oppressors, the Nazis and the fascists. As grassroots revolutionary forces, one could expect them to be the protagonist of the constitutional revolution, but in reality things were much more complex than that.

In 1945 – before the referendum and the elections for the Constituent Assembly – Piero Calamandrei, one of the standout voices of the 'Action Party', which championed the 'revolution', wrote that the liberation committees:

> [A]fter the liberation from the foreigners, shall have the constitutional task to complete the liberation of Italy from fascism. They are new bodies, born of historical need. Outside of any preconceived doctrinal scheme, they naturally rallied all the forces ready to hold their own against the oppressors and to rebuild the State based on the principles of democracy … Only these forces are entitled to rebuild the new Italian state.

> Only these forces … This is the great, unaccomplished function of the liberation committees. To ensure that the Constitution is the exclusive task of the revolutionary forces.[28]

Yet their role in the reconstruction of the country did not match up to these expectations. The role of the Resistance and of the National Liberation Committees did not go this far. A number of different forces played a role in the composite and tortuous liberation process: the monarchy, the allies, the trade unions, the Catholic Church and, yes, the parties of the National Liberation Committees.

In 1942, Great Britain believed that the existing anti-fascist leaders in Italy or in exile would not be able to create a movement that would succeed in countering fascism. On 30 November 1942, a note from the Foreign Office to the State Department said that, at that point in time, there was no leader in Italy able to oppose fascism, nor was there any person abroad who could take on the role.[29]

The Resistance movement covered a limited time period, spanning only from 9 September 1943 to the last days of April 1945. Anticipating or extending the terms of that period would entail the distortion of its exact definition and historical significance.[30] According to the protagonists of the guerrilla struggle, the men who fought in the Resistance never thought they were the winners. It was the Allied armies who won – the English army first and then the Russians and the Americans. The contribution of the Resistance amounted to 20 months of suffering and armed conflict[31] within the context of a more complex process: 'The famous sentence "a Constitution born out of the Resistance" remained little more than an empty slogan.'[32]

ii. From the Revolutionary Approach to the 'Provisional Constitutions'

The transitional period was a theatre in which a variety of forces were at play, moving in different directions. A number of factors suggests that, upon closer analysis, the two great leaders of the constituent momentum, De Gasperi and

[28] My translation from Piero Calamandrei, *Funzione rivoluzionaria dei Comitati di Liberazione*, I(2) Il Ponte 138–40 (1945) (now republished in *Andrea Mugnai, Storia e Costituzione. Radici politiche e tradizione culturale nella Costituzione italiana del 1948* 33–37 (1998)): 'dopo avvenuta la liberazione dallo straniero hanno la funzione costituzionale di portare a termine la liberazione dell'Italia dal fascismo. [Essi] sono appunto gli organi nuovi, partoriti dalla necessità storica, nei quali si sono spontaneamente raggruppate, fuor da ogni preconcetto schema dottrinario, tutte le forze decise a resistere agli oppressori ed a ricostruire lo stato secondo i principi della democrazia … A queste stesse forze, e ad esse sole, spetta oggi il compito di ricostruire il nuovo stato italiano. Ad esse sole … Questa è la grande funzione, non ancora esaurita dei comitati di liberazione. Per garantire che la Costituente sia opera delle sole forze rivoluzionarie'.

[29] See Lepre, *supra* note 22 at 15.

[30] Paolo Emilio Taviani, Politica a memoria d'uomo 69 (2002). Taviani is one of the main protagonists of the entire lifetime of the Christian Democratic Party and had the chance to fight in the final months as a guerrilla fighter in a communist brigade.

[31] *Id.* at 73.

[32] My translation from Paladin, *supra* note 19 at 35: '[L]a celebre formula della "Costituzione nata dalla Resistenza" rimase poco più che uno slogan.'

Togliatti, at different stages of the transitional process refused all *revolutionary* stances in favour of a more *evolutionary* approach. Both decided to support the government led by Marshal Badoglio in the wake of the fall of fascism and supported the two 'provisional constitutions' issued by the royal regency in 1944 and 1946,[33] calling for a Constituent Assembly after a general election.

After Victor Emmanuel's decision to have Mussolini apprehended, following the resolution of the Grand Council of Fascism on 25 July 1943 to dismiss Il Duce from his role as the leader of the Fascist Party in Italy, a discussion about the form of collaboration to extend to Marshall Badoglio's government and to the monarchy occurred amongst the leaders of the parties of the National Liberation Committee and among their popular base, mostly in northern Italy, where opposition to the Nazis was stiffer.

At that very moment, as De Gasperi would later recall in his address at the first congress of the Christian Democrats on April 1946, the parties were facing two options: *uprising or the Constituent Assembly.* At first, the Socialist Party, the Action Party (which was the second group of the Resistance in terms of the number of people involved) and the Communist Party were in favour of the first option, while the Christian Democrats were in favour of the second. When Palmiro Togliatti, leader of the Communist Party came back from Moscow to Naples on 27 March 1944, immediately after the recognition of Badoglio's government by the Soviet Union, the first of the Allied forces, on 14 March, his first statements concerned the willingness of the Communist Party to be an active part of Badoglio's government, much to the surprise of the Communist popular base and much to the anger of the Socialist Party and the Action Party. These parties later accepted this turn of events, though reluctantly and only under the condition that the king abdicated in favour of his son. They worked under a 'veil of ignorance' as Ackerman notes.

In his report, De Gasperi also recalled himself saying:

> I am not afraid of the word revolution, rather it bothers me, after twenty years in which fascism, always citing the rights of the revolution, committed so many abuses and violated the rights of citizens. In any case, the Constituent Assembly is the true revolution … The Christian Democrats are in favour of a democratic solution … The words 'Constituent Assembly' did not come later; they were born during the conflict of those days as a democratic propensity over and against any insurrectionist ambitions … Our work in the government, which went forward amid shoals and difficulties of many kinds, was able to ensure that the Constituent Assembly and the referendum were part of the agreement.[34]

[33] Royal Regency Decree 16 March 1946, n. 98 (Integrazioni e modifiche al decreto-legge Luogotenenziale 25 giugno 1944, n 151, relativo all'Assemblea per la nuova costituzione dello Stato, al giuramento dei Membri del Governo ed alla facoltà del Governo di emanare norme giuridiche). It changes the Royal Regency Decree 25 June 1944, n. 151 (Assemblea per la nuova costituzione dello Stato, giuramento dei Membri del Governo e facoltà del Governo di emanare norme giuridiche), which originally left the choice between monarchy and republic to the Constituent Assembly.

[34] My translation from Alcide De Gasperi, Linee programmatiche delle Democrazia Cristiana, National Secretary's address at the I Congress of the Christian Democrat Party, April 24–28. 1946, http://s3-eu-west-1.amazonaws.com/dellarepubblica.it/Legislature/1943-46/1946/Dc-%201cong%2046/Popolo%20Icongresso%2046/De%20Gasperi.pdf: 'Non temo la parola rivoluzione, ma ne ho piuttosto

iii. Monarchy or Republic?

As for the referendum of 2 June 1946, it was indeed a clear-cut break with the past. The Italian people put an end to the monarchy that had been involved with the fascist regime and chose to establish a democratic republic. But here too, a proper understanding of this historical fact requires careful interpretation. In reality, the referendum can hardly be considered 'revolutionary', since it was the outcome of an agreement among government parties and not the result of an uprising. The agreement was then adopted by an act of the royal regency and is usually referred to as 'provisional constitution'.[35]

The number of votes in favour of the Republic did not amount to an overwhelming majority: the republic gained 12,717,923 million votes and the monarchy 10,719,284 million, so that the difference was about two million votes. However, 1,498,136 million votes were invalid. The votes in favour of the monarchy came mostly from the south of the country; the Christian Democrats, the largest political party at the time, were split on this basic choice.

A legal dispute was brought before the Supreme Court of Cassation as to the interpretation of the majority required to grant victory to one or other of the two options – the controversial clause referred to 'voters' rather than to 'valid votes'. The Supreme Court was expected to announce the poll results on 10 June, but the pronouncement was postponed, leaving the country in a dangerous state of suspense for weeks. Before the results were officially communicated, the king left the country. Under the guise of a subtle legal dispute, a major political conflict was raging.[36]

All things considered, the country had chosen in favour of the Republic, but the polls showed that Italy was a split country from a political point of view. And this division cast its shadow on the constituent process, which had to take into consideration the conservative soul of a significant part of the Italian people: if the new Republic was to be established on solid ground, the Constitution had to represent the whole Italian people, including those who were still nostalgic for the monarchy.

iv. The Unexpected Convergence of a Polarized Political System

The Constituent Assembly was made up of a very fragmented political body: out of the 552 members at the end of its mandate, 209 were Christian Democrats, 104

fastidio dopo venti anni che il fascismo, richiamandosi ai diritti della rivoluzione, ha commesso tante soperchierie e violato i diritti dei cittadini. A ogni modo la vera rivoluzione è la Costituente … I democratici cristiani sono per la soluzione democratica … [L]a parola Costituente non è venuta più tardi, ma è nata nel conflitto d'allora ed è nata soprattutto come tendenza democratica contro velleità di carattere insurrezionale … La nostra opera di Governo, che seguì fra scogli e difficoltà diverse, ha portato ad assicurare la Costituente nell'accordo stesso delle parti in causa e ad introdurre anche il referendum.'

[35] See Cassese, *supra* note 26.

[36] Battaglia, *supra* note 25 at 21 ff.; Paladin, *supra* note 19 at 30.

were Communists, 65 were Socialists, 49 were Workers Socialists, 25 were Republicans, 22 were Liberals, 20 were members of the Common Man's Front and the others were members of five further groups. None of the political groups received a majority of the votes. Moreover, none of the parties could imagine whether, at the next elections, they would be able to govern the country or would instead be the opposition. Nevertheless, the final text of the Constitution was the result of broad agreement – 453 votes in favour and 62 against – on which all the political parties had made their mark. This agreement was a remarkable result, considering that by the time of the final vote on the Constitution, the Communist Party had just been ousted from the government coalition. The Constituent Assembly took a very inclusive stance. None of the many voices tried to impose its own view on the others. The Constitution was not the result of a single ideology. Consider, for example, the fact that Article 7 of the Constitution – regarding the privileged position of the Catholic Church regulated by a concordat signed by Mussolini – was supported by Palmiro Togliatti, the leader of the Communist Party, together with the Christian Democrats. Social peace and re-unification of the country prevailed over divergent ideologies. For similar reasons, in every constitutional clause, the footprints of different, and even competing, political ideas can be easily recognised.

The constitutional principles were phrased in such a way that they were open to development in many directions. Consider those relating to the economic model, a very sensitive issue at the time: 'Property is public or private. Economic assets may belong to the State, to public bodies or to private persons' (Article 42 of the Constitution). 'Private enterprise is free' (Article 41), but 'economic activity may be oriented and coordinated for social purposes'. Principles like these were susceptible to leaving room for a liberal free market or for state control of the economic sector – or, again, for a 'third' model, championed by the Christian Democrats.

As has been said, the Italian Constitution was a 'compromise constitution'. In fact, one can hardly say that, in the Italian experience, the new Constitution was the result of the constitutionalisation of a unique revolutionary ideology. Firmly rejecting fascist ideology, the Constitution set the basis for future, undetermined developments. The revolution was not an accomplished fact, nor was it translated into coherent legal principles.

Given this historical and political background, the question arises as to whether the Italian Constitution was born out of a *revolution* or was, rather, at the origin of a 'gentle', 'incremental' *evolution*. For sure, the Italian constitutional transition was not an abrupt change; the Constitution triggered a new beginning that brought about a 'slow release' transformation. Discontinuity with the past was remarkable, but not immediate. Many constitutional principles were open-ended and left many things undecided.[37] It would take decades after the

[37] See Cass R. Sustein, *Foreword: Leaving Things Undecided*, 110 Harv. L.R. 6 (1996).

entry into force of the new Constitution to implement the new principles, give birth to the new institutions and remodel the whole legal system.[38]

III. The Meandering Implementation of the Constitution

The ambivalent origins of the Constitution and the open-ended result of many constitutional principles accounts for its difficult and uneven implementation.

The old principles and institutions received swift implementation. A new Parliament was elected in 1948, a new President of the Republic was elected and a new government was nominated. On the contrary, it took almost a decade to establish the Constitutional Court (1956) and the Supreme Council of the Judiciary (1958), an essential security measure for the independence of the judiciary. It took more than 20 years to put the ordinary Regions and the referendum (abrogative and constitutional) into place (1970). And some of the constitutional provisions – like Article 39 on the trade unions and Article 46 on 'the rights of workers to collaborate in the management of enterprises' – have yet to be implemented. In a word, the Constitution was enforced at different speeds and some of its provisions were simply ignored.

What is even more remarkable is that – as Ackerman recalls – an attempt was made to downplay the legal value of the Constitution, in particular its more innovative principles on social rights, healthcare, working conditions, and pension and social assistance, (dis)qualifying them as political provisions to be left to the political bodies rather than legal ones and not susceptible to enforcement by the judiciary. The most innovative features of the Constitution as higher law, which was normative and rigid, as opposed to the political and flexible Albertine Statute, were at risk.

A very dangerous attack on the authority of the Constitution was, in fact, launched by a landmark decision of the Supreme Court of Cassation on 7 February 1948[39] (a few weeks after the entry into force of the Constitution), which drew a distinction between preceptive rules and mere programmatic principles, which were to be treated as non-justiciable, and the binding force of which was conditional upon legislative implementation. The Supreme Court of Cassation was giving voice to a very conservative position that was circulating among some legal scholars (VE Orlando[40] and many others) and in the judiciary, where the vast majority of the judges were those who had served under the previous regime.

[38] See Maurizio Fioravanti, *Per una storia della legge fondamentale in Italia: dallo Statuo alla Costituzione, in* Il valore della Costituzione. L'esperienza della democrazia repubblicana 17 (Maurizio Fioravanti ed., 2009).

[39] Court of Cassation, Criminal United Sessions, February 7, 1948, 2 Foro ital, 57 ff. (1948).

[40] Vittorio Emanuele Orlando, *Studio intorno alla forma di governo vigente in Italia secondo la Costituzione del 1948*, 1 Riv. trim. dir. Pubb. 5 (1951). See also Francesco Gentile & Pietro Giuseppe Grasso, eds., La Costituzione criticata 137 ff. (1999).

Had this doctrine taken root, the innovative driving force of the Constitution would have been neutralised. Had the implementation process been left to Parliament, the translation of the constitutional framework into practice would have been distorted or, at least, incomplete.

In reality, the political landscape had dramatically changed in the meantime, with the Communist Party having been excluded from government since May 1947. After the election of 1948, when the Christian Democrats won more than 48.5 per cent of the votes and the parties on the left lost the competition, it became clear that the Communist Party would not return to government for a long time, also considering the unwritten agreement on the implicit *conventio ad excludendum* following De Gasperi's visit to the US in 1947. The Parliament and the political institutions were dominated by the Christian Democrats. This was the reason why the parties on the left turned to the judiciary to have their voices heard in the implementation of the Constitution.

There are two relevant facts to be recorded: the establishment of the Constitutional Court and the Congress of the Associazione nazionale magistrati (National Association of Judges) that took place in 1965 at Gardone.

Whereas most of the politicians on the Constituent Assembly were sceptical about all forms of judicial review of legislation, after the first electoral turn, the opposition parties endorsed the idea of the Constitutional Court as an institution capable of counterbalancing a very powerful majority in the government. The Communists, who had strongly resisted the idea of judicial review of legislation because it could impair the idea of parliamentary democracy, later became the main supporters of constitutional adjudication. Conversely, the Christian Democrats, who in the Constituent Assembly had pushed for its provision within the Constitution, became more hesitant after winning the 1948 election, and the implementation of the Court was postponed.

As a matter of fact, starting with decision 1 of 1956,[41] the Constitutional Court, instead of taking sides in the then current political disputes, emerged as a defender of the anti-fascist Constitution that was hammered out at the founding through an agreement between all the political parties. Despite the personal and professional records of some of its members,[42] the Constitutional Court was able to do its job and to disseminate the new constitutional principles in a legal system that was very much in need of renovation. As has already been mentioned, the new Republic took its first steps in a legal environment that was shaped under fascism. From its inception, the Italian Constitutional Court started a long-standing project

[41] Ackerman, *supra* note 2 at 173; see also Vittoria Barsotti, Paolo G. Carozza, Marta Cartabia & Andrea Simoncini, Italian Constitutional Justice in Global Context (2015).

[42] Giuseppe Capograssi, Costantino Mortati, Tommaso Perassi, Gaspare Ambrosini, Nicola Jaeger and other members of the first Constitutional Court belonged to an older generation: they were born at the end of the nineteenth century or at the start of the twentieth century and had spent their careers under the monarchy and the fascist eras. The most astonishing example is probably Gaetano Azzariti, President of the Constitutional Court from 1957 to 1961, who had held the post of President of the 'Race Tribunal' under the fascist regime.

of renovating old legislation, cutting away all the pieces of legislation that bore the imprint of fascist culture. The Court soon became one of the most influential authorities in the Italian institutional architecture, quickly gaining the respect of all the other branches of government. Since its very origins, the Italian Court has shown solid self-awareness and a high level of esteem for its own mission of implementing the new constitutional principles, while, at the same time, it has maintained an open and cooperative approach towards other actors, both political and judicial.

This last remark on the cooperation with the judiciary brings us to another step. The judicial implementation of the Constitution in Italy was the result of a joint effort between the judiciary and the Constitutional Court. First, the Constitutional Court could not act alone[43] because the main avenue to bring cases before it is the incidental procedure of review, which implies cooperation with lower courts. Second, in 1965, the national congress of the judiciary marked a turning point in the very idea of the judicial function. In the final document of that Congress (where, for the first time, the judges of the Magistratura Democratica – Democratic Judiciary – the progressive 'current' of the judiciary, gained the majority) three principles were spelled out. First, the Constitution has direct effect and every court is required to apply constitutional norms to the cases and controversies under their jurisdiction. Second, parliamentary legislation which is in contrast with the Constitution is to be referred to the Constitutional Court for judicial review. Third, a new method of interpretation is to be followed, ie, interpretation in conformity with the Constitution. In American legal terminology, this method would say that where a statute is susceptible to two constructions, one that gives rise to doubtful constitutional questions arise and one that is able to avoid such questions, a court's duty is to adopt the latter.[44]

The old assumption of the Court of Cassation of 1948 on the programmatic nature of the Constitution was utterly rebuffed. And this 'Gardone congress' soon became a milestone in the evolution of the judicial function in Italy.[45]

La bouche de la loi turned out to be the voice of the Constitution as well in a constitutional framework where the judges are still defined as 'subject to the law' (Article 101 of the Constitution).

IV. Difficult Consolidation

'Revolutionary constitutionalism' describes a four-stage process in which, after some phases where the Constitution is in the hands of the political actors that

[43] See Elisabetta Lamarque, *It Takes Two to Tango, in* Corte costituzionale e giudici nell'Italia repubblicana 101 ff. (2012).

[44] See, eg, Jones v. United States 526 U.S. 227, 239 (1999), quoting United States ex rel. Attorney General v. Delaware & Hudson Co 213 U.S. 366, 408 (1909).

[45] Meniconi, *supra* note 27 at 312 ff.

lead the fundamental change, the judiciary emerges on to the stage. This evolution is easy to see in Italian constitutional history. However, the Italian experience provides some food for thought if one considers what happened after the founding period.

Before the end of the 1970s, the struggle for consolidating the Constitution was heading towards success. The time of constitutional freezing had come to an end. The implementation process was almost completed and the Constitutional Court, together with all the judicial bodies, had developed all the tools necessary to keep the Constitution alive. The most important pieces of social legislation come from these years. The reform of middle schools was approved in 1962,[46] thus implementing Article 34 of the Constitution, which provides that: 'Primary education, given for at least eight years, is compulsory and free of tuition.' In 1970, the 'Statute of the Workers' was passed by Parliament, establishing a long list of safeguard measures for workers that implemented Articles 1 and 35 ff of the Constitution and, around the same time, new legislation implemented Article 38 on social assistance for people unable to work and on pensions. In 1978, the public universal health care service was established,[47] adding another pillar to the welfare system related to Article 32 of the Constitution, which states that: 'The Republic safeguards health as a fundamental right of the individual and as a collective interest, and guarantees free medical care to the indigent.' These and other pieces of legislation passed by the Parliament, together with some crucial decisions of the Constitutional Court, were able to translate some of the promises stipulated by the Constitution in social matters into reality.

However, at the same time, a new crisis was looming, and the political institutions began showing symptoms of weakness and vulnerability. During the 1970s, social legislation was translating into reality even the more 'revolutionary' – ie, progressive – constitutional principles, but the political parties, together with all the political institutions, began experiencing new problems, along with increasing political fragmentation and governmental instability.[48] Long before the present-day populist challenges, Italy underwent a number of political crises, which reached an acute phase in the early 1990s with a massive anti-corruption investigation that implicated the vast majority of political leaders, to the extent that the period is commonly referred to as the beginning of the 'second republic'. This was not an ordinarily difficult time: for a number of historical reasons, all the political forces that had led the constituent process – and notably the Christian Democrat Party and the Communist Party – were wiped away, and a new difficult transition began.

This political instability prompted a debate on constitutional reform. Over the last 40 years, an unending and perennially incomplete debate on the *reform of the Constitution* has produced a number of drafts that were ultimately not approved

[46] Law of 31 December 1962, n. 1859 (Istituzione e ordinamento della scuola media statale).
[47] Law of 23 December 1978, n. 833 (Istituzione del servizio sanitario nazionale).
[48] Fioravanti, *supra* note 38 at 28 ff.

by the Parliament or were subsequently rejected by the people in referendums (as happened with the constitutional reform promoted by the Berlusconi government in 2006 and again, 10 years later, with that promoted by the Renzi government in 2016). None of these projects was able to overturn the original Constitution. However, this prolonged debate has put the republican Constitution under stress and has had detrimental effects on its legitimating authority.

V. A Revolutionary Agreement

Bearing in mind the Italian experience, a tentative remark could be added to the four-stage analysis of revolutionary constitutionalism. Time Three and Time Four – the normalisation of the revolutionary – cannot be exclusively judicial or purely political. A proper balance between the two poles is always a necessary condition in order for the constitution to work. The judicial 'guardians of the Constitution' – to recall a Kelsenian expression – cannot do the whole job, nor can the political actors do it alone in any of the phases, and much less so in the time of consolidation. In order for the constitution to reach stability in time, the judicial and the political bodies should work together in the implementation of the new principles enshrined in the founding text, and should do so in a contextual rather than a sequential pattern. Italian experience shows that one should avoid a reading of Ackerman's 'four-time' model as if it were suggesting that 'there is a time for the people, a time for the parliament, [and] a time for the judiciary' (echoing Ecclesiastes)[49] as distinct segments of a linear idea of time.

Constitutions are not mere political documents, nor are they ordinary legal rules. At the constitutional level, politics and law are strictly intertwined. Their effective legitimating capacity rests on the converging contributions of *gubernaculum* and *iurisdictio* alike.

The new constitutional values are polysemic and lay out a pluralistic understanding of society susceptible to a plurality of interpretations. With such a symphonic composition, none of the interpreters can play alone. Whereas in many revolutionary experiences, the constituent process is founded on an act of will of a *minority* strong enough to oust the political forces in power and willing to change the historical development of the country according to a new ideology,[50] the legitimation of the Italian Constitution rests, to a great extent on *agreement*. In the fight against the totalitarian regime, there was no single winner, nor may De Gasperi be considered the only charismatic leader of the constitutional momentum. The Christian Democratic Party had many souls; there was a strong Communist Party

[49] See Ecclesiastes 3.

[50] See Paolo Pombeni, La questione costituzionale in Italia 56 ff. (2016); see also Harold J. Berman, Law and Revolution, the Formation of the Western Legal Tradition (1983).

and, again, there were strong leaders from the right-wing parties. No one questions the fact that the Italian Constitution was forged through agreement. In a way, it can be considered a 'revolutionary agreement' – to remain in accordance with Ackerman's doctrine – because it involved all the anti-fascist political forces that were determined to counter fascism and any form of dictatorship. However, in the absence of any single winner, the Constitution does not codify a univocal new vision of civil life. Pluralism is the stamp of the constituent process and of the Constitution itself. Therefore, in the founding of the Italian Republic, the new and the old, the people and the elites, the discontinuity and the continuity, the political and the legal, the revolutionary and the evolutionary are all bound together in a historical dynamic, where opposite poles are connected in a 'et-et' rather than an 'aut-aut' relationship.

17

Constitutional Strategy for a Polarised Society

Learning from Poland's Post-revolutionary Misfortunes

MACIEJ KISILOWSKI

After playing first fiddle in the struggle to bring down communism, Poland seemed slated for a relatively minor and bland role in the grand 'end of history' post-1989 narrative: it was supposed to become like the West. Not only did this not happen, but the West is actually becoming more like Poland. For its much of its modern history, Poland has been deeply divided along progressive-conservative lines, although the precise meaning of each of these terms obviously depended on a particular historical context. Polish progressive tradition has always been strong. But Polish conservatives have, likewise, traditionally been much more vocal and emboldened than, until recently, in the West.

I suspect Professor Ackerman's insightful chapters on the troubled story of Poland's post-1989 constitution-building will enter the canon of comparative constitutionalism not only for the reasons emphasised by the author. Ackerman rightly sees the Polish story as an elaboration of one of his three paths to constitutional development – the 'revolutionary' ideal-type. But Poland's (post-) revolutionary constitutionalism emerged in the conditions of a Polarised Society. Since I expect that the coming decades will bring even more polarised societies than political revolutions, the Polish experience may become particularly relevant as a cautionary tale for constitutional strategists operating in divided countries.

I. Constitutional Challenges of a Polarised Society

From a narrow rational choice perspective, in a system of two political camps repeatedly competing in close elections, politicians should have a strong incentive to impose 'significant legal constraints on top decision makers'.[1] After all, in such a system, all politicians face a near-certainty of spending large swaths of their careers in the opposition. Creating rules to prevent abuse of power by the other side seems to be in everyone's best interest.[2]

Well, not so fast. Polarised Society is not just a system of close electoral competition. Indeed, as the Polish case shows, a Polarised Society does not even need to be a two-party system. By 'Polarised Society', I mean a society in which a decisive majority of the electorate is divided into two roughly equal groups: let us call them Group A and Group B. Members of each group not only favour different policy proposals, they also endorse mutually exclusive concepts of good society and, indeed, of good life, and have different sets of moral authority figures and preferred historical narratives. As Amy Chua recently observed, members of such warring 'political tribes' are divided by identity and culture as much as by policy preferences.[3] Furthermore, members of each group harbour particularly strong negative views about the policies and values of the other group. The rational choice concept of 'preference ordering' does not quite capture the dynamics here. The other group's policies are not merely less preferred, they are associated with an intolerable wrong. The other group's values are not only 'misguided' – key virtues of Group A are often among the top vices for members of Group B, and vice versa.

Three important qualifications need to be mentioned here. First and most important, neither group is internally homogeneous. Factions and internal conflicts inevitably emerge within each group. Moreover, even in a Polarised Society, members of Groups A and B often have some important values and interests in common. Finally, a significant minority of voters do not associate themselves clearly with either group.

These factors could potentially mitigate the ideological tribalism of a Polarised Society. However, their impact is more than offset by the realities of political competition. No politician can win without the support of one of the groups. Electoral success is mostly dependent on mobilising one's base. Because Group A's and Group B's policies, values and even facts are mutually exclusive as a matter of logic, 'moderate' voters do not have a coherent platform. Unlike in the early rational choice literature, politicians cannot anchor their message to the 'preferences of the median voter'[4] because voters around the median oscillate between the mutually exclusive worldviews fed to them by Groups A and B. In effect, the areas of mutual enmity between the groups come to define Polarised Society's political life.

In a Polarised Society, the very role of constitutionalism is in question. A standard assumption here is that, while constitutions and their interpretation may be

[1] Bruce Ackerman, Revolutionary Constitutions: Charismatic Leadership and the Rule of Law 6–7 (2019).

[2] See, eg, Viktor Vanberg & James M. Buchanan, *Interests and Theories in Constitutional Choice*, 1 Journal of theoretical politics 49 (1989).

[3] Amy Chua, Political Tribes: Group Instinct and the Fate of Nations (2018).

[4] Anthony Downs, An Economic Theory of Democracy (1957).

contentious, their uncontroversial purpose is to create the most broadly accepted, stable set of rules of the game. Ackerman's constitutional moment is not complete until the opposition accepts a new settlement.[5] In the context of democratic transitions, a consolidated democracy has routinely been defined as a system in which democracy becomes 'the only game in town'.[6] But in a Polarised Society, the calculus of both groups is dramatically different. Constitutions are not viewed primarily as ways to cement areas of mutual agreement of Groups A and B; on the contrary, they become tools to embed the most controversial policies and institutional arrangements in which any agreement cannot be possibly reached. That is fully rational: in closely divided countries, the most contentious aspects of Group A's and Group B's moral and political platforms are unlikely to become a reality through ordinary legislation. Even if Group A wins power and adopts its preferred policies, Group B will undo these changes as soon as it takes over. Since constitutions are more difficult to change, constitutionalisation of favoured policies and institutional outcomes becomes the main realistic avenue for achieving lasting policy impact. In a Polarised Society, Ackermanian constitutional moments give way to a constitutional opportunity: a fortuitous set of circumstances that puts Group A in a position to change a constitution in a way that will never be accepted by Group B. During the constitutional opportunity, Group A's objective is emphatically not to 'convince an extraordinary number of … fellow citizens'[7] to their favoured constitutional changes; instead, it is to legally lock their policy and institutional agenda so that Group B cannot reverse it when it comes to power.[8] In a Polarised Society, the constitution is the opposite of the common rules of the game; it is the primary tool for stacking the political deck against the opposite tribe.

II. Polarised Society: A Case Study

In Ackerman's book, Poland's post-1989 constitutional debacle becomes evident in the summer of 1990, only a year after the historic Round Table Accord that dismantled Poland's communist regime. A seemingly inexplicable rift emerged between Lech Walesa and his handpicked Prime Minister, Poland's first non-communist head of government, Tadeusz Mazowiecki. Mazowiecki, a Warsaw intellectual who for years had acted as Walesa's top advisor, was increasingly frustrated with Walesa's ambition of becoming the country's first popularly elected president. In early October, Mazowiecki decided to officially challenge the iconic Solidarity

[5] Bruce Ackerman, We the People, Volume 1: Foundations (1993).

[6] Juan J. Linz & Alfred Stepan, *Toward Consolidated Democracies*, 7 Journal of Democracy 14 (1996).

[7] Ackerman, *supra* note 1 at 6.

[8] This chapter is certainly not the first attempt to suggest alternative paths to constitutional change within Ackerman's dualist framework; see, eg, Andras Sajo, *Constitution without the Constitutional Moment: A View from the New Member States*, 3 Int'l J. Const. L. 243 (2005).

leader for the presidency. Adam Michnik, Solidarity's leading progressive thinker, supported Mazowiecki in a well-known op-ed that was soon reprinted in English by the liberal *New York Review of Books*. Michnik did not mince his words. He predicted that 'Walesa's presidency may be catastrophic for Poland' and posed a fundamental question:

> What path do we wish to follow? Is it a path to the Europe of contemporary, democratic standards, or, on the contrary, a path of return to bygone traditions symbolized by authoritarian regimes, the hell of national conflicts, and extreme cases of religious intolerance? The position of Poles in Europe depends on the answer to this question.[9]

Note how aptly this quote encapsulates the above-mentioned features of Polarised Society. In the short passage, Michnik indicates that the progressive Poland – represented by Mazowiecki and Michnik himself – was a political project fundamentally different from Walesa's conservative Poland. For the progressive camp, a potential electoral victory of the conservatives was not simply a temporary upset – it amounted to a 'catastrophe'. The 'others' in this struggle were not merely competitors; they were enemies. During the 1990 presidential campaign, Walesa referred to Mazowiecki's team as 'eggheads' and 'Jews',[10] while Michnik called Walesa's supporters 'swine'.[11]

This stark choice between two dramatically different visions of the state and society haunted Poland for all its (relatively brief) periods of modern independent existence. Unlike in many other non-Western countries, Polish progressives have been anything but an irrelevant, tiny elite. In 1791, they passed Europe's first written constitution (inspired by the US Constitution). In 1918, just after regaining independence, they introduced unconditional suffrage for women and built a liberal, parliamentary democracy. Throughout the communist era, they gave the world scores of serious philosophers and writers (including, prominently, Adam Michnik) contesting the authoritarian status quo. And after 1989, they have democratically governed the country for most of the last 30 years.

However, at the same time, Poland's regressive forces have always been much stronger and bolder than – until recently – in the West. The proponents of this conservative Poland have always been represented among the nation's elite, despite the anti-establishment myths that the camp frequently cherishes. A year after the above-mentioned progressive constitution was passed in the late eighteenth century, a group of influential aristocrats from the eastern parts of the country organised a Russian-backed rebellion to defend their 'uniquely Polish' way of life. A few years after the progressive parliamentary state was reconstituted following the First World War, a growing threat from far-right nationalist movements led to a

[9] Adam Michnik, *My Vote against Walesa*, New York Review of Books, Dcember 20, 1990.
[10] *Id.* at 47.
[11] Minutes of the Meeting of the Citizen's Committee (June 24, 1990), https://nowahistoria.interia.pl/prl/news-24-czerwca-1990-r-koniec-solidarnosci-od-dzis-roznimy-sie-fu,nId,1841117.

military coup and an authoritarian state. In 1968, during the communist-instigated anti-semitic purge, many Poles opposed the insanity of stirring xenophobia in the land where much of the Holocaust happened, but many others (including those otherwise opposed to the communists) enthusiastically joined the mob.[12] Last but certainly not least, right-wing nationalists have been methodically dismantling Poland's liberal democracy after gaining a razor-thin parliamentary majority in 2015.

III. Polarised Society and Revolutionary Struggle

Revolutionary struggle against an authoritarian regime complicates an already fragile state of constitutional politics in a Polarised Society. An authoritarian regime can be a direct historical outgrowth of Group A or B; even if it is not, it is inevitably associated with one or other set of values. In Poland, homegrown support for the Soviet-style communists was miniscule and the Communist Party's authority was almost entirely imposed by the Red Army. But the communist ideology, with its emphasis on secularism, economic equality and women's rights, was obviously more aligned with the progressive side of Poland's ideological split. In fact, most of the leaders of the liberal fraction of the Solidarity, including Michnik, Bronislaw Geremek and Leszek Balcerowicz, the author of economic reforms, were themselves disillusioned former communists. Tadeusz Mazowiecki was a long-time member of the façade parliament of the People's Republic from a regime-approved liberal Catholic grouping.

At some stage, ideological affinities give way to moral outrage over state violence propagated by an authoritarian regime. The anti-communist alliance of the ideologically progressive intellectuals led by Mazowiecki with ideologically conservative workers led by Walesa was what made Solidarity so formidable. At the same time, the communists (proving that all ideology is subject to interpretation) started to reach out to Polish nationalists, particularly with the above-mentioned anti-semitic purge of 1968. When communism fell in 1989, the political fault lines seemed complicated. However, it turned out that the return to the essential logic of Polarised Society would not take long.

Today, for instance, former communist nationalists are actively engaged in an effort to dismantle liberal democracy by conservative Poland. Like his counterparts in the US, Jarosław Kaczyński and his ruling Law and Justice party see the replacement of high judges as the quickest path to constitutional revolution. To be sure, Kaczyński's methods are far cruder than those of Mitch McConnell (though Merrick Garland might beg to differ). However, what is remarkable is that the key person coordinating Kaczyński's sweeping judiciary reforms in

[12] Dariusz Stola, *Fighting against the Shadows: The Anti-Zionist Campaign of 1968*, *in* ANTISEMITISM AND ITS OPPONENTS IN MODERN POLAND 284 (Robert Blobaum ed., 2005).

Parliament was Stanisław Piotrowicz, a former communist prosecutor deeply embroiled in repression against the Solidarity movement in the 1980s. Piotrowicz's case is far from unique in the top ranks of Law and Justice.[13]

If the conservative camp recognises the prevailing importance of ideological affinity over conflicting biographies, it is because the progressive side went down this path much earlier. Poland's 1997 Constitution, which in truth was the constitution of progressive Poland, was passed by a coalition of the post-communist Democratic Left Alliance and Mazowiecki's Democratic Union. The formation of this coalition was inevitable given the deep divisions within the Solidarity movement. Already in 1990, during the 'last chance' talks between Walesa and Mazowiecki's teams, one of Walesa's aides observed that 'after 45 years, the Polish Nation has enough of the leftist rule and its horrific consequences. That is why, the left [ie, Mazowiecki's team] promotes the idea of the big-tent Solidarity'.[14] The conservatives, in other words, were not willing to let a relatively small group of progressive intellectuals play an outsized role in the Solidarity movement. From that point on, it was mathematically impossible for Solidarity progressives to win elections – much less to reach a constitutional majority – against Solidarity conservatives without reaching out to the three million former communist party members; the active electorate in Poland was at the time about 13 million.

Distasteful as this marriage had to be for Geremek, Mazowiecki and Michnik, it was evolving in a certain context. Poland's post-revolutionary constitutionalism was taking place during the liberal 'end of history' of the 1990s. With Bill Clinton in the White House and the post-Maastricht European Union (EU) inching ever more closely towards a liberal federation, the progressive side of Poland's divide had ample fuel to build its legitimacy. Every Pole, progressive or conservative, wanted to make sure that the country would never again fall under the Russian sphere of influence. Joining what at the time was unquestionably the progressive West seemed to be the only way. As was evident in Adam Michnik's essay quoted earlier, progressives framed the choice that the voters faced in terms of a Westward or elseward direction for Poland.

Moreover – and not only in Poland – the elites believed that the remnants of religious, nationalist, intolerant, patriarchal society would soon dissolve into the past. Take a telling viral social media campaign, organized by a Law and Justice opponent as recently as 2007 and entitled 'Steal Your Grandma's ID'.[15] The call, made (hopefully) in jest, illustrates the deep belief that conservative support is quite literally witnessing its last breaths. For the Democratic Union, the 1997 constitutional deal with the communists could be viewed as a little like 'Stealing Your Grandma's ID' – an unholy trick that simply accelerated the inevitable triumph of progressive Poland.

[13] See Martin Mycielski, *PiS Off*, POLITICO, December 18, 2015.
[14] Minutes of the Meeting of the Citizen's Committee, *supra* note 11.
[15] *Akcja 'Zabierz Babci Dowód' Do Prokuratury*, TVN24, October 2, 2007.

The powerful liberal winds also weakened the resolve of key conservative leaders. The most important case here was that of Lech Walesa. Walesa's split with the conservatives was truly bizarre and it partly illustrates the right's worldwide penchant for conspiracy theories. It took less than a year after Walesa's 1990 victory over Mazowiecki for Jarosław Kaczyński – the future leader of Law and Justice who at the time was Walesa's top aide – to abandon his boss. Ever since, Kaczyński has argued that Walesa had always been a traitor of (conservative) Poland due to his alleged contacts (as a young worker and a decade before his involvement in Solidarity) with the communist secret police. Obviously, the very fact that Poland's conservatives enthusiastically endorsed this accusation forced Walesa to distance himself from his base. This, in turn, has been viewed by the right as decisive evidence that Walesa had been compromised all along by the communist 'deep state'.[16]

But Kaczyński and his associates did not appreciate, or did not want to appreciate, the impact of the above-mentioned international liberal narrative on Walesa. Revolutionary leaders not only play for the domestic audience but also care deeply about how their legacy is viewed abroad. Walesa loved his international status of the freedom icon; upon his retirement from the presidency, he joined the lucrative international speaking circuit.[17] Today's fall from grace of Aung San Suu Kyi shows the reputational costs that Walesa would have suffered had he fully endorsed the role of the standard bearer of regressive nationalist Poland.

It is worth noting that the second right-wing President, Jarosław Kaczyński's own brother Lech Kaczyński, was likewise a reluctant conservative revolutionary. Before being elected in 2005, he had been a prominent member of Poland's powerful legal academic establishment. As Walesa's deputy in the Solidarity movement of the late 1980s, Lech Kaczyński also developed personal ties with key progressives in the union.

It was only the third protégé of Jarosław Kaczynski who won the country's presidency and was then willing to go all the way down the revolutionary path. Only 17 years old in 1989, Andrzej Duda was not part of the Solidarity story. Almost entirely unknown when Jarosław Kaczyński picked him as a presidential candidate, Duda is living proof of Poland's consolidation as a Polarised Society. Revolutionary myths, narratives, expectations and friendships do not enter his

[16] The lengthy expose of this theory, published by the right-dominated, governmental Institute for National Remembrance, is Sławomir Cenckiewicz & Piotr Gontarczyk, SB a Lech Walesa: Przyczynek Do Biografii (2008).

[17] See, eg, *Walesa Bares His Lip but Refuses to Speak*, Guardian, August 8, 2002; *Walesa, Havel Shine Again in Crisis*, The Globe and Mail, November 24, 2004. Walesa's first post-presidency book, published in the mid-2000s, literally *illustrates* this evolution with a selection of photos from Walesa's political career. They include meetings with American presidents, Vaclav Havel, Mikhail Gorbachev, Boris Yeltsin, Queen Elizabeth II, appearances at the World Economic Forum and the European Council, as well as speeches and honorary degree award ceremonies around the world. A reconciliatory handshake with the post-communist President Aleksander Kwaśniewski is also included in the collection; Lech Walesa, Moja III RP (2007).

calculus. 'It is impossible to be the President of all Poles', Duda remarked with a level of candour worthy of a rational-choice academic paper. 'Because it will never be the case that everybody will vote for you.'[18]

IV. Constitutional Opportunity

However, perhaps all the philosophising about the legacies of the revolutionary struggle is superfluous. Perhaps President Duda's understanding of democracy in Polarised Society is, at least descriptively, the most accurate because, all the moral objections notwithstanding, the Democratic Union made a deal with the progressive wing of post-communists at the first opportune moment – after the conservatives were battered in the 1993 general election and Walesa lost the presidency to progressive post-communist Aleksander Kwaśniewski in 1995. In 2005, the first time when Jarosław Kaczyński had a real shot at power, he did not hesitate to break the widely expected coalition with Solidarity progressives from the Civic Platform (the heir to the Democratic Union) and instead formed an alliance with two smaller nationalist parties filled with former communist apparatchiks and regime collaborators. In 2015, when Jarosław again gained the parliamentary majority *and* a pliant president, he wasted no time before trying to constitutionalise his nationalist, regressive rule.

Both in 1997 and 2015, Poland shows us how constitutions are changed in a Polarised Society. This mechanism of constitutional change has, so far, been somewhat of a loose end in the model I introduced earlier. After all, if Polarised Society is marked by close electoral competitions of two camps representing drastically different worldviews, then the following question emerges: how is a constitutional change possible at all? If the very purpose of Group A's constitution is to prevent Group B from changing it, how could Group A have attained the power to pass 'its' constitution in the first place?

Constitutional opportunity is Poland's answer. It is luck and hardball politics mixed, in varying proportions. In 1997, for the progressives, it was mainly luck. The 1993 parliamentary election was the first one that included a five per cent electoral threshold for parties and an eight per cent threshold for coalitions. The hurdle – a significant modification of the PR electoral system first adopted in post-Second World War Germany[19] – eliminates all the candidates of parties that do not reach a certain level of support nationwide, distributing their mandates proportionally among the winners. The goal is to allow a formation of the more stable parliamentary majority. However, in 1993, it led to an indiscriminate purge

[18] Ludmiła Ananninkova, *Duda: Nie Da Się Być Prezydentem Wszystkich Polaków*, Gazeta Wyborcza, May 3, 2017.

[19] Kathleen Bawn, *The Logic of Institutional Preferences: German Electoral Law as a Social Choice Outcome*, 37 American Journal of Political Science 965 (1993).

of numerous conservative parties; as much as 34.5 per cent of votes were cast for various right-wing factions that did not meet the threshold. In effect, a coalition of two post-communist parties along with the Democratic Union and a smaller leftist group were able to pass the new basic law with a 90 per cent parliamentary majority, even though they represented only 53 per cent of the electorate.

But this did not mark the end of the progressives' luck. Abandoned by Jarosław Kaczyński and much of his conservative base, Lech Walesa lost his 1995 re-election bid to post-communist Aleksander Kwaśniewski. Kwaśniewski – a young and polished avowed agnostic – was a perfect partner for Geremek in designing a progressive constitution and signing it into law.

However, we should not underestimate the hardball aspect here. Most importantly, the progressive constitutional coalition chose to essentially ignore the vast, conservative swaths of the Solidarity movement that became deprived of parliamentary representation because of the electoral threshold. Incidentally, Solidarity itself very quickly began to re-integrate Balkanised right-wing fractions, presenting a comprehensive conservative constitutional counter-proposal. This proposal was never given a serious hearing by the 1993–97 Parliament, which passed its own version of the basic law in April 1997. Less than half a year later, Solidarity prevailed over the post-communists in the general election.

Another hardball tactic used by the progressives was their insistence that no turnout requirement was needed for the referendum to be valid. The argument here was bizarre, as the provisional Constitution passed in 1992 provided for a general requirement of 50 per cent in order for any referendum to be binding. As Ackerman rightly points out, the logic of why a *constitutional* referendum should have less stringent turnout requirements than an ordinary referendum is difficult to comprehend. The turnout in the 1997 referendum ended up being just 43 per cent. Fifty three per cent of those voting supported the Constitution – precisely the same support that the progressive parties forming the constitutional coalition received in the general election three and a half years earlier. Still, it was clear whose feelings about the document were stronger. Among 31 districts where turnout was below average, only five voted against the Constitution. Among 18 districts where the turnout was above average, the constitution lost in 11.

The current, conservative constitutional revolution is also built on a fair amount of luck. In 2015, the conservatives got their payback for the 1993 debacle – two leftist parties failed to meet the ill-fated electoral threshold, wasting 15 per cent of the votes and giving Jarosław Kaczyński's absolute majority of parliamentary seats with merely 37.5 per cent of the actual popular support. In addition, the presidential and parliamentary ballots both took place in 2015 – a rare occurrence given the four-year parliamentary term and a five-year presidential mandate. The surprising victory of Andrzej Duda, a young and energetic conservative handpicked by Jarosław Kaczyński, challenging a tired liberal Catholic incumbent, created a momentum that helped Law and Justice in the later general election. Finally, just around the turn of parliamentary terms, five out of 15 Constitutional Tribunal judges were set to retire.

This should not distract our attention from the truly breathtaking level of lawlessness that President Duda, and the Law and Justice party, are guilty of in using those fortuitous circumstances to radically change Poland's constitutional system. Key to their strategy has been the complete takeover of the Constitutional Tribunal.[20] By introducing long, nine-year terms of the 15 Tribunal judges, the 1997 Constitution clearly intended to prevent a single election winner to abruptly alter the Tribunal's composition. In the first two years of its parliamentary term (2015–17), Law and Justice was widely viewed as entitled to appoint five new judges. Through a combination of sometimes grotesque manoeuvres, considered illegal both by local legal authorities and the international community,[21] it ended up filling nine seats, including that of the chief judge.[22] Incredibly, three other holdover liberal judges have been barred from hearing cases by the Law and Justice-appointed chief judge based on the purported doubts about the procedural correctness of their 2011 appointment.[23] This politically plaint Constitutional Tribunal is now being used to radically re-interpret the 1997 Constitution and to allow Law and Justice to purge all independent institutions of progressive incumbents.[24]

V. Constitutional Ethics in a Polarised Society

Against this background, Ackerman makes two important observations. First, constitutional revolutionaries like Walesa need to act fast. Fortuitous circumstances to 'constitutionalize the high-energy politics of [Solidarity] commitment'[25] were, in his view, extremely short-lived. Second, the prospect of the presidential system, agreed upon at the Round Table Talks with the communists, was the main reason why the desired fast-paced constitutional development failed to take off. Presidentialism was detrimental specifically because it slowed things down.

Ackerman expresses hope that if future revolutionaries understand these two lessons from Poland's tragedy, they will be led 'toward more constructive constitutional options'.[26] I hope that my earlier analysis sets the stage for a crucial

[20] For a recent overview, see Kriszta Kovacs & Kim Lane Scheppele, *The Fragility of an Independent Judiciary: Lessons from Hungary and Polandeand the European Union*, 51 Communist and Post-Communist Studies 189 (2018).

[21] Maciej Kisilowski, *Poland's Democracy Is Crumbling*, Politico, December 24, 2015; Bruce Ackerman & Maciej Kisilowski, *Obama Is Poland's Only Hope*, Foreign Policy, January 21, 2016; European Commission for Democracy Through Law, Opinion of March 11-12 on Amendemnts to the Act of 25 June 2015 on the Constitutional Tribunal of Poland (March 11, 2016).

[22] Maciej Kisilowski, *Poland: A Country without a Constitution*, EU Observer, January 6, 2017.

[23] *Prof. Marek Zubik Apeluje Do Przyłębskiej O Szybkie Rozpatrzenie Jego Sprawy*, Onet.pl, July 15, 2018.

[24] Maciej Kisilowski, *Poland: Authoritarian Not Patriotic*, Politico, November 28, 2017.

[25] Ackerman, *supra* note 1 at 298.

[26] *Id.* at 258.

rejoinder: 'More constructive for what?' If, in Polarised Societies, constitutions are used by either Group A or B against their ideological enemies, is our role as constitutional scholars to help one of the sides stack the deck more effectively? Or should we try to help escape the political-economic Catch-22 described so far and facilitate a pan-tribal settlement that both groups can accept, or at least live with?

Ackerman decidedly supports the second option – his explicit goal is to develop pathways to 'the construction of a constitution that the overwhelming majority would [embrace]'.[27] But is this such an ethically obvious choice? Imagine you are a progressive constitutional drafter in a Polarised Society. By definition, the fundamental values of your conservative compatriots are not only foreign to you, they deeply terrify you. Furthermore, imagine that, like Michnik, Mazowiecki and Geremek in the 1990s, you see the triumph of progressive values as an inevitable historical trend; the liberal end of history seems truly in sight. Even if Ackerman is right and, by moving fast, you can use the post-revolutionary momentum to hammer out some deal with the conservatives, should you really do so? Such a compromise constitution may petrify a lot of morally questionable arrangements. With every passing year, the carrot of joining the EU combined with the expected global normalisation of progressive values will make your job of spurring a progressive constitutional opportunity easier. In addition, after months of Round Table talks with young communist reformers, you may recognise that – awful as it sounds – they are soon likely to become better progressive Europeans than your fellow Solidarity dissidents of a nationalist bent.

To make the ethical dilemma of a constitutional compromise even more concrete, perhaps we should add a few more words about the conservatives in our story. Walesa, who, as we discussed, was not right-wing enough for Poland's conservatives, re-appeared in international headlines as recently as 2013 with a suggestion that, in the Parliament, 'homosexuals should sit behind a wall, and not somewhere at the front. They must know they are a minority and adapt themselves to lesser things'.[28] On the campaign trail before the 2015 parliamentary election, Jarosław Kaczyński tried very hard to convince his support base that 'migrants have already brought diseases like cholera and dysentery to Europe, as well as all sorts of parasites and protozoa'.[29] During the run-up to the 1997 constitutional referendum, the conference of Polish Catholic bishops let their faithful know that the enacted document 'raises serious moral doubts', among other things because it opened a possibility for raped women to legally receive abortions (abortion was already illegal in almost all other cases).[30] The Preamble, meticulously drafted by Mazowiecki to emphasise the equal rights of 'both those who believe in God as the

[27] *Id.* at 298.

[28] *Lech Walesa Accused of Hate Speech after Gay Rights Criticism*, The Guardian, March 3, 2013.

[29] Jan Cieński, *Migrants Carry 'Parasites and Protozoa,' Warns Polish Opposition Leader*, Politico, October 14, 2015.

[30] *Konkordat, Konstytucja, Wierzący Obywatele*, Gazeta Wyborcza, May 5, 1997.

source of truth, justice, good and beauty, as well as those not sharing such faith', was denounced by the Polish Catholic primate as 'equating God and non-God'.[31]

The Polarised Society is not merely an academic concept; it is a tortuous moral reality of sharing a country with people whose values you find deeply unsettling. It is worth re-emphasising that the feeling is mutual, and so surely was the strategy of buying time. It is remarkable how confident conservatives like Kaczyński were about Poland's ability to challenge Europe's liberal consensus.[32] History proved them right: the strict conditionality imposed by the EU as part of Poland's accession process ended as soon as the country joined the EU. As we now realise, the EU has almost no legal means to influence policy choices of authoritarian, nationalist and religiously fundamentalist governments of already admitted Member States.[33] Last but not least, the conservatives could have counted on the vast increase of influence of the Catholic Church after it was freed from the constraints imposed upon it by the communists. As early as 1991, Poland introduced universal religious training in all public schools. The Polish pope was still full of energy and able to inspire new generations of the faithful. As we know, on balance, the historical dynamics ended up initially favouring progressives, but both sides had reasons to look to the future with some optimism. Most importantly, if constitutional opportunity always involves luck – a chance event – then (to use a concept borrowed from modern finance) there always exists an 'option value of waiting'.

Indeed, as I have already mentioned earlier, using rational choice or game theory terminology of deals and pay-offs obscures the moral urgency of the choices in Polarised Societies. For the conservatives, defending their values was not a 'deal', but a heroic battle against godless evil. Solidarity's official declaration before the 1997 referendum compared the campaign against the new Constitution to the 1920 defence of Warsaw against the Bolsheviks – a battle that, in right-wing historiography, was won by Poles owing to the divine intervention of the Virgin Mary.[34] Progressives likewise felt like they had a real chance, perhaps for the first time in Poland's history, to trigger the final Westward civilisational leap, broaden protection of essential human rights and force the regressive camp, quite literally, into extinction. Adam Michnik admits this in the passage quoted earlier in this chapter when he describes the Walesa's election as a choice of whether Poland will be 'on the path to Europe'. Everything pales into comparison with such moral and historical imperatives, including Ackerman's quest for an 'enduring Constitution'.[35]

[31] Jan Turnau, *Prawica, Kościół, Pan Bóg*, GAZETA WYBORCZA, April 29, 1997.

[32] In 2005, in a speech in the Polish branch of the Open Society Foundation, Kaczyński mentioned the 'far-reaching and hasty European integration' as one of Poland's key 'challenges'. 'We want to respond to these challenges because we want the existence of the Polish nation to continue'; Jarosław Kaczyński, O Naprawie Rzeczypospolitej ['on Repairing the Republic'], Lecture, Batory Foundation (February 14, 2005).

[33] Kovacs & Scheppele, *supra* note 20; Maciej Kisilowski, *In Defense of a Multispeed Europe*, POLITICO, March 24, 2017.

[34] Mikołaj Lizut, *Krzaklewski, Bolszewicy I Opatrzność*, GAZETA WYBORCZA, April 24, 1997.

[35] ACKERMAN, *supra* note 1 at 296.

It comes as no surprise that Ackerman's harsh evaluation of the 1990–97 constitutional development as a 'disastrous experience'[36] is worlds apart from the absolutely standard self-congratulatory narrative of Polish constitutional lawyers. Both Ackerman and Polish constitutionalists have access to the same facts, but they simply evaluate them against radically different yardsticks. Ackerman's objective is a constitution that forms a 'collective memory'[37] of the divided nation. The goal of Polish legal elites has always been the forced enlightenment of the 'other Poles'.[38]

VI. Avoiding the Authoritarian Equilibrium

The real threat in Polarised Society is that democracy itself, even in its thinnest electoral form, is no longer a stable equilibrium.[39] Both Groups A and B look at a constitution as the only effective tool to marginalise and eventually eliminate the deplorable other group. But both are also aware that even constitutional norms can be changed when a constitutional opportunity emerges. When the hardball techniques of constitutional revolution become increasingly shameless, constitutionalisation of a group's policy preferences no longer offers much. Group A can reasonably expect that Group B, upon assuming office, will proceed with (formal or informal) constitutional changes just as it would change undesirable ordinary legislation. At that point, the only alternative for Group A is to use the next constitutional opportunity to introduce an authoritarian form of government that will all but prevent Group B from competing for power.

That authoritarian threat is perhaps the best argument why constitutionalists should continue to search for constitutional pathways that go beyond reinforcing Group A's or Group B's ideological agenda in Polarised Societies. But even against the backdrop of authoritarianism, the above-mentioned ethical dilemmas must be taken seriously. To be blunt, in a Polarised Society, it should not be taken for granted that the preservation of democracy is *necessarily* more important

[36] *Id.*

[37] *Id.* at 295.

[38] A telling example here is a 2004 commentary of Piotr Winczorek, the Chairman of the Committee of Experts of the Constitutional Commission of the 1993–97 Parliament and – before 1989 – an active member of one of the Communist Party's satellite factions (*id.* at 252). Written in Poland's major daily merely six weeks after the country's accession to the EU and reprinted in 2006 as the introductory chapter of the author-approved collection of his most important essays, it responds to Jarosław Kaczyński's early calls for a constitutional reform. Winczorek does not even attempt to engage with what he calls 'the political-ideological' critics of the Constitution, bluntly admitting that 'it is doubtful that [they] can be presented with arguments that, for them, will be more convincing than their own'. Instead, as his very first argument, Winczorek offers that 'after joining the European Union, the freedom to shape our constitutional system is relatively constrained'; Piotr Winczorek, Polska Pod Rządami Konstytucji Z 1997 Roku 14 (2006). Exactly like in Michnik's essay quoted at the beginning of the chapter, Winczorek treats 'Europe' in general, and the EU in particular, as both the destination point for Poland's constitutional development and the pressure lever that would ensure a grudging acceptance of the basic law by the conservatives.

[39] Compare Alvin Rabushka & Kenneth A Shepsle, Politics in Plural Societies (1972).

for members of Groups A and B than advancing their worldview. Imagine that President Bernard Sanders declares martial law and indefinitely suspends elections in order to complete a programme of massive wealth redistribution, building a European-style safety net and ending the mass incarceration of African Americans. Are we absolutely sure that an overwhelming majority of American progressives would fight 'their' president in defence of the current version of American constitutional democracy? Perhaps,[40] but the closeness of that call should motivate constitutional democrats to, above all, think about constitutional models that would make democracy attractive in the realities of Polarised Society. If we are to ask a Kaczyński supporter to stand against conservative authoritarianism, he or she (most likely he)[41] needs to be given a democratic alternative that is significantly more enticing than the 1997 Constitution.

Here is where I disagree with Ackerman most strongly. In his chapters, he uses French and Italian constitutional history as proof that when the process is right, the 'ideological splits between Christian nationalist and secular liberals' can be 'hammer[ed] out'.[42] The comparison to constitutions developed in the 1940s and 1950s misses a key variable. Owing in large part to thinkers like Ackerman himself, the progressive cause has advanced tremendously since the mid-twentieth century, while conservatives have changed only a little or not at all. The French Fourth Republic could have its major crisis over public aid to parochial schools[43] because postulates such as true gender equality, including workplace equality and the eradication of sexual violence, full human rights for the LGBT community and genuine racial justice were by and large not even on the table. Today, they form a standard platform of the progressive movement. In the upcoming 2020 presidential election in Poland, Andrzej Duda's major contenders will likely include Robert Biedroń, a popular openly gay former mayor of a city of Słupsk in northwestern Poland.[44] In Polarised Societies, Groups A and B are much further from each other today than was the case 70 years ago.[45]

VII. Presidential and Parliamentary Polarised Republics

Ackerman is certainly right that an early commitment to presidentialism in a post-revolutionary environment leads to an immediate crystallisation of the warring

[40] But see David M. Faris, It's Time to Fight Dirty: How Democrats Can Build a Lasting Majority in American Politics (2018).

[41] In 2015, the gender differences were notable but not huge. A total of 56 per cent of men supported Andrzej Duda, compared to 50.1 per cent of women; Dorota Kowalska, *Wyniki Wyborów 2015: Jak Rozłożyły Się Głosy Ze Względu Na Płeć*, Głos Wielkopolski, May 25, 2015. A total of 54 per cent supported PiS and smaller nationalist or populist parties, compared to 47 per cent of women; Marcin Danielewski, *Wybory 2015: Pis Zwycięstwo Totalne*, Gazeta Wyborcza, October 25, 2015.

[42] Ackerman, *supra* note 1 at 294.

[43] *Id.* at 182.

[44] Claudia Ciobanu, *Gay Polish Mayor Becomes Opposition Icon*, Politico, May 10, 2016.

[45] As is often the case, the most definite data confirming that intuition comes from the US; see Pew Research Center, The Partisan Divide on Political Values Grows Even Wider (October 5, 2017).

ideological camps. We can argue, along with the classic argument of Juan Linz,[46] that the presidential system makes the already tense reality of a Polarised Society even more unbearable. There is only one president, who invariably emerges as a standard bearer of either Group A or B. If the leader of Group A emerges victorious, every symbolic trapping of the presidency – solemn inauguration, official honours, military salutes, the very title of the 'head of state' – add to the spectacle of Group B's humiliation. The president's fixed term and strong re-election prospect take away hope for a quick change in the unbearable status quo. And the significant prerogatives of a president, combined with an outsized sense of legitimacy stemming from a popular mandate, make the holder of the office prone to continuously reinforcing the sense of utter worthlessness and exclusion among members of the defeated group.

Worse yet, all these real and symbolic consequences of holding the presidency are known in advance for the leaders of both groups. This is why ceding the presidency is so difficult, even in the context of a broader constitutional deal. In Poland in 1990, the real surprise was not that Walesa decided to run for office, but that Mazowiecki chose to challenge Solidarity's unquestioned leader. The quote from Michnik offered at the beginning tells you why. For the Solidarity liberals, it seemed inconceivable that a progressive 'European' Poland can emerge under a conservative Walesa presidency. That these fears proved ill-founded – Walesa ended up not being as conservative as expected, and progressives did, until 2015, win the day – is even more telling, for it shows us that a presidential system evokes an *exaggerated* sense of fatalism in both Groups A and B.

Yet Poland's history of the last 20 years should make us cautious about putting the blame entirely on presidentialism.[47] The 1997 Constitution seriously weakened the presidency and strengthened the prime minister along the lines of Ackerman's favourite constrained parliamentarism.[48] The symbolic break with the Gaullist model took place on 23 October 2005. On that day, Lech Kaczyński defeated liberal Donald Tusk in the presidential election to succeed post-communist Aleksander Kwaśniewski (initially elected, we may recall, in the pre-1997 Gaullist set-up). Remarkably, the next day, Tusk showed up to work in Poland's parliament as if nothing had happened. He went on to become a highly successful prime minister two years later and then the president, but of the European Council. Speaking about the Polish presidency, Tusk derisively called a holder of that office 'the protector of the chandelier'[49] – the term that became part of Warsaw's standard political jargon. Since 2005, no top leader of either political bloc has occupied the presidency. Both formal competences and the symbolic allure of the office have been dismantled.

[46] Juan J. Linz, *The Perils of Presidentialism*, 1 Journal of Democracy 51 (1990).

[47] My arguments here are similar in spirit to those in Scott Mainwaring & Matthew S. Shugart, *Juan Linz, Presidentialism, and Democracy: A Critical Appraisal*, 44 Comparative Politics 449 (1997.

[48] Bruce Ackerman, *The New Separation of Powers*, 113 Harv. L. Rev. 633 (2000).

[49] *Nałęcz Odgryza Się Tuskowi*, TVN24, March 9, 2015.

And yet the political polarisation has only become more pronounced. Yes, major parties must normally enter into coalitions with smaller fractions, which often try to find a niche with the message of 'ending the Polish-Polish war'. Yes, the parliamentary electoral campaigns are slightly less obsessed with personifying the progressive-conservative divide in two warring candidates, but the fundamental problem remains: the national winner still takes is all.

Indeed, it is clear the last remnant of the Gaullist model – the popular election of the (now weak) president – has played an important role in *stabilising* the 1997 Constitution. Since presidential approval is needed for a constitutional change and especially for a constitutional revolution that does not involve a formal amendment, independent presidential and parliamentary elections have become one of the most important reasons why a conservative constitutional opportunity emerged only in 2015. Without Aleksander Kwaśniewski in the presidential palace, the right's parliamentary victory just half a year after the enactment of the 1997 Constitution would have likely led to attempts to revise or at least weaken the document that the conservatives despised. Likewise, the electoral victory of the liberals two years into Lech Kaczyński's presidency closed off any option for him to go down the path of a conservative constitutional revolution.

I would be very cautious, to be sure, of treating this blocking function of (weak) post-1997 presidentialism as a 'constitutional benefit'. The key dilemma here is again our ultimate objective. The blocking power of Group A's president is advantageous *to that group*, assuming of course the country is currently governed by Group A's constitution. For a progressive constitutional scholar, it is surely difficult to despair about Poland's regressive forces being unable to impact the 1997 Constitution for nearly two decades. But if we are serious about the Ackermanian constitutional ambition (as I have argued we should), we must admit that entrenching Group A's constitution does nothing to ensure the acceptance of the constitutional settlement by Group B.

VIII. The Overlooked Solution

The appreciation of the independent, causal role that comparative constitutional thought plays in affecting post-revolutionary constitutional developments is one of Ackerman's most insightful observations in his book. The Polish case indeed suggests that in a post-revolutionary setting, constitutional development is not a purely technical exercise of designing rational rules of the game from an open-ended palette of institutional options.

This is perfectly rational. The effectiveness of constitutional arrangements cannot be tested *ex ante*. The stakes are high. The players involved, including local legal elites, must thereby have a sense that the solution on the table is 'serious', which means that it must be perceived as a success in some other countries and also backed by coherent legal and moral theory endorsed by international authority figures. In Poland in 1989, Ackerman rightly observes that the French Gaullist model gained this aura of intellectual seriousness. By 1997, German constrained parliamentarism was quickly catching up in this influence game.

From this perspective, it is unfortunate that Poland's Polarised Society could draw so little inspiration from what is clearly the most effective and tested constitutional solution to managing national diversity: federalism. Like no other real-life constitutional model, federalism holds a promise of dealing with the key underlying problems that tear countries like Poland apart, namely the combination of the winner-takes-all political competition and the prevalence of unsolvable moral and ideological identity clashes.

The pros and cons of federalism are widely discussed, though mostly in the context of two distinct types of circumstances.[50] On the one hand, federation seems to be an attractive option for countries formed through a merger of pre-existing political units. The classic case of this 'coming-together federalism'[51] is the US, but this framework has also been applied to the development of the EU.[52] On the other hand, federalism has been offered as a 'post-conflict' solution for 'plural' or 'divided' societies. This second 'holding-together federalism' may at first glance seem almost synonymous with my preceding analysis in this chapter, yet there is one fundamental difference. The post-conflict literature has widely adopted the definition of a plural society that focuses on '*objective* social differentiation',[53] in particular 'linguistic, ethnic, religious, or cultural conflict'.[54] Special attention is paid to those types of objective differentiation that have already led to violence or secession attempts.

Neither approach explicitly excludes the possibility of federalism in countries like Poland, which does not have a strong tradition of regionalism and is among the world's most ethnically, religiously and linguistically homogeneous nations. As a matter of logic, federalism's success in managing ethnic, religious and linguistic differences, or situations when regional sovereignty pre dates that of the nation, cannot possibly be the basis of an argument *against* the use of the same model in managing other types of politically relevant cleavages. And yet this tacit assumption about the certain uniqueness of 'federalist circumstances' is widespread.

[50] Sujit Choudhry & Hume Natham, *Federalism, Devolution and Secession: From Classical to Post-Conflict Federalism*, *in* Comparative Constitutional Law 356 (Tom Ginsburg & Rosalind Dixon eds., 2011).

[51] Alfred Stepan, *Federalism and Democracy: Beyond the US Model*, 10 Journal of Democracy 19 (1999).

[52] Kalypso Nicolaidis & Robert Howse, The Federal Vision: Legitimacy and Levels of Governance in the United States and the European Union (2001).

[53] Arend Lijphart, Democracy in Plural Societies: A Comparative Exploration 3, 5 (1977) (emphasis added); quoting Harry Eckstein, Division and Cohesion in Democracy: A Study of Norway (1966).

[54] Sujit Choudhry, *Bridging Comparative Politics and Comparative Constitutional Law: Constitutional Design in Divided Societies*, *in* Constitutional Design for Divided Societies: Integration or Accommodation? 3 (Sujit Choudhry ed., 2008).

Figure 17.1 The territorial dimension of Poland's political polarisation

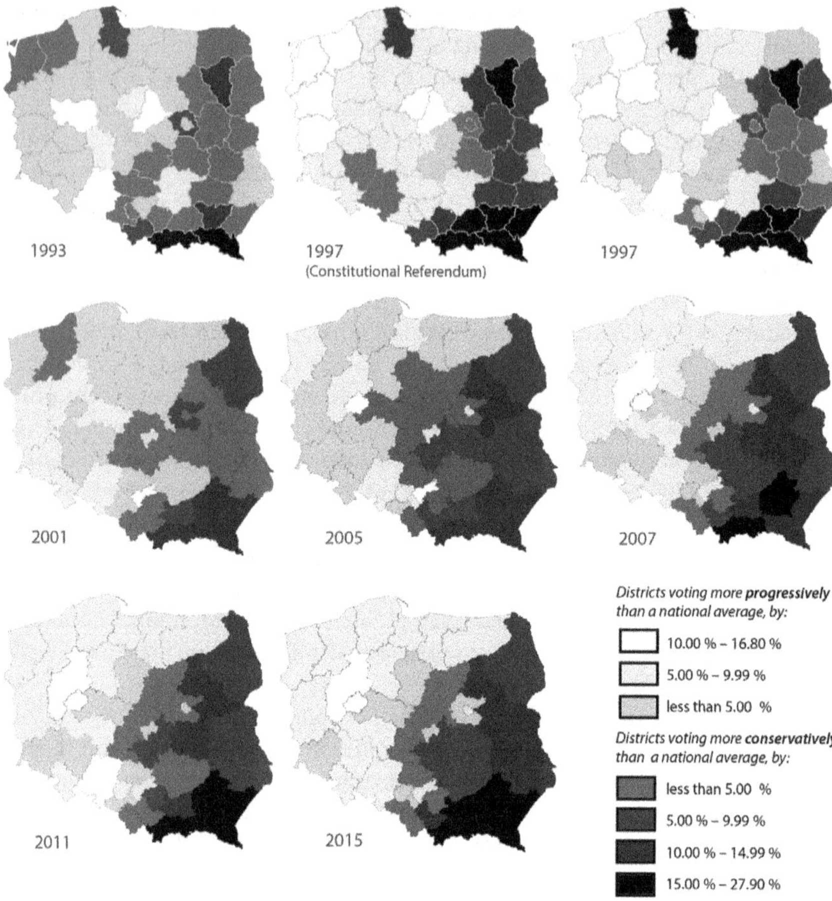

Source: Results of 1993–2015 parliamentary elections and the 1997 constitutional referendum.

Why? Both above-mentioned trends in the literature, I would argue, focus on federalism as a *centralisation* doctrine – the fact made evident by the American practice of calling the *opponents* of a strong central government 'anti-federalists'. Federalism is understood as a vehicle for bringing together communities that used to live separately or that are clearly on their way to such separation. In both cases, the goal of federalism is to avert a national break-up – to make political power *more* centralised compared to the next available alternative.

Neither in the early 1990s nor now is Poland on the verge of breaking up. The most staunchly conservative Pole would choose the rule of Donald Tusk over that of Vladimir Putin, while even a diehard progressive will prefer Jarosław Kaczyński over Angela Merkel. And yet, a careful look at the last 30 years of Poland's democracy demonstrates a significant territorial dimension to the country's political polarisation. Figure 17.1 presents voting patterns in seven parliamentary elections between 1993 and 2015 as well as in the 1997 constitutional referendum. Darker shades represent districts where conservative parties – or the vote against the Constitution – fared better than the national average. Lighter shades depict stronger support for progressive parties or the Constitution.

The results are notable. Poland, a country with no recent democratic tradition, undergoing a host of fast-paced social, economic and political transformations, had every reason to exhibit wildly volatile distribution of voters' preferences. As already mentioned, the legacies of the communist past further complicated ideological fault lines. And yet Figure 17.1 shows us that, with all those confounding factors, southeast Poland has been notably, consistently and perhaps growingly more conservative than the northwest Poland. The regional differences are not only stable but also tend to be rather sizeable; for instance, the 1997 Constitution won 65 per cent of support in the Westernmost Lubuskie region and only 27 per cent in southeastern Podkarpackie.

Polish post-revolutionary leaders would have been lucky if the federalist thinking had developed more as a *decentralisation* doctrine – as a way to constitutionalize a partial devolution of central government's power and legitimacy. Such an alternative understanding of federalism was brilliantly illustrated by Akhil Amar at a 1990 conference on Eastern Europe's democratic transitions. 'Just as competition among firms protects consumers from monopolistic exploitation', Amar pointed out, 'so too a healthy competition between federal and local officials can help protect against government tyranny'[55] – a tyranny of a government captured by either Group A or B, I might add.

We can only imagine how potent that free market analogy could have been for the Solidarity leaders in late 1980s. Just as the break with the discredited centrally planned economy was needed to bring economic prosperity, so too the swift departure from the grotesquely inefficient 'democratic centralism' of the People's Republic could have formed an attractive constitutional part of the Solidarity platform. If we want to understand why such ideas did not develop in Geremek's or Mazowiecki's heads, we do not need to look further than Amar's paper. Right after offering his perceptive analogy, Amar inexplicably ignores it and, falling back on the bringing/holding-together tracks, suggests that federalism was of relevance either for multi-ethnic states that were already federal under socialism (Czechoslovakia, Yugoslavia and the Soviet Union – all dissolved soon after) or for the further development of NATO and the EEC (soon to be renamed the EU). Taking his analogy seriously, should we also conclude that a competitive economy is suited only for a narrow category of ethnocultural circumstances?[56]

[55] Akhil Reed Amar, *Some New World Lessons for the Old World*, 58 U. Chi. L. Rev. 483, 498 (1991).

[56] *Id.* at 498. Amar goes even further and argues strenuously against treating federalism as a decentralisation strategy. The futility of this fight is again best seen through the prism of his own free market analogy. Certainly, the preservation of competitive markets often requires monopolies to be broken up.

IX. The Federalist Imagination

One of the most fascinating stories *not* included in Ackerman's chapters is that, already in 1981, a group of experts completely separate from Mazowiecki and Geremek developed an actual *plan* to decentralise the Polish state. The group was led by Jerzy Regulski, who in many ways was the opposite of Walesa's intellectual advisors. A Stalinist political prisoner in the late 1940s and, in the 1980s, an urban planning professor at the Polish Academic of Science, he had much less appetite for revolutionary philosophising and much more for substantive policy work. During the 1980s, he led a team of experts producing tens of detailed policy papers on how the local government could be implemented.[57]

When, in December 1988, Geremek invited Regulski to the Citizens' Committee that was being formed around Walesa, the latter was fully aware that 'local government was considered as entirely unimportant' by the leadership of Solidarity.[58] During the Committee's first meeting, Regulski announced the establishment of the working group on the topic; of the 120 members, only one person joined.[59] '[Geremek] did not quite get the purpose of the local government', Regulski recalled bluntly. 'He wanted to include me in the [Round Table] talks mostly because he knew that I have a fully developed program and that I can present concrete demands to the [communist side].'[60] Regulski's experts were merged into a section that also negotiated the future status of professional associations and non-governmental organisations. The Solidarity leadership did not even pick up the interest in the topic when the regime proved surprisingly adamant about keeping the local governments under party control. Unlike Walesa and Geremek, the communists clearly understood that local governance was much more than a technical, administrative issue.

The fall of the Iron Curtain rendered the Round Table agreement moot. In September 1989, Mazowiecki appointed Regulski as a cabinet's representative to organise local elections. 'You demand local government in Poland; build it', he reportedly said.[61] Ackerman discusses these elections in some detail; let me add a few additional bits of context. In merely eight months, Regulski – still with hardly any political clout within the Solidarity movement – managed to introduce sweeping reforms to Poland's 2,400 municipalities. These included transferring state property and administrative staff, delimitating governing powers, developing rules for everything from decision-making to financing, and organising the election of more than 50,000 local councillors – the first entirely democratic election in

[57] Jerzy Regulski, Reforma Samorządowa: Materiały Źródłowe 1980–1990 (2000).

[58] Video recording of the statement by Jerzy Regulski (June 14, 2014), http://senat.atmitv.pl/SenatConsole/TransmissionArchiveItem.go?code=8konfKSTAP1306141.

[59] According to Regulski, the one member who did join, Andrzej Celiński, told him 'he was curious what that "local government" is'; Jerzy Regulski, Życie Splecione Z Historią 391 (2015).

[60] *Id.* at 389.

[61] *Id.* at 471–72.

post-communist Poland. Municipal governments created by Regulski ended up being consistently the most trusted elected institutions of the Polish state.[62]

And yet, Regulski's team repeatedly chose to curtail their ambitions by refusing to implement, or even argue for, a decentralised governance beyond the level of small municipalities. Regulski reports that even before the start of the Round Table talks, his team was firmly *against* the establishment self-governing regions. His main stated reason concerned the administrative division of the country, which in 1975 was split by the party into a large number (49) of weak regions or 'voivodeships'.[63] This logistical challenge could have been overcome, for instance, by creating larger provinces made up of several voivodeships. But the true obstacle was clearly Regulski's lack of awareness that a federal model could even potentially be of relevance.

Professor Ackerman finishes his analysis with a counterfactual, asking us to imagine the fate of Solidarity's constitutional development without the early commitment to presidentialism. I would like to add to this counterfactual: imagine that constitutional thinkers of the 1970s and 1980s would have paid more attention to the essential role that federalism plays in successful constitutional democracies. Imagine, for instance, that the French–German constitutional distinction would have been primarily defined as that between a unitary and a federal state, as opposed to the standard focus on the presidency. Imagine that a myth of the supposed narrow applicability of federalism as a centralisation tool in bringing-or-holding-together situations would not have become part of international constitutional conventional wisdom.

Imagine, in short, that the Solidarity intellectuals had come to power keenly aware of the possibility of federalism. If Regulski, with a narrow group of experts, was able to almost singlehandedly introduce highly popular municipalities, then surely a committed Solidarity leadership could in the similar timeframe have added powerful self governing provinces to the mix. Many Solidarity leaders would have chosen to run for the provincial governorships instead of creating insignificant political parties in Warsaw. These powerful provincial leaders, supported by the new municipalities and perhaps by the 49 voivodeships that could have formed an intermediary governance level, would suddenly have had a real interest in constitutionalising the new settlement. The debate with so many stakeholders would have been long, but at least the eventual constitution would no longer have been hostage to the one-dimensional ideological polarisation. Indeed, it is highly likely that many, if not most, ideologically controversial issues would have simply been devolved to the provincial level again, especially if the negotiators had been aware of such a possibility.

[62] According to a long-running survey of trust in institutions, in 2018 65 per cent of Poles trusted their municipality government compared to 34 per cent who trusted the parliament. These figures are not that different from 2008 (68 per cent and 39 per cent, respectively), and in 1998 (61 per cent and 33 per cent); CBOS, O Nieufności I Zaufaniu (March 1, 2018).

[63] Jerzy Regulski, Local Government Reform in Poland: An Insider's Story (2003).

We should blame it all on political scientists. Their inability to see the coming (re-)emergence of regressive conservatism as a 'viable, systematic alternative to Western liberalism'[64] is just as embarrassing as their earlier failure to predict the end of the Soviet communism. We, lawyers, have a plausible excuse: we have not been given fair warning to develop tools for the brave new world. But we should at least acknowledge the urgency of catching up with the history that refuses to end. If my story about the breathtakingly successful Polish conservative constitutional insurgency sounds distant, let us imagine a 7:2 US Supreme Court majority made up of judges who only a decade ago were dismissed as 'radicals in robes'.[65] Given that perspective, much of what we have learnt about constitutional law may soon be all but irrelevant.

Ackerman's work introduces a highly effective comparative methodology for an accelerated process of constitutional innovation that is now much-needed in response to the new challenges. But even more impactful than Ackerman's methodology is his courage – the courage to highlight tragic shortcomings of a well-intentioned progressive constitutional project. Such intellectual courage will be essential to develop outside-the-box solutions to liberal democracy's growing crisis.

[64] Francis Fukuyama, *The End of History?*, 16 The National Interest 3, 1 (1989).

[65] Cass R. Sunstein, Radicals in Robes: Why Extreme Right-Wing Courts Are Wrong for America (2005).

18

Choosing to Have Had a Revolution

Lessons from South Africa's Undecided Constitutionalism

JAMES FOWKES

I. Introduction

History sometimes takes a long time to have happened. And like the earnest account of the child next to the inexplicably vanished cake, there is always the possibility that history can suddenly turn out to have happened differently.

In this first part of his planned trilogy, Bruce Ackerman encourages us to retell the history of a number of countries with the benefit of an account of constructive, revolutionary constitutionalism.[1] It is an aspirational exercise. It is aspirational in a general terminological way, seeking to displace the primacy of violence with which most people associate the term 'revolution'. It is also aspirational because, in many or all of these countries, Ackerman often seeks to stitch events together in ways they are not normally stitched.

Both things are true of the South African case, on which I have been asked to focus here. But in the South African case, Ackerman's account is aspirational in an additional way, one that raises important questions about his account and can serve to deepen our understanding of his project. Ackerman's account is aspirational in South Africa, not only in trying to tell a revolutionary story in a way that few South Africans currently would, but also, more basically, in trying to give a definite answer to what in South Africa remains a question. We do not yet know whether South Africa had a revolution, in the sense in which Ackerman describes.

To offer 'we don't yet know' as an answer can seem like the worst kind of academic cop-out, as well as an odd thing to say about events that began over a generation ago. But it is neither. Revolutionary constitutionalism is a theory of legitimacy, and legitimacy is about the stories a constitutional system tells about

[1] Bruce Ackerman, Revolution Constitutions: Charismatic Leadership and the Rule of Law (2019).

itself. Ackerman is, of course, correct that some societies simply lack the option of telling a revolutionary story about themselves to legitimate their constitutional project. A case like Japan in the late 1940s simply does not have the right kind of facts (and too many of the wrong kind) for a revolutionary story to get off the ground. But if a society does have the right kind of facts, is that determinative? If a constitution is produced in factually revolutionary conditions, and if it endures and succeeds, is it that constitution's destiny to be a revolutionarily legitimate constitution?

To see why it might not be destiny, consider England.[2] Although debates could be had, the factual basis for a revolutionary account of the events in England around 1688–89 is arguably present. But the English have not chosen to tell their story that way. The Glorious Revolution, despite its name, is usually remembered as a *restoration*, in which the existing system and its ancient values were preserved against the threat of James II, a would-be Louis XIV. As a result, Ackerman plans to tell a very non-revolutionary 'insider reform' story about English constitutional legitimacy in his later volumes. This is plausible – but plausible *despite* the presence of potentially revolutionary facts at the founding moment of the modern English constitution. Instead, it is plausible because of the story the English have subsequently chosen to tell about that moment, with Macaulay leading the way.

It is in this sense that describing the presence of revolutionary facts in South Africa in the late 1980s and early 1990s is such an aspirational exercise – a point made even stronger by the fact that it is one of Ackerman's youngest case studies, whose evolution through his stages remains incomplete. South Africans might indeed come to tell the kind of constructive revolutionary story that Ackerman urges. Plausible factual materials are undoubtedly present and such an account certainly has its attractions. If they do, Ackerman will have been right all along about how the history happened. But South Africans might also decide to tell different stories about those facts, including, as we will see, ones that are much closer to the other, alternative paradigms in Ackerman's picture. Revolutionary constitutionalism, to date, is a perfectly feasible story with significant fit and appeal that none of the key political and constitutional actors in South Africa have really adopted as their narrative – and need never adopt, especially as the years go by without it happening.

II. An Undecided Revolution: A Summary of the Argument

Since the aim here is to respond to Ackerman's account of the South African story rather than to tell that story myself, I start with a summary of my response and will

[2] See, eg, Steven Pincus, 1688: The First Modern Revolution (2009); Patrick Dillon, The Last Revolution: 1688 and the Creation of the Modern World (2016).

thereafter elaborate only on the parts of the story that response makes relevant. While Ackerman's account is not factually accurate in all respects, I approach it in the spirit of a difficult comparative law exercise where the interest lies in the broader ideas and perspectives it offers. I focus on these and on what the South African case might tell us about them.

To an extent, the stories South Africans tell about their constitution (to date) are those Ackerman's account would expect. When revolutionary legitimacy is invoked in South Africa, it is most likely to be in the service of the African National Congress (ANC) as the movement party of national liberation. The party understands itself to be the custodian of the National Democratic Revolution, which has not ended. It is the ANC's ongoing responsibility and source of authority. In ANC theory, and often also in ANC practice, the revolutionary movement party is primary, above state or constitution; if the constitution has revolutionary authority, it is only via the ANC's revolutionary authority.[3]

This Ackerman would see as normal during the first stages of his timetable of revolutionary constitutional development, when the movement party still takes primacy. He will simply await the shift of revolutionary legitimacy from party to constitution, or constitution-in-court. It is in connection with this forecast that the deeper questions arise.

The first deeper question is that, for a generation, defenders of the South African Constitution who have sought to establish its supremacy have most commonly done so by invoking things other than South Africa's revolutionary politics. This has much to do with the ANC's continuing dominance of the revolutionary narrative. To those seeking to establish the status of the Constitution as independent of the ANC and as an independent check on the party, it has seemed unwise to appeal to mass-mobilised authority while the ANC still wields it. Instead, these defenders have reached for arguments from history and morality that are often more normative than political: the Constitution has authority not because of its mass-mobilised origins but because it is good and repudiates a very bad past.[4]

The question this raises for Ackerman's account is simply this: what if this pattern does not change when the ANC movement party gets weaker? Ackerman's account will not be surprised that constitutional defenders' use of revolutionary argument is subdued while the movement party stays strong. But what if events continue and constitutional defenders still do not *try* to claim revolutionary authority for the constitution, and instead continue with their less political, more normative arguments? Even if South Africa has revolutionary facts and a case like Germany does not, what if South African constitutional defenders nonetheless

[3] See the key 2012 discussion document: African National Congress, The Second Transition (February 27, 2012), https://www.sahistory.org.za/archive/2012-anc-national-policy-conference-second-transition-building-national-democratic-society. The terminology 'second phase of the transition' was preferred, but the (long-standing) core logic was adopted; see African National Congress, A Second Phase, Not a Second Transition (July 2, 2012), https://www.politicsweb.co.za/documents/a-second-phase-not-a-second-transition--anc.

[4] A distinction emphasised during the conference by Alon Harel.

choose to make legitimacy arguments that look more like German ones? (As we will see, there are indeed some interesting resemblances in this regard between arguments in these two systems.) Ackerman himself, after all, at least at one time thought it preferable to have a constitution built on normative moral foundations like Germany rather than revolutionary authority that could potentially be invoked in all kinds of directions, as in the US.[5] So South Africans might, in the abstract, have good reasons to choose this route. But how much do they have a choice? Are revolutionary facts of such power and primacy that South African constitutional defenders will find themselves inescapably drawn to them once the movement party's primary grip on them fades? Ackerman's work in the US context makes space for the ongoing democratic agency that comes with a revolutionary constitution tradition. But does that agency extend to the choice of tradition itself?

This question sharpens in South Africa because of a second source of complexities. South Africa's founding facts are not straightforwardly about the mass-mobilised authority of a movement party. The ANC, at the crest of its revolutionary authority, chose to sit down and talk, and negotiate and make compromises. This has placed a lasting question mark over the claim that the South African Constitution speaks in the name of the ANC as the rightful voice of We the South African People. And this doubt manifests itself in the fact that Ackerman's other, non-revolutionary paradigms also have real purchase in the South African case and are locally invoked much more often than, to date, revolutionary constitutionalism is.

Ackerman is right that National Party (NP) political leaders tried the insider reform model during the 1980s and failed.[6] But insider reform fits much better if we focus not on those NP efforts, but on white leaders more broadly who gave up their monopoly on political power as the price for maintaining much of the social and economic position of the white community. His other paradigm, elite construction, also offers a promising fit once we understand the events of the early 1990s (as many do) as the response by several groups of leaders to sit down and work out a way forward in response to the crisis of the apartheid state. Nor should we forget that the paradigm of *violent* revolution, whose primacy Ackerman wants to challenge but that he naturally accepts exists, also has a strong presence in these years.

Those who invoke these other paradigms in South African practice today are largely doing so for negative purposes: to argue that the (righteously violent) revolution was betrayed by a negotiated constitution that was the work of political and/or economic elites serving their own interests. It is for this reason that, despite its store of constructive revolutionary facts, constitutional defenders in

[5] Bruce Ackerman, We the People, Volume 1: Foundations 15–16 (1993); see also his relieved comments on the failure of the Reagan revolution: Bruce Ackerman, We the People, Volume 2: Transformations 419–20 (1998).

[6] James Fowkes, Building the Constitution: The Practice of Constitutional Interpretation in Post-Apartheid South Africa 110–12 (2016) and the sources cited therein.

South Africa face the authenticity problem diagnosed by Ackerman in cases he sees as non-revolutionary, like Spain.[7] And this is a strong reason why constitutional defenders may continue to find it more prudent to defend the Constitution in more abstract terms. To use constructive revolutionary arguments would be to rest the Constitution on political foundations many have regarded as cracked from the beginning.

Of course, Ackerman's claim is not that revolutionary legitimacy arguments necessarily succeed. As such, his account will not be embarrassed merely because such arguments face some political obstacles in a given case. But the deeper challenge to his claims about South Africa arise for the same reasons that these other paradigms are so effective as criticisms in South Africa today. These non-revolutionary paradigms have real purchase because, during the Founding, these ideas were sometimes presented as *positive defences* of the constitution-drafting and its surrounding politics. In the late 1980s and early 1990s, whatever their other merits, revolutionary arguments were inflammatory things for the ANC to make. Ideas of negotiation and compromise and reaching out certainly had their critics, but they were strategically valuable and were a useful source of legitimacy arguments. This is why non-revolutionary arguments of this sort were, at the time, quite often a matter of *celebration*, presenting the idea of a peaceful multi-party transition as the central idea of the constitutional developments of those years and not mass mobilisation. In their rosiest hue, these were arguments for a national coming together. They might recall cases like Benin's National Conference of 1990 or perhaps the Colombian constitution-drafting of the following year, influential paradigms whose position in Ackerman's account to date is unclear. If this is a more local and participatory version of elite construction, for example, that paradigm may fit South Africa much better than cases of *externally imposed* elite construction constitutions such as Japan would make us think.

Therefore, the first two points come together. The currently muted status of constructive revolutionary arguments about the South African Constitution might only reflect that the country is still working its way through Ackerman's stages. But it might also reflect that constitutional defenders have often chosen, and may continue to choose, to rely on different, non-revolutionary arguments, for reasons that include the presence of other legitimacy paradigms in the South African case. These alternatives either contradict the revolutionary account or simply offer alternatives with their own basis in Founding-era fact.

This chapter's third point is to ask whether it is true that, the longer the constitutional constructive revolutionary argument lies in limbo in this way, the less likely it is that it will ultimately establish itself as the master legitimacy argument in a given system. Ackerman emphasises the parallel between South Africa and India, which is undoubtedly important. But by the time India had moved as many

[7] Ackerman, *supra* note 1 at 6–7, 18.

years from its Founding as South Africa has now moved from its own, India had been experiencing full-blown constitutional tussles for years, both within Congress and between the Congress government and the Supreme Court. It is in the context of that contest that Ackerman sees revolutionary authority transferring from the movement party to the constitution and the court. He is too quick to see the same dynamic in South Africa. Even today, South Africa has yet to experience a comparable constitutional conflict. Of course, it still might. But if it does not, revolutionary arguments that a contest might have kept alive may simply fade as the movement party does, without ever being transferred – especially because defenders, by that time, may have constructed the authority of the constitution and the court on some other basis, such as the idea that the court is the pro-poor defender of a social justice constitution. *This* parallel to how the Indian Supreme Court constructed its post-Emergency legitimacy using its Public Interest Litigation model, which Ackerman does not mention, might prove to be the real parallel to India.

In these three arguments, we see the real stakes of the question whether revolutionary facts are destiny or whether in subsequent telling, the constitutional history can turn out to have happened differently. I now turn to add some flesh to this skeleton.

A. South African Revolutions

In the late 1980s, the ANC leadership had to make a strategic choice. One choice was embodied in the People's War, a strategy of violence borrowed chiefly from the Vietnamese on which the ANC leadership had embarked in 1979.[8] The People's War was one major way in which South Africans living through this time understood the idea of revolution and experienced it, directly or indirectly. It was also a major way in which the rest of the world experienced it in relation to South Africa. What remained of the apartheid regime's international standing was severely damaged by its actions under the states of emergency declared by the Botha government in the second half of the 1980s. As a result, some of the deepest ideas about the South African case are rooted in these events. Their presence has much to do with the status of the subsequent negotiated transition as a 'miracle' and as 'peaceful' – for a transition that in reality killed thousands was miraculously peaceful only in comparison to the countrywide bloody conflict the People's War threatened to become. It is the reason why so many South Africans understand their history as a (violent) revolution that could have happened, but did not.

The ANC's other choice, at the end of the 1980s, was a peaceful negotiated strategy. At this time, while the ANC was still isolated in exile, the Mass Democratic Movement had firmly established itself within the country. The Movement was

[8] Anthea Jeffery, People's War: New Light on the Struggle for South Africa (2014).

a broad tent encompassing the painstakingly negotiated alliance of the Confederation of South African Trade Unions (COSATU), committed to non-racialism, non-sexism and democracy, and the broad anti-apartheid alliance of churches and other civil society groups known as the United Democratic Front (UDF).[9] The ANC's other option was to cement itself as the leader of this movement – some of whose members were also involved in the People's War – and direct it along a non-violent route to apartheid's demise. This would include drafting a constitution, and Ackerman emphasises this strand of the story accordingly. While internal party thinking about constitutionalism dated back to 1985, it was only in 1992, when serious negotiations with the NP government and other groups got under way, that the ANC began to articulate detailed, public constitutional proposals.[10] In the fact that the ANC's constitutional proposals mostly emerged in the context of negotiating and writing a constitution with others lie the roots of the indecision South Africans have felt ever since about what exactly their constitutionalism rests on and whether that foundation confers legitimacy or not. Much depends on how the negotiations are interpreted. I discuss three different perspectives, each in themselves incomplete, but each vital to build up an understanding of this point.

i. The Rainbow Nation: Constitutionalism as a National Coming Together

First of all, we might understand the decision to negotiate as a decision by the ANC to use its mass-mobilised power, not merely to write an inclusive constitution, but to underwrite an inclusive constitution-writing exercise. ANC statesmen, seeing that the only alternative to a bloody civil war was to find a way to live with the white minority, chose to include their oppressors in the design of a shared future, alongside representatives of other groups.

The rainbow nation interpretation takes the rosiest view of this decision as a national moment of coming together. This view had real if optimistic purchase in these years. Leaders in labour and big business contemplated a future of significantly collaborative planning, replacing the harsher confrontations of previous decades. This produced the National Economic Development and Labour Council (NEDLAC), a permanent bargaining forum for unions, industry and government to maintain and expand their 'social pact'.[11] In Archbishop Desmond Tutu's vision,

[9] Ackerman cites several of the key works, including the standard text, Jeremy Seekings, The UDF: A History of the United Democratic Front in South Africa (2000); see also Ineke van Kessel, 'Beyond Our Wildest Dreams': The United Democratic Front and the Transformation of South Africa (2000).

[10] The development of the ANC's constitutional thinking from 1985 is now being more carefully studied; see Heidi Brooks, *Merging Radical and Liberal Traditions: The Constitution Committee and the Development of Democratic Thought in the African National Congress, 1986–1990*, 44 J. of Afr. Stud. 167 (2018).

[11] Adam Habib, South Africa's Suspended Revolution: Hopes and Prospects 111–18 (2013).

all South Africans were damaged by apartheid, and a Truth and Reconciliation Commission (TRC) was needed to heal all by truth-telling, face-to-face meetings and forgiveness.[12] Mandela's nation-building, based on a message of inclusive citizenship, is famous. However, the foremost written statement of the idea may well be Thabo Mbeki's inclusive 'I am an African' speech, made to mark the Constitutional Assembly's vote in favour of their constitutional draft on 8 May 1996.[13]

All revolutionary moments fade, and the rainbow nation was always going to have the fleeting quality that rainbows do. However, its presence in the South African story matters because it was a crucial part of how leaders in these years presented to the nation what they were doing. They talked about the constitution as an exercise in national coming together and sometimes asserted its legitimacy in those terms. This is central to the moral statesmanship, embodied by Mandela, that the ANC claimed at the time. But, crucially, this also created an incentive to downplay the ANC's mass authority, as a matter of public presentation. Instead, the negotiations were sometimes framed as a coming together of different stakeholders to draft a text that would be acceptable to all – not as the ANC speaking for We the People of South Africa, on the strength of its extraordinary mass-mobilised following and Mandela's unmatched authority at the head of it, but as a coming together of various leaders who *collectively* spoke for We the *Peoples* of South Africa.

In actual fact, many of the earlier key decisions were really bilateral agreements between the ANC and the NP government rather than broader multilateral agreements. The ANC's mass authority also gave it more and more unilateral control of the drafting as time went by.[14] But given the fear of ANC majority power, mass-mobilised authority was a threatening thing for the ANC to invoke. Doing so was sometimes counter-productive in building the nation or securing constitutional agreement. The ANC therefore had incentives to sometimes acknowledge the authoritative authorship of other groups. The other political groupings themselves, of course, had even more incentives to talk in these terms – to support the fragile agreement and to rise to meet the extraordinary moment, but also to tell their nervous supporters that they were doing the utmost to secure their future interests.

As mentioned above, we might understand this using something like Benin's National Conference as an alternative paradigm: a national coming together of different groups committed to working together on a new constitution in order to avoid slipping back into violence (in Benin's case, its history of military rule).[15]

[12] Desmond Tutu, No Future without Forgiveness: A Personal Overview of South Africa's Truth and Reconciliation Commission (2012).

[13] Thabo Mbeki, *Statement of Deputy President TM Mbeki, on behalf of the ANC, on the occasion of the adoption by the Constitutional Assembly of The Republic of South Africa Constitution Bill 1996*, May 8, 1996.

[14] The standard texts are Hassan Ebrahim, The Soul of a Nation: Constitution-Making in South Africa (1999); Richard Spitz with Matthew Chaskalson, The Politics of Transition: A Hidden History of South Africa's Negotiated Settlement (2000).

[15] See, eg, Babacar Kante, *Models of Constitutional Jurisdiction in Francophone West Africa*, 3 J. of Comp. L. 158 (2008); Bruce A. Magnusson, *Democratization and Domestic Insecurity: Navigating the Transition in Benin*, 33 Comp. Politics 211 (2011).

Seen in that way, this aspect of the South African case might fit Ackerman's elite construction paradigm as much as his constructive revolutionary one. Alternatively, we might defend the revolutionary understanding by seeing the ANC's collaborative moves as one inclusive way in which revolutionary authority could be used (as Indian Congress leaders also attempted to use it). In that case, this coming-together image matters not because it is descriptively inconsistent with the constructive revolutionary account, but because it has made it harder to make revolutionary arguments in South Africa subsequently. The bid to erect the Constitution on a broader base meant that some of its foundations, from the beginning, were rested on something other than the ANC's mass-mobilised support. This has made it harder to tell a mass-mobilisation story thereafter.

It also became a potential liability when the joint enterprise, which was never very solid to begin with, began to crumble, as it did even before the 1996 Constitution came into force. NEDLAC's cooperative intent soon collapsed and divisions rehardened.[16] Other areas in which power-sharing had been planned fell apart even quicker. The NP, claiming that the ANC had marginalised it in the Government of National Unity, walked out in 1996 – not as planned, as Ackerman argues,[17] but three years before the negotiated arrangement was supposed to expire at the 1999 elections. The TRC's achievements were not negligible, but they rapidly faded. White people were angered to discover that the past was not forgiven or forgotten – and black people that white people expected it to be. Mbeki, taking over as ANC leader, was among those deliberately shifting to a less conciliatory stance – to some, a cynical removal of the conciliatory mask once the transfer of power was done.

ii. The Strategic Democrat: Constitutionalism as a Means to Power

From this second perspective, the decision to negotiate came from ANC strategists more than moral saints, which threatens to relegate the Constitution to the status of a means at the end of a chain of strategic logic. To end apartheid, went the argument, ANC military options were honourable, but would not be effective anytime soon, if at all, and it was better to avoid bloodshed in any case. A negotiated solution was therefore the way forward. This meant not directing revolutionary violence against white people (a large concession for many), it meant talking to the apartheid regime (another large concession) and offering guarantees to that regime and to the white population more generally (yet another). At this point, and in this context, the Constitution entered the strategic picture and here began its association with what had to be conceded in order for the ANC to get into power.

Part of this association is a product of political talk from other political groups. Seeking to bolster their own credibility with constituencies nervous of being sold

[16] Habib, *supra* note 11 at 118–37.

[17] Ackerman, *supra* note 1 at 101.

out, those negotiating with the ANC had strong incentives to tell their supporters they were driving a hard bargain. The inevitable ANC rebuttals, to *their* supporters, served to reinforce the impression of a contentious deal with winners and losers. The rosier view of the process as an exercise in giving something to all sides also strengthened the impression of a deal; as the rainbow faded, it was merely perceptions of the quality of that deal that changed. Minority groups expressed anger that their leaders had not obtained greater concessions. De Klerk, who had led the NP into the negotiations, was sometimes called *volksveraaier*, a traitor to his people. And some of those with whom ANC leaders had negotiated came to feel that they had been used and were treated as expendable now that the transfer of power was irreversible.[18]

If we associate the rainbow interpretation with Mandela, this more cynical, strategic interpretation is most often associated with Mbeki. Mbeki sometimes alarmed his ANC colleagues during negotiations with his willingness to make concessions.[19] But he often did not see the terms of the constitutional bargain as the crucial issue; what mattered was getting the ANC into power. This did mean that the constitution had to tick certain boxes. It had to satisfy basic post-Cold War ideas of constitutional legitimacy, establish the parts of a functioning democratic state and – very crucially – not unduly hamstring the legitimate democratic authority of the ANC once it got into power. But otherwise, the precise terms of the deal mattered far less than getting it signed and done, and getting into power.

We should not mistake this for blunt constitutional instrumentalism. Mbeki certainly understood the ongoing importance of constitutionalism to the ANC government's legitimacy.[20] Instead, we should understand this in terms of the very familiar tension between democracy and constitutionalism, with a locally South African twist. Here is how.

Ackerman is right to reject the insider reform of the British nineteenth century as a paradigm for the 1996 Constitution, but other aspects of the British model have had a bigger impact. Before 1994, South Africa's constitutionalism was strong-form parliamentary supremacy, including the firmly limited judicial power of the Westminster system. This was combined – the local South African twist – with a strong sense of racial constituencies. British rule, which began at the start of the 1800s, favoured English-speaking white people for more than a century. After 1910, white Afrikaans-speaking leaders then sought to use the power of the state, in their turn, to uplift *their* own, economically and culturally. It is in this respect that black South African thinkers sometimes drew on the NP's record as an *inspiration*. Many ANC supporters had this expectation of what it would mean for the ANC to come to power, and many non-ANC supporters feared ANC rule for exactly the same reason.

[18] Mark Gevisser, Thabo Mbeki: The Dream Deferred (2007) ch. 32.
[19] See, eg, *id.* at 614–21.
[20] Fowkes, *supra* note 6 at 277; Edwin Cameron, Justice: A Personal Account 199–200 (2014).

For ANC members thinking along these lines, its government needed the same power as its predecessors and, given its superior moral and democratic credentials, it surely deserved it. The revolution and its principles were to be expressed at least as much in democratic parliamentary government, led by a black majority perfectly capable of running its own country, as in a constitutional text (or in the decisions of unelected judges). From this perspective, it is more than little jarring, that South Africa's first genuinely democratic government was also the first that had to give up parliamentary supremacy and accept constitutional supremacy – and as a concession, no less, to the leaders, supporters and beneficiaries of the previous unjust and democratically illegitimate regimes.

Of course, tensions between constitutionalism and democracy are an enduring feature of many societies, including revolutionary ones like the US. This very fact might suggest that we should not treat this tension as an important obstacle to telling a constructive revolutionary story in South Africa – except that the South Africa tradition of parliamentary dominance by one racial/cultural group after another gives the argument special edge when constitutional supremacy is invoked against the ANC. And what has made that edge cutting is not the familiar tension between democracy and constitutionalism; it is the third and final interpretation of the founding – the perception that the ANC not only bargained in drafting the constitution, but that it bargained *badly*. While the idea of bargaining is in some arguable tension with the idea of revolution, the idea of bargaining the revolution away holds nothing but flat betrayal.

iii. The Sell-outs: Constitutionalism as the Revolution's Betrayal

As the story is often told, including by Mandela himself, the place where he went out ahead of his party and his mass following was in the decision to negotiate. This is an exaggeration. Instead, for better or worse, the principal site of going out ahead was in economic policy. Debates about South African constitutionalism cannot be understood without this piece of the puzzle.[21] The key ANC leaders took much greater care to explain the decision to negotiate to their followers than they did the shift in economic policy (as Mandela himself acknowledged soon afterwards).[22] A degree of secrecy and elite decision-making can of course be part of a revolutionary constitutional story; again, we need look no further than the US case. But once again, the point takes on a special significance in the South African context because of the way it maps on to local racial divisions.

[21] Standard texts include Alan Hirsch, A Season of Hope: Economic Reform under Mandela and Mbeki (2005); Jeremy Seekings & Nicoli Nattrass, Class, Race and Inequality in South Africa (2005); Antoinette Handley, Business and the State in Africa: Economic Policy-Making in the Neo-liberal Era (2008); Gevisser, supra note 18 at 663–73, 690–94.

[22] See, eg, his speech at the 6th National COSATU conference, 1997, noted by Habib, *supra* note 11 at 118; see also 78–79.

Once ANC leaders began talking seriously to their counterparts in the NP government in the early 1990s, they learned how fragile South Africa's economic position was. Once they began talking to foreign political and economic leaders, as the heirs apparent to the South African government, they realised what the post-Cold War international community expected of governments in emerging markets. Leaders from China, Vietnam and Malaysia, whose commitments to communism had by this point become distinctly selective, urged their ideological cousin to join the free market consensus. Adding to the pressure, both the NP government and the Inkatha Freedom Party (IFP), an ANC rival for a section of the black African vote, took strong pro-market stances and were internationally applauded for it.

Led internally by Mbeki, the ANC redid its calculations. The socialist or communist thinking that had often predominated was swiftly sidelined, though often with regret. A few years later, the same thing happened to the mixed approach exemplified in the Macroeconomic Research Group (MERG) proposal, which included market elements, but emphasised state-led planning and redistribution. MERG was to have been the ANC's policy centrepiece. Instead, to the dismay (and often enduring anger) of those involved with MERG, it was steadily replaced by more neo-liberal, market-driven thinking prioritising growth over state-controlled redistribution. But far more serious than the resentment of some policy-makers was the fact that this shift was not reflected in the ANC manifesto for the April 1994 election. This manifesto emphasised the Reconstruction and Development Program (RDP), which was more or less based on MERG. It was only after the ANC took power that the new direction of economic policy under Mbeki, on behalf of the Mandela administration, become publicly clearer. The Cabinet's formal adoption of Growth, Employment and Redistribution (GEAR), a much more neo-liberal, market-based policy, came in June 1996. The ANC's constituency, to the extent that it had been consulted at all, was mainly sold the promise of the future fruits of ANC economic policy, without the ideologically tricky details.

If spectacular growth had followed, the economic miracle would have swept away what might otherwise have been significant legitimacy questions. But South Africa has not proved to be Germany in this regard. Mbeki's economic leadership produced impressively steady but stubbornly low rates of growth. South Africa has not ceased to be a place where a black majority lives in poverty. Whites relinquished their grip on political power, but largely held on to their privileged social and economic position. That black South Africans are on many measures better off in absolute terms and that the black middle class is now larger than the white one does not affect what is a complaint about relative inequality and about the impunity with which white South Africans are seen to have retained their ill-gotten gains.

The feeling is that this state of affairs must be linked to the Constitution as a negotiated bargain. Something must have gone wrong if the ANC had so much mass-mobilised power in its hands and yet so much, apparently, stayed the same.

It must be that the ANC leaders were out-negotiated or duped by their white counterparts, or that they sold out, or that for some rainbow-coloured reason they were simply more generous to whites than they needed to be. This is the feeling of those who will say that South Africa did not have a revolution, but with the bitterness of a moment missed and a following betrayed.

From this perspective, despite the presence of mass mobilisation in its history, South Africa's constitutionalism is not revolutionary. We might call it an exercise in insider reform, provided we do not mean that NP leaders successfully co-opted moderates from other racial groups. This they tried and failed to do. But if we mean that white elites more generally gave up their monopoly on political power to preserve their social and economic power, insider reform is a far better fit. Big business got much more of what it wanted from the transition than the NP government did or than the Afrikaans-speaking white community did as a cultural minority.[23] However, given the way in which he defines the terms, Ackerman's other paradigm, of elite construction, may be an even better fit. When the apartheid regime entered its crisis phase, white society's leaders wanted to make a deal to preserve their social and economic position, and black leaders wanted to get into power without fighting. The natural result was a compromise in which whites gave up political power far more than they gave up social and economic power. Many white business leaders effectively switched allegiance from an apartheid government that could no longer provide stability, including fiscal and market stability, to a black government that now announced its intention to do so. The top-down, expert-designed features of this recall the part of the Polish case that Ackerman describes as an elite construction element amidst other more revolutionary features.[24]

As a matter of fact, white control over the transition is often greatly exaggerated, including in relation to economic policy. The presence of a right to property in the 1996 Constitution is often treated as a symbol of black concessions to white interests. But it is crucial not to assume that something many whites welcomed is something they wrung from the ANC as a negotiated concession. South Africa's course has been overwhelmingly charted by the ANC leaders. Informed critics of GEAR criticise it as a bad ANC policy choice rather than as a policy coup by other elites. That ANC leaders were firmly in charge can be seen in the fact that they reaped the market-reassuring benefits of including a property right, which suited their neo-liberal economic thinking, while packing the actual text of it with carve-outs to ensure that the ANC retained an open hand in government. The reason these carve-outs do not have a higher doctrinal profile is because they have never really been tested. The ANC, to date, has adhered to policies which have almost certainly been more solicitous of property rights than they would need to be to

[23] Fowkes, *supra* note 6 at 112.
[24] See Ackerman, *supra* note 1 at 222–23, 244–45.

pass constitutional muster. This, too, reflects where the real decisions on the issue have been made, from the drafting to the present.[25]

However, for all this, the property right has never stopped being a symbolic liability, linked to the persistence of white privilege and black poverty. Those who make this criticism often do not trouble themselves with what the text and its carve-outs actually say, or with the details of the ANC economic policy story, or with the fact that the Constitutional Court has never once restrained an ANC government policy, under the property right or anything else, on the substantive basis of its redistributive effects in relation to white people.[26] This omission of crucial facts is regrettable. But it is also unsurprising in an argument that is really about perceptions of the Constitution and the limits of social change in South Africa to date. It is for this reason that South Africa is currently seriously debating a constitutional amendment to the right to property to permit expropriation of land without compensation.[27] Given what the carve-outs in the existing wording would probably already permit, this might well be largely symbolic, but no less important for that.

In this respect, the property right is very like the revolutionary constitutional argument more generally. Legitimacy is about perception and so, notwithstanding the facts, it is easy to see why things can look bad. It is easy to see why both the property right and the Constitution of which it forms part continued to labour under the weight of perceptions that they represent something far from revolutionary, in Ackerman's or any other sense.

B. Constitutional Arguments among Constitution- and Court-Defenders

The nature of the arguments just discussed has had a powerful influence on the arguments of defenders who want to ground the Constitution rather than the ANC as ultimate. They have had to find legitimacy arguments that do not only work via the ANC's authority or that are not too vulnerable to the Constitution's potential weakness as a negotiated deal.

Several disparate groups have had reason to try and position the Constitution as primary. Some have wanted the Constitution to serve as a check on the dominant party, and therefore to be above it. Some, including some ANC members, have simply believed it is better to construct a state in which the Constitution and not the party is primary. Some, who view the ANC government's efforts at transformation as inadequate, have wanted to use the Constitution to pursue these

[25] South African Const., s 25; Fowkes, *supra* note 6 at 112–15 and the sources cited therein.

[26] Fowkes, *supra* note 6.

[27] See, eg, Paul Vecchiatto & Nkululeko Ncana, *South Africa's ANC Resolves to Change Constiution on Land*, Bloomberg, July 31, 2018.

goals in different and often more radical ways than the ANC has done. Naturally, these different groups do not always argue in the same terms, but for present purposes, it is the broader patterns that matter.

The most common conceptual move among constitutional defenders in South Africa draws on the moral and world historical rejection of apartheid, and the associated embrace of ideas of dignity and equality, and inclusivity and pluralism that have sought not merely to reverse apartheid but to transcend it, as a shining example to the world. These ideas, of course, are to be found in ANC party narratives too, but defenders use them much more abstractly. Of course, they do not do so in an entirely free-standing manner. No one pretends that the great constitutional change is not linked to the ANC or the struggle *historically*. But after 1997, once the text was duly drafted by the Constitutional Assembly and installed as supreme law, it is easy enough to de-link these principles from the party if one wishes to do so. Now the Constitution is supreme (why? Because it says so) and one can make these principled arguments based on the text and its many value provisions, without needing to refer to anything so concretely political as a constructive revolution.

This is perhaps most obvious in relation to arguments from history. The way in which history is used in South African constitutional arguments can bear a strong resemblance to its use in the paradigmatically non-revolutionary case of Germany. Both, of course, are making arguments about a past evil of world historical proportions, to which the new constitutional order is presented as a reaction and a contrast. Of course, there are differences: German historical arguments are more often about 'never again', where South African ones add a greater note of transcendence, of using the act of rejecting the past to build a better future.[28] But details aside, South Africa and Germany share a deep form of constitutional argument here, notwithstanding the starkly different place of mass mobilisation in the two cases.

The most important reason for this similarity, aside from the shared experience of past evil, is that in both systems the Constitutional Courts and their defenders have deployed the historical argument in a broadly similar way to broadly similar ends. Both have been seeking to establish the authority of the Constitution and the Court as a great principled mechanism against the evils of the past, having authority as against party politics accordingly.[29] The German Court obviously could not have invoked a story of mass mobilisation to support this argument, while the South African Court could have. But the felt need to establish the authority of the South African Constitution and the Court independently of the dominant party of revolution has led it to tell a story that takes the German line more than,

[28] See the forthcoming work of Justin Collings (Scales of Memory: Constitutional Justice and the Burdens of the Past) on constitutional arguments from history.

[29] On the basis of German constitutional authority, see further Michaela Hailbronner, Traditions and Transformations: The Rise of German Constitutionalism (2015).

say, that of the US. Just as Germans today will sometimes see Weimar and the rise of National Socialism as the reason to be suspicious of appeals to mass political authority, so those in South Africa who fear the ANC, or simply the mob, will worry that moves to link the Constitution's authority to mass political mobilisation will just serve to weaken the Constitution's defences.

This is not the only reason why South African constitutional defenders have found it tempting to de-politicise their arguments. The potential political liability of the negotiations can be a reason not to rely too much on a political story that might have fatal cracks in it. South African legal culture, as it stood in the early 1990s, also accepted formalist legal arguments far more than it did political ones.[30] And many constitutional defenders have held more progressive political opinions than those of the population at large, or have suspected that they do, and so they have found it appealing to use arguments that move quickly from actual political commitments into more abstract principles. As a result, the most common kind of argument made by constitutional defenders to date is more or less that of Ronald Dworkin, especially in his later phase.[31] The first premise of this kind of argument is a politically enacted constitution in a political context, but the abstract moral extrapolation of its rich store of rights and value terms quickly takes over thereafter.

More critical (and Critical Legal Theory) accounts have also had a place in South African discussion since the beginning. But these scholarly accounts, even today, are often focused on the negative project of attacking South Africa's traditional legal culture, or liberal constitutionalism more generally – or it is in that guise that they have their greatest impact. The seminal 1998 article by US scholar Karl Klare is remembered and cited much more often for its criticisms of common law legal culture than it is for its positive suggestions like the call for more candidly political judging, which are often forgotten and have seldom been followed.[32] Subsequent writing in this vein has not altered this pattern, often because it has not tried to. If change is seen as inadequate, defended by reactionaries and betrayed by its supposed leaders, criticism (or more practical activism) will seem more important.[33] This body of work is much more likely to criticise South African legal culture for its hostility to a constitutional argument as political as Ackerman's than it is to *make* an argument like Ackerman's, not least because the constructive revolutionary account has an implication of achievement.

[30] Karl E. Klare, *Legal Culture and Transformative Constitutionalism*, 14 S. Afr. J on Hum. Rts. 146 (1998).

[31] See Drucilla Cornell & Nick Friedman, The Mandate of Dignity: Ronald Dworkin, Revolutionary Constitutionalism, and the Claims of Justice (2016); Drucilla Cornell & Nick Friedman, *The Significance of Dworkin's Non-positivist Jurisprudence in the Post-colony*, 4 Malawi L.J. 1 (2010).

[32] Klare, *supra* note 30.

[33] See, eg, Sanele Sibanda, *Not Purpose-Made! Transformative Constitutionalism, Post-Independence Constitutionalism and the Struggle to Eradicate Poverty*, 22 22 Stell. L.R. 482 (2011); Joel M. Modiri, *Law's Poverty*, 18 Potchefstroomse Elektroniese Regsblad 224 (2015).

In short, then, constitutional argument outside the ANC tends *either* to defend the Constitution as ultimate *or* to be open to more overtly and concretely political appeals, but not both. This position, at this stage in South Africa's development along Ackerman's timetable, could fit well enough with his account. Ackerman expects tension between the existing legal culture and the new constitutional regime. But it also supports two deeper arguments. First, while South Africa has undoubtedly been experiencing an adjustment phase where the new constitution meets the old legal culture, this is not an experience confined to revolutionary cases. To take just one example, Germany experienced – and is still experiencing – something similar, and I refer to the German example again because South Africans have borrowed German ideas about applying constitutional values throughout the legal system, including to traditionally separated topics in private law.[34] Second, this brief survey illustrates why it can by no means be taken for granted that scholarly South African constitutional talk will switch to constructive revolutionary arguments after a generation of approaches that are, in their different ways, often based on suspicion of any such thing.

C. Constitutional Arguments and the ANC

India and South Africa share a pattern in which the movement party dominates politics for many years after the constitution is drafted. But South Africa is not following the Indian path as closely as Ackerman's argument suggests, and a different interpretation of the analogy between the two systems might be at least as instructive.

i. Orchestration: ANC Succession Dynamics

As Ackerman tells the Indian story, Nehru's death prompted a succession crisis within the Congress Party in the form of a competition about the Constitution. A competition also arose between the party and the Supreme Court over who could invoke ultimate authority in the system. Indira Gandhi won the internal Congress struggle, but her radical challenge to the Constitution ended with her electoral defeat after the violations of the Emergency, and the Court's vision of constitutional supremacy triumphed. In this way, revolutionary authority in India shifted from being embodied in the movement party to the constitution-in-court. On Ackerman's account, ANC succession dynamics have been following this track since Mandela stepped down in 1999.[35] In fact, once again, it remains to be seen

[34] See, eg, Reinhard Zimmerman, The New German Law of Obligations: Historical and Comparative Perspectives 21–30, 207–08 (2005); Olha O. Cherednychenko, *Subordinating Contract Law to Fundamental Rights: Towards a Major Breakthrough or towards Walking in Circles?*, *in* Constitutional Values and European Contract Law (Stefan Grundmann ed., 2008).

[35] Ackerman, *supra* note 1 at 104–05.

how much South Africa will follow this pattern, as a brief sketch of local succession dynamics shows.

In fact, when Mandela retired, there was no succession struggle akin to the post-Nehru one. Mbeki had been the heir apparent since his defeat of Cyril Ramaphosa in the vote for ANC Deputy President in 1994 (although his victory was not quite sealed until his election as ANC President in 1997). The care devoted to ensuring an orderly succession is a reflection of the ANC's concern to maintain the discipline of a united movement, and their success in this during the 1990s marks a crucial point of contrast with Solidarity and the Polish case.

However, what Mandela's succession did not provoke, Mbeki's certainly did. Mbeki's deputy, Jacob Zuma, was again chosen early, in the same 1997 process that elevated Mbeki to the ANC presidency. But Mbeki's 2005 decision to fire Zuma as South African Deputy President, following corruption allegations, broke the orderly pattern. Since Zuma retained the elected position of *ANC* Deputy President – Mbeki had no power to fire him from *that* position – Zuma was still in line to succeed Mbeki to the *ANC* presidency and then, in the usual ANC way, as South African President. It was to head off this possibility and to select a different successor that Mbeki sought to run for a third term as *ANC* President.

It is essential to keep the two presidencies separate because there is no clear two-term limit tradition within the ANC. Oliver Tambo, Mandela's revered predecessor, served as ANC President from 1967 until 1991. Tambo's predecessor, in turn, was Albert Luthuli, the first African to win the Nobel Peace Prize, who was President from 1952 to 1967. Mbeki, then, was breaking no George Washington-style precedent by running for a third *ANC* term, and Ackerman's view to the contrary leads him to see Mbeki as an authoritarian threat to *the Constitution*'s two-term limits on the *national* presidency.[36] Mbeki, of all people, would have resisted conforming to the stereotype of the African leader gone wrong by trying to amend the Constitution to permit a third national presidential term. Instead, he was simply making a bad party political calculation because contesting the ANC leadership handed anti-Mbeki votes to Zuma that Zuma might not have won against another candidate. Nor did Mbeki's internal unpopularity have much to do with competing visions of the Constitution within the ANC. Mbeki had become isolated as an aloof, authoritarian leader ruling as the country's expert-in-chief, where Zuma presented a more accessible figure. Mbeki's economic policies had come under attack. And the contest was also about patronage, including along tribal lines.

Ackerman emphasises Zuma's subsequent concerns about the manner of Mbeki's dismissal in order to show that Zuma was the constitutional defender to Mbeki's authoritarian threat.[37] Mbeki, instead of completing his second presidential term, was effectively fired by his party ahead of time. In itself, this raises no

[36] *Id.* at 106.
[37] *Id.* at 108–09.

constitutional concern. Mbeki resigned under party pressure, which is a familiar and perfectly constitutional way for a presidential term to end. However, he did send his resignation letter to the ANC party leadership and not to Parliament, and critics see this technicality as a sign of a broader ANC's tendency to subvert the Constitution by treating itself rather than the formal constitutional institutions of state as paramount. But whatever one thinks of this concern, it was almost certainly not Zuma's. His concern, instead, was with the ANC's tradition of managing leadership transitions in ways that kept disappointed leaders, and their supporters, within the party. Zuma was thinking of avoidable public humiliation and breakaways, not constitutional law niceties.[38]

The most recent succession battle in 2017 saw a resurgent Rampahosa win out narrowly against Zuma's preferred candidate, Nkosazana Dlamini-Zuma, an ANC heavyweight since 1994 (and his ex-wife). Soon afterwards, Zuma was himself forced out early as South African President, as Mbeki had been. But if that contest had greater constitutional stakes, it was because Zuma by that point represented a greater threat to the Constitution. The ANC's internal battle was once again heavily about patronage and the sins of an individual leader.

There are signs this might be changing. The emergence of the Economic Freedom Fighters (EFF) to the ANC's left has brought more radical economic proposals into general discussion. It is producing a debate about the right to property that is more about constitutional fundamentals than any since the drafting era. But it not yet clear how fundamental it is. The open-ended South African property clause represents much less of a textual obstacle to radical redistribution than was true in India in the 1960s. There is a substantial constitutional space for more redistributive policies before the Constitutional Court might feel compelled to resist, and even then that resistance might well be about procedures and details rather than head-on invalidation. The current conflict has much more to do with the solidity of the ANC broad-tent governing coalition and its economic policy choices than it has to do with any deep clash *between* those positions and the Constitution (or the courts). Even today, then, the Indian dynamics remain an uncertain guide to South Africa ones.

ii. Running Late on the Revolutionary Timetable?

As a reply to Ackerman, the argument just made could have quite limited import. It could amount to no more than the claim that South Africa is moving somewhat more slowly along Ackerman's stages than his account suggests – and the signs of

[38] These issues, and not constitutional concerns, are what are mentioned in Ackerman's cited authority for the claim that 'Zuma was well aware of the constitutional significance of self-restraint' (id. at 108 fn. 52): see Mark Gevisser, A Legacy of Liberation: Thabo Mbeki and the Future of the South African Dream 335 (2009). On ANC institutional practices, see, eg, Susan Booysen, The African National Congress and the Regeneration of Political Power (2014).

growing constitutional contestation, for instance, might suggest that South Africa is indeed moving in the direction that Ackerman's argument would expect (in the May 2019 elections, the ANC's 57 per cent of the vote dipped, for the first time, below the comfortable mid-60s percentage band). But they could also support a different hypothesis, which connects the discussion of ANC succession dynamics with the preceding sketch of South African scholarship: is South Africa taking *too* long?

Dominant party cases are an interesting variant of Ackerman's account because in these cases, the revolutionary tide that lifts the constitution does not retreat soon thereafter. Instead of the entrenched constitution soon being left out of reach as the extraordinary revolutionary moment gives way to ordinary politics, in a case like South Africa the dominant party retains extraordinary political control and a two-thirds majority remains in easy reach. The tide stays high and the constitution has to try and swim along in it.

In India, this produced a high-stakes tussle over constitutional authority. Constitutional conflict between Congress and the Supreme Court began almost immediately when Nehru's administration began the practice of trying to put matters into schedules purportedly beyond the reach of judicial review. The ANC briefly attempted something similar, but the attempt was struck down in the *First Certification* judgment in 1996 and has not been tried since.[39] That it has not been retried reflects, above all, that relations between the ANC and the Court have often been characterised by broad agreement and sometimes partnership, notwithstanding that the Court has been a meaningfully independent check on the party throughout.[40] As noted, there is also not in South Africa the same sharp textual conflict between the property clause and the government's redistributive policies that, in India, led to the great constitutional challenge of Indira Gandhi and the articulation of the basic structure doctrine in reply. This conflict was well under way within two decades of the Indian Constitution's drafting. In South Africa, the clock is on the way towards three decades and there are, at most, only early possible signs of such a conflict. The key battle is still the one for the soul of the ANC, not for final authority over the Constitution or its meaning.

The longer this is true, and the longer revolutionary arguments are still being made about the party rather than the constitution in its own right, the longer those who want to establish the constitution's independent authority will be doing so on other foundations. This goes double for a South African context, where, as we have seen, the negotiated nature of the Constitution can make concretely political arguments seem risky in any case. As I suggested, the late 1970s rebrand of the Indian Supreme Court as a pro-poor, accessible institution of social justice may seem a more appealing model for South African defenders.[41]

[39] Certification of the Constitution of the Republic of South Africa, 1996, [1996] ZACC 26, paras. 149–50.

[40] An argument I advance generally in Fowkes, *supra* note 6.

[41] See James Fowkes, *How to Open the Doors of the Court: Lessons on Access to Justice from Indian PIL*, 27 S. Afr. J. on Hum. Rts. 434 (2011).

Whether this will happen remains to be seen; for now, the comparison between India and South Africa raises at least as many questions as it answers. Of these, the most interesting is whether one needs to have a fundamental conflict about constitutional authority, of the sort India saw in the 1960s and 1970s, before defenders are moved to try and claim revolutionary legitimacy from their movement party antagonists. If so, South Africa may yet reach that point, and the ANC or a coalition with forces like the EFF may regain sufficient political momentum from the battle to have the strength to fight it. But South Africa's movement party may also have already become too weak to launch that kind of sustained fight – and this might be the most important reason why it is possible for a dominant party system with revolutionary facts in its history to run *too* late on Ackerman's timetable.

III. A Concluding Thought: What Legal Revolution Looks Like

There are, then, a number of ways in which Ackerman, and South Africans, will find it complicated to tell a constructive revolutionary story about South Africa. While any case study is more complex in real life than theory must pretend, the complexities discussed show that even an apparently good case for Ackerman's theory raises important questions for it. But in conclusion, it is worth asking seriously just how much skin what I have said really takes off the theory's nose.

Constructive revolution may be able to shrug off some of the questions. For example, I have noted the paucity of constructive revolutionary arguments being made by constitutional defenders. But expecting Ackerman to display evidence of lawyers making constructive revolutionary arguments is in some sense unfair: if he is trying to change the way we understand the word 'revolution', we should expect that not many people would currently speak that way. Put crudely, South Africans might not make many constructive revolutionary arguments yet because they have not read Ackerman's book yet.

But it might also be unreasonable to expect this in a deeper and more interesting way. One way to understand Ackerman's core project is as an attempt to show how something as politically rampaging as a revolution can lead to something as staidly legal as a constitution.[42] But if that is the process we are looking for, we might expect that constitutional talk that starts out in revolutionary terms will necessarily get less revolutionary-sounding as the constitution gets built into institutional structures and takes on the more formal working languages of the bureaucrat and the doctrinal lawyer.[43] A lack of revolutionary-sounding evidence,

[42] A point emphasised during the conference presentation of Dieter Grimm.

[43] A point also relevant to the bureaucratised constitutional issue that arose in the discussion of Ackerman's French case study.

especially later on in the process, may make it harder to Ackerman to prove that his timetable fits practice, but it may also, perversely, show that on his core claim he is right. A revolution that produces something as legal as a constitution, and succeeds in establishing it in the doctrines and mechanisms of a governing system, might necessarily look and sound less revolutionary the more it achieves its goal.

The presence of rival constitutional paradigms in the South African case might also appear to be something the constructive revolutionary account can shrug off, at least partly. Certainly, there are other forms of constitutional legitimacy argument in play in the South African case. But isn't that always going to be true? Even a paradigm revolutionary case like the US is hardly one from which other kinds of (il)legitimacy arguments have been absent. We await Ackerman's discussion of some of these other forms, but surely what defines revolutionary cases should be the presence of mass mobilisation and the availability of revolutionary arguments, not the absence of any other paradigms.

But in that case, what is it that justifies our describing a particular system as a revolutionary one, even as an ideal type? This may be the hardest question the South African case poses for Ackerman's approach. If I am right that the South African case shows how revolutionary facts might not be determinative because people might not choose to invoke them (or that the English case shows this historically), then the mere presence of revolutionary facts does not suffice. Some sort of predominance of revolutionary arguments in the practice of the system would have to be shown. The focus would have to shift from what happened at the Founding to ongoing practice – at least in a system that had not already turned the revolutionary facts of its history into the legitimacy arguments of its working constitutional regime. Ackerman's paradigm would not manage to be a guide to how revolutionary constitutions become established (if they do), thus allowing us to detect and understand their distinctive challenges across the global range of cases. It would instead be a guide to how they *could* do so, which does not rule out the possibility that they could turn out more like his other paradigms, and so display the different challenges he associates with those.

I am a defender of more constructively political accounts of South African constitutionalism and an admirer of the ongoing positive constitutional contribution that is part of the ANC record. I would welcome a world in which South Africans told a constructive revolutionary account about themselves and their past constitutional achievements. Ackerman and I alike hope it may yet happen. But just as the possibility of revolution lies underneath any system, if leaders try to invoke it and We the People choose to accept their presumption, so the choice can run the other way. The legitimacy of the constitution will stand or fall on the story, and the version of their history, that We the People choose to listen to and to tell.

19

The Race against Time

BRUCE ACKERMAN

Revolutionary Constitutions is organised around a four-stage dynamic of legitimation. Time One analyses the period of revolutionary insurgency against the entrenched regime. During this period, it is irrelevant whether the insurgents choose to play by the old regime's rules. If there is a constitution at Time One, 'it is the constitution of the enemy', as Dieter Grimm rightly remarks. The decisive question is the insurgents' willingness to join in a collective struggle to sweep the existing government from power.

This is the common feature linking Alcide De Gasperi to Nelson Mandela to the Ayatollah Khomeini. Together with other revolutionary leaders, they all sacrificed greatly to build a broad popular movement to repudiate the old regime. They had the courage to risk imprisonment or death, even though they could have achieved success within the existing system – so long as they played the game according to the rules laid down by the existing system. Their willingness to sacrifice self-interest *earned* them a distinctive claim for integrity as they called upon their fellow citizens to join the insurgency.

Such displays of revolutionary courage will frequently end in crushing defeat by the forces of 'law and order'. However, my book deals with a very different scenario — in which the insurgents at Time One propel themselves to power at Time Two. In these successful takeovers, the ascendant revolutionaries confront a distinctive problem in legitimating authority: now that they are in command, how can they prevent themselves from engaging in the very same abuses of power that led them to rebel against the old regime in the first place?

Call this the *problem of betrayal* and a revolutionary constitution an effort to solve it. To be sure, these commitments 'never again' to repeat past abuses serve as only part of the 'new beginning' proclaimed by the revolutionary constitution at Time Two.[1] The breakthrough at the Founding will also include principles and institutional practices to one-or-another 'vision of progress' as the nation moves

[1] I am indebted to Jed Rubenfeld, whose reflections on 'never again' commitments in his book Freedom and Time (2001) gave me a sense of the high importance of this aspect of constitutional development.

forward to Times Three and Four. I will be considering these forward-looking visions shortly, but the backward-looking 'never agains' serve as a key to my Time Two analysis.

I. Never Again

The content of 'never again' commitments depends on the character of the evils that motivated the revolutionaries' earlier struggle. Consider the case of Italy. As Marta Cartabia explains, the different political parties which joined the resistance to Mussolini advanced very different visions of progress. But they all endorsed a common diagnosis of the failures that permitted the dictatorship to arise in the 1920s. In their view, it was the 'flexibility' of the Royal Constitution of 1848 which allowed King Victor Emmanuel III to transfer power to Mussolini in 1922, instead of appointing a prime minister, supported by liberal democratic parties in parliament, who would forcefully resist Il Duce's 'March on Rome'. It was therefore imperative to create a 'rigid Constitution', which included the judicial protection of fundamental rights, to prevent this tragedy from recurring.

In contrast, Charles de Gaulle advanced a different diagnosis of the fall of the Third Republic. As Denis Baranger makes clear, de Gaulle was firmly convinced that the pre-war parliamentary system was to blame for France's military defeat and Vichy's disgraceful collaboration with Hitler. On his view, parliamentary government allowed party leaders in the Chamber of Deputies to engage in petty political manoeuvring rather than confront the rising threat posed by the Nazis. When the founders of the Fourth Republic sought to reinvigorate the parliamentary system, de Gaulle vigorously campaigned against their post-war Constitution. But his efforts to repudiate their constitutional initiative were defeated at the polls in 1946.

Nevertheless, de Gaulle continued his efforts to overthrow the system, and finally succeeded in sweeping it away during the Algerian crisis of the late 1950s. He then moved swiftly to win a popular referendum for a Constitution of the Fifth Republic creating a super-strong presidency that would enable its incumbent to transcend petty party bickering and lead France to regain its former greatness. As a consequence, France's Gaullist-inspired Constitution contains very different 'never again' provisions from its Italian counterpart. The Italian Constitution attempts to prevent another Mussolini by repudiating a strong presidency and insisting on judicially enforceable limits on parliamentary power. The French Republic attempts to prevent another Marshall Petain by repudiating parliamentary government and authorising its super-strong president to initiate wide-ranging 'states of emergency' when the Republic is in danger.

Alessandro Ferrara's chapter advances a conceptual scheme which clarifies the distinctive character of these 'never agains'. He distinguishes between Type A provisions, containing generic lists of rights and principles prevailing at the time a constitution is enacted, Type B provisions, containing similarly conventional understandings of institutional choices between parliamentarianism, presidentialism and the like, and Type C provisions, which 'the framers of revolutionary constitutions [deploy to] convey their '"message to the world" and claim the unique place that "the People" deserve to take, and be recognised for, in the "space of constitutions"'.[2]

In Cartabia's account, the Italian Republic's 'rigid' protections of fundamental rights by a constitutional court operate as Type C provisions containing post-war Italy's 'message to the world', while its construction of a parliamentary system is largely built out of Type B provisions. In Baranger's account of the Fifth Republic, the 'never agains' are reversed: the super-powerful presidency is Type C, while the provisions defining individual and social rights are Type B.

Similarly, the equal voting rights guaranteed to all inhabitants of South Africa or India may seem, at first glance, as if they were Type A, since they do not differ textually from provisions prevailing elsewhere. But they are better understood as being of Type C, since they represent a revolutionary repudiation of the previous regime's commitment to apartheid or the caste system, and establish that the newly constituted Republics of South Africa/India will be built on the equal rights of all citizens, regardless of their radically divergent religious convictions, cultures and castes.

Ferrara's trichotomy may well, as he suggests, prove a fruitful source for the analysis of 'constitutional patriotism'. But for the present purposes, my simpler dichotomy between backward-looking and forward-looking provisions will suffice for the next stage of my Time Two argument – which develops 'the race against time' as an organising perspective on revolutionary Foundings.

My argument is straightforward: although a particular movement's 'never agains' provide the ideological glue which unite its diverse factions in their revolutionary struggle during Time One, these bonds begin to dissolve as soon as the revolutionaries take over at Time Two. Now that they have real power, they will want to use it to shape the country's future. But their different ideologies and expectations will inevitably lead them to disagree on the best path forward. These forward-looking disputes threaten to split the revolutionaries into rival factions and prevent them from collaborating together to enact a constitution which codifies the 'never agains' that had unified the movement during Time One.

If this happens, the revolutionaries will lose their race against time. Once factional divisions come to dominate the political stage, it will be very hard to recover the broad popular support required to anchor the legitimacy of their 'never again' constitution.

This is precisely what happened in Poland. Despite their collaboration in leading Solidarity to victory in 1989, Lech Walesa and Tadeusz Mazowiecki split their triumphant movement apart when they chose to compete with one another for the presidency in 1990. Once Solidarity disintegrated into competing factions, rival party leaders were unable to come together to endorse a 'never again' Constitution that expressed their joint commitment to liberal democracy.

[2] FERRARA, ch. 9 in this volume, at 172.

Maciej Kisilowski rejects my analysis. Before considering our disagreement, I will begin with James Fowkes' analysis of South Africa's success in constitutionalising its 'never agains', since he provides a conceptual framework that will clarify the Polish problematic.

Fowkes identifies three different positions held by disparate elements of the African National Congress at Time Two. Some activists took up the rainbow nation position and tried to hammer out a document which expressed the core principles of the Time One struggle. In contrast to these idealists, other insurgents took a more strategic view. They looked upon the constitutional project merely as a useful technique for inducing white Afrikaaners to give their reluctant consent to the new regime. From their vantage point, the key element in the new Constitution was its (ambiguous) protection of property rights because it helped to reassure white South Africans that they might well keep the vast riches they had seized during apartheid.

However, it was precisely the property provisions that led more radical elements of the ANC to condemn the Constitution. These Betrayalists insisted that South Africa should 'never again' be the site of white economic domination, and condemned both Rainbowers and Strategists as sell-outs.

Fowkes insightfully describes how the struggles between these three factions shaped the early years of constitutional construction and how they have continued to divide the country since Mandela left the presidency.[3] But I want to take his analysis a step further and contend that these three views will *necessarily* be generated in the process of constitutionalising *any and all* revolutions on a human scale.

After all, we are dealing with movements which refuse to promise some totalising vision of heaven on earth, but unite their followers behind a joint commitment to liberate the country from the very real oppressions imposed by the old regime. Some will take the Rainbow View and see the Constitution as repudiating precisely the right features of the old regime. But others will find these targets too modest or too ambitious – and will denounce the Constitution as a betrayal.

In South Africa, for example, the Betrayal View was held by two very different groups. Fowkes emphasises the Leftists from the Democratic Front and the Spear of the Nation, who condemned the property provisions as a sell-out. But there were also conservative black groups who denounced the ANC's Constitution as a betrayal of their own struggle against apartheid. Led by Mongosuthu Buthelezi, they formed a rival movement party, Inkatha, which aimed to sweep away the puppet governments that the apartheid regime established in the black homelands and force the whites to accept genuine self-rule in native regions. While Fowkes recognizes Inkatha's political significance, he de-emphasises it and sometimes views betrayal as exclusively a Leftist position. For me, it is perfectly predictable that there will be conservative, as well as radical, revolutionaries who will cry betrayal.

[3] Fowkes develops his arguments further in his breakthrough book, Building the Constitution: The Practice of Constitutional Interpretation in Post-apartheid South Africa (2016).

Fowkes' distinction between Rainbow and Strategic positions is also very valuable, but once again, I understand their relationship differently. He seems to view Rainbowers and Strategists as if they were necessarily antagonistic to one another. But so long as revolutions remain on a human scale, it will often make sense for Strategists and Rainbowers to join forces to win the legitimation contest against Left and Right Betrayalists.

To see why, put yourself in the position of a thoughtful Rainbower. While securing 'never again' commitments is of primary importance, you are also very interested in the visions of progress that gain constitutional endorsement. However, you recognise that if you push your own particular vision too aggressively, this may propel lots of your fellow revolutionaries into the Betrayalist camp. As a consequence, you will pay attention when hard-headed Strategists point out that, by making some concessions to former enemies, their support can help compensate for Betrayalist defections and allow your Rainbow Constitution to gain broad popular support.

Such advice will, of course, put Rainbowers in a very uncomfortable position. In the case of South Africa, Fowkes shows how Mandela's concessions to De Klerk led his Rainbow Constitution to take on a Strategic appearance to important ANC constituencies. But in demonstrating this point, he writes as if there was a sharp line dividing the two camps and that the Betrayalists also constituted an equally distinct group.

I disagree. Mandela and his comrades are better understood as making an appeal to idealistic Rainbowers to recognise that Strategic concessions were necessary to avoid a worse fate – in which their entire effort to gain broad acceptance of their 'never again' Constitution would be shattered by a successful countermobilisation of Left and Right Betrayalists. By the same logic, he called upon committed Strategists to compromise their future-oriented aims if they hoped to prevent the repudiation of their constitutionalist initiative by the Betrayalist camp.

The picture of constitutional negotiations that emerges from this modification of Fowkes' approach looks something like this. The construction of a pro-constitution coalition involves an alliance of different Rainbow-Strategic revolutionary groups who are willing to compromise with each other about future-oriented commitments to sustain broad popular support for key 'never again' terms of their proposed Constitution. They are opposed by a coalition of Left and Right Betrayalists, who threaten to mobilise their followers in a sustained effort – which may include violent as well as civil forms of resistance – to defeat the coalition's proposal unless their concerns are more adequately expressed in the constitutional initiative.

In response to these real-world dilemmas, Rainbow-Strategists make serious efforts to include potential Betrayalists in the bargaining process and, if this fails, they will still be obliged to take their concerns seriously in drafting a constitution that will undercut the Betrayalists' grassroots campaign against its adoption.

We have, in short, arrived at a view that begins to converge with the kind of game-theoretic analysis that Tom Ginsburg and other leading comparatists have pioneered over the last generation – but with an important difference. In developing his arguments, Ginsburg focuses on the future-oriented strategies of political actors. As a consequence, he emphasises the ways in which a constitution serves an 'insurance function' for party leaders who find it hard to predict how they will fare in the electoral competition emerging under the new regime. But in the case of revolutionary constitutions, the game-theoretic analysis must be broadened to include the need to redeem the backward-looking commitments generated in the course of the revolutionary struggle.

Ginsburg's chapter tries to do justice to this point by conceding that although 'charisma can explain the really big things, it cannot explain ordinary politics, which fall into Weber's other category of rational-legal authority'.[4] But he fails to consider my claim that the study of modern revolutions must move beyond Weber's emphasis on the *personal* 'charisma' of particular leaders to the *organisational* charisma expressed by millions of grassroots activists who have also sacrificed much for the revolution.

It is the decisions made by these mobilised citizens which will determine the constitutional fate of the new republic. On the one hand, they may choose to channel their energies into a broad-based campaign to gain broad public acceptance of the *authenticity* of the Constitution's claim to express the 'never again' principles that united them in their common struggle at Time One. On the other hand, they may follow Betrayalist leaders and reject the initiative of the Rainbow-Strategic coalition.

Ginsburg fails to recognise this point in claiming that 'constitutional politics are ordinary politics' once revolutionary leaders start bargaining over the terms defining their 'new beginning'.[5] In revolutionary settings, the bargaining power of these leaders *depends on their relativity ability to mobilise their supporters around the country* – either in a positive or negative direction. 'Personal' charisma is not enough – competing leaders must also enlist the 'organisational' charisma of activists on the regional and local level. If Rainbow-Strategic negotiators misestimate their relative 'organisational charisma', their Betrayalist opponents can successfully appeal to millions of grassroots activists to repudiate the proposed Constitution – either by rejecting it at the polls or resisting its imposition through massive demonstrations of civil or armed resistance. Such mistakes can readily lead to an irreversible fragmentation of the revolutionary coalition, making it impossible for the triumphant insurgents to win their 'race against time'.

II. Revolutionary Failures

My revised version of the 'Fowkes-Ginsburg model' leads to a distinctive perspective on Poland's tragic failure to gain mobilised support for a Solidarity constitution

[4] Ginsburg, ch. 7 in this volume, at 121.
[5] *Id.*

in the aftermath of its decisive triumph in 1989. This failure is particularly remarkable because the movement's rise to power during Time One seemed remarkably free of many sharp divisions that plagued other twentieth century revolutions on a human scale.

For starters, virtually all Poles spoke Polish and worshiped the same God in the same way. In contrast, India was a country whose inhabitants spoke hundreds of different languages and were split between a Hindu majority and a Muslim minority. Nevertheless, as Menaka Guruswamy demonstrates, the Congress Party managed to transcend these divisions on behalf of a revolutionary Constitution that vindicated the equal citizenship of all citizens despite their radically different castes, cultures and religions.

To be sure, Solidarity did have a problem incorporating the energies of deeply religious Catholics and emphatic secularists within its common enterprise. But these inevitable tensions were greatly diminished by Pope John Paul II, who was then reaching out to non-Catholics along the lines marked out by Vatican II. Since the Pope was Polish himself and strongly supported Solidarity, his ecumenical pronouncements were a priceless resource in bridging the secular–religious divide.

Similarly, Solidarity faced a far more tractable problem in dealing with ideological conflict. The movement was split between free-market liberals and social democratic union leaders, but this division pales in comparison to those arising in my French and Italian studies of the immediate post-war period. In these cases, hardline communists had been a powerful force within the French/Italian Resistance during Time One, with many Marxists remaining deeply sceptical of the entire project of 'bourgeois constitutionalism'. Yet communist leaders managed to join forces with social democrats and liberals long enough to win the 'race against time' before the Cold War made further close collaboration politically impossible.

In contrast, during the 1980s, very few Polish communists continued to remain fervent believers in the 'dictatorship of the proletariat' – the two million Communist Party members were largely apparatchiks. It was the ideal of 'constitutional democracy' which was inspiring tens of millions of grassroots activists to create a remarkable network linking local, regional and national levels of the Solidarity movement.

What is more, Solidarity's first Prime Minister, Tadeusz Mazowiecki, had been one of Lech Walesa's closest advisers throughout Time One, providing him with essential expertise that the under-educated union leader considered essential for his success. Moreover, Mazowiecki was well aware that his bland self-presentation made it impossible for him to compete with Walesa's charismatic personality. Rather than challenging the union leader's symbolic centrality, there was every reason to expect the prime minister to continue collaborating with Walesa now that they had led Solidarity to victory in 1989.

As a consequence, I cannot endorse Maciej Kisilowski's analysis of Poland's ongoing constitutional crisis. On his account, Poland is a *permanently* divided society, whose polarised politics precluded constitutional success from the very beginning. However, at no point does he place Poland's ideological and religious divisions into comparative perspective. Rather than recognise their relatively modest character, he merely shows that different political parties regularly command majority support in different regions of the country – with urban areas voting 'liberal' and rural areas 'conservative'. But similar urban/rural splits are common in democracies throughout the world. It is only during revolutionary times that citizens – and sometimes their leaders – find it imperative to transcend such differences to join in a common struggle for a 'new beginning'.

As a result, my book looks elsewhere for an explanation for Solidarity's surprising failure to constitutionalise its charisma. I argue that it was the ill-considered acceptance of a Gaullist-style transitional constitution which is largely responsible. The Polish version of this neo-Gaullist system set up a particularly intense form of competition between president and prime minister – encouraging Mazowiecki, if he wished to sustain his political power, to gamble on beating Walesa in the race for president in 1990. It was this 'war at the top' that led the two candidates to break up Solidarity into competing political parties to support their rival campaigns in this decisive election. Once Solidarity split apart, it proved impossible to reunite the rival factions in support of a Solidarity constitution codifying the movement's Time One commitment to liberty and democracy.

Kisilowski fails to undertake a sustained critique of my competing analysis. That said, at one point, he is willing to entertain my hypothesis, but nevertheless defends Mazowiecki's decision to enter the presidential race against Walesa. In making his case, he rightly reports that Walesa was a strong critic of Mazowiecki's neo-liberal economic policies, which endorsed the sweeping privatisation of state-owned enterprises. On Walesa's view, this was unacceptable unless the government took strong steps to protect workers thrown out of their jobs by the new entrepreneurs who were assuming power over their lives. In taking this position, Walesa was adopting a familiar social democratic position associated with the centre-left. Nevertheless, Kisilowski is a neo-liberal himself; he calls Walesa's position 'conservative' even though it was emphatically supported by Solidarity unions and rural cooperatives throughout the country:

> Even if Ackerman is right and, by moving fast, you can use the post-revolutionary momentum to hammer out some deal with the conservatives, should you really do so? Such a compromise constitution may petrify a lot of morally questionable arrangements.[6]

In making this move, Kisilowski is failing to distinguish between his neo-liberal 'vision of progress' and the 'never again' principles that unified Solidarity during Time One. As a neo-liberal, he would *of course* disagree with the 'conservative' Walesa, and social democrats backing Walesa would, *of course*, disagree with his neo-liberal commitment to free enterprise and the separation of Church and State. But the point of a revolutionary constitution is not to resolve all important

[6] Kisilowski, ch. 17 in this volume, at 343.

disputes over the future; it is to legitimate an overarching framework that *both sides* recognise as an *authentic* expression of popular sovereignty – and thereby encourage rival partisans to respect the rules of the game in their ongoing effort to gain popular support for their competing 'visions of progress' during Times Three and Four. This precious resource was sacrificed by the combination of the Gaullist-inspired constitutional design and the failed statesmanship of the Solidarity leadership.

But is the Polish tragedy really so exceptional? Here is where Stephen Gardbaum and Aziz Rana make important contributions. Gardbaum argues that the Polish case is by no means a special case and that revolutionary leaders in many other countries have failed to translate the 'never agains' of Time One into constitutional commitments at Time Two. Analysis of these 'leaderless revolutions', as Gardbaum calls them, is clarified further by Rana's emphasis on the role of Western imperial powers in disrupting the constitution-building efforts of revolutionary movements.

This is hardly the place for a full discussion of such worldwide developments, but I will illustrate Rana's point by pointing to two countries, emphasised by Gardbaum, in which his emphasis on imperial intervention has indeed played a key role in creating 'leaderless revolutions': Mexico and the Philippines. In both countries, it is perfectly possible to identify charismatic leaders who were very self-consciously attempting to constitutionalise their charisma – until foreign imperialist interventions killed them off.

In Mexico, the story begins in the nineteenth century, when a liberal revolutionary movement won a military victory over conservative forces, enabling President Benito Juarez to gain increasing recognition for a breakthrough republican Constitution by the time he occupied Mexico City in 1861. But this triumph was overwhelmed by the invasion of Spanish and French forces during the American Civil War. The foreign invaders' effort to transform the Austrian Archduke Maximillian into the Emperor of Mexico also proved a failure, creating a vacuum filled by Porfirio Diaz and his military supporters in the late 1860s. Over the next generation, Diaz gained legitimacy by convincing the political elite and many ordinary Mexicans that only a centralised bureaucratic government, under his own autocratic leadership, could save the nation from further foreign interventions. But when the 80-year-old dictator announced that he would be running for yet another presidential term in 1910, his grim determination to hold on to power provoked a massive counter-mobilisation which succeeded in forcing him out of office.

At this point, American Ambassador Henry Wilson conspired with Diaz's supporters to murder Francisco Madero in 1913, the revolutionary leader who had succeeded Diaz as President. Wilson's intervention was followed by an outright American invasion in April 1914 aimed at preventing Mexico from allying itself with Germany if Woodrow Wilson later chose to join France and Britain in their battle against the Triple Alliance in the First World War. The American attack split the revolutionary movement into fragments, even though it did not prevent important factions from hammering out the world's first social democratic constitution in 1917.

Nevertheless, imperialist intervention once again initiated a chaotic period which came to an end with the rise of autocratic rule in the late 1920s. Only in the 1990s did Mexico embark on a sustained effort at genuine multi-party democracy – this time, in a decidedly unrevolutionary fashion. However, this step-by-step transition to democracy failed to deliver on its promise. Instead, it degenerated into a corrupt plutocracy over the course of the next quarter of a century. The remarkable presidential victory of Andres Manuel Lopez Obrador (AMLO) in 2018 marks a new effort to reinvigorate Mexico's revolutionary constitutional tradition. Whatever else may be said about AMLO, he is very much a leader who, like Madero in the twentieth century and Juarez in the nineteenth century, is calling upon Mexicans to struggle together for a decisive break with the entrenched corruption of the old regime. It remains to be seen whether the Trump Administration, or its successors, will once again respond to this 'populist' threat by killing off its leaders.[7]

The Philippines displays a similar pattern. During the 1890s, Filipinos launched a successful struggle for independence against Spanish domination, with the rebels gaining control over the entire country (except Manilla Bay) by June 1898. However, when the US won the Spanish-American War, President William McKinley insisted on replacing Spanish imperialism with one of his own devising. He refused to recognise the emerging Philippine Republic and launched a three-year campaign of bloody repression which finally succeeded in establishing the semblance of 'law and order'. The American military then handed over power to the colony's first civilian governor, William Howard Taft, who developed a constitutional order which successfully co-opted wealthy Filipinos into the day-to-day government of the colony.

Once the country gained formal independence in 1946, these same propertied elites relied on American power to crush the Huq Rebellion of the 1940s and 1950s which could well have inaugurated a classic communist dictatorship. But a generation later, the People Power Movement of the 1980s had the makings of a very promising revolution on a human scale, with grassroots activists organising for a broad range of democratic initiatives for social and economic justice. Once again, however, this bottom-up movement was crushed by propertied elites backed by American military forces.[8]

These inter-generational dynamics put a different perspective on President Roderigo Duterte's recent power grabs, which have culminated in utterly lawless

[7] See generally, Richard N. Sinkin, The Mexican Reform, 1856–1876: A Study in Liberal Nation-Building (1979); Friedrich Katz, The Secret War in Mexico: Europe, the United States, and the Mexican Revolution (1981); Diego Valadés & Miguel Carbonell eds., El proceso constituyente mexicano: a 150 años de la Constitución de 1857 y 90 de la Constitución de 1917 (2007).

[8] See Brian Tiojanco, People Power Republic: The Rebirth of Philippine Democracy (2020).

acts of mass murder and oppression. According to Duterte, his assertions of arbitrary power serve as the only realistic means of purging the old regime of its entrenched corruption. In this single respect, Duterte is renewing the aspirations of generations of Filipinos – from the revolutionary Republic of the 1890s through the People Power Movement of the 1980s – to sweep away the oligarchic inheritance of Spanish and American colonialism. Yet it is the repeated failures of these earlier movements which have led many contemporary Filipinos to accept Duterte's claim that only strong-man tactics can realistically destroy the deeply entrenched corruptions of the established regime. Worse yet, the US under President Trump is trying to maintain its alliance with Duterte despite his outrageous conduct.

I strongly oppose Trump's current course – and give my wholehearted support to 'populist' counter-movements seeking to reinvigorate the People Power effort at constitutional revolution in the name of social justice. Yet *Revolutionary Constitutions* is not concerned with my hopes, but with realities. And the reality is that America's imperialist interventions have been a major factor in the failure of the country's 'leaderless' revolutions over the course of the twentieth century, and that these earlier failures help explain why so many Filipinos have accepted Duterte's claim that only brute lawlessness can serve as an effective battering ram against the inherited privileges of the post-colonial establishment.

In short, Rana's imperialism thesis provides powerful insights into the dynamics of Gardbaum's 'leaderless revolutions'. Yet Rana has even greater ambitions. So far as he is concerned, Gardbaum's pathologies are merely special cases of a larger crisis generated by the 'breakdown of the great European empires', and 'the explosion of new states and new constitutional enterprises'.[9] So far as he is concerned, the big problem is *economic imperialism*: while the de-colonising Europeans granted formal independence, they were grimly determined to maintain their economic hegemony over the newly independent nations. This predictably splits the successful revolutionaries into two broad camps, with strong egalitarians demanding the expropriation of foreign assets, while more moderate forces want to pursue prosperity by developing established trading relationships. To put the point in Fowkes' terms, redistributionists will accuse moderates of betraying the great sacrifices of Time One by offering a Rainbow Constitution that accepts too much of the economic status quo. If the Betrayalists win this struggle, the resulting legitimacy vacuum can create an opening for redistributionists to establish a dictatorship in the name of victims of economic oppression – issuing a paper constitution that mocks the realities of top-down rule.

I entirely agree that this totalitarian dynamic poses a clear and present danger. But it is not an inevitable feature of revolutionary liberation from Western imperialism – as the cases of India, South Africa and Iran demonstrate. While Rana offers up Kenya as a counter-example, his sketch only serves as an

[9] Rana, ch. 5 in this volume, at 88.

invitation for further scholarly explorations of the worldwide fate of revolutionary constitutionalism during the post-war period. The challenge is to learn from these successes and failures and to provide a richer framework for a thoughtful confrontation with the crises of the twenty-first century.

I do part company with Rana when it comes to another feature of his diagnosis. On his account, the Western imperial legacy also included an ethnocultural ideal of the state, in which a dominant majority could claim that minorities could rightly be treated as second-class citizens or worse. Rana emphasises how this ideal shaped the thought of Woodrow Wilson, but he fails to consider how the Nazi catastrophe led to its emphatic repudiation by overwhelming majorities in Great Britain, France and Portugal during the post-war period when their empires were disintegrating. Whatever else Europeans might have found objectionable about leaders like Nehru and Mandela, they applauded their efforts to lead a multiplicity of ethnic groups into a constitution-building project committed to Enlightenment principles of political equality of all citizens, regardless of their more particularistic cultural identities. To be sure, ethnocultural nationalism is on the rise today, but it is anachronistic to project it backwards in time and suppose that it was a driving force during the post-war era of decolonisation.

III. Broader Perspectives

Up to this point, I have been focusing on a critical point in the revolutionary life cycle – the transition from Time One to Time Two. But many commentators take a broader view. Not only do they place the 'race against time' within the context of later developments at Times Three and Four, they also compare the four-phase revolutionary dynamic with the 'establishment' and 'elitist' pathways that other countries have travelled over the course of the twentieth century.

In 'establishmentarian' countries, the political order is organised by pragmatic insiders, not revolutionary outsiders. When challenged by insurgent movements for a 'new beginning', these insiders respond with strategic concessions that split the outsiders into moderate and radical camps. When this strategy works, the 'sensible' outsiders enter parliament to join the insiders to enact landmark legislation that codifies the establishment's pragmatic reforms, permitting the broader public to retain confidence in the ongoing system.

This achievement will be viewed as an act of betrayal by more radical elements of the outsider movement. Nevertheless, once the establishment manages to co-opt 'sensible' reformers, remaining radicals will be pushed to the fringe of political life, where their revolutionary sloganeering only serves to emphasise their political powerlessness. During the two centuries since the French Revolution, the British establishment has – at least until Brexit – repeatedly demonstrated extraordinary skill in this co-optation strategy. But many other countries – both within and outside of the British Commonwealth – have moved down this track during more recent times. However, my new book only presents a few brief sketches of establishmentarian success in its introductory chapter, since it is the job of the next volume to supply intensive case studies.

I take the same approach in presenting my 'elitist' ideal type. In this scenario, the establishment is not swept from power by a mobilised movement of outsiders, but collapses for other reasons. Spain's peaceful 'transition to democracy' after the death of Franco serves as a paradigm case. Franco had crushed insurgent movements during his decades of authoritarian rule. While the collapse of his regime did provoke strikes and protests, these bottom-up movements played a secondary role in constitutional negotiations with the old regime. Instead, the emerging power vacuum was filled by political and social elites which Franco had previously excluded from power. The post-Franco Constitution emerged from secret negotiations between representatives of these rising elites and members of the old guard who recognised that the authoritarian system was disintegrating.

When they emerged to present the terms of their 'new beginning' to the broader public, the document they produced superficially resembled revolutionary constitutions, establishing a set of institutional checks and balances in the name of We the People. Nevertheless, the governing parties which took charge of the Spanish government had no deep anchor in lived revolutionary experience. As a consequence, governing elites could not take advantage of the distinctive resource supplied by the 'constitutionalisation of charisma' in gaining broad and deep popular support at Time Two.[10] They would have to legitimate their 'new beginning' by other means, which I will elaborate upon in a later volume.

For now, it is enough to say that while Spanish-style legitimation confronts predictable difficulties over time, these problems pale in comparison with elitist constitutions constructed in the aftermath of military defeat – as in Saddam Hussein's Iraq or Gaddafi's Libya. In both countries, the governments installed by the American military have spectacularly failed to gain broad legitimacy for their 'new beginnings'. Nevertheless, the cases of Nazi Germany and imperial Japan show that the post-war constitutions initially imposed by Allied occupying forces have gradually won recognition by local residents as *legitimate* frameworks governing their democracies. Is it possible to elaborate a multi-stage dynamic that helps account for such remarkable transformations?

My preliminary discussions of these matters have encouraged my commentators to join the hunt in search for answers. Several have focused on the ongoing crisis of the European Union (EU) and whether my trichotomy between revolutionary/establishment/elitist ideal types provides distinctive insights.

Broadly speaking, current scholarly discussion is dominated by two camps: one believes that the EU is broadly comparable to the US and other great federations;

[10] Though some political elites – ranging from communists to devout Catholics – did have roots in the Spanish Civil War of the 1930s, culminating in Franco's military victory. I discuss the Spanish case at greater length, together with scholarly sources, in BRUCE ACKERMAN, REVOLUTIONARY CONSTITUTIONS: CHARISMATIC LEADERSHIP AND THE RULE OF LAW 3–6, 405 (2019).

others believe it to be unique. My commentators rightly see that my trichotomy pushes me into the uniqueness camp, but for a distinctive reason.

The leading nations of Europe come to the EU along different paths: the constitutions of Germany and Spain are elite constructions; France and Italy have their roots in revolutions on a human scale; Great Britain emerges from the establishment tradition of pragmatic adaptation. Little wonder, then, that these countries have trouble finding a common pathway to a more perfect EU. French and Italian constitutional cultures are open to revolutionary appeals to We the People of Europe, but Great Britain and Germany emerge from traditions which are deeply sceptical of the very notion that a mobilised movement could plausibly exercise 'popular sovereignty' on a continental scale. For the British, the right way to fix the EU is by negotiating pragmatic solutions to particular problems; for the Germans, a Euro-wide populist movement creates an intolerable risk that demagogues will re-enact the Nazi tragedy and shatter the entire liberal tradition. Given these historically rooted differences, it will take genuine acts of statesmanship to move the continent forward in a constructive direction.

Neil Walker challenges my diagnosis, because the EU 'is not a state'. It is instead 'unique' in 'its successful assertion of some … areas of final authority … without making the monopolistic claim to comprehensive … and *self-limiting* sovereign authority peculiar to a state'.[11] Since my trichotomy only addresses the way in which 'states' gain constitutional authority, Walker believes it to be categorically inapplicable to the EU's legitimation crisis.

I disagree. In contrast to Walker, I believe that the EU resembles the US at a comparable phase of its historical development. After all, the EU is a relative youngster compared to the US. It only came into existence just over 60 years ago with the Treaty of Rome in 1957, while the US has been around for 220 years since 1789. However, if we focus on the first 60 years of American development, we will find that it displays the very same features which Walker supposes are unique to the European experience.

As my book's treatment of the American Founding suggests, Jefferson and Madison famously denied, in their Kentucky and Virginia Resolutions, the 'monopolistic claim' to 'sovereign authority' advanced by the federal government during the 1790s and defended by the Marshall Court in later decades. Moreover, once Jefferson and Madison won the White House, they forced the Marshall Court to retreat repeatedly from *Marbury v Madison*'s aggressive assertions of federal supremacy.

The same thing happened a generation later when Andrew Jackson refused to execute the Court's nationalising pronunciamentos: 'John Marshall has made his opinion; now let him enforce it'.[12] The pattern repeated itself yet again in the

[11] Walker, ch. 12 in this volume, at 226–27.

[12] It is not quite clear whether Jackson actually made this remark, which has been attributed to him by legal legend. But there can be no doubt that it accurately describes his defiance of the Court in 31 U.S. 6 Pet. 515 (1832).

1850s. For present purposes, the Lincoln/Douglas debates can serve as a symbol of a profound disagreement as to whether the citizens were members of the United *States* of America or the *United* States of America.[13] This is precisely the same question of 'sovereign authority' which currently divides We the People of Europe. If there is something unique about Europe's post-war development, Walker has not identified it. He seems to be taking *Marbury* at face value in supposing that the EU is *sui generis*.

This is not to say that *Marbury* was decisively repudiated during the first 60 years of American development. It is only to remark upon a striking parallel between the two Unions. On both continents, high courts sitting in Luxembourg/Washington repeatedly asserted the supremacy of Union law and often succeeded in gaining recognition for their claims, but their interventions also generated repeated backlashes from Member States and the politically responsive branches of the EU/US in Brussels and Washington. The challenge is to identify salient differences, as well as striking similarities, between the ongoing conflicts between judicial and political authority in the two Unions.

Mitchel Lasser's chapter points in a promising direction. In his view, it is the rise of a bureaucratic elite in the EU which has greatly contributed to the ascent of the European Court of Justice (ECJ). In contrast, the Marshall and Taney Courts could not rely on a bureaucratic ally in the justices' efforts to impose their constitutional will upon resistant political institutions. It was only the New Deal Revolution which created a strong bureaucratic apparatus which permitted the Court to override the resistance of Member States during the Civil Rights Revolution and other moments of crisis.

Lasser is especially illuminating in dealing with the paradoxical rise of the ECJ after 1989. The Western European powers in control of the Court did not close their doors to justices appointed by the newly independent Eastern governments, but they did not open them wide either. Instead, the Westerners tried to assure the new states that, once they were admitted to full membership of the EU, the Easterners' judicial appointments would not sabotage the Court's efforts to intervene if their fledgling governments assaulted fundamental principles of human dignity and democratic self-determination. As Lasser shows, the bureaucratic elite in Brussels was the driving force behind reforms which stripped the Easterners of their ability to appoint justices unilaterally and replaced it with a system which gave the existing members of the Court a central role in deciding on their replacements. Moreover, Lasser demonstrates that these reforms have also deprived powerhouses like Germany and France from appointing justices to the ECJ who would reliably protect their own sovereign prerogatives. These sweeping changes will predictably generate a judiciary which will increasingly favour EU-wide principles

[13] For (much) more on this period of contestation in the US, see Bruce Ackerman, We the People, Volume 2: Transformations (1998); and Bruce Ackerman, The Failure of the Founding Fathers (2000).

when they conflict with claims to national self-determination by Member States. Since this balancing act is already authorised by the Court's 'margin of appreciation' doctrine, there will be plenty of room for the ECJ to defer to national interests in particularly exigent circumstances, but Lasser demonstrates that the balance of judicial statesmanship has decisively shifted in the direction of the EU as a consequence of bureaucratic initiatives.

Daniel Halberstam's chapter adds an additional dimension to this centralising dynamic. In contrast to Lasser, he does not focus on the ECJ itself, but on the transformation of the judicial system in a key nation-state: France. Until the beginning of the twenty-first century, the Conseil constitutionnel played an important, but limited, role in the country's arrangements. It could only invalidate legislative initiatives at the time they were initially passed by parliament. If the Conseil affirmed the law's constitutionality at that point, it lacked jurisdiction to reconsider the matter after the new law made it on to the statute books. From then on, it was up to the country's traditional supreme courts – the Court of Cassation and the Council of State – to determine whether laws were unconstitutionally applied in particular cases.

All this changed with France's sweeping constitutional reform of 2008, which authorised the Conseil to engage in judicial review of concrete controversies after the law's initial enactment. This allowed the Conseil to incorporate Euro-court doctrines into French constitutional law on an ongoing basis. Halberstam demonstrates that this big change did not come out of nowhere, but that the traditional courts had paved the way during the preceding decades by incorporating Euro-doctrines into their own jurisprudence. Indeed, he goes so far as to claim that these earlier doctrinal developments made the dramatic enhancement of the Conseil's role in 2008 merely 'symbolic' and that the advocates for a formal constitutional amendment, led by President Sarkozy and Prime Minister Fillon, 'did not have to push hard' for its enactment.

But this is an exaggeration. In fact, the necessary constitutional amendment passed by a single vote only after intensive lobbying by Fillon and Sarkozy.[14] Ever since 1789, the French tradition had rejected the legitimacy of 'government by judges'; the 2008 amendment represented a radical revision of the country's core constitutional identity, and all the protagonists recognised this point, which is precisely why the move was deeply contested.

If Fillon and Sarkozy had lost their amendment, French constitutional resistance to recent rounds of Euro-court aggrandisement would have been profound. Given the country's strategic and cultural position on the continent, the 2008 amendment played a critical role in propelling the European project forward, giving it significant support as it confronted the bitter struggles of the coming decade. Nevertheless, Halberstam is surely right in emphasising that the judicial dynamics of previous decades played a major role in setting the stage for the epochal French decision of 2008.

[14] For further elaboration, see Ackerman, *supra* note 5 at 221–22, 423.

Perhaps there are similar dynamics at work in one or another American constitutional development. But at present, I cannot think of any cases – can you?

There is a lot more to be said about the EU/US comparison, but it is better to turn to commentaries which reflect more broadly on my 'three pathways' framework.

Richard Albert tries to clarify its concrete implications by unpacking the legalistic category of 'constitutional amendment'. This one-size-fits-all label, he rightly insists, disguises the very different ways in which the technique is deployed in countries travelling down different pathways. His general framework is especially valuable in highlighting amendment dilemmas encountered in places that otherwise look very different from one another. Under Albert's instruction, Canada's efforts to reconcile British-style pragmatism with French-style revolutionary constitutionalism bear a family resemblance to the ongoing efforts by the EU to generate amendment procedures that can plausibly permit its 28 members to find a suitable way of resolving their current crisis. I would be delighted if other scholars tested his approach in their future work, but my own responses must await my next volume's detailed case studies of the elitist and establishmentarian traditions.

Stephen Gardbaum's chapter advances a very different, but no less illuminating, insight, which builds upon my discussion of 'succession crises' that are characteristic of revolutionary development at Times Three. Gardbaum suggests that similar crises also arise in totaliatarian revolutions that categorically reject the principle of checks and balances.

He is absolutely right. We have much to learn, for example, from disciplined comparisons between the Congress Party in India and the Communist Party in China as they rose to power during the course of the twentieth century. During the 1930s and 1940s, both Nehru and Mao led their revolutionary movements to victory (Time One) and then used their movement parties as the organisation basis for a sustained period of charismatic leadership (Time Two). As in India, Mao's death precipitated a bitter succession crisis, with the 'Gang of Four' trying to continue Mao's 'permanent revolution' and a rival group, led by Deng Xiaoping, struggling to end it.[15] Deng came out on top at Time Three, sealing his triumph over his party rivals by promulgating a new Constitution in 1982. However, during the early years of Deng's ascendancy, this text served as a typical communist fig-leaf, without operating as a real-world constraint on party rule. But over succeeding decades, the judiciary has increasingly played a serious role in forcing the regional party organisations to heed the legal commands issued from Beijing, although legalists have failed thus far to impose comparable checks and balances at the apex of the system (Time Four).[16]

Obviously, there are big differences, as well as surprising similarities, in the Indian and Chinese patterns of development. But serious scholarly comparisons

[15] James Palmer, The Death of Mao (2012).

[16] Tom Ginsburg & Taisu Zhang, *Legality in Contemporary Chinese Politics*, 58 Va. J. Int'l L. (forthcoming 2019).

should prove exceptionally rewarding, not only in understanding the past, but also in confronting a twenty-first-century future in which these two great Asian powers will play a crucial role in determining the fate of world constitutionalism.

IV. Fundamental Critiques

In his chapter, Roberto Gargarella takes a very different approach. Rather than locating my revolutionary 'success stories' within a broader framework, he denies that places like India should count as 'successes' at all. He argues that I am wrong in claiming that the Indian Supreme Court has in fact preserved crucial aspects of their Founding legacies during Times Three and Four. Instead, his review of judicial performance convinces him that the justices have 'tend[ed] to work for the *normalisation of domination*,' legitimating deeply entrenched economic and social inequalities by their endless talk of human dignity.[17]

Menaka Guruswamy presents a very different view of the Indian Supreme Court. Rather than reinforcing political compromises with entrenched injustice, she presents a compelling account of the Court's support of rising social and economic movements demanding judicial vindication of the Founding's dignitarian principles to meet twenty-first-century demands for justice. Even if Gargarella disagrees, he should recognise that Guruswamy's analysis of India's 'movement court' requires him to include an additional factor in his equation.

To see my point, let us assume that Gargarella is absolutely right in emphasising that the justice's ongoing invocation of the Founding legacy does indeed lull some groups into passive acceptance of the status quo. Nevertheless, the movement court's developing jurisprudence not only provides legalistic affirmations of the continuing relevance of Founding principles to twenty-first century realities; it also reinforces the broader efforts by civil society groups to organise in defence of the Nehruvian Constitution against Modi's current assault on its basic structure.

This does not mean that this defence will ultimately succeed in defeating Modi's constitutional revolution, but the counter-mobilisation will deprive him of a quick and easy victory. Instead, he will only emerge triumphant if his movement party, the Bharatiya Janata Party (BJP), wins a *series* of electoral victories in which its candidates gain a sustained popular mandate for a revision of the 'basic structure' after a self-conscious and mobilised debate amongst the general public. It is the Founding achievement at Time Two which makes this judicial contribution at Time Four more likely, and thereby serves to enhance the ongoing project of revolution on a human scale.

Contrast this ongoing process with the very different scenario now taking place in countries like Israel and Poland, which failed to constitutionalise their

[17] Gargarella, ch. 4 in this volume, at 68.

revolutionary charisma at Time Two. In both cases, the Israeli and Polish courts did manage to carve out a strong role for themselves at Times Three and Four. Yet they have been far less successful in appealing to the 'constitutional patriotism' of their fellow citizens when confronting the assaults against Enlightenment principles of the Zionist/Solidarity revolutions launched by Benjamin Netanyahu and Jaroslaw Kaczynski.

This suggests that the debate between Gargarella and Guruswamy is not only important in itself; it also has profound implications for future revolutions – and there will be many – in the twenty-first century. If 'populist' movements follow Gargarella's advice, they will not waste their time trying to win broad popular consent for revolutionary constitutions during Time Two. They will instead focus all their political energies on urgent questions of socio-economic justice and military security. Yet this decision to defer constitution-building to some future time can come at a heavy price, as the examples of Poland and Israel suggest.

The Gargarella/Guruswamy debate also casts light on Alon Harel's more general reflections on the varieties of constitutional development displayed over the course of the twentieth century. He wants to complement my 'three path' thesis with a cross-cutting dichotomy between two distinct modes of legitimation: 'representational' and 'reason-based'. His first ideal type 'rests upon the conviction that the constitution … is constitutive of their collective identity, that it promotes their distinct values as a nation and that it is being sustained by the active engagement of citizens with the constitution'. In contrast, '[l]egitimacy is non-representational or reason-based if it rests upon the conviction that the (procedural, institutional or substantive) aspects of the constitutional order promote justice, the protection of rights, stability and/or well-being'.[18]

This dichotomy leads Harel to a different diagnosis of the current 'populist' wave. On his account, the 'current conflict between populists … and liberals … can be better understood as a debate between advocates and opponents of representational constitutionalism', with liberals arguing for 'reason' against the populist demand for the representation of the 'will' of the People.[19]

I reject Harel's diagnosis. Indeed, my book aims to show that his stark dichotomy between 'reason' and 'will' is misconceived, and that some of the greatest constitutional triumphs have been based on a revolutionary synthesis of *both* elements into a compelling whole. At each stage of my Four-Time cycle, I have been emphasising how reason *and* will enter into the revolutionary dynamic. During Time One, it is not enough for insurgents to engage in high-energy resistance; they also advance reasoned appeals which explain why the existing regime is illegitimate and why their fellow citizens should risk their lives to join in the struggle in order to overthrow it. From the American Declaration of Independence to the South African Freedom Charter, these statements of principle have provided

[18] Harel, ch. 2 in this volume, at 21.
[19] *Id.*

the foundation for efforts, at Time Two, to hammer out a *reasoned* basis for a constitution that could gain the *self-conscious* consent of the wider public. This is precisely why the distinctive collaborations of Nehru and Ambedkar, de Gaulle and Debre, Mandela and Sachs are central in their victory in 'the race against time' – and why their Founding syntheses of reason *and* will have played such a central role in the legitimation of the judicial effort to preserve the revolutionary legacy through reason-giving and statecraft at Times Three and Four.

In emphasising this point, I do not suggest that constitutional courts have not managed to achieve an important role in polities travelling down other pathways. However, for the present, it is more important to emphasise the enduring significance of the failure to win the 'race against time' and why future revolutionaries should think twice before following the examples of David Ben-Gurion or Franklin Roosevelt or Lech Walesa, and reject the very effort to gain broad popular consent after a self-conscious public debate over the fundamental principles guiding their revolutions on a human scale.

Yasuo Hasebe is also a sceptic, but he launches his critique from a different perspective. In his view, it is not judicial reason-giving, but the judges' appreciation of 'common-sense morality', which serves as the foundation for checks and balances. He emphasises that his appeal to 'common-sense' should not be confused with HLA Hart's 'rule of recognition', or other forms of legal positivism. According to Hasebe, it is only if high courts effectively vindicate 'common sense' that revolutions will stay 'within a human scale rather than degenerating into a totalising version'.[20]

I have two problems with Hasebe's thesis. For one thing, there are many countries in which there is *no* version of 'common-sense' morality which can hope to express the dominant social mores throughout the nation. Consider India, with its multitude of different cultures, castes and ethnicities. Within this extraordinary diversity, *any* version of judicial 'common sense' would seem like a top-down imposition to hundreds of millions whose intuitions lead them in very different directions. Nevertheless, despite Hasebe's prediction, India has not 'degenerated' into totalitarianism, precisely because Indians owe their identity as equal citizens, endowed with fundamental rights, to the revolution on a human scale constitutionalised by the Congress Party at Time Two and sustained by the Supreme Court and civil society, during Times Three and Four.

Hasebe's thesis is problematic even when applied to countries like Japan, where a single form of 'common sense' morality arguably prevails throughout the nation. Consider, for example, the current Japanese crisis provoked by Prime Minister Shinzo Abe's campaign against the Peace Article of its Constitution, which commits the country to 'renounce war' and the 'threat of force'. Despite this 'never again' commitment emerging from the country's catastrophic defeat in the Second World War, Abe is on a campaign to grant the military full legal authority to engage in

[20] Hasebe, ch. 10 in this volume, at 193.

pre-emptive attacks against China or foreign terrorist groups before they actually launch an attack on the homeland.

The Japanese Constitution provides a straightforward way to accomplish this objective. It puts the burden on the prime minister to gain a two-thirds vote from both branch of the legislature and then appeal to the people to adopt his initiative by majority vote at a special referendum.

But Abe has refused to take this path. Instead, the Prime Minister announced, in May 2014, that the executive branch had 'reinterpreted' the Peace Article that effectively erased its ban on the 'threat' of force, and then rammed through legislation that authorised the Japanese military to engage in pre-emptive strikes for the first time since the Second World War.[21]

Abe's blatant end-run around the Constitution's express provisions for its amendment represents a fundamental breach, but not because the Peace Article is a matter of 'common sense morality'; instead, it is a 'never again' provision emerging out of the country's disastrous defeat in the Second World War. Moreover, it is now an open question whether the Peace Article should remain a centrepiece of Japanese constitutional identity. For many decades after Hiroshima and Nagasaki, it seemed clear that the country could depend on the American military to defend its territorial integrity, but this is no longer obvious. As a consequence, the Peace Article now confronts Japan with a hard choice: should it repeal the Peace Article and authorise its own military to pre-empt attacks from abroad before they endanger the homeland?

There is no 'common-sense' answer to this question, which is precisely why the Constitution *requires* the prime minister and a parliamentary supermajority to gain the self-conscious consent of We the People of Japan before risking a repeat of the tragedy culminating in Hiroshima and Nagasaki.

Hasebe's conflation of constitutional law with common-sense morality makes it impossible for Japanese jurists to raise, let alone analyse, the profound questions of legitimacy raised by Abe's constitutional coup, or to assess the ways in which his 'reinterpretation' of the Peace Article serves as a precedent for further assaults on the basic structure of the post-war constitutional regime.

While Harel invokes public reason and Hasebe appeals to common sense, Andrew Arato mounts an all-out assault on the very foundations of my position. In his view, my project is basically indistinguishable from Carl Schmitt's notorious effort to legitimate Hitler's Nazi dictatorship as the incarnation of popular will. His critique is quite complex, but depends on two premises. The first is easy to deal with; the second requires more elaborate treatment.

[21] Bruce Ackerman & Tokujin Matsudaira, *Cry Havoc and Let Slip the Dogs of War*, Foreign Policy (2015), https://foreignpolicy.com/2015/09/28/japan_constitution_war_peace_article_self_defense_force_shinzo_abe_obama. Bruce Ackerman & Tokujin Matsudaira, *A Militarized Japan?*, L.A. Times, Jan. 11, 2013, http://articles.latimes.com/2013/jan/11/opinion/la-oe-ackerman-japan-constitution-20130111. See generally Craig Mark, The Abe Restoration: Contemporary Politics and Reformation (2016).

Taking first things first, Arato cites a passage from my discussion of Iran to crystallise his fundamental critique. So I will begin with my text, before considering his response:

> Constitutional regimes … deny [that] any single power-center can legitimately impose its commands in a top-down manner. Even the most powerful incumbents must instead engage in on-going competition with institutional rivals for the final say over the future course of political development.
>
> Iran passes this test; many other parts of the Middle East don't. They are poorly disguised despotisms.
>
> This is not a point which should be forgotten amidst the tweets and tragedies of the current day.[22]

Arato rejects my point about Iran on the ground that its Constitution places 'Kompetenz-kompetenz … in the hands of the Supreme Leader, *whether or not in all political moments he is capable of exercising it*'.[23] His appeal to 'kompetenz-kompetenz' signals his commitment to the mainstream German notion that every constitution must, as a conceptual matter, designate a *single* institution as the authoritative judge of the law-abiding character of the remaining actors within the system. But the entire point of my book is to substitute a checks-and-balances definition for this dogmatic search for the super-competent authority which can lord it over all the others.

To put my argument in comparative terms, just as the Supreme Islamic Jurist asserts his kompetenz-kompetenz in Iran, so do the jurists sitting on the US Supreme Court assert their constitutional supremacy over the political branches. Nevertheless, since the days of John Marshall, the justices have not proved 'capable of exercising' this authority 'at all political moments' because the system of checks and balances has enabled popularly elected presidents and Congresses to *earn* greater legitimacy in the eyes of their fellow citizens. When this happens, judges have repeatedly retreated in recognition of the popular mandates of the democratic rivals. But such retreats have not prevented the Court from regaining the initiative once it has revised judicial doctrine to incorporate the most recent principles that have gained the support of We the People.

For all its differences from the US, my Iran case study shows that a similar pattern of constitutional contestation emerged once Ayatollah Khomeini departed from the scene at Time Three. Since his death, a democratically elected president has been locked in an ongoing struggle with the divinely inspired Supreme Leader for real-world legitimacy. During the past 30 years (Time Four), the balance between democratic and religious authority has swung repeatedly from one side to the other.

It is perfectly possible that this cycle will continue for the next generation, with elected presidents, backed by their supporters in the legislature, engaging in an

[22] Ackerman, *supra* note 5 at 385.
[23] Arato, ch. 6 in this volume, at 99 (emphasis added).

ongoing struggle for legitimacy against future Guardian Jurists. Or perhaps the presidents will gain a repeated popular mandate to dramatically limit the effective power of jurists to veto democratic initiatives. Or vice versa. It is impossible to predict how such a point-counterpoint will play itself out over time.

Only one thing is clear. If future Iranian presidents do succeed in winning a series of popular mandates for the enhancement of democratic liberty in the Islamic *Republic*, this should serve as evidence that the promise of revolutionary constitutionalism has not been exhausted by the success stories of the twentieth century, and that 'populism' may well continue to be a powerful force for constitutional government in the future.

INDEX

Please see individual entries for information relating to particular countries